BUSINESS PRINCIPLES
AND MANAGEMENT

By

BERNARD A. SHILT

Supervisor of Secondary Commercial Education
Board of Education
Buffalo, New York

AND

W. HARMON WILSON

Lecturer on Management
University of Cincinnati
and Editor of The Balance Sheet

Published by

SOUTH-WESTERN PUBLISHING COMPANY

Cincinnati   New York   Chicago   Dallas   San Francisco

G22

H240

*Printed in the
United States of America*

PREFACE

BUSINESS PRINCIPLES AND MANAGEMENT is a new type of book based upon some important new developments in business education. It is designed for courses commonly referred to as business principles, business management, business organization, advanced business training, business administration, or business organization and management.

There has been a growing demand for a more general type of business-training textbook involving the principles of business management and containing a reasonable amount of information on business organization. In many schools this type of course has already been established, and in many other schools it is taking the place of more technical courses that have not proved very satisfactory. It introduces many topics not covered in other specific business courses and ties together much of the subject matter found in other separate courses. It helps to give the student a practical working understanding of business organization, business management, and business procedure.

In the development of BUSINESS PRINCIPLES AND MANAGEMENT, particular attention has been given to the specific details of organizing and operating a small business. At the same time a sufficient amount of background information is given with regard to large organizations so that the student going into those organizations will have a better understanding of their functions and procedures. As many types of small businesses are retail establishments, considerable emphasis is placed on those organizations.

Particular care has been taken to avoid a theoretical development of the principles of management and organization; therefore specific details of procedure, organization, and management are discussed. For instance, when forms of business organization are considered, specific examples are used to clarify the explanation. In the discussion of purchasing procedure, concrete examples are used. The chapter on business risks and insurance includes some theory, but, for the most part, deals with concrete examples and information.

Although one specific chapter is devoted to ethics, there are numerous references to good business ethics throughout the various chapters. One chapter is devoted to the relations of business with government, but many of the other chapters also touch upon this important subject. Legal relations in business are discussed wherever they are appropriate in the various chapters, but one special chapter is devoted to this subject.

This course has a very broad value. It not only provides a much-needed background for every student who goes into business, but it also provides invaluable training for the person who may eventually manage a business of his own. As an advanced general business course, it is rich in content that will be interesting and valuable to everyone.

The textbook is divided into logical units. The longer chapters are broken into sections to provide for reasonably uniform assignments. The student starts with the organization of a business and proceeds through the problems of managing and operating a business. This type of presentation has been used because it is realistic and provides a logical sequence of topics.

We gratefully acknowledge the ideas and suggestions obtained from many teachers and the generous contributions of illustrations that were made by various business institutions. We particularly acknowledge the assistance given by William Polishook, head of the department of business education, Clifford J. Scott High School, East Orange, New Jersey, in reading one of the early drafts of the manuscript.

BERNARD A. SHILT
W. HARMON WILSON

TABLE OF CONTENTS

Unit I. Problems of Organizing a Business

Unit II. Getting Started

Unit III. Management Problems

CHAPTER I

OPPORTUNITIES AND REQUIREMENTS OF STARTING IN BUSINESS

Purpose of the Chapter. Almost everyone experiences, at some time or other, the desire to start in business for himself. This desire is based on the hope of becoming independent. It is easier to start in business in the United States than in most other countries, although it is true that organizing a new enterprise becomes more difficult as our economic and financial relations become more complicated. Many businessmen fail and lose what money they have put into their enterprises; yet every day stories of the success of new business projects are heard. The purpose of this chapter is to seek answers to many questions, some of which are:

1. What are the fundamentals necessary for the success of a new business enterprise?
2. What are some of the essentials of organizing a new business enterprise?
3. What are some of the pitfalls to be avoided in organizing a business?
4. What are the chances of success?
5. What are some sources of information?

Place of the Small Business. When conditions are favorable, large and efficiently managed corporations operate smoothly, but they are not always immune from financial difficulties. During times of rapidly changing conditions, a small business organization may find it possible to change management policies more quickly than a large organization. A small business may therefore have this distinct advantage over a large one.

Small business is a title applied to a single retail store, a dry-cleaning establishment, a machine shop, a restaurant, a filling station, a service station, or some other type of

1

business that can be operated conveniently by one or a few individuals. Although combinations and monopolies in some branches of industry and business have made it difficult for small enterprises to begin operations, there are constantly new opportunities to start into business. Local, state, and Federal legislation has tended to protect the operator of a small business by eliminating unfair competition and by preventing certain types of combinations.

Many of our present large businesses have started from small beginnings. One needs only to study the histories of some typical American businesses to discover the importance of the individual in the establishment of a new business.

Opportunities are opening every day. As long as people need to buy food, shelter, clothing, and amusement, there will be opportunities in business. Every group of ten thousand people requires about thirty grocers, ten or fifteen bakers, ten or twelve restaurants, and a smaller number of other businesses, including tailor shops, furniture stores, garages, and drugstores. Service stations and garages are becoming more numerous largely because of the increase in the number of automobiles. The number of drugstores is also increasing because of the greater variety of articles that such stores can now offer for sale.

A recent survey made by the United States Department of Commerce discloses that there are almost one million small-scale retail stores in operation and that the number tends to increase. The report also offers the opinion that small stores will continue as long as they provide services for which society is willing to pay. The elimination of these small stores would result in a shortage of retail facilities for many consumers. Apparently, therefore, opportunity still exists for the small businessman.

Responsibilities Assumed in Business. Some persons are inclined to look upon a businessman as a capitalist who profits at the expense of others. There is sometimes a feeling that a businessman is successful merely because he had money enough to go into business. The fact that so many businessmen fail proves, however, that to be successful the businessman must have many desirable qualities. In most cases he must not only work hard, but, because of his ownership in the business, he must also take certain risks.

For instance, an employee who drives a truck for a delivery business has certain definite tasks. He must pick up loads at different places and deliver the loads rapidly but with care. He may have to see that the truck is properly greased and may sometimes be required to make small repairs. If this man buys a truck and goes into business for himself, he must not only continue to look after those tasks but must also take on others. He may be able to run the business from his home, but he probably must incur some additional expense for an office or a garage. He must assume the responsibility of finding customers who will do business with him; he must persuade those customers to pay a fair price, and he must collect the bills; furthermore, he must assume responsibility for damage that may occur to the merchandise hauled.

In other words, if this workman goes into business for himself, he must do some things that his employer formerly did. He must perform some additional functions. If the truckman does not have the ability to do all these tasks reasonably well, he will probably earn less money in his own business than he got when he worked for someone else. If he is not careful, he may, in the end, lose his truck and all his savings. It is therefore evident that a businessman performs certain functions that are not performed by the average worker. Any additional income that he obtains from performing these functions pays him for the risks he assumes and the added work he performs.

Originating New Businesses. People are willing to pay a reasonable price for having ordinary problems solved or simplified. If a person who wants to go into business will think in terms of solving a common problem or simplifying that problem, he will more likely be successful than if he were to think in terms of developing some ingenious scheme or novelty. In the pages of almost every newspaper, there are stories of new businesses that have been originated as a result of solving old problems or simplifying those problems.

The parking lot and the parking garage in our cities have helped to solve a common problem that has arisen out of parking restrictions. Filling stations have taken the place of the old storage tank that every automobile owner used to have in his back yard, garage, or basement. Traveling libraries built in motor busses, stores on wheels, and special demonstration busses have solved common problems or have simplified them. The theater-ticket brokerage business is reported to have been started by a person with only a small amount of capital. He discovered that people were willing to pay a fee if someone would simplify the problem of obtaining good theater seats.

The examples given above are typical of the ways in which enterprising individuals have started new businesses. A writer in *Nation's Business* [1] recommends that any person thinking of originating a new business should ask himself the following questions:

1. What do the people I know need?
2. What things are they doing that they dislike doing?
3. What new problems do they face?
4. How could I save their time for them?
5. How could I add to their peace of mind?
6. How could I protect them from something they dread?
7. What could I make or do for them that would save them money?

Selecting the Type of Business. Entering business involves many serious problems, the first of which is to decide what kind of undertaking it will be best to follow.

Not all people are qualified to enter the same types of businesses. People differ in education, experience, personal preferences, habits, and ability. No one should enter a business just because he believes that it is a good one. On the other hand, a person should not be so determined to start

---

[1] Updegraff, Robert R., "So You'd Like to Be Your Own Boss," *Nation's Business,* July, 1938.

in business that he will choose an unprofitable type of enterprise just because he likes it.

Before selecting a certain type of business, a person should consider the following questions:

1. Does my education qualify me to enter this business?
2. What experience have I to qualify me?
3. Why have others become successful in this kind of business?
4. Am I willing to work harder than some other businessman to make my enterprise a success?
5. Are my home conditions such that I can devote to the business the amount of time required?
6. Are the prospects for success permanent or only temporary?
7. Is the business one that is liable to be displaced by some other type?
8. Are the financial requirements within my means?

Qualifications for Success. Every person who starts in business and expects to be successful should have some fundamental advantage over his competitor. His advantages may consist of knowledge, skill, or personal qualities. Other advantages may be location, personal prestige, economy, or the ability to give superior service or quality.

One who plans to start a business enterprise should study the opportunities in the community. He should notice which types of businesses are profitable and which are not profitable. There may be six grocery stores in a small town, but not one of them may be making a good profit. On the other hand, there may be ten grocery stores, two of which are making unusually good profits while the others are not successful. The reasons for such difference in success should be investigated.

Suppose, for example, a person who contemplates starting a dry-cleaning business discovers that in his community there are only two establishments of this type, one of which is making a good profit although the other is not making any. He should therefore answer the following questions while he considers the advisability of starting an establishment of his own:

1. Why is one establishment making a profit while the other is not?
2. What qualifications have I to start in this business?
3. What reasons have I to believe that I could obtain enough business to make a profit?
4. How could I render unusual service and introduce new ideas that would bring new business?
5. In what ways are the services and the prices of the existing establishments unsatisfactory?
6. How can the quality of work be improved?
7. How much money would be required to start the business?
8. Where could a good location be found?
9. Where could equipment and experienced help be obtained?

In other words, complete estimates of the prospects and the financial obligations must be considered carefully.

Sometimes entirely new types of businesses provide opportunities. As such businesses may, however, be only temporary, they should be distinguished from permanent types. The Tom Thumb (miniature) golf course was popular as an amusement for only a short time in most parts of the country. On the other hand, many roadside fruit stands have proved to be profitable business enterprises. The automobile has created new business opportunities by requiring more garages and service stations. The airplane and many other inventions may also bring new opportunities.

Chances of Success. One's chances of success in starting a new business enterprise are based largely on education, experience, the amount of money that may be put into the enterprise, careful management, and economic conditions. The time for starting a new business enterprise is very important. There is a great advantage in starting an enterprise after a period of falling prices, that is, when prices have reached their lowest point. While prices are decreasing steadily, many men quit business or fail. As a result there is less competition after such a period. After prices have reached their lowest point, they begin to rise and the demand for goods becomes correspondingly greater. On the other hand, the most unfavorable time to start an enterprise is when prices are falling and many people are losing employment. A more complete discussion of this problem is given in Chapter XXV.

Studies made by the United States Department of Commerce disclose that about 70 per cent of all commercial failures occur in the retail-trade group. In many recent years there have been more than 200,000 failures a year in retail businesses. It is estimated that, of the total number of businesses in existence each year, 1 to 2 per cent of these businesses fail during the year.

Illustration No. 1 covers a study of 570 cases of businesses that became bankrupt. This table shows the apparent causes of the failures. It is important to notice that insufficient capital ranks very high in the opinion of both the owners and the creditors. This factor should serve as a warning that it is important to have adequate capital before starting a business. More than 51 per cent of the businesses studied had no accounting records. Out of a total of 570 bankrupts, 360 reported that they had not obtained any business information or advice from such sources as credit bureaus or trade associations. In more than 68 per cent of the bankrupt businesses, the owners or the managers had not completed a high-school education. This fact is evidence that a good education is a prime essential in successfully operating a business.

Such a study of bankruptcies illustrates the fact that too many people who are not qualified go into business. In some types of retail businesses as many as 60 per cent of those who start never succeed. This fact should not necessarily be a discouragement against entering business, but it should be a warning that the person who does enter must be qualified. Furthermore, anyone who starts an enterprise assumes an important obligation, for his welfare is closely related to that of the entire community in which he operates and of the people with whom he deals. Any failure in business is an economic loss that must be borne by society.

Causes of Failure (Owners' Opinions)	Percentage of Enterprises Affected	Causes of Failure (Creditors' Opinions)	Percentage of Enterprises Affected
Business depression	67.7	Inefficient management .	58.7
Insufficient capital	48.2	Dishonesty and fraud ..	33.7
Competition	37.9	Insufficient capital	32.9
Adverse domestic and personal factors	35.1	Business depression	29.1
Decline in value of assets	31.6	Adverse domestic and personal factors	28.1
Bad-debt losses	29.8	Bad-debt losses	17.6
Inefficient management .	28.2	Competition	9.1
Excessive overhead expenses	24.0	Excessive overhead	8.9
Poor business location ..	14.6	Too rapid expansion ...	7.2
Losses from speculation.	11.6	Decline in value of assets	5.8
Unfavorable changes in trading area	11.2	Losses from speculation.	5.8
Excessive interest charges on borrowed capital	11.1	Buying too much on credit	3.9
Too rapid expansion ...	10.5	Poor business location..	2.7
Losses from signing notes with recourse ..	9.6	Decline in rental income.	2.3
Buying too much on credit	9.5	Lack of adequate books.	2.1
Real-estate losses	6.1	Excessive interest charges on borrowed capital	2.1
Lack of adequate books.	5.6	Unfavorable changes in trading area	1.9
Automobile-accident losses	2.5	Signing notes with recourse	1.4
Failure to carry sufficient insurance	2.3	Real-estate losses	1.4
Unusual expenses	1.8	Unusual expenses	1.4
Inefficient and dishonest employees	.9	Failure to carry sufficient insurance	.7
		Automobile-accident judgments	.6
		Inefficient and dishonest employees	.6

Illustration No. 1—Causes of Failure in Bankrupt Businesses

For example, when a retail merchant fails, he probably owes money to several wholesalers or manufacturers and to other creditors, who must absorb part of the loss. When there are many such losses, business in general is seriously affected. In fact, several such losses may cause additional failures because certain individual creditors may suffer so badly.

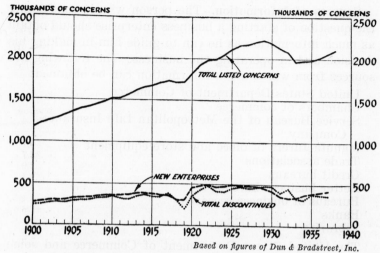

Based on figures of Dun & Bradstreet, Inc.

Illustration No. 2—United States Business Population

Obligations of the Businessman. One of the executives of the Chamber of Commerce of the United States has pointed out the following obligations of a businessman:

1. To *customers:* That they may have the best at the lowest cost, consistent with fairness to all those engaged in production and distribution.
2. To *workers:* That their welfare will not be sacrificed for the benefit of others, and that in their employment relations their rights will be respected.
3. To *management:* That it may be recognized in proportion to its demonstrated ability, considering always the proper interest of others.
4. To *competitors:* That there will be avoidance of every form of unfair competition.
5. To *investors:* That their rights will be safeguarded, and that they will be kept so informed that they can exercise their own judgment respecting their interests.
6. To the *public:* That the business will strive in all its operations and relations to promote the general welfare and, without yielding its rights of petition and protest, to observe faithfully the laws of the land.

Sources of Information. The person who is considering the question of starting a business enterprise should obtain as much information as he can to guide him in making his decision and in operating the business. The following are sources from which much information can be obtained:

United States Department of Commerce
Chambers of commerce
Service Bureau of the Metropolitan Life Insurance
    Company
Manufacturers of office and store equipment
Trade associations
Credit bureaus
Better business bureaus
Bureaus of business research
Banks
Libraries

The United States Department of Commerce and some of the other Federal departments issue bulletins designed to help the man who is organizing or operating a business. A catalogue of these publications can be obtained from the Department of Commerce or from the United States Printing Office.

The United States Chamber of Commerce, state chambers of commerce, and local chambers of commerce are interested primarily in promoting better business relations, the welfare of business enterprises, and civic improvement. These organizations either supply information on business conditions and operations or give directions as to the sources of such information. Some chambers of commerce act as branches of the United States Department of Commerce. Many local organizations of this type give advice and aid in the development of new business enterprises.

The Service Bureau of the Metropolitan Life Insurance Company co-operates with many business concerns and trade associations in making available information on accident prevention, budgetary control, better accounting methods, new products, sales outlets, and many other matters. Printed information is available free or at a reasonable price.

Manufacturers of office and store equipment, as well as trade associations such as the National Retail Grocers' Association and the National Retail Furniture Association, publish magazines and bulletins on business practices, business conditions, merchandising, and advertising. Some of these publications are available free; others are sold at a nominal price.

Credit bureaus are organized locally and nationally. Some are operated by trade associations. Bureaus of this type are in a position to give business advice and should be consulted in organizing and operating a business enterprise.

The National Better Business Bureau and local better business bureaus are equipped to give business advice pertaining largely to promotional schemes and the improvement of business relations. The services of the National Better Business Bureau are discussed in Chapter XXIV.

Many of the large universities operate bureaus of business research. The Bureau of Business Research of Harvard University is one of the best known. This particular bureau and some of the others have available bulletins and reports pertaining to business management, costs of operation, business failures, budgeting, accounting methods, advertising procedure, selling procedure, and many other business problems. Some of these bureaus issue monthly or quarterly publications on business conditions.

Banks offer important services to those who are organizing or operating businesses. Every prospective businessman should expect to have friendly and confidential relations with his banker. Before he starts in business, he should consult his banker for advice and for the purpose of reaching some preliminary understanding with regard to credit relations. A banker may often, from experience with other businessmen, make suggestions that will be very worth while in financing and starting a business.

Libraries in cities, schools, and universities provide current books and periodicals that should be consulted in solving many of the problems incidental to starting a business. Many important libraries are also operated by large corporations, business associations, and chambers of commerce.

QUESTIONS FOR DISCUSSION

1. Are large businesses more efficient than small ones?
2. Name some examples of small businesses in your local community.
3. Are there increasing or decreasing opportunities for starting a small business?
4. Instead of trying to think of some novel idea for a business, suggest a sound basis for a new type of business.
5. What factors should be considered in selecting the type of business?
6. Do most new businesses eventually succeed?
7. In the opinion of the owners what are some of the most important reasons for failure?
8. In the opinion of creditors what are some of the reasons why businesses fail?
9. When a person starts a business, to whom is he obligated in conducting the business on an ethical and sound basis?
10. From what sources can one obtain information that will be helpful in starting a business?
11. Are there any laws protecting businessmen?

PROBLEMS AND PROJECTS

1. How would you estimate the possibilities of starting a candy shop in a school?
2. How would you estimate the possibilities of starting a student dry-cleaning shop on a campus?
3. Make a study of a particular bankruptcy in your community to find out why the business failed.
4. From the local credit bureau, chamber of commerce, or some other source, find out the trend of recent bankruptcies and the reasons for those bankruptcies.
5. Make a list of the new businesses that have started in your community during the last twelve months, and see if you can draw any conclusions with regard to new types of businesses and the reasons for them.
6. From some local businessman find out the following information:
   (a) If business is good, why is it good?
   (b) If business is bad, why is it bad?
   (c) What is the situation with regard to new businesses of that same type?

CHAPTER II

FINANCIAL REQUIREMENTS OF STARTING
A BUSINESS

Purpose of the Chapter. A serious problem to consider in starting a business is to estimate the financial requirements so that sufficient capital may be obtained to start and to operate the business. One must either have a sufficient amount of money to start a business, or he must obtain money by borrowing or by selling part of his interest in the business. The discussion in this chapter will be based largely upon the problems of an individual in starting a sole proprietorship type of business. The following are some of the questions that will be answered in this chapter:

1. From what sources can money be obtained?
2. How much money will be required to start the business?
3. How can the estimated requirements be computed?
4. How soon can the business be expected to make a profit?

Problem of Working Capital. In a study made by the United States Department of Foreign and Domestic Commerce, lack of sufficient capital is given as one of the important reasons for business failures. An otherwise good business may fail because of lack of sufficient capital. *Capital,* or *working capital,* as referred to in this sense, means money. In general, working capital is the term used to refer to the cash available from day to day, week to week, or month to month, that can be used to pay for wages, rent, purchases, and other current expenses.

In starting a business, a person should not be too eager to own his own building or to buy expensive equipment. This caution applies equally well to the person who has already established a business, for there have been many

13

businessmen who, considering themselves successfully established, were ready to buy a building or expensive equipment. After buying the building or the equipment, they found that, because of a lack of working capital, they could not operate their businesses profitably.

It is therefore evident that it is important to conserve capital for use in operating the business. If all the funds are put into assets that cannot be sold readily, the money will not be available in an emergency. Until the business produces enough earnings to ensure plenty of money for operating purposes, it is unwise to put more than a minimum amount into a building or equipment. A building can be rented, and frequently equipment can be obtained on some plan of payment that does not require the immediate payment of the total amount in cash.

Some Financial Requirements. In starting a business, there must be enough money to buy necessary equipment and supplies and to leave a sufficient amount of cash available for operating expenses during the period in which the business is being organized. No profits can be expected from the average new enterprise until the organization has been completed. Some types of businesses require only a few days in which to become established; others require weeks, months, or even years. If there is not a sufficient amount of money available to operate the business during the time when little or no profit is made, failure is almost certain.

The following are some of the expenses that must be estimated in calculating the amount of money that will be required to operate a business during the period of organization:

Rent	Telephone and telegraph service
Taxes	Heat, light, power, and water
Insurance	Advertising and sales promotion
Interest	Delivery service
Wages and salaries	Installation service
Supplies	Printing and stationery
Repairs	

Illustration No. 3 shows the average expenses of different types of stores. These figures were compiled by the United States Department of Foreign and Domestic Commerce. A table such as this, or other similar tables, may be used in estimating the financial requirements of a business. For instance, let us assume that a person is contemplating going into the retail furniture business. The table shows the percentage of net sales represented by each of various expenses incurred in operating a furniture store. After estimating the sales, it is possible to estimate the approximate requirements of cash needed for the various expenses. In such an estimate the expenses should be considered at a rather high rate and the sales at a rather low figure. For instance, generous allowances should be made for all items such as rent, taxes, and advertising.

Making the Estimate. Many failures and bankruptcies that occur in business are the result of the failure of the businessman to analyze the financial requirements of the business. Optimism takes the place of sound judgment.

After one definitely determines the potential possibilities of the business, he should estimate the financial requirements of starting and operating the business until the time when there will be sufficient income to ensure a profit. The initial amount of money or capital should be sufficient, with the assistance of what loans are available, to carry the business conservatively through the stages of its infancy.

Illustration No. 4 shows an example of a sheet that can be used for estimating the cost of equipping a sandwich shop and bookstore. Illustration No. 5 is a form for estimating the expenditures of the first month, and Illustration No. 6 shows an estimate of the profit or the loss for the same month. In this particular case it is assumed that the sandwich shop and bookstore should establish itself during the first month. Other types of businesses will take a much longer time, and some will require less. From the three tables it is possible to estimate the amount of cash that will be necessary to carry the business through the first month of operation. The owner can therefore judge

ITEMS	PERCENTAGE OF NET SALES									
	Grocery, and Grocery and Meat Stores	Drug Stores	General Stores	Furniture Stores	Department Stores	Dry-Goods Stores	Hardware Stores	All Clothing Stores	Shoe Stores	Jewelry Stores
Rent	2.7	4.7	2.5	5.2	3.0	1.7	4.0	4.3	4.2	5.6
Heat, light, and power	.8	1.5	.3	.6	.7	.4	.4	.9	.6	1.1
Taxes and licenses	.7	1.4	.8	1.0	.9	1.0	1.4	.7	.8	1.6
Insurance	.3	.5	.3	.6	.7	1.3	.8	.8	.7	.5
Interest	.6	.5	.4	1.0	.7	2.7	1.2	.9	.8	1.4
Telephone and telegraph	.3	.4	.2	.5	.4	.3	.4	.3	...	.4
Boxes, wrapping, and other packing material	.4	.3	.3	.2	.3	.3	.1	.2	.2	.6
Postage, including parcel post	.1	.3	.04	.1	.5	.2	.3	.2	.3	.5
Maintenance and depreciation of delivery equipment, etc. (exclusive of labor)	.9	.8	.5	1.8	.2	...	1.1	.2	...	...
Depreciation other than that on delivery equipment; repairs	.6	1.0	.3	1.3	.5	.8	.8	.7	.2	1.9
Collection costs, including credit association dues	.9	.1	.3	1.1	.1	...	.03	.1	...	.2
Advertising	.4	.7	.4	1.0	1.7	.5	1.4	1.2	1.9	1.7

Illustration No. 3—Average Expenses of Different Types of Stores

in advance how much money must be borrowed, and should have some reasonable idea of whether this money can be paid back on schedule.

COST OF ITEMS NEEDED IN EQUIPPING THE BUSINESS	MINIMUM	MAXIMUM
Cash Register	$ 60.00	$150.00
Tables	40.00	75.00
Chairs	40.00	75.00
Lamps	20.00	25.00
Rugs	10.00	12.00
Redecoration	25.00	35.00
Dishes	40.00	70.00
Silverware	40.00	60.00
Glasses	12.00	15.00
Stoves	75.00	100.00
Cooking Utensils	30.00	45.00
Grill	10.00	15.00
Toaster	20.00	25.00
Uniforms for Waiters	40.00	48.00
Linens	35.00	40.00
Paper Napkins	10.00	10.00
Others:		
Desk	25.00	30.00
Shelves	40.00	50.00
Miscellaneous	50.00	75.00
TOTAL	$622.00	$955.00

Illustration No. 4—Form for Estimating the Cost of Equipment

Time Required to Make a Profit. The figures in the preceding example are estimates. After the first month definite figures on the operations of that month are available. It is then possible to study the actual figures to see how they compare with the estimates. If, for instance, the total income is $2,100 and the total expenses are $1,600, there is an actual profit of $500 for the first month of operation. The actual figures are consequently more favorable than

EXPENSES OF FIRST MONTH	MINIMUM	MAXIMUM
Salary Expense	$ 200.00	$ 220.00
Rent Expense	50.00	50.00
Heat, Light, and Water	30.00	40.00
Telephone Expense	5.00	5.00
Books	500.00	700.00
Candy	100.00	120.00
Stationery	60.00	75.00
Bakery Goods	150.00	210.00
Dairy Products	120.00	180.00
Meats	150.00	240.00
Groceries and Vegetables	180.00	240.00
Canned Goods	90.00	120.00
Laundry Expense	30.00	40.00
Others:		
TOTAL	$1,665.00	$2,240.00

Illustration No. 5—Form for Estimating the Expenditures

INCOME AND EXPENSE	MINIMUM	MAXIMUM
Income:		
Lunch Counter	$ 800.00	$ 950.00
Books	625.00	950.00
Candy	120.00	160.00
Stationery	70.00	90.00
TOTAL INCOME	$1,615.00	$2,150.00
Expenses (Deduct from Total Income)	1,665.00	2,240.00
Estimated Profit or Loss	$ 50.00 LOSS	$ 90.00 LOSS

Illustration No. 6—Form for Estimating the Profit or the Loss

the estimates. If the business is profitable during the first
month of operation, it should be profitable during succeeding months.

Let us now assume that during the first month of operation the sales amounted to $1,600 and the expenses to
$1,650. Hence there is only a $50 loss, which is not a
serious loss for a new business. Suppose, however, that
during that first month there was a certain unfavorable
factor, such as a week of vacation in a neighboring school,
that deprived the business of some customers. Let us
assume that the business during its first month of operation
has shown a steady increase in volume each week with the
exception of the week of vacation. It could naturally be
assumed then that during the succeeding month, under
normal conditions, the business should make a profit.

One must recognize that there is a strong possibility that,
during the early experiences in operating a business, there
will be very little, if any, net profit. Part of the expenses
must be paid out of the original capital until the business
begins to pay a profit.

In many types of retail businesses it is necessary to
operate at least two or three months before the business
becomes established. Occasionally a business may become
established within a few weeks and become profitable almost immediately, although in certain extreme cases the
business must operate for probably six months before it
becomes profitable. Many businesses never become profitable; and if a small retail business has not begun to make
a little profit within three or four months, the owner should
think about changing his methods or discontinuing the
business before he loses much money.

Influence of Turnover. It is important to estimate sales
carefully and conservatively. The actual cost of the building and the equipment can be computed accurately, but the
amount of sales must be estimated. If one is going to sell
on credit, his money will be tied up until he can make collections. It is therefore important to have a sufficient
amount of capital available to finance the business until

collections can be made. For instance, if most of the sales will be made on credit of thirty days and if purchases are made on the same basis, the accounts can probably be collected from customers in time to pay creditors. If sales are to be made on a cash basis, the cash to pay creditors will be available earlier.

The table in Illustration No. 7 shows the approximate rate of turnover of merchandise for various types of businesses. This ratio indicates the number of times the merchant will buy and sell all the merchandise in his store during the year. Naturally a business with a high rate of turnover needs less capital than one with a low rate of turnover because the former has a smaller amount of money invested in merchandise.

TYPE OF BUSINESS	TURNOVER
Retail grocery stores	9 to 13
Building materials stores	3 to 4
Department stores	2 to 5
Drugstores	2 to 4
Electrical supplies stores	3 to 5
Furniture stores	2 to 4
Hardware stores	1 to 2
Jewelry stores	.5 to 1
Men's furnishings stores	1.5 to 3
Meat markets	50 to 70
Restaurants	30 to 50
Shoe stores	1.5 to 2
Wholesale groceries	4.5 to 5

Illustration No. 7—Approximate Rate of Turnover

A turnover of three times a year means that the merchandise is on the shelves an average of four months from the time it is bought until it is sold. If the turnover is twelve times a year, the merchandise is on the shelves an average of thirty days. This table will therefore help in estimating the financial requirements based upon turnover. For instance, if one is contemplating starting a business in which the turnover is four times a year, with most of the goods sold on thirty days' credit (the average collection period being thirty days), the estimated time from the purchase of merchandise until the collection of cash from sales will be about four months (3+1). On the other hand, a businessman may buy merchandise on thirty days' credit. He therefore must have enough cash available to operate for three months $(2+1)$.

Problem of Obtaining Funds. To supplement his own funds in financing a new business enterprise, a person may obtain capital through a loan from a friend, a bank, a building and loan association, or an insurance company. In some cases capital is obtained through the sale of stock or of a part interest in a partnership. A friend may lend money without security, whereas a bank usually requires security except on some small loans. Money ordinarily cannot be obtained from an insurance company except as a loan on an insurance policy or a mortgage loan on real estate. Wholesalers frequently aid in the establishment of new businesses by granting credit on merchandise that is ordered. The period of credit may be thirty, sixty, or ninety days, depending upon the circumstances.

The advantages and the disadvantages of forming a partnership or a corporation as a means of obtaining funds for a business are discussed in Chapter III. When another person shares in the operation of a business, however, the profits are decreased for the originator of the enterprise. This sacrifice must be made in order to obtain financial assistance.

QUESTIONS FOR DISCUSSION

1. What is meant by working capital?
2. Why is working capital important?
3. What is the danger of investing money in a building when a business is being organized?
4. In what way is wholesale credit helpful in starting a new business?
5. What are some sources of funds for financing a new small enterprise?
6. What expenses should be taken into consideration in estimating the amount of money that will be required to operate a business?

7. What is turnover and how does it affect the profitableness and the working capital of a business?

8. Which type of business is likely to have the greater turnover of merchandise, a jewelry store or a grocery store? Why?

9. Suggest how you would determine the cost of equipping a new business.

10. How can one estimate the profitableness of a new enterprise?

11. How can one determine whether he has enough working capital to last until there is sufficient income to ensure a profit?

PROBLEMS AND PROJECTS

1. Using a table similar to the one in Illustration No. 4 on page 17, prepare minimum and maximum estimates of the cost of equipment for some particular small business in which you are interested or with which you are acquainted.

2. Assume that the following are the actual monthly expenses of a sandwich shop and bookstore:

Salary expense	$200.00
Rent expense	45.00
Heat, light, and water	35.00
Telephone expense	4.00
Books	550.00
Candy	100.00
Stationery	65.00
Bakery goods	175.00
Dairy products	125.00
Meats	185.00
Groceries and vegetables	210.00
Canned goods	100.00
Laundry expense	30.00

Assume that the proprietor has $2,000 invested in the business. How much monthly income must the business earn in order to pay him a salary of $2,400 a year plus a profit of 6 per cent on the money that he has invested in the business?

3. Problem No. 2 on page 12 required the making of an estimate with regard to starting a dry-cleaning shop. Using the same situation, estimate (a) the cost of equipping the business, (b) the expenditures of the first month, (c) the profit or the loss for that month. On the basis of these figures how much working capital (cash) should be available when the business is started?

4. Using the percentages in Illustration No. 3 (page 16) for a shoe store, prepare a statement showing the estimated monthly profit of a shoe store you plan to operate. Assume that a study discloses that you can sell in your community $2,000 worth of shoes a month and that the cost of goods sold will represent 60 per cent of the selling price.

5. Obtain an actual financial statement of a business represented in Illustration No. 3 (page 16), and compute the percentages to see how the actual figures compare with those shown in the table.

6. Ignoring the possibility of any income being made during the first month of operation, determine the exact amount of money that will be needed to start a business and to operate it for a month. Assume the following expenditures: rent, $100; insurance paid in advance for three months, $17.50; wages of a helper, $80; wrapping paper and miscellaneous supplies, $20; telephone service, $8.50; heat, $15; light and power, $26; water, $2.50; advertising, $40; delivery expense, $20; purchases of merchandise, $1,350; down payment on equipment, $354; installation costs, $125.

7. On the basis of Problem No. 6 assume that during the first month the cash sales totaled $200 and the purchases of merchandise amounted to $160. Assume also that $500 was borrowed for thirty days from a bank at the beginning of the month, interest at 6 per cent having been deducted in advance. What is the minimum amount of cash that was needed for the month?

8. The total sales of a store during one month amount to $4,165.15, and the costs of operation total $3,044.12. (a) How much rent will the proprietor pay if he is required to pay a rent of 4 per cent of net profit? (b) How much will he pay if he is required to pay 4 per cent of sales?

CHAPTER III

FORMS OF BUSINESS ORGANIZATION

Purpose of the Chapter. Many small businesses are started by a single individual and operated as sole proprietorships, but some are originally organized as partnerships or corporations. Some businesses that start as sole proprietorships are later changed to partnerships or corporations. Some that are organized as partnerships may be changed to corporations. Corporations are sometimes changed to partnerships or sole proprietorships.

The advantages and the disadvantages of the various forms of organization are discussed in this chapter. To make the study of business organization complete, this chapter also includes a study of the co-operative form of organization. The chapter will disclose answers to the following questions:

1. Shall the business be organized as a sole proprietorship, a partnership, or a corporation?
2. What are the advantages and the disadvantages of the different types of business organization?
3. What type of organization is best for a small business?
4. What are the characteristics and the functions of various types of business combinations, such as mergers and holding companies?
5. What are the fundamental characteristics of co-operative forms of organization?

Section I

Sole Proprietorships and Partnerships

The Sole Proprietorship, a Business Owned by One Person. An enterprise that is owned and operated by a single person is known as an *individual proprietorship,* an *individual enterprise,* or a *sole proprietorship.* Under this form of

24

organization one person usually owns the business, manages it, and is the sole recipient of the profits. The sole proprietor may thus perform the functions of a capitalist, a landowner, and a laborer. He is a capitalist because he owns the business and receives profits from it. He may be a landowner by owning the land on which the place of business is located. He is a laborer because he performs at least part of the labor in operating the business.

Financial Status of the Sole Proprietor. On the sole proprietor rests all the responsibility for the successful operation of the business. Provided he does not owe any debts, he has full claim to all the assets of the business. If he has debts, however, his creditors have claims against the assets. The following illustration is a simple financial statement of Mr. B. S. Davis, who operates a retail grocery as a sole proprietor:

ASSETS		CLAIMS AGAINST ASSETS	
Cash	$ 1,000	B. S. Davis, Proprietor-	
Merchandise	3,000	ship	$13,000
Equipment	1,000		
Land and Building	8,000		
		Total Claims Against	
Total Assets	$13,000	Assets	$13,000

This simple financial statement, which is known as a balance sheet, shows that the assets of the business are valued at $13,000. As Mr. Davis owes no debts, he has full claim to all the assets. If there are any earnings, he gets the total amount. Since he owns the land and the building, he does not have to pay any rent, although he must pay taxes on his property.

Advantages of the Sole Proprietorship. The fact that there is still a great number of individual enterprises indicates that this form of organization has definite advantages. Some of these are:

1. When one is the sole owner of a business, he usually has a certain pleasant feeling that he is his own "boss" and is responsible only to himself. He feels that he has more of a chance to be inventive or creative in

working out his own ideas. This feeling stimulates him to work hard to make his business a success.

2. Very closely related to this first advantage is the fact that all the profits belong to the sole proprietor. As he is the sole gainer, he is more likely to work overtime and to think continually of how his business can be operated more efficiently.

3. Because most proprietorships are small, the proprietor and his employees get to know each other personally. This relationship is conducive to a better understanding and a greater mutual interest between employer and employees. These same benefits should result from the close touch that the sole proprietor has with his customers.

4. The sole proprietor is not hindered in making decisions. As he need not consult business associates, he can act promptly in emergencies. If an unusual opportunity to buy merchandise or equipment arises, or if there is a desire to change the location of the business or to sell on credit terms rather than on a cash basis, there are no dissenting partners to hinder such action. Thus the management of an individual enterprise is flexible and can adjust itself easily to changing conditions.

5. One can usually commence or cease business activities as a sole proprietor without legal formality. One does not need to consult a lawyer and go through a large amount of "red tape" in order to organize an individual enterprise. In some types of businesses, however, such as a restaurant, it is necessary to obtain a permit or license before operations can be begun.

Disadvantages of the Sole Proprietorship. Although there are many advantages, there are also some disadvantages that confront the sole proprietor. Among the disadvantages are:

1. Each individual usually has a particular aptitude or ability. In one, it may be to sell merchandise; in another, it may be to purchase goods; in another, it may

be to keep records. All these activities are important to the success of a business, but the sole proprietor is likely to be deficient in judgment or ability in one or more of them. It is therefore easy to understand why many proprietorships end in failure within a short time.

2. Often there is need of additional capital for emergencies. Financial assistance on a large scale may be difficult to obtain when so much depends upon one person. The expansion of the business may be retarded because of the lack of capital of the sole owner. The size of the business may, then, be limited to the capital available.

3. The sole proprietor assumes a great amount of risk. It is true that he receives all the profits of the business, but likewise, he bears all the losses if the business is not successful. Should the business fail and be unable to pay its debts, the creditors have a claim against any of the assets of the proprietor. He may therefore lose not only the money he has invested in the enterprise but also his personal property, such as his automobile (and in some states, his home).

Kinds of Businesses Suited to the Sole Proprietorship Form of Ownership. This type of ownership is quite common, the majority of businesses being classified as sole proprietorships. The kind of business that is primarily concerned with rendering personal service is well suited to this type of ownership. Dentists, accountants, auctioneers, landscape gardeners, carpenters, painters, tourist camps, barber shops, beauty parlors, shoe repair shops, radio service stores, and automobile repair stations are examples of this class.

Another type of business that seems to be well adapted to the single proprietorship is the one that sells merchandise and service, principally of one kind, and does not require a large amount of capital. Newspaper and magazine stands, roadside markets, rental libraries, tearooms and restaurants, flower shops, gasoline filling stations, retail grocery stores, retail meat markets, dress shops, automobile parking lots, movers of household goods, and dry-cleaning establishments are examples of this type. In general, the type of business that can be operated suitably as a sole proprietorship is one (a) that can be managed by the proprietor or by persons hired by him and (b) that does not require a great amount of capital. There are, of course, exceptions to this general class.

The Partnership, a Business Owned by Two or More Persons. Mr. Davis, who operates the sole proprietorship mentioned in the preceding discussion, is confronted with the problem of expanding his business. He is now fifty-five years old and has operated the business successfully for many years. He sees new opportunities in his community for increasing his business, but he does not wish to assume full responsibility for the undertaking. He realizes that the expansion of the business would place considerable additional burden on him. He also realizes that in order to expand the business he needs additional capital, but he does not wish to borrow the money. Because of these reasons he decides to take a partner into his business.

Mr. W. H. Baker operates an adjoining meat market. He is a younger man than Mr. Davis and has proved to have both honesty and considerable business ability. It is thought that the combining of the two businesses should result in more customers for both groceries and meats. Customers who have been coming to the meat market will possibly become grocery customers also, and those who have been buying at the grocery of Mr. Davis may become meat customers. A discussion between the two men leads to a tentative agreement to form a partnership, provided a third person can be found to invest $13,000 in cash. In that case Mr. Baker will invest in the partnership the net assets of his business and an additional amount of cash to make his investment equal to $13,000. Each of the three partners will then have a net ownership of $13,000.

Mr. Davis and Mr. Baker finally find a young accountant, J. W. Miller, who has $5,000 and is able to borrow the remaining amount. As a result the articles of copartnership shown in Illustration No. 8 are written and signed by the three men.

Financial Status of the Partnership. Under the partnership agreement each partner is to have the same investment in the business. The money invested by Mr. Miller is to be used in joining the stores of Mr. Baker and Mr. Davis to form one large store. The following is a financial statement of Mr. Baker's business:

ASSETS		CLAIMS AGAINST ASSETS	
Cash	$ 500	Accounts Payable (Debts)	$ 100
Merchandise	200	W. H. Baker, Proprietor-	
Equipment	1,500	ship	7,100
Land and Building	5,000		
		Total Claims Against	
Total Assets	$7,200	Assets	$7,200

The net worth of Mr. Baker's business is $7,100. In other words, after deducting the amount of his debts from the total value of his assets, he has a net ownership of $7,100. As Mr. Baker's share in the new partnership is to be equal to that of Mr. Davis, Mr. Baker is required to invest $5,900 in cash in addition to the net assets of his business. Mr. Miller invests $13,000 in cash.

After the partnership is formed, the financial statement of the business appears as follows:

ASSETS		CLAIMS AGAINST ASSETS	
Cash	$20,400	Accounts Payable	
Merchandise	3,200	(Debts)	$ 100
Equipment	2,500	B. S. Davis, Proprietor-	
Land and Buildings	13,000	ship	13,000
		W. H. Baker, Proprietor-	
		ship	13,000
		J. W. Miller, Proprietor-	
		ship	13,000
		Total Claims Against	
Total Assets	$39,100	Assets	$39,100

Operation of the Partnership. In operating the partnership, Davis, Baker, and Miller divide the responsibilities. Mr. Davis supervises the grocery department; Mr. Baker

ARTICLES OF COPARTNERSHIP

This Contract, made and entered into on the first day of February, 1939, by and between B. S. Davis, of Buffalo, New York, party of the first part, W. H. Baker, of Buffalo, New York, party of the second part, and J. W. Miller, of Kenmore, New York, party of the third part:

WITNESSETH: That the said parties have this day formed a copartnership for the purpose of engaging in and conducting a retail grocery and meat store under the following stipulations, which are made a part of the contract:

FIRST: The said copartnership is to continue for a term of ten years from date hereof.

SECOND: The business shall be conducted under the firm name of Davis, Baker, and Miller, at 239 Fillmore Avenue, Buffalo, New York.

THIRD: The investments are as follows: B. S. Davis: Cash, $1,000; Merchandise, $3,000; Equipment, $1,000; Land and Buildings, $8,000; Total Investment, $13,000. W. H. Baker: Cash, $6,400; Merchandise, $200; Equipment, $1,500; Land and Buildings, $5,000; Total Assets, $13,100, less Accounts Payable, $100, equals Net Investment, $13,000. J. W. Miller: Cash, $13,000.

FOURTH: All profits or losses arising from said business are to be shared equally.

FIFTH: Each partner is to devote his entire time and attention to the business and to engage in no other business enterprise without the written consent of the others.

SIXTH: Each partner is to have a salary of $200 a month, the same to be withdrawn at such time or times as he may elect. No partner is to withdraw from the business an amount in excess of his salary without the written consent of the others.

SEVENTH: The duties of each partner are defined as follows: B. S. Davis is to supervise the grocery department. W. H. Baker is to supervise the meat department. J. W. Miller is to have charge of finances and records.

EIGHTH: No partner is to become surety or bondsman for anyone without the written consent of the others.

NINTH: In case of the death, incapacity, or withdrawal of one partner, the business is to be conducted for the remainder of the fiscal year by the surviving partners, the profits for the year allocated to the withdrawing partner to be determined by the ratio of the time he was a partner during the year to the whole year.

TENTH: In case of dissolution the assets are to be divided in the ratio of the capital invested at the time of dissolution.

IN WITNESS WHEREOF, The parties aforesaid have hereunto set their hands and affixed their seals on the day and year above written.

Bernard Stanley Davis
William Harry Baker
James Warren Miller

Illustration No. 8—Articles of Copartnership

supervises the meat department; and Mr. Miller has charge of finances and records.

During the year the three partners remodel the stores and combine them. They also buy some new equipment. At the end of the yearly fiscal period the following financial statement is prepared to show the status of the partnership:

ASSETS		CLAIMS AGAINST ASSETS	
Cash	$ 5,800	Accounts Payable	
Merchandise	11,500	(Debts)	$ 800
Equipment	10,000	B. S. Davis, Proprietor-	
Land and Buildings	16,500	ship	13,000
		W. H. Baker, Proprietor-	
		ship	13,000
		J. W. Miller, Proprietor-	
		ship	13,000
		Undivided Profits	4,000
		Total Claims Against	
Total Assets	$43,800	Assets	$43,800

Has the partnership had a successful year? Each partner has received a salary of $200 a month (according to the terms of the partnership agreement); and, in addition, the profits for the year have been $4,000, which is a return of approximately 10 per cent on the proprietorship. Such a return on an investment is usually considered very good. Mr. Miller, who had to borrow some of the money he used for his investment, probably had to pay 6 per cent interest. As he received a return of approximately 10 per cent, the investment was profitable to him also.

Other Purposes for Which a Partnership May Be Formed. In addition to the advantages previously explained, there are other reasons for the formation of partnerships. Some of them are:

1. In order to eliminate competition, two or more sole proprietors may combine their businesses by organizing a partnership.
2. An owner who wishes to retire from active management without retiring from the business may admit a partner to take over the active management.

3. By the combining of two or more businesses, an economy may be effected through the reduction of certain overhead expenses, such as advertising, supplies, equipment, fuel, and rent.

Advantages of the Partnership. The following are some of the advantages of the partnership form of business organization:

1. The business is likely to be operated more efficiently than a sole proprietorship because two or more persons share in the management. One partner may have special sales ability; another may have an aptitude for buying the right kind, quality, and quantity of merchandise. One partner may propose a change in the business, and the other partner may be able to point out disadvantages in or modifications of the plan that were not apparent to the one who made the original proposal. The combined abilities of the partners should result in more efficient operation than there would be if each were conducting a business as a sole proprietor.

2. When a business is started, more capital can be supplied through the investments of two or more people than could be obtained ordinarily by one person. Some businesses require a greater amount of capital for equipment and merchandise than one person might be able to supply; but sufficient initial capital can be obtained if several persons enter into a partnership. As a rule, the additional capital needed for expansion is obtained more easily if there are several partners.

3. Because it has several owners who are responsible for the ownership and the management, the partnership usually has better credit than the sole proprietorship.

4. Each partner is likely to have a large personal following that he can bring to the business.

5. Because of their financial responsibilities, the partners will take a greater interest in the business than would be taken by employees hired by the business.

Disadvantages of the Partnership. The following are some of the disadvantages of the partnership form of business organization:

1. According to law each member of the partnership has an *unlimited* financial liability for all the debts of the business. Each partner is responsible for his share of the business debts; but if one or some of the partners are unable to pay their share, one partner may have to pay all the debts. Suppose that the partnership of Davis, Baker, and Miller should fail and that, after all the business assets have been converted into cash and the liabilities paid with that cash, there is still $9,000 due the creditors of the partnership. Each partner should contribute $3,000 to the partnership so that there will be enough money to pay the remaining business debts. If both Baker and Miller, however, are unable to contribute their $6,000, but Mr. Davis has enough property, the law can compel him to contribute the entire $9,000. In such a case Mr. Davis would then have a *right of contribution claim* against each of the other partners for $3,000; that is, he would have a claim against these partners and might, if necessary, sue them individually or jointly for the amount that he had had to pay in their behalf.

2. There is always danger of disagreement among partners. The majority of the partners may want to change the nature of the business but are unable to do so because of the refusal of one partner. For example, a partnership may have been formed for the purpose of conducting a retail piano business. After a while the majority of the partners feel that it would be wise to discontinue selling pianos and handle radios. As one partner disagrees, however, the partnership cannot make the change, although the change may seem very desirable.

3. Each partner is bound by the contracts of other partners if such contracts pertain to the ordinary operations of the business. There is always the possibility

of friction and hard feeling between partners if one partner makes a contract that turns out to be unprofitable to the partnership. Furthermore, if there are many partners, certain ones may feel that they are not having their proper share in the management while others have too much authority. This situation may cause disagreements and impair the efficiency of the business. Such a condition may be partly prevented if the articles of copartnership specifically state the duties of each partner.

4. The life of a partnership is uncertain. Usually, when the contract for a partnership is drawn up, a definite length of time, such as ten years, is fixed for the existence of the business. If one partner dies, however, there must be a dissolution of the partnership. The deceased partner may have been the principal manager, and, as a result of his death, the business may suffer. Or the heirs of the deceased partner may demand from the surviving partners an unfair price for the share of the deceased partner; or they may insist upon the complete liquidation of the partnership so that they can obtain the share belonging to the deceased partner. In the latter case, the assets that are sold usually do not bring a fair price, and consequently all the partners suffer a loss. Under the laws of most states the bankruptcy of any partner, the entrance of a new partner, and the incapacity of a partner are other causes that may bring a sudden termination of the partnership just at a time when the business is beginning to prosper.

5. The amount of funds that a partnership may obtain is limited by the contributions of the partners, the earnings of the business, and the amount that can be borrowed. It is difficult for a partnership to obtain enough capital to carry on a large enterprise unless the members of the partnership are individually wealthy or unless they are many in number. Too many partners, however, may cause inefficiency in operation.

6. Sometimes there is not a satisfactory distribution of the partnership profits according to the ability and the efforts of the individual partners. The profits are shared on the basis of the partnership agreement. If no provision is made in the agreement, the law requires an equal division of the profits. Some of the common methods of distributing profits among partners are: equally; in ratio to the capital of each partner; according to some other agreed ratio, such as 40 per cent to one partner and 60 per cent to the other partner; with interest allowed on the capital of each partner and then the remaining profits divided equally or in some other ratio.

Limited Partnership. In an ordinary partnership each partner is liable for the entire debt contracted by the partnership. Under the laws of some states a partnership can be formed that has at least one general partner and one special, or *limited,* partner whose name does not appear in the firm name. In some states the name of the limited partner is included in the firm name. The limited partner is the only one who is not liable for the debts of the partnership in case of bankruptcy. This type of partnership is known as a *limited partnership.* In some partnerships of this type the word *Limited,* or the abbreviation *Ltd.,* must be used after the name. Usually the law requires that a certificate of limited partnership be filed in a public office of record and that proper notice be given to each creditor with whom the limited partnership does business. If these requirements are not fulfilled, the limited partners have unlimited liability in the same manner as a general partner.

Joint-Stock Company. The so-called joint-stock company is a form of partnership. The ownership of such a company is represented by shares, or certificates, of stock that ordinarily may be sold at will by the owners, or partners, without consulting the other owners. A change in ownership does not dissolve the joint-stock company as it would an ordinary partnership. The management of a joint-stock company is in the hands of a board of directors, who are elected by the individual shareholders. The board of directors may operate the business or may hire the necessary individuals to manage the business.

The shareholders of a joint-stock company have essentially the same liabilities as the partners in an ordinary partnership. In other words, they are individually or collectively liable for any debts or any acts of the company. This type of company is not particularly common, although some partners prefer to change the form of their organization to a joint-stock company rather than to a corporation.

Kinds of Businesses Suited to the Partnership Form of Ownership. The partnership form of ownership is found in many businesses that furnish more than one kind of product or service. Each partner usually looks after some phase of the business in which he has special ability. Some examples of businesses that are well suited to this form are automobile sales and repair companies; retail grocery and meat markets; restaurants; radio stores with both sales and repair departments; barber shops and beauty parlors; automobile repair and painting shops; camera stores

Underwood & Underwood.

Illustration No. 9—Businesses Commonly Operated as Partnerships

with film developing and printing services; men's clothing
stores and tailor shops; laundries with dry-cleaning departments; and landscape gardeners rendering tree sur-
gery service. For instance, in the case of an automobile
company having separate sales and repair departments,
one partner may handle sales and the other partner repairs.
Some garages have a new-car sales department, a used-
car sales department, and a service department, with a
partner in charge of each of the three departments.

QUESTIONS FOR DISCUSSION

1. Name at least two advantages of a sole proprietorship.
2. Name at least one disadvantage of a sole proprietorship.
3. What are some common types of businesses operated as
   sole proprietorships?
4. Name two or more advantages of a partnership.
5. Name at least two disadvantages of a partnership.
6. What is a limited partnership?
7. What is a joint-stock company?
8. What are articles of copartnership?
9. How is a partnership affected when a partner withdraws
   from the business?
10. If a partnership that fails and ceases operations is unable to
    pay all its debts, what may the creditors do?
11. If one partner in a business signs a contract to buy mer-
    chandise for the business and the two other partners object,
    is the partnership responsible for the contract?
12. If a person who is operating a sole proprietorship wishes to
    retire, what is the advantage of forming a partnership to
    continue the business?
13. Discuss the advantages of a joint-stock company as com-
    pared with an ordinary partnership.
14. What types of businesses are suited to the partnership form
    of ownership?
15. Analyze the financial statement of W. H. Baker on page 29
    and explain the financial interest which Mr. Baker has in the
    business.

Section II

Corporations and Corporate Combinations

The Corporation, a Business Owned by Stockholders. Davis, Baker, and Miller, of the partnership mentioned previously, have learned from reading and observation that a large number of small businesses and nearly all the very large businesses are corporations. They believe that there is an opportunity to expand their business by purchasing two small stores and operating the two new stores as branches. They make a study of the corporation as a form of business organization and find that it is an association of individuals organized under a charter granted by the state. It is, in a sense, an artificial person created by the laws of the state.

The essential characteristics of a corporation are found to be as follows:

1. The ownership is divided into equal parts called shares of capital stock.
2. The stockholders own the business. (There must be at least three.)
3. The stockholders elect directors.
4. The directors formulate general plans and policies and appoint the officers.
5. The officers in a small corporation usually consist of a president, a secretary, and a treasurer.
6. The officers have charge of the active management of the business.
7. The officers have the privilege of employing additional persons, if necessary, to operate the business.

The corporation is permitted to make contracts, to borrow money, to own property, to sue and to be sued in its own name. Any act performed for the corporation by an officer or an authorized employee is not done in the name of the officer or the employee, but in the name of the corporation. For example, the treasurer of a corporation has the power to borrow money for the corporation. As he acts for the corporation, he signs his name as agent of the corporation.

After consulting a lawyer who is experienced in corporation law, and after studying the disadvantages of the partnership and the advantages of the corporation, Davis, Baker, and Miller decide to incorporate. The capital of the corporation will be $50,000, and consist of 500 shares of par-value common stock. (Common stock is explained in detail later.) As the partners have an investment of $13,000 each, or a total of $39,000, plus $4,000 of undivided profits, they decide to leave the undivided profits in the business. They effect a tentative organization, and each subscribes for a number of shares of stock equal to his investment in the partnership (130 shares each). They then submit to the secretary of state (or the state securities commission) the articles of incorporation shown in Illustration No. 10 and apply for a charter.

The charter of the corporation is granted by the state. The three men are issued 130 shares each. The remaining 110 shares are unissued, but may be issued later whenever the stockholders decide to sell them in order to expand the business. The corporation is to assume the liabilities of the partnership. After the corporation has been formed, the following financial statement is prepared:

ASSETS		CLAIMS AGAINST ASSETS	
Cash	$ 5,800	Accounts Payable	
Merchandise	11,500	(Debts)	$ 800
Equipment	10,000	Capital Stock Outstand-	
Land and Buildings	16,500	ing	39,000
		Undivided Profits	
		(Surplus)	4,000
		Total Claims Against	
Total Assets	$43,800	Assets	$43,800

The ownership of the corporation is in the same hands as was the ownership of the partnership. The ownership of the corporation, however, is evidenced by the outstanding stock. Each former partner has in his possession stock certificates indicating that he owns 130 shares of stock at $100 each.

Certificate of Incorporation

OF THE

State of New York, } ss:
County of Erie

We, the undersigned, of full age, being desirous of associating ourselves together for the purposes hereinafter mentioned, pursuant to and in conformity with Acts of the Legislature of the State of New York, relating to Membership Corporations, do hereby certify and declare that we are all of full age, two-thirds of us are citizens of the United States and......all......of us....are....resident of the State of New York.

We do further certify and declare as follows:

First.—That the particular objects for which said Corporation is formed are as follows, viz.:

To operate two or more retail grocery and meat stores.

Second.—That the name of said Corporation shall be......Davis, Baker, and Miller, Inc.

Third.—That the territory in which the operations of said Corporation are to be principally conducted　　　　Buffalo, New York

Fourth.—That the principal office of said Corporation shall be located in the......City...... of......Buffalo......County of......Erie......and State of New York.

Fifth.—That the number of Directors of said Corporation shall be......three......

Sixth.—That the names and places of residence of the persons to be the Directors of said Corporation until its first annual meeting are:

B. S. Davis, 736 Hartman Avenue, Buffalo, New York

W. H. Baker, 1210 Robinson Street, Buffalo, New York

J. W. Miller, 458 Dayton Street, Kenmore, New York

Seventh.—That the annual meeting of said Corporation shall be held on the......first...... day of......April......in each and every year.

In testimony whereof, we have made and signed this Certificate in duplicate this ......fourth......day of......February......one thousand nine hundred and......forty......

Bernard Stanly Davis

William Harry Baker

James Warren Miller

Illustration No. 10—Articles of Incorporation

Management of a Corporation. As only the three stock-holders own the business, they become the directors. Among themselves they elect officers. Mr. Davis is elected president; Mr. Baker, vice-president; and Mr. Miller, secretary and treasurer. A simple organization chart of the new corporation is shown in Illustration No. 11.

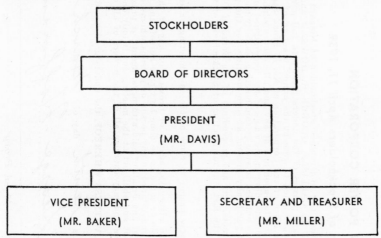

Illustration No. 11—An Organization Chart of a Corporation

Each stockholder will have 130 votes on matters arising in the meetings of the stockholders. Voting stockholders usually have one vote for each share owned. Should Mr. Miller sell 66 of his shares to Mr. Baker, Mr. Baker would own 196 shares, or one share more than 50 per cent of the total 390 shares of stock that have been issued. Then Mr. Baker could control the corporation.

The law usually requires a corporation to send each stockholder, at a specified time in advance, a notice of a meeting to be held by the stockholders. If a stockholder cannot attend the meeting personally, he may be represented by a proxy. A proxy is a written authorization for someone to vote in behalf of the person signing the proxy. It is a common practice for a blank proxy to be included in the letter announcing a stockholders' meeting. A form of proxy is shown in Illustration No. 12.

NIAGARA HUDSON POWER CORPORATION

Proxy for Annual Meeting of Stockholders April 11, 1939

KNOW ALL MEN BY THESE PRESENTS: That the undersigned stockholder of Niagara Hudson Power Corporation hereby constitutes and appoints FLOYD L. CARLISLE, GEORGE H. HOWARD and RANDALL J. LE BOEUF, JR., and each of them, attorneys, agents and proxies of the undersigned, with full power of substitution, for and in the name, place and stead of the undersigned to vote at the annual meeting of stockholders of Niagara Hudson Power Corporation, to be held at the office of the Corporation at No. 15 Broad Street, New York, N.Y, on Tuesday, April 11, 1939, at 11:00 o'clock in the forenoon and at any and all adjournments thereof, all of the shares of the Common Stock of the said Corporation standing in the name of the undersigned on March 3, 1939, the date of record for the determination of stockholders entitled to vote at said meeting, as fully and with the same effect as the undersigned would, might or could do if personally present at such meeting, for the purpose of:

1. Ratifying, approving and confirming all contracts, acts and proceedings of the Board of Directors, Executive Committee and officers of the Corporation since the last Annual Meeting of Stockholders of the Corporation as set forth in the minute book;

2. Electing a Board of Directors;

3. Considering and transacting any other business proper to come before said meeting or any adjournment or adjournments thereof;

hereby ratifying and confirming all that said attorneys, agents or proxies, or any of them, or their substitute or substitutes, may lawfully do or cause to be done by virtue hereof, and hereby revoking all proxies heretofore given by the undersigned to any person or persons whomsoever in respect of such shares of stock. A majority of any or all of said attorneys, agents or proxies, or substitute or substitutes, who shall be present and shall act at the meeting (or if only one shall be present and act, then that one) shall have and may exercise all of the powers of all of said attorneys, agents and proxies.

IN WITNESS WHEREOF, the undersigned has duly signed this proxy this *tenth* day of *March*, 1939.

George Hoffman ... L. S.

Illustration No. 12—A Proxy

Closed Corporations. A *closed corporation* is one that does not offer its securities for public sale. It is frequently owned by just a few stockholders, some of whom may be actively engaged in operating the business in the same manner as partners operate a business. Davis, Baker, and Miller, Incorporated, is an example of a closed corporation. The three former partners own all the stock and operate the business.

A closed corporation, under the laws of most states, does not need to make its activities known to the public, for its securities are not offered for general sale. It must, however, submit reports to the state from which it obtained its charter, or for tax purposes must submit reports to all states in which it operates.

Open Corporations. An *open corporation* is one that offers its securities for general sale. For the benefit of prospective investors an open corporation must furnish to the public information regarding its earnings, assets, and liabilities. These reports must be furnished in accordance with Federal and state laws and the rules of the stock exchanges.

Such corporations often have a very large number of stockholders, some having as many as several hundred thousand. Most of the stockholders in these large corporations own only a few shares; but, because of the great number of stockholders, such a corporation has a very large amount of capital. Naturally, these large corporations are not so simple in organization as Davis, Baker, and Miller, Inc. The form of organization becomes more complicated as the business becomes larger.

Capital Stock. The ownership of a stock certificate of a corporation is evidence of part ownership in the corporation. A stockholder of a corporation does not have the same responsibility as a partner in a partnership; that is, he has no liability beyond the extent of his ownership. If the corporation fails, he may lose the money that he has invested in the corporation, but the creditors cannot collect any additional amounts from the stockholders.

Common Stock. The two kinds of stock most frequently issued by a corporation are known as *common stock* and *preferred stock*. So far as profits are concerned, the owners of common stock are in much the same position as the partners in a partnership. They participate in the management of the business and share in the profits if there are any. They do not obtain earnings, however, until all other investors have been paid. Furthermore, there is no fixed rate of earning on common stock. The stock issued to Davis, Baker, and Miller is common stock. Their ownership of the stock permits them to operate the business.

Illustration No. 13—A Common-Stock Certificate of No Par Value

Preferred Stock. Preferred stock, as its name indicates, has some kind of preference over the ordinary, or common, stock. A point of distinction applicable to all preferred stock is preference in the distribution of profits. Whenever profits are distributed, the preferred stockholders must receive their dividend first. A corporation must, of course, pay its regular debts and interest on borrowed money before any dividend can be paid. Holders of preferred stock usually receive a fixed dividend, ranging from 5 to 7 per cent of the face value of the stock.

Let us see just how this plan works out. Suppose that a certain corporation has issued $50,000 of 7 per cent preferred stock and also $50,000 of common stock, and that the profits for a certain year are $4,000. The preferred stockholders will receive their 7 per cent of $50,000, which is $3,500. Then there is only $500 remaining, which is available for the common stockholders. But suppose that the same corporation should earn $12,000 in profits during a certain other year. In this case the preferred stockholders would be paid their fixed rate of dividend (7 per cent), or $3,500; and there would be $8,500 left for distribution to the common stockholders. If this whole amount were distributed, the common stockholders would receive a dividend of 17 per cent. It is, however, usually not a good policy to distribute all the profits. It is better to keep some of the profits as a reserve (or surplus). If all the profits are paid out in the form of cash, a company may later need to borrow money in order to carry on its operations. Some corporations prefer to leave a surplus in the business so that, if no profit is earned during a particular period, they may still pay a dividend out of the surplus that was previously earned. If a corporation pays out all its earnings and profits, it may have serious difficulty if a loss is suffered during any particular year. It is therefore considered good practice for corporations to build up a surplus.

Ordinarily the preferred stockholders do not participate in the management of the business, although the ownership of certain types of preferred stock does permit such activity in case dividends are not declared and paid regularly. Some kinds of preferred stock carry a special privilege with regard to claims against the assets. For instance, if the corporation ceases operations, the preferred stockholders must be paid before the common stockholders.

For example, suppose that a corporation has outstanding $50,000 of common stock and also $50,000 of stock that is preferred as to assets. During the ensuing liquida-

*Illustration No. 14—A Preferred-Stock Certificate
of Par Value*

tion process all the assets are converted into cash and all
the creditors are paid. There then remains $80,000 in cash.
The sum of $50,000 must be paid to the stockholders whose
stock is preferred as to assets. Consequently the holders
of common stock receive only $30,000. Thus the common
stockholders receive only 60 per cent of the full face value
of their stock. Had there been no preference as to assets,
all the stockholders, both common and preferred, would
have shared equally, each group receiving $40,000.

When a corporation goes out of business, however, the
preferred stockholders seldom get much from the assets
because the assets usually are sold for much less than
their value on the books of the corporation and often do
not bring enough to pay the creditors.

Preferred stock may be *cumulative* or *noncumulative.* If
it is cumulative, the owners are entitled to the payment of
a dividend for each year, even though the dividend for any
particular year was not paid during that year. If, for instance, profits are not distributed for a year or more, all
the dividends on preferred stock that were due in the past
must be paid to the preferred stockholders before the common stockholders begin to receive any dividends again.

Suppose, for example, a corporation has $50,000 of 7 per cent cumulative preferred stock. During one year there are no earnings and no dividends are paid. During the following year the earnings are large. In this second year a dividend of 14 per cent, or $7,000, must be paid to the holders of the cumulative preferred stock before a dividend can be paid to the common stockholders.

There is a common misunderstanding that the rate of dividend specified on preferred stock is guaranteed. It is not guaranteed in any sense of the word, but the preferred stockholders must be paid dividends before the common stockholders have a right to any.

If the stock is noncumulative, the preferred stockholders are not assured their income in case the corporation ceases temporarily to pay dividends. If the corporation does not earn a profit or have a surplus, it may not declare dividends. In such a case the preferred stockholders begin to receive their regular dividend when the company makes profits again, but they do not receive dividends for the time when no profits were earned.

Preferred stock may also be classified as *participating* or *nonparticipating*. Ordinarily the common stockholders share in the profits after the preferred stockholders have been paid. If the common stockholders have a right to all the earnings beyond a fixed percentage paid to the preferred stockholders, the preferred stock is said to be nonparticipating; but if the preferred stockholders share in the excess earnings under some predetermined plan, the preferred stock is said to be participating. In other words, this stock participates with the common stock in the earnings beyond the fixed rate of dividend paid to the preferred stockholders.

There are many ways in which the preferred stock may participate. For instance, the fixed rate for preferred stock may be given to both the preferred and the common stockholders, and then all the remainder of the profits may be distributed to the preferred stockholders. In another case the preferred stockholders may receive their fixed rate, the common stockholders the same rate; then the preferred stockholders 4 per cent, the common stockholders 2 per cent; and finally the preferred stockholders the remainder.

Which Kind of Stock to Issue. One of the problems that must be decided in organizing a corporation is the amount of capital stock to be issued and the kind or kinds. When application for a charter is made, information must be given as to whether all the stock of the proposed corporation is to be common or whether part is to be common and part preferred, and which kind or kinds of preferred are to be issued. The charter issued to the corporation states the kind or kinds of stock and the amount of each that may be issued. No other kinds can be issued unless authorization is received from the government.

In starting a business, it is usually a good plan to issue only common stock. Even though profits may be made from the very beginning, it is often desirable to use those profits in the expansion of the business. If preferred stock is issued, the corporation is under an obligation to pay the specified dividend. If the company begins business with common stock and later finds it desirable to expand the business, it may then issue preferred stock in order to induce others to invest in the company.

Par-Value and No-Par-Value Stock. In many states, corporations have the privilege of issuing par-value stock or no-par-value stock. Illustration No. 13 (page 44) shows a certificate for no-par-value stock; Illustration No. 14 (page 46), a certificate for par-value stock.

Each certificate of stock must show the number of shares that it represents. If the stock has a par value, the certificate must indicate that value. The par value of a share may be almost any amount, but it is usually $100, $50, or $10. Many corporations prefer to issue stock with a low par value, such as $10, in order that they may induce a large number of small investors to buy the stock. For example, if stock sold at $1,000 a share, there would be fewer people who could buy it than if the stock sold for $10 a share. With a large number of people owning stock in a company, there should be many "boosters" for that company. But, on the other hand, a large number of stock-holders will mean more clerical work in keeping the records of the various stockholders, in sending out many more notices of stockholders' meetings, in computing dividends, and in writing dividend checks.

Dividends on par-value stock may be declared in terms of a percentage of the par value, but they are required by most stock exchanges to be specified as a certain amount on each share. Dividends on no-par-value stock are always quoted as a certain amount a share.

The value indicated on a stock certificate should not be confused with the *market value,* which is the value at which the stock is bought and sold on the stock exchanges. A share of a certain stock may have a par value of $50; but, because the company that issued it has been prosperous and has been paying large dividends, certain people may be willing to pay $60 for it. If a corporation has not been successful financially, the market value of its stock is likely to be less than the par value.

No-par-value stock is essentially the same as par-value stock, except that the former bears no statement that pro-fesses to indicate its value at the time it is issued. Its use is intended as a means of avoiding the inference that the stock is worth a certain amount.

Another term, *book value,* is often used in connection with the value of a share of stock. The book value of a share is found by dividing the net worth of the corpora-tion by the total number of shares outstanding. Thus, if the net worth of a corporation is $75,000 and the number of shares of stock outstanding is 1,000, the book value of each share is $75, regardless of whether the stock has a par value of $50 or $100, or whether it has no par value.

Corporate Bonds. Illustration No. 15 shows another means by which a corporation may obtain additional money. By reading the face of this corporation bond, you will see that the bond is a written promise to pay a defi-nite sum of money at a specified time. It also contains an agreement to pay interest at a specified rate at certain in-

Illustration No. 15—Coupon Bond

tervals. Bonds do not represent a share in the ownership of the corporation; they are evidence of a debt owed by the corporation. All bondholders have a preferred claim against the earnings of the corporation, for they must be paid before stockholders share in the earnings.

There are two general types of bonds: (a) *mortgage bonds* and (b) *income,* or *debenture, bonds.* The issuer of

mortgage bonds pledges some specific assets as a guarantee that the interest and the principal will be paid according to the terms specified in the bonds. The assets
that are commonly used as security for such bonds are
land, buildings, or machinery. Debenture bonds have no
specific assets behind them. They are secured by the faith
and the credit of the corporation that issues them. Public
corporations, such as city, state, and Federal governments,
usually issue debenture bonds when they need to borrow
money. Private corporations usually find it difficult to sell
debenture bonds, although they probably prefer to issue
debenture bonds instead of mortgage bonds. If the latter
type is issued and the corporation is unable to meet some
of the interest payments as they fall due, the bondholders
may start foreclosure proceedings against the corporation.
Such proceedings are usually instituted through the trustee
of the bondholders. The trustee is ordinarily a bank that
holds the mortgage representing the security for the mortgage bonds.

There are two general forms of bonds: (a) *coupon bonds*
and (b) *registered bonds*. As coupon bonds are generally
payable to the bearers, the corporation that issues them
has no way of knowing who are the owners at the time
interest payments are due. Because of this fact, coupons,
one for each interest-due date, are attached to such a bond.
The owner of the bond may collect the interest by clipping
off a coupon and cashing it at the office of the corporation
or at a bank on or after the date specified. For example,
the interest on the coupon bond illustrated is payable on
June 1 at the Chase National Bank, of New York. The
coupon may be presented at this bank for payment, or it
may be given to any other bank for collection. If the owner
of the bond lives in Buffalo, he may turn the coupon over
to his local bank for collection from the bank in New York.
The bank in Buffalo will charge a fee to the owner of the
bond. The corporation that issued the bonds will settle
with the Chase National Bank, of New York.

If registered bonds are issued, the corporation keeps a
record of each owner and pays the interest and the prin-

cipal by check to the registered owner. This type of bond means more clerical work for the corporation, but it is preferred by many people who buy bonds.

Sometimes *convertible bonds* are issued. The holder of such bonds has the privilege of exchanging them for a definite number of shares of stock. This feature is attractive to the holder. He receives a fixed rate of interest as long as he holds the bonds; and later, if the corporation should begin to earn large profits and to pay large dividends, he may exchange the bonds for stock and begin receiving dividends instead of interest.

Expansion of a Corporation. Davis, Baker, and Miller, Inc., decide to carry out their original plan to expand the business by buying the land and the buildings for two additional stores. They have investigated carefully the stores that they wish to buy. They find that the two stores can be bought for $30,000, which they believe is a fair price. They are now confronted with the problem of raising sufficient capital to make the purchase and add $10,000 to the cash operating fund. Although they realize that they will have to pay a higher rate of earnings on preferred stock than they would on bonds, they decide to sell preferred stock, for it will place on them no obligation to repay to the stockholders the original amount of the investment. If they were to issue bonds, however, the bondholders would at a specified time have to be repaid the principal of their investment. If business conditions were to continue to be good, the bonds could probably be paid off easily; but if business conditions were to become unfavorable, the corporation might not be able to pay the principal of the bonds. The issuing of preferred stock is therefore the more advisable procedure.

The officers of the corporation obtain permission from the secretary of state to issue $40,000 worth of preferred stock with a fixed dividend rate of 7 per cent a year. The stock is offered for sale at $100 a share. The officers succeed in selling only 110 shares of the stock, which bring them only $11,000 in cash. They therefore decide that their only alternative is to issue bonds. They obtain permission from the secretary of state to issue $30,000 worth of bonds in denominations of $100 with interest at 6 per cent a year. The corporation closes the sale after selling $29,000 worth of bonds at the par value. With the proceeds from these sales it purchases the two stores. The financial statement of the corporation then appears as follows: (It is assumed that no time has elapsed between the date on which the previous statement was prepared and the date on which the following statement was prepared.)

ASSETS		CLAIMS AGAINST ASSETS	
Cash	$15,800	Accounts Payable (Debts)	$ 800
Merchandise	11,500	Bonds Payable	29,000
Equipment	10,000	Preferred Stock	11,000
Land and Buildings	46,500	Common Stock	39,000
		Undivided Profits (Surplus)	4,000
Total Assets	$83,800	Total Claims Against Assets	$83,800

A more conservative procedure for this corporation would have been to rent the store buildings. If funds were then needed to buy additional merchandise and equipment, and the officers did not wish to obtain a short-time loan from the bank, the corporation could have issued the preferred stock and the bonds.

Suppose that, at the end of another fiscal period, the financial statement of the corporation appears as follows:

ASSETS		CLAIMS AGAINST ASSETS	
Cash	$18,500	Accounts Payable (Debts)	$ 500
Merchandise	13,000	Bonds Payable	29,000
Equipment	12,500	Preferred Stock	11,000
Land and Buildings	46,000	Common Stock	39,000
		Undivided Profits (Surplus)	10,500
Total Assets	$90,000	Total Claims Against Assets	$90,000

The directors declare and pay the 7 per cent dividend on the preferred stock. This payment reduces the cash by $770 and the undivided profits by a like amount. A 6 per cent dividend is also declared and paid on the common stock. This dividend reduces the cash by $2,340 and the undivided profits by the same amount. A financial statement prepared at this time appears as follows:

ASSETS		CLAIMS AGAINST ASSETS	
Cash	$15,390	Accounts Payable (Debts)	$ 500
Merchandise	13,000	Bonds Payable	29,000
Equipment	12,500	Preferred Stock	11,000
Land and Buildings	46,000	Common Stock	39,000
		Undivided Profits (Surplus)	7,390
Total Assets	$86,890	Total Claims Against Assets	$86,890

Advantages of the Corporation. The corporation has a number of advantages as compared with the sole proprietorship and the partnership. Some of these are:

1. Except in a few cases the owners (stockholders) are not legally liable for the debts of the corporation beyond their investments in the stock. Thus persons, whether they have only a few dollars to invest or whether they have thousands of dollars, may invest in a corporation without incurring a liability.

2. The corporation is a more permanent type of organization than the sole proprietorship or the partnership. It may continue to operate as long as the term stated in the charter, without danger of interruption because of the death of an owner or because of other changes in the ownership.

3. The corporation can accumulate money from several sources. This advantage makes possible large-scale business operations and the hiring of expert management.

4. It is easy to transfer ownership in a corporation. A stockholder may sell his stock to another person and transfer the stock certificate, which represents the ownership, to the latter. When shares are transferred, the transfer of ownership is indicated in the records of the corporation and a new certificate is made out in the name of the new stockholder.

5. A corporation may be able to attract a large number of stockholders, who, in turn, will help to advertise the business and will recommend its products or services.

Disadvantages of the Corporation. Although we have seen that there are several distinct advantages to the corporation, there are also a number of disadvantages. Some of the most significant disadvantages are:

1. A corporation is permitted to engage only in those activities that are specified in its charter. Should Davis, Baker, and Miller, Inc., wish to add to their business a department selling hardware, they would be unable to do so unless they went through the legal formality of obtaining a new charter. As a partnership they could have added the other department without governmental consent, provided the expansion was agreeable to all the partners.

2. A corporation cannot do business wherever it pleases. Davis, Baker, and Miller, Inc., are granted permission to conduct their business only in the state of New York. Should they wish to do business in adjoining states, they would probably be required to obtain in each state a license as a foreign corporation and to pay a fee for the privilege of doing business in the state.

3. A corporation must make special reports to the state from which it obtained its charter, as well as to other states in which it may be doing business. There is consequently an increased need for detailed financial records and reports.

4. Large corporations are seldom managed by men who take the personal interest of a sole proprietor or a partner. Stockholders who own only a few shares ordinarily are not interested personally in the management of the corporation. The corporation is therefore managed largely by a small group of stockholders.

5. The corporation is usually subjected to more taxes than are imposed on the sole proprietorship and the

partnership. Some taxes that are special to the corporation are: a filing fee, which is payable on application for a charter; an organization tax, which is based on the amount of authorized capital stock; an annual state franchise tax, which is usually based upon the profits; a Federal income tax. The first three of these vary in the different states.

6. The regulation of corporations by states and by the Federal Government is becoming more strict and burdensome.

7. Large corporations that have many stockholders have an added expense in the great amount of clerical work required, particularly in keeping the records of stockholders and in paying dividends.

Types of Businesses Organized as Corporations. A survey of businesses would show that almost every kind of business may exist as a corporation; but there are two particular kinds that are generally organized as corporations:

1. Those businesses that require large amounts of capital, such as railroads, companies that supply power and electricity for large cities, automobile manufacturing concerns, iron and steel manufacturing industries, large hotels, and office buildings.

2. Those businesses that have uncertain futures, such as amusement parks, makers of amusement devices, publishers of new magazines, and manufacturers of novelty articles. Persons who organize these types of businesses do not wish to assume the additional risk that falls upon a sole proprietor or a partner in case of failure of the business.

Holding Companies. A *holding company,* as its name implies, holds a sufficient amount of the stock of subsidiary corporations to control the management of those businesses. In some cases, if a holding company can obtain possession of only 30 or 40 per cent of the stock of another corporation, it can exercise managerial control over that corporation, for the ownership of the remainder of the stock may be so scattered that no other group of persons owns enough of the stock to exercise control. A holding company therefore does not necessarily own all the stock of the corporations that it controls. Its success depends upon its ability to own a sufficient amount of stock to control the operations of all its subsidiaries.

The American Telephone and Telegraph Company is an example of a holding company. It does not own the physical assets of its various subsidiary corporations, but it owns enough of the stock of each corporation to control the management.

Mergers. New ways are constantly being found to avoid antitrust laws. The merger was a very popular plan of combination during the period that was climaxed with the depression of 1929. Under this plan of combination several companies may actually be combined (a) by discontinuing one or more of the companies and operating under the name of one of the merged companies, or (b) by forming a new company under a new name. For example, in the first case the Williams Company and the Jackson Company merge, and the entire business is operated in the future as the Williams Company. In the second case the Williams Company and the Jackson Company merge, and the entire business is operated in the future as the Frontier Supply Company. The transfer of ownership is accomplished (a) by paying cash for the property or (b) by exchanging the stock of the new company for the stock of the old companies that were merged.

Advantages and Disadvantages of Combinations. There are numerous forms of combinations besides the mergers mentioned above. Some of the objectives and advantages that are claimed are: (a) to consolidate in one location manufacturing operations so that manufacturing will be more economical; (b) to gain economy by specializing in manufacture in each of two or more plants instead of manufacturing a variety of products in several isolated plants; (c) to eliminate duplication of management; (d) to eliminate duplication in the sales organization.

From these statements it can be seen, therefore, that the objectives are greater economy, greater efficiency, and greater competitive advantage. Some of the combinations result in monopoly and price-fixing. Sometimes, after the elimination of competition through combination, the newly formed corporation is successful in operating to better advantage. On the other hand, many new businesses often spring up to take the place of those that have been merged. In some cases merged corporations have disbanded and have gone back to the original plan of operation.

QUESTIONS FOR DISCUSSION

1. If an investor does not care to participate in the management of a business, which is the more satisfactory type of organization in which to invest his money, a partnership or a corporation? Why?
2. Who elects the directors of a corporation?
3. Must the directors of a corporation manage the business, or may they hire others to operate it?
4. What are the two general classifications of stock?
5. Does the par value of a stock indicate its real value?
6. What is cumulative stock?
7. What are articles of incorporation?
8. (a) What is a bond? (b) What are the two general types of bonds?
9. What is a registered bond?
10. List at least two advantages of a corporation from the point of view of the management.
11. Name at least two disadvantages of a corporation from the point of view of the management.
12. What is a closed corporation?
13. What are supposed to be the advantages of mergers and combinations in business?
14. What authority is granted by the proxy that is illustrated on page 42?
15. In what ways do preferred stockholders usually have a preference?
16. The shares of stock of a corporation have a par value of $100 each and are offered for sale for $10 a share. Is the stock a bargain? Why?

Section III

Co-operative Form of Organization

What Is a Co-operative Enterprise? Co-operation is a familiar word that applies to many situations. It means teamwork. When there is co-operation, there is unified effort for a common benefit. Everyone on a football or a basketball team must co-operate for the success of the team. Members of society must co-operate to assure the successful functioning of society.

A co-operative may be defined as an organization owned and operated by the so-called members of the co-operative. It is operated for the purpose of serving the members. If there are any profits, these are distributed among the members. A co-operative is a type of business organization that differs from those previously discussed. Some of the most common types of co-operative business enterprises are discussed in the following paragraphs.

Consumers' Co-operatives. One of the simplest forms of co-operatives is found where two or more people make purchases jointly. Several housewives may jointly purchase a crate of oranges or a case of soap, each taking a portion of the goods purchased. By making one large purchase, they are usually able to buy the goods at a lower price than if each made a purchase of a smaller quantity. In the farming section of our country it is quite common for several farmers to purchase jointly carloads of fertilizer, oil, and coal.

Retail Co-operatives. From the simple type of consumers' co-operatives, it is relatively easy to form a larger organization as a kind of buying club. Some of the organizations having large memberships begin to operate stores to serve their members better. According to the United States Bureau of Labor Statistics, there were, in 1936, 3,600 retail co-operative associations all over the country operating stores for their 677,000 members and doing a $200,000,000 business.

Illustration No. 16 gives a general picture of the various types of retail activities carried on by a number of these co-operatives.

SALES OF REPORTING DISTRIBUTIVE CO-OPERATIVES
(BY MAJOR TYPE OF BUSINESS)

Major Business	Number of Associations Reporting	Amount of Sales	Average per Association
All associations	1,802	$146,153,418	$ 81,106
Store associations	858	71,027,638	82,783
Groceries[1]	259	11,612,935	44,838
General merchandise ..	194	15,701,165	80,934
Students' supplies	12	1,884,310	157,026
Fuel	56	5,515,885	98,498
Farm supplies	322	35,441,276	110,066
Miscellaneous[2]	15	872,067	58,138
Buying clubs	79	415,991	5,266
Petroleum associations ..	720	50,781,102	70,529
Distributive departments of marketing associations	132	20,360,534	154,246
Bakeries	6	595,680	99,280
Creameries	4	2,954,121	738,530
Water-supply associations.	3	18,352	6,117

1 This group includes those handling meat also.
2 This group includes mail-order, artists' supplies, clothing, and "other household supplies" associations.

Illustration No. 16—Distributive Co-operatives

Of the whole group of distributive associations, 48 per cent fell in the sales range of $25,000 to $100,000, as the table in Illustration No. 17 shows.

The leading distributive associations in point of sales in 1936 (omitting three students' associations) were: The Franklin Co-operative Creamery Association, Minneapolis, Minnesota, with sales of $2,827,560; the Cloquet Co-operative Society, Cloquet, Minnesota, with sales of $1,125,714; the Co-operative Trading Company, Waukegan, Illinois, with sales of $709,736; and the New Co-operative Company, Dillonvale, Ohio, with sales of $639,476.

THE BUSINESS DONE BY DISTRIBUTIVE CO-OPERATIVES

Major Business	Number Reporting	Number of Associations Doing Classified Amount of Business in 1936							
		Under $10,000	$10,000 and under $25,000	$25,000 and under $50,000	$50,000 and under $100,000	$100,000 and under $250,000	$250,000 and under $500,000	$500,000 and under $1,000,000	$1,000,000 and over
All associations	1,802	249	279	447	421	334	55	10	7
Store associations	858	114	137	208	189	168	32	5	5
Buying clubs	79	74	3	...	...	2	...	...	...
Petroleum associations	720	49	117	207	197	128	19	3	...
Distributive departments of marketing associations	132	10	19	29	33	35	3	2	1
Bakeries	6	...	1	2	1	1	1	...	...
Creameries	4	...	1	1	1	...	...	...	1
Water-supply associations	3	2	1	...	...	...	...	...	...

Illustration No. 17—Volume of Business of Distributive Co-operatives

Consumers' Guide.

Illustration No. 18—Retail Co-operative

The greatest amount of co-operative business is still concentrated in the north central states, more than 70 per cent of the total in 1936 having been done there.

Wholesale Co-operatives. The natural next step, when a number of retail co-operative societies are functioning in a region, is the formation of a co-operative organization for wholesale buying. About one half of the 3,600 local retail co-operatives are joined in some 30 wholesale buying associations. Most of these are regional wholesale associations, taking all or parts of several states as their trading areas. Some of them overlap because their member societies are sponsored by competing farm organizations—Farm Bureau, Grange, Farmers' Union. In most European countries one national wholesale co-operative serves all the local retail co-operatives of the country.

Local retail member co-operatives do not buy all their goods from the wholesale co-operatives. One reason for not doing so is that the local retail co-operative usually likes to shop around to get the best possible price on the goods it buys. Another reason is that the wholesale co-operatives are not in a position to supply all goods. Some commodities, like fresh fruits and vegetables, milk, and meats, must be purchased locally.

Approaching a national status are two interregional wholesale co-operatives. One buys petroleum products for co-operatives in nine states and operates its own oil-blending plants. Ten wholesale co-operatives pool their purchasing power in National Co-operatives. This organization, founded in 1933, acts as a broker. It negotiates master contracts under which goods—so far, chiefly oil, automobile accessories, electrical appliances, tractors, farm machinery—are put under the co-operative label and delivered directly by the manufacturers to the member regional wholesale organizations.

In a few cases the consumers' co-operatives, the retail co-operatives, or wholesale co-operatives also operate production or manufacturing businesses.

Producers' Co-operatives. A common type of producers' co-operative is one that is organized by workers. The workers combine their own capital and either rent or purchase a plant. They manage the plant among themselves and do the work themselves. They share in the profits or the losses. Hence a producers' co-operative is operated in some respects just as a partnership. The theory of the producers' co-operative is that the workers will share in the profits of the enterprise, as well as earn wages.

Some of the advantages claimed for the producers' co-operative are:

1. There are no labor troubles because the workers own and operate the business for common profit.
2. The workers are stimulated to do their best because they are part owners and thus share in the profits.
3. There is less waste because the workers take a personal interest in the enterprise.
4. Society benefits because middlemen are eliminated and the product can be sold more cheaply.

Consumers' Guide.

Illustration No. 19—Producers' Co-operative

Some of the disadvantages of the producers' co-operative are:

1. There is a lack of experts among those who are members of the association.
2. It is difficult to obtain enough capital from members of a co-operative association to operate the association successfully.
3. There is no centralized responsibility because all members are equally responsible. Because of the lack of centralized responsibility, the management is frequently lax and outside capital with which to finance the enterprise is often difficult to obtain.

Co-operative Marketing. Co-operative marketing has been more successful than most of the other types of co-operative enterprises. Growers of cotton, fruit, tobacco, and many other crops co-operate in the harvesting, storing, and marketing of their products. Some of the fruit-growers' associations present interesting examples of co-operative marketing. After the fruit is grown, it becomes the property of the co-operative association. It is harvested, packed, and marketed by the association. If there is a surplus of production, the fruit of one grower may not be harvested, but the grower is paid in the same proportion as the other members of the association.

Some of the advantages of co-operative marketing are:

1. Enlarged facilities make it possible for the association to handle and store products better and more cheaply than the individual producer could.
2. By regulating the supply, the association can obtain better prices and a better profit for the growers.
3. Any agent of the association has a personal interest in the welfare of the association.

Some of the disadvantages of co-operative marketing are:

1. Co-operative marketing associations are frequently hard to control because of their widespread membership and the variation in membership. Members sometimes drop out and leave the burden on the remaining members.
2. Storing and holding products for higher prices sometimes leads to a serious oversupply of particular products.
3. It is difficult to obtain good management in a co-operative marketing association. Some of the members want to become the salaried managers, and others want expert help from the outside. This condition sometimes leads to dissension.

Management of Co-operatives. There are many variations in the ownership and management of co-operatives, but most of these organizations are patterned along the following plan. The local retail co-operative is composed of members who buy shares in the organization. These shares are usually of a small value, such as $1, $5, $10, or $50. On the shares they hold, members receive a modest interest rate. The policies of the co-operative are controlled by votes cast at membership meetings. One vote is allowed to a member regardless of the number of shares owned. Any profits the organization makes for its members are divided periodically in proportion to the purchases made by the members from the retail co-operative.

The ownership and management of the wholesale co-operative is controlled by the local retail co-operatives. In some wholesale co-operatives the voting control is on the basis of one vote to each member retail co-operative, regardless of the number of shares held or the amount purchased through the wholesale co-operative. In others the retail co-operative gets additional votes in the wholesale co-operative in proportion to its membership or its purchases from the latter. The control of National Co-operatives rests with its stockholding wholesale co-operatives in proportion to the volume of their purchases through it.

The average number of members in a distributive co-operative association is about 250. The largest number of members is found in such co-operative businesses as bakeries and creameries, in which the membership is usually over a thousand.

From the point of view of net worth, the majority of co-operative organizations is still small. Statistics published by the United States Department of Labor show that almost 50 per cent of these organizations have a net worth of less than $10,000.

QUESTIONS FOR DISCUSSION

1. What is a co-operative enterprise?
2. Name some relatively common types of retail co-operatives.
3. In what section of the United States are retail co-operatives most common?
4. In what fields are wholesale co-operatives particularly common?
5. What are some of the advantages claimed for producers' co-operatives?
6. What are some of the disadvantages of producers' co-operatives?
7. In what fields has co-operative marketing been common?

8. State some of the advantages of co-operative marketing.

9. Name some of the disadvantages of co-operative marketing.

10. To whom are the profits of a co-operative paid?

11. Compare the voting power of members of a co-operative with that of stockholders of a corporation.

PROBLEMS AND PROJECTS

1. In the financial statement of the partnership of Davis, Baker, and Miller on page 31, there is an item of $4,000 of undivided profits. If these profits are distributed, (a) how much will each partner get, and (b) how will the financial statement appear after the distribution?

2. Assume that in the partnership of Taylor & Williams the capital of Taylor is $15,000 and the capital of Williams $10,000. How should $3,500 of profits be divided if earnings are distributed in proportion to the capital of the partners?

3. Suppose that in the partnership of Davis, Baker, and Miller the death of Mr. Miller occurs on May 1 of a certain year. Referring to Article Nine in the articles of copartnership on page 30, state how the profit of $3,600 for the entire fiscal year ending on the next January 31 should be divided.

4. Assume that you and four other classmates decide to form a corporation. Write the articles of incorporation.

5. Obtain an organization chart of a local corporation, and make a report explaining the chart. If it is impossible to obtain such a chart, collect what information you can and draw a chart on the basis of this information.

6. Investigate the requirements in your state for (a) organizing a corporation, (b) obtaining a charter, (c) selling and issuing stock, and (d) making reports to the proper state authority. Write a report of your findings.

7. Investigate the requirements in your state for forming a partnership. Find out whether it is possible to organize a limited partnership, and in what respect the liabilities of the partners are limited.

8. On the basis of the corporation financial statement on page 39, assume that at the end of the first year the assets of the corporation formed by Davis, Baker, and Miller are as follows:

Cash	$ 8,800
Merchandise	11,300
Equipment	9,500
Land and Buildings	16,500

The accounts payable amount to $500. The earnings for the first year are $2,600. This amount may be added to the undivided profits or distributed among the stockholders. It is decided, however, to let the undivided profits remain at $4,000 and to distribute the earnings for the latest year to the stockholders as a dividend. How much is paid on each share?

9. By referring to the following balance sheet, answer the questions given below.

THE EMPIRE CORPORATION
BALANCE SHEET

ASSETS		LIABILITIES AND CAPITAL	
Cash	$15,500	Accounts Payable	$ 2,000
Accounts Receivable	5,000	6% Bonds Payable ...	20,000
Merchandise	20,000	Common Stock:	
Equipment	4,500	Authorized . $50,000	
Real Estate	45,000	Unissued ... 10,000	
		Outstanding	40,000
		7% Preferred Stock:	
		Authorized . $50,000	
		Unissued ... 30,000	
		Outstanding	20,000
		Undivided Profits	
		(Surplus)	8,000
Total Assets	$90,000	Total Liab. and Capital	$90,000

(a) What was the organization tax if the rate was 50 cents on each $1,000 of capital stock?

(b) If the par value of each kind of stock is $50, how many shares of each kind are outstanding?

(c) What is the book value of each share of stock?

(d) If the directors decide to distribute $3,400 as dividends, how much will be paid to the common stockholders and to the preferred stockholders? How much should Mr. Goodman receive if he owns 10 shares of common stock and 25 shares of preferred stock?

(e) Suppose that the preferred stock is cumulative and that the corporation was unable to pay any dividends last year. How should $6,000 of undivided profits be divided?

10. The net profit of a retail co-operative is $2,000, and the purchases made by members amount to $50,000. If the profits are divided in proportion to the purchases, how much should be given to a member who had made purchases of $500?

CHAPTER IV

PROBLEMS OF SELECTING A BUSINESS LOCATION

Purpose of the Chapter. The location of a business, in most cases, is an important factor in determining whether the business will be a success or a failure. The discussion in this chapter will answer many questions with regard to location, some of which are:

1. What are the criteria of a good location?
2. What are the possibilities of particular locations?
3. How do automobile and pedestrian traffic affect locations?
4. What are some of the common errors in selecting locations?
5. What are some of the factors that affect the location of manufacturing industries?

Section I

Factors in Locating Retail Establishments

Importance of Selecting the Proper Location. Selecting a location should not be a matter of guesswork. The proper location is frequently the factor that determines the success of a business. The United States Department of Commerce has conducted studies that disclose the importance of the proper location of stores. Some types of businesses do well in one kind of location, whereas other types would not succeed in such a location. Some of the large chain-store organizations have a special department that selects the locations for stores. Some companies have found that the elimination of unprofitable stores and the relocation of the remaining stores increase sales and thereby increase profits. What is true for a company that operates several

69

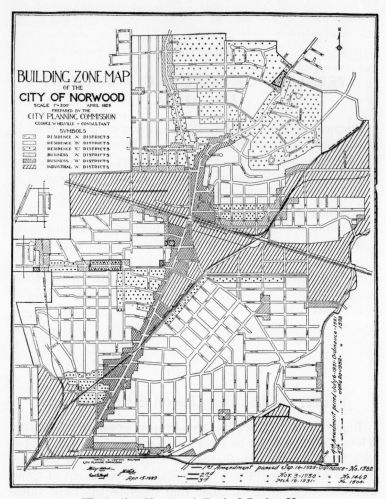

Illustration No. 20—A Typical Zoning Map

stores is true for the business that consists of only one store; that is, each location must be studied as a distinct problem.

Selecting a Location. As transportation facilities improve, businesses tend to congregate. There was a time when single stores were common in rural districts. Although such stores may still be found, they are gradually clustering together in small communities because of the improvements in transportation facilities. As a result of the use of the automobile, people in a rural community ride to a larger town to buy instead of patronizing a neighboring store. One who contemplates operating a store in a small town must recognize the fact that some of the customers will prefer to go to larger communities for their important purchases. The success of a store will, to a large extent, depend upon the owner's ability to interpret the particular wants of the people in the surrounding community, to fill those wants, and to encourage the people to buy at home. In other words, a good merchant is one who serves as a good purchasing agent for the people whom he serves.

In cities, stores congregate in groups, forming what are commonly known as *shopping centers*. Neighborhood stores and neighborhood garages are still common, but such businesses are usually fairly well concentrated in location. A shopping center that includes a dry-cleaning establishment, a drugstore, a meat market, two grocery stores, a garage, a barber shop, an electric supplies shop, a beauty parlor, and a motion-picture theater is reasonably well balanced. If it included four drugstores, however, instead of one, it would not be a particularly attractive business location for a new drugstore. While there are advantages in congregation, there may be a disadvantage because of too much competition in one particular type of enterprise.

Downtown locations in cities are good for department stores, hotels, restaurants, and parking lots. Large complete food stores are also commonly found in the downtown sections of cities. Such a section can support, however, only a limited number of grocery stores and meat markets. These accommodate the people who live in this part of the city and some who buy on their way home. The average town or city can support only a few fresh produce markets where merchants and farmers congregate to sell their products. These naturally must be located in some central downtown area to be accessible from all parts of the city.

Downtown locations are ordinarily preferred for the sale of products that are not purchased so frequently as food products. The purchase of furniture, for instance, is sufficiently important for the customer to be willing to make a special trip. Many housewives, however, prefer to buy food supplies near their homes and thus to save time.

Corner locations have the advantages of accessibility and effective display, but they usually cost more than other locations.

The manufacturer has problems of location that are distinct from those of the merchant. His market is not always close to him. In fact, he frequently serves a wide area, whereas the retailer serves a relatively restricted area.

The person who sets up a simple roadside stand must follow an intelligent plan of selection if he expects to be successful. For instance, he must consider (a) the amount of traffic that passes the location; (b) the type of traffic; (c) the habits of the people with regard to buying from roadside stands; (d) the convenience of location for stopping and parking; (e) the appearance of the stand; (f) the location with respect to a large community; and (g) the location with respect to competitors. If a desirable location has been selected, the success of the roadside stand will depend upon practices of courtesy, honesty, efficient service, and good quality. Such an enterprise usually thrives upon a good reputation, but fails upon a bad one.

Selecting a location for a manufacturing enterprise is quite a complicated procedure if it is done scientifically. Such an enterprise must consider carefully such factors as (a) the extent of the market; (b) the location of the market; (c) labor conditions; (d) the supply of proper labor; (e) the sources of materials; (f) transportation costs; (g) transportation facilities; and (h) production facilities and costs. Several locations should be compared with a view to selecting the proper one. These problems are discussed in Section II of this chapter.

Estimating the Prospects of the Location. In addition to the transportation facilities, zones, and other factors, the population of the particular community should be studied to find the location of customers. For example, Illustration No. 20 on page 70 provides some information about the characteristics of a community. A study of census figures, local welfare figures, statistics from the United States Department of Commerce, and information from the local chamber of commerce will frequently disclose the characteristics of the community. Chain-store organizations make these studies in a scientific manner. One chain-store organization covers the following factors in its study of store locations:

1. Age and sex of the prospective customers
2. Habits of the prospective customers
3. Racial characteristics
4. Conveniences demanded
5. Needs of the people
6. Occupations of the people

Influence of Traffic on the Location of Stores. The traffic problem is a serious one for stores. Merchants have found that a scarcity of parking facilities discourages shopping, for people often buy at stores that can be reached easily. Some merchants have found it profitable to provide free parking space for customers or to make arrangements with the managers of garages and parking lots to reduce rates for the customers of the stores. Some stores that are not located in the shopping district provide special transportation facilities, such as busses. If all merchants in the same kind of business provide similar service, no merchant gains any particular advantage, but all gain some advantage because shopping has been made easier. Nevertheless, the cost of the added service must be included in the selling price of the merchandise.

Another important aspect of traffic has to do with what is called the *traffic count*. This term refers to the number of vehicles or the number of people that pass a specific location. Real-estate firms, large stores, and chain-store organizations conduct traffic counts to determine the relative values of different locations. For example, if a person is considering two locations for a women's shoe store, he may have a traffic count made of each location. If the traffic count shows that three hundred women pass one location in an average day, whereas five hundred pass the other location during the same time, the latter is to be considered the better location. If a count of automobile traffic were made, it might show that one hundred women pass the first location in automobiles during an average day, whereas only fifty pass the second location. The latter would still be considered the better location because the number of people who walk by a store is more important than the number who ride by.

A high automobile traffic count is more important if there are parking facilities in the immediate vicinity than it is if there are no parking facilities. Many people may pass a location in automobiles; but if they cannot stop and park their cars, the location has no particular advantage from the point of view of shopping, although it does have an advantage from the point of view of publicity. The traffic count of automobiles is, of course, more important than the pedestrian count in the case of determining a location for a garage or a filling station.

What Is a Good Location? The rent to be paid for a location should have a satisfactory ratio to the anticipated sales volume. The tables in Chapter VI show satisfactory ratios. As good locations usually have high rents, rent should be considered only as a percentage of the anticipated sales volume. In other words, a location that is poor requires only a low rent because the anticipated sales volume in such a location will be lower than it would be in a better location.

In comparing one business location with another, it is necessary to consider other factors. If automobile parking lots are near, people can park their cars and shop conveniently. A location near apartment buildings should be favorable for a food store. Locations near bus terminals should be favorable for restaurants. Grocery stores, meat markets, and drugstores attract customers to a shopping center. Such a shopping center should therefore be favorable for a hardware store.

An automobile sales district is ordinarily not a satisfactory location for a retail store. A location near public buildings or in a manufacturing district is not favorable for such a store because it is inconvenient to large numbers of potential customers.

Sometimes one side of a street may be a good location, whereas the other side may be undesirable. For instance, the character of the businesses on one side of a street may attract certain types of customers. The sunshine on one side of a street may be so hot in the summer that people will walk on the shady side. One side of a street often has more pedestrian traffic than the other and may therefore be a better location for certain types of businesses.

Some Common Errors in the Location of Stores. When people go into a retail business or when retail merchants change their location, they frequently make mistakes. Some of the most serious mistakes are:

1. The retailer is influenced too much by vacant space and low rent, and the expectation that customers will come to him. He bases the selection of his location on cost rather than on suitability. His business consequently fails because it is located where too few customers pass.

2. The fact that several stores are already located in a section encourages the retailer to select the same location. The volume of business available in this section is not sufficient, however, to support all the merchants there.

3. The location may be suitable for one type of business but unsuitable for another.

Fitting into the Community. In studying the suitability of a location, the retail merchant should give careful consideration to the type of community. There is a general tendency for all merchants to improve the appearance of their stores. It is natural, however, to expect a store in a better residential section to be more modern and better equipped than a store in a neighborhood in which the people are interested mainly in obtaining the most value for their money. These factors of location will govern the decoration of the front and the interior, the arrangement and display of the merchandise, and the types of service offered. Well-to-do customers are frequently willing to pay a little extra in order to have their merchandise delivered, whereas persons in meager circumstances are not willing to pay for this extra service.

QUESTIONS FOR DISCUSSION

1. Why are stores usually found in groups commonly known as shopping centers?
2. Name an advantage and a disadvantage of a corner location for a business.
3. Why are rents in a downtown district higher than those in an outlying district?
4. If you were making a traffic count to determine the suitability of a particular location for a beauty parlor, to which of the following factors would you give most consideration: (a) the number of women who pass the location, (b) the number of men who pass the location, (c) the number of automobiles that pass the location, or (d) the number of men and women who pass the location in couples?
5. Name several common errors made in selecting locations for retail stores.
6. Competitors in many departments of retail business try to obtain store locations near one another. Can you explain the reason for this practice?
7. What do you think are some factors that should be considered before establishing a beauty parlor in a town with a population of five hundred?
8. What factors do you think would help to determine a good location for a filling station?
9. What are some of the factors that would govern the selection of a location for a roadside fruit stand?

Section II

Major Factors in Locating Manufacturing and Wholesale Industries

Regional Markets. Many businesses that operate in local markets eventually extend into regional markets that take in more than one state. For instance, some ice-cream manufacturers expand from one city to another until they cover a regional market, such as New England, the Ohio Valley, or the West Coast. Seldom, however, does an ice-cream manufacturer extend marketing into a particularly large area. Some candy manufacturers who start as small enterprises eventually expand into regional markets, and a few of these expand into national markets. Numerous food products, as well as other products, are sold in regional markets; but often no attempt is ever made to market them nationally.

A business can expand within certain limits set by competition, financial support, economy in distribution, and efficiency in service. Producers and distributors often find that they cannot reach out into national markets without establishing branches. They hesitate to establish branches because the problem of management then becomes more complicated and expenses increase. Many manufacturers have found that the most profitable plan is to confine activities to a reasonably restricted area. When they attempt to expand into larger markets, competition and the costs of service make increased sales unprofitable.

National Markets. Many businesses, such as book publishing companies and manufacturers of automobiles, steel, and breakfast foods, have developed what are called national markets. In other words, they sell products in all states. In catering to a national market, a business enterprise must take into consideration the location from which it can produce and distribute its products most economically. Some of the factors that influence the location are discussed later in this chapter. It is obvious, however, that

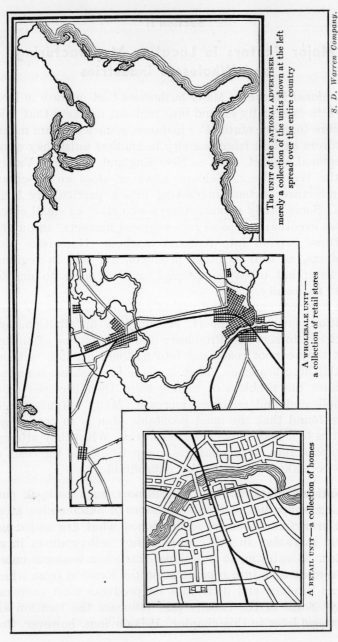

The UNIT of the NATIONAL ADVERTISER — merely a collection of the units shown at the left spread over the entire country

A WHOLESALE UNIT — a collection of retail stores

A RETAIL UNIT — a collection of homes

S. D. Warren Company.

Illustration No. 21—Relationship of Markets

the producer who expects to sell in a national market must give very careful attention to his location in relation to the market. For example, a company that manufactures a breakfast food largely from wheat with a national market for its products would not find it economical to be located in the northern part of Maine or in New Mexico. In either of these locations the company could not serve its market advantageously. In many cases, however, raw materials, power, and labor may be more important factors than the location in relation to the market.

Concentration of Markets. The concentration of a market is an important consideration. Illustration No. 22 on page 80 shows the wholesale trade centers of the United States. The concentration of wholesale activity is similar to that of population. Population attracts business activities, and vice versa. The interrelation of these two factors is responsible to some extent for the dense population of some sections.

A state may have a large geographic area, but a small population and small buying power. Many businesses are therefore interested in knowing the relative buying power of various states and counties. They divide their sales areas on the bases of wealth, income, and population. Wealth and income may be determined in any one of several ways. It is sometimes computed on the basis of (a) the number of people who pay income taxes; (b) the value of products; (c) the amount paid in wages; (d) the per capita wealth; (e) the per capita income; (f) the number of people who have subscribed to various publications; (g) the number of automobiles that are registered; (h) the post-office receipts; (i) the increase or the decrease in population; (j) savings deposits; (k) bank transactions; or (l) a combination of these factors. Statistics such as these may be obtained from the United States Department of Commerce and from many private service agencies.

Source of Supply of Raw Materials. The source of supply of raw materials is extremely important in some industries,

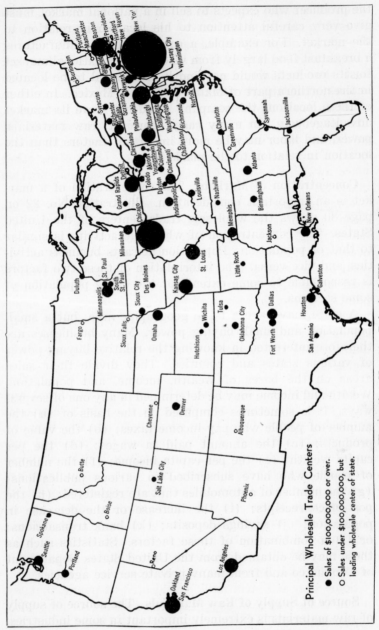

Illustration No. 22—Principal Wholesale Centers

whereas it is not important in others. If the raw material is used in small quantities and has a very high unit value, the source of supply is not so important as in the case of raw material that is used in large quantities at a low unit cost. For instance, the jewelry business is not so much interested in the source of its supply of gold as it is in other factors. It would be foolish for a manufacturer of fine jewelry to locate his plant near a source of gold. If he did, his plant would be situated somewhere in the mountainous sections of the West, in Alaska, or in some other place away from large centers of population that provide markets.

Many companies, however, find it very desirable to become located at the immediate source of supply of the raw material. For example, a manufacturer of cement finds it necessary to locate his plant in the center of a large deposit of a certain grade of limestone. Additional materials used in smaller quantities can be shipped from distant points. As the basic raw material is limestone, it is easier to ship the cement to distant markets than it is to bring the basic raw material from a distant source and then manufacture the cement and distribute it to neighboring markets.

Focal Points for Raw Materials. The location of iron and steel mills is a good example of care in the selection of producing points. Coal, from which coke is made, iron ore, and certain amounts of limestone are the principal raw materials used in the production of iron and steel. Some mills are located near iron deposits, while many others are located near coal deposits. The ideal location is one near a good grade of iron ore and a good grade of coal. The coal in the South is not so good as some of the grades in Pennsylvania. In the South, however, the iron and steel mills have the advantage of relatively near supplies of the basic materials, coal, iron ore, and limestone.

Some iron and steel mills are located at points that are not near the source of supply of coal, iron ore, or limestone. They are located at what might be called focal points for all these materials. From these focal points the mills have easy access to their markets for the finished products of iron and steel. The steel mills of Ohio, Pennsylvania, West Virginia, Illinois, and Indiana are not located at original sources of all the raw materials. None is at the source of iron ore. Some are located at the source of coal, and others at the source of limestone; but a few of them are not located near any of the raw materials. They operate successfully, however, because they are situated at focal points in areas where they are able to serve large markets economically.

Quality Standards of Raw Materials. The supply of raw material may be totally adequate in quantity and, from the point of view of production, may be located in a strategic position; but if the material is not of good quality, the company that uses it may not be able to produce economically. For instance, neighboring deposits of a low grade of coal might not be an advantage to a manufacturer. It might be more economical to ship a high grade of coal from another source or to move the plant to a location near a better grade of coal. On the other hand, some manufacturers can use a low grade of coal satisfactorily if the price is reasonable. A low grade of coal at a sufficiently low price may therefore be an advantage in some cases.

There may be large deposits of gold in a mountainous section of the West; but unless the ore is rich enough, it cannot be mined profitably. If gold increases in value, however, the mining of low-grade deposits may become profitable. Price is therefore helpful in determining the profitableness of the use of low-grade materials.

Assured Supply of Raw Materials. Just what would happen to a canning factory, built in a rich farming section, if the farmers ceased to produce the fruits or the vegetables used in the cannery? It is obvious that the cannery would have to cease operations or obtain supplies from a long distance. Canneries usually depend, however, upon receiving supplies from short distances because most fruits and vegetables cannot be hauled long distances economically.

A constant and reasonably definite supply of materials of a uniform quality is desired. Many canning factories will not begin operations without having some definite assurance from surrounding farmers that they will be furnished a supply. For instance, a factory may be established to can tomatoes. The managers of the cannery will contract with surrounding farmers to furnish tomatoes, and in some cases will establish a definite price and make agreements as to grading the tomatoes. These contracts help to assure the supply, but do not necessarily guarantee the quality. The cannery runs the additional risk of a poor productive season.

Some coke plants stand today as ghosts of the past. They were located near profitable coal mines; but the supply of coal in the mines became exhausted, and the coke ovens were then abandoned. Some paper factories were constructed along streams, from which the owners obtained an adequate water supply for power. After the owners expanded the factories, however, they discovered that the water supply was not adequate in some dry seasons. This condition placed a handicap on production because water is, in this case, an important raw material.

The rayon industry needs large quantities of water that must be free of certain chemical impurities. If the water contains many impurities, the cost of purifying it is excessive. An adequate supply of water of the right type is therefore important to this industry. In fact, the water supply is usually more important than the source of supply of the basic material, cellulose, for this material can be shipped long distances more easily than water could be transported.

Inducements for Moving Businesses. Industries that create employment in a community are in demand, for every community is anxious to see its people working. Businessmen and civic organizations encourage new factories and other business enterprises to locate in their cities. There have been periods during the last fifteen years when the chambers of commerce of many large cities have launched active campaigns to induce business organizations to move plants to their cities. The chambers of commerce of many cities have boasted of bringing in many industries from other cities. Special inducements are offered by some cities and states to new industries. Free sites are offered. Sometimes new buildings are furnished free for at least a few years. Tax exemption is granted for a specified number of years, or the tax rate is reduced.

There are two potential disadvantages in the practice of offering inducements to a business to locate in a particular community. The first one is that a business enterprise may be drawn away from an economically favorable location into one that is not so favorable. In other words, the owners may make an unwise decision to move merely in order to take advantage of the offer in the new community. The second disadvantage is that a business has no assurance that it will be successful in its new location. Businesses have frequently not been prosperous after moving to a different community.

It is a recognized fact that the business enterprises which are most willing to move are those that have been looking for some financial assistance because they have been experiencing difficulty in operating at a profit. If the industry is of the proper type for the community, if it has good management, and if conditions are satisfactory in the community, the inducements will be justified. The fact cannot be overlooked, however, that even under these circumstances many businesses that will consider moving are not desirable.

Types of Power. Power is an extremely important factor in modern industry. It may be derived from waterfalls or from some fuel, such as coal, oil, gas, or wood. Power that is generated by a waterfall is usually converted into electricity, whereas that derived from fuels is used to generate steam. The steam may operate engines directly and thus furnish the power for manufacturing processes, or it may operate engines that convert the mechanical power into electric energy.

Many manufacturers buy electricity from a public-utility company. Others have their own power plants, in which they generate steam to be used in steam engines or to be converted into electrical energy. Still other plants generate electric power through the use of Diesel engines, which burn crude oil. The generation of steam power depends upon good supplies of coal and water. The generation of electric power through the use of Diesel engines depends upon obtaining a supply of crude oil at a reasonable price.

Surplus Power. Some large manufacturing plants develop their own power and have a surplus that they can sell. The sale of this surplus power has a bearing on the profit to be expected from the operation of the plant. For instance, a paper mill uses great quantities of hot water and steam. The mill generates steam, which can be used, in turn, to generate electric power. In a process such as this, the steam is first used to operate steam engines or turbines, which produce the electricity. The exhaust steam from the engines or turbines is then used in the paper manufacturing process. But in order to supply enough exhaust steam for the manufacturing process, the company sometimes produces a surplus amount of electricity. If the electricity can be sold, the company makes a profit on its power plant. Some large manufacturing plants sell their surplus electric power to cities and to other industries.

Sources of Power. Power developed by a natural waterfall is sometimes, but not always, cheaper than that developed by a steam plant. Some plants cannot make use of waterfalls in this respect because they are located at too great a distance from the source of the power. The low cost of fuel helps many steam plants to operate economically and to compete with water-power plants.

Power plants are operated by individuals, corporations, cities, or the Federal Government. The power developments in the Tennessee Valley and along the Colorado River are important examples of Federally controlled plants. These and other power developments tend to encourage new industries.

Illustration No. 23—Norris Dam and Power Plant, TVA

Cost of Power. The cost of power is one of the most important elements in determining the location of various types of industries. Many plants that consume large amounts of electrical energy are located in a place such as Niagara Falls, New York. The advantage of locating near these waterfalls is that the power developed at this particular source is very low in cost. Obviously, a steam plant located at such a point could not compete with an electric plant because its coal or other fuel would have to be shipped a long distance. If all other conditions are equal, an industry that consumes a large amount of electric power will choose the location where it can obtain the right kind of power at the lowest cost.

Dependability of Power. The dependability of power is extremely important. The voltage and the frequency must be kept constant if the machines are operated by motors that require electrical energy of a known power and frequency. If there is any great variation in current, the productivity of the machines is affected. If the power is shut off occasionally, a lapse in production, and consequently a loss, is caused. In figuring the cost of power, the manufacturer must therefore consider dependability first.

Kinds of Transportation and Communication. Everyone is familiar to some extent with our modern means and methods of transportation. The most important ones are steam railway, electric railway, ocean vessel, lake vessel, canal boat and barge, river boat and barge, railway express service, postal service, air express, and motor truck. Some businesses use all these forms of transportation, whereas others use only a few.

The most common forms of communication are letter, telegraph, telephone, and radio.

Dependability of Transportation and Communication. A location on a small railway that affords freight service only two or three times a week would not be satisfactory for a business establishment that had to make daily shipments. In that case incoming and outgoing shipments might have to be hauled by truck for a considerable distance to another railway. This procedure would add to costs, however, and would therefore decrease profits.

Before locating their factories, manufacturers who must ship large quantities of material by freight investigate carefully the freight service in and out of all cities. They find that freight moves more quickly from one city than it does from another. This small difference in time is frequently important in selecting a location.

The dependability of transportation and communication is therefore extremely important. Water transportation and air transportation have their handicaps in this respect. Water transportation is cheaper than most other forms, although it is not quite so dependable nor so fast. Sometimes shipments are made, for example, from the East Coast to the West Coast through the Panama Canal; but they may be delayed by storm or other unforeseen difficulties. Air express is usually the fastest type of transportation, but it too is sometimes undependable because of stormy weather. Weather conditions affect other forms of transportation, but usually to a lesser degree.

A business that is located where it has access to all types of transportation service is in a desirable situation provided other conditions are satisfactory.

Speed and Service. In studying suitable locations for their establishments, businessmen must consider how they can best serve their customers. Mail-order houses, for example, have found Chicago and St. Louis good locations from which to serve the entire United States. These cities are near the center of population, near the geographic center, and have good transportation facilities radiating from them. As they expand, they place branches in other cities. Service is one of the most important elements in the success of a mail-order house.

Shippers usually need to know how soon they can expect deliveries to be made to their customers. Illustration No. 115 (page 306) in Chapter XIII shows the time that it takes freight shipments of less than a carload to be delivered in various areas surrounding a particular shipping point. If this map is compared with a similar map of another city, it is possible to discover the relative merits of the two locations with regard to freight service.

Cost Versus Service in Transportation. The cost and the reliability of transportation service must be considered together. Some businesses could operate more profitably by maintaining a single large plant, with a central office in one city, and shipping to all customers from this point. The cost could then be kept at a minimum. Service is, however, extremely important. For example, a textbook publisher with a central office in Chicago may find it necessary to establish branches in San Francisco, Atlanta, and New York in order to serve the entire United States. From the central point in Chicago supplies must be sent to each branch. From each branch supplies are shipped in smaller lots to customers. This type of organization often adds to the cost of distribution, but it accelerates service. A customer in San Francisco would not want to wait until his order was shipped from Chicago.

Businesses that have to make many heavy shipments give very careful consideration to the location of branches because they want to provide a maximum amount of service at a minimum cost. If there is a choice between two locations, and if all other conditions are the same, the location selected will be that which will enable the business to serve its customers in the area at the lowest possible transportation cost.

Access to Markets. Chicago has developed as a great meat-packing center because it is a focal point for railroads. Cattle, sheep, and hogs are shipped from the West over many railroads. The livestock is assembled in Chicago and prepared for consumption. From this logical distributing point meat is shipped to all parts of the United States. Packing companies located in Chicago have branches in many other cities, to which they ship meat for further distribution. Other packing centers less important than Chicago have developed for the same reason. They too are within access of producing areas and markets.

Businesses that have a large export business usually find it more economical to have their plant, or at least a branch, at a port or at a point where they can obtain good transportation to a port. Some businesses located in the Middle West send shipments down the Ohio and the Mississippi River for transfer to ocean-going vessels. Others located within the interior of the United States ship by rail to the East or the West Coast for transshipment by water.

Supply of Labor. Some industries require highly skilled labor, whereas others can use unskilled labor. Still others require a combination of the two. Producers of machine tools, jewelry, musical instruments, and watches require a large number of highly skilled workers and but a few unskilled workers. In selecting a location, such a manufacturer finds that the supply of labor has an important bearing unless workers can be "imported" easily. In some instances highly skilled labor is moved from one location to another.

Most industries have no difficulty in obtaining large supplies of unskilled labor. Some of the textile plants moved to the South so that they could obtain large supplies of unskilled labor at low prices and, at the same time, be near the raw material and cheap power. When new plants are organized in small communities, however, labor is frequently imported. Unskilled workers are sometimes encouraged to move to a new location in order to increase the supply of labor and thus to keep the price of labor low.

Some manufacturers are interested only in seasonal labor, whereas others are interested in permanent labor. For instance, canneries that pack fruits, vegetables, and fish need labor only during their canning seasons. They therefore find it necessary to use a small percentage of skilled labor and a large percentage of unskilled labor. Seasonal workers cannot be expected to be skilled.

Types of Workers. The age, sex, race, or nationality of workers is important to some employers. In many types of work employers do not wish to hire older people because younger people are more efficient. The heavier industries, such as the steel and lumber industries, usually require men; whereas others are more suitable for women than for men. The textile industries, for example, use a good percentage of women workers because no great physical strength is needed. Women handle some types of work better than men.

The traditions of workers are sometimes important. Through several generations the families in New England have become accustomed to making such products as hats, shoes, and other clothing, as well as small mechanical parts. They are therefore traditionally qualified for these kinds of skilled work.

Weather Conditions. Geographic environment is important in some industries, whereas it is negligible in others. Weather, for example, has an important bearing on the production of certain types of cigars. One notable manufacturer has created artificial weather within his factory in order to reproduce the conditions under which cigars are made in the Mediterranean districts.

It is obvious that an individual who intends to raise citrus fruits will want to establish his business in California, Florida, or in one of the newer producing areas, such as Texas. It is commonly known that soft drinks are produced and sold in larger quantities in the South than in other regions because of the element of temperature.

Seasons. Seasons and weather are closely related as factors relating to business. Seasons are the regular changes in weather conditions. In Florida there is no winter season, and in parts of California there is no winter season comparable to that experienced in the North. One would therefore not select Florida or California as a manufacturing or distributing point for winter clothing. A retailer in the North would be just as foolish to try to sell straw hats in the wintertime as a southern dealer would be to try to sell heavy clothing in Florida in the wintertime.

Traditions and Customs. Traditions and customs have important influences on business operations. It is difficult to explain exactly why the rubber industry has become centered largely in Akron. The main explanation is that the rubber industry started there and has stayed there. There are other locations that would be more economical; but because the business has been established, it cannot be transplanted easily to another area. There are large investments in buildings and equipment in Akron. Thousands of workmen in Akron have spent their entire lives in the rubber industry. Hence they understand it and are traditionally qualified to work in this industry.

Kindred Industries. Industries tend to group themselves into "families." Woodworking industries of various types frequently congregate. Machine industries also group themselves together. Cincinnati, Ohio, for instance, is one of the most important machine tool centers. This fact has led to the manufacture of a great many other types of machinery in Cincinnati. In Detroit and surrounding cities a large percentage of our automobiles are made. Because of the automobile industry in this area, there are many factories that make automobile accessories, tools, and equipment.

The supply of labor in kindred industries can be transferred from one enterprise to another without serious difficulty. Another advantage of the grouping of such industries is the fact that the necessary service agencies are developed in the same community. For instance, if a factory needs some kind of repair, the service can be obtained without difficulty provided the factory is located in a community in which there are many kindred industries and also service agencies that aid these industries.

Operating Costs of Two Locations. The following table shows how the Osborn Manufacturing Company has reached a decision between two suitable locations, A and B. The managers of this company have carefully considered the more important factors mentioned in the foregoing discussion. Their expert engineers and accountants have calculated the relative costs of operating a plant for one year in each of the two locations on the same production schedule. From an analysis of this table it is evident that location A is more desirable, provided the other considerations mentioned in this chapter are favorable to it.

FACTORS IN COST	LOCATION A	LOCATION B
Rent and upkeep	$ 4,800.00	$ 5,200.00
Power	6,250.00	7,963.00
Incoming transportation ..	1,250.00	1,100.00
Outgoing transportation ...	2,200.00	2,000.00
Taxes	460.00	520.00
Wages	10,450.00	9,980.00
Insurance	240.00	300.00
Total costs	$25,650.00	$27,063.00

In addition to the costs analyzed in the preceding table, it is necessary to evaluate such factors as speed and facility in serving customers, climate, labor supply, and others mentioned in this chapter. A slight saving in the cost of operating in one location may be offset by other undesirable factors. For example, if a company is located in a place where it cannot serve its customers promptly, it may not be able to compete effectively with other businesses of the same type. Very often companies find it necessary to incur additional expense in order to serve customers promptly.

QUESTIONS FOR DISCUSSION

1. What types of goods are usually confined to a local market, such as a central city or town?
2. What is a regional market?
3. What is a national market?
4. Is the source of supply of raw material for an industry such as the manufacture of jewelry an important or an unimportant factor?
5. Is the source of supply of raw material important or unimportant in determining the location of a cement manufacturer? Why?
6. Explain briefly what is meant by a focal point for obtaining raw materials in manufacture.
7. How does the adequacy or the inadequacy of the supply of raw material affect the location and the successful operation of a business?
8. What are some of the unfortunate results of making inducements to encourage industries to locate in particular communities?
9. Name some types of businesses and professional services that are restricted to local markets. Exclude those mentioned in the textbook.
10. Which do you think are restricted largely to local markets, and which have the greatest opportunity to sell in national and international markets: (a) retailers, (b) wholesalers, or (c) manufacturers?
11. Would you expect a manufacturer of artificial silk to consider a location in Kansas or Oklahoma? Why?
12. In what ways must electric power be dependable for some types of industry?
13. Why do some companies have branch offices and warehouses when they could operate more economically from a central point?
14. Explain why Chicago has developed into an important meat-packing center.

15. Name some types of industries that require more skilled labor in proportion to unskilled labor.

16. Explain the statement that the rubber industry has become centered in Akron because of tradition.

17. What bearing do kindred industries have upon the location and the operation of a business?

18. Name some of the natural resources that give certain sections of the country an economic advantage over other sections that do not have them.

PROBLEMS AND PROJECTS

1. Select what you consider to be a good business location in your community. Study the type of business for which you think the location is suitable, and list the reasons why you think so. In your report give the specific location to which you have reference.

2. (a) If you live in a city or town, make a map of the business district showing the various streets. Mark on the streets, by code or letters, the various types of businesses located there. (b) Then add the number of each type, and comment on what you consider a satisfactory or an unsatisfactory concentration and placement of these businesses.

3. (a) Make a pedestrian count for a certain location within the center of a block. Make this count during a particular time. The longer the time, the better. (b) On the same day a week later, and at the same hour, make a pedestrian count for an adjacent corner location. In each case tabulate the number of women, children, and men who pass the location. (c) Draw some conclusions with regard to the value of each location.

4. Select some type of business that you would like to enter. (a) Decide what would be a suitable location. (b) Make a study to show the amount of money that would be needed to pay the expenses for the first month and to buy equipment for cash. (c) Give your reasons for selecting the location and for believing that you would be successful in that particular business enterprise.

5. Make a study of some local industry that your teacher suggests. Write a report giving logical reasons why the industry is located in your community. Indicate what other locations you think would be better.

6. Select one location in your community that you think would be suitable for a new gasoline station. Give reasons why you think it would be a good location.

CHAPTER V

HOUSING FACILITIES FOR A BUSINESS

Purpose of the Chapter. A major problem in starting a business enterprise is the finding or the constructing of a suitable building. Several factors must be considered, such as building ordinances, construction, layout, lighting, and ventilation. The study of this chapter will answer many questions, some of which are:

1. What are desirable types of material for building construction?
2. How many entrances should there be, and where are the best locations for them?
3. What is the best type of floor, walls, and ceiling for the particular business?
4. What type of lighting will be the best?
5. Shall an air-conditioning system be installed?

What Kind of Building? Naturally, the general type of building to house a business will be determined primarily by the question of expense. In many businesses it may be desirable to have a certain elaborate type of building, yet a less costly one is used because the businessman feels financially unable to pay more. Elaborate buildings are not necessary for many businesses.

The outside appearance of the building is more important for some businesses than for others. Wholesale businesses are less concerned about the outside appearance of their buildings than are retail stores. The same is true of factories. These two types of businesses are more concerned with the location of their buildings in relation to transportation facilities and rental costs or taxes. Probably outside appearance is most important to retail stores that wish to attract the attention of passers-by. In such cases it is desirable that the outside appearance suggest to the customer the nature of the store. For example, an exclusive retail shop should be housed in a building that suggests exclusiveness. A stone building or one faced with granite or marble, liberally trimmed with bronze, may suggest this quality. Illustration No. 24 is a picture of the store front of Dennison's New York City store, which is located on exclusive Fifth Avenue. Stores and shops that carry ultramodern styles of merchandise should, if possible, be housed in a building of ultramodern architecture.

American Brass Company.

*Illustration No. 24—A Building that Harmonizes
with Its Surroundings*

Glass blocks are now being used to make buildings distinctive. They may be used for unusual architectural designs, as well as to improve the lighting. Glass blocks used in building construction draw attention night and day. They have a clean, sanitary appearance that gives them added value for restaurants and food shops. Illustration No. 25 indicates the attention-getting value of translucent glass building blocks when the interior is illuminated at night.

Owens-Illinois Glass Company.

Illustration No. 25—Attention-Getting Value of
Translucent Building Blocks

Businesses that require a great deal of light for efficient working conditions are finding glass building blocks desirable. Illustration No. 26 shows the walls of a printing plant constructed of translucent glass blocks. A certain type of glass block is a good insulator, keeping out noises, heat, and cold. Recently it has been used in the construction of many factories.

A building is distinctive if only the ground floor or even the front side of the ground floor is faced with stone and the rest of the building is constructed of brick that harmonizes with the stone. Less expensive, but still attractive, is a brick building of a well-chosen style of architecture. The buildings discussed so far are usually of fire-resisting construction, a feature that, unless the cost is prohibitive, is desirable because it lessens the chance of loss by fire. Thus the cost of insurance on the building, the merchandise, and the equipment is decreased. Stone and brick buildings usually require much smaller expenditures for repairs and upkeep than do wooden buildings. Warehouses for furniture storage and the like should be of fire-resisting construction not only for the sake of greater safety but also for a proper psychological effect upon customers.

Owens-Illinois Glass Company.

Illustration No. 26—Translucent Glass Blocks in the
Walls of a Printing Plant

Many businesses, especially in small communities, are
carried on in frame or wooden buildings. Whether buying
or leasing, one should attempt to find a structure suitable
for the particular business. A frame building can be attractive if the style of architecture is good, if the building
is of a pleasing color, and if it is in excellent condition.
Freakish or loud colors are usually undesirable. If the
paint is old, faded, and scaly, customers will not be at-
tracted to the place of business. Often a frame building
can be improved greatly in appearance by the construction
of a brick or stone veneer front. There is a growing tendency to make factory buildings attractive to passers-by
and to eliminate unsightly buildings and grounds.

Building Codes. Many states and most large cities have
established *building codes,* which are rules and regulations
as to the construction, equipment, arrangement, and maintenance of buildings. Before one may erect a building, it is

necessary to submit the plans and specifications to the proper authorities. If the plans comply with the requirements of the code, a building permit is issued. Architects and building contractors should be familiar with the requirements of the code.

A few excerpts from the New York state code for mercantile establishments are given here as an indication of what a building code is:

Rule 1302. No mercantile establishment shall be conducted in any building erected after April 1, 1924, unless the building is so constructed that the several floors or parts of floors throughout the building, to be used as mercantile establishments, shall be capable of safely sustaining the load which it is to carry, but at least one hundred (100) pounds per square foot, uniformly distributed, and more whenever so prescribed by local building laws or ordinances.

Rule 1303. No mercantile establishment shall be conducted in any building hereafter erected, more than four stories in height, unless the same is of fireproof construction. A basement as defined in these rules shall not be considered a story in determining the height of a building.

Rule 1304. No mercantile establishment shall be conducted in any building hereafter erected, more than twenty-five feet in height, nor more than five thousand (5,000) square feet in area, unless the exterior walls of the same are constructed of masonry, and the roof is covered with incombustible material, or that that part of the building occupied as a mercantile establishment be of fireproof construction.

Rule 1306. No mercantile establishment shall be conducted in any building hereafter erected unless the clear height of any story or part of story so occupied, except for storage, is at least nine feet.

Rule 1307. From every floor area there shall be not less than two exits remote from each other. . . . No point in any floor area shall be more than one hundred feet distant from the entrance to one such exit at that floor, and in a sprinklered building not more than one hundred fifty feet distant from such exit. . . . Every door leading to or opening on a required stairway or other required exit shall be not less than forty-four inches wide.

Rule 1309. Every boiler room, machinery room, regular packing room, rooms where inflammable material used for packing is stored, shipping room, refuse room, bakery, kitchen, garage, or stable in a building occupied as a mercantile establishment, shall be completely enclosed on all sides by fireproof partitions, fireproof floors, and incombustible ceilings, except for the necessary windows to the outer air, and necessary doorways equipped with fire doors.

Also in this code are detailed specifications as to what is meant by fireproof floors and roofs, fire doors, fireproof windows, etc. Similar codes provide specifications for plumbing and electrical work.

How Many Entrances? The size and the location of a building determine to a large extent the number of entrances. For a small retail store that fronts on only one street and is thirty feet or less in width, one entrance, such as that shown in Illustration No. 27, is all that is needed. As shown in this illustration, it is desirable to avoid having a step at the entrance. A step is a handicap for children and old people. It is a hazard that may cause injury to a person and result in a lawsuit for damages. Even if, in the case of an accident, no lawsuit is involved, ill will may be created and customers may be lost.

For stores with a frontage of more than thirty feet, two entrances are often desirable to permit a little more freedom for entrance and exit. Stores occupying corner locations may advantageously have an entrance on each street so that customers can enter conveniently from either.

Congestion and accidents are prevented if the entrance is sufficiently wide to allow customers to enter and others to leave at the same time by means of two swinging doors. Large stores usually prefer not to have revolving doors as such doors cannot take care of crowds easily and may be dangerous if a large number of people attempt to use them hurriedly.

Space for unloading and loading merchandise should also be considered in selecting a building. Many small businesses in the city must have incoming merchandise un-

General Electric Company.
Illustration No. 27—A Small Store Front with a Single Entrance

loaded on the sidewalk in front of the building and then carried or carted through the store. Such inconvenience could be avoided if there were at the back or the side of the building an entrance where trucks could unload merchandise. Another possibility would be the installation of an elevator from the basement to the sidewalk. The latter method, however, would involve a risk to pedestrians.

In congested city areas, indoor loading and unloading platforms are used so that the delivery trucks do not block traffic. These platforms are built to such a height that the bed of the truck is on a level with them. Goods can therefore be loaded or unloaded easily by either hand or small hand trucks. Outdoor loading platforms are usually covered in order that materials being loaded or unloaded are not damaged by the weather. Illustration No. 28 shows a loading platform.

The Starchroom Laundry Journal.

Illustration No. 28—A Loading Platform

Manufacturing establishments located on railroad spurs have doors on that side of the receiving or shipping room which is adjacent to the tracks. Here goods that have arrived by train or are to leave by such means are taken care of. Frequently, on the other side of the room, there are doors and a loading platform for goods arriving or departing by motor truck. In large businesses it is usually desirable that there be separate entrances for goods being received and exits for goods being sent out.

Awnings. Stores so located that the sun shines into the windows may find it profitable to have awnings. In addition to making the interior of the building cooler on hot days, the awnings aid in protecting goods from the effects of the bright sun, which may cause the fading or bleaching of textiles or the spoilage of candies and fruits.

Walls. The walls have a great deal to do with the interior appearance of a store. To be attractive, the interior should be bright and cheerful, for people avoid visiting stores that are dingy. Light-colored walls are generally preferred to dark ones, as they aid in making the store light. For the same reason, as well as for the fact that they are easier to clean, walls with a smooth finish are preferred to those of rough plaster. Extremely smooth finishes, such as enamel, may be undesirable, however, because the high gloss produces a glare when the lights are turned on.

There are available many types of wall materials, such as plaster, wall board, wood, tile, linoleum, and numerous other composition materials. With such a great variety it should be easy to select the type that is best suited for the particular store. For example, notice how the walls of the candy store in Illustration No. 29 are suggestive of cleanliness. The walls, as well as the floor, are washable.

The colors of the walls and the furnishings should harmonize. For example, a millinery store that caters to women should have an appropriate feminine setting. Coral, gray, and blue seem to harmonize well and create a feminine atmosphere. Walls of coral and gray, a blue rug with a modern design of gray and rust, silver-gray natural hardwood furniture and display cases, and blue and gray upholstering on benches and chairs might prove an attractive and inviting setting.

Sound-Absorbent Ceilings. It is now possible to install ceilings that deaden noise. The owners of restaurants and soda fountains should find it profitable to install such ceilings in order to minimize the clatter of dishes and glasses. Customers like quiet and restful eating places. Stores in which machinery is in operation, such as shoe repair shops and optical shops, might profit by such ceilings.

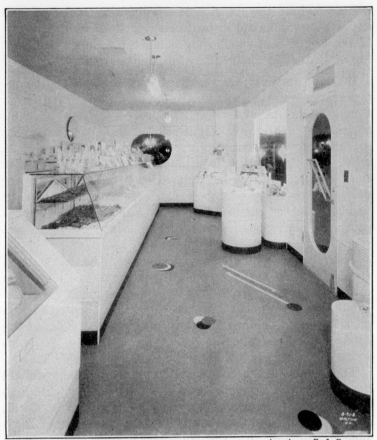

Armstrong Cork Company.

Illustration No. 29—A Building with Walls Suited to the Business

What Type of Floors? Wooden floors easily show marks and signs of soil. They are difficult to keep clean because dirt collects in the cracks. Boards often become loose and squeak when walked upon. Wooden flooring is therefore not considered desirable for stores having a large amount of customer traffic.

Many stores have certain floors or departments that are carpeted. Many specialty stores, such as men's clothing stores, ladies' dress shops, and luggage stores, have carpeted floors. Carpets give a springiness under foot that

adds to the tone or atmosphere of the store. Shoe stores
frequently use linoleum or tile floors covered partly by
rugs. A customer trying on shoes feels that the shoe is
soft and comfortable as he walks across deep-pile carpets
or rugs. Such covering also reduces the amount of scuffing
that a shoe receives in being tried on by the customer.
Carpets and rugs are easily soiled, stained, or spotted and
need cleaning frequently.

In the past few years great advances have been made in
the production of attractive designs in linoleum. Repro-
ductions of trade-marks or other symbols desired by architects or owners are inlaid into the linoleum floor covering.
Illustration No. 30 shows the design of a clock in the floor
of a department selling clocks. Even the circular shape of
the room is suggestive of a clock.

Linoleums vary in thickness and quality. The better
quality has the designs running through the linoleum from
the surface to the base so that the designs are not broken
when the linoleum begins to wear. Small stores and some
departments in department stores find linoleum-covered
floors to be satisfactory. Such floors are cleaned easily;

Armstrong Cork Company.

Illustration No. 30—A Floor Design Suggestive of the Goods Sold

but, when damp, they are slippery and are liable to cause a customer or an employee to fall.

Other Floors. Marble floors, because they add an atmosphere of quality and elegance, are usually found in exclusive retail shops. A popular composition material called *terrazzo* is made from a mixture of cement and marble chips. The floor is divided into tilelike forms by means of brass strips, and the mixture is then poured into the forms and leveled off. The marble chips give a marbled appearance to the floor. Rubber, asphaltic, cork, and clay tiles are also used in floors. Many new floor coverings are being made from plastic materials. Laundries, dairies, and automobile washrooms make extensive use of waterproofed cement floors. Factory floors that receive a great deal of hard wear from small trucks and heavy materials are usually made of concrete or wood blocks.

Importance of Window Display Space. The display windows should be the most valuable part of a retail store. They are considered so valuable by large department stores that the various departments are charged for the window display space used by them. The simple plan of displaying merchandise to the people who pass the store should serve the purpose of telling them that the store handles those items and should result in increased calls for the things shown. To the small store located in a large city, the window display is the chief means of advertising.

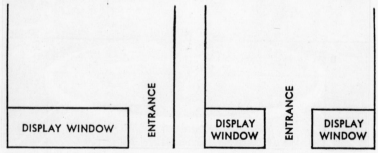

Illustration No. 31—Arrangements of Window Display Space

Window Construction. Window construction should provide a proper amount of display space. This space should be in proportion to the items that are to be displayed. Such items as furniture and stoves require much space, whereas small items, such as watches or neckties, can be displayed to the best advantage in relatively small space. For instance, if the window is large and some small items are to be displayed, the space should be divided into various sections for the merchandise. Such window display space could be made more suitable by the relocation of the entrance to the store. Instead of a single large display window with the door at one side of it, there might be one small window on each side of a center entrance. Illustration No. 31 shows the two arrangements. If the store front is very narrow, however, the entrance at the side is probably the better arrangement.

If a store has a minimum of window display space because of a narrow front, more space can be provided by recessing the entrance in various ways. Additional space may be obtained by the construction of island display cases in recessed areas, such as those shown in Illustration No. 32.

In selecting a building as the location of a business, it is important to consider the possibilities of window displays.

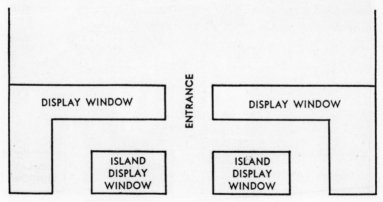

Illustration No. 32—Island Display Cases

A tenant may be able to get the owner to remodel the store front if the present one appears unsuited for display purposes. Building contractors and architects can be consulted as to the details of designs and plans.

Window Lighting. A well-lighted store window attracts people. For example, notice the contrast between Illustration No. 33 and Illustration No. 34, which shows the same store window after it was redesigned. Some businessmen believe that it is well worth the added expense to make their display windows more brilliantly lighted than those of adjacent stores.

Various types of lighting can be used. Concealed lights are most effective as they do not shine in the eyes of people who stop to look at the display. Spotlights or floodlights placed on the floor and focused at close range on a featured part of the display draw special interest to that

General Electric Company.
Illustration No. 33—A Poorly Lighted Store Window

part. Such equipment can be concealed behind placards or pieces of merchandise. Colored lights may be effective in displaying certain kinds of merchandise. In the arrangement of goods and lights care must be taken to prevent undesirable shadows.

Some stores use artificial light during the day to provide adequate lighting for their window displays. Even if such displays are lighted during the day, however, they usually do not require so much light then as they do at night. During certain hours of the night when very few, if any, people are passing, the displays need not be lighted or they may be lighted only slightly. Small stores may use time-clock devices for turning on and off the lights in their display windows. In large stores the night watchman can turn off the lights during the hours when there are few passers-by.

General Electric Company.

Illustration No. 34—A Well-Lighted Store Window

Care of Window Displays. Many window displays repel rather than attract because the window glass is not kept clean or because dust, dirt, and soot are allowed to remain on the goods or on the floor of the display space. It is quite important that the window glass be washed and the goods be dusted carefully and freshened as often as needed. Stores located in climates where the winters are very cold should guard against the display windows becoming frosted and thus losing their advertising value. An electric fan may be used to prevent frost from forming on windows.

Does Sufficient Illumination Pay? When a customer enters a place of business, the general appearance of the store interior makes a strong impression. If the store seems dark and gloomy because of lack of sufficient light, or if the lighting is glaring and spotty, an unfavorable impression is immediately received by the customer. Notice how unattractive the store in Illustration No. 35 appears, and what a difference there is (Illustration No. 36) after

General Electric Company.

Illustration No. 35—A Dark and Gloomy Store

the store has been well lighted. The light-colored walls, ceiling, counters, and display cases aid greatly in showing the interior to advantage.

A customer may feel that the merchandise carried by a poorly lighted store is of inferior quality. Proper lighting makes it easier for the customer to read labels and price tags; to examine the merchandise better; to see corners of display cases, steps, and other obstructions over which he might trip and fall.

Proper lighting in a factory means fewer accidents resulting in personal injuries and less spoilage or damage to the goods being handled by employees. In addition to the general lighting of the factory, it is often desirable to have special lights placed where very close work is being done. For example, special lights are needed over a bench where the small parts of a watch are assembled.

Kinds of Lighting. Broadly speaking, there are two kinds of general illumination. *Direct lighting* is the name given

General Electric Company.

Illustration No. 36—The Same Store Well Lighted

to the method in which all or the greater part of the light is sent directly downward from the lighting fixture. *Indirect lighting* is the term given to the method in which all or most of the light is directed from the fixtures to the ceiling, where it is reflected evenly without any severe glare.

A direct lighting scheme is likely to produce light so bright and glaring that it is difficult to see the merchandise properly. Diffusing globes or panels may be used to lower the brightness and glare. Modern overhead or ceiling lights are recessed in glass boxes. Illustration No. 37 shows some examples of direct lighting.

When indirect lighting is used, bright lamps are concealed from view so that the light is spread over the entire ceiling. The light is thus diffused from many directions; and, as a result, there are no sharp, annoying shadows. Illustration No. 38 shows some examples of indirect lighting.

As all the light must be reflected from the ceiling when indirect lighting is used, the ceiling should be of a very light color. It should also be kept clean and repainted when necessary. For example, notice how the white walls and ceiling aid in lighting the dairy products shown in Illustration No. 39.

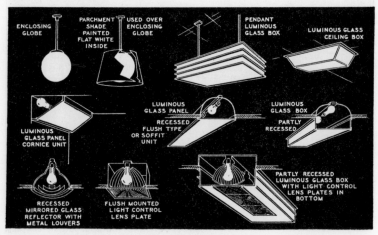

Illustration No. 37—Examples of Direct Lighting

Indirect lighting fixtures must be cleaned often, for all the light comes out of the top of the fixtures, where the dust falls and collects.

A new type of lighting called *fluorescent,* which gives off a proportionately smaller amount of heat than other types, is becoming popular for showcase lighting in candy stores, fruit markets, bakeries, and florist shops.

Large lighting companies and manufacturers of lighting equipment are glad to give advice on lighting problems to interested people.

Ventilation. Because natural ventilation is inadequate in most stores, artificial means are used to pump in and circulate fresh air. In basements that are used as selling space, it is especially important that proper ventilation be provided. Stale and foul air is not inviting to customers and is not healthful to employees. When the ventilation is poor, employees become fatigued easily and render poor service. The management should therefore give consideration to the proper ventilation of the business building.

In automobile repair shops in which motors are frequently being run, the danger from the effects of the exhaust is lessened by placing special connecting pipes from

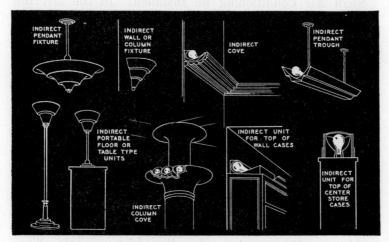

Illustration No. 38—Examples of Indirect Lighting

General Electric Company.

*Illustration No. 39—A Dairy Products Store with
Indirect Illumination*

the exhaust pipes of the automobiles to a central ventilating outlet. Many machines in factories have specially constructed suction devices to collect the fine dust and dirt resulting from manufacturing processes.

Shall Air Conditioning Be Installed? In the last few years we have heard much about air conditioning and have observed that many businesses, as well as homes, have had air-conditioning systems installed. United States Department of Commerce figures show that in 1937 some 7,000 installations costing approximately $31,000,000 were made in this country. This number was almost three times as many installations as were made in 1935. Modern air-conditioning systems cool and dehumidify the air (take out the moisture) in summer, and heat and humidify the air in winter. The air is filtered (dust, dirt, and pollen are removed) and made to circulate.

Surveys show that air conditioning brings more customers to stores, especially during the hot summer months. The cool air comes as a welcome relief to the customer who has been walking on hot sidewalks and pavements. Since the doors are not kept open for ventilation as they are in nonair-conditioned stores, the street noises and dust are kept out. Hence the store is quiet and inviting. Customers usually stay longer and buy more in air-conditioned stores, whereas customers hurry out of uncomfortably hot stores without doing much extra purchasing.

Merchants claim that air conditioning reduces stock losses. Candy stores and groceries handling fresh fruits and vegetables have greatly reduced the spoilage due to hot weather by the installation of air conditioning. Less merchandise is soiled from the perspiring hands of customers and salespeople. Clothing, linen, and decorations stay cleaner with air conditioning. The store employees benefit too. Air conditioning keeps them full of vitality throughout the entire day. Likewise, workers in offices and factories that have been air conditioned find that they are less fatigued at the end of the day's work. Drugstores with soda fountains and luncheonettes, restaurants, beauty parlors, barber shops, doctors' and dentists' offices, and theaters lead in the installation of air-conditioning systems.

Installation costs vary because of such factors as the size of the store, the number of windows, the number of customers entering and leaving, the thickness and the type of walls in the building, and the wattage of the light bulbs. Many small stores have been satisfactorily air-conditioned for less than $1,000. The cost of operation also varies. Small stores in New York, New Jersey, and Pennsylvania report $90 to $120 as operating expenses for a three months' season. Installation costs doubtlessly will continue to decrease as equipment is produced in larger quantities. Refinements and improvements will also mean a decrease in operating costs.

There are many types of so-called air-conditioning systems. Some are merely ventilating systems and some are merely cooling systems. Those which serve only as cooling systems may be very detrimental to the health of employees because the air may not contain the proper amount of moisture.

QUESTIONS FOR DISCUSSION

1. Why is the outside appearance of a building that houses a business usually more important in the case of a retail store than it is in that of a wholesale or a manufacturing business?
2. What are some advantages of using glass blocks in a building?
3. Discuss the reasons why business buildings in various communities need a distinctive appearance.
4. What is meant by a building code?
5. What location is desirable for the receipt and the shipment of merchandise by a small business?
6. What is the purpose of awnings over the windows or the front of a store?
7. Why are light-colored walls usually desirable?
8. Suggest types of businesses that might profit by installing ceilings that deaden noise.
9. What are some of the disadvantages of wooden floors?
10. Explain the chief purpose of window displays.
11. How may a store with a small front increase its window display space?
12. Why should the articles on display in a window be approximately on a level with the eye of the passer-by?
13. What is meant by (a) direct lighting? (b) indirect lighting?
14. What are some of the beneficial results claimed for air conditioning?
15. What are some of the possible disadvantages of certain types of air-conditioning systems?
16. Discuss the advantages of indirect lighting.
17. It is contended that it pays to have good lighting in business. Discuss this point.
18. What are some of the advantages of special floor designs?
19. Why, in your opinion, are heavy wood blocks desirable for floors in some factories?

PROBLEMS AND PROJECTS

1. Compare the number of retail stores on each side of a certain street that have awnings over their store fronts.
2. Visit several businesses and make a report on the different kinds of floors found in their buildings.

3. Draw diagrams showing the entrance or entrances and window display space of three retail stores you have observed.

4. If possible, visit a newly built or remodeled store and compare its lighting with that of some older store. Give a report.

5. A certain business uses for lighting fifteen 200-watt bulbs, ten 100-watt bulbs, and ten 60-watt bulbs. To provide better lighting, the business replaces the 200-watt bulbs with 300-watt bulbs, the 100-watt bulbs with 200-watt bulbs, and the 60-watt bulbs with 100-watt bulbs. If the bulbs are lighted approximately 10 hours daily and the current cost is 5 cents a kilowatt hour (1,000 watts), what is the increased cost of electricity for a month of 26 days?

6. Make a survey of your community to find out what businesses have installed air-conditioning equipment.

7. The cost of installing air-conditioning equipment in a certain store is $1,800. The estimated depreciation is 10 per cent a year, and the operating expenses are approximately $45 a month. What is the total annual cost of operation if 6 per cent interest on the investment is included?

8. If the total annual sales of the business in the preceding problem are $33,120, what percentage of the sales is the total cost of operating the air-conditioning equipment?

CHAPTER VI

PROBLEMS OF OBTAINING HOUSING FACILITIES

Purpose of the Chapter. Obtaining satisfactory housing facilities for a business may involve buying, leasing, or renting a building, constructing a new building, renting or leasing space in a building, or leasing a department in a store. Many of the problems of acquiring housing facilities are discussed in this chapter. Some of the important questions that are answered are:

1. How much can a business afford to spend for housing facilities?
2. Is it more desirable for a person starting in business to lease or to buy the necessary building?
3. What are the principal legal points in connection with leasing property?
4. What are some types of lease contracts?
5. What things should be investigated before buying a building?

How Much to Spend for Housing Facilities. As one of the large operating costs in most businesses is the cost of providing proper housing facilities, the prudent businessman must determine how much he can afford to pay. The amount that can be safely spent for space to house a business will depend upon how much profit can be made from operating the business in that location. The factors that influence the cost of rent were discussed in a preceding chapter. Rent is charged largely on the basis of the demand for the property. Obviously, therefore, rents in downtown sections are higher than those in outlying areas of the city. The rent for a location in a small town is usually lower than the rent for a similar location in a larger city. The rent for a building on a rural road, however, is less than that for a similar building in a small town.

118

A study made by the United States Department of Commerce in a typical large city discloses that some types of businesses can be operated more profitably in the central shopping district than they can in locations outside this district. The central shopping district is considered to be the heart of the city; that is, the place where buildings are concentrated and traffic is congested. This is also the place where rents are highest because more people, who are potential customers, pass locations in this part of the city than locations in other sections.

The results of the study made by the Department of Commerce are shown in Illustration No. 40. This table indicates the percentage of sales that each type of store spent for rent in each location. Notice, for example, that candy and confectionery stores found it cheaper to operate

Kind of Business	Percentage of Sales Spent for Rent	
	Stores Located in Central Shopping District	Stores Located in Other Parts of City
Candy and confectionery stores	5.5	10.7
Fruit and vegetable stores	28.7	6.4
Department stores	2.8	3.7
Dry goods stores	9.8	6.0
Variety stores (5¢–10¢–$1)	6.2	6.5
Automobile accessories stores	4.1	4.6
Men's clothing stores	5.8	6.9
Men's specialty shops	14.7	8.0
Family clothing stores	4.9	2.9
Dressmaking establishments	6.7	9.7
Men's shoe stores	11.7	4.6
Women's shoe stores	10.6	8.9
Furniture stores	4.0	5.1
Household appliance stores	5.0	3.7
Radio shops	5.9	3.3

Illustration No. 40—Percentage of Sales Spent for Rent in Different Parts of a Typical City

in the central shopping district than they did in other locations. Men's specialty shops found it more expensive to operate in the central shopping district, whereas men's clothing stores found rent less expensive there.

Leasing Rather than Buying. Seldom will a person starting in business want to buy a piece of property. In the first place, he should be careful to have available for operating purposes as much cash as possible. If he invests his cash in a building, he may later run into difficulty through a lack of funds. When a person starts into business, it is rather difficult to anticipate exactly the needs of the business. Furthermore, he may buy a building in the wrong location or one that is too small or too large. If he leases or rents, he can rectify a mistake in a reasonably short time and without any great cost.

Relations of Landlord and Tenant. When a person allows his property to be occupied and controlled by another, he is called a *landlord*. The one who occupies the property with the consent of the landlord is the *tenant*. Although the tenant has possession of the property, he has certain duties and obligations with respect to the rights of the landlord. These are explained later. After the expiration of the agreement the landlord has the right to regain possession of the property.

Explanation of Tenancy. The agreement between the landlord and the tenant is known as a *lease*. The landlord is the *lessor*, and the tenant is the *lessee*. Unless there is a law prescribing that a lease must be written, the lease may be oral. In all cases, however, it should be written in order to avoid any misunderstanding. A written lease is desirable in many cases because it clearly defines the rights of the landlord and those of the tenant. As will be seen later, the period of occupancy may be definite or indefinite. In some states the lessor and the lessee must sign their names before a witness, such as a notary public.

The lessor grants the lessee the privilege of using the property for lawful purposes and without interference, provided the terms of the contract are properly carried out. The lease states specifically the rights of each party to the contract. A typical lease is shown in Illustration No. 41. Some of the particular rights of the lessee and the lessor are mentioned later in this chapter.

This Lease Witnesseth:

THAT Harry F. Warner
HEREBY LEASE TO James A. Barnet
the premises situate in the   City   *of*   Lincoln   *in the County of*
Lancaster   *and State of*   Nebraska   *described as follows:*

Store Building, No. 732 Highland Avenue, Lincoln, Nebraska

with the appurtenances thereto, for the term of   two years   *commencing*
March 1   194 ; *at a rental or*   sixty
dollars per   month   *, payable* monthly.

SAID LESSEE AGREES *to pay said rent, unless said premises shall be destroyed or rendered untenantable by fire or other unavoidable accident; to not commit or suffer waste; to not use said premises for any unlawful purpose; to not assign this lease, or under-let said premises, or any part thereof, or permit the sale of* his *interest herein by legal process, without the written consent of said lessor ; to not use said premises or any part thereof in violation of any law relating to intoxicating liquors; and at the expiration of this lease, to surrender said premises in as good condition as they now are, or may be put by said lessor , reasonable wear and unavoidable casualties, condemnation or appropriation excepted. Upon non-payment of any of said rent for* ten *days, after it shall become due, and without demand made therefore; or if said lessee or any assignee of this lease shall make an assignment for the benefit of his creditors; or if proceedings in bankruptcy shall be instituted by or against lessee or any assignee; or if a receiver or trustee be appointed for the property of lessee or any assignee; or if this lease by operation of law pass to any person or persons; or if said lessee or any assignee shall fail to keep any of the other covenants of this lease, it shall be lawful for said lessor ,* his *heirs or assigns, into said premises to re-enter, and the same to have again, re-possess and enjoy, as in* his *first and former estate; and thereupon this lease and everything herein contained on the said lessor behalf to be done and performed, shall cease, determine, and be utterly void.*

SAID LESSOR AGREES *(said lessee having performed* his *obligations under this lease) that said lessee shall quietly hold and occupy said premises during said term without any hindrance or molestation by said lessor ,* his *heir or any person lawfully claiming under them.*

Signed this   first   *day of*   March   A. D. 194

IN PRESENCE OF:

Walter S Lange   Harry F. Warner
Louis M. Stevens   James A. Barnet

Illustration No. 41—A Lease

The formal type of lease usually embodies the following information:

1. The date
2. The names of the landlord and the tenant
3. A description and an identification of the property
4. The length of the tenancy period
5. The amount of the payment
6. The manner of payment
7. A statement of the conditions and the agreements
8. The signatures of the tenant and the landlord

A tenant may occupy property as (a) a *tenant for years,* (b) a *tenant from year to year,* or (c) a *tenant at will.* A tenant for years occupies property under an agreement for a definite period. A tenant from year to year, like a tenant from month to month, occupies property under an agreement for an indefinite period. A tenant at will is one who occupies property for an indefinite period, the agreement being terminable at will by either party. A tenancy at will is commonly referred to as *renting.* This term is a somewhat indefinite one that most people use in reference to the occupancy of property without a written contract.

Rights and Duties of the Tenant. The tenant of a piece of property is entitled to the peaceful possession of it. If he is deprived of that, he may recover damages through a lawsuit. The tenant is also entitled to use the property for any purpose for which it is adapted, unless he is forbidden by the agreement. The wording of the lease should therefore cover the use of the property. Under no circumstances is the tenant allowed to use the property for unlawful purposes.

The tenant is under obligation to make minor repairs but not improvements. He must pay his rent when it is due. Unless the lease states otherwise, the rent is not due until the end of each month.

If the lease is for a definite period of time, the tenant is not obligated to give notice when he vacates the property. The lease may be terminated, however, before the expiration of the period if an agreement is reached with the landlord. If the lease is for an indefinite period of time, the tenant must notify the landlord of his intention to give up the lease. The form and the time of notice are regulated by the customs or the laws of the community in which the tenant is located. The following is an example:

Billings, Montana,
December 1, 19—

Mr. Andrew Walker:

I hereby give you notice that I will quit and deliver possession, January 1, 19—, of the premises at No. 945 Hamilton Avenue, in the city of Billings, Montana, which I now hold as tenant under you.

Martin Arnold

Illustration No. 42—Tenant's Notice of Intention to Terminate a Lease

The tenant should inspect carefully the property that he rents or leases. In the absence of any agreement with the landlord, he accepts the property with the risk of any defects (except defects hidden by the landlord) that may be present. In most states the tenant is liable for injuries to guests resulting from defects he should have remedied.

Length of Lease. If one is starting into business, he should not lease for any longer than is absolutely necessary for his own protection. In other words, he should not obligate himself so that he cannot move if he finds that he has made a mistake in the selection of the property or that the business is not going to be successful in its present location. If he finds it necessary to move, he will not want to be obligated to pay on the original lease. If the business fails, he will not want the obligation of a long lease.

On the other hand, an established business can afford to take a longer lease. In the first place, it is possible to determine the probable volume of business and amount of profit. In the second place, previous experience will indicate the value of the location. In times of anticipated increases in the value of real estate, it is advisable to arrange for a long lease. In times of anticipated decreases in the value of real estate, it is advisable to arrange a short lease.

Lease with Privilege of Purchase. If a businessman is reasonably sure that he has found a desirable location that he may wish to buy later, it is sometimes advisable for him to lease the property with the privilege of purchase. Under such a contract the tenant may have the right at any time or at a specified time to obtain the property at a price agreed upon in the contract. In some cases part of the rent may apply as a down payment if the property is purchased. Such a plan is a more conservative one than an outright purchase. It at least gives the tenant an opportunity to be sure that the property is what he wants and needs. It also gives him an opportunity, if he does not have the money available, to wait until the business has earned enough money for him to buy the property.

Percentage-Income Leases. Some rental leases are based upon a percentage of sales rather than upon a fixed price. In other words, the person who rents property agrees to pay to the owner a certain percentage of his sales. The theory of a percentage-income lease is that, if a business is not successful in a particular location, the tenant should not be burdened with a high rate and the landlord is not entitled to such a rate. If the business is successful, the tenant can afford to pay a greater rent and the landlord is entitled to a larger amount. The following are the five general types of percentage leases:

1. The minimum-maximum form. This type of lease provides a minimum guaranteed rental and also specifies a fixed maximum rental that the owner may realize under any circumstances, no matter to what extent the volume of the tenant's business may grow. This type is rare and is considered to be neither equitable nor sound.

2. No-guarantee form. This type carries a clause giving the owner the right to cancel the lease after a reasonable time if the tenant fails to accomplish the predetermined volume.

3. Regular percentage form with minimum guarantee. This is the most simple and common type.

4. A combination of fixed-rental and percentage form, in which a certain portion of the term calls for a regular rent and the balance of the term has a percentage basis with a minimum amount. This type actually amounts to two leases running consecutively: one, a fixed-rental form; the other, a percentage form. This type is not common, and few good reasons may be advanced for its use.

5. A flat percentage of net sales for an initial period, followed by a minimum amount for the balance of the term.

Amount of Rent Paid under Percentage-Income Leases. The percentage of his sales that a businessman pays under a percentage-income lease depends upon the type of business and upon his success in negotiating a satisfactory lease. A percentage lease, if the rate is reasonable, is fair to the tenant and to the landlord. Under such a plan, however, it is advisable for the landlord to be sure that the tenant is the kind that will produce the greatest maximum income in the location.

The table in Illustration No. 43 shows the results of a study made in a large city to determine the percentage of income paid as rent under percentage-income leases during a particular year.

Clauses in Percentage-Income Leases. The ordinary type of printed lease form is used in drafting a percentage lease. This form stipulates the usual rights and duties of the landlord and the tenant, but also includes a clause stipulating the basis on which payments are to be made. The landlord usually also inserts some additional clauses for his own protection. The following are examples of those clauses:

1. A clause to the effect that the lessee shall not own, operate, become financially interested in, or lend any type of support to a store selling like merchandise within so many blocks of the location.

2. A clause whereby the lessee agrees to carry insurance on his life, the benefits from which are to accrue to

the lessor for rental payments applicable to the balance of the lease in the event of the lessee's death.

3. A clause whereby the lessee agrees to carry and to display merchandise of a certain described type, decided upon in advance as being proper, and further agrees to sell such merchandise at a price not in excess of that at which like products may be obtained.

Type of Store	Percentage of Income Paid as Rent
Art goods and gifts	10%
Automobile parking lots—parking only	50%
Automobile parking lots—accessories (and 1 cent a gallon on gasoline)	15%
Automobile sales	5%
Bakery goods	7%
Barber shops—street	15%
Beauty shops—merchandise	10%
Beauty shops—service	15%
Books and stationery	8–10%
Books—secondhand	10–12%
Candy	10–12%
Cigars	8–10%
Drugs	8–10%
Flowers	8–10%
Furniture	5%
Furs	7–8%
Groceries	5%
Haberdasheries	10%
Hosiery	8–10%
Jewelry—quality and popular price	10%
Jewelry—novelty, costume, etc.	12%
Linen	8–10%
Lingerie	10%
Liquor—packaged goods	6–8%
Men's clothing	7–8%
Men's hats	10–12½%
Millinery	12½–15%
Optical goods	10–12½%
Paints—specialty goods	10%
Radios, musical instruments, etc.	6%
Restaurants and taverns	8–10%
Shoes, women's	8–10%
Shoes, men's	8–10%
Shoe repair, valet service, etc.	15–20%
Sporting goods	7–10%
Stationery (15 per cent on legal blanks)	10%
Trunks and leather goods	10%
Women's wearing apparel	8–10%

Illustration No. 43—Percentage of Income Paid as Rent under Percentage-Income Leases

4. A clause whereby the lessee agrees to expend a certain percentage of his gross annual sales for advertising in local newspapers, on the radio, and in other established advertising mediums.

5. A clause whereby repossession of the property may be had by the landlord if the rent paid over a certain period has not averaged or equaled a certain amount.

6. A clause whereby the lessee agrees to operate his business continuously during certain set hours, or at least during the hours generally considered to be those established for that type of business. (This clause is particularly important in percentage leases for theaters.)

7. Other clauses that may be inserted are: a clause regarding use and occupancy insurance (explained in Chapter XVIII), a clause regulating the type of fixtures to be used in the storeroom, and a clause requiring the lessee to employ adequate help so that the maximum potential business may be taken care of. These clauses, however, are employed only in extreme cases.

Escalator Clauses. Regular leases and percentage-income leases may contain so-called escalator clauses. For example, during the first year under an ordinary lease, a certain amount may be paid each month; during the second year and succeeding years the amount may be increased until a fixed maximum is reached. Likewise, percentage-income leases may require the tenant to pay 4 per cent on the first $10,000 of sales, 5 per cent on the next $10,000 of sales, and so on.

Subleasing. There is a common practice of subleasing business property. For example, a tenant may lease a piece of property and find later that it is not desirable or that it is not large enough. He may therefore sublease the property to another tenant and obtain for himself another piece of property.

It is desirable that the tenant have a lease contract that gives him the privilege of subleasing. It is equally desirable that the landlord be protected in such a case by some clause in the lease. In other words, the landlord will probably want to insert a clause prohibiting the tenant from subleasing the property without the approval of the landlord.

The subleasing of property constitutes an additional business risk. For example, if the businessman is working on a small margin and decides to sublease a piece of property and obtain another piece, there is a possibility that his tenant, the person to whom he has subleased, may go out of business and have to give up the property. The loss of this income may therefore be a serious handicap.

Department Leasing. One who is operating, or contemplating operating, a small retail store in a city may find it advantageous to arrange with some established store to lease a part of it. For example, one may be able to lease, from the owner of a grocery store, space for a meat department in that store. It is a common practice for department stores to lease departments. For instance, such a store may operate all its major departments, but may sublease some of the others. Some department stores make

Rike-Kumler Company.

Illustration No. 44—A Leased Department

a practice of leasing most of their departments. Those most commonly leased are as follows:

Millinery	Wallpaper
Hair goods, hair dressing, and manicuring	Shoes
	Furs
Crockery and glassware	Sewing machines
Carpets and linoleum	Dress patterns
Furniture or house furnishings	Men's clothing
	Cleaning and dyeing
Optical goods	Restaurants
Musical instruments	

The lease arrangements of departments are quite similar to the agreement made between a businessman and any other landlord, with the exception that the leased department operates, so far as the public is concerned, as an integral part of the store. It is usually impossible for the customer to determine whether he is buying from a regular department of a store or from a leased department. All the policies are governed by the store.

Advantages and Disadvantages to the Department Lessee and Lessor. Among the principal advantages to the lessee of a department are:

1. Obtaining a location in a developed market where a certain volume of trade is already waiting.
2. Gaining the prestige of the lessor's name and goodwill.
3. Receiving the advantages of the accounting and collection systems of the department store.
4. Participating in giving his customers many store services that he would not be able to give if he were located in a separate building.

Some of the disadvantages to this type of lessee are:

1. The tenure may be impermanent. Often the lessor may terminate the contract on short notice.
2. As there may be considerable demand for leased departments, the rentals may be high.
3. The lessor controls the store policies.

Leased departments have advantages and disadvantages also for the store, or lessor. For instance, the store may have difficulty in controlling the policies and the conduct of miscellaneous leased departments, as well as the quality and the appearance of the merchandise handled in those departments. On the other hand, the leasing of departments eliminates the problems of buying and merchandising for those departments.

One who leases a department should have a clear understanding of his rights and privileges. He should also have a definite knowledge of the customs and practices of the store. For example, if each department records its own sales and collects its own money, no particular problem is involved; but if charge accounts are handled through the store management, the department must depend upon the store for collections, returns, exchanges, and adjustments. In some cases exchanges and adjustments are handled by the individual departments, but in most cases they are handled by the management of the store so that all policies are uniform.

Rights and Duties of the Landlord. A landlord does not have a right to enter the premises of a tenant except to do what is necessary to protect the property. He must not interfere with the tenant's right of possession. If the tenant abandons the property, however, the landlord may take possession. At the expiration of the lease the landlord may enter the property and take possession through legal proceedings.

The landlord is entitled to receive the rent specified in the lease. In some states, through legal proceedings, he may seize the tenant's personal property and have it sold to pay the rent that is in arrears.

In some states the landlord is under no obligation to make repairs or to pay for improvements on the property unless an agreement has been made with the tenant. In most states, however, he is obligated to keep the house in habitable condition. Unless the lease specifies otherwise, taxes and assessments must be paid by the landlord.

When a tenant occupies property for an indefinite period of time, the landlord may obtain possession of it by giving notice. The form and the time of the notice are regulated by local customs or laws. Illustration No. 45 is, however, a typical notice from a landlord.

When the landlord retains control over a part of the property, as in the case of a landlord who leases part of a building to a tenant, he is liable for certain injuries that may be caused by the defective condition of the part of the property over which he has control. For instance, Mr. A owns a store building and rents part of it to Mr. B. Mr. B and his customers must pass through a section of the building controlled by Mr. A. Should any injuries occur to Mr. B or to his customers as they are passing through Mr. A's part of the building, Mr. A may be liable for damages.

Alterations and Fixtures. The tenant or the landlord may agree to make alterations or to install fixtures. It is more customary, however, for the landlord to make the alterations and for the tenant to install fixtures. The lease should cover these provisions very specifically.

Guides in Buying Property. It was pointed out previously that it is usually undesirable for a man starting in business to purchase a building or buildings to house his business. Sometimes a businessman may be unable to lease a suitable building; or, after operating for a while in leased property, he may decide that it is more desirable to buy than to continue to lease. Should he decide to buy, there are many things that must be considered. Some of them are discussed here.

Time to Buy. A person cannot always choose the exact time at which it is most profitable to buy; but if he keeps certain points in mind, he will be able to make a good purchase. Generally, real-estate valuations are lowest near the end of business depressions when many real-estate mortgages are being foreclosed; they are highest near the peak of the prosperity phase of the business cycle. Valuations are also likely to rise as the surrounding property begins

LANDLORD'S COMPLAINT.

To_____ **Paul H. Martin** _____, a Justice of the Peace in and for
the Township of_____ **Fairfield** _____, County of_____ **Butler** _____ and State of Ohio.

The undersigned_____ **Robert P. Miller** _____, a resident of
the County of_____ **Butler** _____ and State of Ohio, do **es** hereby make _____ **his** _____ complaint against
_____ **Gordon B. Matthews** _____

for this: That the said_____ **Gordon B. Matthews** _____

_____ ha **s** _____, ever since the _____ **fifth** _____ day of _____ **January** _____ , 194

and do **es** still unlawfully and forcibly detain from the undersigned, possession of the following premises,
situated in the Township of_____ **Fairfield** _____, in the said County of
_____ **Butler** _____ and described as follows:

_____ **House and lot, No. 155 Maple Avenue** _____

_____

_____

_____

_____

_____

_____

_____

_____

_____

_____

_____

The said_____ **Gordon B. Matthews** _____
entered upon said premises as the tenant _ of the undersigned. The lease thereof expired at the time
herein first mentioned, and from that time the said_____ **Gordon B. Matthews** _____

ha **s** unlawfully and forcibly held over_____ **his** _____ said term.

On the _____ **second** _____ day of _____ **February** _____ , 194 , the undersigned duly served upon the
said _____ **Gordon B. Matthews** _____
as required by law, notice, in writing, to leave said premises.

The undersigned asks process and restitution.

Dated this _____ **second** _____ day of _____ **February** _____ , 194

Robert P. Miller

*Illustration No. 45—Landlord's Notice Requesting Tenant
to Vacate Property*

to be developed and improved. Naturally, the best time to buy is when valuations are low. It is difficult to determine the end of a depression. If a businessman wishes to buy real estate at the most opportune time, however, he should not buy it when prices are relatively high and many people are buying, but should buy it when prices are low and few people are buying property.

Conditions of the Property. Before one buys, the property should be inspected thoroughly. Instead of relying upon a real-estate agent's glowing account of the property, one should engage a building expert to check the details of construction and the present condition of the building. A detailed list of needed repairs and their cost should be made. Likewise, a careful search of the title to the property should be made by one trained in such work. Many a person who purchased property believed that he had received a clear title, only to find at some later date that there were other claimants to the title. A careful investigation should be made to see if there are any special assessments, such as for paving and sewers, against the property. The assessed valuation of the property and the tax rate also should be considered.

QUESTIONS FOR DISCUSSION

1. What should be the principal consideration of a businessman in deciding whether the rent demanded for a prospective location of his business is suitable?
2. Illustration No. 40 shows that the operators of furniture stores found their rent to be a smaller percentage of their sales when they were located in the central shopping district, whereas the owners of radio shops found it to be smaller when they were located in other parts of the city. Suggest reasons for this difference.
3. Why is it usually more desirable for a new business to lease rather than to buy housing facilities?
4. Who are the lessor and the lessee?
5. Why is it desirable to have a written lease?
6. What are the principal items that should be included in a lease?

7. Distinguish between a tenant for years and a tenant from year to year.

8. Is a tenant under obligation to make repairs to the property?

9. Why is a short-term lease preferable for a new business?

10. What is meant by a percentage-income lease?

11. State three general types of percentage-income leases.

12. What is the average charge under percentage-income leases?

13. What is subleasing?

14. Explain department leasing.

15. Give some advantages and disadvantages to the lessee of a department.

16. What are some factors to be considered in buying housing facilities for a business?

PROBLEMS AND PROJECTS

1. According to the figures given in Illustration No. 40 (page 119), fruit and vegetable stores located in the central shopping district spend about 28.7 per cent of their sales for rent, whereas similar stores located in other parts of the city spend approximately 6.4 per cent. Using these figures, determine what the monthly sales of such a store should be to justify (a) a monthly rental of $143.50 for a location in the central shopping district; (b) a monthly rental of $35 for a location in another part of the city.

2. It is possible to lease a certain building for $200 a month or to buy it for $20,000. Considering the following factors, determine whether it is better to lease or to buy and by how much per year: The assessed valuation is $15,000, and the tax rate is $25.50 a $1,000; insurance for $16,000 at a rate of 75 cents a $100 must be taken out for three years; the estimate for annual repairs is 1 per cent of the purchase price; the estimated annual depreciation is 2 per cent; interest on the investment is 5 per cent.

3. A percentage-income lease requires a tenant who operates a drugstore to pay an annual rental of 8 per cent on the first $10,000 of sales, 9 per cent on the next $10,000 of sales, and 10 per cent on all additional sales. If the sales during a certain year are $25,500, what should be the amount of the annual rent?

4. Suppose that you wish to lease a certain piece of property for the operation of a business you are starting. Find out the probable rent you would have to pay for that particular property, and then draw up a lease that you think the owner of the property would ask you to sign.

CHAPTER VII
EQUIPMENT PROBLEMS

Purpose of the Chapter. The term *equipment* is a very broad one and includes a large number of items. In this chapter the discussion of equipment will be limited to a few of the more common types in order to illustrate some of the equipment problems that confront a business. The following important problems in connection with equipment will be discussed in this chapter:

1. What are the advantages and the disadvantages of the various kinds of display and storage fixtures?
2. What kinds of equipment should be used for the handling of money and the keeping of records?
3. What particular make of equipment should be purchased?
4. What terms do the sellers of equipment give to a purchaser?

Equipment in Selling Departments. It is important that the fixtures used in a selling department be in keeping with the merchandise being sold. If ultramodern merchandise is being sold, the fixtures should also reflect the ultramodern style. Cheap and old-style fixtures will detract from high-priced merchandise. In men's stores, heavy, rugged furniture and dark-colored fixtures may be used to give an effect of masculinity. In women's stores, there should be light colors and artistic fixtures to create a feminine atmosphere. The fixtures in a rural store should not be too expensive because, if they are, they are likely to give the impression of high overhead expenses.

Display and Storage Fixtures. Formerly merchandise for display and immediate use was stored in the cardboard boxes in which the goods arrived from the manufacturer or the distributor. In retail stores these boxes were placed under the counter or on shelves back of the counter. This antiquated method is still used in thousands of small stores and even in some large stores, but it does not meet adequately the requirements of modern merchandising. Modern merchandising demands display, protection, and speedy service from its fixtures. If cardboard boxes are placed under the counter, they are easily broken by the foot of a salesclerk or the broom of a person sweeping and cleaning. Covers may be torn easily or may not be replaced tightly by the clerk. It is therefore possible for the contents to be soiled by dust and dirt. Constant handling makes the cardboard boxes soiled and unattractive. When a clerk places such boxes on the counter and prepares to show the merchandise stored in them, a customer may be influenced against buying. There are often health ordinances that require the business to keep certain products in closed, and sometimes in refrigerated, display and storage fixtures. Special fixtures are available for practically every kind of merchandise, whether it be spools of thread or expensive fur coats.

The preceding discussion with regard to the use of shipping cartons does not apply, however, in handling reserve stock. The original shipping cartons are usually quite convenient for storing reserve stock. In fact, the merchandise often can be kept better in these cartons than in any other way.

A customer usually enters a store to buy one or two articles, but he may buy others if they are brought to his attention. One of the simplest ways to bring additional merchandise to his attention is to have it displayed attractively in full view. Glass fronts on stock drawers, glass showcases, glass tops on counters, and glass doors on wardrobes containing delicate and dainty clothing are means by which goods are given proper display, as well as protection. Food products not only are displayed attractively in glass cases, but also may be kept from spoiling by means of refrigerated display cases. Illustration No. 46 shows how baked goods can be displayed attractively through the use of the proper fixtures. Notice how the design in the floor

Illustration No. 46—Baked Goods Attractively Displayed

is planned to draw the customer to the back part of the
room. The ovens are located in the rear of the salesroom.

Quicker service is possible by the use of proper storage
and display equipment. Steaks, chops, roasts, and other
cuts of meat can be prepared in advance of actual sale and
then placed in refrigerated display cases. When a customer
wishes a steak or chops, it is not necessary for him to wait
until the butcher goes into the storage refrigerator, brings
out a large portion of meat, places it on the cutting block,
sharpens a knife, cuts off a part, and then returns the large
portion to the storage refrigerator. Likewise, service to
the customer is accelerated when the salesman of men's
hats pushes open a glass door on a wall display case of
hats and selects one for the customer. Such a procedure
is quite in contrast to that of storing hats in cardboard
boxes, many of which must be opened before the customer
gets an idea of what hats are being offered for sale. Illustration No. 47 shows both wall display cases and a counter
display case for men's clothing.

General Electric Company.

*Illustration No. 47—Display Cases Protect the Goods and
Permit Quicker Service*

As a general principle, goods should not be displayed above the average eye level. Goods in large display cases on the floor should be arranged so that the customer need not stoop to get a good view of them. If there are shelves in the display case, they should be so arranged that the upper shelves do not hide the goods on the lower shelves. Narrower upper shelves may be used. Some of the glass cases in Illustration No. 46 of the Duane Bakery show this feature of display cases.

Low Store Fixtures. Fixtures, including counters, display cases, and cabinets, should be low enough so that a customer standing in one part of the store may have an unobstructed view of the other parts of the store. This practice is desirable because it brings to the customer's attention merchandise displayed in other departments. The customer may therefore be induced to make further purchases. Fixtures against side walls may be higher as they will not obstruct the view of customers.

Many of the modern fixtures are of metal instead of wood. Such fixtures are lighter in weight than the old-fashioned ones made of wood. Wooden fixtures are liable to develop rough edges, which easily damage delicate fabrics.

Open Display Fixtures. In some types of businesses the open display fixture is very popular. Tables, racks, and bins that make it possible for the customer not only to see but also to handle and examine the goods are known as *open display fixtures*. Variety stores, such as Woolworth's, use them almost to the exclusion of other types of fixtures. Hardware stores also make use of this type of fixture. Grocery stores are beginning to put more of their merchandise on open display tables. Roadside stands, fruit and vegetable markets, and gift shops make extensive use of open displays. Making it easy for the customer to come into personal contact with the goods usually results in greater sales than if the goods are hidden away in drawers or on shelves back of counters. There is, of course, the disadvantage of soilage and damage resulting from the handling and examining of certain types of goods by customers. Illustration No. 48 shows an open display of fresh fruits and vegetables. Notice that the display fixture has devices for emitting a fine spray of water over the vegetables. This moisture keeps the vegetables looking fresh and reduces loss from spoilage.

Many stores make use of *bargain* or *special tables*. A grocer may have a special price on a brand of canned peaches that he is discontinuing; or a clothing store may have a table of second-quality, slightly defective, or soiled men's shirts marked to be sold at bargain prices.

Comfort and Convenience of Customers. The modern business depends upon more than quality goods at fair prices to build the goodwill of customers. It strives particularly to make the customer comfortable while shopping. At glove counters, in shoe stores, rug departments, and millinery stores, comfortable chairs and seats are provided for not only customers but also friends who might

Illustration No. 48—A Display Fixture for Keeping
Vegetables Fresh

be accompanying the customers. In most cases chairs are
more desirable than seats or stools fastened to the floor
because they can be moved quickly to wherever they are
needed. At lunch counters and soda fountains, however,
the stools are usually fastened to the floor. Such stools
formerly were quite high, and the customer had to climb
awkwardly on and off them. Recently counter stools have
been made the height of ordinary chairs, and the counter
has been lowered accordingly, for the purpose of making
the customer more comfortable. Metal chairs and stools
are to be preferred to wooden ones because there is less
danger of damage to the hosiery and other clothing of customers. Gasoline filling stations and large stores provide
washrooms for the convenience of customers.

Self-service grocery stores provide baskets into which
customers may place purchases selected from shelves and
tables. The large supermarkets provide deep wire baskets
mounted on wheels for the convenience of customers. Some

of these large self-service stores have a continuous track, waist high, running around the store in front of the shelving. On this track the customer sets the market basket with four small wheels and pushes it along easily, like a tray on a cafeteria rail, as he selects his purchases.

Lighted Display Fixtures. Wall cabinets and counter display cases have their attention value greatly increased when lighted. Where heat from the lighting unit would affect merchandise, such as candy, meats, and dairy products, the lighting equipment may be mounted outside the front of the case, provided the equipment is ventilated to keep customers from touching the hot reflector; may be placed inside the case in a special ventilated built-in compartment; or may be suspended above the glass top of the case, over the front edge and high enough above the floor

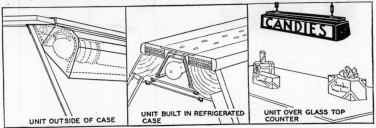

Illustration No. 49—Methods of Lighting Display Cases

so as not to obstruct the view of the customer or of the clerk. Illustration No. 49 shows these three plans of lighting display cases.

The entire face of open stock on shelves can be lighted effectively by placing lighting units in concentrating trough reflectors across the top of the shelves and from eight inches to twelve inches out from the shelving.

Mirrors form an important part of the equipment in such places as millinery stores, dress shops, shoe stores, beauty parlors, and men's clothing stores. They should be arranged and lighted so that the customer can get a good view of himself and the article being tried on. Manufacturers can furnish catalogs and information as to the types of mirrors suitable for various purposes.

There are many types of illuminated signs that may serve to decorate as well as to illuminate the interior of a store. The signs should harmonize with the general decorative plan. The following are a few examples of types of lighted interior signs:

CUTOUT LETTERS SILHOUETTED AGAINST CURVED WHITE BACKGROUND

LUMINOUS PANEL WITH CHANGEABLE CUTOUT LETTERS

SPECIAL SALES BOOTH WITH CANOPY AND TRANSLUCENT SIGN ILLUMINATED BY INDIRECT TORCHIERE

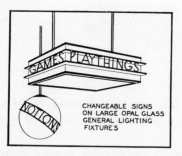

CHANGEABLE SIGNS ON LARGE OPAL GLASS GENERAL LIGHTING FIXTURES

LUMINOUS WEDGE SIGN LIGHTED FROM PARABOLIC TROUGH REFLECTOR AT WIDE END

LETTERS ETCHED IN CLEAR PLATE GLASS EDGE LIGHTED BY LUMILINE LAMPS

BAND CONCEALING LUMILINE LAMPS FOR SILHOUETTE EFFECT

FLAT SIGN LIGHTED BY LUMILINE LAMPS

Illustration No. 50—Interior Signs

Interior Signs. Lighted signs in the store can be used to call attention to merchandise being featured and also to help the customer find departments easily. These signs may be permanently fixed, such as a lighted sign over the entrance to a special department or shop; or they may be temporarily placed on the wall above merchandise on display. Temporary signs may be cut from cardboard or thin metal and fastened around light globes. Various types of interior signs are shown in Illustration No. 50.

Signs at Store Fronts. A suitable electric sign at the store front may be used to attract new customers and to serve as a reminder to present patrons. A vertical projecting sign is usually most effective as it can be seen clearly from both sides. A sign across the face of the store building sometimes may be more in keeping with the general treatment of the store front.

Modern store signs, such as neon signs, make possible the use of color and varied designs. The design, color or colors, and size depend largely upon the signs used on neighboring stores. To stand out, such a sign should be different from those used by neighboring stores, and should be so placed that it can be seen from many angles by passers-by. Bright, flashing signs that are liable to be annoying should not be used. Most cities have building codes regulating the size, location, types, and fastening of outdoor signs. In such cases a permit must be obtained.

Measuring Equipment. To ensure greater accuracy and to give better service to the customer, many kinds of measuring equipment are being used by the businessmen of today. Gasoline was formerly pumped by means of a hand pump into one-gallon or five-gallon containers and then transferred to the fuel tank of the automobile. Modern pumps, electrically operated, now transfer the gasoline directly to the fuel tank of the automobile. A dial on such a pump indicates to the customer the exact quantity and the total cost, even if a fractional part of a gallon is pumped. Another dial shows the total gallons pumped during the day.

Stores selling yard goods, such as ribbons and dress and drapery materials, have found that, when measuring machines are not used, the salesperson has a tendency to give the customer "good measure." Suppose that a salesperson gives an average of three inches "good measure" on each sale of yard goods and that he makes an average of twenty-four sales daily. The loss from the inaccurate measurement would be computed as follows:

24 sales a day
3 inches
——
72 inches, or 2 yards, of extra cloth given away each day

300 working days in a year
600 yards (300 × 2) given away each year
$.50 average cost of goods per yard (There is, of course, a great variety of prices for different kinds of yard goods.)
$300 the loss caused to the management in one year by the inaccurate measurement of one salesperson (600 × .50)

Careless and dishonest salespersons may, on the other hand, give customers too little by undermeasuring. This

The Measuregraph Co.

Illustration No. 51—A Cloth-Measuring Machine

practice may cause the store to lose customer goodwill. Modern machines measure yard goods accurately and make a small cut or notch in the material at the point where the clerk should start cutting the goods with a scissors. The machine also may have a mechanical calculator that figures the price automatically and thus eliminates errors that clerks might make in figuring such amounts as 4⅜ yards at 17 cents a yard.

Illustration No. 51 shows a cloth-measuring machine.

Weighing scales that automatically compute the total cost of the items being weighed are desirable fixtures for businesses that sell bulk products.

A common type of scale is shown in Illustration No. 52. The long, white movable pointer, shown pointing at 0, has on it certain numerals from 10 to 125. These are the prices per pound or other unit. To determine the selling price of a quantity of butter being weighed, the salesperson finds the numeral on the long, white movable pointer that corresponds to the selling price per pound and then determines at what numeral

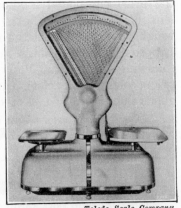

Toledo Scale Company.
*Illustration No. 52—A Self-
Computing Pointer Scale*

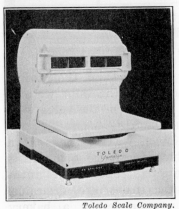

Toledo Scale Company.
*Illustration No. 53—A Self-
Computing Scale with
Magnifying Lenses*

on the large scale the pointer is resting.

The average net profit of food stores is under 5 per cent. Five per cent of one pound is four fifths of an ounce. If every customer were given one ounce overweight with each pound, there would be a resulting loss instead of a 5 per cent profit. In order to prevent profits being given away through errors in reading the scale, certain models contain powerful optical lenses to magnify the figures on the computing chart of the scale. Illustration No. 53 shows such a model.

The four lenses in this type of scale are carried in a sliding frame. By a simple shift of the frame the visible surface of the chart is changed. The result, as shown in Illustration No. 54, is a double price range, one for low prices and one for higher prices. Price ranges can be obtained to fit the particular business. In this illustration

the price per pound is shown across the bottom of each
lens (4, 5, 6, 7, 8, 9, etc.). The reading line shows the
weight of the goods in the right-hand column of each lens
(approximately 6 pounds 4 ounces in this illustration). By
following the reading line across the chart to the proper
price column, the clerk can determine the value of the
goods being weighed. For example, in this illustration, if

LENSES AT LOW PRICE RANGE POSITION

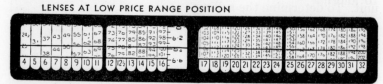

LENSES AT HIGH PRICE RANGE POSITION

Illustration No. 54—Reading a Self-Computing Scale

the value of the goods were 4 cents a pound, the reading
line would show a total of 25 cents; if the value were 20
cents a pound, the total would be $1.25; if the value were
34 cents a pound, the total would be $2.12.

Toledo Scale Company.
*Illustration No. 55—A Photo-
Electric Control Scale*

In many businesses in
which the same quantity is
weighed repeatedly, auto-
matic scales are desirable.
For example, in a bakery
quantities of flour will be
weighed for each batch of
mixture. Accurate weight is
important if uniform quality
is to be had. For such a situation photo-electric control
scales are available. Illustration No. 55 shows such a
scale. A beam of light falls
on an electric eye located in

the dial housing. The indicator has two arms, one pointing to the dial graduations and the other acting as an interceptor of the beam of light. As the interceptor passes in front of the electric eye, it blocks off the beam of light, causing an electrical reaction that controls gates, valves, and conveyors. The illustration shows an overhead track on which a hopper can be moved easily from one mixer to another.

Cash Registers. Most businesses of today use cash registers entirely or partially in handling cash. Such registers have been designed for almost every need that a business may have in handling cash. Most cash registers perform the following operations at one time:

1. Indicate on a large dial the price of the article sold.
2. Print a receipt to be given to the customer.
3. Accumulate totals of sales by departments, such as meats, groceries, fruits, and vegetables.
4. Give the totals of sales made by various salespeople.
5. Give the number of transactions by departments and the number of sales made by each salesperson.
6. Indicate the total sales.
7. Provide a place for keeping money.

Cash registers make possible speedy service in connection with cash sales. Money can be received from the customer; change made and returned with a receipt; and the customer started on his way in a very short time.

At soda fountains, registers that print the amount of the sale on a ticket are often used. The soda clerk gives a ticket to each customer, and the latter then pays his bill at a cashier's desk. This system speeds up service and eliminates the actual handling of money by the soda clerks. It also serves as a check on sales made by the clerks.

Illustration No. 56 shows a cash register that is used by retail stores. As there are four individual cash drawers, one may be assigned to each of four salespeople so that responsibility is placed upon each for all the money he handles. This model has transaction counters in the dials just above the money drawers. These counters keep an

National Cash Register Company.
Illustration No. 56—A Cash Register for Retail Stores

accurate record of the number of customers, charge sales, cash sales, amounts received on account transactions, amounts paid out, and the number of times "No Sale" was registered in order to open a cash drawer for some purpose other than a sale or receipt or payment of cash. There are also counters to show the number of transactions handled by each of the four clerks. The totals of eight different items, such as cash sales and charge sales, are accumulated inside the register. At the end of the day the register can be unlocked and these totals taken off for the financial records. The machine also provides a printed receipt, a detailed audit strip, and a means of imprinting the amount of a charge sale on the charge slip at the same time the amount is recorded in the machine.

The Cash Tube System. Many large department stores make use of pneumatic tubes for handling the cash in certain departments where the amount of each sale is usually large. The money received from a customer, together with the sales slip, is placed in a carrier; the carrier is then sent by means of compressed air through a tube to a central cashier or tube room. The change is returned in a similar manner. This system affords greater protection to large amounts of money, but is much slower than the cash-register system.

Change-Making Machines. To accelerate the change-making process, restaurants, soda fountains, and theaters make use of change-making machines. There are two types of these machines. Let us suppose that a customer made a purchase of 55 cents and handed a one-dollar bill to the cashier. If one type of change-making machine is used, the cashier must determine the amount of change to be given the customer, in this case 45 cents. Then, by depressing a key labeled "45," the cashier causes one quarter and two dimes automatically to drop out of the machine. If the other type of machine is used, the cashier depresses the key that corresponds to the amount of the sale, in this case "55," and causes the correct amount of change to drop out.

Accounting and Record-Keeping Machines. Many machines have been designed to aid in accounting and record-keeping. Only a few are explained here. Illustration No. 57 shows an accounting and analysis machine used by laundries and examples of records made by it. Notice that the machine, by means of one operation, certifies the laundry list in three places, on the routeman's stub, the office stub, and the customer's list. It also prints the date, the amount, the identification number, the class of service (symbol after the amount), the route number (number after the kind of sale, such as charge or cash), and the kind of sale. A statement of the customer's charge account is posted at the same time that the entries are made on the laundry list. The machine accumulates totals of many kinds, such as the totals of the different types of sales, the totals of various routes, the total amount of business, and an analysis of the different kinds of sales made by each routeman.

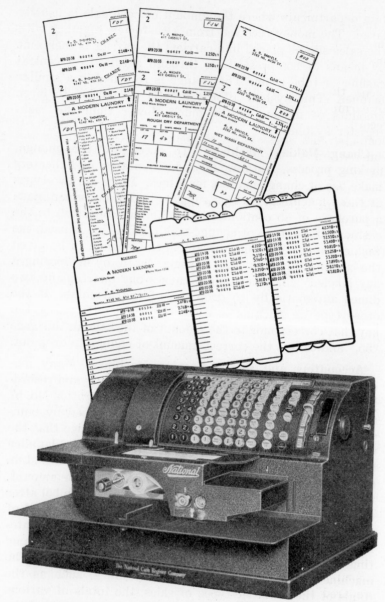

National Cash Register Company.

Illustration No. 57—An Accounting Machine for Laundries and Records Made on It

Illustration No. 58 shows a typewriter-bookkeeping machine and how it can be used for pay-roll records. On the machine illustrated, five records are made in one operation by the use of carbon paper. The five records are the pay check, the employee's statement (the stub on the check), an earnings record card, a pay-roll summary, and a check record. The net amount of each check is automatically computed and printed. The totals of the various items accumulate in the machine. This machine may be used also for general bookkeeping work, such as posting accounts receivable, accounts payable, and the general ledger. This type of machine can also be used for straight tabulating and listing.

A check-writing, signing machine with automatic deduction computation is shown in Illustration No. 59. Examples of work done by this machine are also shown. Notice that the machine can be used for several kinds of checks. Various totals of gross amounts, discounts, deductions (savings, insurance, and old-age pensions), and net amounts accumulate in individual locked totals. The signature plate is removable, and the compartment for it can be locked to prevent fraudulent use of the plate.

Some businesses make use of an alphabetic electric bookkeeping and tabulating machine when they desire to show names, addresses, and descriptions printed in full on finished reports. Illustration No. 60 shows such a machine. The basic units of this method are cards, such as those shown in Illustration No. 60, that are designed to contain all the data pertinent to a given subject. Holes are punched in the cards at various points to represent the information to be handled. By inserting these punched cards into the machine, it is possible to have the detailed information automatically printed on forms such as the one shown in Illustration No. 61. This illustration shows an invoice (usually made in duplicate by the use of carbon paper) prepared for a wholesale grocery. Many chain groceries make similar use of this machine. The punched cards that have been used can be automatically sorted and counted by a special machine in order to provide financial and statis-

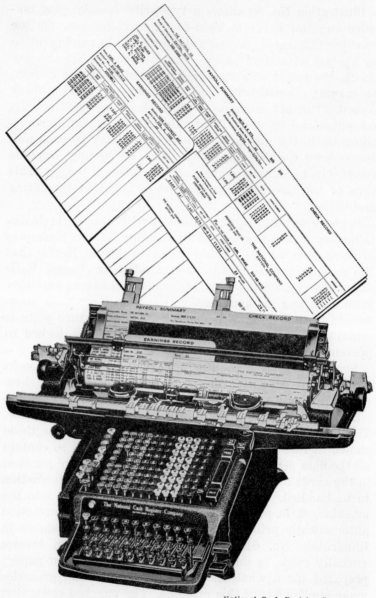

National Cash Register Company.

*Illustration No. 58—A Typewriter-Bookkeeping Machine
and Pay-Roll Records Made on It*

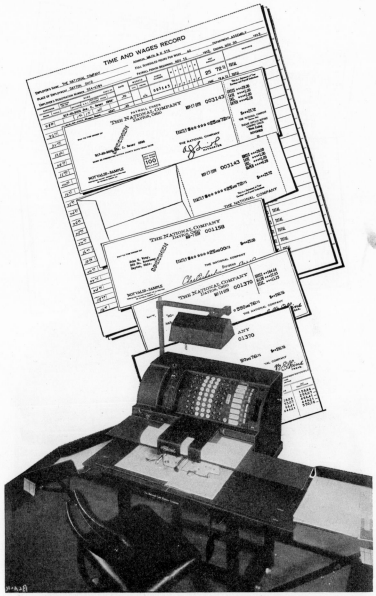

National Cash Register Company.

Illustration No. 59—A Check-Writing, Signing Machine and Work Done on It

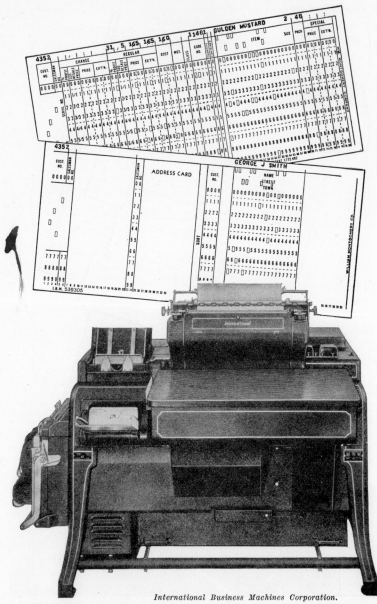

International Business Machines Corporation.

Illustration No. 60—An Electric Bookkeeping and Tabulating Machine and Cards Used on It

DELIVERY RECEIPT

DATE ____________

RECEIVED OF INTERNATIONAL WHOLESALE GROCERY CO.

DRIVER ____________

____ PIECES OF MERCHANDISE IN GOOD CONDITION ____________

SIGNATURE

DATE JULY 26 1938

TO GEORGE J SMITH
2342 ST JAMES AVE
ELIZABETH N J

CUST. NO. 4352

PIECES	ITEM	SIZE	PACK	CODE	% PROFIT	S. R. P.	PRICE	EXTENSION	
1 CS	GULDEN MUSTARD	2 OZ	48	1148	31	5	1.65	1.65	1.60
1 CT	MABCO ICE CR CONES		250	1232			.65	.65	.50
1 CS	SCHIM JELLY GRAPE	16 OZ	24	1274	17	.15	3.00	3.00	2.70
1 CS	HIRES ROOT BEER	26 OZ	12	1616	33	.15	1.40	1.40	1.28
1 CS	WELCHS GRAPE JUICE	QT	12	1646	21	.42	4.00	4.00	3.90
1 CS	S SWT PRUNE JUICE	32 OZ	12	1718	23	.19	1.75	1.75	1.65
3 CS	CAMP TOM JUICE	14 OZ	48	1760	26	8	2.85	8.55	8.19
1 CS	PHILLIPS STG BEAN	2	24	2326	30	8	1.35	1.35	1.25
3 CS	WILDEY SW PEAS	2	24	2556	29	.17	2.90	8.70	7.35
2 CS	GREAT NORTH PEAS	#303	24	2562	28	.13	2.25	4.50	4.00
1 CS	STANDARD TOMATOES	2	24	2700	30	8	1.35	1.35	1.25
1 CS	WHEATLEY TOMATOES	1	48	2706	19	5	1.95	1.95	1.70
1 PK	DERBY ANCHOV ASST	2 OZ	20	2733	30	.15	2.10	2.10	2.00
1 CS	MORTON BEEF STEW	1	24	3058	27	.12	2.10	2.10	1.[illegible]0
1 CS	CLAPPS BEEF BROTH	4½ OZ	12	3080	28	9	.78	.78	.73
1 CS	RED HEART ASST	1	48	3182	26	9	3.20	3.20	3.06
6 UN	CAMP VEG SOUP	10½ OZ	12	3343	21	.10	.95	5.70	5.52
1 CS	HORMEL VEG SOUP	16 OZ	24	3356	21	.10	1.90	1.90	1.70
1 CT	KELLOGG ALL BRAN	11 OZ	24	3462	18	.13	2.55	2.55	2.47
1 UN	CREAM OF WHEAT	14 OZ	12	3479	17	.15	1.50	1.50	1.3[illegible]
1 UN	YELLOW MEAL GRAN	10 LB	1	3565	18	3	.25	.25	.20
1 CS	BISQUICK	20 OZ	12	3736	21	.18	1.70	1.70	1.65
1 CT	FRENCH INSTANT TAP	8 OZ	24	4090	22	.10	1.90	1.90	1.85
1 CS	KINGS CORN STARCH	1 LB	24	4506	20	.11	2.10	2.10	1.90
1 CS	JELLO CHERRY		36	4659	26	6	1.60	1.60	1.55
1 CS	JELLO LIME		36	4662	26	6	1.60	1.60	1.55
1 CS	JELLO STRAWBERRY		36	4668	26	6	1.60	1.60	1.55
1 CT	JUNKET TABLETS		12	4786	23	.13	1.20	1.20	1.15
1 CS	MORTON DATE PUDDING		24	4802	23	.10	1.85	1.85	1.55
39				1015				72.48	66.95

Illustration No. 61—A Report Prepared by an Electric Bookkeeping and Tabulating Machine tical records for the business and then used again when needed at some later date.

Time-Recorders. In nearly every business it is desirable to have an accurate record of the time worked by the individual employees. There are many types and makes of time clocks. A simple one is shown in Illustration No. 62. Each employee is given a card which must be stamped by the clock when he comes to work and when he leaves.

International Business Machines Corporation.

Illustration No. 62—An Automatic Time-Recorder

Special Mailing Equipment. Businesses having a large amount of outgoing mail usually make use of some special mailing equipment such as postage meters. These meters print the postage on mail matter instead of affixing adhesive stamps. Such a meter is taken to the local post office, where it is set for the amount of postage that has been paid for. When the meter has printed the full amount for which it was set, it automatically locks and prevents further operation. Some models, such as the one shown in Illustration No. 63, can be adjusted by a simple shift of a lever to print postage in any amounts from ½ cent to $99.99 (with a total setting capacity of $99,999.99). This type of postage meter is desirable in the shipping department of a business that sends out small packages requiring various amounts of postage. The postage and the postmark are printed on a gummed tape that can be affixed easily to the package. When not needed for parcel post, the machine can be used to stamp, seal, and stack the regular mail.

Postage Meter Company.

Illustration No. 63—A Small Postage Meter and Mailing Machine

Some advantages of using such a machine are:

1. It speeds mail delivery by eliminating time-consuming operations at the post office. Stamps printed on this machine do not have to be canceled at the post office.
2. It safeguards the postage account by eliminating the mutilation, waste, and misuse of postage.
3. Daily or departmental costs for postage are available by reading the registers, which show the number of pieces mailed, the amount of postage used, and the balance still on hand.

4. Such a machine saves time in the preparation of mail because it both affixes the postage and seals the envelope.

5. It gives the mail a uniform and neat appearance.

6. Special advertising can be printed on the mail at the same time that the postage is printed.

Postage Meter Company.

Illustration No. 64—A Parcel-Post Scale

The parcel-post scale shown in Illustration No. 64 is an automatic device for determining the amount of postage needed on a parcel. The parcel is placed on the platform. Then, when the proper zone lever is pressed, the correct amount of postage necessary appears on an indicator.

Businesses that send out large amounts of mail matter to the same people or businesses from time to time find that addressing equipment is desirable. The telephone company in a large city, for example, sends out monthly bills to its subscribers. If each bill and each envelope had to

be addressed on a typewriter or by hand, it would be a
gigantic task to get out the many thousands required. A
permanent printing plate is made by embossing the subscriber's name, address, and telephone number on a metal
plate. This embossing is done on a machine known as a
Graphotype. These plates can be arranged and filed alphabetically according to the names of subscribers, or they
may be grouped according to locations in the city. For
instance, the plates of all customers served by a particular exchange may be filed together alphabetically. When
monthly bills are to be sent out, the plates are run through
a machine called an *Addressograph,* which prints the name
and the amount on each bill. Any additions required on the
bills are done by hand. Various models of the Addressograph can imprint approximately 3,000 forms an hour.
Illustration No. 65 shows an Addressograph.

Some of the work that may be done on Addressograph
equipment is as follows:

1. Addressing envelopes, cards, and booklets
2. Filling in the names and the addresses on letters
3. Making lists of dealers, agents, jobbers, and salesmen
4. Printing pay-roll cards, envelopes, and receipts
5. Imprinting the names and the numbers on time cards
   and salary checks
6. Listing pay-roll sheets with name, department, and
   rate of pay

Such businesses as insurance companies, department
stores, gas and electric companies, concerns doing installment sales business, and tax offices probably could use
addressing equipment to good advantage.

Equipment for Special Businesses. Special types of equipment have been developed for many different kinds of businesses, especially manufacturing businesses. A dairy, for
example, will need such specialized equipment as clarifiers,
pasteurizers, coolers, bottling machines, bottle washers,
and can washers. Illustration No. 66 shows several pasteurizing machines, each of which is glass-lined for sanitation.

Illustration No. 65—An Addressograph and Printing Plates

United Dairy Machinery Corporation.

Illustration No. 66—Milk-Pasteurizing Equipment

Determining the Kind of Equipment. When a businessman has decided that it is desirable to purchase equipment for a certain purpose, he must next determine the exact make of equipment needed. By consulting trade papers, directories, and other businesses using similar equipment, one can obtain the names of equipment manufacturers. From these manufacturers one should obtain literature descriptive of the equipment that will probably best fit the needs of the business. The next step should be to interview representatives of the equipment manufacturers and let them offer suggestions with regard to the most suitable kind of equipment. Most manufacturers will give demonstrations and furnish technical data on the operation of machines. Some of them will leave equipment on trial so that a thorough test may be made. Often it is possible to observe the equipment in use in other plants. Comparisons as to the original cost, the probable life, the rate of depreciation, and the repairs or services required should be made of similar equipment manufactured by competing businesses.

Standardization of Equipment. So far as possible, it is desirable that a particular type of equipment be selected as a standard for use in all similar work. If display cases are of the same size and make, it is easy to shift a display case from one part of the store to another during special sales or busy seasons without breaking up the harmony of the entire store display. Furthermore, a neat appearance is given to the store if all the equipment is alike. If all the cash registers in a store were manufactured by the same company, it is easy to obtain service on them and for employees to shift from one machine to another. Likewise, if all the typewriters in an office are of one make, the service problem is simple and employees can use any machine.

Another advantage of standardization is that one can usually purchase a large number of the same articles at a lower price per article than if a small number is purchased. If equipment is purchased in large quantities, better repair and maintenance service is ordinarily available. For example, there are four typewriters in an office, each of which was made by a different typewriter manufacturer. Two of them need repairs. It is necessary that two service men, each from a different company, make a trip to take care of the repairs. If all four of the typewriters were of the same make, one service man could make the trip to take care of all the repairs.

Less variety in supplies, which means less cost per unit, is necessary when equipment is standardized. When all the typewriters in an office, for instance, are of the same make, only one kind of typewriter ribbon need be carried in stock. If various kinds of display cases are used in a store, it may be necessary to stock a variety of electric light bulbs for the proper illumination of each kind.

Determining Whether to Purchase Equipment. Businessmen have often purchased equipment because it seemed to be desirable, but they did not stop to consider whether such a purchase would be advantageous from a financial viewpoint. Before buying equipment, one should consider the following factors:

Depreciation
Repairs
Increased operating costs, such as electricity and insurance
Rental charge for space occupied
Interest on capital invested

All the possible costs resulting from the purchase and the maintenance of the equipment should be added and then compared with the probable financial income resulting from the use of the equipment. Then, one is more likely to purchase equipment only when it is definitely advantageous to do so. Sometimes it is not economical to continue to use old equipment, but in other cases it is economical to purchase new equipment to replace the old.

A certain public utility (gas and electricity) company found it necessary to have photostatic copies made of some 10,000 sheets of handwritten, typed, and printed records. The cost of having the work done by a commercial photocopy company would have been $5,000. After investigating the cost of buying equipment to do the work, the company determined the following facts:

Cost of Equipment
Photostat $1,200
Dryer 180
Lamps 160
Washer 35
Trimming board 25

    Total $1,600

Cost of Materials
Paper, chemicals used in the developer and in the fixing bath, etc. 350
Labor (two months) 300
Rental value of space occupied by the equipment ($15 a month), including heat and light costs 30
Interest on equipment cost (2 months at 6 per cent) 16
Depreciation (1 per cent a month) 32

    Total cost $2,328

As a result of these figures the company decided it would be advantageous to purchase the equipment and materials and to do its own photostatic work.

Leasing Equipment. Some equipment manufacturers do not offer certain of their products for sale. Instead they lease such equipment to users, believing that better service will be given under such conditions. The equipment leased is usually of the type that needs frequent servicing. The maker of the equipment maintains a corps of service mechanics to keep the equipment in proper order. For example, the United Shoe Repairing Machine Company leases to shoe repair shops a cement press for an initial rental fee of $35 and a monthly rental of $1. It leases a stitching machine on a different basis. The initial license fee is $450 on a new machine or $200 on a rebuilt machine. In addition, it gets a royalty of 12 cents a thousand stitches, with a guarantee of $5 a month. If these machines need servicing, however, the shoe repair shops need not pay for the repairs. All that the manager of such a shop has to do is to notify the local service office.

Some examples of other equipment that is leased are:

Electric bookkeeping and accounting machines
Proof machines for banks
Postage meter machines
Registers used in streetcars, busses, and the like

Rental for Short Terms. Frequently a business may wish to rent equipment for a short period of time. For instance, a company may rent long-carriage typewriters for the making of annual reports. During certain peak seasons a business may find it desirable to rent additional typewriters, Addressograph equipment, or calculating machines. The rental charges paid by the lessee may often be applied toward the purchase of the machine should the lessee decide to buy it. A clause governing such a situation is contained in the rental order in Illustration No. 67.

Terms of Purchase. The terms given to purchasers of equipment vary with the different kinds of equipment. In most cases a substantial down payment is required, and the unpaid balance will be financed for a charge of from 4 to 6 per cent. Companies that finance their own sales frequently add a carrying charge of 4 per cent on the

RENTAL ORDER
(SHORT TERM)

To ADDRESSOGRAPH-MULTIGRAPH CORPORATION, Euclid Branch P. O.
ADDRESSOGRAPH DIVISION   Cleveland, Ohio   Date July 1

Please enter { my / our } order for rental equipment and supplies listed below.

Invoice to   C. K. Richards & Company
                       NAME

1132 South Broad Street, Dayton, Montgomery, Ohio
STREET AND NO.   CITY   COUNTY   STATE

Ship to   C. K. Richards & Company
                    NAME

1132 South Broad Street, Dayton, Montgomery, Ohio
STREET AND NO.   CITY   COUNTY   STATE

Ship via   Freight   Shipment Promised August 1

SALESMAN	CODE NO.
A. R. Jones	A31
AGENCY	CODE NO.
SALESMAN'S ORDER NO.	
15340	
AGENCY ORDER NO.	
726	
LESSEE'S ORDER NO.	
954	

TERMS FOR PURCHASE of machines or supplies. Net 30 days. Prices F.O.B. Cleveland

TERMS FOR RENTAL of machines only. Net 30 days. Rental Charges F.O.B. Cleveland

Minimum rental charge $ 20.00 per machine for first two weeks, $ 4.50 per machine each week thereafter. Machines may be recalled at option of Addressograph-Multigraph Corporation (Addressograph Division) at any time after minimum rental period has expired.

It is agreed that these machines will be only used by one shift of clerks in any one day and Lessor reserves the right to immediately charge, and lessee agrees to pay, double the rental stipulated above for any machine used by more than one shift of clerks in any one day for the period that the machine is so used; the minimum additional amount to be billed in any such case being one week's rental.

Rental charges paid by lessee not in excess of ten weeks charges may be applied toward the purchase of the rental machine at the price shown below, but not toward the purchase of any other machine, equipment or supplies.

Lessee agrees to pay transportation charges for shipment from Cleveland and return.

Rental charges accrue for entire time machine is in lessee's possession. Lessee agrees to notify Addressograph-Multigraph Corporation (Addressograph Division) promptly in writing when use of machine will be completed and when machine is to be returned.

Title to machine remains with Addressograph-Multigraph Corporation (Addressograph Division) and lessee assumes responsibility for any damages to machine other than ordinary wear and tear while in his possession or during transportation from or to factory or authorized shipping point or return to destination. Lessee agrees to pay for replacement of parts and breakages of punches and dies.

Lessee agrees that machines covered by this order shall be used only in connection with address plates or other standard Addressograph supplies purchased from Addressograph-Multigraph Corporation (Addressograph Division) or one of its authorized agencies.

Rental charges cover use of machine only and do not include special parts or attachments which must be made to fit lessee's requirements, and do not include any charge for mechanical service or other service by Addressograph-Multigraph Corporation (Addressograph Division) or its authorized agents.

It is agreed that any assessments of State and/or Local Taxes paid by Lessor on equipment covered by this agreement shall be borne by the Lessee.

QUANTITY	MODEL	DESCRIPTION	PRICE	
1	6283	Graphotype	$525	00
		Total $	525	00

C. K. Richards & Company
1132 South Broad Street
Dayton, Ohio
Print name and complete address for permanent customer records in space above.

SIGNED C. K. Richards

By

WITNESS D. H. Jackson

Addressograph-Multigraph Corporation.

Illustration No. 67—A Rental Contract for Equipment

unpaid balance. Those equipment companies that finance their sales through commercial finance companies usually add a carrying charge of 6 per cent. Illustration No. 68 shows a contract for the purchase of some dairy equipment on the deferred-payment plan. It includes an allowance for a used piece of equipment being traded in. Read carefully the purchaser's obligation, which is printed in small type.

It is understood and agreed that there are no conditions whatever, verbal or otherwise, except as written herein	**UNITED DAIRY MACHINERY CORP.** 1023 JEFFERSON AVE., BUFFALO, N. Y.		

Date_____December 1,_____193 9

Ship to the undersigned Purchaser___Purity Dairy Products Corporation
Street___126 River Street___City___Buffalo___State New York
R. R. Sta.____Same____R. F. D._____Co.
NOTE: WHERE SHIPMENT IS TO BE DIVIDED, BE SURE TO SPECIFY HOW EACH ITEM SHALL BE SENT

Parcel Post	
Express	
Freight	
Truck	x
Will Call	
Via	

QUANTITY	DESCRIPTION	UNIT PRICE	TOTAL
2	200 gal. Pfandler Glass Lined Pasteurizers with motor (3 phase, 60 cycle) complete	$980 00	$1,960 00
	Allowance 1 - 100 gal. pasteurizer		160 00
			1,800 00
	Cash with order		300 00
			1,500 00
	6% Finance charge on balance		90 00
			1,590 00
	Settlement in 12 equal notes to be made within 30 days after delivery.		

For which Purchaser will pay Seller $ 1,800.00 , as follows: Cash with this contract $ 300.00 , Cash on delivery $ none and balance of $1,590.00 as follows: on the first of each month for 12 months in equal payments of $132.50.

Full settlement shall be completed by Purchaser within 30 days from date of shipment.
All notes shall bear the same date as the last cash payment and draw interest, and be payable at a bank, optional with purchaser.

1. The above described property shall be and remain the property of the seller until the purchase price, including any notes which may be accepted by the seller in part payment or temporary settlement of the above debt, shall be fully paid, and the acceptance of a note for the whole or any part of the indebtedness shall not be deemed payment, and the purchaser agrees to do all acts necessary to protect and maintain seller's title and to keep said equipment insured in the name of the seller in an amount and in a company satisfactory to the seller.
2. In event of refusal of the purchaser to accept, when tendered, any of the equipment herein described or to make any payment falling due when same is due and payable, or if the purchaser remove or attempt to remove, sell or transfer possession or ownership of said equipment without the written consent of the seller, in any such case the purchase price of said equipment or the balance remaining unpaid shall forthwith become due and payable and the seller may take possession of said equipment and sell the same in accordance with the statutes in such cases made and provided.
3. In the event of the seller agreeing to erect equipment herein described, it shall be understood that steam and water lines shall be brought within a distance of 6 (six) feet unless otherwise specified herein. All sewer and electric connections including electric fixtures and wiring shall be promptly provided for and furnished by purchaser, unless otherwise specified herein.
4. This order and contract subject to acceptance by the seller at Buffalo, N. Y.

Signature of Purchaser
___Purity Dairy Products Corporation___ Date_____December 1,_____193 9
(Individual—Partnership—Corporation)   Mailing address of purchaser
By___Frank L. Smith___ Title___President___ Address 126 River St. City Buffalo State N. Y.
Signed and delivered in the presence of
1_____

Location of plant or building in which machinery is to be installed

_____
Address   City   State

Accepted and Signed this___first___ day of___December_____193 9
                                                    UNITED DAIRY MACHINERY CORP.
By___C. L. P.___

Rediform SPEEDIGRAPH BOOK   (TRADE MARK)—MFD. AM SALES BOOK CO., INC., NIAGARA FALLS, N. Y.

United Dairy Machinery Corporation.

Illustration No. 68—An Installment Sales Contract for Equipment

There are many forms of contracts under which equipment may be purchased. In some cases the contract may be a conditional sales contract, but in others it may be a chattel mortgage contract. These are explained in Chapter XIV. In the case of the conditional sales contract, the equipment does not become the permanent possession of the purchaser until it has been paid for. In the case of the chattel mortgage contract, it becomes the property of the purchaser at the time it is delivered, but the seller holds a mortgage claim against it until the amount specified in the contract is paid. Occasionally, for a small unpaid balance, the seller does not require any special contract. The buyer is merely billed on open account.

QUESTIONS FOR DISCUSSION

1. Why should the fixtures in a selling department be in keeping with the merchandise being sold?
2. Give some disadvantages of using cardboard boxes for the storage of merchandise on the selling floor.
3. Why is it desirable to have low store fixtures?
4. What are open display fixtures?
5. What is the main purpose of having display cases lighted?
6. State some advantages of mechanical or automatic measuring equipment.
7. Explain the principal functions performed by a cash register.
8. Where is the cash tube system ordinarily used?
9. What is a typewriter-bookkeeping machine?
10. What is the purpose of using a time clock?
11. Explain the operation of a postage meter machine.
12. What is an Addressograph?
13. State how one may determine the exact kind of equipment to buy.
14. Give some of the probable advantages resulting from the standardization of equipment.
15. How can a businessman determine whether it is advantageous from a financial viewpoint to purchase equipment?
16. What are some types of equipment that are leased instead of sold?
17. Who pays for the repair service needed on leased equipment?
18. What is the average finance charge made when equipment is sold on the deferred-payment plan?

PROBLEMS AND PROJECTS

1. Visit at least two stores, such as a grocery store and a drugstore, and make a list of items found in closed display cases (not windows). Give reasons for such goods being displayed. Observe if there are other goods that might have been displayed to advantage in cases.

2. Make a list of metal fixtures you have observed in various business houses.

3. Visit four of the newest grocery stores that sell fresh fruits and vegetables, and observe if they have special fixtures for keeping the fruits and vegetables fresh. Report on the kind of fixtures used.

4. Write a report concerning the sign of some store front that you have observed. State the features that you think are good and also any that are not desirable.

5. In weighing butter by the bulk, a retail salesperson gives an extra ounce to each customer buying a pound. (a) If there is a daily average of 50 customers during a year of 304 working days, how many pounds of butter are given away during the year? (b) If the retailer pays an average of 24 cents a pound for the butter and sells it at an average of 32 cents a pound, what are the wholesale value and the retail value of the butter given away?

6. Bring to class envelopes on which a postage meter machine printed special advertising at the same time that it printed the postage.

7. A certain model of the Addressograph sells for $385 on terms of net 30 days. If the deferred-payment plan is desired, the customer may make 12 monthly payments but must pay a finance charge of 4 per cent on the balance remaining after the down payment. If a customer makes a down payment of $80, what will be the amount of each of the 12 monthly payments?

8. A shoe repair shop leases a cement press and one rebuilt stitching machine. Using the figures given on page 164 for the United Shoe Repairing Machine Company, determine the total rental cost for the first year of operation. The stitching machine does the following amount of stitching:

January	35,000	May	70,000	September	75,000
February	60,000	June	63,000	October	70,000
March	65,000	July	55,000	November	62,000
April	60,000	August	50,000	December	53,000

CHAPTER VIII

ARRANGEMENT AND LAYOUT

Purpose of the Chapter. After the building and the equipment have been selected, the management must decide how to make efficient use of the space and the equipment. While each type of business has its own particular problems in this respect, many businesses do have common problems. The following are some of the important questions that are answered in this chapter:

1. How shall the selling space be divided so that each division will pay its share of the overhead?
2. How can a study of customer traffic and attitudes be of value in planning the layout of a business?
3. Where shall related and unrelated items of merchandise be placed?
4. Is it possible to arrange supplies, equipment, and departments so as to enable employees to give prompt and efficient service to customers?

Making Efficient Use of the Selling Space. The term *selling space* is used to denote the store space from which merchandise is sold. Regardless of the kind of store, certain portions of the selling space are more valuable than other portions. That part of the store near the entrance contains the most valuable selling space because people pass through this section when entering or leaving the store. As it has been found that customers tend to go to the right, the space to the right of the entrance is usually considered more valuable than that to the left. If the store is quite deep, one hundred feet or more, the extreme rear is not valuable as selling space, for customers dislike walking so far. If each end of the store has an entrance, however, there is not much difference in value between the front and the rear space, unless the rear entrance is on a street traveled by few customers.

169

Whether he pays $30 or $300 a month for rent, the efficient businessman should draw a map or floor plan of his store and divide it into sections. Then he should apportion a certain percentage of the rent to each section, the percentage being based upon the experiences of other similar businesses as well as upon his own experience and study. The percentage of total rent assigned to each section of the store will depend upon a number of factors, including the size and the shape of the building as well as the nature of the business. The diagram in Illustration No. 69 shows a division of selling space that might apply to many small retail stores.

The management might make this application: Suppose that the rent paid for this floor space is $100 a month. Then the division labeled 20% should be charged with 20

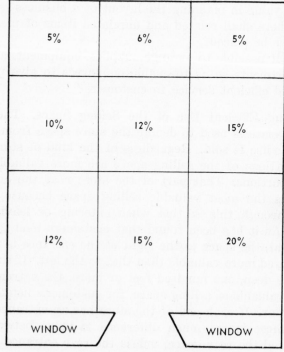

Illustration No. 69—Making Efficient Use of Space

per cent of $100, or $20. The department that occupies
that particular space should be one that can afford to pay
$20 rent. The application of this method to the other divi-
sions of the floor space should result in assigning the proper
locations to the various types of merchandise. In a small
store, such as the one just illustrated, the office space might
be in a rear corner that has the least value as selling space.

If the store has several floors, the businessman should
evaluate each one. The first, or street, floor is most valuable because many customers walk around the street floor
and go out without visiting the other floors. The second
floor is easy to reach by stairway without waiting for elevator service; hence it is next in value. There is probably
not much difference in the value of the other floors as customers riding on the elevators can reach any of them conveniently. The value of the selling floors in a three-story
building generally is: first floor, 60 per cent; second floor,
30 per cent; third floor, 10 per cent.

Effect of Customer Traffic. As customers tend to turn
to the right when entering a store, especially if there is no
large center aisle, the space at the right of the entrance is
the place where the owner should display merchandise that
yields large profits or that might otherwise be overlooked
by the shopper. For example, in a grocery store, the fresh
fruits and vegetables or fancy groceries might be placed at
the right of the entrance into the front part of the store;
in a jewelry store, the diamond jewelry; in a drugstore,
the cosmetics; and in a camera shop, the movie cameras.

If there is a large center aisle leading from the entrance,
most of the traffic will be confined to this one aisle, and
customers may not see other parts of the store. A large
center aisle is therefore undesirable unless the store is very
narrow. Even a store that has a width of only twenty-five
feet may be arranged without a center aisle. Illustration
No. 70 shows a possible arrangement of a small grocery.

In large stores having elevators, there are also rather
definite traffic routes taken by customers. Such routes are
usually the most direct aisles between the entrance and the

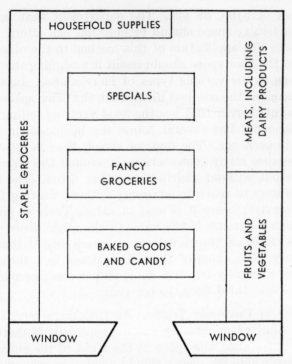

Illustration No. 70—Arrangement for a Retail Grocery

elevator. Along such lanes it is desirable to place items that customers are likely to purchase as the result of impulse upon seeing them, rather than merchandise that is usually purchased because of definite buying plans. Toiletries, perfumes, costume jewelry, and neckwear usually sell better if they are placed along these main traffic routes. On these routes the merchant often places aisle tables containing merchandise that he wishes to move quickly. The elevators should be so situated that customers must walk past as much display as possible in order to reach them.

As people usually follow the widest space offered them upon entering a store, it is possible to get customers to turn to the left if the aisle on that side is wider than the one at the right. Some studies show that customers tend to turn to the right if the aisles are equal in width.

Effect of Customer Attitudes. The attitudes of customers toward various types of merchandise and services should be given much attention in planning the layout of a place of business. When buying items classed as staples and necessities, the customer usually enters the store with a definite plan to buy. For that reason such items may be placed in less desirable and less accessible parts than other items. For example, household cleaning supplies, such as laundry soaps, may be placed in the rear part of a grocery store; the prescription counter of a drugstore may be located similarly; the furniture department of a large store may occupy an upper floor; the repair shop of an automobile dealer may be located in space at the rear of the display room.

Some articles are purchased mainly as the result of an impulse upon seeing them displayed, rather than because of definite plans to buy them. Such goods are known as *impulse goods.* For instance, as a customer is paying a restaurant cashier for his meal, he sees chewing gum, small packages of candy, or cigarettes and cigars, and immediately purchases some with part of the change being given him by the cashier. Experience proves that people at that particular moment are more inclined to make such an additional purchase than at other times. Furthermore, such items are usually consumed immediately after a meal.

The salads and the desserts are usually placed at the front of the service table in a cafeteria. Customers see the salads first and are tempted to buy them before they have obtained the rest of their food. Should the salads be placed near the cashier end of the service table, customers will probably have meat, potatoes, and other vegetables before reaching the salads and will likely decide to do without a salad.

Bottles of meat sauces and horseradish are placed on the top of meat display cases so that customers may buy them on impulse. For the same reason some items are displayed at eye level; some, below eye level; and some, above eye level. For instance, on the lowest shelf of an open display fixture, there may be placed the best selling kind of bread; on the next shelf, the special breads; on the next, the cookies; and on the top shelf (about eye level), the cakes. Wrapping counters and places near cash registers are valuable places for arranging impulse goods. Displays near the entrance of a store are usually effective as they may be a last-minute reminder to the customer.

When customers are shopping for goods that represent a large expenditure of money, they usually do not want to hurry in making their decisions. Such goods should not be placed on congested aisles. For example, when buying dresses, women do not want to be hurried in making their decisions. Department stores therefore find it undesirable to have their dress departments on the street floor. Such a department is frequently made into a sort of store with a main entrance of its own. It then has more seclusion and quietness than it would have if it were just open space on a floor with other departments. Illustration No. 71 shows such a department. Notice how the lighting adds to its attractiveness.

Arrangement of Related Items. Whenever possible, it is a good plan to arrange *related,* or *complementary, goods* near each other. When men's ties are placed near men's shirts, the purchaser of a shirt is likely to see the ties and to purchase a new tie to wear with the new shirt. Such arrangement also makes it easy for the salesperson to suggest related goods. In like manner it is proper to place hosiery near shoes, patterns near dress goods, toothbrushes near tooth paste, fountain pens and desk sets near stationery. If one is operating a book store, he may find it desirable to group books on travel in the same section of the store, fiction books in another section, and biographies in still another section. Should it be a magazine and newspaper stand, it is possible to carry out the same principle even though the business is very small. Financial magazines may be grouped together; out-of-town newspapers together; and fiction magazines together.

During various seasons a merchant should adjust the arrangement of those goods that are in particular demand at such times. For instance, during the jelly-making season, sugar, jelling ingredients (such as pectin), paraffin, and jelly glasses should be arranged together; during the house-cleaning seasons, the various articles used in cleaning should be grouped together.

Illustration No. 72 shows an effective arrangement of related items. By displaying flowers in various glass and pottery holders, the florist increases the sale of both flowers and holders. The arrangement of his merchandise suggests to the shopper ideas on using flowers in the home. No doubt many shoppers who had never thought of using certain flowers in such ways were stimulated to buy them when they saw how attractively they could be arranged.

Arrangement of Unrelated Items. Businesses often carry merchandise not usually associated with their types of stores. For instance, books, magazines, and stationery are usually not associated with drugstores, but are commonly sold in them. These unrelated items should be displayed

General Electric Company.

*Illustration No. 71—An Arrangement for Customers Who
Desire Much Time to Reach a Decision*

prominently in the store. Stationery may be arranged on center tables. Books and magazines may be placed near the entrance, where they will be seen by customers entering or leaving the store. At a roadside fruit market, cut flowers may be sold in season. They should be given prominence in the display, probably by being arranged at the front and in the center of the stand. A shoe repair shop may have rubber overshoes for sale. They should be placed at the front of the store. An optical shop that sells barometers and binoculars may display these items similarly. A public garage used mainly for the parking of cars may display such merchandise as heaters, windshield wiper blades, and horns in the room where customers wait for their cars.

Convenience of Customers. In planning the arrangement of a business, one must consider the customer. A characteristic of practically every person is a desire for convenience. This fact explains why the motorist does not stop

Armstrong Cork Company.

*Illustration No. 72—An Effective Arrangement in a
Florist's Shop*

at a roadside market that lacks an adequate entrance drive and ample parking space. A roadside market that wishes to sell its produce on rainy days will find it profitable to have a large projecting roof, under the shelter of which customers may drive and make their purchases without getting wet.

A dry-cleaning company opened a branch on a main traffic street in a downtown section of a large city. It provided curb service by having a man in uniform take the garments from the cars at the curb and also deliver the cleaned garments from the building to the customer in the car at the curb. This service eliminated the inconvenience to customers that would have resulted from their attempting to find a place to park their cars in the congested area.

Many roadside refreshment stands have been successful because they provided a large, inviting parking space for automobiles. Even city refreshment stands can be made highly profitable by establishing curb service, which means that the customers are served while they remain in their cars. One such business in Indianapolis employs 30 waitresses and 12 men to take care of the needs of some 2,000 cars and 6,000 persons daily. All this business is taken care of from only a small building, shown in Illustration No. 73.

Self-service groceries make it convenient for their customers by placing heavy items, such as molasses, flour, salt, and sugar, near the checking counter. To gain attention, new or special items are placed close to those which are frequently purchased.

Many customers are in a hurry when making their purchases. For that reason the soda fountain in a drugstore should be located at the front of the store. If a customer has to walk to the rear of the store for a soda, he probably will do without it or stop at some other store that has a more conveniently located soda fountain.

Men usually like to make their purchases where it is quite convenient. They dislike crowded stores. If a store is large and has departments in addition to that for men's clothing, it is desirable that there be a separate entrance

The Coca-Cola Company.

Illustration No. 73—A Refreshment Stand Providing
Curb Service

to the men's department. If the store is very large, the men's department should be located at the front so that it is readily accessible.

The aisles in a store should be wide enough to allow plenty of room for customers to pass around the displays without crowding. Upon finding the main aisles crowded, many people will walk out of a store and buy elsewhere. If the aisles are narrow, some items may be damaged as a result of being knocked off their display fixtures by passing customers.

Checkrooms, public telephones, and branch post offices, maintained for the convenience of customers, are usually located toward the rear of stores in order to get customers to walk past several displays of merchandise. In large stores there is usually a rest room and lounge for women. This is situated on an upper floor so that persons using it may see as much of the store as possible. As the elevator stops at the different floors, the customer may get a view of each floor which may suggest certain purchases to her. Some stores have a mezzanine floor, which would make a desirable place for chairs to be placed for customers who wish to rest. While resting, they would get a view of the entire street floor and, seeing certain items on display, might make purchases.

Illustration No. 74 shows the arrangement of the interior of a shoe repair shop. Booths, chairs, and a radio are provided for the convenience of the customer who wishes to wait while his shoes are being repaired. Magazines are probably also available for the customer to read. The shoe-shining equipment is located in a prominent place to remind the customer to have his shoes shined after he has had them repaired.

United Shoe Repair Machine Company.

Illustration No. 74—An Arrangement of a Shoe Repair Shop

Arrangement for Prompt and Efficient Service. Paper bags, boxes, wrapping paper, cord, and other supplies used in preparing goods for the customer's convenient handling and carrying should be placed under counters near the place where they will be needed. Sufficient thought given to this detail will save many extra steps on the part of the salesperson and will give the customer prompt service. All store supplies, such as paper bags, should, of course, be arranged according to size so that a clerk can select the proper size quickly.

Counters and display cases can be so arranged as to facilitate service on the part of employees. Placing three of these fixtures together in the form of the letter *U* and then placing opposite them another three in the same form, so that the open ends of the *U's* are near each other, as shown in Illustration No. 75, permits salespeople to serve customers at six counters or display cases more quickly and easily than they could if the six were arranged end to end in one long line. It might be desirable in some instances to include as one of the six fixtures a counter that could be used for wrapping and as a place for a cash register. A few special items can also be displayed on this counter.

If part of the equipment is a special counter for wrapping merchandise that the customer will take with him, it should be placed near the items that are wrapped most frequently. If the counter is used chiefly for wrapping goods that will be sent out by delivery trucks, it should be placed as near as possible to the place where the trucks are loaded.

Location of the Cash Register. Most small businesses use a cash register rather than the overhead carrier system or the pneumatic tube system in handling cash sales. Each type of business may have a slightly different place for the location of its cash register, but there are principles that can be used as a guide in selecting a good location.

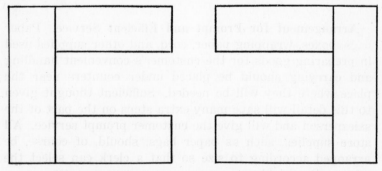

Illustration No. 75—Arrangement of Display Cases

If a business is large enough (that is, with respect to the size of the floor space and the number of salespeople) for more than one cash register, each register should be placed where it will be most accessible to the employees. The registers might be placed by departments. For example, a drugstore that has a soda fountain and a luncheonette might have one register for the fountain and the luncheonette and one for the drugs and the toilet goods; a grocery store might have one for fresh fruits and vegetables and another for the other groceries.

In most small businesses one cash register will be sufficient. The problem then is just where it should be placed. If customers are given saleschecks by the various salespeople and are to make payment at a cashier's desk, the cashier and the cash register should have a place near that where the customers will leave the store. Restaurants, large shoe stores, meat stores, barber shops, beauty parlors, soda fountains, and tearooms are examples of businesses that ordinarily use this arrangement.

In businesses having only a small number of salespeople, the central cashier system need not be used, as it is possible for the cash record of each salesperson to be kept separately by the one cash register. In such a situation the register should be placed in that part of the store where the most cash sales are made. For instance, in a grocery store it should be placed near the staple groceries rather than near the fancy groceries; in a magazine and newspaper store it should be near the daily newspapers rather than the weekly or monthly magazines.

The factor of safety should not be overlooked in selecting a location for the cash register. When a cashier is not at the machine constantly, it is better to have a counter or a display case between the machine and customers. In a small store it is not desirable to place the cash register too near the front as someone may walk into the store and open it while the proprietor is at the rear. Businesses that receive a large amount of cash find it a good policy to remove quantities of the money from the cash register at intervals and store it in a safe.

Armstrong Cork Company.

Illustration No. 76—An Arrangement of a Beauty Parlor

Location of the Office. For small stores doing a retail business, only a small space is needed for an office. As selling space is valuable, it should not be sacrificed for a large office that will be used very little. A small space in a rear corner may be used for a desk, a filing case, and other office fixtures. Many small stores in cities have the office located on the mezzanine floor, toward the back part of the store.

Other Arrangements and Layouts. The arrangement of a beauty parlor is shown in Illustration No. 76. Notice that the cashier's desk is near the entrance. The fixtures and equipment suggest cleanliness and sanitation.

Illustration No. 77 is a diagram showing the arrangement of a dairy. The dotted line with arrows shows the path taken by the milk from the time it is unloaded from the milk trucks until it is bottled and loaded onto the delivery trucks. There is a large window between the dairy store and the plant so that customers may see into the plant. (Outside windows are not shown in the illustration.) The chillroom has insulated walls, and the floor is at the same height as the bed of the delivery trucks so that loading is facilitated. The refrigeration coils are located under the floor.

The layout of a laundry is shown in Illustration No. 78. The first step is the sorting of incoming laundry and identifying it by tag, pin, or pen markings. The second step in the laundry process is the washing. From the washers the laundry is placed in extractors to take out most of the water. Up to this point all goods have gone through the same processes. From this point, however, various kinds of laundry are handled differently. Sheets, pillowcases, and napkins are put through the flat ironers for their finishing. Bath towels and mats, as well as wearing apparel such as bathrobes, socks, and sweaters, are put through airway dryers, the process being known as tumbling. Wearing apparel such as shirts and dresses is put through the pressing process.

Straight-Line Production. The two following diagrams that illustrate the arrangement of a dairy and a laundry are examples of the routing of materials by what is known as the *straight-line production method*. This method is usually the most economical because the goods do not back-track, but move steadily forward from operation to operation with a minimum of handling. The term *straight-line method* applies even though the goods do not move forward exactly in a straight line.

Straight-line production is important because it will usually save space as well as cause economy in production. Space is often saved by eliminating unnecessary steps and by joining together the various related functions. Efficiency in production is automatically obtained by eliminating wasted motion. For example, in some factories materials are moved from one bench to another or from one department to another on trucks. Using trucks requires wider aisles, causes confusion, and requires more time. By joining the tables or the departments together so that the production flows smoothly from one step to another, there is more efficiency.

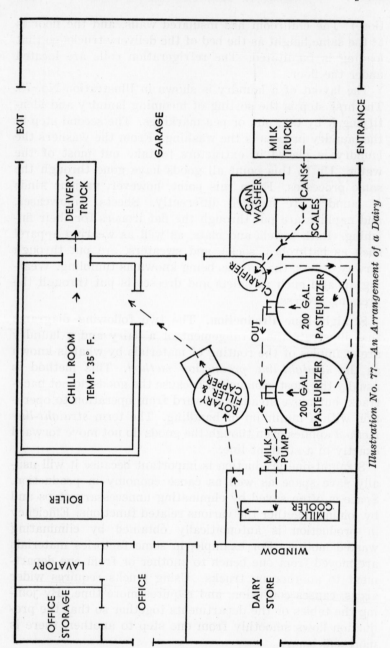

Illustration No. 77—An Arrangement of a Dairy

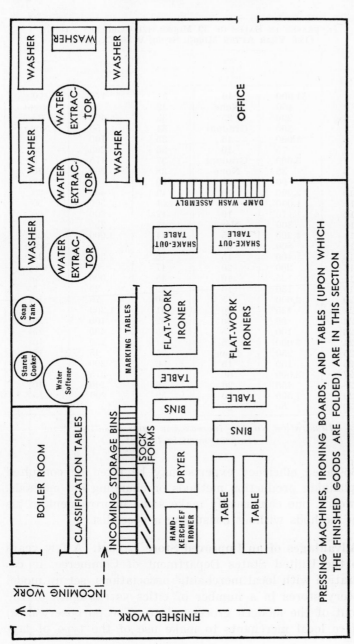

Illustration No. 78—An Arrangement of a Laundry

INCREASES IN SALES OF 59 MODERNIZED GROCERY STORES,
ONE YEAR AFTER MODEL STORE WAS EXHIBITED

Store No.	Cost of Improvements	Sales Increase (per cent)	Store No.	Cost of Improvements	Sales Increase (per cent)
1	$4,000	40	31	$ 170	10
2	450	None	32	50	None
3	200	25	33	400	25
4	300	Gradual	34	50	None
5	1,000	15	35	100	5
6	75	10	36	200	20
7	3,000	Gradual	37	175	5
8	35	None	38	200	20
9	90	50	39	100	10
10	2,000	10	40	300	25
11	1,000	5	41	500	50
12	1,170	10	42	200	60
13	300	None	43	250	10
14	4,200	25	44	1,000	20
15	800	65	45	25	None
16	400	15	46	2,500	15
17	200	20	47	50	20
18	125	10	48	1,000	35
19	130	10	49	25	5
20	2,000	15	50	75	10
21	125	20	51	1,200	None
22	90	40	52	100	20
23	100	15	53	400	15
24	3,000	25	54	150	10
25	250	None	55	45	15
26	150	15	56	300	5
27	3,000	60	57	375	40
28	450	20	58	100	10
29	1,500	50	59	200	15
30	50	25			

*Illustration No. 79—Increases in Sales Resulting from
Improvement in Layout*

So-called efficiency experts may be hired or consulted
in planning production methods or changing old methods.
However, one can usually make some improvement in his
own methods without consulting a specialist.

Advantages of an Improved Store Layout. A few years
ago the United States Department of Commerce, in co-
operation with local merchants' associations, set up model
grocery stores in a number of cities as examples of the
layout of the modern grocery store. The purpose was to
inspire local merchants to make use of the type of lay-

out exemplified. Many did. One of these model stores was set up in Jacksonville, Florida. One year later a survey was made to discover the effects of the improved modern layout. Illustration No. 79 indicates the results of that modernization.

In every community there are usually examples of businesses that have lost patronage because they have "gone out of date." A little improvement will often retain or regain customers.

QUESTIONS FOR DISCUSSION

1. Why is that part of a store near the entrance the most valuable selling space?
2. Explain a method of making efficient use of the selling space in a store.
3. Suggest the probable selling values of the different floors of a large department store.
4. Why is a wide center aisle undesirable in a large store?
5. Where might it be desirable to place items classed as (a) staples or necessities? (b) impulse goods?
6. What might be a good location for goods that customers usually take a great deal of time in buying?
7. What is meant by related, or complementary, goods?
8. Where should items that are carried by the merchant, but usually not associated with his type of business, be displayed?
9. What are some of the services and conveniences that various types of businesses provide for their customers?
10. Where is a good location for the wrapping counter if customers usually carry their purchases?
11. Discuss the probable best locations for the cash register in various types of businesses.
12. Suggest a good location for the office of (a) a small retail store and (b) a department store having six floors.
13. Do you think that the layout of the dairy shown in Illustration No. 77, whereby the customers of the dairy store may see into the plant, is desirable? Explain your answer.
14. What is meant by the straight-line production method?
15. The figures in Illustration No. 79 show that most of the stores that spent money in modernizing had increases in their sales. What is probably the reason for those increases?

PROBLEMS AND PROJECTS

1. Suppose the values of the selling floors in a three-story building are: first floor, 60 per cent; second floor, 30 per cent; third floor, 10 per cent. How should an annual rent of $30,000 be apportioned by floors?

2. Assume that the annual sales of the business mentioned in Problem 1 are: first floor, $250,000; second floor, $100,000; third floor, $50,000. What percentage of the sales of each floor did the rent for that floor represent?

3. What conclusions might be drawn from the results shown by the preceding problem?

4. A restaurant serves daily an average of 250 persons. If, when paying their checks at the cashier's desk, where chewing gum, cigars, and cigarettes are on display, one person in 25 buys a 5-cent package of chewing gum, one person in 20 buys a 15-cent package of cigarettes, and one person in 10 buys a 5-cent cigar, what are the average total sales of these three items in one year (365 days)?

5. Visit a small retail business and observe the arrangement of the different kinds of goods. Draw a diagram of the floor, showing where the various kinds are displayed.

6. Visit several businesses and observe the location of the offices. Give a report.

7. What percentage of the stores given in Illustration No. 79 showed an increase in sales after modernization?

CHAPTER IX

INTERNAL BUSINESS ORGANIZATION

Purpose of the Chapter. Chapter III explains the various legal forms of business organization. After a business has been organized, the problems of internal organization, important in managing a business, must be considered. This chapter is therefore devoted to a study of methods of internal organization. The following are some of the questions that will be answered in this chapter:

1. What are the fundamental types of internal organization?
2. What are the advantages and the disadvantages of the various types of internal organization?
3. In a small business how can the procedures be advantageously organized?
4. What are the functions of an organization chart?
5. How do organization charts help to disclose some of the weaknesses of an organization?

Types of Organization Charts. A one-man organization may operate smoothly because that one man performs the duties of the head of the organization, the purchasing agent, the salesman, and the treasurer. All these activities are therefore correlated. As the business expands, it usually becomes necessary to delegate duties and responsibilities to someone else. The control should, however, be retained by the head of the organization. As an organization becomes large and complicated, no one person in it can readily visualize all the lines of control, duty, and responsibility. It therefore proves advisable to construct organization charts to show not only lines of control but also duties, responsibilities, departmental organization, and functions. Several of these charts are shown later in the chapter.

189

The various forms of organization for the purposes of control and administration are: (1) line type, (2) staff type, (3) line and staff type, and (4) committee type. These various methods are explained in the following paragraphs. One should realize, however, that probably not one of these methods is adhered to strictly without involving some of the aspects of the others.

Line Type of Organization. The so-called line type of organization is referred to sometimes as the military type. It obtains its name from the fact that all authority and responsibility may be traced in a direct line from the manager down to the lowest administrative unit in the organization. For instance, in a military organization the line of authority runs from the colonel down to the lieutenant colonel, to the major, to the captain, to the first lieutenant, to the second lieutenant, to the sergeant, to the corporal, to the private. As orders are passed along, the responsibility for carrying out the instructions is delegated to successive officers; but the final responsibility rests upon the officer who originated the order.

Illustration No. 80 shows an example of a line type of organization. For instance, it shows that the president has authority over the sales manager. The sales manager in turn has authority over the merchandise manager; and the merchandise manager, over a staff of salespeople. The president has direct control over all functions of the business, but responsibilities are passed along from one person to another down to the lowest level of the organization. Under this form of organization each person is responsible to only one superior executive, who in turn is responsible to someone else. Very little red tape is involved because the line of action is direct. This type of organization can be quite efficient if the manager is capable, for new ideas can be put into effect immediately.

Staff Type of Organization. There are numerous forms of the so-called staff type of organization. Probably no particular company, however, uses this type without some

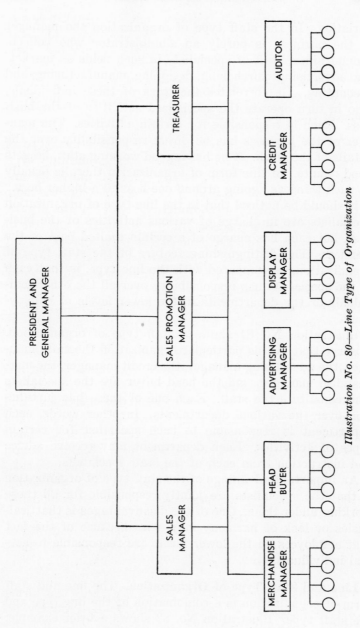

Illustration No. 80—Line Type of Organization

variation. In the staff type of organization the manager of the business is purely an administrator who collects around him a staff of specialists in such fields as marketing, advertising, purchasing, designing, manufacturing, and accounting. He correlates the work of these individuals, who in turn operate the specialized activities of the business. Each is responsible for certain activities. The manager of the business has no direct responsibility over the details of the work. If he has a good working staff, he gets good results. In this form of organization there is usually no such thing as "going around one boss to a higher boss."

It should be noticed that in the line type of organization specialists are in charge of various activities of the business, but each has charge of a certain limited part of the business. The distinguishing feature of the staff type of organization, as compared with the line type, is that each of the specialists has responsibility over all the other individuals or the departments in the lower levels of employment.

Illustration No. 81 shows a staff type of organization. Observe that in this particular organization the sales manager, the advertising manager, the credit manager, the merchandise manager, and the head buyer are the specialists who constitute the staff. Each one of these has jurisdiction over the various departments. In other words, each department is responsible to each specialist for certain types of activities. Each department may receive advice and instruction from each of the staff specialists.

An important advantage of the staff type of organization is that the specialists are jointly responsible for all those working under them. One of the disadvantages is that jealousies or lack of harmony may arise because of the fact that employees on the lower levels are responsible to several individuals.

Line and Staff Type of Organization. The line and staff form of organization is a combination of the line type and the staff type. Illustration No. 82 shows a brief example. Observe, for instance, that the line type of organization is

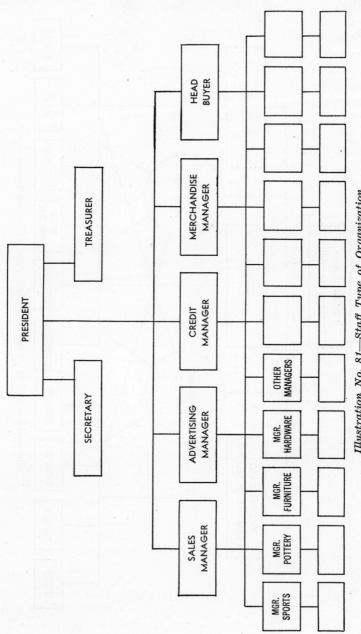

Illustration No. 81—Staff Type of Organization

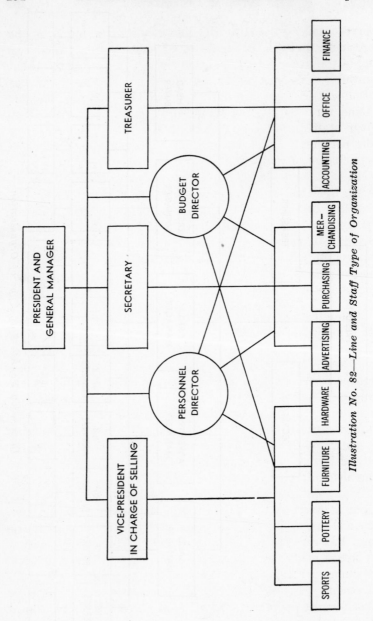

Illustration No. 82—Line and Staff Type of Organization

represented by the authority and control running from the
president through the treasurer to various other employees,
or, in the other direction, from the accounting department
through the treasurer to the president. In this particular
organization there are, however, two staff officers, the personnel director and the budget director. These officers perform staff duties. The personnel director has control over
the personnel in all departments, and the budget director
has charge of budgeting in all departments.

In this particular organization the executives, the president, the vice-president, the secretary, and the treasurer,
are line officers, whereas the personnel director and the
budget director are staff officers. It is possible in such an
organization as this for the personnel director and the
budget director to have authority over the vice-president,
the secretary, and the treasurer; but such an arrangement
is usually not likely.

Committee Type of Organization. The committee type
of organization somewhat approximates the staff form of
organization or the line and staff form. The real difference
arises in the method of administration. Under the committee form the staff members serve as an administrative
and policy-setting group. The general manager merely correlates the activities of this group and sees that the decisions of the committee are carried out. In many respects
a partnership is often operated as a committee type of
organization. Each partner has an equal voice in the management of the business.

Many authorities in the field of business assert that seldom, if ever, is the committee form of organization successful. Its weakness lies in the fact that it is cumbersome
and has no direct line of authority. The theory is that
it keeps everyone happy; but sometimes, when numerous
opinions are asked and when everyone shares in the management, there are too many opportunities for dissension.
Authorities point out that some of the desirable results of
the committee type of organization can be obtained through
the line and staff type of organization. In other words, such

results can be obtained when the staff members are specialists who give advice to the manager, but the manager is finally responsible for rendering a decision.

Functional Organization. Organization charts are of two kinds: (a) one shows individuals and departments; (b) the other shows the functions performed. The preceding illustrations show largely individuals and departments, but the chart in Illustration No. 149 in Chapter XVI shows an analysis of functions. Such a chart is particularly useful in making clear to employees various functions that are performed and in tracing the responsibility for these.

Departmentalized Organization. In large organizations it is quite desirable to organize departments so that the duties of everyone and the lines of authority are clearly determined. Illustration No. 83 shows an organization chart for a sales department. Observe, for instance, that the sales manager and the assistant sales manager have direct control over the branch offices; but that the advertising manager, the sales promotion manager, and the district sales managers have no direct control over the branch offices. They do, however, have a certain amount of authority over the salesmen.

Production Organization. The organization of production involves not only an organization of personnel but also an organization of routine. Two charts are therefore necessary to depict such an organization. Illustration No. 84 shows a simple organization for a production department. Illustration No. 85 shows an organization of the routine of a production department. In some businesses the routine of manufacture is quite complicated. For such a business a chart of production procedure can be drawn, and through its use certain inconsistencies in the operation may be determined. The chart might, for example, show the possibility of combining the inspection service of several departments and might lead to an improvement in the physical layout of the plant. Charts of production procedure therefore serve a very useful purpose.

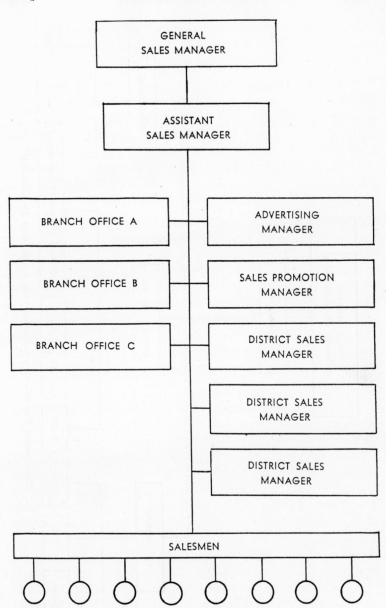

Illustration No. 83—Organization of a Sales Department

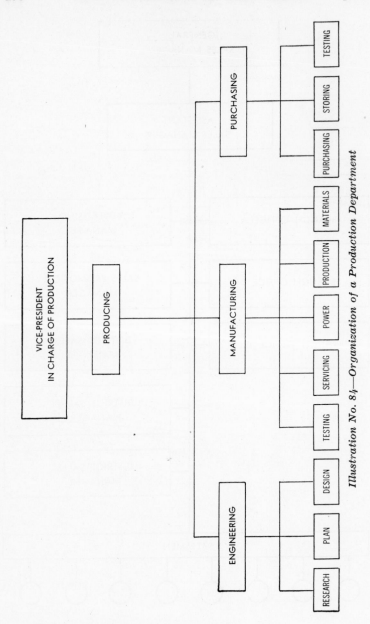

Illustration No. 84—Organization of a Production Department

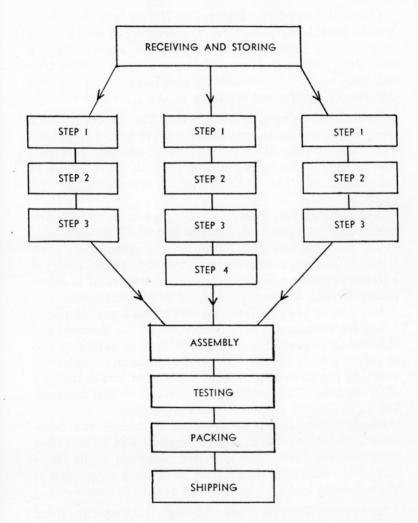

A chart of this kind, when compared with the physical layout of a factory, will often help to plan so-called straight-line production. Straight-line production involves moving from one step to another without wasting time and effort. A chart of this type is often referred to as a functional chart.

Illustration No. 85—Organization of Production Routine

Chart of Procedure. Illustration No. 86 is a chart tracing the purchasing procedure. The drawing of such a chart may disclose some unnecessary steps or some necessary new steps. Often the construction of a chart of this type will help employees not only to understand the procedure but also to analyze the efficiency of the procedure.

Functions of Organization Charts. The important functions performed by an organization chart are: (a) to indicate lines of responsibility; (b) to co-ordinate functions and to make those functions clear; (c) to indicate lines of promotion; and (d) to bring out an opportunity for job analysis.

An organization chart showing personnel and departments definitely places responsibility and shows authority. When responsibility and authority are understood, overlapping functions can be eliminated easily. By pointing out authority, such a chart can also be instrumental in eliminating friction between individuals and departments.

Many large organizations present to each new employee a booklet explaining the organization of the business and showing an organization chart with lines of authority and of promotion. If an individual understands an organization chart, he has some idea of what is ahead of him in the way of promotion. This aspect is important in any business. The right type of personnel seeks promotion.

Organization charts, by depicting processes and functions, make it possible to analyze various jobs, to establish standards for them, and to select personnel to fit those jobs. The personnel department in a large organization has a definite idea of what kind of person is needed.

Large-Scale Organizations. Through the corporate form of organization many huge businesses have been developed in the United States. It is particularly necessary in such corporations to have charts that show the kind of organization. Illustration No. 87 is an organization chart of the General Electric Company. Notice how the lines of authority are traced from the stockholders down to the smallest parts of the corporation.

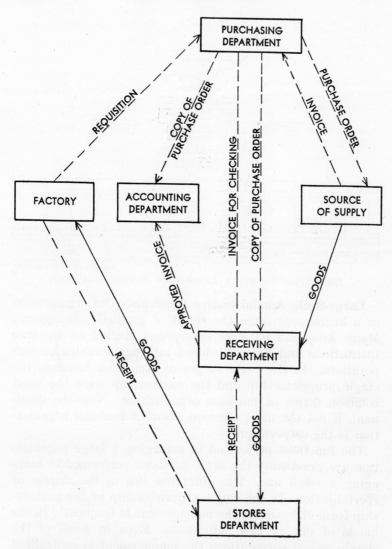

There are other possible variations in this procedure. For instance, after the receiving department checks the purchase order with the invoice and with the goods delivered, the invoice may be referred back to the purchasing department and then to the accounting department. Or, before sending the purchase order, the purchasing department may send to the source of supply a request for a quotation.

Illustration No. 86—A Chart Tracing the Purchasing Procedure

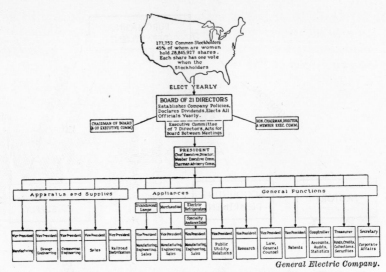

General Electric Company.

Illustration No. 87—A Large-Scale Organization Chart

Large-Scale Administrative Problems. The organization of a business is often the result of gradual development. Many American business enterprises started as one-man institutions and later developed into partnerships or corporations. In the early stages of American business the single proprietorship and the partnership were the most common forms of business organization. Now the dominant, if not the most common, form of business organization is the corporation.

The functions performed in managing a large organization are practically the same as those performed in managing a small one. The difference lies in the degree of specialization. In the single proprietorship or the partnership form of business, the management is frequently in the hands of one or two individuals. Even in some of the closely owned corporations the management is centralized in the hands of a few people. In The Ford Motor Company, for example, the management is controlled by Mr. Ford.

Generally, when businesses become large as the result of natural expansion or through combination, the owners and managers gradually delegate authority to subordinates and devote their time to specialized phases of management or to general supervision. Illustration No. 88 shows how the managerial functions of a large organization are delegated to subordinates under the control of executives.

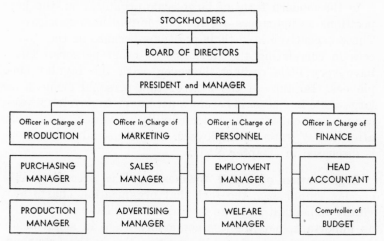

Illustration No. 88—Delegation of Managerial Functions

Specialized Functions in Large-Scale Business. The most common branches of management in a large corporation are those pertaining to accounting, credit, finance, buying, production, and selling. Personnel management is sometimes considered a separate function. Purchasing and selling are sometimes combined under one executive.

Each department of a business has its individual problems. The functions of the various departments are correlated through the good management of the executives. The accounting records and the budgets help to correlate finance, buying, production, and selling. Although responsibility for the various functions is delegated to several executives, these executives must co-operate in making a profit for the business. The problem of the purchasing department is to buy the proper quantities at the right price. Furthermore, in order that the production department can produce economically, the goods must be available at the proper time. The sales department must sell enough goods at prices that will assure a profit. The problem of the finance department is to correlate income with expenditures. If sufficient funds are not available, money must be borrowed.

In the modern form of large-scale organization, the key positions as managers are held by highly paid executives. These executives hold their positions because of their success in correlating the functions of other persons. They have very little contact, however, with the regular employees. Because of the lack of this personal element in large-scale business, it becomes necessary to develop a personnel department, the responsibility of which is to look after the welfare of employees. Personnel administration is discussed in Chapter XVII.

Organization of Small Businesses. The preceding discussion emphasizes the fact that organization charts are vitally important in large organizations. They are equally as important, but are less commonly used, in small businesses. The reason for this situation lies in the fact that the manager of a small business is able to visualize the organization and the procedure, and therefore assumes that everyone else has the same understanding. In such a case, however, the manager overlooks the fact that many of the employees may not thoroughly understand the lines of authority and of procedure.

In a small business the manager usually assumes too much responsibility. If he should die or become ill, the business would suffer severely. It is therefore desirable to delegate at least certain responsibilities to others. The manager might, for instance, delegate to someone the responsibility for making part or all of the purchases; to a second person a part or all of the responsibility for supervising sales; and to someone else all the responsibility for keeping the records and preparing financial statements. Although all these persons would report to him, they would at least share in the responsibility of managing the business. The manager could go away on a vacation without disrupting the business.

QUESTIONS FOR DISCUSSION

1. Explain briefly the line type of organization, and state its main advantage.
2. Explain the chief advantage of the staff type of organization.
3. What is the committee type of organization?
4. What danger sometimes exists in a one-man business with the line type of organization?
5. What is the value of an organization chart?
6. What are the advantages of having a chart of the procedure of some particular department, such as a purchasing department or a manufacturing department?
7. Are organization charts necessary in small businesses?

PROBLEMS AND PROJECTS

1. Obtain a chart showing the internal organization of some neighboring business. Write an explanation of the chart.
2. Assume that you and two of your friends are going into a retail shoe business. Draw an organization chart showing how the three of you will manage the business.
3. Draw your conception of a good organization chart for a garage and filling station, taking into consideration the following facts: (a) The owner of the business is Mr. A. J. Stevens. (b) The business consists of a filling station, a new- and used-car sales department, a repair and service department, and a parts department. (c) Mr. Stevens' son, John, acts as his assistant, but also manages the parts department and supervises to a certain extent all the other functions. (d) Mr. O. P. McGuire and three assistants have charge of the repair and service department. (e) Mr. H. A. Anderson has charge of the new- and used-car sales department, but a young man by the name of R. A. Smith spends most of his time with the used cars. (f) A nephew, Mr. Mac Stevens, takes care of the filling station with the assistance of two young boys.
4. Prepare a chart of production procedure for some kind of business, showing the various steps in production. After drawing the chart, recommend some improvements in the processes if you can see possibilities of improvement.

CHAPTER X

PURCHASING AND STOCK PROBLEMS

Purpose of the Chapter. In operating a business, there are two main problems involving merchandise and materials. One is purchasing these and the other is taking care of them after they have been purchased. This chapter deals with these two problems. It will answer such questions as follows:

1. How many different items should be handled in a retail store?
2. What quality of goods should be handled?
3. When should one buy?
4. Where can purchases be made most advantageously?
5. How much should be purchased?
6. What are various credit terms of purchasing?
7. What procedure is followed in ordering merchandise for a large business?
8. How can overpurchasing and underpurchasing be avoided?
9. How may the prices of various types of merchandise be indicated?
10. What is a good system for taking and keeping an inventory?

Section I

Purchasing Problems

What to Buy. Anyone who enters business should remember that his existence can be justified only on the basis of the service that he renders to the community. He should therefore consider himself as serving in the capacity of purchasing agent for his community. If he has that attitude, he will study the people he is to serve; he will find out their wants, their tastes, and their methods of living.

If the store is located in the middle-class section of a city
and customers are expected from that section, it should not
be stocked with only the highest-priced goods. Stocking
medium-priced goods would probably be better. Should the
goods of the store be bought only by women, the management should study feminine likes and dislikes before deciding what to buy.

If the climate is cool, the merchant buys goods suitable
to the needs of people in a cool climate. If a certain percentage of his customers like bright colors or a certain type
of goods, he buys with the thought of obtaining goods that
such customers will want.

The customer of today is a much different person from
the customer of twenty years ago. Formerly the customer
allowed the stores to choose the articles and then was content to buy whatever the stores had for sale. The customer
of today reads magazines, attends movies, and travels. As
a result he is a better educated person and a keener judge
of values; he is more discriminating in his selection of
goods and more critical if the article is not satisfactory.
In other words, it is now the problem of the merchant, not
to try to force something on his customers, but to attempt
to satisfy their individual wants. For instance, chain stores
have discovered from their operations that a product that
will sell well in one community sometimes will not sell in
another.

Attempts to buy merchandise at a central headquarters
and to distribute it through various outlets have met with
failure in many cases. Even chain-store managers therefore have to admit the desirability of acting as purchasing
agents for the communities in which their stores are operated. The individual who owns his own store has an advantage in the flexibility with which he can select what his
customers want.

The business cycle will have an effect on what the merchant should buy. In times of prosperity his customers
will be inclined to buy higher-priced goods, whereas in the
depression phase of the business cycle they will probably
want lower-priced merchandise. During hard times the

merchant should buy high-priced goods cautiously. When times are prosperous for the customers, he may buy a higher grade of merchandise and carry more extensive lines of style goods.

Chapter XXVI contains a detailed discussion of ways to keep informed on business conditions, both national and local. The merchant should utilize these sources of information in planning purchases. It is especially important for him to recognize local conditions. For example, business conditions as a whole may indicate prosperous times; but in a certain locality, where mainly one type of industry is carried on, there may be hard times because the one particular industry that furnishes employment to a large percentage of the people has shut down or operates only for short periods of time.

Policies in Buying. Many businesses have failed because the one in charge of buying knew very little about the quality of merchandise. In starting a new enterprise for himself, a person is likely to know little about the quality of goods. To have a better chance of operating his business successfully, he should have associated with him someone who has the ability to judge properly the quality of goods, or he must become efficient in judging quality for himself. Buying from reliable business concerns, buying on specifications, and buying warranted goods will also be an aid. The merchant must learn, however, to buy the best that he can obtain for his money.

Many merchants have wrecked their businesses by thinking more about quantity than quality. They have been anxious to give greater quantity than their competitors without regard to quality. In other words, the price factor has been uppermost in their minds. Winning the confidence of the public and holding it is the primary factor in the success of any business. A customer may be fooled for a short time; but when he finds that he has been fooled, he will look for another place to buy.

The purchasing of merchandise involves more than merely giving an order for a certain amount of goods at the lowest price. When prices are too low, the buyer can reasonably suspect that something is wrong. For instance, the package may contain less than the standard amount or the product may be adulterated. Prices that are too low should arouse suspicion and should encourage a thorough investigation. The fact that prices are high is no indication of the quality of merchandise.

The businessman who is just beginning an enterprise is confronted with the problem of deciding what brand or brands of goods to handle. Well-known or nationally advertised brands are probably the best for a new business. After the business is well established and has earned a good reputation, the customers might be induced to try private brands.

A decision must be made as to how many different brands of similar products are to be carried in stock. For instance, the grocer must decide just how many different brands of canned corn he should handle. A study of the customers and the community should be of aid. He must serve his community by attempting to give customers what they wish; but if he carries five or six brands instead of two, he will have a larger amount of his capital tied up. Most stores do not find it necessary to carry more than three brands. When little advertising has been given to particular goods, one brand should be sufficient.

National advertising is a big factor in creating demand. The retailer who sells advertised goods should take full advantage of the manufacturers' advertising campaigns. For example, if a dealer sells nationally advertised goods, he can often obtain special window displays, samples to distribute, and literature to hand out. Sometimes national advertisers will share in local advertising campaigns. At least the advertising campaign of the local dealer should be timed to correlate with that of the national advertiser. A fuller discussion of this problem is included in Chapter XV.

Just how many different items should be handled cannot be answered definitely, for the number will vary with each business. Should the person who is opening a men's clothing store handle suits only, or should he also stock shoes, shirts, underwear, socks, neckties, and hats? There are two factors that should influence him in reaching a decision. The amount of competition is one. If there are already sufficient stores conveniently located that carry the same quality of merchandise, the proprietor of the men's clothing store would probably find it unwise to handle all the related items. If, in a survey, he found that there was seemingly a lack of such stores selling hats, then he might find it desirable to handle hats in addition to suits. The other factor is the financial ability of the business to handle many items in addition to suits. Keeping in mind these two factors, the merchant should handle as many related items as possible. However, he probably will not want to sell every related item.

When to Buy. Merchandise should never be bought because of inducements. New products offered at attractive prices should not be bought in large quantities until the merchant has proved to himself that they will sell at a profit.

Purchasing merchandise in dull seasons for use in active seasons is a dangerous process because prices may change considerably. A merchant who follows this process is gambling, unless he has an assurance from the wholesaler or the manufacturer that he will be protected from loss caused by a price change.

Buying too far ahead is not wise. For instance, if ten dollars' worth of baking powder, which will last one month, can be purchased on terms of 2 per cent discount in ten days, it will probably be wiser for the average merchant to buy in this quantity than it would be to buy one hundred dollars' worth and thus get a discount of 4 per cent. In the latter case the merchant would have his money invested in merchandise that would last for ten months, but he would be getting only an additional 2 per cent discount on his purchase. This is not a high rate of discount when one considers the length of time that it would take to sell the merchandise.

In many businesses an attempt is made to find out the wishes of customers. Whenever a customer asks for an item that the store does not have in stock, the salesclerk fills out a *want slip*. Such a form is shown in Illustration No. 89. Some businesses use a want slip for each item, but the one shown in Illustration No. 89 is a daily report.

From a careful study of these slips the management may get a better idea of what and when to buy. Of course, care must be used in such a study. If only one or two calls are made for merchandise not carried, it may not be wise to stock such goods. On the other hand, if a number of cus-

THE WILLIAMS COMPANY

IMPORTANT

Please list below every call made by a customer for goods not in stock, even though the merchandise is on order. Do this *immediately* after your customer has left.

Articles asked for	Number of calls *	Article you were able to substitute
Half-inch silk bias binding (orange)	2	Cotton binding
Glove stretchers, size 6	1	Nothing
Boxes A. and B. assorted darning floss	4	Single spools

* If more than one call was made for any one article, state the number of calls for it

Dept. Notions_____   Clerk *Alice Palmer* Date December 15, 1939

Illustration No. 89—A Want Slip

tomers ask for merchandise that is not stocked, sales are lost and the disappointed customers go to a competitor to purchase the goods and may purchase others while there.

Another guide to buying is found in the records of past purchases and sales. These records, which also show factors that affected sales of past seasons, can be interpreted in connection with new circumstances that may have an important effect in the future season. For instance, the records may show that during the last three seasons the average number of men's white linen suits sold was four hundred. But the fashion news for the coming season indicates that men's summer suits are to be characterized by color, and even two-color suits (trousers and coat of different colors) will be in vogue. So it probably would be unwise for the store to plan to purchase four hundred white linen suits for the coming season. There are many publications that will aid the buyer in forecasting the demands of a season.

Making a study of what other stores are doing may help the businessman with his purchasing problems. He may study the advertising and examine the merchandise displayed in the windows of competing stores. Many of the larger stores in cities send someone to competitors' stores to find out what merchandise, prices, and services are offered by those stores. This person is usually known as a *comparison shopper*. He may actually buy goods in a competitor's store and bring them back for comparison with the goods of his own store.

Where to Buy. Through trade papers and other magazines, businessmen should be able to obtain information as to important sources of supply. The leading methods of buying are: (1) ordering goods through traveling salesmen; (2) making personal trips to the market; and (3) ordering by mail by means of a catalogue. The last method is used mainly for repeat orders of staple goods when the merchant finds his stock getting low and the representative of the manufacturer or the wholesaler will not call again for some time. The operators of small stores often cannot afford to take the time and incur the expense of making personal trips to large markets to buy their goods, so they usually order their goods from traveling salesmen. The buyers for large stores usually go to the chief markets, such as New York City. One advantage of such a method is that it gives the buyer a chance to visit a large number of businesses and to compare their merchandise. Making personal trips to the market is the usual procedure followed in buying clothing for women, most of which is sold on a style basis. Wholesalers do not like to handle such goods because of the great risk of loss due to style changes. Direct contact between the buyers for retail stores and the manufacturers of women's clothing is also advisable so that a style that is proving popular can be manufactured quickly and placed on sale in the stores. Unless the clothing is produced quickly, there may be no demand for it when it is placed on sale.

Whether to buy most of his goods from a few concerns or whether to scatter his orders among many business concerns is a problem that the businessman must decide. Most successful businessmen believe that to concentrate buying among a few concerns is the better plan. The businessman who follows this plan usually develops friendly and personal relations with the manufacturer; and the manufacturer consequently gets to know the merchandise, store, methods, and needs of the businessman. Better prices and better credit terms, as well as better service, is likely to result.

One should buy only from reputable businesses. Such businesses handle quality merchandise because they have a reputation to maintain. For example, suppose that Mr. Taylor decides to buy some goods from a business that is not reputable but that claims its goods are "just as good" as those made by reputable businesses and are sold for less. When a customer buys the goods from Mr. Taylor and later finds them to be of inferior quality, he will be dissatisfied and form the opinion that all the goods sold by Mr. Taylor are of inferior quality. He will therefore probably go elsewhere to buy his goods in the future. He may even advise other people not to buy their goods from Mr. Taylor. Thus it is easy for a businessman to lose both his customers and his reputation by buying goods from concerns that are not reputable.

The businessman should not be misled, however, by an argument that merchandise is good just because the price is a little high. An elaborate label, a strong advertising campaign, and a forceful salesman may create the impression that an article available at a high price is superior to similar articles sold at lower prices. The only way for the businessman to be sure is to make definite comparisons of the products.

As the transportation cost, whether prepaid by the seller or paid by the buyer, affects the total cost of the purchase, the merchant should buy his goods from concerns located as near as possible to his place of business, other factors being equal. Buying from neighboring businesses also results in orders being filled more quickly.

How Much to Buy. After the businessman has decided what to buy, when to buy, and where to buy, there is still the problem of how much to buy. The increasing amount of attention paid in recent years to stock turnover has greatly changed buying policies. Formerly a six months' supply of goods was bought at a time. Such a policy would result in the money of the business being tied up in merchandise for a long time. For example, a clothing merchant might estimate that he could sell 3,000 suits of clothes during the spring and summer season. If all the suits were purchased at one time at a cost of $20 a suit, the merchant would have $60,000 of his capital tied up in suits for a considerable time. It would be better for him to purchase approximately 1,500 suits at one time, 1,000 suits at a later date, and the other 500 at a still later date. By that method he would require only about $30,000 (1,500 suits at $20) to finance the purchase.

A good practice to follow is to buy in small quantities, for this permits a minimum investment in merchandise. If only small quantities of merchandise are kept in stock, the danger of loss from obsolescence, spoilage, shrinkage, or

changes in demand will be small. When the stock of merchandise is large, there is a greater chance of loss.

The merchant should be careful in purchasing new items.
He should plan to buy a very small quantity the first time
in order to try out the sales possibility of the item. With
our rapid transportation systems it is usually easy for the
businessman to get his orders for merchandise delivered
quickly. Consequently there is less need for purchasing a
season's supply at one time.

Many merchants cannot resist the temptation to buy
large quantities of merchandise when they are offered a
discount for buying such a quantity. A clothing store may
be quoted a price of $20 for 100 pairs of men's socks or a
price of $18 for 100 pairs on a purchase of 1,000 pairs. If
the store should buy 1,000 pairs at one time, the cost would
be $180 instead of $200 for 1,000 pairs purchased at the
rate of 100 pairs each time. But suppose the store were
able to sell only 800 pairs during the season. The remaining 200 pairs would have to be stored until the next season.
In that case capital would be tied up; there would be danger of deterioration and moth damage; and styles might
change during the next season. As a result the store would
probably suffer a larger loss on the 200 pairs than the $20
($200 — $180) that would have been saved in buying the
larger quantity.

Speculation. Many merchants have learned, to their dismay, the inadvisability of speculation in commodities. Good
guesses with regard to prices are profitable, but one poor
guess may disrupt an otherwise sound business. If a merchant purchases an unusually large supply of merchandise
in anticipation of a rise in prices, he is fortunate if the rise
does occur. On the other hand, he is unfortunate if prices
fall.

Dating and Terms. As the dating and the terms offered
by sellers vary a great deal, the businessman should be
familiar with the more common ones in order to know
which are the most advantageous to him when he purchases merchandise.

When purchases are made, a free delivery point is indicated. Ordinarily merchandise is bought *f.o.b.* (free on board) *shipping point*. The seller then pays only the expense of delivering the goods to the carrier, such as a railroad, in the city in which he is located. *F.o.b. destination* means that the seller will pay the transportation charges. These transportation charges to the destination do not include charges for trucking the goods from the railroad to the purchaser's place of business. As will be seen, however, in Chapter XIII, store-door delivery can be obtained at no extra cost under some conditions. Most trucking lines provide store-door delivery.

As an example of shipping practices, consider the following case: Mr. Jones, who operates a store in Buffalo, orders an electric washing machine from a Chicago business, the price being $60, f.o.b. Chicago (the shipping point). The transportation charges from Chicago to Buffalo are $5. Mr. Jones therefore pays the transportation company $5 and the seller in Chicago $60. Suppose that Mr. Jones wanted the machine shipped f.o.b. destination. In that case the Chicago business would probably ask a price of $65 because it would have to pay the $5 to the transportation company.

There is a legal point in connection with these two situations that the buyer should keep in mind. In the first situation, when goods are purchased f.o.b. shipping point, the title to the goods passes to the buyer as soon as the seller delivers the goods to the carrier in his city. Thus, if the goods sold to Mr. Jones should be damaged en route to Buffalo, the loss would fall upon Mr. Jones, the buyer. In some cases Mr. Jones might be able to collect damages from the transportation company. In the second situation, however, when goods are sold f.o.b. destination, the title to the goods remains with the seller until the goods reach their destination. So it is usually to the advantage of the buyer to order goods f.o.b. destination.

Regardless of the responsibility for damage to goods, it is usually good practice for the seller to make whatever adjustment is necessary and to handle the claim with the transportation company. If there is a justifiable claim against the transportation company, the seller can usually collect damages readily.

A common way for the terms of a purchase or sale to be stated is "net 30 days," which means that payment is to be made within 30 days from the date of the invoice. The date of the invoice is usually the date of shipment of the goods. Some businesses offer longer terms, such as net 60 days. The longer the terms, the better for the buyer as he will have a chance to sell some or all of the goods by the time he is to make payment for them.

In order to encourage buyers to purchase in advance, that is, to place their order for goods several months before they will actually sell them, some businesses offer *advance datings*. Under such a dating the date of payment is computed from a particular day in advance of the date of shipment. For example, goods may be shipped in February but have a dating of April 1. If the terms are net 30 days, payment need not be made until May 1.

Another form of dating is *E.O.M.* (end of month). The time of payment is then computed from the end of the month in which the merchandise is purchased. If goods are shipped on May 14 with E.O.M. terms of net 30 days, payment need not be made until June 30.

When the buyer is located a great distance from the seller, *R.O.G.* (receipt of goods) terms may be given.

The businessman is often offered *discounts* on goods that he purchases. There are two general types of discounts: (a) trade and (b) cash, or time, discounts. *Trade discounts* are special deductions made to buyers such as wholesalers, retailers, or jobbers. For example, the price of a certain article is $12 a dozen; but if five gross (60 dozen) are purchased, the buyer receives a discount of 20 per cent. Sometimes a series of trade discounts may be offered. For instance, in the catalogue of a manufacturer a particular article may be quoted at $40, less 25 per cent, less 10 per cent. The net cost would be figured as follows: $40 less $10 (25 per cent of $40), or $30, less $3 (10 per cent of $30), or $27.

Most manufacturers and wholesalers offer a discount if payment is made within a given time. This is known as a *cash,* or *time, discount.* It may be offered with various advance datings and credit terms. The terms of a purchase may be net 30 days with a 1 per cent discount for payment within 10 days. If the invoice is dated May 1, the buyer will be permitted to deduct 1 per cent provided he pays for the merchandise on or before May 11; otherwise he must pay the full amount by May 31. It is customary in business to express such terms as "1/10, n/30."

If a discount is to be granted for payment within a 10-day period, the remittance should be in the hands of the seller before the close of the tenth day of the credit period, or the envelope should bear a postmark indicating that it was mailed within that period. It is not considered ethical to attempt to claim a discount after the discount period has expired.

If a cash, or time, discount is offered, the buyer should attempt to make payment in time to get the discount because (a) discounting purchase invoices gives the merchant a good credit rating and (b) such a practice effects a saving. For example, under the terms 1/10, n/30, the saving amounts to approximately 18 per cent on an annual basis. In other words, if 1 per cent is saved by making payment 20 days before the due date, there is an equivalent saving of approximately 18 per cent in 360 days.

The following table gives the approximate annual saving on several discounts:

TERMS	APPROXIMATE SAVING
½% in 10 days, net 30 days	9% a year
1% " 10 " " 30 "	18% " "
2% " 10 " " 30 "	36% " "
2% " 10 " " 60 "	14% " "
2% " 30 " " 120 "	8% " "
3% " 10 " " 120 "	10% " "
3% " 10 " " 60 "	21% " "

The foregoing figures show that a businessman will actually profit by borrowing money at 6 per cent annual interest in order to take advantage of cash discounts. It is quite apparent that he should keep his finances in such a condition that he can discount invoices.

Businesses that have sufficient working capital may sometimes be granted *anticipation discounts*. As an example, suppose that the terms on a $400 invoice are net 90 days. The buyer has sufficient funds to make payment at the end of 30 days. As he will be paying 60 days before the due date, he may deduct interest for the 60 days anticipated. Sixty days' interest at 6 per cent on $400 is $4, the anticipation discount. The buyer accordingly makes a payment of $396 to settle his account. An anticipation discount should not be taken, however, unless the option is granted by the seller or unless the granting and taking of such discounts is an established practice within the particular industry. Taking an anticipation discount without having the privilege is certainly unethical.

QUESTIONS FOR DISCUSSION

1. What thought should be kept uppermost in mind by the businessman in deciding what goods to buy?
2. Why is the customer of today more discriminating in his purchases?
3. Why is the buyer for a large chain of stores often unable to purchase wisely for all the stores?
4. What type of merchandise do customers tend to buy in times of business depression?
5. For a new business what brand or brands of goods should be carried?
6. Why should a business avoid carrying too many brands of the same product?
7. It is a good policy not to buy too far ahead. Explain this statement.
8. (a) Name three articles that quickly deteriorate physically. (b) Name two that are subject to sudden style changes.
9. Explain the term *comparison shopper*.
10. Is it usually a better plan to buy from many business houses or from only a few?
11. Who pays the charges for transportation when goods are shipped (a) f.o.b. shipping point? (b) f.o.b. destination?
12. What is meant by an advance dating?
13. Distinguish between trade discounts and cash discounts.
14. What is an anticipation discount?

Section II

Purchasing Procedure and Stock Control

Organized Purchasing Procedure. Much of the preceding discussion was based upon simple examples of purchasing for retail stores. Those principles also apply to the purchasing problems of other types of businesses. In large retail stores and in manufacturing businesses, it is often necessary to have a purchasing department or at least one person in charge of purchasing. A scientific procedure is therefore desirable. Various steps in an efficient procedure are indicated in Illustration No. 90. An organized purchasing procedure involves obtaining and keeping detailed information on supply, consumption, quality, and prices. For each product that is purchased and consumed, there should be detailed information with regard to sources, specifications, quantity consumed, quantity purchased in the past, time required for delivery, the satisfaction obtained from previous purchases, prices, and price trends.

Much of this information can be obtained from the catalogues of the various manufacturers and distributors. There

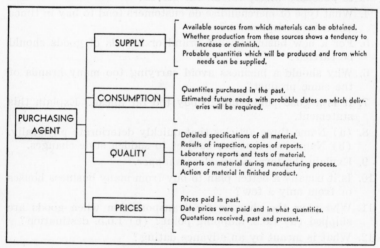

*Illustration No. 90—Information Needed by a
Purchasing Department*

should be a systematic method of filing and indexing such catalogues or the information obtained from them. For instance, each catalogue should be analyzed according to the different kinds of goods listed in it. A separate card showing all pertinent facts for each class of goods can then be prepared and placed in a convenient file.

The Purchasing Department. Many businesses have a large staff of skilled employees who do nothing but handle the purchases. Each person has specialized duties to perform. Illustration No. 91 shows the organization of a purchasing department.

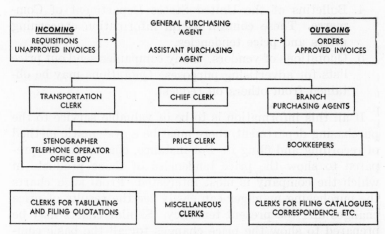

Illustration No. 91—Organization of a Purchasing Department

Information Concerning Prices. The purchasing department should have information concerning the prices of all the commodities it buys so that it can judge the fairness of the prices quoted by salesmen. There are many sources from which information concerning prices may be obtained. The following are the most important:

1. Commercial and financial newspapers such as those published in large cities. These give quotations of prices on all the basic materials. The purchasing department will probably be in the market for some of

these materials. The prices of other materials will be useful in indicating the general price level.

2. Trade journals, which are published in many lines of industry. These usually contain price quotations. The purchasing department should subscribe for those journals covering the types of products in which it is most interested.

3. Statistical organizations that sell their services to businesses on an annual basis. Several of these collect data concerning prices in general and publish this information in a convenient form. This information is also useful in judging price tendencies.

4. Bulletins of the United States Department of Commerce. These contain useful information concerning prices and price tendencies.

5. Quotations of vendors. Many companies send out price lists for advertising purposes. Quotations may be obtained from others on request.

If all this information is to be of valuable service to the purchasing department, there must be a systematic method of recording and filing it. For instance, charts may be prepared to show the price tendencies of those products in which the company is most interested. From such charts the purchasing manager can easily see the results of price changes and the present tendency. Similar charts may be prepared to show the price changes for all the basic commodities. The purchasing manager can then see the general market conditions. Such charts may be provided by the statistical agencies for whose service he subscribes. If they are, he need only keep them in a convenient file.

Information of a general nature obtained from periodicals and similar sources may be filed under appropriate headings so that it can be found easily when desired. Information concerning commodities purchased most frequently may be tabulated and kept in a card file for ready reference. It is also important to keep a card record of each source of supply, providing information in regard to previous purchases, quality standards, and delivery service.

Information on Quality. In a business having an organized purchasing department, there should be established methods of making certain simple tests within the scope of the management. It is also possible to have tests made by outside agencies. A list of these testing agencies can be obtained from the United States Department of Commerce, National Bureau of Standards. The list is entitled "A Directory of Commercial Testing and College Research Laboratories." Many merchants and manufacturers use the facilities of these various testing agencies to determine quality.

Information with regard to standards, which can be used as a guide in buying, can be obtained from the American Standards Association. Details on the services of the association are given in Chapter XXVI.

Control of Merchandise Stock. Every businessman should have some definite means of controlling his stock so that he knows which items are selling best, how rapidly the various items of stock are being turned over, when goods should be reordered, and in what quantities repeat orders should be placed. Too many businessmen depend on their memories and, because of the lack of records, are compelled to guess about the most important facts of their business.

A practical policy is to fix high and low stock limits for every item carried in stock. In a retail store the low limit, or point below which the management does not wish the supply to fall at any time, is a safeguard against being unable to supply items called for by customers; in a manufacturing business it is a safeguard against there being a lack of supplies needed in the process of manufacturing. In a manufacturing business a shortage of supplies will hold up production and consequently cause a serious loss.

From the point of view of a retail business, empty shelves give the customer a very bad impression. His observation may lead him to believe that the merchant carries an incomplete stock. A merchant should not allow his shelves to appear as those in Illustration No. 92.

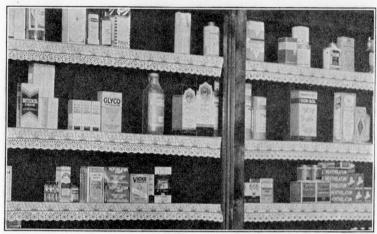

Illustration No. 92—Empty Shelves May Give a Bad Impression

The low point is determined largely by the time required to have more goods delivered and made ready for resale or use. The high point is established to serve as a check against buying too large a quantity and thus overstocking with probable bad results.

A simple plan for securing proper attention to the low limit is to place a strip of ordinary gummed tape, such as that used for packing and wrapping, around the group of items that is considered the low-limit quantity. For example, the low limit for a certain brand of tooth paste may be four dozen tubes. The gummed tape is placed around a group of four dozen tubes, together with a gummed label, or "sticker," that contains information about the article. When, days or weeks later, a clerk sells the last loose tube of that particular brand of tooth paste and is confronted with the taped group of four dozen, he tears off the tape and gives the "sticker" to the one who does the buying.

Many businesses use *stock cards* as an aid in making purchases and as the basis of their perpetual-inventory record. Individual stock cards are kept for all items. Illustration No. 93 shows one form of stock card. This type of card is quite useful in a manufacturing enterprise, in a department store, and in some specialized stores, such as a shoe store. In a small grocery store, however, too much detailed work would be involved in keeping a record of this kind for each individual product.

Placing the Order. The proprietor of a small business can easily discover that the stock of certain items is getting so low that additional orders should be placed. As a check or reminder he should list his purchase needs in a memorandum book of some kind as he discovers them. As the orders are placed, he can check off the items ordered.

Article _Black Kid Shoes_						Stock No. _503_		High _30 pr._ Low _10 pr._		
Maker	Ordered		Received		Unit Cost	Selling Price	Sold		Balance		Remarks
	Date	Quantity	Date	Quantity			Date	Quantity	Quantity	Value *	
W. R. Co.	1939 Oct.15	30	1939 Oct.30	30	$4.00	$6.00	1939 Nov. 2 4 5	3 2 4	30 27 25 21		

* This column may be used for either cost value or retail value. Usually the value column is used only at the end of a fiscal period, as at the end of a month.

Illustration No. 93—A Stock Record Card

It is impossible for the owner or even the purchasing department of a large business to know when goods should be ordered. For that reason *purchase requisitions* are used. These are forms requesting the purchasing agent to buy the items listed. A department head or the chief stock clerk usually fills out and signs the requisition. Illustration No. 94 shows a purchase requisition. At least one carbon copy is made. The original is sent to the purchasing agent, and one copy is kept by the person requesting the purchase of the goods. An example of purchasing procedure is shown in Illustration No. 86 (page 201).

THE EMPIRE COMPANY
SYRACUSE, NEW YORK

PURCHASE REQUISITION

Requisition No. 25B

Date December 8, 1939

Date Goods Wanted January 2, 1940

To: Purchasing Agent

Please order the following for delivery to ___Advertising___ Department

QUANTITY	DESCRIPTION
25M	White buckskin O. E. envelopes, 6" x 9"
50M	#10 Postage saver envelopes, 28 lb.
5M	#80 clasp envelopes

Signed _E. Staub_

Approved _C. R. Smith_

MEMORANDUM FOR PURCHASING DEPARTMENT

Purchase Order No. 38376 ___ Goods ordered from Hamilton Supply

Dated December 8, 1939 ___ Company, Hamilton, Ohio

Illustration No. 94—A Purchase Requisition

The Purchase Order. The proprietor of a small business places his order for goods by writing a letter, while a large business makes use of a business form, known as a *purchase order,* to accomplish the same result. Such a form is shown in Illustration No. 95.

Several copies of a purchase order are made. The original is sent to the company from which the goods are being ordered. One copy is kept in the files of the purchasing department; another is sent to the person who made out the purchase requisition so that he will know the goods have been ordered; one copy is sent to the receiving department; and still another is sent to the accounting department. These copies are usually made on paper of different colors so that the proper copy will be sent to the proper department or person.

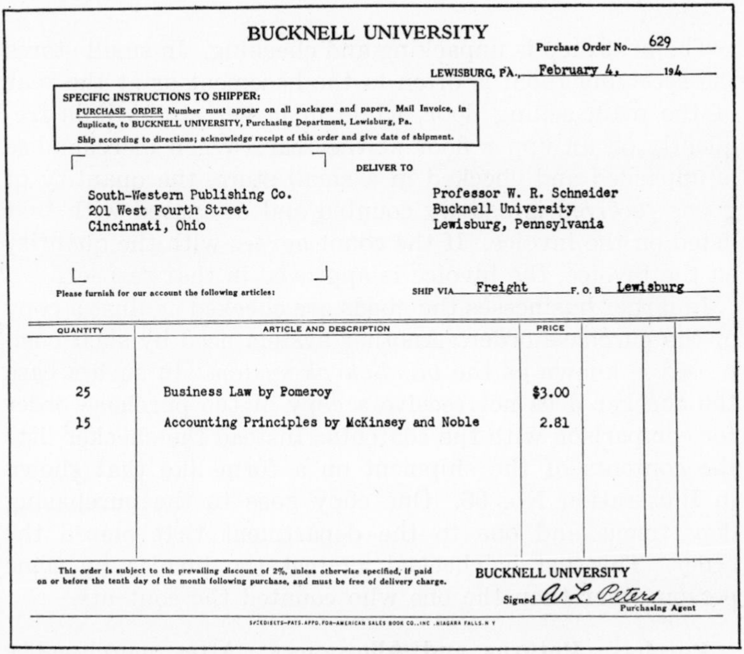

BUCKNELL UNIVERSITY

Purchase Order No. 629

LEWISBURG, PA., February 4, 194

SPECIFIC INSTRUCTIONS TO SHIPPER:
PURCHASE ORDER Number must appear on all packages and papers. Mail Invoice, in duplicate, to BUCKNELL UNIVERSITY, Purchasing Department, Lewisburg, Pa.
Ship according to directions; acknowledge receipt of this order and give date of shipment.

South-Western Publishing Co.
201 West Fourth Street
Cincinnati, Ohio

DELIVER TO
Professor W. R. Schneider
Bucknell University
Lewisburg, Pennsylvania

Please furnish for our account the following articles:

SHIP VIA Freight F. O. B. Lewisburg

QUANTITY	ARTICLE AND DESCRIPTION	PRICE			
25	Business Law by Pomeroy	$3.00			
15	Accounting Principles by McKinsey and Noble	2.81			

This order is subject to the prevailing discount of 2%, unless otherwise specified, if paid on or before the tenth day of the month following purchase, and must be free of delivery charge.

BUCKNELL UNIVERSITY
Signed A. L. Peters
Purchasing Agent

SPEEDISETS—PATS. APPD. FOR—AMERICAN SALES BOOK CO., INC. NIAGARA FALLS, N. Y.

Illustration No. 95—A Purchase Order

Handling Incoming Goods. After goods have been ordered for a store, other fundamental operations must be carried out in preparation for the resale of the goods. All incoming shipments should be received at a specified point, and a complete and correct record should be made here. Before signing the receipt of the transportation company, the receiving clerk should examine each shipment to see if the case or the wrappings are damaged, wet, or broken. If the shipment is not in good order, a statement of the condition in which it is received should be written on the receipt. This precaution will aid in establishing a claim if some of the contents are found to be damaged or lost. Before signing the receipt, the receiving clerk should also check to see that the shipper's name and the number of packages received agree with the statements on the receipt. It is desirable that a detailed record be made of the shipment received.

The next step is unpacking and checking. In small stores the receiving room is often in the basement or at the rear of the main selling floor, while in larger stores it is frequently on an upper floor at the rear. When merchandise is unpacked and checked in a small store, the quantity of goods received is usually counted and compared with that listed on the invoice. If the count agrees with the quantity on the invoice, the invoice is approved in that respect.

In larger businesses the goods are checked against a copy of the purchase order. Another system used by such businesses is known as the *blind-check system*. In such a case the checker does not receive a copy of the purchase order for comparison with the contents. Instead the checker lists the contents of the shipment on a form like that shown in Illustration No. 96. One copy goes to the purchasing department and one to the department that placed the order. This list is checked against the invoice by some person other than the one who counted the contents.

Purchase Returns and Allowances. After merchandise has been checked for quantity, it should be inspected to see if it is of the same size, color, and quality as that ordered. The buyer is usually responsible for this work. If goods are received in a damaged or defective condition or are not of the kind ordered, the business may either return them for credit or keep them and ask that an allowance be made.

The proprietor of a small business ordinarily asks for this adjustment by means of a letter. Larger businesses make use of a form known as a *charge-back invoice,* such as the one shown in Illustration No. 97. Several copies

Comptrollers Form
No. 33   10M 8-38

COMPTROLLER'S STORES

INDIANA UNIVERSITY
RECEIVING MEMORANDUM

Date_____ April 10,_____ 194___ No. **10068**

Received from____ South-Western Publishing Co.

Address__201 West Fourth St., Cincinnati, Ohio

PURCHASE ORDER NO.	515	HOW SHIPPED	PRO. NO
REQ. NO.	146	Freight	71

COLLECT	PREPAID	DRIVER
	x	A. S. Edwards

QUANTITY	DESCRIPTION OF SHIPMENT
24	College Law by Peters
20	Accounting Principles by McKinsey and
	Noble

Remarks_____

Delivered to____ Professor James Lawson
Rec'd at   Rec'd for Book Store
Stores Room by_ O. W. Banning _Dept. by_ C. A. Case
FOR DEPARTMENT

FLATPAKIT PATENT NO.1,534 478—AMERICAN SALES BOOK CO.,INC.,NIAGARA FALLS,N Y

Illustration No. 96—A Receiving Memorandum

are usually prepared. The original is sent to the vendor. One copy is kept by the purchasing agent, who filled out the charge-back invoice; another is sent to the shipping department and serves as an order for the goods to be shipped back to the seller; ordinarily still another is sent to the accounting department.

THE WILLIAMS COMPANY

BUFFALO, NEW YORK

February 6, _____, 19 40

To Highlight Manufacturing   Our Pur. Order No. 36360

Company, Buffalo, New York   Your Invoice No. 21123

We are charging your account as indicated. Please credit our account.

QUANTITY	ITEM AND EXPLANATION	AMOUNT
1	Table lamp, shade crushed and base scratched	$ 5.00
10	Bed lamps, wrong kind, see our order	20.00

C. H. Young _____ Purchasing Agent

Illustration No. 97—A Charge-Back Invoice

Care of Merchandise Stock. Marking the prices on the merchandise is the next step. In a department store this procedure becomes a great task. All major items are marked individually. Whenever it is feasible, a price ticket should be placed on every article. Items such as handkerchiefs can be grouped together with one price notation applying to each item in the group. These items are, however, often marked individually. In grocery stores, of course, it is impossible to mark each individual item, as in the case of oranges or cookies. The price is usually placed upon the carton or the display compartment. All prices should, however, be marked plainly, as they are in Illustration No. 98.

The practice of marking prices on merchandise in retail stores advertises the merchandise to those who are hesitant about asking the price. It avoids the misquoting of prices to customers. The price ticket may also aid in taking a physical inventory. The retail price should be marked in large, plain figures. Price tickets may be stitched to clothing, tied to some articles, or pasted on others.

National Cash Register Company.

Illustration No. 98—Goods with Plainly Marked Prices

The efficient merchant wants to know which stock is old and which sells slowly, so that he can better decide about his future purchases and also make plans to dispose of the older merchandise. Information of this and other types can be indicated on the price tag. An example of a tag containing various items of information is shown in Illustration No. 99. Tags of this general type are made so that a stub can be torn off and turned in by the salesperson to the department head or to the stock room. Such stubs not only indicate how well particular articles are selling, but also serve as a check on the supply of each item. In other words, as each item is sold, the management gets a stub

The Williams Bros. Company	
45	828
117	W 1118
2.89	
....	
45	828
117	W 1118
2.89	

Information on the tag:

45	department
828	style number
117	business from which the article was purchased
W 1118	date of purchase
W	1939
11	November (11th month)
18	18th day
2.89	selling price

Illustration No. 99—A Duplicate Price Ticket

and can watch the inventory of that item. Many businesses, however, do not use a price ticket with a stub.

Ticket machines, used in larger stores, print the desired information on each ticket. In small stores the marking of the price tickets is done by hand.

Many kinds of tags, tickets, or labels are used. The most common types are:

1. Gummed labels for towels, handkerchiefs, and books
2. String tags for jewelry, dresses, and large articles
3. Pin tickets for hosiery, underwear, and other articles that pins do not damage
4. Tickets that are fastened to cloth goods by looping part of the goods into a slot on the ticket

When new merchandise has been marked and is ready to be placed on sale with other goods of its kind, it should be so placed that the merchandise already in stock and still in good condition will be disposed of first. Should the new merchandise be placed on top of or in front of the old merchandise, the latter becomes shopworn and depreciates greatly before it is sold.

Taking an Inventory. At the close of each fiscal period an inventory of the merchandise is taken primarily to determine the amount for the financial records and also to discover what merchandise is moving slowly. Either of two general methods may be used in taking an inventory. Under the *cost method* the values of the items on hand are computed at the prices paid for the articles. It is therefore necessary that the cost price of each item be known. The price can be determined by hunting up the invoice for each item, but this plan is laborious and therefore little used. The cost price is usually marked in code on each item at the time of purchase. Then, as each item is counted, the cost value is determined by the code mark. If the market value of the goods being inventoried is less than the cost price, the former is used. The cost method is used in manufacturing businesses and in some retail stores.

The *retail method* of taking an inventory is the listing of all the items on hand and determining their value on the basis of the retail prices marked on them. Thus it is easier to inventory goods by the retail method. The total value of the goods arrived at by this method cannot, however, be used on the balance sheet because on this statement the assets are to be listed at their cost, not their sale, value. To adjust this retail value to cost value requires that detailed records be kept, especially when a large number of items are handled. The costs of the merchandise received are accumulated along with the retail values. Then, at the end of a fiscal period, the average margin figure (the margin is the selling price minus the cost of any item) can be applied to the retail value of the stock in order to adjust the inventory to cost value. This method is satisfactory for income-tax purposes.

Explanation of the Retail Inventory Method. The following example will explain briefly how the retail method is used in taking an inventory:

Beginning inventory (at retail)		$ 4,500
Merchandise received during the period (at retail)		7,600
Retail-price advances (goods marked higher than the original retail price)		200
Total stock available for sale		$12,300
Sales made during the period (both cash and charge)	$8,550	
Retail-price reductions, spoilage, etc...	350	
Total deductions from stock		8,900
Retail value of the stock that should be on hand		$ 3,400

Lyon Metal Products, Inc.

Illustration No. 100—Stock Carefully Arranged

When an actual physical inventory is taken (that is, when the merchandise is counted), it should show approximately the same amount, $3,400, the retail price. Suppose, however, that the actual physical inventory amounts to $3,100. There is consequently a shortage of $300 worth of merchandise. This discrepancy should be investigated. One of the purposes of taking a physical inventory is to discover shortages or other discrepancies in the retail method.

Let us assume, therefore, that the final retail valuation on the merchandise is accepted as $3,100 and that the average margin of profit used in setting the retail price is 20 per cent. The value of the merchandise at cost price is therefore approximately $2,480. This figure will be used on the financial statements as the value of the merchandise in stock.

It is a difficult task to take a physical inventory frequently, that is, to make an actual count of the merchandise on hand. If the retail method is used, however, financial statements can be prepared frequently without a count of the merchandise. Occasionally, however, as was indicated above, a physical inventory should also be taken in order to make any necessary adjustments.

Perpetual Inventory. A *perpetual-inventory system* is one that provides records showing the amount of merchandise or raw materials on hand at any particular time without the necessity of making a physical count. Illustration No. 101 shows a perpetual-inventory card used in a manufacturing business. A card record is kept of each item in the stock rooms. Whenever a purchase of any item is made and the material is received, an entry is recorded on the appropriate card. Whenever a quantity of an item is withdrawn from stock, it is recorded on the card. The balance on hand at any time is always shown in the last column.

This particular type of card shows only the quantity and does not indicate value. When it is used, the market price of each item is considered the value at the time an inventory is taken, but the actual monetary value of the quantity in stock must be computed. Some perpetual-inventory

| PERPETUAL-INVENTORY CARD | | | | |
| Item: #12 bolts | | | | |
Date	Pur. Req. or Stock Req. No.	Put in Stock	Withdrawn	Balance
2/3/39	2192	1200		1200
2/10/39	126		100	1100
2/12/39	128		500	600
2/26/39	2198	1000		1600
3/1/39	140		300	1300

Illustration No. 101—Perpetual-Inventory Card

records provide for not only the quantity but also the unit cost and the total cost. When withdrawals are made, it is considered that the first items placed in stock are the first ones taken out. It is therefore possible to keep a perpetual balance computed on a monetary basis as well as on a physical-quantity basis.

Explanation of Terminology Used by Retail Businesses. Retail stores also keep so-called perpetual inventories. In order to understand the method of keeping a perpetual inventory for a retail store, it is first necessary to understand some of the terms involved. The following explanations of terminology are necessary before one particular method of keeping such an inventory is explained:

Net profit is the net amount of money a business earns, that is, the amount over and above all costs and expenses. The expenses include the owner's salary.

Selling price is the price at which merchandise is sold to customers. The price should be sufficient to yield a net profit in addition to covering the cost of the merchandise and the operating expenses.

Operating expenses are the expenses incurred in operating the business. The cost of merchandise is not included in operating expenses.

Margin, or gross profit, is the sum of the operating expenses and the net profit, or the difference between the

operating expenses and the net loss. The term *spread* is
sometimes substituted for *margin* and means the difference
between the cost of the merchandise and the selling price.

Markup is the percentage by which the cost of an article
is multiplied to arrive at the amount that, added to the
cost of the merchandise, gives the selling price.

Markdown is any amount by which the original selling
price is reduced.

The selling price rather than the cost of the merchandise is the basis for figuring the value of a perpetual inventory. The merchant who has been in business for some
time tries, at the beginning of a year, to estimate his sales
on the basis of past experience. If a merchant is starting
a new business, he estimates his sales for the first year as
carefully as possible. An estimate is also made of the operating expenses and the percentage of profit that is anticipated. For example, if a merchant estimates that his net
sales in a year will be $75,000 and that his operating ex-
penses will be $12,000, how much should he add to the cost
of the merchandise in order to have a net profit of 4 per
cent on sales? The following is the computation necessary
to find the markup of the merchandise that will be purchased for resale:

Operating expenses	$12,000.00
Add net profit (4% of sales)	3,000.00
Margin	$15,000.00

The merchant must determine next what percentage of
sales is represented by the margin. By dividing $15,000 by
$75,000, he finds this percentage to be 20. In other words,
in order to cover the operating expenses and to earn a net
profit of $3,000, or 4 per cent of sales, he must operate on
a 20 per cent margin. The cost of the merchandise must
therefore be no more than 80 per cent of the selling price.
That is, if an article costs $1.20 and if that cost can be no
more than 80 per cent of the selling price, the selling price
is found by dividing $1.20 by 80 per cent. The selling price
is therefore $1.50. As proof of this figure, 80 per cent of
$1.50 is $1.20, the cost price. The margin on the particular
article is 30 cents.

The markup is the percentage by which the cost of an article is multiplied to get the amount that, added to the cost of the merchandise, gives the selling price. The percentage of markup is determined by dividing the margin by the cost. In the case of the article mentioned above, 30 cents (the margin) divided by $1.20 (the cost) equals 25 per cent, the rate of markup. In other words, as the rate of markup is 25 per cent, it is merely necessary to add 25 per cent to the cost of the merchandise in order to arrive at a retail price that will result in a margin of 20 per cent of sales.

Figures have been compiled by departments of the government and by trade associations to show the average markup for various classes of merchandise and various sizes of stores. The same markup is not applied to every article. Competition has much to do in setting selling prices on merchandise. For example, a merchant may decide on 30 per cent as his markup, but competition may cause him to mark up certain merchandise only 20 per cent. If his markup for the entire store is to average 30 per cent, some merchandise must have a markup of more than 30 per cent. In a business in which detailed departmental records are kept, it is possible to determine the markup and the profit for each department. The markup in various departments is often not the same.

Frequently it is necessary to mark down the price of merchandise because it gets too old or becomes soiled. An efficient store, however, has very few markdowns. Any markdowns, or reductions from the original selling prices, result in losses that reduce the intended percentage of markup. Whenever merchandise is marked down, a record should be kept of the reduction so that this amount can be deducted from the retail inventory shown by the perpetual-inventory records.

Perpetual-Inventory Record for a Retail Store. Illustration No. 102 is an example of a perpetual-inventory record for a retail store. This form illustrates the use of markups and markdowns.

PERPETUAL-INVENTORY RECORD					
Date of Invoice	Cost of Mdse.	Markup (25% of Cost)	Selling Price (Cost + Markup)	Mark-downs	Net Yield
4/7/39	$101.75	$25.44	$127.19	$10.05	$117.14
4/25/39	260.50	65.13	325.63		325.63
5/4/39	180.15	45.04	225.19		225.19
5/28/39	375.00	93.75	468.75	30.15	438.60
6/1/39	262.40	65.60	328.00	18.75	309.25

Illustration No. 102—Perpetual-Inventory Record

If the store is accustomed to taking discounts, the cost of the merchandise entered in the perpetual-inventory record should be the amount of the invoice minus the discount. In determining the inventory at any time, it is necessary merely to make the following computation:

To the merchandise inventory, as determined by the actual count at the beginning of the year, add the selling price of the merchandise received and deduct the amount of markdowns. Then deduct the amount of merchandise sold. In the markdowns should be included the amount of any merchandise stolen or destroyed. Many stores keep a separate account called "Shrinkage," in which are recorded any losses of merchandise.

In a larger store in which departmental records are necessary, a separate analysis similar to the one described above is kept for each department.

Taking an Inventory. Even when perpetual-inventory records are kept, it is desirable occasionally, usually once a year, to make an actual count of all goods available to see whether the actual inventory agrees with the records. When a perpetual-inventory system is not used, it is more important to take an inventory at least once a year and sometimes more often. An inventory is taken by counting or estimating the quantity of each item. The price marked on the goods may be used or the current market price may be used in computing the value of the inventory.

QUESTIONS FOR DISCUSSION

1. What is a purchasing agent?
2. Give a general classification of the information needed by a purchasing department.
3. Referring to Illustration No. 91 on page 221, explain to whom each party is directly responsible.
4. What are some sources of information as to prices?
5. Suggest a method of keeping information on prices.
6. State two methods of determining the quality of materials purchased.
7. What is meant by low and high stock limits?
8. What is a stock card?
9. Distinguish between a purchase requisition and a purchase order.
10. Why should the receiving clerk examine incoming goods before signing the receipt for the transportation company?
11. When purchased goods have been received, should the purchasing department be responsible for inspecting them to see whether they are of the right quality? Explain.
12. What is a charge-back invoice?
13. Suggest information that it is usually desirable to indicate on price tags.
14. What are the two general methods of taking an inventory?
15. Explain the general procedure in determining the retail value of an inventory at any time without taking a physical inventory.

PROBLEMS AND PROJECTS

1. A retail grocer sells an average of 65 cans of peaches weekly, and pays an average of 15 cents a can. He buys in case lots (24 cans to the case) each week. What will be the minimum amount of capital invested in his inventory if he stocks 10 different brands of peaches? if he stocks 3 different brands? (Assume that he sells the same quantity regardless of the number of brands.)
2. Visit a small clothing store and observe how many different kinds of wearing apparel are stocked. Also observe if there are neighboring stores that stock similar items.
3. A retail grocer is offered a crate of 150 oranges for $2.25. If two crates are purchased, however, the price will be $2.20 a crate. Suppose that he buys two crates. Twenty-four

oranges spoil, and the remainder are sold at 23 cents a dozen. If he had bought one crate at a time, he would have had only 6 oranges in a crate to spoil, because the oranges would have been sold more quickly. Which would be the better buying plan to follow? How much better?

4. A dealer is offered an article by the X Company at a list price of $200, less discounts of 25 per cent and 20 per cent. The M Company offers him the same type of article for $200, less a discount of 45 per cent. Is one offer better than the other? Explain.

5. What is the percentage of approximate annual savings effected by taking advantage of each of the following discounts: 1/10, n/60; 2/10, n/90; 3/10, n/90?

6. An invoice of March 5 for $625, with terms of net 60 days, is to be paid on March 17. If an anticipation discount of 6 per cent a year is taken, what amount is necessary to pay the invoice?

7. On March 1 you make a purchase of $400 on terms of 2/10, n/30. Suppose you do not have the money to take advantage of the discount, so you borrow at 6 per cent for 20 days the amount needed to pay the invoice on March 11. What is the net saving you make by borrowing to take advantage of the discount?

8. Draw a diagram showing the parties involved, the business forms used, and the movement of goods in connection with a purchase made by a purchasing agent as a result of a request from the stock clerk.

9. Bring to class several price tags on articles purchased by you or by members of your family. Explain on what articles they were used and how they were attached. Attempt to explain the information on the tags.

10. From the following information find the value of the merchandise stock to be reported on the financial statements: beginning inventory (retail value), $10,000; purchases made during period (retail value), $28,000; sales made during the period, $30,000; markdowns, $500; average margin of profit, 25 per cent.

CHAPTER XI

MARKETING AND MERCHANDISING PROBLEMS

Purpose of the Chapter. In most businesses the problems of selling, merchandising, and marketing are very important because sales are the lifeblood of business. In a single chapter it is impossible to cover all these problems; but among other points that are discussed in this chapter, the following questions will be answered:

1. What factors affect the selling prices of goods and services?
2. What items are included in the cost of doing business?
3. How does one compute the markup and the markdown in establishing the price of goods?
4. How can a businessman find and obtain new customers?
5. What types of training should be given to salespersons?
6. What are some of the problems of selling?
7. What is the effect of merchandise turnover?
8. What special services should be offered to customers?

Section I

Determining the Selling Price

Price Policies. As a business is operated for profit, it is obvious that the owner will obtain for each item that he sells a price that is as high as is practicable. A businessman may establish high prices and sell very few articles; but as a result of that policy he may make very little profit or may actually lose money. On the other hand, some businessmen establish very low prices in the hope of selling merchandise in quantities large enough to result in a desirable profit, even though the percentage of profit is low. Let us consider, for instance, the following two examples:

Example A: An article that costs a businessman $50 is offered for sale at $100. The businessman sells three of these in a month, making a gross profit of $150.

Example B: Another businessman, having the same or a similar item costing $50, decides to attempt to sell a greater quantity at a lower price. He therefore offers his item for sale at $60. During a month he sells ten of these at a gross profit of $100.

If we assume that all other factors are equal, the businessman in Example A makes a greater gross profit than the one in Example B, although each may fail to make a net profit. In many cases more expense will be involved in selling ten items than in selling three. The cost of doing business will therefore be greater when the larger volume of business is handled. It is probable, however, that in each of the preceding cases the price is wrong. In one case it is so high that a sufficient quantity will not be sold to ensure a fair net profit; in the other it is so low that a sufficient gross profit will not be made. Between these two extremes there is probably a reasonable price; but there are many factors influencing the establishment of that price. Some of these factors are discussed in the following paragraphs.

Competition Affects Prices. The amount of competition among businesses handling similar goods or giving similar services is an important factor in establishing prices. If one business asks a higher price than a competitor, some of its customers are likely to do business with the competitor. Even businesses in neighboring localities are influenced by competition. If prices are too high in one locality, many people will travel to adjacent localities for the purchases of goods or services. For example, if a filling station in one neighborhood is selling a certain brand of gasoline for 18 cents a gallon and a station in another locality one mile away is selling the same brand for 16 cents, the customer is likely to buy where he can get it for 16 cents. Often a business must offer some of its merchandise at a price below that which will yield a fair profit because some competitor has established a similar low price.

In businesses in which competition is keen, prices have a tendency to cover only the actual costs of the average business. Net profits are made therefore only by the most efficient businesses. Even if there is little or no competition, a business that fixes its prices too high finds that people do without its products or services, or find substitutes, rather than pay the prices that seem to give that business an unduly large profit. For example, a laundry that asks too high a price for its services will find that many of its customers will go to another laundry or will do their own laundry at home.

Fixed Prices during Long Periods of Time. Many businesses, especially in the retail trade, have a tendency to fix a price for a certain item and to keep the item at that price for a considerable period. For example, a store has been selling women's hosiery at $1.19 a pair for several years, even though the cost of the hosiery to the store has varied from time to time. As the customers have become accustomed to paying $1.19, they naturally expect to continue to buy their hosiery at that price. Should the store raise the price to $1.29, the customers are liable to resent the increase, thinking that the store is attempting to make an unfair profit. On the other hand, should the price be lowered to $1.09, they are liable to become suspicious of the quality. The same situation applies to the dentist, the barber, the shoe repairman, and other businessmen who have had fixed prices for their services over a considerable period of time. Even though operating costs vary, customers may resent price changes.

Consumer Demand. The owner of a business that carries fashion goods knows that at certain times the goods will be in great demand and at other times the demand will be greatly diminished. As an illustration, a milliner will find that spring hats sell readily early in the season but that later in the season it is almost impossible to sell them unless the prices are much lower. As the exact number of hats that will be sold cannot be estimated accurately, the milliner will, at the beginning of the season, fix a selling price that should ensure a net profit on the entire lot of spring hats, even though prices may have to be reduced drastically late in the season in order that no hats need to be carried over to the next spring season.

Sometimes a businessman may buy a group of similar items at the same price; but, because there are variations in the designs, the colors, and the styles, he may charge different prices for the various items. As certain colors or designs will be more attractive than others, customers will be willing to pay higher prices for them.

A manufacturer of a novelty article that suddenly becomes popular finds it necessary to sell at a high price while the demand is great. When new competitors come into the field and the demand begins to subside, the original manufacturer either sells the product at a much lower price or ceases production. For instance, a game that has become suddenly popular is sold at a high price by the manufacturer. Before long, many other manufacturers come into the field. Then the demand soon begins to subside. The original high price cannot be maintained. In such cases the manufacturer should be careful not to overproduce, and the retail store not to overbuy.

The introduction of new products on the market (for example, an electric shaver) presents an interesting study in price policies. During the process of introducing a product of this type, large amounts of money are needed for advertising and promotion. In the early stages there are few, if any, competitors. The price that is established may therefore be the highest price at which the manufacturer feels he can sell a reasonable quantity. Sometimes when production facilities are limited, a high price is established because, even at that price, buyers will consume all that is produced. As the manufacturer increases his production facilities and develops more economical methods, he can reduce the price and, in many cases, make a greater gross profit. As new competitors come into the field, there is usually a tendency to readjust prices on a lower basis. The additional sales promotion of several competitors will help to create a greater total demand. With this greater demand there often will result a larger volume of sales. But, in spite of the greater volume, a severe reduction in price may curtail profits.

Perishability of the Product. In determining his selling price, the owner of a small store who purchases a crate of strawberries must consider, in addition to his usual operating expenses, the probable loss due to spoilage. For example, he pays $4.80 a crate (20 cents a quart) and establishes a selling price of 30 cents a quart. If he sells all the strawberries, his net profit is:

$7.20 = sales (24 quarts at 30 cents)
4.80 = cost

$2.40 = margin, or gross profit
1.08 = operating expenses (15% of sales)

$1.32 = net profit

But if 6 quarts should spoil, the result would be:

$5.40 = sales (18 quarts at 30 cents)
4.80 = cost

$ .60 = margin, or gross profit
.81 = operating expenses (15% of sales)

$ .21 = net loss

The merchant should have figured the approximate loss due to spoilage, and made the selling price slightly higher (probably 34 or 35 cents a quart) so as to have made a satisfactory net profit in spite of the spoilage of part of the strawberries.

Likewise, the baker must consider the loss that will result from unsold baked goods that soon become stale. The owner of a cider press who sells sweet cider, the vendor with his popcorn and peanut-roasting cart, and all other businessmen handling perishable products should be careful in determining their selling prices.

Fragile articles that are easily broken by handling, such as glassware, chinaware, toys, and eggs, should be considered in much the same manner as the perishable products just mentioned. The manufacturer of or dealer in ice and liquids that evaporate easily has a similar problem.

Sometimes the problem to be considered in establishing a price is, not to obtain the greatest net profit, but to avoid as much loss as possible. In other words, the problem is to establish a selling price that will permit a minimum loss. A merchant, a distributor, or a manufacturer may discover that he has on hand perishable merchandise that, if not sold soon, will become a total loss. Sometimes if style merchandise is not sold quickly, it will become so out of style that it can be sold only at a great loss. After a price has been established it may become necessary to reduce it in order to sell the goods. Good judgment and past experience are therefore important in establishing prices.

Effect of Turnover. Articles that sell slowly usually are marked at higher prices than articles that cost the same but sell more rapidly. For example, one article that cost $4 remains in stock for approximately six months and then is sold at a price of $6. Another article that cost $4 and remains in stock for approximately two months is sold for $5.50. Because of the greater rate of turnover, the latter article may yield a larger net profit to the business at the end of a year. Stores often attempt to increase the rate of merchandise turnover by establishing lower prices.

As was disclosed previously, it is often dangerous for a businessman to attempt to sell too great a volume because the gross profit may not be sufficient to yield a net profit.

It is difficult to predict in advance what one's rate of turnover will be, but average figures have been computed for many types of businesses. Some of these figures are given in Chapter II. Turnover is computed by dividing the average inventory (the merchandise on hand at the cost price) into the cost of goods sold, or by dividing the average inventory (at the selling price) into the net sales. If, for example, a businessman discovers that he has a turnover of two times a year, it will be good management for him to increase this figure if he can do so without lowering his prices or increasing his costs.

The theory of obtaining from goods with a low turnover a higher profit than from goods with a high turnover is based upon two facts: (a) If money is invested for a long period of time in merchandise with a low turnover, a high rate of profit should be obtained; (b) if merchandise moves slowly, it is necessary to obtain a high percentage of profit in order to make a net profit for the business. For instance, the merchandise in a jewelry store is not sold and replenished at the rate of more than once a year. This rate may even run as low as once in two years. Under such circumstances the jeweler therefore finds it necessary to obtain a very high gross profit of 50 per cent or more.

Retail Prices Fixed by Contract. Under the Sherman Antitrust Act it is fundamentally unlawful to fix prices by agreement. The fixing of prices is considered restraint of trade. Nevertheless the new Miller-Tydings Amendment to the Sherman Antitrust Act permits manufacturers of branded, nationally advertised goods to fix the resale prices. The details of this legislation are discussed in Chapter XXII. The important point to consider in this chapter is that the resale prices of some branded items are definitely fixed by the manufacturers, while those of other branded items are controlled through agency agreements. For instance, if a businessman accepts an exclusive agency for a certain product, he must sell that product at the price prescribed by the manufacturer.

As will be seen in a later discussion, the agreements fixing the prices of certain nationally advertised brands also prevent price-cutting. Some retailers prefer to sell brands on which the prices are not fixed.

Prices Affected by Store Services. A business that has a policy of extending credit to its customers and of delivering goods may have larger operating expenses than one that sells on a cash-and-carry basis. Larger operating expenses mean that a higher selling price must be received to ensure the same net profit as that earned by a store doing a cash-and-carry business. The attitude of a merchant toward goods returned by customers also has its influence. If a store is liberal in making adjustments, it usually has high original selling prices. Other services, such as free parking space, free checkrooms, and rest rooms, also have an effect on the prices at which goods are marked for sale.

In establishing a price, a manufacturer or a wholesale distributor should consider all the services that must be performed. The price should not be far out of line with the prices of competing items, but it should be sufficiently high to provide a gross profit that will cover all distributive costs. For instance, a certain amount must be allowed for advertising. Sometimes an amount must be allowed for the installation of the product sold. In the case of some kinds of equipment it is necessary to provide for service either free of charge or upon a fee basis. If such service is to be provided free, the cost must be considered in establishing the selling price.

Terms Used in Connection with Determining Selling Prices. The diagram shown in Illustration No. 103 explains the component parts of the selling price of an article.

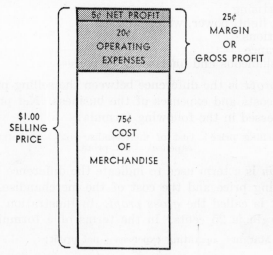

Illustration No. 103—Component Parts of the Selling Price

The basic factor in determining the selling price of goods is the *cost of the merchandise*. To determine the total cost of merchandise, it is customary to add the transportation charges to the purchase price of the merchandise. For example, if the cost price of an article is 70 cents and the transportation charge is 5 cents, the total cost of that article is 75 cents.

Operating expenses are the costs incurred in operating a business. The following items are those that make up the operating expenses in most businesses:

Rent
Taxes
Interest paid on money borrowed
Repairs and painting
Salaries
Stationery, bags, paper, twine, and other wrapping materials
Telephone and telegraph service
Allowance for shrinkage due to theft, spoilage, or breakage
Depreciation of furniture, fixtures, and delivery equipment
Bad accounts and collection expenses
Delivery costs
Advertising
Heat, light, power, water, and ice
Donations
Insurance
Miscellaneous and unclassified expenses

Net profit is the difference between the selling price and all the costs and expenses of the business. Net profit can be expressed in the following formula:

Selling price — cost of merchandise sold — operating expenses = net profit.

Margin is a term used to indicate the difference between the selling price and the cost of the merchandise. Sometimes it is called the *gross profit*. In Illustration No. 103 the margin is 25 cents. In the terms of a formula it is:

Margin = operating expenses + net profit;
or
Margin = selling price — cost of merchandise sold.

In trade papers and magazines the margin is often referred to as a percentage of the selling price. In the preceding case it would be 25 per cent ($.25 ÷ $1.00).

Markup is similar to margin. When both are spoken of in dollars and cents, they are identical; but when used in terms of a percentage, they are quite different. The markup is usually referred to as a percentage of the *cost* of the merchandise, in order that it will be easy to determine the price at which the goods should be marked for sale. The markup in Illustration No. 103 would be 33⅓ per cent (25 cents ÷ 75 cents). On the other hand, when margin is spoken of in terms of a percentage, it is based on the *selling price*. In the same illustration the margin would be 25 per cent ($.25 ÷ $1.00).

The Selling Price as the Base. In order to compare figures that are related to sales, it is necessary to have a common base for the computations. If the salaries were figured as a percentage of the cost of the merchandise sold and the net profit as a percentage of the sales, it is quite obvious that a fair comparison could not be made. As the selling price includes everything (the cost of the merchandise, the operating expenses, and the net profit), it is the whole amount and should be used as the base, or 100 per cent. Then the cost of the merchandise, the various operating expenses, the sales returns, the net profit, the margin, and practically all financial items can be stated as percentages of the sales of the business.

The modern businessman thinks in terms of sales. He figures what percentage of his sales are such items as salaries, advertising expense, delivery expense, loss on bad debts, taxes, net profit, cost of goods sold, margin, sales returns, sales discount, interest, and many others. He plans his budget and adjusts expenditures upon the basis of these percentages.

Another important reason why a businessman should use his selling price as the base, or 100 per cent, is that all discussions and statistical reports in trade magazines and government bulletins use the selling price as a base. Let us

assume that a writer in a magazine discusses the following
margins of profit: (a) 25 per cent on cheese, (b) 30 per
cent on tea, (c) 12½ per cent on cereals, and (d) 20 per
cent on canned tomatoes. These percentages are based on
selling prices. Let us take the example of tomatoes, on
which a margin of 20 per cent is proposed. Here is the
way the profit is computed:

                100% is the selling price
                 20% is the margin (20% of 100%)

Therefore   80% of the selling price = the cost of the goods
Let us assume that $400 = the cost of the goods
Then   80% of the selling price = $400
                  1% of the selling price = $5 ($400 ÷ 80)
                100% of the selling price = $500

The margin (20 per cent) is composed of two elements,
the net profit and the operating expenses. As 2 per cent is
a good average net profit, the operating expenses will be
18 per cent. The final result will therefore be:

                $500 = sales
        18% of $500 = $90, operating expenses
         2% of $500 = $10, NET PROFIT
        80% of $500 = $400, cost of goods

But let us assume that the margin of 20 per cent is figured on the cost of the goods. The following will then be
the result:

                        $400 = the cost of the goods
        20% of $400 =   80 = the margin
                        ─────
                        $480 = the selling price
The operating expenses will be   90, or the same amount as in
                                       the preceding situation
                        $ 10 = NET LOSS ($90 — $80)

It is evident from these calculations that, when one
attempts to utilize published figures on costs and profits,
one should know how these percentages are computed. For
instance, if a man starts a new business with the assumption that he should have a 20 per cent margin of gross
profit, and if he figures that margin on the cost price, he
probably will lose money.

The cost of selling different kinds of merchandise varies.
Competition and other factors, which were mentioned in the
first part of this chapter, affect the prices of many kinds
of merchandise. These factors make it impossible to have

the same margin on all items. It is necessary therefore that the businessman keep records of sales and operating expenses by departments or by kinds of merchandise. Only when such information is available is it possible to mark each kind of goods so that each will be sold profitably.

The Markup Table. We have already seen how to compute the selling price when the cost price and the margin are known. Because it would be a laborious task to compute the selling price for many different items at various rates of margin, most businesses have margin, or markup, tables prepared to simplify the process. Illustration No. 104 shows a markup table for a number of margins. Some businesses have more elaborate tables.

Suppose an article costs $1.50 and the desired margin is 33⅓ per cent (of the selling price). The table shows us that we should multiply the $1.50 by 50 per cent. This computation gives us 75 cents, which is the margin. We then add this amount to the $1.50 (the cost) and get a selling price of $2.25. Let us now check our work. If the selling price is $2.25, the desired margin of 33⅓ per cent of the selling price is 75 cents. The selling price of $2.25 minus the margin of 75 cents gives a cost of $1.50.

MARKUP TABLE

Find the desired margin in the left-hand column. Multiply the cost of the article by the corresponding percentage in the right-hand column. Add this amount to the cost in order to determine the correct selling price.

DESIRED MARGIN (PERCENTAGE OF SELLING PRICE)	EQUIVALENT (PERCENTAGE OF COST)
10%	11.1%
12½	14.3
15	17.7
20	25.0
25	33⅓
30	42.9
33⅓	50.0
35	53.9
40	66⅔
50	100.0

Illustration No. 104—Markup Table

Markdowns. A *markdown* is any reduction from the original selling price. In many cases a merchant is compelled to mark and sell part of his goods at a lower price than that at which he had been selling them previously. Some of the principal reasons for markdowns are:

Shopworn, soiled, or damaged goods
Style changes
Broken assortments and remnants
Competitors' lower prices
Unseasonable weather
Overproduction or overpurchases
Sudden change in costs

Naturally the amount of markdown varies greatly with different items. Some of the variations are indicated in the following table:

MARKDOWN AVERAGES	
Women's dresses	15.6%
Women's suits and coats	12.6
Blouses and skirts	9.3
Women's shoes	8.3
Silks and velvets	7.2
Men's clothing	7.1
Leather goods	6.4
Jewelry	5.4
Drugs and toilet goods	4.0

Although some markdowns can be reduced by a more careful control of buying, there are some that cannot. By an accurate record of his own past experiences with markdowns, as well as the experiences of others, the businessman should be able to estimate the probable allowance he should make for markdowns in determining his original selling price.

Sometimes a businessman believes that, by reducing the selling price, he will increase the volume of sales and thus earn more profit. His belief may or may not prove true. Let us see how, in the case of a markdown, the unit sales must be increased in order that the gross profit, or margin, will be the same in dollars and cents as the gross profit from the original selling price.

Suppose $10 is the selling price
           6 is the cost

          $ 4 is the margin (10 — 6) or 40% of the sales

Assume   12 articles are sold daily

          $48 is the daily gross profit (4×12)

If the goods are marked down 10 per cent—

       $ 9 is the new selling price
        6 is the cost

       $ 3 is the margin, or gross profit, on one article (9 — 6)

       $48 is the daily gross profit desired

       16 articles must be sold daily in order to yield the same
           amount of gross profit in dollars $(48 \div 3)$

Thus, if goods carrying a 40 per cent margin are reduced 10 per cent, it is necessary to increase the volume of unit sales $33\frac{1}{3}$ per cent $(16 - 12 = 4 \div 12 = 33\frac{1}{3}$ per cent) in order to obtain the same amount of gross profit. The smaller the percentage of original margin, the greater must be the increase in sales to bring about the same gross profit. In the preceding example a 10 per cent reduction on goods carrying a 40 per cent margin necessitated an increase of $33\frac{1}{3}$ per cent. A 10 per cent reduction on goods carrying a 30 per cent margin would necessitate a unit sales increase of 50 per cent, while the same reduction on goods carrying a 20 per cent margin would necessitate an increase of 100 per cent. Another factor to be considered is the probable increase in operating expenses that will result from the increase in volume.

It is obvious from the previous discussion that a reduction in the unit price requires a considerable increase in the volume of sale of individual units in order to maintain the same amount of net profit. So-called cut-rate businesses are therefore not always profitable. To be successful a cut-rate business must be in a location where, through the proper sales promotion methods, a sufficient amount of additional business can be obtained to compensate for the lower unit profit. Supermarkets operate on this plan.

QUESTIONS FOR DISCUSSION

1. How does competition affect prices?

2. A business has very little competition. It therefore fixes the prices of its goods so that it will make a large profit. What will be the probable effect of this policy?

3. Why do some businesses have a tendency to keep the same price on a certain item over a long period of time?

4. Why do prices on novelty goods usually become much lower after a time?

5. The perishability of a product should be considered in determining the selling price. Explain this statement.

6. Can larger net profits be made if the selling price is reduced but there is a greater rate of merchandise turnover?

7. What provision in connection with the selling prices of certain goods is found in the Miller-Tydings Act (Amendment to the Sherman Antitrust Act)?

8. How do store services affect prices?

9. What is meant by the term *margin? markup?*

10. Of what two items does margin consist?

11. Why is the selling price ordinarily used as the base in comparing items relating to sales?

12. What is a markup table?

13. State some of the principal reasons for markdowns.

14. Why is it often necessary in the initial stages of introducing a new product to charge a considerably higher price than is later charged? Why is it possible?

15. Why is the markup higher on fragile articles than on other articles?

16. Why does turnover affect profits?

17. How is turnover computed?

18. Why is it sometimes possible for a cash-and-carry type of business to charge lower prices than another type of business?

Section II

Problems and Policies of Merchandising and Marketing

Finding Prospects. Whether the business be engaged in manufacturing, in wholesaling, in retailing, or in supplying service, one of the biggest problems that confronts the management is the obtaining of customers. Not only must this problem be met at the beginning of a new business enterprise, but it is present all the time. New customers must be obtained to take the place of old customers ceasing to deal with the business because of change in residence, death, change in financial status, or the like.

Prospects for the Wholesaler and the Manufacturer. Advertising in its various forms, as discussed in Chapter XV, is one of the main methods that wholesalers and manufacturers use in obtaining prospects. Manufacturers use various forms of advertising especially to develop demand on the part of consumers. This demand then makes it easier for the manufacturer and the wholesaler to sell to the retailer.

National advertising in certain types of magazines helps to disclose retail prospects. Probably general advertising is most effective in determining consumer prospects when coupons or answers to radio advertising are to be sent to the manufacturer or the wholesale distributor. These may be turned over to representatives, who in turn get in touch with local dealers. The next step is to try to get these dealers to buy merchandise to take care of the local demand.

House-to-house canvassing and sampling are sometimes used to obtain retail prospects. Coupons are given to housewives. These coupons are then taken to a store. The dealers who get them are encouraged to buy the merchandise from the wholesaler or the manufacturer. It can therefore be seen that the problem of finding prospects is intimately tied up with advertising.

Some manufacturers and wholesalers subscribe to clipping services. The latter are agencies that clip news items from newspapers. For instance, a manufacturer or an insurance company might be interested in storm damage and would therefore subscribe for newspaper clippings about cases of such damage. Magazines and newspapers sometimes disclose plans for the construction of new buildings. Some publications specialize in providing such information for clients.

Doctors, lawyers, accountants, or persons of various other classifications can purchase mailing lists giving the names of prospective clients. Some manufacturers sell directly to consumers by mail and therefore want the names of individuals who may be good prospects. Other manufacturers, as well as wholesalers, want lists of dealers of various types. It is possible to obtain such lists through several agencies, including Dun and Bradstreet, Incorporated.

Using Telephone and City Directories. Telephone and city directories contain classified sections from which many businesses may select prospects. A stationery merchant could find in the telephone book a list of local accountants who might be prospects for accounting supplies; a laundry or a linen supply company could obtain a list of all the restaurants and the barber shops in the city; a flour-milling company would be interested in the names of bakers; a list of the beauty shops would furnish prospects for businesses handling beauty-shop equipment and supplies; and carting or automobile trucking companies should make good prospects for truck salesmen and insurance salesmen.

From city directories that have the residents listed by streets, such neighborhood businesses as public garages, delicatessens, beauty shops, gasoline filling stations, and dry-cleaning shops, can obtain a list of prospects who live in the immediate neighborhood. Some city directories indicate whether the person living at a certain address is the owner of the property. The property owners listed might, for instance, be prospects for fire insurance and building repairs.

Lists such as those mentioned can frequently be purchased from businesses that compile commercial mailing
lists and keep them revised.

The Newspaper as a Source of Prospects. The daily
newspaper will aid many businesses in finding prospective
customers. The list of building permits granted and contracts let for buildings, roads, and streets should be valuable information to businesses furnishing contractors with
raw materials and supplies. News items telling of the promotions of people to higher salaried positions may provide
prospects for real-estate companies or life-insurance salesmen. Likewise, the announcements of marriages, births,
and political appointments should provide prospects for
many businesses.

Other Sources of Prospects. The proprietor of a restaurant located in that section of the city occupied mainly by
office buildings could make a list of the people who have
offices near by and use that list for his sales promotion
letters. The landscape gardener, the tree surgeon, the
painting contractor, and other persons who render similar
personal services can find a large number of prospects by
closely observing the condition of shrubbery, trees, and
buildings. Similarly, tire salesmen find prospects by observing the condition of the tires on parked automobiles.
A person who operates an automobile paint shop could
find prospects by observing the paint on automobiles. The
names of new prospects can often be obtained from old
customers and from friends. Usually such prospects become customers.

Obtaining Prospects for a Retail Store. One of the most
important means of getting prospective customers for retail
stores is newspaper advertisements. To attract first customers, a businessman opening a new store may insert an
announcement in a newspaper. From time to time the advertisements of a business are designed to attract additional customers. The display windows are one of the best
means of drawing prospective customers into the store.

The windows should be so attractive that passers-by will observe the goods and be stimulated to buy. Business-promotion letters are often used to convert prospects into customers. For example, a department store may make a practice of sending a letter to all new teachers who have just moved into the city, inviting them to open a charge account.

Do Special Sales Pay? Some businesses conduct many special sales, but others seldom have them. The management must therefore decide the advantages and the disadvantages of special sales and determine which types of sales are most effective for that particular type of retail business. There are many kinds of special sales. In each case the purpose is to discover new prospects who can be brought into the store to buy merchandise. Some of the more common types of special sales are:

Anniversary sales
Pre-inventory sales
Post-inventory sales
Clearance sales
Factory sales
Cash-raising sales
Going-out-of-business sales
Half-price sales
One-cent sales

Frequently the offerings at these sales are not as they have been represented. Customers consequently become rather skeptical of sales in general and doubt the genuineness of a real sale when one is carried on.

Many merchants feel that continuous markdown sales have a strong tendency to turn regular customers into bargain hunters. Such sales build up a sales resistance to the merchandise when it is offered at regular prices. More money is generally made on business done at regular prices than on a greater volume produced by a policy of continual sales. A business may find that winning customers from competing stores by continual sales at low prices may actually make profits less instead of greater because the customers may buy the low-priced goods instead of the items that produce a reasonable profit. A large volume of sales alone does not mean profits.

Reasons for Holding Sales. For every sale that a business conducts, there should be a good reason. It is better to have a few special sales and to see that the customers are given extraordinary values than it is to have a large number of sales. The customers of today are better informed than those of a generation ago and so are naturally curious as to the reason for a special sale. If they are given the real reason for the sale, they are more likely to believe in the worthwhileness of the sale.

There are two general types of sales. Most stores accumulate certain pieces of merchandise that did not sell at the regular prices. In order to make room for new stock and to dispose of the old items before they become unsalable, stores often have *clearance sales*. These are usually held at the close of a season. For example, a women's clothing store may have a clearance sale of summer clothing in August. If a business is careful in its buying, however, there should be little need for clearance sales. In order to avoid general clearance sales, many stores use bargain tables as a means of disposing of excess goods. In some stores the bargain basement serves the same purpose. The bargain basement, however, usually handles lower-priced merchandise than that carried in the other parts of the store, and does not serve as a place for the disposal of slow-moving stock.

The other type of sale is known as the *stimulative sale*. Its primary object is to stimulate business. The following are some of the purposes of stimulative sales:

Introducing a new kind of goods
Offering the customer especially good bargains in new goods purchased at bargain prices
Calling attention to a special department or a special kind of goods that customers have seemingly neglected

Manufacturers sometimes have various forms of sales, or "deals." As part of such a sale the manufacturer furnishes display materials and sometimes co-operates in advertising to help sell the merchandise. In most cases free goods, such as dishes, spoons, and cake pans, that are given with merchandise in retail stores have been obtained by the retailers as special inducements from the manufacturers. For example, the manufacturer may offer ten cases of his product at a special discount and give a certain number of dishes free. The retailer then conducts a special sale and gives away the dishes as an inducement for his customers to buy the merchandise.

Planning Special Sales. If special sales are to be successful, both in immediate financial returns and in building customer goodwill, they must be planned carefully. In large retail stores there is usually a sales promotion manager, who is a specialist in this type of activity. In small businesses the owner is his own sales promotion manager.

Before any sale is started, many factors must be considered. For instance, a special sale may fail if it is promoted at the time that a neighboring competitor is having a similar sale. A merchant must be familiar with the prices of competing merchandise so that when he sponsors a sale his prices will be reasonable in comparison with competitive prices. Business conditons may be so bad that a sale may prove to be a failure. On the other hand, a special sale may be just the thing that is needed to stimulate business.

The advertising should be prepared well in advance of the actual time of the sale. It should be truthful, telling the facts about the merchandise. If the merchandise is slightly soiled from handling or is of second quality, or if the sizes are broken, the advertisement should indicate the fact. Such words as *stupendous, mammoth,* and *colossal* should be avoided. These words long ago lost their power to attract the majority of people. In cities the advertising should appear in the newspapers on the day before the sale. If it should appear too long before the sale, its effect would be lost before the time of the sale. Furthermore, if the sale is announced too far in advance, it may prevent customers from coming into the store for normal purchases because they will wait until the time of the sale.

Regular customers should be mailed notices of the sales event. Illustration No. 105 is an example of such a notice. Special window displays that are dignified rather than gaudy and cheap should be arranged for the goods on sale. The merchandise being featured should be indicated clearly by cards that tell the price and something about the quality and the value of the goods. It may be a good plan to place other attractive goods where customers are likely to see them as they walk through the store looking for the goods on special sale.

Merchandising Services. The problem of providing extra services was discussed previously in this chapter as a factor in determining the selling price. The providing of various services does not necessarily require an increase in selling prices. If a business that is operated economically offers many services, it may make a greater profit than one not offering any. For instance, a cash-and-carry store does not always have lower prices, but it quite often does. In many types of stores it is necessary to offer certain services in order to obtain business. For instance, credit may have to be extended in order to obtain certain kinds of customers. Because of competition many department stores have established restaurants, rest rooms, and beauty parlors. Manufacturers quite often have to furnish engineering service, laboratory testing facilities, and technical advice. From the point of view of retail stores, delivery service is the most important merchandising service. It therefore deserves special attention.

Problems of Providing Delivery Service. The nature of many businesses requires delivery service for customers. For instance, in cases in which the customer purchases heavy or bulky articles, delivery is imperative. In some types of businesses the competition is so keen that delivery service is furnished to build up goodwill in an effort to win and keep customers. Some businesses probably could increase their sales volume if they would furnish delivery service.

THE RIKE-KUMLER COMPANY

DAYTON, OHIO.

Win built your GREATER RIKE'S

February 18, 1939

Just a note to announce the high spot in
Rike's fashion season...a special showing of
Eisenberg dresses in Rike's Better Dress Depart-
ment on Wednesday, February 22.

Mr. Harold Eisenberg will be here in person
with original and exclusive designs in chiffon,
printed crepe and dark sheers for the spring
season. Sizes range from 10 to 20.

Our models will wear the clothes informally
throughout the day and Mr. Eisenberg will be
available to take special orders for colors not
included in the showing. I hope that you can
find time to stop in and see these lovely new
fashions.

Very sincerely,

Rike's Better Dress Department

*Illustration No. 105—Letter Sent to Customers
Announcing a Sale*

If delivery service is provided, many customers use the service when they do not need it, thereby adding to the operating expenses of the business. If the item purchased is small and light in weight, the salesperson may ask, "Will you take it?" rather than, "Shall I send it?" The answer of the customer to the latter question is almost always "Yes," whereas the former question often results in the customer's carrying home her purchase.

Rapidly increasing congestion in city streets makes driving and walking more hazardous and makes parking facilities less convenient. This situation, together with such changed buying habits of people as extensive buying by telephone, has a tendency to increase the demand for delivery service.

Types of Delivery Service. If a business has decided that it will furnish delivery service, its next problem is to decide on the type of service. The two most common types are (a) individually owned delivery equipment and (b) consolidated delivery service.

Individually owned equipment for delivery service is widely used in almost all kinds of businesses. Under this type of service the delivery equipment is owned by the business that has goods to be delivered. The business hires the necessary drivers and pays all the costs of repairs, storage, delivery supplies, and insurance. Some of the advantages claimed for this type are:

1. The delivery personnel, being employees of the business, make a better contact between the business and the customer than there would be if they were employees of a delivery company.
2. The delivery equipment can be used for advertising purposes.
3. The style and the quality of the equipment can be in keeping with the character of the business.
4. This type of service permits more flexibility in delivery routes and schedules.

If this plan of delivery service is used, the personnel should be chosen carefully. The deliveryman is legally a representative of his company, and the company is therefore responsible for his acts. He should have a good personality, as he comes into direct contact with the customer almost as much as does the salesperson. If he is capable, he can do much to facilitate adjustments and to smooth out the complaints of customers.

Consolidated delivery service is used when several stores make a contract with some other privately owned business to take care of deliveries for them. Some of the advantages of using such service are:

1. Large amounts of capital need not be tied up in equipment.
2. This method usually reduces delivery costs, as the contract commonly provides for a charge of so much a unit. Thus, when sales are slack, the delivery costs are low; but if the business owned its own equipment, the depreciation and other overhead expenses would occur just the same. Stores in Detroit found that their delivery expenses were reduced from 15 to 25 per cent after they had adopted a consolidated delivery system.
3. Small businesses can have their deliveries made as promptly as larger ones. It may also be possible for the small businessman to give delivery service to his customers, even though his business is too small to warrant purchasing delivery equipment.
4. Consolidated service eliminates the problems of personnel and management in relation to the employees needed to operate and service the equipment.
5. It shifts the responsibility for damage suits growing out of accidents caused by the delivery equipment.

Other types of delivery service used by businesses include parcel post, express, and freight. They are used profitably when customers live long distances away from the business.

Problem of Returned Goods. A survey of eleven department stores in Boston disclosed that in one year's time approximately $20,000,000 worth of merchandise purchased by customers was returned. This amount represented nearly

12½ per cent of the total sales. In a survey of the large stores in Pittsburgh, Chicago, and New York City, the same condition was found. In some stores the percentage of returns was a little smaller than that found in the Boston stores; in others it was a little larger.

Studies made of the kinds of goods returned showed that dresses were returned most frequently. The following is a list of certain goods and the percentage of returns for each item:

Dresses	25.4%
Women's and misses' wear	10.9
Shoes	10.5
Men's furnishings	6.7
Gloves	5.9
Hosiery	5.7
Furniture	3.3
Notions	3.0
Millinery	2.6
Groceries	2.4

These surveys indicate that the return of merchandise purchased by customers is an important problem to most stores and particularly to those handling clothing.

Manufacturers and distributors have similar problems pertaining to returned goods. For instance, a manufacturer may sell to a wholesaler or a retailer more goods than the retailer can sell. In order to maintain the goodwill of the retailer, the manufacturer may accept the return of some of the merchandise. Sometimes manufacturers will take back perishable merchandise to protect the reputation of the goods. Occasionally a new product is put on the market that sells well for a while and then ceases to sell. The manufacturers and the distributors sometimes have to take back from the retailers the unsold goods. These difficulties often arise from the fact that manufacturers and wholesalers sell to retailers larger quantities than they should.

Effect of Returned Merchandise on Profits and Selling Prices. The handling of sales returns is an expensive activity for a business. Some of the usual activities in connection with a sale and a return are: making the original sale, wrapping the merchandise, recording the sale, delivering the merchandise, handling the complaint (either by telephone or in person), having the article picked up by the delivery truck, recording and inspecting it upon arrival back at the store or the warehouse, making the proper accounting record of the return, and placing the merchandise back in stock for resale. In a typical department store, often as many as twenty different employees are involved in handling these various steps. It is not difficult to understand, therefore, that there is an average expense of approximately 50 cents for each return.

In addition, there is often depreciation (loss of value) due to handling of the merchandise or delaying the return of it. For example, if a woman purchases a new spring dress and keeps it for two weeks before returning it, the delay in making the return may prevent the store from selling the dress to someone else. If a store has a large amount of returns, it must carry a large inventory of goods. Some of the merchandise will always be in the hands of customers; and, although it will be returned eventually, it will not be available to show to other customers.

Let us see which goods, according to price, are returned most frequently. A survey revealed the following facts:

Price of Goods Returned	Percentage of Total Returns		
$ 0.01 to $ 0.50	3.4%	34.8% not over $2	63.2% not over $5
0.51 to 1.00	7.8		
1.01 to 2.00	23.6		
2.01 to 5.00	28.4		
5.01 to 10.00	17.4		
10.01 to 20.00	11.6		
20.01 to 50.00	3.5		
50.01 to 100.00	1.2		
100.01 and up	3.1		
	100.0%		

As 63.2 per cent of the returns represent items that sell for $5 or less, and the cost of handling a return is about 50 cents, it is apparent that in the majority of returns the expense is approximately 10 per cent. This loss greatly affects the prices at which goods must be marked originally in order that the business may make a net profit. If stores that have many sales returned fail to consider this expense, they are liable to operate at a loss.

Reasons for Merchandise Returns. It is good management for a store to attempt to reduce as much as possible the amount of merchandise returned by customers. Before we consider what can be done to bring about a reduction, we should study the reasons for merchandise returns. Naturally the reasons vary a great deal with different kinds of merchandise; but in a study of many kinds of goods the reasons for the returns, as given by the customers, were:

REASONS FOR RETURNS	PERCENTAGE OF ALL THE RETURNS
Wrong size	37.2%
Unsatisfactory merchandise	16.5
Goods that did not match	15.6
Change of mind	15.0
Faulty merchandise	13.0
Misrepresentation of the store	1.2
Disapproval of the person for whom the merchandise was purchased	1.2
Unsatisfactory delivery service	.3
	100.0%

The "wrong size" was the most important reason for returns. This reason is most prominent largely because of the faulty memory of customers who ask for wrong sizes, or because of guesswork when an item is being purchased for someone else. Sometimes the salespersons are to blame because they do not know the correct size to suggest. For example, the customer gives the shoe size of the one for whom hosiery is being purchased, but the salesperson suggests the wrong hosiery size. Salespersons should know that in some brands of clothing the sizes run small while in others they run large. In a few cases it was found that the wrong size was due to incorrect labels or errors in filling the orders.

"Not satisfactory" as a reason for a return is rather vague and indefinite. As it does not refer to faulty merchandise, it probably is an excuse given to cover up the real reason. Quite often the real reason is that the salesperson was too anxious to sell and therefore finally induced the customer to take something against his will.

The excuse that the goods did not match was used mainly in connection with the return of home furnishings and dress accessories, such as gloves or handbags. Greater care on the part of the salesperson in determining the color and the design of the things with which the item is to be matched should reduce somewhat the returns from this cause.

It is the policy of some merchants to encourage customers to take clothing or furniture home on approval. Sometimes salespersons follow this practice against the will of the management. In either case the policy is undesirable.

Probably the excuse of change of mind is due largely to overinsistence on the part of the salesperson. A customer, knowing that she can later return her purchase, finds it easier to agree to take the merchandise than to resist the high-pressure type of salesperson. This excuse probably covers the situation in which a customer decides after the purchase is made that she cannot financially afford it. Her desire for the goods was probably made so intense by the salesperson that she could not resist the purchase.

Educating the Public. In attempting to reduce the amount of returned sales, the retail merchants of a city might cooperate in a campaign to educate customers as to the cost and the effect of sales returns. In one city the plan included:

A series of advertisements in the local newspapers
Billboard posters
Pamphlet inserts in monthly statements and packages
Talks before women's organizations
Direct-mail literature

The percentages of returns made during the five years of the campaign in that city are shown here.

SALES RETURNS (PERCENTAGE OF GROSS SALES)						
Year	Store A	Store B	Store C	Store D	Store E	Store F
Year previous to the start of the campaign	9.0%	10.4%	13.9%	20.9%	9.8%	15.2%
First year	7.3	9.0	12.6	18.7	9.2	12.3
Second year	5.3	7.1	10.5	14.6	7.2	9.8
Third year	6.3	7.1	9.1	13.9	6.2	9.5
Fourth year	6.3	5.9	8.2	13.7	6.0	8.1
Fifth year	5.7	6.8	8.7	15.1	6.2	8.1

QUESTIONS FOR DISCUSSION

1. Why must a business be continually looking for new customers?

2. State some methods used by wholesalers and manufacturers to find prospects.

3. How may directories be used as a source of prospects?

4. Give some of the methods used by retail stores in obtaining customers.

5. Why are many people rather skeptical of special sales in general?

6. Why do some businesses disapprove of many special sales?

7. What is meant by a stimulative sale?

8. What is a sales promotion manager?

9. What are the two most common types of delivery service?

10. Give three advantages of each general type of delivery service.

11. Why does returned merchandise affect profits and selling prices?

12. What are some of the reasons given by customers for returning goods?

13. Give two general types of activity that the management of a store might follow in attempting to reduce the amount of returned sales.

14. What factors will determine whether newspaper advertising or direct-mail advertising will be the cheapest method of getting in touch with prospects?

15. Explain why consolidated delivery service is often more economical than individually operated delivery service.

16. The "wrong size" is given as the most important reason for returning merchandise. What fault in selling is disclosed?

Section III

Problems of Selling

Importance of Personal Salesmanship. In any sale there are four elements: the customer, the business, the merchandise or the service, and the salesperson. The salesperson bridges the gap between the customer and the business. The success of the business depends, to some extent, upon the quality and the price of its goods or services; but its success is more dependent upon good salesmanship.

Every Employee an Ambassador of Goodwill. Every employee in a business has an opportunity to build goodwill for his organization. The salesperson is probably the employee who makes the most contacts with customers and therefore has a good opportunity to build goodwill for his organization; but the other employees also may have a great deal to do with keeping customers satisfied or causing a loss of customers. The delivery boy can easily lose goodwill by poor delivery service. Errors made by employees in the bookkeeping department or in the delivery department also have an undesirable effect upon customers. Even the manner in which telephone calls are handled has its effect. Delay in answering an incoming call, making the customer wait on the telephone unnecessarily until the desired information or person is found, hanging up the receiver before the customer does, and using the wrong tone of the voice can easily cause the loss of customers.

In a survey of several hundred stores the customers who had stopped patronizing the stores gave these reasons:

Indifference of salespeople	9%	
Lack of knowledge of goods and misrepresentation of goods	8	
Haughtiness of salespeople	7	
High-pressure salesmanship	6	63%
Mistakes and poor service	17	
Unwillingness to make adjustments	10	
Tricky methods	6	
Prices too high	14	
Merchandise of inferior quality	10	
Slipshod store methods	13	
	100%	

These figures show that 63 per cent of the loss of customers resulted from the human element in business.

Let us look at the matter from another angle. What do customers like? An investigation as to what the present customers liked about the businesses with which they were dealing showed the following principal items, which are arranged according to their importance as stated by the customers:

1. A sufficient variety of stock from which to choose
2. Prices comparable to the quality of the merchandise
3. Pleasant and helpful employees
4. Truthful statements about the goods and the services
5. An attractive store (including lighting, ventilation, equipment, and arrangement)
6. Willingness to make adjustments in case of errors and returns
7. Service features, such as delivery, charge accounts, and free parking for automobiles

As items 3, 4, and 6 are principally dependent upon the personality of employees, it is evident that the employee has a very important part in the success of a business.

Attractive Personality. If a business is so small that one person can take care of all the phases of operation, it is extremely important that this one individual possess or develop a personality that will build goodwill for the business. Should the business be so large that many employees, in addition to the owner, are needed, it is important that the owner should know what qualities are desirable in his employees, especially his salespeople.

One's personal appearance makes a definite impression on anyone whom one meets for the first time. One may have many desirable personality traits and still not make a favorable impression because of an unfavorable personal appearance. A good personal appearance helps to command the respect of others and also helps to give one self-confidence in meeting people.

One's personal care has a great deal to do with one's appearance. Care should be taken to have clean teeth, clean hands, clean fingernails, and a scalp that is free from dandruff and greasy toilet preparations. Likewise, one should guard against body odors that may offend others.

The clothing of the owner of a business or that of his employees should be in keeping with the position. For example, the clothing worn by a salesman in an exclusive men's apparel store should be of high quality. Many kinds of businesses, such as restaurants, filling stations, laundries, dairies, and beauty parlors, find it desirable to have their employees wear uniforms.

Other physical factors, such as health, physique, posture, and even manner of walking, have an influence on others. The tone and the inflection of one's voice, as well as one's enunciation, have their effect. Some large organizations consider good speech so important that a course of training in speech is given to salespersons.

Courtesy is not only expected but also demanded by customers. One who is courteous will be patient, sympathetic, and always considerate of the feelings of both the customer and the co-workers in the business. He will devote his attention to the customer; will listen attentively without interruption; will become interested in the problems of his customer; and will give respectful consideration to the opinions of others.

Enthusiasm makes work a pleasure instead of a drudgery; it makes one an optimist instead of a pessimist. People like to associate with persons who are cheerful. One can hardly expect customers to be enthusiastic about goods or services unless the salesperson explaining them is enthusiastic. Likewise, the owner or manager of a business cannot expect his employees to be enthusiastic about methods and procedures used in the operation of the business unless he himself is enthusiastic about them. Enthusiasm is contagious. The attractive personality has a plentiful supply of enthusiasm that can be spread to others. Enthusiasm is based upon knowledge. So to develop enthusiasm, one should find out in what way or ways his goods, services, or ideas are better than those of others. He should then emphasize these points.

A *good memory* is a distinct asset to one in business. Remembering the names of customers so as to greet them by name the next time they call makes an appeal to their vanity. Remembering the likes and dislikes of a customer will aid in better serving that customer.

Many persons in business who have some splendid qualities have lost goodwill and customers for their business because they lacked *tact*. They did not have the ability to do or say the proper thing so as not to offend others. The shoe salesperson who comments to a customer, "You have a foot that is unusually hard to fit," displays a lack of tact.

Industriousness is essential to business success. The proprietor who is willing to work many extra hours after regular business hours in planning and taking care of the many details of his business will find that his industriousness pays dividends. The industrious salesperson will never have difficulty in finding things to do between sales. He will rearrange and care for his goods. He will call customers to tell them of merchandise in which he knows they will be interested. He will study his merchandise in order to learn more about it and its possible uses.

Knowledge of the Product. If a salesperson is to be of the most service to his customer, he must understand the wants or needs of his customer. In addition, he must have a thorough knowledge of his goods or services in order that he may be able to suggest that which best fits the needs of the customer. In many cases the customer looks to the salesperson for expert advice. The landscape gardener who suggests the wrong kinds of plants and shrubs for a particular kind of soil in which they are to be planted; the salesperson who suggests the wrong kind of furniture polish for a particular kind of furniture; the oil salesman who suggests the wrong kind of oil for a certain machine; and the hairdresser who uses a coiffure that is not becoming to her customer will quickly lose the goodwill of their customers.

Customers are usually interested in what the articles or the services will do for them and how they can be used.

Hence it is important that the salesperson should have a thorough knowledge of the various uses of his product, as well as its limitations. Even in the simple case of apples the successful salesman will know which apples are best suited for baking, which are to be preferred for making sauce, and which are desirable as eating apples. Likewise, in selling dry-cleaning preparations, the salesperson must know upon what type or types of materials each preparation should be used. He can render a very valuable service to his customers in this way.

In order that the customer will receive a full measure of service, he should be given definite information as to the proper care of the article he is purchasing. The purchaser of a dry-cleaning preparation should be given complete directions for using it. The customer who has purchased a pair of gloves should be told whether they should be laundered or dry-cleaned. If they should be laundered, she should be told the best means of laundering, including the kind of soap to be used, the correct temperature of the water, and the best method of drying. A company selling plants will want to give the customer suggestions as to the best methods of caring for the plants. Failure to give the customer proper instructions on the use and care of the product he has purchased is liable to result in the customer's failing to get the best service from the product. He may therefore become dissatisfied with both the product and the business that sold it, even though the product is of the proper quality.

One of the best ways for a salesperson to prepare himself to render service to the customer is to obtain information concerning the kind, quality, cost, and source of materials used in the manufacture of his product. These factors affect the price, wearing quality, appearance, uses, and the care of an article. For example, the fact that a certain piece of clothing is made of cotton, wool, rayon, silk, or a combination of two or more of these has a decided effect upon the care that should be given the article in laundering. It also has a definite influence upon the wearing quality, the appearance, and the price.

A knowledge of the processes used in manufacturing an article should be valuable to a salesperson. The dyeing of a piece of cloth or clothing may have been done by the process known as *stock dyeing*. Under this method the raw material is dyed before it is spun into yarn and woven into cloth. Thus the cloth will be colorfast because the dyes have thoroughly penetrated the fibers. Another piece of cloth may have been dyed by the process called *piece dyeing*. Under this method the dyeing is done after the cloth has been woven. The piece of cloth is dipped into the dye bath. This method is less expensive, but such cloth is less durable than that which was stock-dyed. Whether a piece of linen has been made from fibers retted by the water process or by artificial (chemical) means is information that a salesperson should find valuable. Knowing that certain products are "handmade" and still others are "not touched by human hands" is important information.

Different items of information about the same product may appeal to different persons. For instance, a safety feature on a washing machine will appeal to the wife and the husband. Simplicity of construction or some novelty feature may appeal to the wife. Sturdiness of construction will appeal to the husband. In order to find out the various features of a product, a successful salesman should study his product as well as competing products and should always be prepared to show why his product is worth the price that is being asked for it.

How to Obtain Information about the Product. For the ambitious salesperson there are many sources of information about his merchandise. One of the best is the merchandise itself. Advertisements in both local newspapers and national magazines should yield much information. Many manufacturers publish booklets which tell much that should aid the salesperson who sells their products. Representatives of the manufacturer, wholesale salesmen, and other experienced salespeople can supply much valuable information. Even comments from customers may be a source of information.

Satisfied Customers. The modern salesman has learned that the best sale is that in which the customer buys, and not that in which the customer is talked into a purchase against his better judgment. The salesperson who organizes the facts about his product, presents them intelligently, and guides the customer to a favorable decision is the one whose customers remain satisfied. He is rendering a service to his customers and to economic society. Therefore his customers will learn to have confidence in him.

National Cash Register Company.

Illustration No. 106—Getting Acquainted with the Customer

Studying the Wants of Prospects and Customers. The salesperson who attempts to sell candy to a child by emphasizing the quality probably will not succeed. On the other hand, the salesperson who emphasizes the quantity of a certain kind of candy that can be purchased for a nickel probably will make a sale because he understands the important reason that causes a child to prefer one kind of candy to another. If one wishes to be successful in satisfying customers, he must study and understand human nature. Why do people buy? What wants do they have, and how can those wants be satisfied?

There are many motives that cause people to buy. Some of the most important of these so-called *buying motives* are:

Imitation	Amusement
Desire for ease and comfort	Desire for bargains (thrift)
Affection	Desire for good health
Appetite	Pride of possession
Love of beauty	Desire to excel
Desire for gain	

To be successful, the salesperson must know what is likely to be the buying motive of a particular customer and then make his sales talk and demonstration appeal to that motive. In many cases appeals can be made to more than one buying motive. For instance, a laundry representative, in attempting to sell the services of his company to a housewife who has a family of three persons and financial means that are a little above average, may talk about the comfort and convenience of having her laundry done by his company rather than doing it herself. He may also explain that it is less expensive to send the laundry to his company because of all the expenses involved in doing it at home. Probably he will mention that having the laundry done by his company would also eliminate the chance of taking cold from working with wet clothes in cold weather.

Suppose that this same laundry representative were calling upon the proprietor of a barber shop or a beauty parlor. In such a case he could emphasize the special sterilizing treatment given to linens and the high degree of whiteness in the laundered linens, both of which factors would aid in keeping customers of the barber or the beauty-parlor operator satisfied and also help in attracting other customers.

When several buying motives may be appealed to, the salesperson can often make brief appeals to different ones and carefully observe the reaction of the customer. He can usually discover which is the most important appeal and can then concentrate upon or emphasize that particular one.

Knowledge of Customers. The more one knows about his product and the more one knows about his customer, the easier it is to decide which probably are the most important motives that should be appealed to. In addition to having a thorough understanding of his product, the salesperson should attempt to find out as much as possible about his prospect or customer. Some of the valuable things to know are:

Approximate age	Social standing
Occupation	Hobbies
Financial ability	Temperament
Family	Buying habits

Naturally some of the specific information desirable will vary with different kinds of businesses. Some salesmen find it desirable to keep an information card for each prospect or customer. On it are recorded any items that should be of value to the salesman in refreshing his memory from time to time. Illustration No. 107 shows such a card used by life-insurance representatives.

Name		Age	Date of Birth		
			Mo.	Day	Year
Residence					
Business Address		Name of Wife			
Occupation	Income				
Hobbies		Names of Children			
Friends, etc.					

Present Insurance							
Company	Date	Kind	Amount	Premium	Prem. Date	Beneficiary	Settlement Option

	Results of Calls	
Date	Remarks	

Illustration No. 107—A Prospect Card Used by a
Life-Insurance Salesman

An information card used by a representative of a textbook publisher might have such detailed information as the various subjects taught in a certain school; the texts being used at the present time; changes in subjects or texts, or both, that are being contemplated; the names of school officials to be seen; and the names of the teachers of the various subjects.

Most companies that follow an organized plan of selling have detailed records of customers. These records provide considerable information with regard to the use of the company's own products, as well as those of competitors. The information has often been accumulated over a long period of time and represents the history of the dealings with the customer. Illustration No. 108 is an example of such a record.

Companies that have traveling salesmen must depend upon detailed reports in order to keep in touch with their customers and to organize a sales program by mail. Illustration No. 109 is one type of daily report that provides useful information for the management. There are numerous forms of this kind. Some organizations require a single detailed report for each prospect and, in addition, a summary report of the day's work.

Training of Salespeople. From the point of view of management, it is important to have well-trained salespeople. Salespeople should be trained not only in the policies of the organization, but also in the principles of personal selling. They should be taught how to get favorable attention, to create interest, to demonstrate, and to obtain favorable action. They should be encouraged to avoid negative suggestions and undesirable tactics. The following paragraphs contain several points on selling that are important in all types of organizations.

Suggestion Selling. Have you had the experience of buying a fountain pen and having the salesman suggest that you buy a mechanical pencil to match the pen? Or have you been with your mother when she purchased some glass jars to be used in canning and the grocery clerk suggested jar rubbers? Such activity on the part of salespeople is

Analysis of Individual Customer's Purchases

Mr. __Benj. Little_____   Date__Jan. 14_____
                        Salesman.

Below is a statement of the total purchases of

Name__Hamlin & Judge_____   Address__Farwell, Texas_____

for the period from__Sept. 1__ to __Dec. 31__

ITEMS					
The purchases are distributed, according to the resale price, in each of our five principal price groups:	50 cents	$1.00	$1.50	$2.00	Over $2.00
Customer's total purchases for the period in dollars	$ 150.	655.	173.	380.	190.
Customer's total purchases for the period in percentages	9.6	43.3	11.1	24.5	12.2
Standard percentages for this type store	23%	40%	11%	19%	6%
Check marks at this point indicate undesirable departures from the standard. Check, in the proper column, that one of the five following statements which, in your opinion, indicates the main reason. If none of these statements apply, write your explanation on line (6).	X				
(1) This customer does not carry our type of merchandise in this price range					
(2) Carries competitive line (give key letter of chief competitor)					
(3) Carries too small stock					
(4) Goods of this price are not adequately displayed					
(5) Proprietor (or clerks) do not push goods at this price					

(6) Or, write principal reason here: *They carry 50c stock in good assortment but usually step up sale to $1.*

Check marks at this point indicate satisfactory adherence to standards, or desirable departures in the sale of higher priced merchandise. Check, in the proper column, the statement below which indicates the main reason or, if none applies, write your explanation on line (11).	50 cents	$1.00	$1.50	$2.00	Over $2.00
				X	X

(7) Carries our goods exclusively at this price

(8) Carries large stock

(9) Stock is well displayed

(10) Proprietor (or clerks) push merchandise at this

(11) Or, write principal reason here: *They get P.M.'s for all sales over small items of dress import and they are enthusiastic boosters of the "Dress-well-and-succeed" campaign*

> ### A FORM THAT PROMOTES BALANCED SELLING
> This form, one employed by a selling organization whose line falls into several distinct price classifications, is used to check up the performance of salesmen in relation to balanced selling. Records covering a considerable period, thus making them representative of the merchant's sales, are used; otherwise, the stock on the merchant's shelves would need to be considered. Only those accounts showing marked departures from the established standards for balanced selling are called to the salesman's attention. In addition to being used periodically with all the salesmen, the form is also used whenever an individual salesman's record shows a falling off from normal in his territory.
>
> The chief result secured by the use of this form has been to equalize the effort the salesman put behind the various classes—to overcome their common tendency to concentrate on certain numbers or price classes. The replies checked by the salesman, also, are valuable.

Return this blank to Sales Department, properly filled in, with your regular mailing on the Wednesday of the week following its receipt.

Hammermill Paper Company.

A FORM THAT PROMOTES BALANCED SELLING

This type of form is valuable as a constant check against the tendency of salesmen to get into a rut. The pressure of getting the order may warp the sales judgment of the salesman at times. This form enables him to see how his sales to a particular customer check against the average for other purchasers in the same general classification.

Illustration No. 108—Analysis of the Purchases Made by an Individual Customer

Salesman's Daily Report for ☑ ☐ ☐ ☐ ☐ ☐ *Jan 16*
Mon. Tues. Wed. Thur. Fri. Sat.

Phila Branch

City *Philadelphia* State *Pa* Salesman *Jack Grey*

If a re-call, write the number of previous calls in the "Re-call" column. Indicate Results of Call (with the exception of Sales, which are indicated by the amount in the "Sale Made" column). Prospect's Rating, and Chief Competition by check marks in the appropriate columns. Check as "Interviews" only those calls in which you succeed in giving an adequate presentation of our machine. If the prospect is "too busy" or makes some other excuse, or grants you insufficient time, check under "Saw prospect, interview refused," unless you are able to make a definite appointment; in that case, check under "Made appointment."

Prospect's name and address

	Prospect	Re-call	Could not see	Saw prospect, interview refused	Made appointment	Interview without demonstration	Interview with demonstration	Sale made (Enter amount of sale)	Live prospect	Future prospect	Doubtful	Discard	B. and W.	Lyons	Diener	A. A. T.	All-Electric
1	R C Andrew 2518 Walnut St.		✓					$									
2	P. B. Battersea 2530 " "		✓					$									
3	Mrs H L Sanders 2551 " "	2				✓		193.00						✓			
4	The Cheltenham 209 So 25th St.			✓		✓		$	✓								
5	James R. Woods 2416 Chestnut	4	✓					$		✓			✓				
6	Chapin Tarr 2533 Market St.			✓				$	✓					✓			
7	Dr A H Graybill 433 Brooklyn St.				✓			$	✓							✓	
8	Victor "								✓					✓			
9																	✓
10																	✓
11																	
12																	
13																✓	
14																	
15																	
16																	
17																	
18																	
	Totals	4	3	4	2			306.00	5	1	1	1		2	3	2	

Remarks: (Refer to prospects reported above, by number)   Posted to monthly summary ☑

4 Prospect for three model W's. Have F.B. arrange for inspection of Hall-Wilks installation

5 Bought A.A.T.

Hammermill Paper Company.

A FORM THAT BUILDS SALES

This form, filled in by specialty salesmen selling an electrical device, accomplishes two definite ends which the newer sales management sees as the main purposes of a daily salesman's report: (a) Each salesman is forced automatically to review the day's accomplishment; (b) The management is furnished data not available from other sources.

This particular form is noteworthy in that it provides a great deal of worth-while information with a minimum of clerical work. The salesman has only to write in each prospect's name and address and then make 2 to 4 check marks after each name. (If he thinks a longer report necessary, it may be sent in separately.)

The adoption of this form was followed by an immediate and marked increase in sales. This increase was evidently due to self analysis, for it preceded the additional results later obtained by the sales management on the basis of their study of each man's record.

The management's study was based on a summary of all the facts recorded in the columns headed: "Re-calls," "Results of Call," "Prospect's Rating," and "Chief Competition." A record of the number of sales made on the first, second, or third call and on or after the fourth call was part of the summary.

This summary (easily tabulated by clerks in the home office), is made monthly and has proved itself a remarkably clear index to each salesman's chief points of strength and weakness—a high percentage of "interviews refused" indicating a poor approach; a large proportion of sales made on the first or second call being generally accompanied by a correspondingly high percentage of sales, and so on. It thus became possible to give each man suggestions and help of individual benefit to him—and to back up the management's recommendations with definite figures.

The data regarding competition were found particularly valuable in determining the slant to be taken in mail promotion and other advertising.

A FORM THAT BUILDS SALES

This form accomplishes two definite ends: (a) Each salesman is forced automatically to review the day's accomplishment; (b) The management is furnished data not available from other sources. This particular form is noteworthy in that it provides a great deal of worth-while information with a minimum of clerical work.

Illustration No. 109—A Salesman's Daily Report Form

known as *suggestion selling*. Suggestion selling takes place when the salesperson calls the attention of the customer to goods not definitely asked for.

A customer has just purchased a can of paint. The sales-man says, "We have just the kind of brush to use with this paint," and hastens to show it to the customer. A woman has just purchased some yard goods for a dress, and the salesperson suggests thread and trimmings to match. These are examples of what is known as the suggestion of *related articles*.

You ask the grocery clerk for a small-sized package of cocoa. He brings you a package that sells for 10 cents and one that sells for 20 cents, and tells you that the larger one contains three times as much as the smaller one and yet it sells for only twice as much. Or you ask for a 15-cent can of a certain brand of corn, and the clerk tells you that you can purchase two cans for 25 cents. This kind of selling is called the suggestion of a *larger quantity*.

You may have asked a salesman to show you medium-priced shirts but he shows you also a higher-priced shirt that has really more quality for its price. This type of sell-ing is called suggestion of *higher-priced goods*.

You may often have gone into a store for a particular brand of goods, but the salesman told you that that brand was not carried. He did, however, show you a similar brand stocked by the store. Or you may have told the salesman the purpose for which you intended to use the particular brand, and he may have suggested that another brand was more suitable for your needs. This type of selling is known as the suggestion of a *substitute*.

In addition to the four kinds of suggestion selling ex-plained in the preceding paragraphs, there is another kind in which the customer's attention is called to merchandise that has been specially priced or that is being featured in the advertising of the store or the manufacturer.

Is Suggestion Selling Desirable? If the salesperson really uses suggestion and does not attempt to force unwanted goods upon the customer, then suggestion selling is desir-

National Cash Register Company.

Illustration No. 110—Suggestion Selling

able from the viewpoint of both the customer and of the store. Calling attention to related goods may save the customer from making an extra trip to the store later to buy the related article. It may also furnish him with related goods that more closely suit his original purchase than would related goods that were purchased elsewhere. Likewise, suggesting to the customer that by purchasing a larger quantity he can get the goods at a lower price, suggesting a higher-priced article when it means more quality for its price, and suggesting substitute brands should be of value to customers and should be considered as a part of the service that a salesman can render.

To a business, suggestion selling has great possibilities for increasing sales by getting customers to purchase related items instead of buying them from competitors. The increased sales should result not only in larger net profits but also in a greater percentage of net profit because the additional sales cause only a little increase in overhead expenses. Let us see the effect.

Suppose that a store served 50,000 customers; it did a business of $40,000 (the average sale amounted to 80 cents) ; and the net profit was $2,000. The figures for the store would be:

Sales		$40,000
Cost of goods sold (75% of sales)		30,000
Margin, or gross profit		$10,000
Expenses:		
Salaries	$3,500	
Other operating expenses	4,500	8,000
Net profit		$ 2,000

Now suppose this store were to increase the average sale only 10 cents; that is, assume customers buy an average of 90 cents instead of 80 cents. The figures would be:

Sales		$45,000
Cost of goods sold (75% of sales)		33,750
Margin, or gross profit		$11,250
Expenses:		
Salaries	$3,500	
Other operating expenses	5,000	8,500
Net profit		$ 2,750

The operating expenses have been increased slightly because of the extra cost of wrapping and delivery, but most of the expenses of the store would not increase.

Guides in Suggestion Selling. All suggestions should be based on a thorough knowledge of the merchandise and on a sincere desire to be of service to the customer. To be effective, the suggestions should be positive, not negative. "Will this be all for this time?" "You wouldn't like some nice strawberries today, would you?" and similar questions are likely to be futile in increasing sales. It would be more effective to say, for instance, "These Tennessee strawberries have an exceptionally fine flavor." The suggestion should be made in an enthusiastic manner, and the salesman should attempt to show or demonstrate the suggested article. In suggesting substitutes, one should avoid such indefinite statements as, "This is just as good as the X brand." If the X brand is a shirt that gained its reputation because of its fast colors, the salesperson might say, "This shirt carries a money-back guarantee that its colors are fast. It also has a collar that needs no starching when being laundered."

QUESTIONS FOR DISCUSSION

1. What four elements are involved in a sale?
2. Every employee is an ambassador of goodwill. Explain this statement.
3. Give several reasons why customers stop patronizing certain stores.
4. State several reasons why customers like certain stores.
5. Explain the importance of a good personal appearance to a salesperson.
6. State five personal traits that are desirable in salespeople, and give a specific example of the importance of each.
7. Of what importance is a thorough knowledge of the product to the person who is selling it?
8. Where can a salesperson obtain information about the products he sells?
9. What is meant by a buying motive?
10. What are some of the most common of the so-called buying motives?
11. Why is it desirable for a salesperson to find out as much as possible about his customers or prospects?
12. What two general types of training should be given salespeople?
13. What is meant by suggestion selling?
14. Name three kinds of suggestion selling.
15. Is suggestion selling desirable? Discuss.

PROBLEMS AND PROJECTS

1. Make a survey of the retail prices of various brands of gasoline being sold in your community.
2. The business owned by Albert Saylor shows the following figures for a certain year: sales, $50,000; average inventory (at selling price), $20,000; operating expenses, $12,000; cost of goods sold, $35,000. A similar business owned by William Watson shows the following figures for the same year: sales, $30,000; average inventory (at selling price), $20,000; cost of goods sold, $21,000; operating expenses, $7,200. (a) Find the annual rate of merchandise turnover for each business. (b) In each business what percentage of the average merchandise inventory is the net profit?

3. A business has been selling each month an average of 15 items of a certain article that cost $60. The regular selling price has been $100, and the monthly operating expenses have averaged $500. By reducing the selling price to $80, the management is able to sell 25 items monthly. The additional sales increase the operating expenses 10 per cent. By how much have the monthly net profits been increased or decreased?

4. Find the percentage of markup and the selling price in the following cases:

COST PRICE	DESIRED MARGIN (PERCENTAGE OF SELLING PRICE)
(a) $6.00	40%
(b) $ .75	25%
(c) $8.40	20%
(d) $4.50	50%

5. A ladies' dress shop buys 100 dresses at $6.80 each. The dresses are marked to be sold at a margin of 50 per cent. Eighty dresses are sold at that price. The remaining are sold after a markdown of 25 per cent. What is the average percentage of margin on the entire lot?

6. Assume that a shoe store is now selling for $8 a pair a certain style of shoe that cost $4.80. If the selling price is reduced 10 per cent, it will be necessary to increase the number of pairs sold by what percentage in order that the same amount of gross profit will be earned? (Assume a daily sale of a certain number of pairs, such as 30 pairs.)

7. Assume that you are operating a wholesale business handling supplies for barber shops and beauty parlors. Make a list of actual prospects in your community. Give the name and the address of each prospect and the source of the name.

8. Prepare an outline of plans for a special sale to be held during the month of March in order to stimulate trade with your dry-cleaning business.

9. Compare the annual delivery costs under the following plans:
   (a) Individually owned equipment. Cost, $2,000; depreciation, 20 per cent; truck repairs, $30; gasoline, oil, and grease, $380; insurance, $65; storage, $84; driver's salary, $1,250.
   (b) Contract plan. 4,500 packages at 8¢; 5,650 packages at 10¢; 2,200 packages at 15¢; 1,000 packages at 25¢; 440 packages at 50¢.

10. Give a report on some salesperson you have observed, pointing out good characteristics and also any traits that you think are not desirable.

CHAPTER XII

PROBLEMS OF DISTRIBUTION

Purpose of the Chapter. The producer or manufacturer must be acquainted with the various channels of distribution in order to know how to market his goods most effectively. The retailer and various other middlemen must understand the channels of distribution in order to know how they can be served most effectively. In this chapter many questions with regard to distribution will be answered. Some of the important questions are:

1. What is meant by direct marketing?
2. What is meant by indirect marketing?
3. What are the various channels of distribution that are used for different types of products?
4. What are the advantages and the disadvantages of the various methods of distribution?
5. What are some criteria that can be followed in selecting a method of distribution?
6. What are the economic functions performed in distribution?

Trade Channels. How do goods get from the producer to the consumer? Sometimes the producer markets them directly to the consumer without the use of middlemen. Some producers sell their products to retailers; others distribute their goods to wholesalers, to jobbers, or to other middlemen. The various routes taken by goods in getting from the producer to the consumer are known as *trade channels*.

From Producer Directly to Consumer. The shortest trade channel is that in which the goods move directly from the producer to the consumer. The manufacturer of locomotives sells his products directly to railroads. The farmer may sell his produce directly to consumers through his roadside market, by house-to-house canvassing, or by taking his produce to a farmers' market in a city, where he may sell it from his truck. A bakery may have trucks making a direct house-to-house delivery of its baked goods, or it may operate a retail store in the front part of the building in which the baking is done.

There are three methods by which the producer may sell directly to the consumer: by mail, by having salesmen go to the customers, or by having the customers come to the producer. Selling by mail requires a large amount of advertising and correspondence. In the past this method has been used most successfully in selling to people in rural areas where the consumer found it difficult to get to city retail stores. With the extensive building of good roads and the wide popularity of the automobile, the total mail-order sales have decreased greatly. A large number of products of almost every variety and description are, however, still being sold by mail.

There is more success in selling some products by mail than others. A mail-order business is likely to be most successful if—

1. The shipping expenses are not high in comparison with the value of the articles. For instance, if a fifty-cent article would require a shipping expense of twenty cents when marketed directly by mail in shipments of one item each, it would probably not be marketed in that manner, but would be shipped to middlemen in large quantities by freight.

2. The goods sold stand up well in being handled and transported. For example, although eggs have been sold directly by mail, the handling of fragile products by such a method has not proved successful generally.

3. The selling prices of the articles are low. People are afraid to take the risk of investing a large amount of money in articles they cannot see before buying. The largest percentage of buying directly by mail is done by people in the low-income class. They hesitate, however, to send in large sums of money for goods they have not seen.

4. There is a warranty of return and refund in case the purchaser is not satisfied. This warranty must be fulfilled in the strictest sense.

Products that people can do without, but that mean convenience and comfort, are often purchased only when the consumer is urged to buy them. In such cases the producer often sends his salesmen to call directly on consumers in an attempt to intensify the want that is present but inactive. Encyclopedias, household appliances, and magazines are often marketed in this manner.

In some cases the producer has the consumer come to him to get the product. This plan is sometimes followed because the producer does not wish to devote the additional time to marketing, or in order that the customer will feel he is getting a fresher product. In some cases it would be impractical to carry a wide variety of bulky products to the consumer for his selection. The produce of farmers and the trees and shrubbery sold by nurseries are examples of such products.

From Producer to Consumer Through One Middleman. This trade channel is next to the shortest. The middleman is usually spoken of as a *retailer*. Automobiles ordinarily are distributed by this method, the local dealer, or agent, buying from the manufacturer and selling to the consumer. Milk usually follows this trade channel in reaching consumers in cities, the dairy purchasing the milk from the dairy farmer and then pasteurizing, bottling, and selling it to the housewife. Some farmers choose to haul certain products to town and market them directly to the consumer. Others find that, if they let someone else handle the marketing, they can spend their time more profitably at home in producing. This specialization tends to create more efficiency.

The manufacturer who expects to market his product to retailers must be able to maintain a sales organization large enough to contact the retailers. If a producer makes a large group of related products, he will probably find it desirable to sell to retailers. Producers of the following types of goods may also find it desirable to use this trade channel: bulky goods, such as brick, cement, lumber, and coal; style goods, such as women's hats and dresses; perishable goods that need to be made available to the consumer as quickly as possible; goods of such a high value that they justify a large selling expense; or products that have to be pushed a great deal in order to make sales.

From Producer to Consumer Through Two Middlemen. This channel is frequently thought to be the most typical of the trade channels used in distributing merchandise in this country. Illustration No. 111 shows several trade channels with different combinations of two middlemen.

Staples, such as groceries, drugs, and hardware, are frequently marketed through a wholesaler and a retailer. Large department and chain stores, however, usually eliminate the wholesaler by purchasing directly from the manufacturers.

Manufacturers of farm machinery and large meat packers are examples of producers who often have their own branch houses that sell to the retailer. In some cases the branch house is owned entirely by the producer; in other cases it is controlled by the producer, who owns a controlling interest in the capital stock of the branch house. This method is likely to be used when other distribution facilities

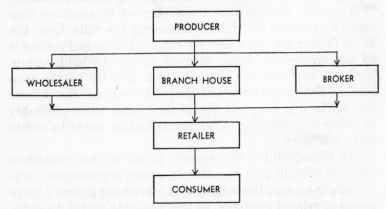

Illustration No. 111—Trade Channels with Two Middlemen

in the form of suitable wholesalers or brokers are inadequate. Also, a manufacturer may feel that if his goods were distributed through wholesalers or brokers, who handle a large variety of goods, his goods might not be pushed so much as they are by his own branch house. Branch houses are usually found only in metropolitan areas.

The output of small coal mines is frequently marketed through a broker, who represents several mines. The coal-mining companies find this method less expensive than that of maintaining their own sales force.

From Producer to Consumer Through Three or More Middlemen. Sometimes when the producer has a small business, such as a small canning factory or a textile mill producing only a few kinds of cloth, he may turn the marketing of the goods over to sales agents or brokers in order to eliminate the need for maintaining a sales and related personnel department. From the agents or brokers the goods pass to the wholesaler and then to the retailer. Likewise, wholesalers who handle a very large variety of articles, such as wholesale hardware dealers who carry a great number of products made by many manufacturers, find it desirable to get their goods through buying agents, who can keep in close touch with the different manufacturers and the daily price changes. Illustration No. 112 shows several trade channels having three middlemen.

Other middlemen, such as local shippers, importers, and auctioneers, may come between the producer and the wholesaler in such a way that there are four middlemen. For example, fruit growers may market their fruit through a local shipper, who sends it to an auction where the wholesaler buys it. It then reaches the consumer through the retailer. Sometimes a large co-operative organization of fruit growers serves as the main middleman, displacing the broker, the sales agent, the buying agent, or the local buyer.

Using Several Channels at the Same Time. Usually a manufacturer finds it best to use only one channel of distribution. Sometimes it is necessary, however, for a manu-

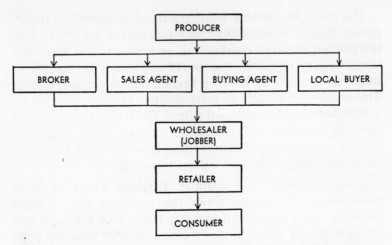

Illustration No. 112—Trade Channels with Three Middlemen

facturer to use more than one if he is to get the greatest distribution. Such goods as fountain pens, razor blades, stationery, and soap are stocked by so many different kinds of retail stores that the manufacturers of them must use different trade channels to get the widest distribution.

A large soap-manufacturing company has its own warehouses in metropolitan areas and sells directly to retail stores in such areas. In rural sections that are served by retail stores in small towns, the same company uses wholesalers to distribute the soap to the retailers. Each plan has its advantages under a different set of circumstances.

For the convenience of customers some businesses use more than one trade channel. For example, a publishing company might desire to have its weekly magazine distributed entirely through news agencies and newsstands; but, because of the wishes of many customers, it will also distribute copies directly by mail.

A business that produces various products may find it desirable to use different trade channels. A good example of such a business is a large meat-packing company. Fresh meat, soaps, fertilizers, glue, hides, and hair each reach the consumer by a different route.

The four diagrams in Illustration No. 114 show trade channels used in distributing four different products. Notice how different trade channels may be used for the same product. For example, the dairy farmer sells his milk to the city dairy, which in turn sells directly to the consumer. This same city dairy also sells milk to the retail grocery or delicatessen, which sells it to the consumer.

Swift & Company.

Illustration No. 113—A Branch Distributor

The Empire Hosiery Company Sells Directly to Consumers. Let us suppose that we are starting a company, known as the Empire Hosiery Company, that will manufacture silk hosiery. We know that already there are many businesses in this field; but we believe that, because of the superior quality of our hosiery, we shall find a ready market, once the hosiery has been introduced sufficiently. We shall start our manufacturing on a small scale, until we can determine to what extent the public will desire our product.

We find it difficult to interest retail stores in our goods because they already carry one or more other brands and are doing a satisfactory business with them. They tell us that adding our brand would mean more of their capital tied up in inventories. Furthermore, if they should induce

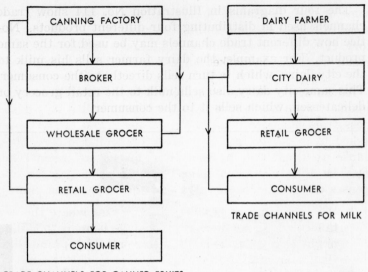

TRADE CHANNELS FOR CANNED FRUITS
AND VEGETABLES

TRADE CHANNELS FOR MILK

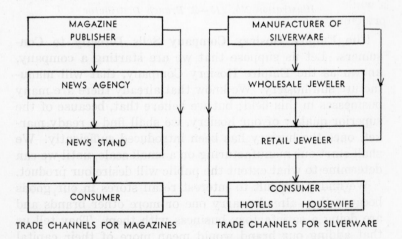

TRADE CHANNELS FOR MAGAZINES   TRADE CHANNELS FOR SILVERWARE

Illustration No. 114—Various Trade Channels

some of their customers to buy our new, untried brand instead of the others, and if the hosiery should be unsatisfactory, they would lose their reputation and customers. As a result we decide to market our goods directly to consumers.

Advantages. In marketing our hosiery directly in this manner, we have to hire salespeople who will solicit business from house to house. We set our prices below those asked by retail stores for hosiery of similar quality, because we think that by this direct-marketing method we may be able to eliminate the profit and some of the expenses of the middlemen. We find that under this plan—

1. We can push our product in territories where the retailers might be unwilling to handle it or, if they did, might have a tendency to push some other brand that they also handle.
2. We can make it easier for the housewife to select hosiery that will match various costumes, for she will be able to match the hosiery with various dresses and suits in her own home.

Disadvantages. After this plan has been in operation for a while, we find there are a number of disadvantages. The principal ones are:

1. Our representatives find it hard to obtain interviews because of the distrust many people have of house-to-house salespeople and because the housewife may be in the midst of other activities when our representative calls.
2. Customers dislike anticipating their wants far in advance. It is much easier for them to stop in a retail store today and get a pair of hose to wear to the party tonight.
3. When adjustments have to be made, the customer resents the delay caused by her having to get in touch with our local representative, who must, in turn, get into contact with headquarters. She says that she can get an adjustment almost instantly at any local store.

4. We find that our delivery expense is very high because of the small size of the orders.
5. In order to get a wide distribution of our product, we find it necessary to employ hundreds of sales representatives. Such a large number increases our problem of hiring, training, and supervising.
6. We also find that the large number of salespeople and the thousands of small orders require an immense amount of correspondence and bookkeeping in relation to the sales volume done.
7. Two trips of our representative are required: one to make the sale and one to deliver the goods at a later date. Often the customer is not at home when delivery is attempted, and still another trip must be made. We try sending the goods C.O.D. but find that many customers object to buying in this way.

The Empire Hosiery Company Sells to Retailers. Now that we have acquainted the public in several localities with our product, and the quality of our product has been proved, we are able to interest retailers in handling our brand of hosiery. Retailers, especially in the localities where our product is well known, become middlemen for our product. As the retailer must have a margin for his operating expenses and his net profit, we have to sell the hosiery to him at a price considerably less than that at which we sold it under the former plan. The lower price that we now receive has, however, some offsetting advantages. We do not have the former salespeople's commissions to pay (we still have a few representatives to call on dealers); we have less packaging and delivery expense because we can ship in large quantities to the retailer; we need less storage space as the retailer now will carry the stock necessary for supplying the wants of customers; we have less record-keeping; and we should be able to increase our volume of sales because many of the reasons why customers did not buy from us when we had house-to-house representatives have been eliminated. This increased volume of sales may result in lower manufacturing costs.

The Empire Hosiery Company Plans for Future Expansion. Once our product is well established in a section of the country, we may wish to expand our business further by marketing our goods in other sections. Either of two general plans may be followed. We might greatly increase our staff of salesmen, who call on retailers, and thus attempt to contact retailers in all parts of the country. As this plan, however, would mean additional personnel problems, as well as delivery and record-keeping problems, we might use another plan, that of selling to wholesale dry-goods merchants, or jobbers. Under this plan our selling price to the wholesalers or the jobbers would be lower than that at which we would sell to retailers, but there would be offsetting features. We would need fewer representatives to contact all the wholesalers than we would to contact the retailers; we would have only a few accounts receivable; we would need to keep less goods in storage for filling orders; we would ship in larger quantities. Under the latter plan the problem of marketing our goods would require little of our time and attention; hence we could concentrate on improving our processes of manufacturing. If we choose this plan, however, we must establish a definite program of advertising to create consumer demand in the new territories and must have a sufficient number of representatives to create wholesale demand by calling on the retailers.

Economic Services and Functions of Middlemen. From the preceding discussion it is evident that a number of services and functions are performed by middlemen. They may be summarized under these general headings:

1. Assembling (bringing the goods together at points where there is a demand for them)
2. Storage
3. Grading and standardizing goods
4. Selling
5. Financing
6. Risk-bearing
7. Record-keeping

Regardless of which channel of distribution the goods follow, these services and functions are to be found. If a certain middleman is eliminated, his services and functions must be taken over by someone else. The services may be consolidated, but nevertheless they are still performed. This fact is well illustrated by the experiences of the Empire Hosiery Company.

Factors to be Considered in Choosing the Trade Channel. Many factors must be considered by a business in deciding what trade channel will be used in marketing its product. A few of the principal factors are mentioned here.

1. *Perishability of the product.* Highly perishable articles, such as baked goods, ice, ice cream, and certain fruits and vegetables, are usually marketed directly to the consumer or by means of few middlemen.
2. *Distance between the producer and the consumer.* Ordinarily the greater the distance from the producer to the consumer, the more middlemen will be involved in handling the product.
3. *Financial condition of the producer.* The better the finances of a producer, the more likely he is to sell to retailers or directly to consumers. Should he be restricted in finances, he will want less money tied up in inventories and can less afford to have a large number of accounts receivable with comparable losses due to bad debts.
4. *Need for special facilities for handling the product.* If the product requires costly fixtures or equipment for handling, it is likely to pass through as few middlemen as possible. For that reason gasoline, which needs special tanks and tank trucks for handling, is marketed directly from refiner to the retailer. Often the retail outlet is owned by the refiner.
5. *Number of users.* The greater the number of users of a product, the more middlemen there probably will be. For instance, the manufacturer of steel is likely to sell directly to users, whereas the manufacturer of shoes usually sells to retailers.

6. *Number of various products produced.* A manufacturer who has only one product, such as an electric
iron, will probably sell his product to a wholesaler as
he would find it too expensive to maintain a sales force
large enough to contact all the retailers. But if a
manufacturer has a large number of electrical products, such as clocks, toasters, waffle irons, heaters, and
heating pads, he will probably have salesmen call on
retailers because the expense of this plan will be distributed over many products.

Changing Trade Channels. It was pointed out previously
that some producers change from one trade channel to another in marketing their products and that other producers
use more than one trade channel at the same time. There
is also the growing tendency for certain products to be
marketed through trade channels different from those that
were used ten, twenty, or thirty years ago. For instance,
the co-operative marketing organizations of farmers are
often eliminating one or even two middlemen and are selling directly to city wholesalers. In the past the usual trade
channel for eggs, for example, was: poultry farmer to
country buyer (huckster or country store), to shipper
(packer), to wholesaler (jobber), to retailer, to consumer.
Now the egg-producers' co-operatives are selling directly
to wholesalers.

With the growth of chain stores and supermarkets of a
great many kinds, there has been a tendency to eliminate
the wholesaler in many lines of goods. Increased efficiency
in transportation also has tended to change trade channels.
Good roads and automobiles have resulted in many products being marketed through retailers instead of directly
by mail or by peddlers canvassing from farmhouse to farmhouse. Likewise, the retailer need not depend upon some
neighboring wholesaler for goods, but can get them directly
from the manufacturer in almost the same time that it formerly took him to buy from the wholesaler.

Market research, which is growing in importance, is
showing more efficient methods of marketing products.

This research has its effect on trade channels and probably will continue to cause changes in the years ahead. Legislation also has an effect on trade channels. For example, many laws that have been passed during the last few years tend to eliminate some of the chain-store systems.

QUESTIONS FOR DISCUSSION

1. What is meant by trade channels?
2. Which is the shortest trade channel?
3. What are three methods that may be used by the producer in selling directly to the consumer?
4. Under what conditions is mail-order selling likely to be most successful?
5. When goods pass through the hands of only one middleman, what is the middleman usually called?
6. What is meant by a wholesaler?
7. Name some of the middlemen that may be found between the producer and the wholesaler.
8. Why is it sometimes necessary for a producer to use more than one channel for the distribution of his products?
9. State two reasons why the Empire Hosiery Company decided to sell directly to consumers.
10. Give four disadvantages that were experienced by the Empire Hosiery Company in selling directly to consumers.
11. If the Empire Hosiery Company markets its product through wholesalers, what are the principal advantages it will have?
12. What are the principal services and functions performed by middlemen?
13. When certain middlemen are eliminated, will the price paid by the consumer be less?
14. What are some of the factors that a businessman should consider in deciding which trade channel to use in marketing his product?
15. Name some causes for the changes that have occurred in trade channels.

PROBLEMS AND PROJECTS

1. A farmer has produced 50 bushels of potatoes for sale. He could sell them in their ungraded condition to a city wholesale produce business at 70 cents a bushel. Instead, he de-

cides to market them directly to housewives by a house-to-house canvass. He finds that it requires 15 hours to clean, grade, and put the potatoes into containers. He is compelled to make a trip to the city, which requires two hours, to purchase the containers (bushel baskets). The cost of the containers is 12 cents each. The time spent in making a house-to-house canvass to dispose of the 50 bushels is 10 hours. He sells 40 bushels, which are the large size, at $1.10 and the remainder, which are the small size, at 75 cents. Assume that the expense of operating the truck for the two trips to the city is $4 and that the farmer's time is worth 30 cents an hour. Did the farmer receive more or less by marketing the potatoes directly than he would have by selling them to the produce business? How much?

2. Select some product, such as clothing, machinery, flour, or canned goods, that is produced locally and find out the various channels of distribution through which it goes from the time of its production until the time of its final use. Draw a diagram showing the specific types of outlets through which the product is sold.

3. Surveys show that the consumer's dollar paid for canned tomatoes is divided approximately as follows:

Grower	18.7 cents
Canner	45.9 cents
Broker	3.9 cents
Wholesaler	11.5 cents
Retailer	20.0 cents
	100.0 cents

From these figures determine the percentage of margin received by (a) the retailer, (b) the wholesaler, and (c) the broker.

4. Referring to the preceding problem, compute the number of cents received by each person for his services if the retail price of a can of tomatoes is 15 cents.

5. Visit some retail store and find out if all the products carried are purchased from wholesalers. If some are not, from what sources does the retail store obtain them? Find out from what source or sources the store equipment has been obtained. Make a report.

CHAPTER XIII

SHIPPING AND TRANSPORTATION PROBLEMS

Purpose of the Chapter. Every businessman is confronted with certain problems of shipping and receiving goods. It is therefore important to know some of the problems of the one who ships and the one who receives. The following are questions that will be answered in this chapter:

1. What are the advantages and the disadvantages of different methods of shipment?
2. How can one compare the costs of shipment by various methods?
3. How may shipments be sent C.O.D.?
4. What is the difference between a private carrier and a public carrier?
5. How should one file a claim for the loss of a shipment?

Railway Freight and Express Shipments. Railway transportation is probably the most common form of shipping in the United States. It includes carload freight (C.L.), less-than-carload freight (L.C.L., or package car), and express. Express shipments are carried in special cars on passenger trains or on special fast trains. Such shipments are therefore faster than other railway shipments, but they are also more expensive. Ordinarily large, bulky material is not shipped by express because the express rate is higher than the freight rate; but when speed is a factor more important than cost, express is preferable to freight. Less-than-carload shipments, or package-car shipments, cost less than express but more than carload freight. Under this plan the shipments of several companies are placed in the same car for the same destination. Carload freight is self-explanatory. One shipper uses a complete car at a fixed rate for the car, the rate depending upon the destination.

As carload shipments are routed through from the point of origin to the destination, they are handled speedily. It is a common practice in large cities to pack less-than-car-load shipments in one car for through shipment to another city. For instance, a car of miscellaneous merchandise may be packed in Chicago for shipment directly to Cincinnati. This car will be routed through without interruption. Not all less-than-carload shipments, however, can be handled in this manner. For instance, a train leaving New York may have a car of merchandise for distribution to Buffalo, Pitts-burgh, Chicago, Cincinnati, and Indianapolis. In such a case the train stops at transfer points, where the less-than-carload shipments are unloaded from the original car and reloaded into other cars according to their final destination. Such a process delays shipment.

Some railroads arrange for so-called store-door pickup and delivery service on small freight shipments. In some cases there is no charge for this additional service, but in most instances there is an extra charge. In some localities the express company is permitted to ship some merchandise by express at freight rates. Under such circumstances the charge for the pickup and delivery service is included in the rate. The chart in Illustration No. 115 shows the de-livery service that can be expected on less-than-carload shipments from a certain point.

Freight Forwarding Companies. Several so-called freight forwarding companies have been organized specifically for the purpose of gathering together small shipments and packing them in cars, each car going to a particular destina-tion. The companies obtain the cars from the railroad at the full car rate. Essentially a less-than-carload shipment service is provided, but an attempt is made to give more prompt service than could ordinarily be obtained on freight shipments. A few of these freight forwarding companies are owned by railroads, but the others are independent.

Railway Express Agency. There formerly were several express companies in operation in the United States, but there now is only one express company. That is the Rail-way Express Agency. It is affiliated with the American Express Company; but the Railway Express Agency is

Illustration No. 115—Delivery Service on Package-Car Shipments

engaged only in the handling of shipments, whereas the American Express Company is engaged in financial and travel service.

Shipment by Water. Canal, lake, river, or coastwise shipping by boat is cheaper than railway freight, but it is much slower. This type of shipping is usually considered economical for heavy, bulky merchandise that does not need to be delivered promptly. For instance, some shippers on the East Coast send merchandise by boat through the Panama Canal to the West Coast and thus save money in comparison with railway freight rates. Bad weather may, however, delay a shipment and cause serious difficulties.

Motor Freight. Motor trucks are considered most advantageous for shipments to be sent two or three hundred miles. Within this radius the truck competes favorably with railway freight because it can pick up the merchandise at the door of the shipper and deliver it at the door of the consignee in the destination city. Trucks, in many cases, can give more prompt service than that obtained by railway freight, but sometimes traffic congestions, bad weather, and breakdowns cause this form of transportation to be undependable. Trucks are used for both packaged goods and bulk shipments. In handling bulk shipments, the truck has the disadvantage of having less capacity than the freight car. For most of the bulky, cheap freight the railroad can compete more effectively than the truck.

In some cases railroad lines have been discontinued, and trucks have been substituted. Some railroads own truck transportation companies. At least one nationwide trucking company has a plan whereby truck trailers are loaded upon railroad flatcars for transportation over long distances. At the destination the trailer is lifted from the car, and the shipment is delivered to the consignee by a truck.

Air Express. Commercial airlines and private airlines do not yet carry any great volume of express shipments. This means of transportation is too costly for most types of shipments. It does provide the greatest possible speed, although in bad weather the delivery service may be questionable.

The Air Express Division of the Railway Express Agency operates over the main transport airlines, covering the United States and reaching into Canada, South America, Hawaii, and other foreign countries. Through arrangements made with the Western Union Telegraph Company, a messenger will pick up at one's home or office a package to be sent by air express. Any Western Union office will accept a shipment. Illustration No. 116 provides examples of air express rates. The rates include insurance up to $50 for each shipment. Additional insurance may be obtained at the rate of 10 cents for each additional $100 in valuation.

EXAMPLES OF AIR EXPRESS COSTS
RATES BY AIR MILES (MINIMUM CHARGE, $1)

Air Miles	2 lbs.	3 lbs.	5 lbs.	10 lbs.	25 lbs.
200	$1.00	$1.04	$1.12	$1.32	$ 2.00
500	1.12	1.28	1.60	2.40	5.00
1,000	1.32	1.68	2.40	4.20	10.00
2,000	1.72	2.48	4.00	8.00	20.00
3,000	1.92	2.88	4.80	9.60	24.00

Illustration No. 116—Air Express Rates

Parcel Post. Parcel-post shipments get essentially the same handling as express shipments, except that they are handled by the Post Office Department. They are often hauled on the same train with express shipments. A single parcel-post package must not exceed 100 inches in length and girth combined or 70 pounds in weight. If merchandise in a large quantity is therefore to be sent by parcel post, it must be shipped in packages of the appropriate size and weight.

Costs of Railroad Freight Shipping. Railroad freight rates are determined on (a) a classification basis and (b) a commodity basis. More than 25,000 articles and commodities are divided into groups referred to as classes. All items within each class are shipped at the same rate. The classification books contain information describing articles in each class and giving special rules pertaining to packing, marking, quantity, billing, and rights and obligations of the carrier, the shipper, and the consignee.

Commodity rates are established largely on products that are shipped in great volumes, such as coal, sand, and iron ore. In general, a lower rate per 100 pounds is charged under commodity rates than under class rates. If a class rate, as well as a commodity rate, is established for a certain product to be shipped between two points, the commodity rate is used. From the point of view of tonnage most freight is shipped under commodity rates. These rates are established by setting for a particular commodity, such as coal, a flat rate per ton between the point of origin and the destination. The exact mileage is not considered. For this reason a railroad having a long haul can compete with a railroad having a short haul between the same two points. However, one route may provide faster service than another.

Illustrations Nos. 117 and 118 show two pages from a freight rate book. The first page shows the rate classifications in the various freight zones, and the other shows a table for computing the actual first-class rates between points. After determining the first-class rate on a certain item between two points, another table is used to compute the rates for other classes.

The Interstate Commerce Commission has divided the United States into three classification territories, known as the official, the southern, and the western. Each territory has a committee appointed by the railroads. These committees propose their own classifications, which must be approved by the Interstate Commerce Commission.

The minimum charge for a freight shipment is the charge for one hundred pounds. If a shipment weighs only fifty pounds, for instance, the rate is that for one hundred pounds. If a shipment weighs more than one hundred pounds, the charge is based upon the actual weight and the distance. The rates are not the same, however, for all products shipped the same distance. From an analysis it can be seen that freight rates are based upon what the traffic will bear. For instance, commodities of a high unit

CONSOLIDATED FREIGHT CLASSIFICATION

Publishing the Ratings, Rules and Regulations of the Official, Southern, Western and Illinois Classifications

Item	ARTICLES	Official/Illinois	Southern	Western
1	Furnace Coils, iron pipe bent in U shape, in boxes:			
	L. C. L.	3	3	3
	C. L., min. wt. 36,000 lbs.	5	6	5
2	Furnace Parts, Blast or Open Hearth, iron or steel:			
	L. C. L.	4	4	4
	C. L., min. wt. 36,000 lbs.	5	6	5
3	Furnace Radiators, House Heating, iron, see Note:			
	L. C. L.	3	3	3
	C. L., min. wt. 36,000 lbs.	5	6	5
4	Note—Ratings apply on so-called Radiators or Indirect Flues used on hot air furnaces to prevent loss of heat into chimney.			
5	Furnace or Kiln Lining or High Temperature Bonding Mortar or Cement, N.O.I.B.N., see Note:			
	In pails, L. C. L.	3	3	3
	In metal cans or pails in boxes or crates, L. C. L.	R26	4	4
	In cloth or double or multiple-wall paper bags, or in bulk in barrels or boxes, L. C. L.	4	4	4
	In packages named, C. L., min. wt. 40,000 lbs.	6	A or 8	C
6	Note—Ratings apply only on material of the kind used in kilns or industrial furnaces.			
7	**FURNACES:**			
8	Assayers', in barrels, boxes or crates:			
	L. C. L.	2	2	2
	C. L., min. wt. 24,000 lbs., Rule 34	45	5	A
9	Clay, pail-shaped:			
	With steel jackets, loose, L. C. L.	1	3	1
	With or without jackets, in boxes or crates, L. C. L.	2	3	2
	In boxes or crates or loose, packed in excelsior, hay, straw or similar material, C. L., min. wt. 30,000 lbs.	5	B or 7	5
10	Foundry Cupola:			
	S. U., L. C. L.	1	1	1
	K. D., or in sections, L. C. L.	4	1	1
	C. L., min. wt. 20,000 lbs., Rule 34	4	5	A
11	Metal Heating or Melting, N.O.I.B.N.:			
	Wheeled, S. U., loose, L. C. L.	2	1	1
	Not wheeled, S. U., loose or on skids, L. C. L.	3	1	1
	Wheeled or not wheeled, in boxes or crates, or K. D., in packages, loose or on skids, L. C. L.	3	2	2
	C. L., min. wt. 24,000 lbs., Rule 34.	5	5	A
12	Plant Bed:			
	S. U., with or without wheels	1½	1½	1½
	K. D., in packages	2	2	2
13	Plumbers' or Tinners' Charcoal (Tinners' Stoves), Gas or Gasoline, in barrels, boxes or crates.	1	1	1

Item	ARTICLES	Official/Illinois	Southern	Western
14	**FURNACES, HOUSE HEATING, AND HOUSE HEATING FURNACE CASTINGS, IRON:**			
15	Castings, House Heating Furnace:			
	Weighing each less than 25 lbs., loose, L. C. L.	1	1	1
	In packages, or if weighing each 25 lbs. or over, loose, L. C. L.	3	3	3
	C. L., min. wt. 36,000 lbs.	5	6	5
16	Furnaces, House Heating, Hot Air, see Note 1:			
	L. C. L.	3	3	3
	C. L., min. wt. 24,000 lbs., Rule 34	5	6	5
17	Note 1—Ratings also apply on Air Conditioning Apparatus when forming an integral part of furnaces which they accompany, not in excess of 20% of weight upon which charges are assessed, and equipment of Stove Cement or Firing Tools, consisting of Pokers, Scrapers, Slice Bars or Wire Brushes.			
18	Furnaces, House Heating, Hot Air, House Heating Furnace Castings or House Heating Furnace Casing Parts (House Heating Furnace Jacket Parts), iron or steel, and Air Registers, iron or steel, Air Duct Grating, wooden, see Note 3, Asbestos Sheathing Paper, including Felt Paper, Cement, liquid or paste in cans, Dry Flour Paste in barrels or boxes, or Heating Furnace Pipe or Elbows (Air or Smoke Flues), iron, steel or tin, or Sheet Steel, see Note 2, loose or in packages as provided for straight C. L. shipments, mixed C. L., min. wt. 24,000 lbs., Rule 34	5	6	5
19	Note 2—The weight of House Heating Furnace Castings, Air Registers, Asbestos Sheathing Paper, including Felt Paper, Cement, liquid or paste, or Dry Flour Paste and Heating Furnace Pipe or Elbows (Air or Smoke Flues), single, side seams not closed, nested, or Sheet Steel, must not exceed 33½ per cent of total weight of shipment.			
20	Note 3—The weight of Air Duct Grating, wooden, must not exceed 500 lbs. in each carload.			
21	**FURNITURE, see Notes 1 and 2:**			
22	Note 1—Furniture Packing, unless otherwise provided, must conform to the following:			
23	(a) Articles of furniture for which ratings are provided "wrapped" must be prepared for shipment as follows: All finished surfaces and upholstered parts must be protected against damage and articles must be wrapped in material indicated in individual items, i.e., burlap, fibreboard, straw matting or two or more thicknesses of paper. If wrapping material is not designated, article may be wrapped in any of the materials above named.			
24	(b) Articles of furniture for which ratings are provided "in crates" must be in crates complying with Rule 40, Section 2, and space between crate slats covering glazed or finished surfaces must be close enough to protect such finished surfaces. Crates of wire-bound construction must not exceed 108 united inches.			

(Continued)

Illustration No. 117—Rate Classifications in a Freight Rate Book

First Class Freight Rates in cents per 100 lbs.

For rates on other classes see Pink Pages, using first class rate below as index number

O—OFFICIAL CLASSIFICATION   S—SOUTHERN CLASSIFICATION

Block	FROM— TO	Albany	Atlanta	Baltimore	Boston ①	Buffalo	Chicago	Cincinnati	Cleveland	Columbus	Dayton	Detroit	Indianapolis
		O	S	O	O	O	O	O	O	O	O	O	O
844 O	Akron	109	189	102	126	76	94	82	39	64	72	70	87
944 M	Alliance	109	192	99	126	75	96	82	45	66	75	75	89
943 C	Ashland	113	182	107	128	82	89	73	51	55	64	67	79
845 A	Ashtabula	99	194	102	117	62	99	87	45	73	79	76	92
1043 M	Athens	123	174	101	139	93	96	67	72	52	64	82	82
844 O	Barberton	109	189	102	126	76	94	82	39	64	72	70	87
945 O	Bellaire	113	208	94	129	82	101	84	64	66	76	82	92
942 I	Bellefontaine	123	173	111	140	92	82	58	64	45	45	67	66
843 I	Bellevue	113	182	107	128	82	84	72	48	56	64	58	76
842 K	Bowling Green	121	185	120	136	89	79	70	62	60	62	52	73
841 K	Bryan	121	182	120	136	92	70	72	69	67	64	58	69
943 A	Bucyrus	114	180	114	130	84	84	67	54	48	58	62	73
944 O	Cambridge	117	185	99	133	87	96	73	62	53	67	82	84
944 C	Canton	109	189	99	126	76	94	79	46	62	73	73	87
941 F	Celina	130	173	123	145	99	75	60	70	58	49	67	58
1041 O	Cheviot	129	166	119	145	98	87	84	82	64	51	84	58
1043 I	Chillicothe	125	171	104	140	94	92	56	72	43	52	78	72
1041 O	Cincinnati	132	154	116	148	99	87	..	79	60	45	82	58
1043 E	Circleville	125	173	104	140	94	92	58	69	37	51	75	72
844 K	Cleveland	105	189	102	122	72	92	79	..	64	72	69	87
1042 D	Columbus	120	173	106	138	89	87	60	64	..	49	72	70
845 B	Conneaut	99	197	102	117	60	99	89	49	75	82	79	94
944 I	Coshocton	118	182	101	135	84	94	72	58	49	64	75	82
943 B	Crestline	114	180	114	130	82	84	69	52	48	58	64	75
844 P	Cuyahoga Falls	109	189	102	126	75	94	82	39	64	73	72	87
1041 D	Dayton	126	166	114	144	94	82	45	72	49	..	73	58
841 L	Defiance	121	180	120	136	92	72	70	66	64	62	58	69
942 M	Delaware	114	175	110	130	87	84	62	60	36	51	67	72
941 C	Delphos	125	178	123	140	95	73	64	67	58	54	64	66
944 L	Dennison	113	185	99	130	82	96	76	55	55	70	76	84
944 G	Dover	113	187	99	130	82	96	76	53	58	70	76	87
945 F	East Liverpool	113	208	94	129	82	101	84	58	66	76	82	92
945 B	East Palestine	105	194	94	122	70	99	87	54	70	79	78	92
843 M	Elyria	113	187	107	128	75	89	78	37	62	69	64	82
842 O	Findlay	121	180	114	136	87	78	67	60	54	58	58	70
842 P	Fostoria	114	180	114	130	84	79	70	56	54	60	55	72
842 M	Fremont	114	182	120	130	82	82	73	52	58	64	54	75
943 E	Galion	114	180	110	130	84	87	67	52	46	58	64	75
1143 D	Gallipolis	129	172	104	141	97	101	70	79	62	67	89	84
845 O	Girard	105	194	94	122	70	99	87	48	70	79	78	92
1042 L	Greenfield	123	169	111	140	96	89	36	73	45	48	79	69
941 O	Greenville	129	171	119	145	98	76	54	73	55	58	73	55
1041 K	Hamilton	132	164	116	148	99	82	37	76	58	39	79	56
1143 F	Ironton	131	157	107	146	99	99	64	84	56	62	89	82
1043 O	Jackson	125	172	104	140	94	96	64	78	54	60	84	78
844 P	Kent	109	189	102	126	75	94	82	39	66	73	72	87
942 F	Kenton	121	175	114	136	89	79	64	62	46	52	62	69
844 F	Lakewood (Cleveland)	105	189	102	122	72	92	79	..	64	72	69	87
1043 F	Lancaster	120	175	106	138	92	92	62	69	39	55	78	75
941 H	Lima	121	175	114	136	92	75	62	66	54	51	62	64
1041 O	Lockland	132	154	116	148	99	87	..	79	60	45	82	58
1043 G	Logan	123	176	101	139	93	94	66	72	43	60	78	78
1042 C	London	123	171	111	140	94	87	55	69	37	42	75	67
843 M	Lorain	113	187	107	128	75	89	78	37	62	70	64	82
1041 O	Madisonville	132	154	116	148	99	87	..	79	60	45	82	58
943 B	Mansfield	113	180	107	128	82	87	70	52	51	60	66	76
1044 L	Marietta	117	181	99	133	94	101	75	72	62	72	87	87
942 H	Marion	114	178	110	130	87	82	64	58	43	53	64	72
945 O	Martins Ferry	113	208	94	129	82	101	84	64	66	76	82	92
944 B	Massillon	109	187	99	126	78	94	78	48	60	72	72	87
1041 G	Miamisburg	132	166	116	148	99	82	45	73	53	34	76	60
1041 G	Middletown	132	164	116	148	99	84	39	75	54	36	76	60
943 L	Mt. Vernon	113	178	107	128	87	89	67	60	42	60	70	78
841 M	Napoleon	121	182	120	136	92	73	70	66	62	60	55	70
1043 M	Nelsonville	123	176	101	139	93	94	67	73	48	62	82	79
943 P	Newark	118	180	103	137	89	92	66	64	39	58	73	76
1143 E	New Boston	131	157	107	146	99	99	58	84	56	62	89	82
944 L	New Philadelphia	113	187	99	130	82	96	76	53	58	70	75	87
845 N	Niles	105	194	94	122	70	99	87	46	70	79	78	92
845 O	Norwalk	113	185	107	128	70	94	75	46	58	66	60	78
1041 O	Norwood	132	154	116	148	99	87	..	79	60	45	82	58
843 M	Oberlin	113	187	107	128	78	89	78	42	62	69	64	82
94 A	Orrville	113	187	107	128	79	92	78	46	58	70	70	84
844 G	Painesville	102	192	102	121	67	96	84	37	69	76	73	89
1043 A	Pickerington	120	180	106	138	92	89	64	67	34	54	73	73
941 Q	Piqua	125	171	114	140	94	79	53	70	51	37	70	60
1043 Q	Pomeroy	129	178	104	141	97	101	70	79	62	67	89	84
1143 E	Portsmouth	131	157	107	146	99	99	58	84	56	62	89	82
844 Q	Ravenna	109	192	102	126	73	94	82	40	66	75	73	89
1041 O	Reading	132	164	116	148	99	87	..	79	60	45	82	58
1041 O	St. Bernard	132	154	116	148	99	87	..	79	60	45	82	58
941 G	St. Marys	130	173	123	145	99	78	62	69	55	49	66	60

Illustration No. 118—Table for Computing First-Class Rates

value, such as silk, have higher rates than commodities of a low unit value, such as coal.

The preceding discussion indicates that a shipper should be acquainted not only with the proper classification rate or commodity rate under which he may ship his product, but also with any other conditions that affect the rate. For instance, furniture and some large toys are usually shipped unassembled because they can then be sent at a lower rate than they could be if they were assembled.

Comparison of Methods of Shipping. When one is deciding upon a method of shipment, he must consider (a) speed, (b) carefulness in handling, (c) convenience in pickup and delivery, (d) packing requirements, and (e) insurance. Insurance may be obtained on all forms of shipments. It is included in the rates on some shipments but must be carried separately on others.

A person can usually decide readily whether he prefers to send a shipment by freight, express, parcel post, or some other method; but, without having available some definite figures, he cannot easily make a decision based upon cost. The costs of the various methods must be compared to determine the most economical method. The table in Illustration No. 119 shows a comparison of the costs of shipping one commodity, ruled paper, between two points. The costs are shown for freight, express, and parcel post. Three different shipments are used as examples. In the first case freight is the cheapest method; in the second, parcel post; and in the third, express. This table emphasizes the importance of comparing costs along with service.

In the case of the first shipment of 150 pounds, it is assumed that the ruled paper will be packed in cartons. As the shipment is going into the southern classification zone, it will be sent as third-class freight with a maximum weight per carton of 65 pounds. Larger cartons could be used provided they passed the Mullen test (a test of the strength of the carton). It is assumed that the shipment will be packed in three cartons of 60 pounds, 40 pounds, and 50 pounds, respectively. If a wooden crate were to be used

Item	Value	Weight	Destination from Cincinnati	Freight [1]		Express [2]		Parcel Post [3] (Fourth-Class Mail)		
				Rate	Amount	Rate	Amount	Rate	Amount	Insurance
Ruled Paper	$100	150 lbs.	Spartansburg, South Carolina	$1.19 a 100 lbs. Third Class	$1.79	$3.25 a 100 lbs.	$4.88	4th zone	$5.46	$ .25
Ruled Paper	$ 20	25 lbs.	Hancock, Michigan	$1.26 a 100 lbs. Third Class	$1.26	Less than 100-lb. rate	$1.22	4th zone	$ .94	$ .10
Ruled Paper	$ 35	35 lbs.	Ocala, Florida	$1.72 a 100 lbs. Third Class	$1.72	Less than 100-lb. rate	$1.70	5th zone	$1.92	$ .15

[1] Insurance is included in the rate.

[2] Insurance on a valuation up to $50 is included in the rate; a charge of 10 cents is added for each additional $100 in valuation or fraction thereof.

[3] The shipper may carry his own insurance or assume the risk alone.

Illustration No. 119—Comparison of Shipping Costs

as the container, all the paper could be packed in one crate.

In the second example, if the shipment were made by freight, it would go into the official classification zone as third-class freight.

If the 150-pound shipment were to be made by parcel post, each carton would be limited to 70 pounds in weight. The paper would therefore be packed in three cartons of 60 pounds, 40 pounds, and 50 pounds, respectively.

The freight charge for a shipment between two points is based upon a certain rate per hundred pounds given in the freight rate book for shipments between those points. If an express shipment weighs more than 100 pounds, the charge is based upon the 100-pound rate. If an express shipment weighs less than 100 pounds, a special table of rates is used in computing the charge according to the actual weight. In the case of parcel post the rate is determined by the parcel-post zone and by the weight of each package. The total postage of the parcel-post shipment in the first example of Illustration No. 119 was computed as follows:

		POSTAGE
First carton, 60 pounds	....	$2.17
Second carton, 40 pounds	....	1.47
Third carton, 50 pounds	....	1.82
Total	....	$5.46

Insurance is included in freight and express rates. In the case of express, however, the amount of insurance is only $50. When an express shipment exceeds $50 in valuation, there is an extra charge of 10 cents for each additional $100 in valuation or fraction thereof. The Government makes a separate charge for the insurance of parcel-post shipments. If the shipper wishes, he may assume his own risk or may insure his shipment through a private agency.

Forms Used in Freight Shipments. The bill of lading is probably one of the most commonly used forms in shipping. It represents a contract between the shipper and the railroad company. There are two forms, the *straight bill of lading* and the *order bill of lading,* or negotiable bill of lading. Examples of these are shown in Illustrations Nos. 120 and 121.

The straight bill of lading is sent by the shipper to the consignee (the one who receives the merchandise). Upon presenting the bill of lading and signing for the merchandise, the consignee can obtain his shipment. The order, or negotiable, bill of lading requires the railroad to withhold the shipment until the original bill of lading has been endorsed to show that payment has been received for the merchandise. A draft usually accompanies an order bill of lading. If it is a sight draft, the merchandise is released when the draft is paid. If it is a time draft, the merchandise is released when the draft is accepted (or signed), for the acceptance (or signing) converts the draft essentially into a note that will become payable on an agreed date.

Freight charges may be prepaid by the shipper or collected from the consignee. If they are prepaid, the receipted *freight bill* is often attached to the bill of lading. The freight bill (page 318) is merely an itemized statement of the railroad covering the charges for handling the shipment.

The *waybill* is a routing card or sheet of instructions accompanying the shipment. It is made out by the consignor (the shipper).

The *notice of arrival* is sent to the consignee by the railroad when the shipment has reached its destination.

When a carload shipment arrives at its destination, the consignee is given a certain amount of time to unload the shipment and to release the car. After the lapse of this specified time, a charge known as *demurrage* is assessed against the shipment. The consignee cannot obtain the shipment until he has paid the demurrage charge in addition to all other charges.

Numerous other forms are used in shipping by express, parcel post, truck, or boat. These forms serve essentially the same purposes as those used in shipping by railway freight.

C.O.D. Shipments. C.O.D. shipments may be sent by any form of transportation. When a shipment is sent C.O.D.,

Illustration No. 120—A Straight Bill of Lading

(Uniform Domestic Order Bill of Lading Adopted by Carriers in Official, Southern and Western Classification Territories, March 15, 1922, as amended August 1, 1930.)

UNIFORM ORDER BILL OF LADING—ORIGINAL.

Shipper's No. _____

THE PENNSYLVANIA RAILROAD Company   Agent's No. _____

From   Frank's Electric Company

RECEIVED, subject to the classifications and tariffs in effect on the date of the issue of this Bill of Lading.

at Philadelphia, Pa., December 18, 1939

The property described below in apparent good order, except as noted (contents and condition of contents of packages unknown), marked, consigned, and destined as indicated below, which said company (the word company being understood throughout this contract, as meaning any person or corporation in possession of the property under the contract) agrees to carry to its usual place of delivery at said destination, if on its own road or its own water line, otherwise to deliver to another carrier on the route to said destination. It is mutually agreed, as to each carrier of all or any of said property over all or any portion of said route to destination, and as to each party at any time interested in all or any of said property, that every service to be performed hereunder shall be subject to all the conditions not prohibited by law, whether printed or written, herein contained, including the conditions on back hereof, which are hereby agreed to by the shipper and accepted for himself and his assigns.

The surrender of this Original ORDER BILL of Lading properly indorsed shall be required before the delivery of the property. Inspection of property covered by this bill of lading will not be permitted unless provided by law or unless permission is indorsed on this original bill of lading or given in writing by the shipper.

Consigned to ORDER OF   Frank's Electric Company

Destination   Marietta   State of   Ohio   County of Washington

Notify   American Hardware Company, 15 West Ninth Street

At   Marietta   State of   Ohio   County of Washington

Route   Pennsylvania Freight

Delivering Carrier   Car Initial   Car No. _____

No. Packages	Description of Articles, Special Marks and Exceptions	*WEIGHT (Subject to Correction)	Class or Rate	Check Column	
3	cases Electrical Appliances	1200 lbs.			Subject to Section 7 of conditions, if this shipment is to be delivered to the consignee without recourse on the consignor, the consignor shall sign the following statement: The carrier shall not make delivery of this shipment without payment of freight and all other lawful charges.
					_____ (Signature of Consignor)
					If charges are to be prepaid, write or stamp here, "To be Prepaid."
					Received $ _____ to apply in prepayment of the charges on the property described hereon.
					_____ Agent or Cashier
					Per _____ (The signature here acknowledges only the amount prepaid.)
					Charges Advanced: $

*If the shipment moves between two ports by a carrier by water, the law requires that the bill of lading shall state whether it is "carrier's or shipper's weight."   Note—Where the rate is dependent on value, shippers are required to state specifically in writing the agreed or declared value of the property.   The agreed or declared value of the property is hereby specifically stated by the shipper to be not exceeding _____ per _____

Frank's Electric Company   Shipper,   Per _____

Per   Jack Smith, clerk

Permanent post-office address of shipper 18 North Avenue, Philadelphia, Pa.

_____ Agent,

Illustration No. 121—An Order Bill of Lading

Printed in U.S.A.

(NEW YORK CENTRAL SYSTEM)

NYCS
AR 40-8

THE NEW YORK CENTRAL RAILROAD COMPANY
(EASTERN DISTRICT) (WESTERN DISTRICT) (WESTSHORE DISTRICT) (BOSTON & ALBANY DISTRICT)
(MICHIGAN CENTRAL DISTRICT) (CHICAGO, KALAMAZOO & SAGINAW DISTRICT)
(CLEVELAND, CINCINNATI, CHICAGO & ST. LOUIS DISTRICT)

Dr.

For Charges on Articles Transported:

To

CONSIGNEE....Kramer Shoe Company....

DATE...Dec. 4, 1939....PRO. NO........... CINCINNATI, OHIO, STATION

DESTINATION...16 Findlay St., Gallup, New Mexico....ROUTE...Big Four & Santa Fe

Way-Billed From	Way-Bill Date and No.	Full Name of Shipper (POINT OF ORIGIN TO DESTINATION)	Car Initials and No.
Cincinnati, Ohio	12-1-39 T86392	American Shoe Company, Inc.	NYC 49627
Point and Date of Shipment	Connecting Line Reference	Previous Way-Bill References	Original Car Initials and No.
Cin'ti, 12-1-39			N 306

NUMBER OF PACKAGES, ARTICLES AND MARKS	WEIGHT	RATE	FREIGHT	ADVANCES	PREPAID	TO COLLECT
3 cases Shoes	225 lbs.	2.89			Prepaid	
1 carton Rubbers	50 lbs.		7.95			
					TOTAL	

RECEIVED PAYMENT................

December 4, 19 39

H. J. Warren
AGENT

LOCATION

STORAGE RECORD	
Notice Mailed	........19....
Free Storage Time Expires	........19....

DOOR

FREIGHT BILL

MAKE CHECKS PAYABLE TO THE ORDER OF THE RAILROAD
Original paid freight bills must accompany claims for
overcharge, loss or damage.
All freight will be subject to demurrage or storage
charges or both, as provided in published tariffs.

Illustration No. 122—A Freight Bill for a Prepaid Shipment

the consignee, or receiver, must pay the cost of the merchandise upon delivery to him. In the case of express and parcel-post shipments, an extra fee is charged for this service. The express agent or the postman collects the amount due the shipper, as well as the transportation charges and the C.O.D. fee.

If a freight shipment is sent C.O.D., a sight draft may be attached to a copy of the order bill of lading. This draft, with the bill of lading, is then sent to a bank. The bank presents the sight draft to the consignee for payment. After the consignee has made payment, the railroad company is authorized to release the shipment. In recent years, however, a new method of sending freight shipments C.O.D. has been developed. Under this method the railroad company charges a C.O.D. fee for collecting the amount of the shipment. Collection is made in cash unless some other form of payment is specified on the bill of lading. The letters *C.O.D.* must be marked on each package. The shipment must be sent on a uniform straight bill of lading accompanied by the invoice. All documents must be stamped in a manner similar to the following:

C.O.D. SHIPMENT (SENT FREIGHT COLLECT)

C.O.D. Amount $250.00
Collection Fee .... $ 1.10
Total Charges $251.10

A shipment by automobile truck may be merely billed as C.O.D. and a copy of the invoice given to the driver. The driver collects for the C.O.D. shipment and makes payment to his company, which in turn reimburses the consignor.

Collect and Prepaid Shipments. All forms of freight and express shipments may be sent with the transportation charges collect or prepaid. If a shipment is sent collect, the transportation company collects the transportation charges from the consignee on delivery to him. The transportation charges on a prepaid shipment are paid by the consignor. In order to send a parcel-post shipment collect, it is necessary to send it C.O.D. for the amount of the transportation charges.

Tracing Shipments. If a shipment becomes lost or delayed and a customer complains, everything possible should be done to find the shipment and to assure its delivery. If a lost shipment was sent by insured parcel post, the Post Office Department is responsible. The Department will conduct an investigation and, if the shipment is not found, will make payment for the loss. Even if the shipment was not insured, the Post Office Department will do its best to find the shipment. Under all other forms of shipping it is possible to ask the transportation company to start a tracing procedure. When such a request is made, it is important to present the transportation company with complete information about the original shipment. The customer should be notified that the shipment is being traced. In many cases a new shipment should be sent to replace the original one.

Auditing Freight Bills. Any company handling many shipments should know enough about freight classifications and freight services to be able to check freight bills carefully. As items are quite often sent under the wrong classification, shippers may be paying higher rates than are necessary. For instance, there may be two freight rates on beds. One rate may be for a bed set up; the other, for a bed knocked down. Assume that a manufacturer has been shipping beds knocked down and has been paying the higher rate that is charged for shipping beds set up. If such an error is detected, the shipper can claim a deduction upon furnishing satisfactory proof. Furthermore, there are chances of errors in figuring the amounts of freight bills. For that reason such bills should be checked carefully. There are some companies that specialize in checking the freight bills of various shippers. A flat service charge is made, or a fee is collected on the basis of the adjustments that are made.

Claims. Claims other than those based upon rates arise from the fact that shipments may not be delivered or may be totally or partially destroyed. Such a claim should be presented by the party who possesses the title of ownership. The passing of the title is explained in Chapter XXIII. When a claim is presented, the freight bill, the bill of lading, and the invoice should be presented. A photostatic copy may be used if the original bill of lading cannot be presented. An affidavit of nondelivery should be attached to these papers. The affidavit should be made by the consignee, regardless of whether the consignee or the consignor is filing the claim. When a claim for partial loss is submitted, the affidavit should specifically state the extent of the loss.

When any loss is claimed because of damage, it is important that a representative of the transportation company examine the merchandise to help substantiate the claim.

Common Carriers. A *common carrier* is a company or a person that undertakes to transfer, for some form of compensation, goods for anyone who may desire to use the facilities. In other words, the business of a common carrier involves remuneration and the indiscriminate transportation of goods for all who apply. For instance, a railroad is a common carrier. Such a carrier is often called a *public carrier*. Its rates are fixed by the Interstate Commerce Commission.

Private Carriers. A *private carrier* is a company or a person that transfers goods for others under the terms of individual or special agreements. In other words, a private carrier may carry goods for some persons and refuse to serve others. An example of a private carrier is a local trucking company that establishes its own rates and hauls material from time to time or under contract for anyone whom it chooses to serve.

Duties of Carriers. No legal relationship is established between a carrier and a shipper until the goods have actually been delivered into the possession of the carrier. The goods must be delivered at the time and the place stipulated. The bill of lading signed by an agent of the carrier

150m 10-37 ⓐ 52094
Printed in U. S. A.

NYCS
FCA-146

NEW YORK CENTRAL SYSTEM
Standard Form for Presentation of Loss and Damage Claims

APPROVED BY THE INTERSTATE COMMERCE COMMISSION; FREIGHT CLAIM DIVISION, ASSOCIATION OF
AMERICAN RAILROADS; NATIONAL INDUSTRIAL TRAFFIC LEAGUE, AND THE NATIONAL
ASSOCIATION OF RAILWAY COMMISSIONERS.

Alex T. Brown	November 20, 1939	
(Name of person to whom claim is presented)	(Date)	(Claimant's Number)
New York Central System	121 Vine Street	57321-46
(Name of carrier)	(Street Address of claimant)	(Carrier's Number)
New York, New York	Cincinnati, Ohio	
(Address)	(City and State)	

This claim for $ 55.00 is made against the carrier named above by Smith's Luggage Company
(Amount of claim)   (Name of claimant)
for damage in connection with the following described shipments:
(Loss or damage)

Description of shipment 5 cartons Leather Goods and 1 case Leather Goods

Name and address of consignor (shipper) Johnson's Leather Goods Co., 623 East 51st Street

Shipped from New York City , To Cincinnati, Ohio
(City, town or station)   (City, town or station)

Final Destination Cincinnati, Ohio Routed via New York Central System
(City, town or station)

Bill of Lading issued by Co.; Date of Bill of Lading September 5, 1939

Paid Freight Bill (Pro) Number PD 8431 ; Original Car Number and Initial NYC 23762

Name and address of consignee (Whom shipped to) Smith's Luggage Co., 121 Vine St., Cincinnati

If shipment reconsigned enroute, state particulars:

DETAILED STATEMENT SHOWING HOW AMOUNT CLAIMED IS DETERMINED.
(Number and description of articles, nature and extent of loss or damage, invoice price of articles, amount of claim, etc.)

5 Purses	$6.00 each	$30.00
1 Overnight Case		25.00
	Total Amount Claimed	$55.00

IN ADDITION TO THE INFORMATION GIVEN ABOVE, THE FOLLOWING DOCUMENTS
ARE SUBMITTED IN SUPPORT OF THIS CLAIM.*

(   ) 1. Original bill of lading, if not previously surrendered to carrier.
(   ) 2. Original paid freight ("expense") bill.
(   ) 3. Original invoice or certified copy.
       4. Other particulars obtainable in proof of loss or damage claimed:

Remarks

The foregoing statement of facts is hereby certified to as correct.

J. L. Smith
(Signature of claimant)

‡Claimant should assign to each claim a number, inserting same in the space provided at the upper right-hand corner of this form. Reference should
be made thereto in all correspondence pertaining to this claims
   * Claimant will please place check (x) before such of the documents mentioned as have been attached, and explain under " Remarks " the absence of any
of the documents called for in connection with this claim. When for any reason it is impossible for claimant to produce original bill of lading, if required,
or paid freight bill, claimant should indemnify carrier or carriers against duplicate claim supported by original documents.

Illustration No. 123—Form for Freight Claim

is considered to be the acknowledgment on the part of the carrier of the acceptance of the goods.

A common carrier has the responsibility of shipping goods carefully to the proper persons and of serving everyone alike. The carrier, however, may make rules and regulations for handling goods and has a right to demand reasonable compensation. The carrier is responsible for all damages and losses except those resulting from the intervention of public authority, the fault of the shipper, the interference of a public enemy, riots and strikes, or the nature of the goods. The carrier may also escape responsibility sometimes if damage or loss was caused by an act of God. In other words, if the carrier has done all within its power to protect the shipment; but, because of some unforeseen calamity the goods are damaged, it will probably not be held responsible.

The responsibilities of the carrier and the shipper are printed on the reverse side of the bill of lading. This printing is too small to be read easily; but, as the information represents the terms of a contract between the carrier and the shipper, the shipper should be familiar with it.

The liabilities of a private carrier are somewhat different from those of a common carrier. In all cases the private carrier must assume responsibility for due care and caution in handling the shipment, but it is allowed to make discriminations with regard to its methods of handling. It may enter into any special agreements with shippers.

Public Warehouses. Many businessmen find it advisable to use the services of public warehouses. When merchandise is entrusted to a public warehouse, the owner of the warehouse has responsibilities that are similar to those of a carrier. In other words, he must keep the property safe and deliver it to the proper person at the proper time. He is allowed to set his own regulations and to establish rates.

The public warehouse often provides storage, transportation, and credit facilities. The storage service may include rental, handling of goods, insurance, clerical help, accounting help, repacking, and marking. The transportation service may involve receiving, shipping, and trucking. The credit service may include the handling of all financial transactions involved. For instance, a public warehouse receives merchandise sent on consignment to a business-man. The warehouse releases the merchandise to the consignee in small lots. As the goods are sold, the consignee pays the warehouse, and the latter in turn makes payment to the original shipper. The warehouse in such a case handles all the financial transactions. Freight shipments are often sent to warehouses with a negotiable bill of lading

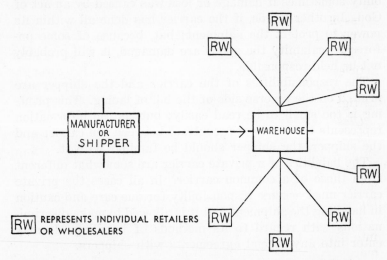

Illustration No. 124—How Public Warehouses Help Distribution

and a draft. When the consignee pays the draft or accepts it, the warehouse is permitted to release the merchandise to the consignee.

Private Storage. Many businessmen find it convenient to use separate storage space so that they need not enlarge their buildings or rent more space in the buildings in which they conduct their businesses. Space can often be obtained in other buildings or in private warehouses. In such a case it may be necessary to arrange for insurance, fire protection, and other services that are normally provided by the public warehouse.

Packing and Shipping. A great deal of damage and loss are caused each year because of the improper packing, labeling, and shipping of goods. Scientific information on packing and shipping can be obtained from such sources as the United States Department of Commerce, the United States Chamber of Commerce, local chambers of commerce, trade publications, and books on the subject.

The following are a few suggestions offered by the United States Department of Commerce with regard to certain types of paper-wrapped packages prepared largely for parcel-post and express shipments:

Curtain rods, umbrellas, canes, golf sticks, and similar articles of a breakable nature must be reinforced throughout their full length with strong strips of wood. They must be tightly wrapped in strong paper and tied.

Glass, crockery, enamelware, fragile toys, musical instruments, and other easily broken merchandise should not be shipped in paper-wrapped packages, but should be carefully cushioned with corrugated strawboard, excelsior, or similar material, and packed in strong wooden, fiber, or double-faced corrugated boxes or other suitable outside containers.

Fabric merchandise (such as dry goods) should be made into a solid package and then wrapped tightly in two or more thicknesses of strong paper.

Wearing apparel (men's or boys' suits, ladies' blouses, dresses, and the like) should be packed in strong boxes. If there is any doubt as to the strength of the box, additional protection should be given by wrapping the box in strong paper.

Sharp-pointed or sharp-edged instruments or tools must have their points or edges protected thoroughly. The whole tool or instrument must be wrapped or suitably crated so that it cannot break through its covering.

Careful attention should be given to the selection of wrapping paper and twine. There are many kinds of paper and twine, several of which are good, but some of which will not stand up satisfactorily under shipping conditions. Some paper, for instance, may tear or crack readily. When it becomes damp, it may pull apart easily. Some kinds of twine made from paper pulp or other materials become weak and break when they are moistened. Therefore, both paper and twine should be tested in a moist as well as in a dry condition.

Illustration No. 125—An Efficiently Arranged Shipping Department

Careful attention should be given to the marking of packages. The following are some simple rules that should be observed:

1. Eliminate all previous marks.
2. Use a stencil, dark crayon, brush, or rubber stamp, or attach a typed or printed label.
3. Packages containing fragile articles should be marked "Handle with care" or "Fragile."
4. Perishable articles should be marked "Perishable."
5. The name of the shipper should be indicated by the word *from* before it; that of the consignee, by the word *to*.
6. Special instructions should be followed on freight and express shipments. These are provided on the forms available for such shipments.

Selecting Packages. In order to select the most satisfactory manner of packaging, information on the best available methods should be collected. Furthermore, as was brought out in a preceding example, it is important to know whether, for instance, a shipment can be sent by freight in one large crate or whether it must be sent in several smaller cartons.

There are numerous types of cartons and boxes appropriate for specific uses. Some of the manufacturers of such containers offer a technical service in selecting the proper kind of carton or box. For instance, assume that it is necessary to pack two dozen packages of a product in the form of powder. The contents of the packages are soft and may be damaged easily. The packages themselves may be punctured easily and thus spill their contents. It is therefore desirable to have an outer container with a high resistance to puncture and crushing. Avoiding excess weight is also important. Good specifications in such a case are:

1. Resistance to puncture—250 pounds a square inch (Mullen or Cady test)
2. Resistance to crushing—top load 900 pounds, side and end load 500 pounds each
3. Weight—not to exceed 1,500 pounds a thousand cases

On the other hand, suppose one is shipping canned goods, such as fruits or vegetables. The resistance of the outer container to puncture and crushing is somewhat negligible. Nevertheless the box must carry the heavy weight of the contents. In such a case the following specifications are recommended:

1. Durability of box—40 falls in a standard drum
2. Thickness of box wall—not over one-eighth inch
3. Weight—not to exceed 1,200 pounds a thousand cases
4. Resistance to puncture—220 pounds
5. Resistance to crushing—top 300 pounds, end 500 pounds, side 500 pounds

These examples are merely cited to emphasize the fact that the proper handling of shipments should be based upon a scientific study of the requirements. If a customer regularly receives damaged goods, he will eventually try to find some more satisfactory source of supply. Improper packaging may therefore spoil all sales efforts.

Manufacturers of cartons and boxes used for shipping purposes can furnish considerable information in regard to the most suitable types of cartons and boxes for particular products. In many cases standard specifications have been set up for different kinds of products. Furthermore, if one has an unusual shipping problem, such as shipping to a foreign country, he should consult the United States Department of Foreign and Domestic Commerce in regard to methods of packing and shipping.

QUESTIONS FOR DISCUSSION

1. What is an L.C.L. shipment?
2. What is a freight forwarding company?
3. What is the advantage of using the services of a freight forwarding company?
4. What are the limits on the size and the weight of parcel-post shipments?
5. Is the rate on a commodity such as coal determined on the basis of actual mileage?
6. Why is it sometimes advisable to send furniture or other similar items unassembled rather than assembled?
7. In what way is it possible to determine the lowest rate on any particular shipment to be sent between two points?
8. What are the essential points of difference between a straight bill of lading and an order bill of lading?
9. What is a freight bill?
10. What is a waybill?
11. What are two ways of sending railroad freight shipments C.O.D.?
12. When a claim is made for a lost freight shipment, what information should be presented?
13. What is the primary distinction between a private carrier and a common carrier?
14. Who is responsible for goods stored in a public warehouse?
15. What are some general suggestions on selecting packages for shipping merchandise?

PROBLEMS AND PROJECTS

1. Select some point at a distance of fifty miles or more from your community, and determine (a) the railroad freight rate on some particular item, (b) the automobile truck rate, (c) the express rate. Take into consideration the cost of delivering the item to the transportation agency, the cost of delivering it to the door of the consignee, and any extra charge for insurance. Draw your conclusions as to the cheapest and most satisfactory method.

2. Consider the following facts and draw your conclusions with regard to the shipping of 125 pounds of merchandise between two points, A and B: The freight rate is $1.25 a hundred pounds. Insurance is included in the rate. The express charge is $3.41 a hundred pounds. From the information in the textbook, compute the cost of the express insurance. The value of the shipment is $90. As the weight limit on parcel-post shipments is 70 pounds, the shipment must be divided into two packages. Assume therefore that the 125-pound shipment is broken up into two packages of 70 pounds and 55 pounds. The parcel-post charge for the 70-pound package is $2.52, and for the 55-pound package $1.99. The cost of parcel-post insurance on $90 is 25 cents. Determine the cheapest method, including insurance.

3. The following table shows the information in a section of the parcel-post zone and rate book:

Pounds	Local	Zones 1 and 2	Zone 3	Zone 4	Zone 5	Zone 6	Zone 7	Zone 8
46	$0.30	$0.58	$0.99	$1.68	$2.50	$3.27	$4.19	$5.10
47	.30	.59	1.01	1.71	2.55	3.34	4.28	5.21
48	.31	.60	1.03	1.75	2.61	3.41	4.37	5.32
49	.31	.61	1.05	1.78	2.66	3.48	4.46	5.43
50	.32	.62	1.07	1.82	2.71	3.55	4.55	5.54

Compute the cost of sending a shipment from your home to a destination in Zone 5. Assume that the shipment comes within the size limit and that it weighs 50 pounds. The value is $50. Insurance on parcel-post shipments is computed from the following information:

INSURANCE FEES

Up to and including $ 5.00 .... 5 cents
   "   "   "   "   25.00 .... 10 cents
   "   "   "   "   50.00 .... 15 cents
   "   "   "   "   100.00 .... 25 cents
   "   "   "   "   150.00 .... 30 cents
   "   "   "   "   200.00 .... 35 cents

What is the total cost of sending the package, including insurance?

4. The following table shows the information in a section of a freight rate book:

First Class	Second Class	Third Class	R25	R26	Fourth Class	Fifth Class	Sixth Class
$1.80	$1.53	$1.26	$1.26	$0.99	$0.90	$0.63	$0.50
1.82	1.55	1.27	1.27	1.00	.91	.64	.50
1.83	1.56	1.28	1.28	1.01	.92	.64	.50
1.84	1.56	1.29	1.29	1.01	.92	.64	.51
1.85	1.57	1.30	1.30	1.02	.93	.65	.51

Compute the cost of sending a freight shipment C.O.D., transportation charges prepaid, from Cincinnati, Ohio, to Topeka, Kansas. Assume that the package weighs 376 pounds and has a value of $425. The material to be shipped carries a third-class freight rate. If the first-class freight rate is $1.83 a hundred pounds, determine from the preceding table the third-class rate. The following is a section of a table for computing the charges that must be made for collecting and remitting the proceeds from freight C.O.D.'s:

AMOUNT COLLECTED	FEE
Over $300, not over $350	$1.30
" 350 " " 400	1.45
" 400 " " 450	1.60
" 450 " " 500	1.75

What is the total cost that the customer has to pay in order to obtain the shipment from the railroad?

5. Obtain the freight rate table of a railway and also the rate table of some other agency such as a trucking company or an express company. Compare the rates on some particular item to be shipped from your community to several other communities at successive distances of approximately 100 miles, 200 miles, 500 miles, and 1,000 miles. Draw some conclusions as to how the rates compare as the distance grows larger.

6. Make a study of the local transportation services available in your community. List the various types of transportation available, and point out their advantages and disadvantages with regard to (a) frequency of service, (b) points served, (c) dependability, and (d) any other factors.

7. Write a theme on (a) the advantages of railway freight shipments over automobile truck shipments or (b) the advantages of automobile truck shipments over railway freight shipments.

CHAPTER XIV

CREDIT AND COLLECTION PROBLEMS

Purpose of the Chapter. The purpose of this chapter is to point out various types of credit and to explain their uses, advantages, disadvantages, and abuses. Suggested policies and procedures are provided for establishing credit and making collections. The following are some of the important questions that will be answered:

1. What types of credit are there?
2. What factors determine the credit standing of a person or a business?
3. Where can credit information be obtained?
4. What is a good credit policy?
5. What is an example of a good collection sequence?
6. How does a statute of limitations affect collection procedure?

Section I

Credit Policies and Procedures

Wholesale Credit. The very nature of the transactions between wholesalers and retailers makes the need for some kind of credit imperative. Requiring retailers to make their purchases in cash would be very inconvenient. Wholesalers therefore usually *sell on account* to retailers who have proved worthy of the extension of credit. The retailer buys merchandise, sometimes in a limited amount, and is expected to pay according to the terms of the sale. The granting of credit by the wholesaler permits the retailer to purchase goods and to sell at least part of them before he is required to make payment.

Retail Credit. Retail credit is ordinarily credit that is extended by the retailer to the consumer, whereas wholesale credit arises in transactions between the wholesaler and the retailer. The average person is more interested in retail credit than in wholesale credit.

Retail credit may be classified roughly as (a) *short-term credit* and (b) *long-term credit.* Short-term credit is credit extended on account. When the customer of a retailer buys merchandise, the sale is charged to his account. At the end of each month he is expected to pay for the purchases made during the month. A retailer usually submits a monthly statement to each customer. In most communities the practice is to require the customer to pay his account by the tenth of the month following that in which the purchases were made. Some stores, particularly food stores, expect customers to pay their accounts weekly. A discount is seldom allowed on retail purchases.

Long-term credit may be extended on account or through an installment plan. In the latter case the customer is required to enter into a formal contract. Such a contract is explained later in this chapter. The principal difference between short-term credit and long-term credit is that in the latter case the customer is given a longer time to pay. He is sometimes required to pay an extra amount for this privilege, and he is often required to make regular small payments on the amount he owes.

Some businessmen require their customers to make a deposit of cash. This cash is credited to the customer's account. As the customer makes purchases, the amount of each purchase is deducted from the cash balance until the amount of cash on deposit has been consumed.

In department stores, furniture stores, and other similar stores, regular customers who have charge accounts may be allowed to purchase some major items on sixty or ninety days' credit without having to pay any additional charge. For instance, a store may permit a customer who has a good credit record to buy furniture amounting to $200 and allow him sixty to ninety days to pay for it without having to pay any extra charge or to sign any installment contract.

The table in Illustration No. 126 shows the results of a study made to determine the average length of time in

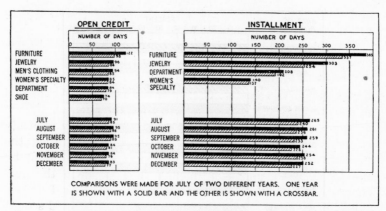

*Illustration No. 126—Average Length of Time in Which
Consumer Accounts Are Paid*

which consumer accounts are paid. This study covered a
period of two years. The solid line represents one year,
and the broken line represents the second year.

Illustration No. 127 is a chart showing the proportions
of cash and credit sales of all retail stores that reported
to the United States Department of Foreign and Domestic
Commerce during a particular year. It will be seen, for
instance, that most furniture is sold on the installment
plan. Less than 10 per cent is sold for cash.

Determining Credit Standing. A commonly recognized
formula for determining the credit of a person or a business is the "three C's"—character, capacity, and capital.

Character is the first consideration. Most people are
honest. Their failure to pay their debts is usually due to
mismanagement of their business affairs. Many businessmen feel that an individual's character is more important
than his capital resources. Character represents a sense of
moral responsibility toward a financial obligation and the
determination to pay according to the agreement. Wealth
alone cannot determine one's credit, nor, of course, can one
get unlimited credit on his character alone. One must have
a capacity to pay; but because of the importance of character, one's reputation must be guarded carefully.

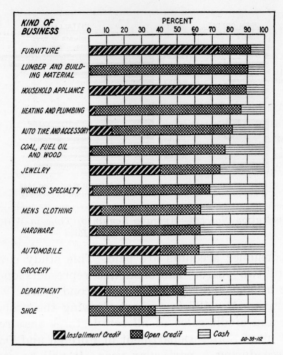

Illustration No. 127—Proportions of Cash and Credit Sales

Capacity is merely another term for earning power. It represents one's ability to earn money and to pay obligations when they become due. An individual may have an honorable character and perfectly good intentions of paying an obligation; but unless he has the ability or capacity to pay, he cannot pay satisfactorily. It is often more difficult to judge character than capacity. Capacity, or earning power, can be measured reasonably accurately, but character is an intangible quality.

The third measuring standard, *capital,* applies only to people who have property. The amount of credit that individuals are entitled to receive varies greatly. A person with a temporary lack of earning power may be entitled to receive credit, provided he has good capital resources and a good character. Capacity and capital without character will, however, usually disqualify any credit applicant. The personal aspect of credit is extremely important.

Sources of Credit Information. The following sources of credit information are available to the merchant who is dealing with individuals:

1. Information may be obtained from the applicant by asking questions and by requiring the applicant to fill out a credit application blank, such as the one shown in Illustration No. 128.
2. Information may be obtained from a local retail credit bureau, which obtains information from all businesses that co-operate in supplying such information. The functions of a credit bureau are explained later.
3. Information may be obtained from other businesses or stores.
4. Information may be obtained from the applicant's bank, employer, neighbor, or some other person who can furnish information for credit purposes.

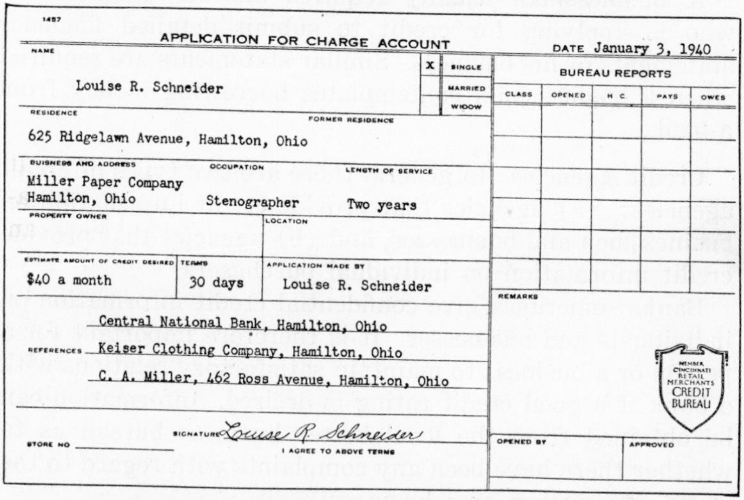
1457

APPLICATION FOR CHARGE ACCOUNT

DATE January 3, 1940

NAME: Louise R. Schneider — X SINGLE / MARRIED / WIDOW

RESIDENCE: 625 Ridgelawn Avenue, Hamilton, Ohio — FORMER RESIDENCE

BUISNESS AND ADDRESS: Miller Paper Company, Hamilton, Ohio — OCCUPATION: Stenographer — LENGTH OF SERVICE: Two years

PROPERTY OWNER — LOCATION

ESTIMATE AMOUNT OF CREDIT DESIRED: $40 a month — TERMS: 30 days — APPLICATION MADE BY: Louise R. Schneider

REFERENCES:
Central National Bank, Hamilton, Ohio
Keiser Clothing Company, Hamilton, Ohio
C. A. Miller, 462 Ross Avenue, Hamilton, Ohio

STORE NO ______ SIGNATURE Louise R. Schneider
I AGREE TO ABOVE TERMS

BUREAU REPORTS

CLASS	OPENED	H C	PAYS	OWES

REMARKS

MEMBER CINCINNATI RETAIL MERCHANTS CREDIT BUREAU

OPENED BY — APPROVED

Illustration No. 128—A Credit Application Blank

Businessmen who deal with other businessmen may obtain information by all the preceding methods and also by the following means:

1. Information may be obtained from salesmen who call on the applicant. Credit information is sometimes contained in the reports of salesmen.
2. Dun and Bradstreet, Incorporated, is a national agency that reports information on businessmen. The services of this agency are explained on pages 340 and 341. There are also special agencies that report credit information within restricted fields. For instance, there are agencies that report on doctors, lawyers, and other professional people. There are also special sources of credit information in fields such as the steel industry and the textile industry.
3. The National Association of Credit Men has a credit-reporting service that is available to businessmen.
4. Banks will sometimes furnish confidential credit information about their patrons. For this reason many credit applications require the applicant to give a bank reference.

A businessman usually requires another businessman who is applying for credit to submit detailed financial statements of his business. Similar statements are required when a businessman contemplates borrowing money from a bank.

Credit Agencies. In general there are two types of credit agencies: (a) agencies that provide credit information on businessmen and businesses, and (b) agencies that provide credit information on individual purchasers.

Banks sometimes give confidential credit information on individuals and businesses. It is therefore important for a person or a business to maintain satisfactory relations with a bank if a good credit rating is desired. Information can be obtained from the local better business bureau as to whether there have been any complaints with regard to the credit of a person or a business.

Private credit agencies collect information and publish confidential reports for the benefit of their subscribers, who are usually retailers. Each subscriber contributes to these reports by furnishing information and periodic ratings. Additional information is gathered from local news-papers, notices of change in address, death notices, and court records. Such information is valuable to the retailer in protecting himself from loss on accounts. If one of his customers moves, he will want to know of the change in address. If a customer dies, he will want to be sure that his claim is presented. If someone is taking court action against one of his customers, he will want to protect his own claim.

Illustration No. 129 shows a form that a credit bureau uses for keeping a record of each retail purchaser. The name of the store is recorded by code number in order that the information in the files of the credit bureau may be kept confidential.

THE CINCINNATI RETAIL MERCHANTS' CREDIT BUREAU COMPANY
INSTRUCTIONS AND CONDITION OF ACCOUNT

NAME			DATE		19
PRES. RES.					
FORMER RES.					
PRES. BUS.					
FORMER BUS.					

CHECK HERE			CHECK HERE		
1		Account Opened Own Investigation	6		Chronic or Unfair Returner of Mdse.
2		Account Closed Months	7		Check Ret. from Bank No Account — N. S. F.
3		In Hands of Col. Agency	8		New Residence Address
4		Fraudulent Pur. on This Acct.	9		New Business Address
5		P. and L..	10		Address Wanted

REMARKS   REPORTED BY
                                           STORE NO.

CB-6   BE SURE TO DATE THESE INSTRUCTIONS

Illustration No. 129—A Record of Individual Purchasers

The National Retail Credit Association is composed of local associations in various cities. These associations are organized to co-operate in furnishing credit information. Illustration No. 130 on page 338 shows a group of Telauto-graph operators in a credit bureau. By means of the Tel-autograph, credit reports can be submitted promptly to any subscriber. Reports can also be submitted over the tele-phone or by letter.

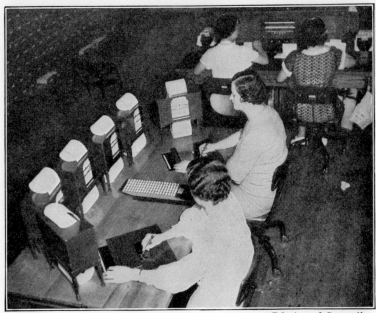

Telautograph Corporation.

*Illustration No. 130—A Group of Telautograph Operators
Giving Information in a Credit Bureau*

The twelve hundred credit bureaus of the National Consumer Credit Reporting Corporation, an affiliate of the National Retail Credit Association, maintain credit records of sixty million persons. These records are kept up to date constantly through the co-operation of local bureaus. The information is at the fingertips of any merchant who is a member of a local bureau. When a person establishes a credit rating, the information is available to merchants even though the person may move from one city to another.

This huge network of credit-reporting agencies is beneficial not only to the merchant but also to the individual who seeks credit. Anyone who is honest and who desires to maintain proper credit should be perfectly willing to have a report submitted on him. Under this system of reporting credit information, it is difficult for any person to establish a bad credit reputation without the information being made available to other merchants who extend credit.

In many communities there are associations of credit men which are a part of a nationwide organization known as the National Association of Credit Men. This national organization operates a credit interchange service. Through the credit interchange service, members report their credit relations with their various customers. This information is assembled and is furnished in the form of a confidential report to any interested member. Illustration No. 131 below is an example of the kind of information furnished in these reports. The various firms which have provided credit information are listed in the first column. The type of business and the location of the business are indicated, but the exact name of the business giving the information is indicated by a code number.

REPORT ON:

X Y Z Company   Cleveland, Ohio   December 11, 1939

BUSINESS CLASSIFICATION	HOW LONG SOLD	DATE OF LAST SALE	HIGHEST RECENT CREDIT	AMOUNT OWING INCLUDING NOTES	AMOUNT PAST DUE	UNFILLED OR FIRST ORDERS	TERMS OF SALE	MANNER OF PAYMENT			COMMENTS
								DIS-COUNTS	PAYS WHEN DUE	DAYS SLOW	
GRAND RAPIDS 326-240 165 MTL	10-37	10-37					COD				
CLEVELAND 324-309 D 66 PNT	*Yrs	3-38	$ 83	$ 58	$ 33		2-10-60			30-90	
CD 170 PNT	Yrs	3-38	816	733	399					3-5 Mos	
C 1 HDWE	Yrs	3-38	1403	687	449		2-10-30			120	
C 258 MISC						12					
C 46 ELEC							COD				
C 218 ELEC		12-37	85	35	35					60-90	
A MISC	Yrs	3-38	50							30	
GRAND RAPIDS CONT'D 86 MTL	Yrs	2-38	240	18						30-60	
NEW ENGLAND 326-342 260 HDWE	Yrs	8-36	40				2-10			30-90	
WHEELING 326-16 104 MTL	1935	1-38	43	19			60			30-60	

* Several years

Illustration No. 131—Report of National Association of Credit Men

ESTIMATED PECUNIARY STRENGTH				HIGH	GOOD	FAIR	LIMITED
*1	AA	Over	$1,000,000....	A1	1	1½	2
	A+	Over	750,000....	A1	1	1½	2
	A	$500,000 to	750,000....	A1	1	1½	2
	B+	300,000 to	500,000....	1	1½	2	2½
	B	200,000 to	300,000....	1	1½	2	2½
	C+	125,000 to	200,000....	1	1½	2	2½
*2	C	75,000 to	125,000....	1½	2	2½	3
	D+	50,000 to	75,000....	1½	2	2½	3
	D	35,000 to	50,000....	1½	2	2½	3
	E	20,000 to	35,000....	2	2½	3	3½
*3	F	10,000 to	20,000....	2½	3	3½	4
	G	5,000 to	10,000....		3	3½	4
	H	3,000 to	5,000....		3	3½	4
	J	2,000 to	3,000....		3	3½	4
*4	K	1,000 to	2,000....		3	3½	4
	L	500 to	1,000....			3½	4
	M	Less than	500....			3½	4

*Numerical Rating — When a numeral *only* (1, 2, 3, or 4) follows a name in the Reference Book, it is an indication that the financial strength, while not definitely determined, is considered within the range of the ($) figures in the corresponding bracket, and that a condition is believed to exist which warrants credit in keeping with that assumption.

Absence of Rating — The absence of *any* rating following a name signifies circumstances which preclude forming a definite decision as to financial strength or credit standing of the individual or concern named, and should suggest to the client the advisability of reading the detailed report.

Divided Partner Liability — Where an *italic d* in parentheses precedes a rating, it is an indication that one or more of the partners in the firm are liable in another or other firms, and the responsibility is in that sense divided, THUS: (d) B + 1.

Illustration No. 132—Dun and Bradstreet Ratings

There is another important source of information on the credit of commercial houses and manufacturers. This agency is Dun and Bradstreet, Incorporated. A book of credit ratings is published regularly by this agency and sold as a service to subscribers. The service covers the entire United States. In addition, a subscriber can obtain a special report on any businessman or professional man

SYMBOLS INDICATING TRADES

Books	=
Butchers	T
Drugs	Z
Dry goods	▲
Filling Stations	⊂
General Hardware	■
General Stores	★
Lumber Dealers	⌐
Machinery	V
Men's Furnishings	+
Plumbers	O
Restaurants	⊏

EXAMPLES:

O The E. C. Arnold Company .... B+2½

This example means that The E. C. Arnold Company has an estimated pecuniary strength of from $300,000 to $500,000 and has a limited credit rating. The symbol before the name indicates that the company is engaged in the plumbing business.

⊂ J. A. Mayer Oil Company .... C 2

This example indicates that this oil company has an estimated pecuniary strength of from $75,000 to $125,000 and has a good credit rating.

★ The Lane General Store 3

The single number (3) given in this example indicates that the financial strength of the store is not definitely determined but is considered to be within the range of from $2,000 to $20,000. A condition is therefore believed to exist which warrants credit in keeping with that assumption.

+ The Gentlemen's Store .... (d) D 1½

The letter d in parentheses (d) in this example indicates that the firm is a partnership and that one or more of the members of the firm are liable in another firm. The estimated financial strength of the firm is, however, $35,000 to $50,000, and the general credit rating is high.

Illustration No. 133—Symbols Used in Dun and Bradstreet Ratings

in any part of the country. The reliability of this agency has been established through many years of effective service to all types of business- and professional men. For examples of Dun and Bradstreet ratings and symbols, see Illustrations Nos. 132 and 133.

Advantages of Extending Credit. As has been stated before, business could not be transacted without some form of credit. Merchants recognize the advantages of credit in dealing with their customers. The following are some of these advantages:

1. Credit develops permanent customers. It makes regular customers and creates a more intimate relationship between the seller and the purchaser.
2. As a rule, credit sales are larger than cash sales, although they are not so frequent as the latter. Customers usually buy in larger quantities when they do not have to pay immediately. The larger quantities last a longer time.
3. Good credit relations develop the customers' confidence in a merchant and build goodwill for the merchant.
4. Customers who have the ability to pay patronize stores that extend credit, whereas bargain-hunters sometimes seek cash stores.
5. Credit permits a larger volume of business without increased selling expense. Credit purchases are usually regular, whereas cash purchases in many types of stores are made periodically when the customers receive their salaries or wages.

The businessman who allows his customers to buy recklessly is not only abusing his credit relations, but also is encouraging his customers to abuse their credit relations. Any merchant who encourages extravagance through urging customers to make thoughtless purchases soon finds that he cannot collect the accounts that are owed him. He fails, and deserves to fail.

Cost of Credit to the Seller. Merchants who sell on open account may be classified as follows: (a) those who have uniform prices for credit and for cash sales; (b) those who charge more for credit than for cash sales.

The extending of credit adds extra costs to every sale. The principal extra costs result from (a) the clerical work necessary for recording credit sales and collecting accounts and (b) interest on the money that is invested or has been borrowed in order to extend credit. Additional costs result from (a) occasional losses due to bad debts and (b) the tendency of credit customers to return goods for exchange.

The extra cost for clerical help is obvious. It is also a known fact that merchants find it impossible to collect all their accounts. Furthermore, a merchant who does a large credit business must have available enough money to provide a stock of goods, to pay his expenses, and to operate his business until collections can be made. In other words, he always has some debts outstanding. If he had all the money that is due him, he could invest it and earn an income from it. He is therefore entitled to some extra income because he is deprived of the use of some of his own money for business or for investment purposes. Most merchants find it necessary to borrow money. They extend credit and at the same time borrow money to finance their own businesses. The interest they must pay on the loans is an added operating cost.

These comments should not be construed to mean that a merchant who sells on credit must necessarily sell at higher prices than a merchant who sells for cash. If selling on credit results in greater sales than selling for cash, the increased sales may produce a greater profit in spite of the additional costs. On the other hand, if a merchant does set his prices higher for credit sales and makes no concessions for cash sales, he may lose many cash customers and may fail to attract many credit customers because the latter will not pay the additional cost of obtaining credit.

Recommended Community Credit Policy. It is desirable to have a uniform credit policy in each community so that all merchants will treat their customers alike and so that customers will become accustomed to the policy. The following credit policy was proposed for use in one rather typical city of 33,000 people:

1. To standardize all terms, classifying accounts as follows:
   (a) Monthly charge accounts (open accounts)
   (b) Budget, or deferred-payment, accounts (time-payment accounts of short duration, not exceed-

ing ten weeks, on which no carrying charge is made)

    (c) Installment accounts (time-payment accounts of long duration on which a carrying charge is made)

2. To state the terms to the applicant for credit, stressing a definite due date.
3. To consider all accounts to be past due on the day following the definite due date.
4. To make no deviation from the terms of credit.
5. When an account has not been paid in full within sixty days following the end of the month of purchase, to use at this point a uniform "term" letter.
6. To charge interest at the rate of not less than one-half per cent a month on all balances of monthly charge accounts that have been due for sixty days.
7. To use a credit application blank requiring the signature of the applicant and carrying a notice of the interest charge.
8. To check *all* applicants for credit through the credit bureau *before* opening any new accounts, and not to open an account when the credit report is unfavorable.
9. To require a down payment of not less than 10 per cent on all installment, lay-away, or will-call sales.
10. To record all installment accounts with the credit bureau if they are not recorded with the county clerk and recorder.
11. To furnish to the bureau each month a complete list of all accounts that have been delinquent ninety days. (Example: January purchases would be reported on May first.)
12. To report promptly to the bureau all accounts that have been closed with cause; to report, at the time of repossession, any merchandise that has been repossessed; to report all unfair claims and any other special information that might affect the credit standing of the customer in the community.

Types of Installment Contracts. Every time-payment contract provides a legal claim upon the merchandise until

THE McALPIN COMPANY
Cincinnati, Ohio

County __Hamilton__ State ___Ohio___ City ___Cincinnati___ Date__January 3, 1939__

CONSIDERATION ACKNOWLEDGED.—I do hereby grant, bargain, sell, convey and confirm unto THE McALPIN COMPANY (mortgagee) or assigns, the following described merchandise, to have and to hold said merchandise forever, provided, however, that I shall pay to the mortgagee or its assigns the full purchase price in installments on the day of each month that the installment becomes due, then this mortgage to be void.

DESCRIPTION AND TERMS

Item __Thor Washing Machine__ Serial No.__625437__ Cash Purchase Price $ __78.00__

_____ $ _____

_____ $ _____

Less Down Payment Received by _Louis P. Morton_ $ __18.00__
(Signature)

Balance to be paid as follows: Principal $ __6.00__ BALANCE $ __60.00__

Carrying Charges $ __.30__

Total $ __6.30__ each and every month.

If I fail to make any monthly payment then all remaining installments may be declared due and payable, and upon failure to make any monthly payment, or all, if all are declared due, I agree to deliver said Merchandise as described, upon demand to the Company, or its assigns, and all payments made and the used Merchandise applied on purchase as described shall be retained by said Company, or its assigns, as stipulated damages. I Further Agree to take good care of said Merchandise and to be responsible for its loss by theft, fire or other casualty, and not to remove it from

__1619 Buckeye Street__ __Cincinnati__ __Ohio__ __Melrose 2235__
Name of Street   City   State   Tel. No.

unless I first obtain the written consent of said Company, or its assigns.

It is Understood and Agreed that no other agreement or guaranty, verbal or written, expressed or implied, shall limit or qualify the terms of this contract.

Not valid unless accepted by Dealer.

Accepted _Paul C. Willis, Treasurer_ Signed _James L. Sherman_
Customer

Date ___January 3,___ 1939 Salesman _Louis P. Morton_
Salesman sign here

Illustration No. 134—A Chattel Mortgage

the obligation has been paid. Security for the deferred payment may take the form of (a) a chattel mortgage or (b) a conditional sales contract. Illustration No. 134 shows a chattel mortgage; Illustration No. 135, a conditional sales contract. In most states the laws specify the particular form that must be used, whereas in a few states either form may be used.

Terms of Payment under Installment Contracts. The percentage of down payment and the length of the credit term vary according to the product, the amount of the down payment, and the policy of the finance company. The table in Illustration No. 136 provides a summary of the usual percentages of down payment and the usual maximum periods for making payment for particular types of merchandise.

Financing Installment Credit. When a merchant sells on open account or on installment contracts, he has a lot of money invested in merchandise that is in the hands of customers. He may therefore need cash with which to operate his business until he can collect these accounts. He may

CONDITIONAL SALES CONTRACT

    This Agreement, Made in duplicate this   eighth   day of   February   , 19 39 ,

between THE MADISON CO., Incorporated, party of the first part, and

     W. W. Woodrough   , party of the second part.

    Witnesseth That, whereas I,   W. W. Woodrough   , now residing at

No   136 Forest Avenue   ~~Street~~, in the City of   Dallas   , State of   Texas

have leased and received from THE MADISON CO., party of the first part, Household Goods described on the list

attached and made a part hereof, in good order and valued at   Two Hundred and   Fifty- - - - - - -

Dollars ($ 250.00   ), which I am to use with care and keep in as good order as received, I agree to pay

Fifty- - - - - - - - - - - - - - - - - Dollars ($ 50.00   ) on receipt of this agreement,

the receipt whereof is hereby acknowledged and accepted as payment for the rent of the first   month   only,

and   Twenty-five- - - - - - - - - - - -Dollars ($25.00   ) on the   first   day of

each   month   until the payments have been completed.

    All payments shall be made at the store of THE MADISON CO., in the City of Cincinnati and the State of Ohio, without notice or demand; but if default shall be made in any of said payments or if I shall sell, remove or attempt to remove the Household Goods from my aforesaid residence without the written consent of said THE MADISON CO., then in that case, or at the expiration of the time for which the Household Goods are leased, I will return and deliver the same to THE MADISON CO., in good order except for reasonable wear, and the said THE MADISON CO. or its agents may resume actual possession thereof; and I hereby authorize and empower said THE MADISON CO. or its agents to enter the premises wherever said Household Goods may be and take and carry the same away, hereby waiving any action for trespass or damages therefor and disclaiming any right to resistance thereto, and I also waive all right of homestead and other exemptions under the laws as against this obligation.

    I FURTHER AGREE to keep the said Household Goods fully insured in the sum of Two Hundred and Fifty- - - - Dollars ($ 250.00   ) against loss or damage by fire, in a solvent insurance company, in the name and for the benefit of the said THE MADISON CO., and I further agree that if the said Household Goods be partially or wholly destroyed or injured by fire or otherwise, by any default or neglect on my part, to pay the said THE MADISON CO. the damages sustained by it thereby. And in default of my making such insurance, the said THE MADISON CO. may do as my agent at my expense.

    I FURTHER AGREE to retain the said Household Goods for my own use, and not to let or underlet the same for any purpose nor allow them to be removed from   136 Forest Ave.   without the written permission of said THE MADISON CO., first obtained, and to allow the said THE MADISON CO. or its agents to examine said Household Goods at all proper times.

    I FURTHER AGREE that should I default in the payment of any one or more of the stipulated payments, or should I part with the possession of the said Household Goods or remove or permit them to be removed from the premises herein set out unless the written consent of the said THE MADISON CO. had first been obtained, then the said THE MADISON CO. shall at its option have the right, either personally or by its agent, to at once reclaim and take possession of said Household Goods wherever found; and such taking of them shall not be subject to any legal proceedings, civil or criminal.

    Any and all payments of rent are accepted simply as rent and are taken as an equivalent for the use of the said Household Goods while in possession of the said party of the second part. Party of the second part agrees to and becomes bound to pay THE MADISON CO. all rent due or to become due for the term herein set out.

    For and in consideration of the sum of Fifty- - - - - - - - - - - - - - - - - - -Dollars ($ 50.00   ), and the prompt payment of rent as herein stipulated, we agree to render a receipted bill of sale to   W. W. Woodrough   for Household Goods herein described when the total amount of rent paid shall equal the cost of the purchases on the list attached.

Witness our hands and seals this   eighth   *day of*   February   , 19 39

Witness: **THE MADISON COMPANY**

Charles H. McConnell   By *Albert B. Thompson*
                                        Credit Manager

    I hereby acknowledge receipt of a duly executed copy of the preceding contract on this   eighth

day of   February   , 19 39.   *W. W. Woodrough*

Illustration No. 135—A Conditional Sales Contract

borrow money from a banking institution by pledging the accounts to the bank as security for the loan. It is more common for him, however, to pledge installment contracts as security for a loan. If the loan is not repaid, the bank may collect the money due on the contracts.

Product	Usual Percentage of Down Payment	Usual Time Allowed the Debtor to Pay (Months)
New automobiles	10 to 33⅓	12 to 24
Used automobiles	10 to 33⅓	6 to 18
Soft goods (textiles and perishables) .	10 to 20	3 to 12
Furniture		
Department stores	10 to 20	6 to 18
Furniture stores	10 to 25	12 to 24
Refrigerators		
Department stores	5 to 10	12 to 36
Electrical appliance stores	5 to 10	12 to 36
Radios		
Department stores	10 to 20	12 to 24
Electrical appliance stores	10 to 20	12 to 24
Washing machines	5 to 10	12 to 24
Ranges	10 to 20	12 to 36
Jewelry	5 to 20	6 to 18
Men's clothing	10 to 25	3 to 12

Illustration No. 136—Down Payments and Time Allowed on Installment Sales

Another practice is to sell, or discount, installment contracts. In the field of installment credit, a particular type of financial institution has developed. It is often referred to as a *finance company.* In a sense, it is a dealer or a bank that purchases from merchants the notes signed by customers who buy on the installment plan. These notes are purchased by the finance company at a discount. For example, a customer may buy a refrigerator on the installment plan and sign a mortgage contract. This contract may then be sold to a finance company for less than the amount that is due on the contract. The finance company collects the full amount of the contract and thereby makes its profit for handling the transaction. In many cases the contract is endorsed *without recourse;* that is, it is endorsed in such a way that the finance company will have no recourse against the merchant if the debtor refuses or is unable to pay. In a few cases, however, contracts are sold to finance companies with the understanding that the merchant is responsible for handling the collections.

QUESTIONS FOR DISCUSSION

1. What is the distinction between short-term credit and long-term credit?
2. What are the "three C's" of credit?
3. Name the sources of credit information that a retail merchant may use.
4. Name the common sources of information that businessmen use in obtaining credit information on other businessmen.
5. If the numeral 2 appears after the name in the Dun and Bradstreet credit reference book, what financial condition is signified?
6. What are some of the advantages that a merchant derives from extending credit?
7. What are some of the added expenses of selling on credit?
8. What are the generally accepted terms of credit on open accounts in retail stores?
9. What is the essential difference between a chattel mortgage and a conditional sales contract?
10. Are the down payments and the periods of payment somewhat uniform in all installment selling?
11. What is meant by selling, or discounting, an installment contract?
12. Explain the credit interchange service of the National Association of Credit Men.
13. What is meant by the statement "credit develops permanent customers"?
14. What is the importance of having a uniform community credit policy?

Section II

Collection Policies and Procedures

Credit Limits. It is customary in extending credit in business to limit the amount. This practice is followed in dealing with consumers as well as with other businessmen. When an account is opened, the credit manager usually indicates the maximum amount of credit that will be allowed. If credit is desired beyond this amount, the customer must make special arrangements. In some cases a note must be signed or some security furnished.

Recording Credit Information on Customers. Every businessman should be very cautious in extending credit. A convenient record of the credit history of every customer should be kept. This record should show the credit experience of the business in dealings with the customer, as well as information obtained from outside sources. A card is often used for this purpose. It may contain space for indicating the dates on which statements and collection letters are sent.

The customer should be classified under some such plan as (a) unlimited credit or (b) credit limit of $100. After there has been enough experience with customers, they should be classified as (a) prompt pay, (b) slow pay but good, (c) slow pay but doubtful, and (d) bad pay.

Those at the upper end of the scale should be treated with more caution than those at the lower end. For the former the collection process should be drawn out longer. Those at the lower end of the scale should be handled with more firmness and promptness so that they will not become too far in arrears. Every account should be studied carefully to be sure it is classified properly.

Collection Procedures. The person who has charge of making collections should bear in mind the two major objectives of the collection procedure: first, to get the money and, second, to retain the goodwill and patronage of the customer. When one considers the second objective, it is evident that much tact is necessary in making collections.

One of the best methods of collecting past-due accounts is through a series of collection letters. Extreme tact must be used; but as the series progresses, the appeals can be made stronger. They should also be varied because not all people will respond to the same appeals.

The telephone is used in many cases when an account is not too long overdue. A gentle and courteous reminder through a telephone call will often prove effective. In urgent cases a telegram will often bring the desired result because it gets prompt attention and emphasizes the urgency of the situation.

Collectors are frequently employed on installment or contract accounts, but they sometimes create ill will. Past-due accounts may be turned over to a collection agency or sold to the agency. Such a procedure may result, however, in ill will because the businessman is at the mercy of the collection agency in handling the matter.

A lawyer may be employed to write letters as a last appeal, threatening to begin legal proceedings for collection. In some cases he may actually begin such proceedings. If a suit is brought against a debtor, it may be possible to attach some of his personal property and hold it until the debt is paid, or to sell the property to satisfy the debt. If the debtor does not have enough money or property to be attached, the businessman may obtain a judgment whereby the debtor is required to pay the debt whenever he gets sufficient money.

Special agencies, such as Dun and Bradstreet, Incorporated, the National Association of Credit Men, and credit bureaus, have services through which accounts can be collected.

Some businessmen follow the procedure of drawing a sight draft on a delinquent customer for the amount of the account. The customer is requested to pay the draft to the bank that presents it for collection.

Example of a Collection Sequence. The preceding discussion has pointed out some general procedures in collection. Each businessman must develop a specific procedure of his own. Ordinarily, the type of procedure used must be varied according to whether the person is slow pay or good pay. Special cases require individual handling. The following is an example of a collection sequence used in a business:

1. An invoice is issued at the time the order is filled.
2. A statement is rendered at the end of the month during which the purchase was made.
3. A statement is mailed at the end of the second month. Some companies follow a practice of attaching to the statement or typing on it some comment, such as "Now due" or "Just a friendly reminder that your account is now due."
4. A statement with a typewritten comment such as the following is mailed on the fifteenth day of the third month: "Did you overlook paying this amount, which is forty-five days overdue?" or "Past due. No doubt payment has been overlooked."
5. A statement with a sticker pasted on it containing a comment such as the following is mailed at the end of the third month: "You must have overlooked this amount because it is sixty days overdue." At this stage a telephone call may be effective, or a letter may be written.
6. On the fifteenth day of the fourth month, a brief friendly letter is written calling attention to the amount due and the length of the overdue period. The letter should point out the advantages of prompt payment and remind the customer of his obligations.
7. At the end of each fifteen days thereafter, another letter is written, each letter becoming stronger in its demand for payment. The first letter of the series, however, is personally dictated and discusses the whole matter.
8. If no collection has been obtained after a certain length of time, a letter is written stating that the account will be placed in the hands of a collection agency. If such a threat is made, it should be carried out.

Of course, if a partial payment is made or some agreement is reached, the collection procedure is stopped. A new similar series is started, however, if payment is not made according to the agreement. The collection procedure that has been explained is a relatively mild procedure. In most businesses the procedure is more forceful.

Statute of Limitations. Nearly every state has in operation a law commonly known as the *statute of limitations*. Under this law a debt is outlawed upon the expiration of a certain period of time unless it has been partially paid or otherwise reinstated during that period. For instance, the law of one state makes it impossible to bring any legal action to collect a debt after five years from the date of the sale. The seller can, if possible, collect the debt after that time; but he cannot resort to legal action in doing so. If the seller has, during the period allowed by the statute of limitations, obtained an additional acknowledgment of the debt, the time allowed by the statute begins again from the date on which the debt was reinstated by the acknowledgment.

There are various ways of reinstating an account. For instance, a partial payment reinstates an account in most states, but not in California, Missouri, Kentucky, North Carolina, Tennessee, or Virginia. A written acknowledgment or a new promise to pay reinstates accounts in most states, and an oral acknowledgment or promise is sufficient in a few states.

Repossession of Property. When merchandise is sold on open account but is not paid for, the only way that a merchant can protect himself is to sue for the amount of the debt. If merchandise is sold under a conditional sales contract, the title to the merchandise does not pass to the customer until full payment of the price has been made. The merchandise therefore still remains the property of the seller and can be retaken by him. If merchandise has been sold under a chattel-mortgage contract, the seller has to go through definite legal proceedings to regain its possession.

Garnishment. If a debtor refuses to pay, the creditor may in most states bring a legal action to force the payment of the debt. By an order of a court the employer of the debtor is required to pay to the creditor a certain percentage of the debtor's wages until the amount of the debt or the amount specified by the court has been paid. This procedure is called the *garnishment,* or *garnisheeing,* of wages. The laws on garnisheeing wages vary in the different states. In some states, only a certain percentage of a person's wages can be collected in this way. In other states a worker cannot be forced to pay small debts through this process.

Bankruptcy. There are two types of bankruptcy through which a debtor may escape some or all of his obligations. One type of bankruptcy is referred to as *voluntary bankruptcy;* the other, as *involuntary bankruptcy.*

Under the Chandler Bankruptcy Act, which became effective on September 22, 1938, creditors may not file an involuntary petition against a wage earner, a farmer, a municipality, a railroad, an insurance company, a bank, or a building and loan association. These individuals and institutions may, however, file voluntary bankruptcy petitions. Under the Act a debtor may file with a court a petition requesting the court to arrange for the settlement or the satisfaction of an unsecured debt, or the extension of the time for payment of such a debt. A debtor may also petition a court for an arrangement affecting debts secured by real property or chattels (such as equipment and livestock). The filing of a petition with a court does not make the debtor a bankrupt. In other words, the court has the power to decide upon a proper settlement or extension of the terms. Under the same law the court is given broad authority to halt or stay actions for the collection of debts and the foreclosure of mortgages.

A debtor may voluntarily declare himself bankrupt by applying to the proper court for a judgment of bankruptcy. If the court finds that the debtor is incapable of paying his debts, it may discharge him from further claims. The assets owned by the debtor (with the exception of certain exempt assets) must, however, be used to pay as large a part of the outstanding debts as possible. For instance, a person may voluntarily declare himself bankrupt, but the court may discover that he has assets of $525 and debts of $3,000. The court will allow him to retain certain assets of a minimum amount, possibly $150; but the remaining assets, equal to $375, must be distributed among his creditors, who hold the claims totaling $3,000. Under the Chandler Bankruptcy Act a wage earner with an annual income of $3,600 or less can provide, under the supervision and control of a court, for the settlement of his debts, secured or unsecured, out of future earnings.

Creditors sometimes force a debtor into bankruptcy in order to collect their claims. They believe that, if they allow the debtor to continue his business, he will go more deeply into debt and will dissipate whatever assets are available; but if they forced him into bankruptcy, they may collect at least part of their claims before it is too late. This process, referred to as involuntary bankruptcy, is therefore a means of protection to the creditors. When involuntary bankruptcy proceedings are started, the creditors assume that they will lose less by forcing the debtor into bankruptcy than they would if they allowed him to continue to operate his business.

Responsibility for Debts. Every individual or businessman should have a sufficient knowledge of law to be familiar with his own responsibilities and the responsibilities of those with whom he deals. For instance, it is important that a husband know to what extent he is responsible for his wife's debts. Let us assume, by way of illustration, that a young married woman opened charge accounts in two stores. Her purchases of household necessaries amounted to $150. The husband became indignant and refused to pay the debts. The stores could, of course, sue for the collection of these debts because in most states the wife has an implied authority to pledge her husband's credit for necessaries of the household.

On the other hand, the husband may give out a legal written notice that he will not be responsible for his wife's debts. He may publish the announcement in a newspaper or may write a notice to the various retail stores in which his wife has charge accounts.

Parents are not responsible for debts incurred by minor children in purchasing luxuries or other unnecessary articles. The laws of most states do place responsibility upon parents for the payment of debts incurred by children in purchasing necessaries of life. In most states a parent cannot be held responsible, however, if the purchases of a minor child were goods or services not necessary for preserving the life or the health of the child. A businessman should therefore always be cautious in dealing with minors.

Employees of businesses, particularly of corporations, often act as agents of the businesses. The authority of an agent is limited by the ordinary functions of his position. For instance, a purchasing agent may purchase goods in the name of his employer, but he usually cannot do such things as collect money or employ workers and thereby bind his employer to the agreements he makes.

If an employee acts in some unusual capacity and a substantial sum of money is involved, the person dealing with him should insist upon proof of the employee's responsibility. For example, a traveling salesman ordinarily does not have the authority to collect accounts. Consequently, if such an employee makes a collection but withholds the money from his employer, it is doubtful whether the payment will be binding on the employer.

Guaranteed Accounts. When it is difficult for a person to establish credit, some merchants require the customer to get some responsible person to guarantee that the account will be paid. If the account is not paid by the customer, the guarantor can be held legally responsible for paying it. The form in Illustration No. 137 shows the kind of contract used for such a purpose.

Loss on Bad Debts. If a businessman follows a vigorous policy in collecting debts and places past-due accounts in

GUARANTY OF ACCOUNT

In consideration of The Mabley & Carew Company, Cincinnati, Ohio, granting credit for merchandise purchased

or to be purchased by or on the account of.................Catherine L. Arnold...at present residing at

...........161 Belle Avenue, Cincinnati, Ohio.., to an amount not exceeding

..........................Twenty-Five...........................Dollars per month, I hereby agree to become responsible as surety for the payment of and will pay on demand said monthly accounts. Notice of separate transactions is waived. This surety is to continue from month to month until revoked by me in writing and the amount due thereon is settled in full to date of receipt of said notice of revocation.

Cincinnati, Ohio...............December 8,...............1939.....   Harold Matthews.....................................
                                                                                                            Signature of Guarantor

Witness: Robert Kennedy...............................   552 Madison Road, Cincinnati, Ohio..........
Property Owned   Address of Guarantor
    by Guarantor.........House and lot at 552 Madison Road, Cincinnati, Ohio...................................

Illustration No. 137—A Guaranty of Account

the hands of a collection agency or a lawyer, he will be able to collect most of his debts; but in doing so, he will probably acquire the ill will of his customers and lose many of them. For instance, a policy that is too vigorous may be unfair to the person who is honest but temporarily unable to pay his debts.

Surveys show that the percentage of net sales resulting in losses ranges from 0.5 per cent to 1.5 per cent. In some businesses there are practically no bad-debt losses; in others the losses run rather high. Illustration No. 138 shows the percentages of bad-debt losses on open-credit and installment sales for all stores reporting to the United States Department of Foreign and Domestic Commerce in 1936 and 1937. It will be noticed, for instance, that most of the open-credit losses do not exceed 1 per cent, whereas many of the installment-credit losses do exceed 1 per cent.

Status of Accounts Receivable. In every business it is important to watch accounts receivable in order that their total does not get out of proportion to the amount of credit sales. For example, if credit sales are not increasing but accounts receivable are gradually growing larger each month, an effort should be made to collect the accounts more efficiently.

The amount of accounts receivable may not show the true picture of conditions. For instance, an analysis of the accounts receivable may show that most of them are only thirty or sixty days old, while only a few are ninety days

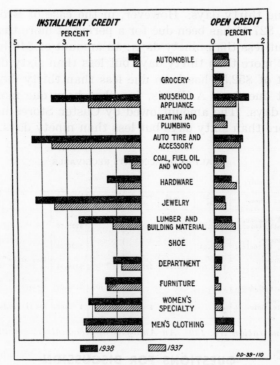

*Illustration No. 138—Bad-Debt Losses on Open-Credit
and Installment Sales*

old or older. The situation may therefore not be particularly alarming. On the other hand, if an analysis of the
accounts receivable shows that most of them are ninety
days old or older, it may prove necessary to have some of
the customers sign notes, to place some accounts with a
collection agency, to start lawsuits for collection, and to
strengthen and speed up the collection procedure generally
so that accounts in the future will not become so old.

A study of accounts receivable is often referred to as
aging the accounts. The form in Illustration No. 139 is an
example of the type of analysis that can be used to show
the true situation. The following is an explanation of the
analysis of accounts receivable: The amounts owed by the
Adams-Jones Company and the Artwell Company have not

been due thirty days. However, in the case of Brown and Brown, $27.41 has been due for a period of more than sixty days but less than ninety days; an amount of $40 has been due for more than thirty days but less than sixty days; an amount of $52.50 has been due less than thirty days. The amount due from A. Davis, Inc., has been due more than ninety days. The amount owed by Custer Stores has been due more than sixty days but less than ninety days.

ANALYSIS OF ACCOUNTS RECEIVABLE						
Date January 2, 1940						
Name and Address	1 to 30 days	30 to 60 days	60 to 90 days	Over 90 days	Total	Explanation
Adams-Jones Company, Cincinnati, Ohio...	$235.00				$235.00	
Artwell Company, Chicago, Illinois..	$426.51				$426.51	
Brown and Brown, Gary, Indiana......	$ 52.50	$40.00	$27.41		$119.91	They wrote "will clear up account this month."
A. Davis, Inc., Detroit, Michigan..				$175.00	$175.00	Account in hands of attorney
Custer Stores, Granville, Ohio....			$76.06		$ 76.06	Now on C.O.D. basis.

Illustration No. 139—An Analysis of Accounts Receivable

QUESTIONS FOR DISCUSSION

1. What is meant by credit limits?
2. What are the common ways of classifying customers who buy on credit?
3. Would it be advisable to turn good accounts over to a collection agency before they become very old?
4. Suggest a collection sequence or series. Explain each item in the series.
5. What is a statute of limitations?
6. What procedure must a seller follow to obtain the repossession of property sold under a chattel mortgage and not paid for according to the agreement?
7. What is garnishment, and how is it used?
8. Name and explain briefly the two types of bankruptcy.
9. What are the average losses from bad debts?
10. What should be done if the aging of accounts receivable indicates that many of them have been past due for a long period of time?

PROBLEMS AND PROJECTS

1. Assume that a merchant who sells equipment on the install-ment plan finds it necessary to borrow money to finance his business. The average amount that he owes to the bank each year is $10,000, on which he pays interest of 5 per cent. He adds 10 per cent to his regular price when merchandise is sold on the installment plan. His costs and losses on in-stallment sales amount to 5 per cent of the sales. If he sells $20,000 worth of merchandise under the installment plan during a year, is the 10 per cent added to the installment contracts sufficient to take care of his losses and the interest on the borrowed money?

2. A department store has sold a refrigerator to Mrs. J. A. Smith for $298. Mrs. Smith has made a down payment of 10 per cent and is to pay the balance in twelve monthly installments. Compute the unpaid balance after the down payment. Compute the equal monthly installments. If the department store sells the contract to the Universal Finance Company at a discount of 5 per cent, what will the store obtain from the contract?

3. Assume that Mr. H. O. Mosby operates a retail store. His net sales are $29,246.30 for one year. During the year he has been unable to collect the following balances of accounts, which he considers total losses and is therefore marking off his books: $23.50, $10.40, $46.75, $63.40. Compute his per-centage of credit loss for the year.

4. The balances of the accounts receivable of the Central Sup-ply Company amount to $36,246.52 at the end of a year. It is the practice of this company to charge as a loss one-half per cent of the outstanding accounts on the assumption that this amount will be uncollectible. How much will the com-pany charge off as the bad-debt loss for the year?

5. The United Range Company sells a stove to Mr. and Mrs. J. E. Harrison on the deferred-payment plan. The price of the stove is $160. An old stove was traded in for an allow-ance of $20. A down payment of 10 per cent of the amount of the sale (the selling price less the trade-in allowance) is required. Compute the net amount, taking into account the trade-in allowance and the down payment. Add 5 per cent to that amount to take care of the extra costs of selling the stove on the deferred-payment plan. Compute the amount of each installment payment, assuming there will be twelve equal installments.

CHAPTER XV

ADVERTISING AND SALES PROMOTION PROBLEMS

Purpose of the Chapter. The businessman must use various means of publicity and advertising to promote the success of his business. Some methods of advertising are useful for a large business operating on a nationwide scale, but are of no value to the person operating a small local business. The purpose of this chapter is to point out and to explain the advantages and the disadvantages of the various types of advertising. No attempt is made to develop skill in writing advertisements. This chapter will answer many questions, some of which are:

1. How much should be spent for advertising?
2. What advertising media may be used?
3. How can advertising be correlated with other sales efforts?
4. What display material can be used effectively?
5. How should an advertising campaign be planned?

Purposes of Advertising. Advertising is one form of selling. There are many types of advertising, but their main purposes may be summarized as follows:

1. To make a direct sale of goods.
2. To create demand.
3. To make the customer more friendly.
4. To familiarize the consumer with the use of the product.
5. To introduce new styles or customs.
6. To induce people to enter a store.
7. To get a list of prospects.
8. To prepare the way for a salesman.
9. To establish the popularity and familiarity of a trade name, trade-mark, or slogan.

Not many single advertisements will attempt to perform all these functions, but many perform more than one. As will be shown later, different types of advertising serve different purposes.

Cost of Advertising. A person engaged in business should know what constitutes a reasonable expenditure for his advertising. Illustration No. 140 contains statistics compiled from various sources by the National Cash Register Company. It shows the average percentage of net sales spent for advertising by various types of businesses; or, in other words, the number of cents of each dollar of sales spent in promoting sales.

The table in Illustration No. 141 shows the results of a study made by the United States Department of Commerce among a large number of stores to determine the practices of profitable and unprofitable stores. The study shows that the profitable stores used sales promotion methods more completely and consistently than did the unprofitable stores.

Advertising Media. The following are the various advertising media that are available to the businessman:

1. Publication advertising: newspaper space advertising and classified advertising; general magazines; class magazines; trade, technical, and professional magazines; directories; and programs
2. Mass advertising: outdoor advertising, streetcar advertising, station posters, point-of-sale advertising, window displays, skywriting, loud speakers, radio advertising, and theater advertising
3. Direct advertising: circular letters, catalogues, booklets, broadsides, folders, package inserts, calendars and novelties, mailing cards, and house organs
4. Store advertising: window displays and counter displays

Some large companies use practically all these forms of advertising, but many small businessmen must be content to use a few of those that are most practical. For instance,

Types of Businesses	Percentage of Net Sales
Automotive Parts and Accessories	1.0
Bakery Shops and Caterers	0.6
Beauty Shops	3.0
Builders' Supplies	0.49
Cleaning and Dyeing	2.5
Confectioneries	1.3
Department Stores:	
Sales under $150,000	2.1
Sales $150,000—$300,000	2.6
Sales $300,000—$500,000	2.75
Sales $500,000—$750,000	2.85
Sales $750,000—$1,000,000	3.4
Sales $1,000,000—$2,000,000	3.55
Sales $2,000,000—$4,000,000	3.7
Sales $4,000,000—$10,000,000	4.0
Sales $10,000,000—$20,000,000	3.9
Sales over $20,000,000	3.4
Drugstores	0.8
Dry Goods Stores	1.0
Electrical Supplies	2.7
Florists	2.5
Food Chains	1.08
Food Stores (Independent):	
Combination (Handle fresh meats and groceries) ..	0.8
Grocery (Do not handle fresh meats)	0.8
Supermarkets (Large, complete food markets)	0.8
Furniture Stores	1.6
General Merchandise	0.6
Gift Shops	3.0
Haberdashery	1.0
Hardware	0.92
Jewelry	1.9
Leather Goods	1.3
Liquor Stores	0.5
Meats	0.8
Men's and Boys' Clothing	1.5
Millinery	1.3
Musical Instruments	2.0
Paint	1.5
Restaurants	1.1
Service Stations	0.4
Shoe Stores	2.9
Specialty Stores:	
Sales under $150,000	2.35
Sales $150,000—$500,000	3.7
Sales $500,000—$2,000,000	4.4
Sales over $2,000,000	4.2
Sporting Goods	1.6
Stationery	1.22
Taverns and Bars	0.4
Tobacco	0.2

Merchants Service Bureau, National Cash Register Company.

Illustration No. 140—Average Percentage of Net Sales Spent for Advertising

Items	Grocery Stores				Drugstores				General Stores			
	Profitable		Unprofitable		Profitable		Unprofitable		Profitable		Unprofitable	
	Number	Percentage	Number	Percentage	Number	Percentage	Number	Percentage	Number	Percentage	Number	Percentage
Methods used in promoting sales:												
Stores reporting	60	100.0	44	100.0	25	100.0	12	100.0	12	100.0	17	100.0
Newspaper advertising	42	70.0	15	34.1	20	80.0	7	58.4	8	66.7	9	53.0
Direct mail	25	13.3	14	9.1	17	48.0	6	50.0	2	16.7	4	23.5
Circulars	26	40.0	10	22.8	13	52.0	10	83.3	4	33.3	4	23.5
Highway signs and billboards	2	3.3	2	4.6	1	8.0	3	25.0	3	25.0	1	5.9
Lantern slides in theaters	2	....	....	....	....	4.0	2	16.7	1	8.3	3	17.6
Movie strips	....	....	....	....	9	36.0	2	16.7	....	....	....	....
Store souvenirs	13	5.0	5	11.4	2	24.0	2	16.7	6	50.0	3	....
Electric signs	13	21.6	....	....	....	8.0	2	33.4	....	....	....	....
Radio advertising	....	5.0	....	....	....	....	4	8.3	....	....	....	....
Personal solicitation	45	75.0	40	91.0	17	68.0	9	75.0	12	100.0	11	64.8
Telephone solicitation	41	68.3	33	75.0	15	60.0	8	66.7	9	75.0	8	47.1
Special sales	40	66.7	16	36.4	11	44.0	5	41.7	1	8.3	5	29.4
Handbills	49	15.0	22	74.6	....	76.0	....	....	1	8.3	1	5.9
Window displays, their own trim	55	91.7	31	70.5	19	....	9	75.0	11	91.6	16	94.1
Window displays, manufacturers' trim	22	36.7	14	31.8	13	52.0	4	33.4	6	50.0	....	29.4
Frequency of change of window trims:												
Stores reporting	57	100.0	38	100.0	21	100.0	11	100.0	12	100.0	16	100.0
Three times a week	12	21.0	7	18.4	....	9.5	....	....	....	....	1	6.3
Twice a week	10	17.5	3	7.9	2	9.5	7	63.6	....	....	1	6.3
Once a week	30	52.7	16	42.1	18	85.7	7	63.6	5	41.7	2	12.5
Every 2 weeks	1	1.8	2	5.3	2	9.5	4	36.4	2	16.7	5	31.2
Every 3 weeks	....	....	....	....	....	....	....	....	....	....	1	6.3
Every 4 weeks	....	....	....	....	....	....	....	....	1	8.3	4	33.3
Every 8 weeks	....	....	....	....	....	....	....	....	....	....	1	6.3
Irregularly	4	7.0	10	26.3	....	....	....	....	4	33.3	1	6.3
Special promotion services received:												
Stores reporting	56	100.0	41	100.0	25	100.0	11	100.0	10	100.0	15	100.0
Special advertising copy	16	28.6	3	7.3	15	60.0	4	36.4	1	10.0	2	13.3
Mats of electrotypes of advertisements	20	35.7	1	2.4	16	64.0	5	45.5	3	30.0	3	20.0
Plans and materials for features or "stunts"	....	....	....	....	2	8.0	....	....	....	....	....	....
Special signs, display racks, floor displays, etc.	55	98.3	40	97.6	22	88.0	9	81.8	10	100.0	15	100.0
Manufacturer's share of retailer's advertising cost:												
Stores reporting	52	100.0	45	100.0	26	100.0	13	100.0	12	100.0	18	100.0
None	38	73.1	43	95.6	15	57.7	9	69.2	10	83.3	15	83.3
Sometimes a small amount	6	11.5	1	2.2	6	23.1	....	....	....	....	2	11.1
Some manufacturers pay 50 to 100 per cent of cost of space devoted to product	8	15.4	1	2.2	5	19.2	4	30.8	2	16.7	1	5.6
Co-operative advertising:												
Stores reporting	62	100.0	52	100.0	26	100.0	14	100.0	12	100.0	18	100.0
Merchants who co-operate	6	9.7	1	1.9	3	11.5	....	....	1	8.3	1	5.6
Merchants who do not co-operate	56	90.3	51	98.1	23	88.5	14	100.0	11	91.7	17	94.4

Illustration No. 141—Practices of Profitable and Unprofitable Stores

a merchant in a small town could not utilize national magazine advertising, but he could use the local newspaper. The classified advertising section in the newspaper would probably not be so good as space advertising with an attractive layout.

When newspaper space is used, the following are considered to be some preferred positions: [1]

> Outside pages
> Special news pages
> Sports page
> Woman's page
> Amusement page
> Top of a column
> Top of a column next to reading matter
> Next to or following reading matter
> Next to and following reading matter

Directories and programs are ordinarily not considered satisfactory media, but some businessmen advertise in these as a matter of policy. In other words, the money is spent in this way because the businessman feels that he dare not refuse. He uses such media somewhat in self-defense because he does not want his competitors' advertising to appear without his.

Billboards, car cards, and local radio programs are considered good advertising for many localized businesses. Such advertising is effective in attracting the general public within a wide area. It is doubtful, however, if, for instance, a grocer in a section of a large city would find radio advertising profitable. The cost would probably be so great that the results would not justify the expense. Radio advertising in this case would not be effective because such a small percentage of the listeners would be potential customers. Nevertheless a billboard advertisement on roads leading into the merchant's section of town might prove profitable.

Almost any businessman, particularly the merchant, can use most forms of direct-mail advertising. The merchant will not use catalogues, but he can use other forms.

---

[1] Edward J. Rowse and Louis J. Fish, *Fundamentals of Advertising* (Cincinnati, Ohio: South-Western Publishing Co.), 1937.

Illustration No. 142—Package Inserts and Direct-Mail Literature

Handbills are a popular means of advertising used by neighborhood stores and by centrally located stores in large cities. In many cities there are agencies that make a business of distributing handbills at a contract price. In a neighborhood, however, the delivery boy or the clerks in the store can sometimes perform this function. One of the bad effects of distributing handbills is the littering of porches and lawns. In some cities there are ordinances against this practice. A substitute for distributing handbills to homes is to wrap the bills in customers' packages. In this instance, however, the handbills do not reach noncustomers. Items of this type enclosed in packages are often referred to as package inserts.

Mailing Lists for Direct-Mail Advertising. Mailing lists can be bought from many commercial agencies. The names on these lists are often classified according to professions and occupations, sex or age. The best mailing lists for a local businessman are, however, those that he compiles on a selective basis. The following [1] are some means of obtaining satisfactory mailing lists for an advertising campaign:

Records of former customers and prospects

Names of prospects supplied by customers

News and society items in papers

Telephone directory

City directory

Classified business directory

Financial and trade directories

Mercantile directories

Voting lists

Assessors' lists

Lists of real-estate transfers

List of automobile owners

Records of business permits issued

Records of marriage licenses issued

Records of charters of incorporation issued

Records of births and deaths

School manuals

Lists of faculty members and students of universities and colleges

Lists of municipal and state employees

Social register

Club membership lists

Convention rosters

[1] Edward J. Rowse and Louis J. Fish, *Fundamentals of Advertising* (Cincinnati, Ohio: South-Western Publishing Co.), 1937.

Space Advertising Versus Direct-Mail Advertising. In some businesses, space advertising in newspapers or magazines is the most economical form of advertising. In other businesses, direct-mail advertising has been found to be most effective and economical. In many businesses it is necessary to use a combination of these types of advertising. The table on page 368 compares space advertising with direct advertising. All these factors should be considered carefully by a businessman in deciding what kind of advertising to use.

Correlating Sales Promotion. To be effective, space advertising should be correlated with direct-mail advertising and all other forms of promotion. The ideal purposes of such correlated advertising are as follows:

1. To have a possible customer pick up a magazine or a newspaper, read the seller's advertisement, and be impressed with a need for the product.
2. To have the prospect receive at about the same moment a folder or a booklet from his or her *favorite* retail dealer, telling the advantages of this same product.
3. To have the prospect go down to the dealer's store and be reminded again of this product by a sign on the window or a display in the window.
4. To have the dealer's clerk suggest to the prospect the purchase of this product, pointing out its advantages and merits.
5. To have the prospect buy the product and, on opening the package at home, find an insert rehearsing the story and the uses of the product.
6. To have the prospect, after reading this information carefully, recommend or praise the product to friends.
7. To have the prospect and friends of the prospect use and reorder the product.

Combining Oral and Printed Salesmanship. There is only one way to find out what combination of oral and printed sales effort will most conserve time and effort in any business. That method is by testing several combinations that

SPACE ADVERTISING	DIRECT ADVERTISING
CIRCULATION: Inflexible. The mailing list is provided by the publisher. The advertiser must use exactly the quantity of the advertising medium offered. He cannot pick and choose except that he can select a magazine or a newspaper.	CIRCULATION: Flexible. The advertiser can select his own circulation or mailing list by communities, by businesses, by professions, by social or executive positions.
MAILING DATES: These are set by the publisher.	MAILING DATES: These can be suited exactly to the work in hand.
TIMELINESS: The closing dates of magazines often prevent taking advantage of items of immediate news interest. The advertiser in the daily newspaper can use copy of immediate news interest.	TIMELINESS: Items of immediate news interest can be put into type and mailed while interest is keen.
UNIT OF SPACE: The advertiser must use the unit of space determined by the publisher.	UNIT OF SPACE: This can be whatever size and shape seems desirable for the presentation of the subject under discussion.
PRINTING TREATMENT: The advertiser must be guided by the publisher's rules regarding ink, type, and paper.	PRINTING TREATMENT: This can be whatever is necessary or desirable for the particular subject being promoted.
COST PER UNIT: The per unit per reader cost of space advertising is low, especially when each one of the entire reader group is a possible purchaser, or influences possible purchases.	COST PER UNIT: The per unit per reader cost of direct advertising may be low or high according to the character of the mailing.
ADVERTISING COMPETITION: Magazines and newspapers carry advertising of competitors and of many other businesses.	ADVERTISING COMPETITION: Direct-advertising pieces usually are devoted exclusively to the business of a single advertiser.
INFORMATION TO COMPETITORS: In a space campaign the scope and the character of the effort are usually apparent to competitors.	INFORMATION TO COMPETITORS: The scope of the effort is not apparent to competitors. It may comprise one hundred names or one million.

S. D. Warren Company.

Illustration No. 143—Space Advertising Compared with Direct Advertising

seem suitable. The following comments suggest combinations of oral and printed salesmanship. Some of these
comments are based upon direct selling through traveling
salesmen, but most of the principles apply also to store
salesmanship.

It is possible that the salesmen may be trying to see too
many people. The question therefore arises as to whether
the territory should be restricted or whether some form of
direct-mail advertising would help the salesmen cover the
territory more effectively.

Because of their lack of training or their habit of not
presenting all the strong points of the product that is being
sold, salesmen may be failing to capitalize all their sales
efforts. It may therefore prove desirable to prepare port-
folios, manuals, booklets, or other printed pieces to help
the salesmen. Some printed literature may be presented
by the salesman during a demonstration or mailed after
the interview. This literature will help to complete the
sales story and clinch certain points.

Sometimes businessmen find that they are trying to cover
too large a territory. They therefore have printed literature
distributed. On the other hand, it may be possible that not
enough territory is being covered. Without expanding his
sales force, the businessman can increase his selling field
by distributing printed literature in new territories and
thus paving the way for salesmen to call.

Particularly in the field of retailing, it is important to
back up new products with campaigns that correlate with
national advertising and local newspaper advertising. The
house-to-house distribution of literature, the mailing of
circulars, or the enclosure of literature in packages often
serve as effective means of increasing sales and introducing
new products. The use of a package insert is particularly
important in giving instructions as to the use of a product.
The satisfaction that a customer enjoys from a product
may depend upon his successful use of it. Printed instructions prove important, therefore, in many cases.

The chart in Illustration No. 144 shows how one manufacturer has organized an advertising program that co-

operates with wholesalers, retailers, architects, and decorators. Part of the program is also directed toward the consumer. This chart illustrates many of the uses of advertising.

Manufacturer and Dealer Aids. The manufacturers and the distributors of many products co-operate with merchants in advertising those products. The following are some of the means of advertising commonly furnished:

> Window displays
> Counter displays
> Handbills
> Layouts for newspaper advertisements
> Mailing pieces
> Co-operative financing of newspaper advertising
> House-to-house canvassing and sampling
> Store demonstrations

The obtaining of such co-operation in advertising is sometimes dependent upon the buying of a certain quantity of merchandise. Overloading one's stock, however, in order to participate in such a plan is undesirable, although buying a certain quantity may often be advantageous. When merchants buy a certain quantity of goods, some manufacturers or distributors agree to provide special window displays that will be set up by a trained specialist.

Timeliness of Advertising. In nearly every type of business there are certain times when advertising can be done more effectively than at others. For instance, manufacturers and sellers of toys advertise widely before the Christmas holidays. Outdoor furniture is advertised in the spring and early summer. Blankets are advertised in the late summer and early fall. Laundries and dry-cleaning establishments feature special advertisements for curtains and draperies in the spring and the fall. Rug-cleaning companies make a special advertising drive at house-cleaning time in the spring. At other times of the year advertising may be wasted to a great extent. One should therefore study his business to determine the most opportune times at which to advertise.

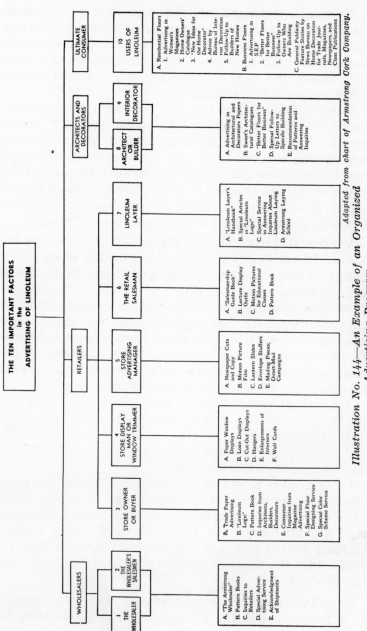

Illustration No. 144—An Example of an Organized Advertising Program

Adapted from chart of Armstrong Cork Company.

Co-operative Advertising. Through co-operative advertising, chambers of commerce, organizations of retailers, or smaller groups have been able to sponsor profitable sales days. Such sales days promote the community as a shopping center and in that respect have a general beneficial effect upon the entire community.

In some communities the mayor issues a proclamation; local newspapers co-operate with special publicity; streetcars and busses co-operate in the publicity program; package inserts, window cards, car cards, posters, billboards, and handbills are used to spread publicity throughout the entire shopping community. During some of these promotional days, special athletic events, fireworks displays, concerts, picnics, and other amusements are arranged.

Window Displays. The Merchants Service Bureau of the National Cash Register Company has made a study of the points for measuring the quality of window displays. These criteria are listed on page 373.

Window displays should be kept clean and should be changed frequently. To a great extent the same people pass the windows daily; and, if the displays are not changed frequently, the passers-by become tired of looking at the same exhibits, which after a while lose their appeal. Furthermore, the merchandise eventually becomes soiled.

A merchant should bear in mind that the windows and the front of his store greatly influence the first impression of the customer. They should therefore be kept attractive and in harmony with the rest of the store and with the merchandise that is being sold.

If one expects to utilize his window display for the most effective presentation, he should decorate it during times when there are few people passing the windows. Illustration No. 146 shows the pedestrian traffic in a central business district and in a neighborhood business district. Notice that the times of inactivity are early morning and late at night.

Store Displays. The special displays within a store should be in harmony with the window displays. If something is

TO ASSURE GOOD WINDOW DISPLAYS

- Make the windows advertise the merchandise to be sold as well as the character of the store.
- Put human interest into displays.
- Suggest the use of the articles displayed.
- Mark prices plainly.
- Display related articles together.
- Display seasonal goods; tie up displays with local events and needs.
- Group merchandise; don't scatter it.
- Tie up displays with advertising.
- Don't crowd the windows.
- Make displays simple.
- Plan displays ahead.
- Get together everything needed before starting to work in the window.
- Improve the window lighting.
- Study and use harmonious color combinations.
- Don't expose to sunlight merchandise that will be harmed by it.
- Change displays frequently.
- Keep the windows and displays spotlessly clean inside and outside.
- Make the displays sell merchandise.

Illustration No. 145—Criteria of Good Window Displays

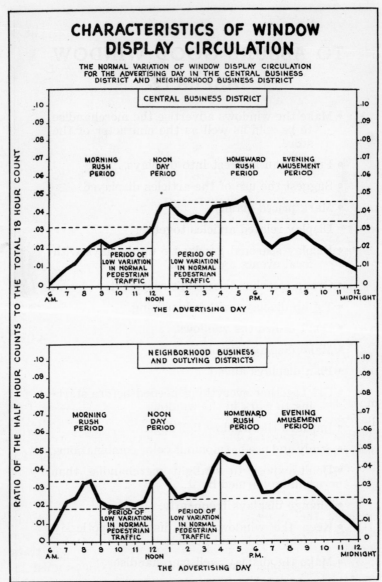

*Illustration No. 146—Characteristic Pedestrian Traffic
Passing Window Displays*

Dennison Manufacturing Co.

*Illustration No. 147—An Attractive Window Display That Can Be
Effectively Tied Up with Other Advertising*

featured in a window, it should also be featured in the
interior of the store.

Above all considerations, the displays within a store
must be neat and clean. They should be changed frequently. The degree of modernity will depend upon the
types of customers, but competition usually forces the
merchant to use modern equipment and modern displays.
The merchant who keeps up to date is usually the one who
gets the business.

Large department stores, chain stores, and associations
such as the International Grocers Alliance have made
studies that disclose the most useful display space for
certain products. For instance, a grocery store has certain
preferred locations. Fresh fruits and vegetables must be
displayed prominently, whereas soap, unless it is on special
sale, may be placed in an obscure place. Condiments and
various luxuries should be displayed prominently because

people do not ask for them as they do for the usual necessities. It is a common practice in restaurants to display chewing gum and candy near the cash register. After eating a meal, customers are usually in a receptive mood for such items and may use some of their change in buying them. Unless such items are within sight, however, they will not be requested.

A maximum amount of display should be obtained with a minimum amount of crowding. Literature and suggestions on displays can be obtained from such sources as the following: the United States Department of Commerce, the United States Chamber of Commerce, the National Cash Register Company.

A merchant can also obtain books on the subject. He can employ the services of professional persons who arrange displays. Some manufacturers help merchants prepare special displays for their goods. Manufacturers of display material, such as crepe paper and other items, also furnish suggestions on arranging displays.

Special Displays. Manufacturers and dealers also make arrangements for other displays. Some of these are the displays placed in bank windows, at county fairs, at state fairs, or in vacant buildings. Banks are often willing to feature home products by granting window-display space. Every producer and distributor of merchandise should be alert for every possible means of attractive display.

Samples and Demonstrations. When producers are introducing new merchandise or a new product into a new territory, they commonly distribute samples. The purpose of this practice is to familiarize people with the product so that there will be a demand for it in local stores.

Producers and distributors also co-operate with merchants by arranging special displays and demonstrations within stores. Samples are given to customers as they enter. This practice usually helps the merchant to sell the new product. He, of course, gives this merchandise a preference over other competing products. Sometimes distributors pay merchants for the privilege of giving demonstrations or offer special inducements for such a privilege. If conducted properly, the demonstration and sampling process is of common advantage to the merchant and to the producer or the distributor. Before granting the privilege, the merchant should be sure, however, that the product is of a quality that he is willing to recommend.

Planning the Advertising Program. The preceding discussion points out the various types of advertising and helps to evaluate their usefulness. Any businessman, however, has an individual problem in determining what kind of advertising program to follow. In many cases the businessman will imitate his competitors or at least follow a similar plan, but he should always be looking for a new and more effective means of advertising. One of the first considerations is to determine a reasonable amount of money that can be afforded for advertising. Some of the figures presented in this chapter will help in estimating the amount that can be spent judiciously.

From the United States Department of Foreign and Domestic Commerce, from some of the cash register manufacturers, and from other sources, it is possible to obtain books, pamphlets, and various other information that show the effectiveness of different types of advertising for various purposes.

Handling the Advertising Program. The small businessman often has to rely on his own ability in making all the advertising plans and in writing the advertisements. The printer may help him in writing the copy and designing the advertisement. Paper supply houses often help in selecting the proper paper. Newspaper publishers will offer suggestions in preparing newspaper advertisements. Radio-broadcasting companies will help to plan radio advertising.

As the business grows larger, the owner has the option of hiring someone to handle the advertising or of placing all his advertising problems in the hands of an advertising agency, which will take care of everything. For their services, advertising agencies usually charge a percentage of the total amount spent for the advertising.

QUESTIONS FOR DISCUSSION

1. What are some of the purposes of advertising?
2. From an analysis of the advertising expenditures given in the table on page 362, what seems to be the upper limit in terms of percentage of net sales?
3. For what types of products or businesses are the highest percentages of net sales spent for advertising?
4. What is meant by publication advertising?
5. What is meant by mass advertising?
6. What is meant by direct advertising?
7. Why is the outside page of a magazine considered to be a desirable advertising space?
8. In your opinion why is radio advertising probably not a desirable advertising medium for a grocery store in a large city?
9. From what sources can a new store in a community obtain a satisfactory list of prospects?
10. Compare the advantages and the disadvantages of publication, or space, advertising as contrasted with direct advertising.
11. Is direct-mail advertising cheaper than space advertising?
12. State briefly how various forms of advertising and sales promotion can be correlated.
13. What are some means that can be used in educating retail dealers how to sell a product effectively?
14. Enumerate some of the advertising aids that manufacturers often provide for retail merchants.
15. What aspect of timeliness in advertising should be considered in planning a program?
16. What is the advantage of a community co-operative plan of sales promotion?
17. Point out some means of judging or measuring the quality of window displays.
18. Name at least three sources from which information on store displays can be obtained.
19. From the point of view of the manufacturer and the store owner, what are the advantages of store demonstrations?
20. What assistance can the small businessman obtain in preparing his advertising?

PROBLEMS AND PROJECTS

1. Take with you a list of the items by which a window display can be measured as to its quality and effectiveness. With this list before you make a study of some window display in your community, evaluate it, and write a report.

2. Obtain a sample of a handbill, a package insert, or a piece of direct-mail advertising literature, and criticize it from the following points of view: (a) attractiveness, (b) specific information, (c) effectiveness, (d) any other points that seem important.

3. Plan an advertising campaign for a small shoe store in your community, being sure that the total expenditures for a year will not exceed $3,000.

4. Plan a national advertising campaign for a company that produces about $300,000 worth of hand-wrought aluminum products each year. These products consist of ash trays, trays, book ends, match cases, and other items that are commonly sold in gift shops, department stores, book stores, and the like.

5. Develop a plan for an advertising campaign for a local grocery store.

6. Obtain a sample of a newspaper advertisement of some nationally advertised product, and explain how it ties in with the local sales campaign of stores that are selling the product.

7. The Midwest Mail-Order House has a mailing list containing the names of 5,000 professional men. The item sold by this company is a leather traveling bag that sells for $30. It costs the company $20. The following table shows the number of pieces of literature in each mailing, the cost of each mailing, the number of answers, and the number of sales. Copy this table and then complete it by placing in the fifth and sixth columns the gross profit from the sales made as a result of each mailing and the net profit or loss after the mailing cost has been taken into consideration.

Number of Pieces in Each Mailing	Cost of Literature	Number of Answers	Number of Sales	Gross Profit on Sales	Net Profit or Loss
5,000	$400	75	60		
4,925	340	60	50		
4,865	300	30	25		
4,835	295	20	15		
4,815	295	10	8		

CHAPTER XVI

OFFICE PROBLEMS

Purpose of the Chapter. The transactions in every business office involve purchasing, selling, transporting, issuing credit, making collections, advertising, accounting, and budgeting. Most of these functions have been explained in preceding chapters. There are, in addition, functions of office operation that are more or less routine and apply to all these other functions. The purpose of this chapter is to point out and explain these additional functions from the points of view of the large office and the small office. The following are some of the questions that will be answered:

1. How may an office be organized?
2. How should mail be handled?
3. How should telephone and interoffice communications be handled?
4. What is an efficient plan for stenographic work?
5. What is an efficient plan for indexing and filing?
6. What is an efficient plan for handling supplies?
7. What office equipment is needed?
8. How can an efficient office layout be planned?

Office Organization. Illustration No. 148 shows the organization of a large office. In a large business the office manager ranks with the managers of such departments as credit, accounting, and sales.

Business establishments differ widely in their methods of fixing responsibility for the management of an office. If the head of the accounting department or of some other department is responsible for the office work, the management of the office is liable to be neglected because under such a plan there is no centralized control and each department carries on its own work.

When the office work is organized as a department of the business, the office manager will contact all the other de-

380

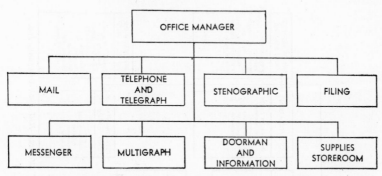

Illustration No. 148—Organization of an Office

partmental executives and work in close co-operation with
them. Under this type of organization much can be done
to promote harmony and efficiency. Furthermore, the duplication of work can be eliminated. For example, there can
be a centralized filing force and a centralized stenographic
force. If, on the other hand, the stenographic force is
divided among the various departments, there is a likelihood that at certain times one department will be extremely
busy while another will be idle, but the busy department
may not be able to call upon the idle department for assistance. Under a centralized system the office help can do
whatever work is necessary at the time.

Office Functions. Illustration No. 149 shows the numerous
detailed functions that are performed in large offices
through the office manager. Not all these functions are
performed in every office, but this chart does give an idea
of most of the functions that are performed.

Handling Incoming Mail. In every office, large or small,
some particular person should be responsible for sorting
and distributing the incoming mail. In some offices it is
desirable to hand to the proper persons the unopened mail;
whereas in many large offices a special mailing department
will open the mail, stamp it with the time of arrival, and
distribute it to the proper persons or departments. Whenever there is any doubt as to who should get a certain piece

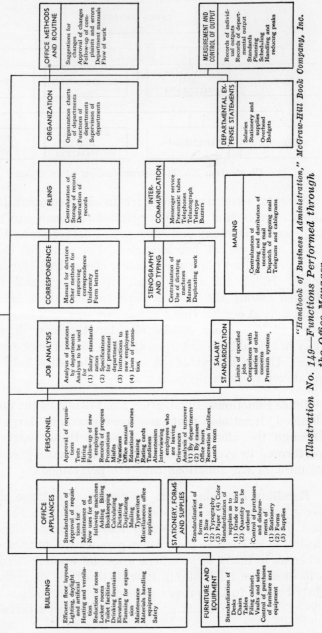

"Handbook of Business Administration," McGraw-Hill Book Company, Inc.

Illustration No. 149—Functions Performed through the Office Manager

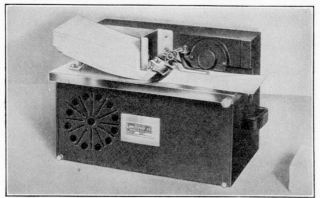

Multipost Company.
Illustration No. 150—A Letter Opener

of mail, the office manager or some other person in charge determines the person. Personal mail or mail marked for certain individuals is delivered to the proper individuals. Mail within the office is usually delivered by means of an organized messenger system.

Particular care should be taken in scanning mail to discover its general contents, to check enclosures, particularly remittances, and to verify any mistakes that might be evident before the mail is distributed. If there is a discrepancy between the statements in a letter and the actual enclosures, this discrepancy should be marked on the mail. Checks and other enclosures should be clipped, or preferably pinned, to letters before the mail is distributed.

Handling Outgoing Mail. The internal messenger system should provide for not only distributing mail but also collecting outgoing mail. Under an organized mailing system the mailing department collects all outgoing mail, checks enclosures, and further prepares the letters for mailing. In some offices the mailing department is responsible for folding, weighing, stamping, and sealing. Hand-stamping machines or permit-stamping machines are commonly used as time-saving devices. It is ordinarily not advisable to allow everyone in the office to handle stamps. If a permit-stamping machine (see page 157) is not used, some one

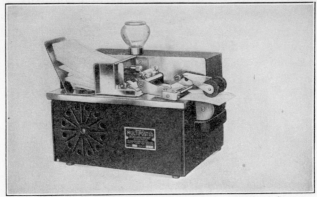

Multipost Company.

Illustration No. 151—A Sealing Machine

person should be responsible for handling the stamps and usually for stamping the mail.

Telephone and Telegraph Services. Every business office must have telephone services. Large offices have a telephone switchboard with connections to the individual desks and departments. All incoming and outgoing calls are handled through this switchboard. Interdepartmental messages are also handled through this switchboard. The management of the telephone switchboard is under the jurisdiction of the office manager.

Multipost Company.

Illustration No. 152—A Hand Stamp Affixer

It is common to have the telephone operator handle all incoming and outgoing telegrams. She can keep a record of the incoming collect telegrams and the outgoing telegrams to be charged to the business. When the monthly statement is received from the telegraph company, it can be checked with this record. The telephone operator is responsible for calling the telegraph messenger. A call box is commonly used for this purpose. Any office of a reasonable size may have a call box installed by the telegraph company. When a messenger is desired, all that is necessary is to signal the telegraph office over the call system.

The telephone operator is also responsible for keeping a record of outgoing long-distance calls and incoming collect calls. This function is important so that the monthly bills from the telephone company can be checked. It is possible, as a convenience, to telephone a message to the telegraph company and to have the message transmitted to its destination by telegraph. The cost of the telegram will appear on the monthly telephone bill.

Information and Reception Clerk. In most offices the telephone operator acts as the information and reception clerk for those who visit the office. In some offices, however, a special reception clerk is used in order to avoid interference with the duties of the telephone operator.

Regardless of who handles this function, the person should have exceptional qualities. She should be calm, pleasant, and courteous. Her diction should be clear and precise. She should have a good working knowledge of the organization so that, if she is questioned about it, she can answer satisfactorily. She should be acquainted with the

> **PHONE CALL**
>
> To...........J. A. Sherman................................
>
> During your absence you were called by
>
> Mr.......Thomas Patterson.............................
>
> ....
>
> ....
>
> Message:...Mr. Patterson will be glad to.....
> see you in his office tomorrow in regard
> to the matter that you discussed with him.
>
> ....
>
>   By........Jane Robinson..........
>
> Date.....January 5, 1940.

Illustration No. 153—A Call Notice

policies of the organization so that she will know what to do in giving information and in handling callers. As this person represents the company to the public, her position is very important. She is not only the reception clerk, but she must also handle many appointments. Illustration No. 153 is a form used for call notices and appointments.

Interdepartmental Communications. In most offices the person who distributes the incoming mail and collects the outgoing mail is also responsible for distributing interdepartmental communications. In some small offices the stenographer or the secretary who types an interdepartmental communication may pass it from one person to another; but in large offices where there are many such communications such a plan will cause considerable confusion, delay, and inefficiency. It is common for each department to have baskets for incoming and outgoing communications. Communications coming to the department are placed in one basket; those that are to be distributed to other departments are placed in the other.

An interoffice note may be directed to a particular individual. In some cases, however, it is advisable to send the same communication to several individuals. In such cases there is a choice of writing duplicate copies of the communication, one for each person, or listing at the top of a single copy the names of those who are to read the communication. After each person has read the communication, he checks off his name and passes the communication on to the next person.

The messenger who handles the interoffice communications should pass through the office at regularly established intervals to collect and to distribute communications. He should also be on call at any other time to handle any messages that are necessary.

The internal telephone system, handled through the switchboard or through another type of speaking system, may also be used for communications within the office. Pneumatic tubes may be used for sending communications from one department to another. Department stores use pneumatic tubes for handling sales tickets, and many offices use them for sending invoices and instructions from the order department to the shipping department.

INTEROFFICE COMMUNICATION

Mr. Baker
Mr. Ralston
To Miss Smith   Date   January 10,   19 40

There will be a meeting in my office this afternoon at 2:30 P.M.

Please be prepared to discuss any problems regarding your work

INTEROFFICE COMMUNICATION

Date   January 10,   19 40

To Mr. Baker

There will be a meeting in my office this afternoon at 2:30 P.M.

Please be prepared to discuss any problems regarding your work.

Copies to: Mr. Ralston

Miss

DATE   January 5,   1940

☒ NEED NOT BE RETURNED
☐ PLEASE RETURN
(TO RETURN CROSS OUT YOUR NAME
AND THE WORD FROM)

MO TO   Miss Overman

FROM   Mr. Ashby

Subject { Opinion on manuscript
           ☒ See attached sheets

Elson

PLEASE TAKE ACTION
INDICATED NOT
LATER THAN

January 7 , 19 40

Please see me ☐
personally

Being sent for ☐
your information

Please furnish ☐
data on material
requested

Please take ☐
action indicated

Please take ☐
up with

_____
_____

Please investigate ☐
and report to

Please express ☒
your judgment

Examine this manuscript and give me your
opinion of it.

PLEASE REPLY BELOW THIS LINE

By _____

*Illustration No. 154—Various Forms of Interoffice
Communications*

Stenographic Department. Businesses differ widely in the extent to which they centralize the responsibility for the preparation of outgoing and interdepartmental communications. In some cases each executive or employee regularly responsible for the preparation of such communications has his personal stenographer. The employees who are only occasionally responsible for the preparation of communications use stenographers detailed for such service. This situation represents the extreme of decentralization.

On the other hand, none of the executives or employees may have personal stenographers. A central stenographic service provides a stenographer on request. A further development of this plan is the use of dictating machines. The executives and employees dictate to these machines whenever they desire. The records are collected at regular intervals and taken to a central typewriting department, where the transcriptions are made. The transcribed material is then returned to the dictators, who inspect and sign it. It is then collected by the mail messengers and distributed. Illustrations Nos. 155 and 156 show the use of dictating and transcribing machines.

Thomas A. Edison, Inc.

*Illustration No. 155—An Executive Dictating on a
Dictating Machine*

In many offices the principal executives have secretaries who do their stenographic work in addition to the performance of other tasks, while the junior executives and employees use the services of a central stenographic department or employ machines. In most business there are some correspondents who handle the routine correspondence. It is unnecessarily expensive to have high-salaried executives devoting their time to answering inquiries and complaints that can be handled just as well by medium-salaried employees. In some cases, too, the use of correspondents leads to the preparation of better letters. Investment banking institutions, for example, have found it desirable to have correspondents not only so that the salesmen can spend more of their time in direct selling, but also because correspondents can be selected who write better letters than does the typical salesman.

At the present stage of development in office administration, no arbitrary rule can be stated concerning the proper degree of centralization. The best plan for any given business can be determined only after a consideration of the nature of the operations and the character of the personnel.

Dictaphone Sales Corporation.

Illustration No. 156—A Stenographer Transcribing Letters That Were Dictated on a Dictating Machine

In most businesses, when the office functions have been developed to any considerable extent, it is expedient to have some centralization of this work. In all cases the office manager should have functional control over this activity in all departments.

Filing Procedures. In most businesses the correspondence and other material appropriate for filing soon reach such proportions that it is not feasible to have separate files for each office, executive, or employee. Both efficiency and economy are promoted by the use of a centralized filing service. As soon as the recipient of any correspondence or other material has completed his present use of it, it is sent to the files. If it is desired later, a memorandum requesting it is sent to the filing department. The filing department supplies the desired material. When it is removed from the file a so-called out card is inserted in its place containing a memorandum of the material that has been removed from the file. If anyone goes to the files for

Remington Rand, Inc.
Illustration No. 157—A Central Filing Department

this particular correspondence, the out card shows who has the correspondence. In some offices a follow-up card is also made when correspondence is removed from the files. This card is put in a so-called tickler file. If the material that has been removed from the files is not returned within a specified time marked on the follow-up card, this fact is brought to the attention of the filing clerks. Follow-up cards placed in a tickler file may also be used for various types of reminders.

The filing department should be located near those departments that make most frequent use of it, or some mechanical means should be employed to transfer material as quickly as possible. If an executive has frequent need for specific material, he may keep this material in a private file.

When a central filing system is used, only the filing clerks should be permitted to file correspondence or to take correspondence from the files. If others are permitted to go to the files, there are too many chances of errors, and no one can be held responsible.

If there are individual departmental files in addition to the files of the central filing department, there should be close correlation between them. If something is filed in a

1 2 3 4 5 6 7 8 9 10 11 12 13 14 15 16 17 18 19 20 21 22 23 24 25 26 27 28 29 30

NAME_____ POSITION_____

ADDRESS _____

_____

_____

HOME ADDRESS _____

REMARKS

Illustration No. 158—A Follow-Up Card

```
School _____
Address _____
Folder requested by _____ Date _____
Remarks _____
_____
_____
```

Illustration No. 159—Out Card: A Memorandum of
Material Removed from the Files

departmental file that has a relation to the general files, a duplicate should be placed in the general files or there should be some other method of cross-indexing.

Indexing and Filing Systems. There are fundamentally four systems of indexing and filing correspondence: alphabetic, subject, geographic, and numeric. However, there are variations of these.

The alphabetic and the subject filing systems are essentially the same. Under the alphabetic system, general alphabetic divisions are indicated on the tabs of the guide cards, and material is filed either by subjects or by names between these alphabetic divisions. Under the subject system of filing, the actual subjects are specifically indicated on the tabs.

The geographic filing system is likewise fundamentally an alphabetic system. The guide cards are arranged alphabetically according to the states, the cities, or the counties indicated on the tabs, and within these geographic divisions material is filed alphabetically according to the names of the correspondents.

Numeric filing requires the classification of correspondence into groups that are numbered. Such a plan necessitates the keeping of a separate card index to indicate in what section of the numeric files particular correspondence can be found, or the numeric system must be memorized so that one will know under what numeric classification correspondence can be found.

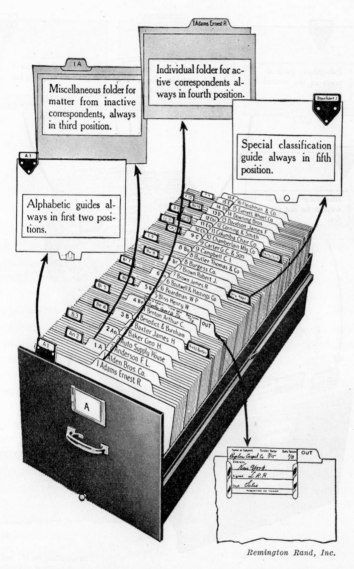

Miscellaneous folder for matter from inactive correspondents, always in third position.

Individual folder for active correspondents always in fourth position.

Special classification guide always in fifth position.

Alphabetic guides always in first two positions.

Remington Rand, Inc.

Illustration No. 160—An Alphabetic Filing System

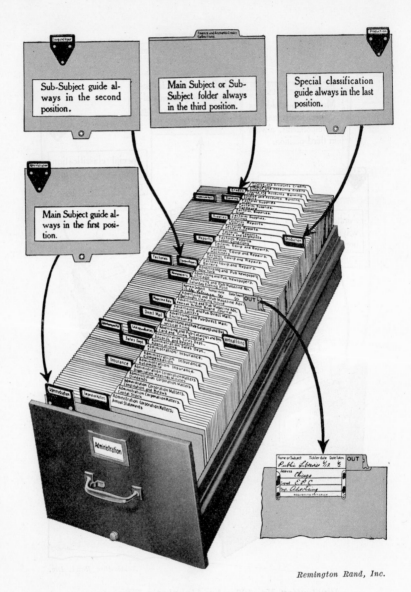

Remington Rand, Inc.

Illustration No. 161—A Subject Filing System

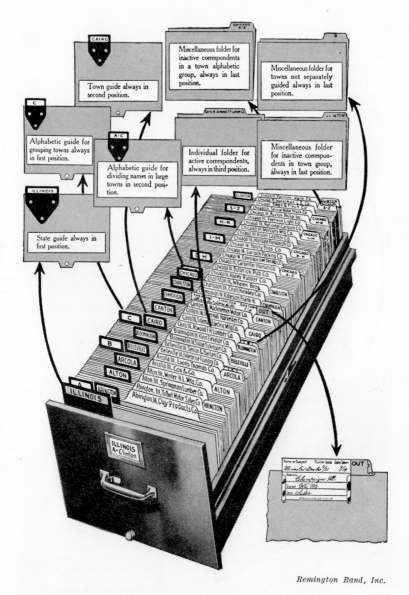

Remington Rand, Inc.

Illustration No. 162—A Geographic Filing System

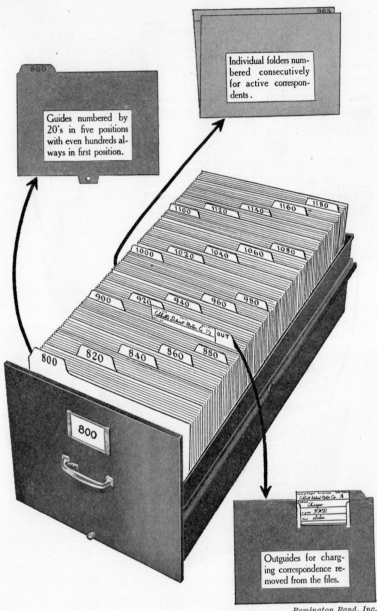

Guides numbered by 20's in five positions with even hundreds always in first position.

Individual folders numbered consecutively for active correspondents.

Outguides for charging correspondence removed from the files.

Remington Rand, Inc.

Illustration No. 163—A Numeric Filing System

Handling Supplies. The modern tendency is to standardize office supplies as much as possible. By standardization is meant the elimination of numerous unusual sizes
and kinds of supplies used in the office. For instance, one
company found that it was using twenty-six different types
of steel pens and finally standardized on three types. It also
found that it was using twelve different kinds of paper and
finally standardized on three. Eight different types of pen-
cils were used. One kind of mechanical pencil was selected
as the standard, and leads of different colors were purchased for this pencil.

Standardization leads to economy in the purchase and
the use of supplies. In order that standardization may be
established, control should be centralized in the hands of
the office manager. Naturally, he must co-operate with
employees and department heads in determining what
should be obtained.

After the supplies have been selected, they are purchased
by the regular purchasing agent. The quantities to be purchased should be determined by the office manager in consultation with the department heads. It is advisable to
establish minimum quantities for stock so that the supplies
will not be exhausted at any time. The maximum quantities
to be purchased will be determined by the savings that can
be made in purchasing. Illustrations Nos. 164 and 165 show
a record for controlling the stock of stationery.

If supplies are to be used economically, they should be
placed in a central storeroom and issued only upon the request of department heads. The quantity each department
is permitted to requisition at one time, or within a definite
period of time, can be established; and the storekeeper can
see that these standards are not exceeded. Requisitions for
supplies may be sent through the controller's department
so that they can be checked against budget appropriations.
This plan brings about an effective control, which is not
possible when each department has the custody of its
supplies. If each department keeps its own supplies, almost
invariably inadequate attention will be given to the care of
the supplies and excessive quantities will be used. The

STATIONERY SPECIFICATIONS AND INFORMATION

Time required to get delivery. . . .	10 days
Sheets consumed each day	50
Minimum quantity	1,000 sheets (2 reams)
Maximum quantity to be ordered . . .	10,000 sheets (20 reams)
Kind of paper.	Uncle Sam Bond
Weight	24 pounds
Color.	White

Illustration No. 164—Front Side of a Stationery-Stock Control Card

Reams

Date	Purchased [1]	Taken out of Stock	Balance [2] in Stock
6/2/39	10		2
6/3/39			12
6/25/39		1	11
7/5/39		2	9

[1] Recorded at time of purchase.
[2] Place order when supply diminishes to 2 reams.

Illustration No. 165—Reverse Side of the Stationery-Stock Control Card

purchasing procedure for supplies is the same as that for merchandise. This procedure is discussed in Chapter X.

Office Equipment. Whenever possible, it is desirable to use standard equipment in all departments of a business. Standardization is especially desirable for furniture, fixtures, and other office furnishings. To that end, the manager of a business frequently selects a standard type of desk, standard typewriters, and other standard machines to be used in all departments of his business.

To obtain the adoption and the continued use of standardized equipment, it is necessary to have a centralized control of all equipment purchases. A customary procedure is to have all requisitions for the purchase of equipment referred to the office manager for approval. They are then sent to the purchasing agent, who makes the purchase. The purchasing agent is sometimes held responsible for standardization.

The various units of the office organization should be in proper relation to one another. Departments that have

From Bowman, *Shorthand Dictation Studies,*
South-Western Publishing Company.   *Ewing Galloway.*

Illustration No. 166—A Well-Arranged Office

frequent relations with each other should be located near each other. The equipment within the various departments should be arranged in such an order that each employee will receive a maximum amount of light and ventilation. It is the function of the office manager to work out a proper layout for all departments and all equipment within the office.

The office manager should be responsible for keeping an accurate record of the condition and the repairs of office equipment. He should make arrangements for servicing and reconditioning, and should also keep himself well informed on new developments in equipment that can be purchased as time-saving devices.

Mechanical Time-Saving Equipment. The mechanical equipment in an office is important. Large offices use many types of time-saving equipment. In some small offices such equipment is used only to a limited extent because not many types are needed. Examples of time-saving equipment are:

Adding machines	Envelope openers
Calculating machines	Envelope sealers
Duplicating machines	Time stamps
Dictating machines	Stamp affixers
Billing machines	Letter folders
Bookkeeping machines	Metered mailing machines
Numbering devices	Addressing machines
Dating devices	Coin counters and sorters
Stapling machines	Coin changers
Check-writing devices	Package tying machines

Duplicating Equipment. In every office, large or small, there are times when a number of copies, ranging from two or three to several thousand, of a letter, a bulletin, or some other communication must be duplicated. There are numerous duplicating devices available. Illustration No. 167 shows the most common devices, with their uses, possible economies, advantages, and disadvantages. The ranking in the last column shows the most expensive process at the top with the least expensive at the bottom.

Office Layout. The layout of an office, large or small, is an important factor in adding to the efficiency of the office.

Duplicating Process	Uses Recommended	Number of Copies for Which Equipment Is Economical (Compared with Typing)	Advantages	Disadvantages	Rank of Relative Cost (100 Copies)
Printing (Letter Press)	Circulars, forms, catalogues, books, pamphlets	500—unlimited	Clear, neat, flexible	Useful only for work than can be done outside the office	1
Typewriting (Typewriters)	Letters and originals of other manuscripts	1—10	Personally typed and individualized	Depends on skill of typist; costly in large quantities	2
Offset Duplicators (Rotoprint, Multilith)	Forms, bulletins, catalogues, letters, circulars	100—10,000	Faithful duplication of original; flexible; economical when typed material is reproduced	Requires photo equipment and a skilled operator	3
Type Duplicators (Multigraph)	Letters, forms, bulletins	100—5,000 (Some will permit longer runs)	Clear reproduction, similar to printing	Not flexible; requires slow process of setting type	4
Automatic Typewriters (Hooven, Autotypist)		25—3,000 (3,000, approximate life of stencil)	Perfectly typed and individualized	Costly equipment and skilled operator	5
Direct Process (Cardograph, Dupligraph, Addressing Machine)	Letters and cards	100—5,000	Addressing to match letter	Not flexible; costly; requires addressing equipment	6
Stencil Duplicators (Mimeograph, Niagara, etc.)	Interoffice forms, bulletins, notices	10—3,000 (3,000, approximate life of stencil)	Flexible; distinct; fair imitation of typewriting	Cannot match clearly the inside address on letters	7
Gelatin Duplicators (Ditto, Speedograph, Fluid, Liquid Process)	Interoffice forms, bulletins, notices	5—100 (100, approximate life of master copy)	Flexible, economical	Indistinct duplication; smearing; not permanent	8

Illustration No. 167—An Analysis of Types of Duplication

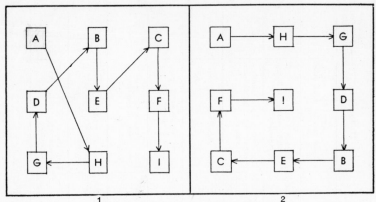

Illustration No. 168—Flow Charts

There are two ways of making a study to determine the proper layout. One is to devise a *flow chart* showing how the normal transactions of the office proceed from one department or person to another. The charts in Illustration No. 168 show the original layout of an office and the improved layout. Notice how the rearrangement in Chart 2 has eliminated the overlapping and confusion.

Another means of checking the layout of an office is through the use of a *relationship chart*. For instance, each department will have certain relationships with other departments each day. The department that has the most relationships with another department during an average day should be nearest the latter department. Of course, certain compromises must be made. Illustration No. 169 shows a chart made to determine these relationships and also the new improved layout. Each line indicates that a relationship or a communication is established between the departments or individuals five times a day. Chart 2 shows a rearrangement to eliminate overlapping and confusion.

Small Offices. In a small office all the functions mentioned previously are performed, but many of them are assigned to fewer individuals. For instance, a small office may have only one stenographer who acts as the telephone clerk, the filing clerk, and the bookkeeper. This individual,

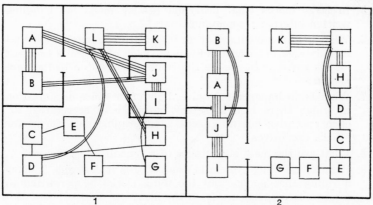

Illustration No. 169—Relationship Charts

however, can organize the office on a small scale in the same way as a large office. Essentially the same procedures can be performed, and exactly the same principles should be followed.

In a small office it is often advisable to send out to agencies certain work, particularly duplication work, that cannot be performed economically by the small staff in the office. There are so-called letter service companies that specialize in typing letters, or in mimeographing, multigraphing, or printing material for small offices that do not have the necessary equipment. Prices on a particular type of service can be obtained from various agencies and can then be compared with the possible cost of doing the work in one's own office.

QUESTIONS FOR DISCUSSION

1. Give some reasons why it is desirable for one person in an office to sort and distribute the incoming mail.

2. If an office has a mailing department that takes care of outgoing mail, what are the responsibilities of that department?

3. Who is usually responsible in an office for keeping a record of incoming and outgoing telegrams?

4. Who is responsible in an office for checking the monthly bills from the telephone and telegraph companies?

5. In large offices what provision can be made for handling written interoffice communications?

6. What is a disadvantage of an interoffice communication that is addressed to several individuals, each of whom is to check off his name as he passes the communication on to the next person?

7. What is an important disadvantage of an office organization in which there is a secretary or group of secretaries for each executive but no general stenographic department for all the executives?

8. What are the main advantages of a central filing system?

9. If a central filing system is used, why is it desirable to have a ruling that no one but the filing clerks be permitted to remove correspondence from the files?

10. What are the main systems of filing used in business offices?

11. What are the advantages of standardizing the supplies for an office?

12. Who should handle the purchasing of supplies in an office?

13. What plan can be used to prevent a shortage of office supplies at any time?

14. Name some examples of time-saving and labor-saving office machines.

15. Name the principal duplicating processes used for office work.

16. Name and explain two types of charts that help to determine good office layouts.

PROBLEMS AND PROJECTS

1. Obtain information on first-class mail, and make a report on (a) material that must be sent as first-class mail and (b) the restrictions on such mail.

2. Make a study of the regulations regarding the sending of registered mail, and explain those regulations in your own words.

3. Prepare a report on the different services offered by telegraph companies.

4. As the manager of an office, write an interoffice communication notifying each member of the executive staff that there will be a meeting in your office at 2:30 P.M. on Friday for the purpose of discussing the summer vacation schedule.

5. Taking into consideration the following facts, compute the cost of each letter that is written during a week:

```
Letters written during the week .................   400
Cost of stationery ............................$  5.00
Cost of envelopes .............................$  6.00
Cost of  postage ..............................$12.00
Stenographers' salaries .......................$37.00
Salary of dictator ............................$50.00 a week
```
(60 per cent of the dictator's time is devoted to dictating.)

Assume that two girls handle the typewriting, each having her own typewriter. The policy of the company is to trade in typewriters once every two years. The usual additional cost of each new typewriter obtained through the trade-in is $30. In determining the cost due to one week's wear on each typewriter, do not take into consideration any other miscellaneous costs.

6. If there are three people in an office who have the responsibility of preparing two hundred pieces of printed literature for mailing, suggest an efficient method of doing so. Assume that the literature must be folded and inserted into the envelopes, but that the stamps are not to be affixed by any of the three employees.

7. Assume the following facts with regard to the hand stamping of mail and to the use of a postage-meter machine for affixing stamps:

```
Rate of hand stamping .............1,000 pieces an hour
Cost of labor for hand stamping .....50 cents an hour
Rate of stamping with a postage-
    meter machine ..................2,000 pieces an hour
Cost of labor for machine stamping ..50 cents an hour
Cost of machine ....................$295
Length of life of machine ..........10 years (trade-in value,
                                               $30)
Rental of meter ...................$7 a month (average, 21
                                               days a month)
```

(a) If the company has an average daily mailing of 5,000 pieces, which method would be the more economical? (b) If the company has an average daily mailing of 25,000 pieces, which method would be the more economical? Assume that in either case the person who handles the stamping will be kept busy at other work when no mail is to be prepared.

8. Draw a plan for a small model office in which the following individuals will work:

Manager of the office, who is out of the office a good portion of the time; assistant manager; secretary to the manager; secretary to the assistant manager; combination bookkeeper and filing clerk; general stenographer; statistical clerk, who also serves as telephone operator.

Make provision for whatever equipment appears necessary, including desks, tables, chairs, and other equipment.

CHAPTER XVII

PERSONNEL PROBLEMS

Purpose of the Chapter. Every business has the problem of hiring and maintaining an efficient working force. Some of the problems that have to do with the human element of a business are:

1. Is it desirable to have a centralized employment bureau?
2. How may new workers be hired efficiently?
3. Why does a business wish to keep down its labor turnover?
4. What are the best methods of compensating employees?
5. How shall employees be trained?
6. What shall be done for the health, safety, and general welfare of employees?
7. Shall the business adopt a profit-sharing plan for its employees?

Section I

Employment and Compensation Plans and Procedures

Importance of Personnel Management. In many businesses the wages and salaries paid to employees amount to 60 per cent or more of the total operating expenses. A typist may be paid $1,200 a year, and the typewriter she uses may have cost $100. This condition, in which the operator is paid wages in excess of the value of the machine, is true in a majority of cases. Yet we find that the managements of most businesses have spent more time and money in studying and planning ways of efficiently caring for their machinery than they have in studying the care of the most important element, the human element, in their businesses.

406

An employee who has the proper mental attitude toward his employer and his position, and who is doing the kind of work that is best suited to his abilities, will be a most valuable asset to the business. If the employee is not interested in his job, does not enjoy his work, and has no pride in the business, he can be very much of a liability to the business. It is therefore essential that the manager of every business make a careful study of what should be done in connection with the selection, training, supervision, and welfare of the employees. This handling of problems in connection with employees is known as *personnel management*.

Who Directs the Personnel Activities? In a business that has only a few employees, the proprietor, or general manager, takes care of the personnel activities. He hires and dismisses employees, as well as trains them for their specific jobs. As he works side by side with his employees, he has a good understanding of them and readily appreciates their viewpoint. Likewise, the employees get to know something about the problems of their employer and, as a result, have a better attitude toward their employer and feel free to discuss their problems with him. Such conditions make for good employer-employee relationships.

Much of our modern business, however, is done on a large scale, and it is common to find businesses with five thousand or more employees. Naturally, this bigness makes it impossible for a close human relationship between the owners and the employees. As these large businesses need employees for hundreds of different kinds of highly specialized jobs, the problem of selecting properly qualified employees, training them for their jobs, providing for their health and welfare, and inciting them to work at their greatest efficiency is one of complexity and magnitude. Because it is of such importance, usually a *personnel department* is organized. The one in charge of this department is given some title, such as *personnel director*.

The principal activities of the personnel department are indicated in the chart in Illustration No. 170.

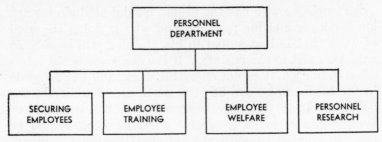

Illustration No. 170—Organization of a
Personnel Department

Centralized Employment Bureau. In a small business the hiring of employees is done by the proprietor. In most large businesses the hiring is done by a centralized employment bureau instead of by each department. Some of the advantages of centralization are:

1. An applicant may be a desirable employee for a job in a department other than the one in which he is applying for work. Under the centralized system the employment manager can place the applicant to better advantage. Under the decentralized system, however, the applicant might be rejected for a certain job in a certain department. That department, not knowing the qualifications for positions in other departments or the needs of those departments, might turn away an applicant who would make a desirable employee in some other department.

2. Because of his training and experience, the employment manager is usually better qualified to select employees for specific jobs than would be most supervisors or department heads.

3. The employment manager has more time to devote to the interview and to a study and appraisal of the applicant's education, training, and previous experience. The department heads are kept busy with the problems of managing their own departments.

4. A centralized employment bureau, with its detailed records, furnishes valuable information when transfers and promotions are being considered.

Employment of Workers. In order to obtain the proper workers, the personnel department must have a thorough knowledge of the job to be filled, information on the sources of labor supply, and a knowledge of the procedure to be used in selecting and placing the new employee. Each of these three essentials will be discussed in some detail.

Knowledge of the Job to Be Filled. The personnel department must have complete and accurate knowledge of the job to be filled before it can properly select an employee to fill that job. One of the best ways to obtain this information is to have detailed specifications prepared for each kind of job. These specifications include information as to the nature of the work done in the particular job, the necessary qualifications of the employee who is to do that work, and the opportunities that the job offers to the employee. This information is usually printed on cards, which are known as *job specification cards*. These cards are kept on

Illustration No. 171—A Job Specification Card

file in the personnel office. When a department is in need of a worker to fill a certain job, it communicates that information to the personnel department. The employment manager selects the proper job specification card from his files and quickly ascertains the type of worker wanted.

Knowledge of the Sources of Labor Supply. If the employment department is to fill quickly the needs of various departments for workers, it must have developed possible sources of labor supply. Some possible sources of labor are:

1. Employees of the company. Often a vacancy can be filled by transferring a present employee from some other job. Personnel records may show that certain employees are well qualified for the vacancy. Such a transfer may give an employee a chance to use his ability to a much higher degree than he did in his previous job. The transfer may therefore result in greater efficiency and a better satisfied employee. This policy also acts as a strong incentive for employees to be efficient and to train themselves for advancement. A detailed personnel record of each employee is therefore valuable. Such a record is usually kept permanently on a large record card. The filling of a vacancy by this means usually creates another vacancy that must be filled from some source outside the company.

2. Friends of present employees. The employees of the business may recommend friends for employment. Such a recommendation is usually dependable because a present employee knows the standards and the policies of the business and would hesitate to recommend friends who would not measure up to the demands of the business.

3. Applications on file. A business that has earned a reputation for excellent treatment of its employees is likely to have many applications on file at all times. From these it may be able to fill most of its vacancies.

4. Employment agencies. Professional, technical, and trade schools frequently maintain employment offices to aid their graduates in obtaining positions. They can furnish lists of suitable candidates for positions. The offices of many trade unions maintain lists of unemployed members and can furnish applicants for vacancies. State and city governments often maintain

employment agencies from which workers can be obtained. The United States Employment Service is sponsored by the Federal Government. Many states have employment service bureaus affiliated with the Federal bureau. These governmental agencies handle both adult and junior workers in all occupational groups and are usually operated without special charge to the persons applying to them. There are also many employment agencies operated by private individuals. These agencies make a charge to the person for whom they find employment. They usually specialize in supplying help of a particular kind.

5. Newspaper advertising. If a business needs employees, it can obtain prospective employees by inserting an advertisement in the daily newspapers. This source is used most frequently when workers are needed in large numbers or immediately.

Selection and Placement. The need for an employee should be anticipated as far in advance as possible so that the personnel department will have sufficient time to find a suitable employee. When the requisition is received from the department in which the vacancy will occur, the per-

Employment Dept.

EMPLOYMENT REQUISITION

Date 11-5-39

-Boy Girl Woman - Man Required in Mail Order Sales Dept. Dept. No._____

Kind Of Work Messenger _____ Specific Qualifications Necessary High School graduate girl about 18 - inexperienced.

To begin work (Date) 11-28-39 Starting Rate $ 12.00 per week Hours of work 40

To increase force no To replace Mary Smith Who was

or will be Released or Transferred to be married on (Date) 12-1-39

Permanent Position yes Temporary until _____

Charge to Acct. No. 1025-A Signed Mary White Dept. Chief

Approved H. J. Stevens Dept. Manager

EMPLOYMENT DEPT'S RECORD | DEPT. MANAGER'S ACCEPTANCE

Name _____ The person named started work

Address _____

was employed transferred to fill this requisition on (Date) _____

To begin work on ____ 193__ Rate $ _____ at _____

Reg. No.____ Acct. No.____ Signed _____ Signed _____ Dept. Manager

Emp. Dept.

Larkin Co., Inc.

Illustration No. 172—An Employment Requisition

sonnel department follows a procedure somewhat like that as follows:

1. The specification card for the job to be filled is examined to determine the qualifications demanded of the worker.
2. The personnel records of present employees are consulted to see if the desired employee can be found among the present employees.
3. Applications on file are examined for properly qualified workers. If there are any suitable applicants, they are asked to report for an interview. If there are no applications on file, a newspaper advertisement is run, employment agencies are contacted, or present employees are asked to recommend friends.
4. The applicant is interviewed to determine whether he has the general qualifications called for by the job specification card. The person doing the interviewing attempts to put the applicant at ease so that the latter can talk in a natural manner.
5. If the applicant passes the preliminary interview, he may be given a test or tests that are designed to show

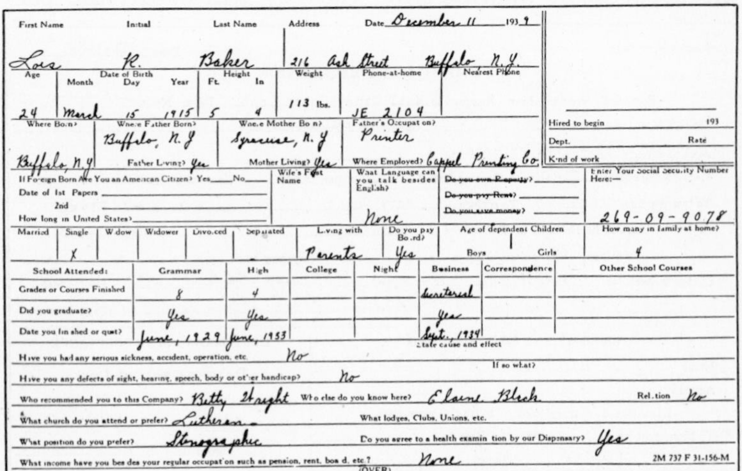
First Name Lois | Initial R. | Last Name Baker | Address 216 Ash Street Buffalo, N.Y. | Date December 11 1939
Age 24 | Date of Birth: Month March, Day 15, Year 1915 | Height: Ft. 5, In. 4 | Weight 113 lbs. | Phone-at-home JE 2104 | Nearest Phone
Where Born? Buffalo, N.Y. | Where Father Born? Buffalo, N.Y. | Where Mother Born? Syracuse, N.Y. | Father's Occupation? Printer
Father Living? Yes | Mother Living? Yes | Where Employed? Cappel Printing Co.
Hired to begin 193 | Dept. | Rate | Kind of work
If Foreign Born Are You an American Citizen? Yes____ No____ | Date of 1st Papers | 2nd | How long in United States?
Wife's First Name | What Language can you talk besides English? None
~~Do you own Property?~~ | ~~Do you pay Rent?~~ | ~~Do you save money?~~
Enter Your Social Security Number Here:— 269-09-9078
Married | Single X | Widow | Widower | Divorced | Separated | Living with Parents | Do you pay Board? Yes | Age of dependent Children: Boys, Girls | How many in family at home? 4

School Attended:	Grammar	High	College	Night	Business	Correspondence	Other School Courses
Grades or Courses Finished	8	4			Secretarial		
Did you graduate?	Yes	Yes			Yes		
Date you finished or quit?	June, 1929	June, 1933			Sept., 1934		

Have you had any serious sickness, accident, operation, etc. No — State cause and effect
Have you any defects of sight, hearing, speech, body or other handicap? No — If so what?
Who recommended you to this Company? Betty Wright | Who else do you know here? Elaine Black | Relation No
What church do you attend or prefer? Lutheran | What lodges, Clubs, Unions, etc.
What position do you prefer? Stenographic | Do you agree to a health examination by our Dispensary? Yes
What income have you besides your regular occupation such as pension, rent, board, etc.? None
(OVER)
2M 737 F 31-156-M

Larkin Co., Inc.

Illustration No. 173—An Application Blank (front)

his general and specific knowledge. For example, the Larkin Co., Inc., of Buffalo, New York, gives its applicants for general office work a test consisting of six parts: (a) mathematics, (b) vocabulary, (c) filing, (d) classifying correspondence, (e) grammar, and (f) observation. Applicants for stenographic jobs are required to take dictation and transcribe letters on a typewriter.

A joint committee representing the National Office Management Association and the National Council of Business Education, after several years of experimenting, has prepared clerical ability tests.[1] These were given first in 1937 and since that time have been given annually in the larger cities in the eastern part of the United States.

Each person taking these tests is tested on his general information and on his knowledge of such fundamentals as spelling, meanings of words, grammar, plurals of nouns, arithmetic, and business informa-

---

[1] Information and sample copies of past tests can be obtained from the Joint Committee on Tests, 16 Lawrence Hall, Harvard University, Cambridge, Massachusetts.

Have you ever worked for Larkin Co Inc. No ? If so when and where?

Check the following lines of work in which you have had training or experience.

___Grocery Clerk	✓ Stenographer	___Elevator Op'r	___Carpenter	___Draftsman	List others ___
___Dept. Store Clerk	✓ Typist	___Telephone Op'r	___Electrician	___Printing	___
___Cashier	✓ Bookkeeper	___Power Sewing	___Upholsterer	___Woodworker	___
Waiter	___Cost Clerk	___Canvassing	___Millwright	___Painter	___
___Nurse	___Comptometer	___Gas Station	___Gardener	___Chauffeur	___

WORK RECORD: Describe positions you have held beginning with the last.

Month and year began and left.	Firm's name and address and kind of business	Who was your supervisor or manager?	Kind of work you did?	Exact Salary Rec'd	Why did you leave?	Do not use this space
From 10-20-34	Wilde Stationery Co.	L. O. Wilde	Stenographic	$18.00 wk	Went out	
To 11-24-35	211 Fourth St., Buffalo				of business	
From 9-24-34	Mc. Alpin Department Store	R. S. Loring	Typing	$15.00 wk	Temporary	
To 10-6-34	902 Seventh St., Buffalo					
From						
To						
From						
To						

May we ask the above employers in regard to your Service? Yes Excepting

Give two names of persons such as business men, ministers or friends to whom we may refer as to your character.

Name	Address	Business	Name	Address	Business
B. R. Steel	19 Ross Ave., Buffalo	Insurance	D. A. Manning	2523 Ida Ave., Buffalo	Printer

Physical

Appearance

Expression

Experience

Larkin Co., Inc.

Illustration No. 174—An Application Blank (back)

tion. Then the testee may choose any one of the following vocational tests:

(a) Stenographer
(b) Machine transcriber
(c) Typist
(d) Bookkeeper
(e) Filing clerk
(f) Key-driven calculating machine operator

These tests are based upon actual jobs that office clerks do as a part of their daily work. They are endurance, as well as speed, tests. A personality rating chart is filled out for each person tested.

Those who are successful receive a certificate of proficiency from the joint committee on tests. (In May, 1939, there were approximately 1,000 successful testees out of the 2,400 who took the various tests in 31 testing centers.) This certificate is evidence that the holder ranks high among a large number of selected people who have taken similar tests.

6. The applicant is usually given a physical examination. Such an examination is required by many businesses and in some cases by government laws. It is wise for a business to require the examination as it should reveal whether the applicant is physically able to do the work expected. It may also protect the business in a lawsuit if the employee later claims disability as a result of his work. The medical department report becomes a part of the permanent record of the employee. It is usually copied onto the permanent record card or is attached to the card.

7. The references are investigated to see if the applicant's previous conduct has been satisfactory.

8. In many cases the applicant who has thus far proved satisfactory to the personnel department is sent to the head of the department where he would work, in order that the department head may judge his fitness.

9. If the applicant is hired, the records for the personnel department are then prepared.

Compensation. One of the most important incentives for an employee to do efficient work is the compensation he receives. If he feels that he is being underpaid for his services or that increased effort on his part will not result in larger pay, he is likely to do the minimum amount of work necessary; but if he feels that he is being paid a just compensation or that he does have a chance to add to his salary by increased effort and efficiency, he is likely to be a better satisfied, more co-operative, and more efficient employee. A major problem of the management is to adopt compensation plans that will bring the best results.

Because businesses vary so greatly in the type of work being done and in the qualifications required of their employees, a great many methods are used in determining the pay of employees. Some of the more common methods in use will be discussed here.

Straight Salary. The payment of a salary or wages on the basis of a year, a month, a week, a day, or an hour is probably the most common method. Wages paid under this method are often spoken of as *time wages*. Some of the advantages of this method are:

1. Only a small amount of clerical work is required to determine the wages to be paid.
2. The employee can budget his personal expenditures better as he knows what pay he is to receive.
3. This method is the only satisfactory way of paying employees who do a variety of work, such as the employee who answers the telephone, serves as information clerk, and does some filing or record work.

The chief disadvantages of this method are:

1. It offers no immediate incentive for extra effort.
2. The conscientious worker feels that he is penalized to the advantage of a lazy fellow worker who receives the same salary.

When this method is used, the employee can be stimulated to greater effort and efficiency by increases in his salary from time to time when he merits them.

Straight Commission. Some employees, usually salespeople, are often paid a given percentage of the volume of business done by them. A similar method of compensation is the so-called *piece-work system,* in which the factory worker's pay is determined by the number of parts turned out. Recently the practice of paying certain office employees on the basis of their individual efforts has been started by some businesses. Billing clerks are paid according to the number of invoices they complete. Some typists and stenographers are having their wages determined by the number of strokes or lines of material they type.

This method has the following advantages:

1. It provides a direct incentive to the employee to do his best.
2. It enables the management to control costs. For example, the salesmen of a wholesaler are paid a straight commission. Thus the selling expense represented by salesmen's salaries becomes a predetermined percentage of the selling price and varies directly with the sales volume.

Some of the disadvantages are:

1. The management cannot control employees on commission as easily as it can employees paid by other methods. For example, wholesale salesmen are likely to feel independent and, instead of working their territory intensively, may do just enough to ensure themselves a reasonable compensation.
2. Employees are likely to be interested in doing nothing except that which will directly increase their wages. They do not want to do missionary work or to perform goodwill activities for their business.
3. Salespeople working on a straight commission are likely to cater to customers who place large orders and to neglect those who do not.
4. The compensation is likely to vary a great deal when there are seasonal fluctuations.

Salary and Commission. Some salespeople are paid a straight salary plus a certain commission on their sales volume. For instance, a salesperson may be paid a salary of $20 a week plus a 2 per cent commission on his sales. Such a method eliminates most of the disadvantages of the straight salary and the straight commission plans. The practice of paying a salary plus a commission is used chiefly for salespeople and managers.

Salary and Bonus. This plan is similar to the salary and commission plan in that the employee is paid a regular salary. In addition to the salary he is paid a bonus based on some quota. The quota is generally an annual or semi-annual volume rather than a monthly or weekly volume. For example, a salesman may receive a salary of $40 a week; and, if at the end of six months, he has made sales of more than $15,000, he will receive a bonus of 1 per cent of his total sales. Sometimes the bonus is graduated so that the last bracket of the goal offers the greatest reward. In the example just mentioned, the bonus might be 1 per cent on all sales up to $15,000; 2 per cent on all sales of $15,000 or more and under $18,000; 3 per cent on all sales of $18,000 or more and under $20,000; 4 per cent on all sales of $20,000 or more. The bonus, however, is not always a percentage; sometimes it is a definite sum of money.

The advantage of this plan is that it keeps the employee working harder over a longer period than he would be if he were being paid a salary plus a commission. Similarly, bonuses are granted on production bases to piece-workers in both factories and offices. Route men for dairies and laundries are often given bonuses for obtaining new customers or for getting a certain volume of sales of all kinds or of a specific kind.

These four methods of compensating employees are the ones most commonly used. There are, however, many variations and also other combinations, such as:

1. Commission and bonus

2. Salary, commission, and bonus

3. Salary plus a commission based on varying quotas that have been adjusted to total costs

In companies in which employees, such as salesmen or supervisors, are compelled to do a large amount of traveling by automobile, the automobiles are often owned by the employees. In such cases the employee is usually allowed a definite sum, such as $5 a day, to cover traveling expenses, or he is reimbursed on a mileage basis.

Piece-Rate Plans. The simplest form of piece-rate plan is based on the *straight piece rate*. Under this plan the employee is paid a fixed sum per unit of production. The chief difficulty encountered with this plan is the establishing of a just rate for each piece. If the rate has been based upon a standard resulting from properly made motion and time studies, the plan has advantages. Some of these are:

1. Workers are paid in proportion to their productive effort.
2. The plan of compensation encourages workers to become more skillful.
3. It is easily understood by employees.
4. Labor costs can be determined with a small amount of clerical effort.

Some of the disadvantages are:

1. The plan does not protect the employee against loss of earning power due to causes beyond his control, such as the breakdown of the machine or the failure of another employee to do his job properly.
2. It tends to sacrifice quality for quantity, although proper inspection can keep the quality up to the standard.
3. The rates of compensation are difficult to establish.
4. The plan is discouraging to beginners.

Another plan, known as the *Halsey Plan*, guarantees a day rate and establishes a standard time for the completion of each job. The workman is paid a premium according to how much he shortens this standard time. This plan requires a great deal of computation to determine the pay of each worker. The Halsey Plan provides a bonus for saving in time on a particular job or on a particular day rate.

A variation of this plan, however, provides for the payment of the premium on the basis of sustained average production over a longer period of time, such as a week or a month. This variation tends to maintain efficiency at a high level over a longer period of time.

This discussion has explained only a few of the more common piece-rate plans. There are many others that are complicated and little used except in special types of work. In some cases individual workers and labor unions have objected to the piece-rate plan. This plan is usually popular if it enables skilled workers to make more than they ordinarily would. When such a plan is used as a device for speeding up production, but the piece rate is then lowered, the plan proves quite objectionable to workers. If the piece-rate plan is operated on a fair basis, it is usually advantageous to the workers as well as to the employer.

Profit-Sharing. Profit-sharing takes many forms. In a very small business the owner may share profits by granting bonuses of a flat sum, such as $25 or $50, to his employees each year, the amount depending upon the success of the business activities of the past year. Some companies share profits by giving to their employees either a lump sum of cash or shares of stock in the company, the amount depending upon the financial success of the company and the length of service of the employee.

A brief discussion of several plans is given here:

1. The features of the profit-sharing plan of the Selby Shoe Company, of Portsmouth, Ohio, are as follows:

> Recognizing the fact that the interests of the company and its employees are largely mutual, and that both depend chiefly for their financial returns on the general success of the business, it is agreed generally that after labor has had fair wages, and capital a fair return, the balance of the net profits be divided as hereinafter provided:
>
> First, there shall be set aside for employees on the general pay roll who have been continuously employed during the previous fiscal year, a sum equal to the total of their average week's earnings;

Second, there shall be set aside for payment of dividends, or additions to surplus, an amount equal to 6 per cent of the book value of the capital stock of the business;

Third, there shall be added to the employees' fund a second amount, equal to 25 per cent of the earnings left after the amount for dividends or surplus has been deducted;

Fourth, the sum of items 1 and 3 shall be divided equally among all qualifying employees on the last Friday in June;

Fifth, qualification requirements for participation in this fund shall be as follows:

(a) The employee must have been on the general pay roll during the whole of the previous fiscal year.

(b) He shall not have been absent more than 30 days at any one time during the year except because of injuries received at work in the plant.

2. The Sears, Roebuck & Co. profit-sharing system is designed to encourage employee savings. The employees contribute 5 per cent of their wages to a fund, and the company contributes 5½ to 7½ per cent of its profits to the same fund. After contributing for ten years, the employee is entitled to make withdrawals from his account.

3. The plan of the Procter & Gamble Co. is to have the employee purchase stock in the company. The employee has 5 per cent deducted from his salary to apply on the purchase of the stock. The company pays in from two to three times that amount. In six years the employee owns the stock; and thereafter, as long as he retains it in his possession, he receives yearly a cash profit-sharing dividend in addition to the regular dividend on the stock that he owns. At the end of the six years the average employee has a paid-up account of approximately $1,600, somewhat more than the average annual wage.

4. The Eastman Kodak Company makes an annual cash payment to employees, the size of which is determined

by the amount of the regularly declared dividend on the company's stock and the earnings of the employee for the five preceding years. In a recent year employees who had been working for the company five years received the equivalent of five weeks' pay.

Employee Security Plans. A great many plans are used by businesses to give greater security to their employees. A few of such plans are discussed here.

1. *Mutual Relief (Benefit) Associations.* Most large businesses have mutual relief, or benefit, associations that pay benefits, usually weekly, to members who are unable to work because of illness or accident. Such an association is financed largely by the employees, but it is sponsored and often assisted financially by the business itself. The contributions of the employees (the members) are usually based upon the salaries, and the weekly benefits to be received are scaled accordingly.

2. *Social Security and Unemployment Insurance.* These two methods of adding to the security of the employee are discussed in a later chapter. In addition to the contributions made by the employee for social security insurance, the employer contributes a like amount. The employer in many states contributes the entire amount for unemployment insurance.

3. *Group Insurance.* Many businesses have made it possible for their employees to obtain life insurance at wholesale rates through what is called group insurance. In some cases businesses pay part of the insurance premium. Life insurance is thus provided for workers who probably would not be able to pay the regular rates. Some group-insurance policies provide for benefits in the case of accidents not incidental to the jobs of the employees (workmen's compensation covers accidents that occur while the employees are working), and other policies provide for benefits when the employees are sick. Another advantage of group insurance is that no physical examination is required.

Some employees would be unable to pass the physical examination required in obtaining insurance on an individual policy.

4. *Pensions.* Some businesses that wish to aid employees who are too old to perform their jobs efficiently have established pension plans. There is much variation in the plans, but the general characteristics are as follows:

(a) The business usually pays the entire cost, but in some cases the employee makes a contribution.

(b) The age for retirement is usually from sixty to seventy. Sometimes retirement is mandatory at a certain age, and at other times it is at the request of either the employer or the employee.

(c) The length of service required before an employee is eligible to retire is usually from twenty to thirty-five years, with adjusted pensions for those who wish to retire sooner.

(d) There is such great variation in the amounts of the pension payments that no attempt will be made to name them. Pension plans usually provide a minimum and a maximum monthly pension based upon the salary of the employee.

Many pension plans have failed because the businesses that established them did not set aside a large enough reserve to meet the pension demands several years later. Businesses often did not keep the fund separate, but used it when regular business operations required further financing, and thus weakened the fund. Pension systems established by businesses for their employees have been better administered when they were handled by insurance companies. The Social Security Act may displace some of these pension plans.

5. On January 1, 1939, the General Motors Corporation put into effect two plans, known as the General Motors income security plan and the General Motors layoff benefit plan, that affect its 150,000 hourly wage workers. These plans are explained below.

(a) *Income security plan.* Employees with 5 years of service or more on January 1, 1939, and who worked any time during December, 1938, will be eligible:

First: If, in any week while this plan is operative, an eligible employee's earnings from the Corporation and/or other regular employment are less than 60 per cent of his standard weekly earnings, as hereinafter defined, the Corporation will advance, at the option of the employee, the difference between his actual earnings and 60 per cent of his standard weekly earnings, less any unemployment compensation to which the employee may be entitled. Thus, for the entire year the eligible employee is assured that in each week his minimum weekly income will be at least 60 per cent of the standard.

Second: Advances are to be repaid without interest by the employee, but only through an opportunity to work. Whenever the employee's subsequent weekly earnings are in excess of 60 per cent of the standard, one half of the excess shall be applied to the reduction of such advances until they have been repaid.

Third: In the event of the death of an employee, any amount due as a result of such advances shall be canceled.

(b) *Layoff benefit plan.* An employee not qualified under the previous plan but who on January 1, 1939, had two years' service or more and was employed at any time during December, 1938, or the year 1939, will be eligible:

First: A credit will be established for each such eligible employee, equivalent to 72 hours' pay at his latest earned hourly rate.

Second: If, during any week while this plan is in operation, an eligible employee's weekly earnings from the Corporation and/or other regular employment are less than 40 per cent of his standard weekly earnings, the Corporation will advance to such employee, at the option of the employee, the difference between his actual earnings and 40 per cent of his standard weekly earnings, until he has exhausted the credit established in his behalf—less the amount of unemployment compensation to which the employee may be entitled for that week.

Third: Advances are to be repaid without interest by the employee, but only through an opportunity to work. Whenever the employee's subsequent weekly earnings are in excess of 60 per cent of the standard, one half of the excess shall be applied to the reduction of such advances until they have been repaid.

Fourth: In the event of the death of an employee, any amount due as a result of such advances shall be canceled.

Employee Representation in Management. It is often helpful for the management to get the viewpoint of its employees on different phases of the operation of the business. By having committees representing the employees meet with committees representing the management, there should be much of benefit not only to the management but also to the employees. Each group will see the problems of the other.

The *Multiple Management Plan* of McCormick & Co., a large food manufacturing company with headquarters in Baltimore, Maryland, was introduced in 1932. Since that time the plan has been adopted by more than one hundred businesses in the United States, Canada, and England. Briefly, the plan is as follows:

1. The Senior Board, directors of McCormick & Co., Inc., is elected by stockholders. This is the governing board that adopts and controls all the company policies and directs the general management of the business.

2. The Junior Board is a clearinghouse through which the views of the office employees go to the management. It really represents the office employees, and its problems are primarily those of administration and office management.

3. The Factory Board is a clearinghouse for the views of factory workers and represents factory employees to the management. Its problems pertain primarily to factory management, and much of its time is given to studying working conditions and employees' sug-

gestions, as well as improving the relationship between the company and the employees.

4. The McCormick Sales Board is the board of the Mc-
   Cormick Sales Company, a subsidiary of McCormick
   & Co., Inc. Six of the members are elected from the
   active division managers in the field who supervise
   the selling of merchandise. The other members are
   sales-minded executives.

Under this system the active management is carried on
through group meetings of more than fifty people instead
of a few executive officers or department heads. All four
boards meet separately at stated intervals to discuss and
act upon their individual problems. Plans passed unani-
mously by the Junior and Factory Boards are submitted
to the Senior Board or the president for final approval. So
practical have been the recommendations of the Junior and
Factory Boards that nearly every one of them has been
approved and adopted.

Group meetings of the Senior, Junior, and Factory
Boards are held every two weeks. Three chairmen preside,
one representing each board and each conducting that part
of the meeting which pertains to his board. The members
of all the boards attend each meeting and are paid a director's fee for attending. The chairman of each board calls
on individuals of his group to report items of interest that
have transpired in his particular department during the
past two weeks and also to outline work of outstanding
interest in which his department will be engaged during
the coming two weeks. In addition, a member of each board
is appointed to give a five-minute talk on some interesting
topic that has been selected beforehand. Guest speakers
are invited to address the group at frequent intervals on
topics of general interest, which may or may not pertain
directly to the McCormick business. There is absolute freedom of speech, and all members are on an equal footing.

Elections to the Junior and Factory Boards are held semiannually. Three new members must be elected to each
board at every election so that the three least efficient

members will be displaced. Elections are by ballot. Office or factory employees showing the most ability are considered for election to the Junior or the Factory Board.

The management wants each and every employee throughout the organization to realize fully that his responsibility under the multiple management plan is to state clearly his views on any conditions pertaining to his own welfare or that of other employees or the business as a whole. Factory executives, junior executives, and Sales Board members are willing to talk over individually with employees under their supervision anything pertaining to management, working conditions, and hours and wages in their respective departments. Such information is immediately placed before the management at the meetings of the various boards, and satisfactory explanations are given the employees after their views have been considered.

Along with the tendency to let employees have some voice in management problems, many large organizations have found it desirable to acquaint employees with the financial conditions and the financial operations of the organization. For example, it has been found that some misunderstandings arise because employees do not understand that a very small proportion of the income is paid as profits to the stockholders. Therefore, when a financial statement is issued at the end of each fiscal year, each employee gets a copy of the financial statement at the time a statement is sent to each stockholder.

The Wagner Act. Recent legislation has tended to give employees much greater freedom in their relationships with their employers. Under the Wagner Act, employees are given freedom to organize as they choose. They may conduct an election, under government supervision, to determine which group or organization shall be empowered to act as bargaining agent for them in dealings with their employer. The minority must abide by the wishes of the majority in relations between the employees and the employer. Recent court decisions have shown that the employer must be very careful in dealing with employees. No employee can be discharged because of activity in a labor union, and any action that could be interpreted as coercion on the part of the employer is forbidden.

QUESTIONS FOR DISCUSSION

1. What is meant by personnel management?
2. Why is personnel management important?
3. Why do large organizations have personnel directors but small businesses do not?
4. What are the four general types of activities carried on by a personnel department?
5. State some of the advantages of a centralized employment bureau.
6. Explain what is meant by a job specification card.
7. Why is it considered a good policy to fill vacancies with present employees?
8. What are some of the sources of labor supply that may be used by a personnel department?
9. What is an employment requisition?
10. What three types of examinations are frequently given to prospective employees?
11. What type of compensation is being received by each of three employees who are paid (a) $25 a week, (b) $3,000 yearly, (c) 80 cents an hour?
12. State two advantages of the straight commission or the piece-work method of compensation.
13. Give the principal disadvantages of the straight commission or the piece-work method of compensation.
14. What are some of the more common profit-sharing plans?
15. What is a mutual relief (benefit) association?
16. Explain the General Motors income security plan.
17. What is the purpose of employee representation in management?
18. What general provision of the Wagner Act is important to personnel management?

Section II

Training and Management of Personnel

Introducing the New Employee to His Work. It is desirable that the new employee be given some information about the business as a whole. He is often given a manual or booklet that states the policies and regulations of the business, especially as they affect new employees. He may also be informed as to lunchrooms, lockers for clothes, and the like. Finally, he should be introduced to his department head or supervisor. The latter will see that he is introduced to other members of the department and given detailed information and directions about his new job.

Follow-up of the New Employee. The personnel department should make a follow-up of each new employee to see whether the right person has been selected for the job. This practice will aid the department in the future selection of employees. By consulting the department head or super-

PERSONNEL DEPARTMENT

REPORT ON EMPLOYEE

The following is recommended with reference to

Date 11-25 193 9

NAME Smith, Mary

DEPT. Mail Order Sales

Describe duties Order Recorder

Reg No. 4042

Release

X.....Quit
......Dismissed
......Laid Off

Last day here........ Dec. 1 ..193 9 Hour 5 p.m.

All Company property, tools, etc. returned to ....

Owes Larkin Co?	Medical	Desirable to re-employ in your Dept?
no	O.K.	YES

Change Rate to $..................beginning..............................193

Present Rate $............. in effect since.................................193

Transfer to.................................... Dept. beginning 193

Reason: To be Married.

Mary White — Dept. Head
H. J. Stevens — Dept. Mgr.
C. O. Morse — Personnel Manager

15C 837 F.31-25

ESSENTIAL QUALITY RATINGS

Rate with reference to particular job person is doing.
Indicate rating with an X in proper space under each quality.
Underline Strong qualities Circle Weak ones. Add figures opposite the Xs to get rating in points.

INTELLIGENCE: Knowledge of duties, ability to learn, mental alertness, initiative, judgment

Dull 8	Fair 12	Good X 16	Excellent 20

INDUSTRY: Energy applied to work day-in and day-out without being urged Accomplishment, interested effort, ambition, stability

Lacking Lazy 8	Fair Spasmodic 12	Good 16	Excellent X 20

QUALITY of work: Freedom from error attention to details Satisfactory results efficiency

Poor 8	Fair 12	Good X 16	Excellent 20

CONDUCT: Proper deportment, cheerful obedience co-operation, loyalty, good habits

Undesirable 4	Fair 6	Good 8	Excellent X 10

ATTENDANCE: Being on the job regularly Good attendance record.

Poor 2	Fair 3	Good 4	Excellent X 5

TARDINESS RECORD: Punctuality

Poor 2	Fair 3	Good X 4	Excellent 5

Past month's record: Absent 0 Day's Tardy...0 .Times

HEALTH: Physical fitness, strength, endurance, appearance, personal neatness.

Unfavorable 4	Fair 6	Good X 8	Excellent 10

TRUSTWORTHINESS: Truthfulness, fairness sincerity honesty, worthiness of confidence

Unreliable Poor 4	Fair Doubtful 6	Good Reliable X 8	Excellent 10

PROSPECTS

Poor	Fair	Good	Excellent X

40 60 80 100

Total Points 67

GENERAL VALUE TO DEPT.

Poor...... Fair...... Good X ...Excellent......

Larkin Co., Inc.

Illustration No. 175—A Report on an Employee

visor, the personnel department can determine the efficiency of the new employee. By consulting the new employee, it can determine whether he is satisfied. After such a follow-up it may decide that, for the best interests of everyone, the employee should be transferred to another job or department.

The department heads should send to the personnel department reports of the work, the attitude, and the attendance of employees. Thus there will be centralized records upon which transfers and promotions of employees can be based. (The term *transfer* is used here to denote simply a change in position, as from typist in one department to typist in another department. By *promotion* is meant an increase in authority and responsibility.) Suggestions as to transfers and promotions often originate with department heads or supervisors.

Frequently the discharge of an employee is not left entirely in the hands of the department head. If the department head wishes to discharge an employee, he must consult the personnel department. Such a consultation may

SPECIAL REPORT ON EMPLOYEE

Date 12-15 1939

NAME	DEPT	DATE EMPLOYED
Lillian Wheeler	Typing	12-11-38

Give position and describe duties as fully as space permits.

Typist

How long on present job? One year

Next positions, in order, to which likely to progress.

Transcriber
Junior stenographer

REMARKS:—Emphasize the particular strength, also weakness of employee. State prospect, ambitions and recommendations here.

Excellent typist. Very alert. Recommended for junior stenographic position.

Mary White H. J. Stevens C. O. Morse

DEPT. HEAD DEPT. MGR. PERSONNEL MGR.

2M 1230 F.31-1512

ESSENTIAL QUALITY RATINGS

Rate with reference to one's particular job.
Indicate rating with an X in proper space under each quality.
Underline strong qualities. Circle weak ones. Add figures opposite the Xs to get rating in points.

INTELLIGENCE: Knowledge of duties, ability to learn, mental alertness, initiative, judgment.

DULL 8	FAIR 12	GOOD 16	EXCELLENT X 20

INDUSTRY: Energy applied to work day-in and day-out without being urged. Interested effort, ambition, stability, accomplishment.

LACKING LAZY 8	FAIR SPASMODIC 12	GOOD X 16	EXCELLENT 20

QUALITY of work: Freedom from error, attention to detail, satisfactory results, efficiency

POOR 8	FAIR 12	GOOD X 16	EXCELLENT 20

CONDUCT: Proper deportment, cheerful obedience, co-operation, loyalty, good habits.

UNDESIRABLE 4	FAIR 6	GOOD 8	EXCELLENT X 10

ATTENDANCE: Being on the job regularly. Good attendance record.

POOR 2	FAIR 3	GOOD X 4	EXCELLENT 5

TARDINESS RECORD: Punctuality.

POOR 2	FAIR 3	GOOD X 4	EXCELLENT 5

PAST MONTH'S RECORD: ABSENT 1 DAYS, TARDY TIMES.

HEALTH: Physical fitness, strength, endurance, appearance, personal neatness.

UNFAVORABLE 4	FAIR 6	GOOD X 8	EXCELLENT 10

TRUSTWORTHINESS: Truthfulness, fairness, sincerity, honesty, worthiness of confidence.

UNRELIABLE POOR 4	FAIR DOUBTFUL 6	GOOD RELIABLE X 8	EXCELLENT 10

PROSPECTS:

POOR 40	FAIR 60	GOOD X 80	EXCELLENT 100

TOTAL POINTS 86

GENERAL VALUE TO DEPT.

POOR ...... FAIR ...... GOOD X ...... EXCELLENT ......

Larkin Co., Inc.

Illustration No. 176—A Special Report on an Employee

result in transferring the employee to some other department. In this way a low rate of labor turnover can be maintained. When the personnel department has a voice in the matter of discharging employees, it can compile statistics that should be valuable to the management of the business in determining labor policies.

Labor Turnover. A certain branch office manager was commenting upon the high rating that the head office had given to reports sent in by his office. Upon being asked to what he attributed the high rating he answered, "Our low rate of labor turnover." Further questioning revealed that the rate of labor turnover in his office was 8 per cent, whereas in most of the other branch offices it was approximately 40 per cent. What did he mean by *labor turnover?*

Several methods are used to compute the percentage of labor turnover. Two of the most common are:

1. $\left\{\begin{array}{c}\text{Number of employees who have}\\ \text{terminated their employment}\\ \text{with the business}\end{array}\right\} \div \left\{\begin{array}{c}\text{Average}\\ \text{number of}\\ \text{employees}\end{array}\right\} = \left\{\begin{array}{c}\text{Percentage}\\ \text{of labor}\\ \text{turnover}\end{array}\right\}$

2. $\left\{\begin{array}{c}\text{Number of employee}\\ \text{replacements}\end{array}\right\} \div \left\{\begin{array}{c}\text{Average}\\ \text{number of}\\ \text{employees}\end{array}\right\} = \left\{\begin{array}{c}\text{Percentage}\\ \text{of labor}\\ \text{turnover}\end{array}\right\}$

Let us suppose that during one year fifteen persons left the employ of a business; twelve new employees were hired to replace those who had left; and the average number of persons on the pay roll was one hundred. According to the first method, the labor turnover was—

$$\frac{15}{100} = 15 \text{ per cent}$$

According to the second method, it was—

$$\frac{12}{100} = 12 \text{ per cent}$$

Because the branch office manager mentioned previously has so small a change in his personnel, most of his employees were experienced and could therefore produce reports of a high quality.

The importance of keeping the rate of labor turnover as low as possible can be seen if some of the costs of labor turnover are considered:

1. It costs money to train new employees.
2. The work of regular employees is disturbed by new workers.
3. There is greater spoilage of goods and materials, as well as increased depreciation of machinery, while new employees are learning their jobs.
4. A large part of the cost of operating a personnel department is the result of labor turnover.

Training Employees. All new workers must receive some training for their jobs, the amount varying greatly in different kinds of work. A typist will probably need very little training as he already has acquired typing skill; but an employee going into the pattern-making department of a manufacturing company will require a great deal of training. Sometimes he serves as an apprentice, but often organized training is given.

As an aid in the training of new employees, most large businesses provide *procedure* manuals. These booklets give definite instructions for the accomplishment of certain operations and tasks. For instance, each new employee who is to type correspondence may be given a printed letter manual describing the various styles of letter arrangement used by the business and including rules on capitalization, punctuation, and the handling of enclosures. The employee can then study the manual and later refer to it whenever he is in doubt.

Manuals ensure a standard procedure of operation and usually provide directions for the most efficient method of doing work. They have an advantage over verbal directions in that they save the time of those employees who would have to give the oral directions. They also prevent much misunderstanding and fix responsibility on the employee.

The employee is held responsible for his job being done according to the printed directions in the manual.

Most business executives believe that much of the training needed by their employees can be obtained more efficiently by formal instruction than by the apprenticeship method. Under the latter method a new employee learns by working as an apprentice for three or four years with an experienced employee. Because of this belief on the part of executives, large businesses are (a) co-operating with public and private schools in developing training programs for prospective employees; (b) encouraging their employees to attend evening schools, sometimes paying the tuition if such is required; and (c) organizing courses for their own employees with teachers and classroom space provided.

Many businesses provide another form of training for their employees by establishing a library and reading rooms. Books and magazines containing information of a technical nature directly related to the particular business are provided. Often related and general information is to be found in the library. The business may also provide free lectures for employees.

Motion and Time Studies. In order to improve the methods used by employees at different jobs, a business should have studies made of the jobs. Such a study should result in an economy of motion on the part of the employee and possibly a simplification of the work. For example, a study was made of a person doing assembly work while seated at a bench with the various parts to be assembled placed in small boxes on the bench. This study showed that the parts to be picked up by the left hand and the right hand should be placed within the semi-circles shown in Illustration No. 177. If the various parts were not placed in those positions, the employee would have to get up from his seat to reach the necessary parts.

Likewise, a study was made of the cutting of felt soles from stock by means of a power press and die. Formerly the right sole was cut, the die was raised and turned, and then the left sole was cut. After the study it was decided to feed the felt stock into the press in two strips placed back to back. Then, by one operation of the die, both the right and the left sole would be cut.

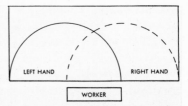

Illustration No. 177—A Motion Study

In making studies, it is usually desirable to determine the actual time required for the different operations performed by the worker. By that means one can determine how much each operation costs. Those operations that cost the most are studied with special care to see if they can be made less costly. Let us take as an example a simple type of work, such as shining shoes. The time study discloses that the employee uses two minutes to fan shoes dry in preparation for the final polishing. After figuring the cost of the employee's time and the increased number of customers that might be taken care of, the owner of the shoe-shining establishment decides that it will be more efficient to purchase an electric drying machine that can do the work in one minute.

Recently the motion-picture camera has been used to record the movements of a worker at a certain job; as the picture is taken, a special clock records the time consumed in each phase of the work. The film is then projected at a slow speed so that each phase of the work can be studied carefully. Such slow-motion pictures are used not only in industry but also by college athletic coaches, who make use of them in training athletes and athletic teams. A study of this type discloses opportunities for improvements. These improvements often cause greater efficiency and less fatigue for the employee.

Employee Welfare. The term *welfare* as used here means the general well-being of the employee. Every employer should consider the well-being of his employees as important. Many Federal, state, and municipal laws provide that certain standards in working conditions must be maintained by the employer in order to safeguard the health

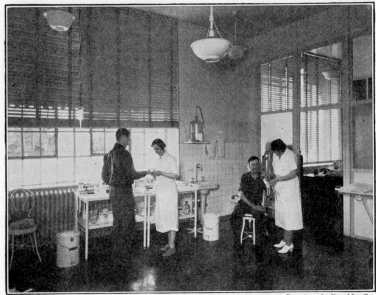

Procter & Gamble Co.

Illustration No. 178—A Factory Hospital

and the safety of employees. The employer who sees that the working conditions of his employees are above the standards required by law will likely have employees who are more efficient and better satisfied than those who work under less favorable conditions.

The Health Program. If the employee is to do his most efficient work, he must be healthy. The person who is suffering from toothache, a stomach disorder, or other illness will not do so much work as he should and is liable to spoil materials or have accidents. Illness may also mean absence from work, which is costly to the business. The health program often has the following features:

1. A physical examination is required at the time of employment and at periodic intervals thereafter.

2. Health education is carried on by means of posters on bulletin boards, booklets, and talks. Employees are thereby taught how to prevent certain kinds of illness and how to look after their physical well-being.

3. Plant sanitation provides healthful surroundings for the employees. This often includes supervision of ventilation, heating, and lighting, as well as care of washrooms, drinking fountains, and toilets.
4. Dispensary service, a first-aid room, and in some cases hospital service are provided. If the business does not maintain its own hospital, it may arrange with a local hospital for service to its employees.
5. Sometimes dental service is provided at a nominal cost for the benefit of employees.
6. The operation of a lunchroom may be considered part of the health program as wholesome food is provided at reasonable prices.
7. Fatigue studies are often made and are used as the basis for a more efficient planning of the employee's work. As a result of these studies many businesses have established rest periods.

The Safety Program. If it were possible to compile the costs of industrial accidents during one year, the sum would be enormous. During every year several thousand workers lose their lives, and many times that number are injured. No doubt many of the accidents could have been prevented. The primary purpose of the safety program is therefore to reduce the number of accidents.

Accidents are due to mechanical, physiological, or psychological causes. The mechanical causes are such as unguarded machinery, defective machinery, slippery floors, and obstructed passageways. They usually can be eliminated if proper care is exercised on the part of the management. The physiological causes of accidents are long hours of work, inadequate lighting, tasks that are dull and monotonous, and the like. These causes cannot always be eliminated, but they can be reduced somewhat by the maintenance of proper working conditions. The psychological causes are ignorance, recklessness, carelessness, inexperience, and the like. To eliminate these causes, there must be a co-operative undertaking on the part of both workers and management.

Illustration No. 179—A Safety Contest Bulletin Board

Part of the work of the personnel department is to determine the causes of accidents and then to attempt to remove those causes. In most cases such work means a continuous campaign. The employees can be reminded constantly of the need for safety by posters on bulletin boards and printed reminders on interoffice forms. (See Illustration No. 180.) Moving pictures and talks may be used frequently to drive home safety lessons. A prize may be awarded to the department making the best safety record over a given period. Pins or certificates of merit may be awarded to "no-accident" employees, such as truck drivers.

It is a good plan to present the awards at dinners or get-together meetings. Such a plan gives the employees who receive the awards proper recognition and makes it possible to have the meeting become a means of further discussion on accident prevention.

SAFETY SAYING

Saving time at the expense of safety doesn't make sense.

Illustration No. 180—A Safety Slogan

Personnel Research. Companies spend vast sums of money on their research laboratories in an endeavor to find new uses for their products as well as better methods of production. It would seem logical, therefore, that research or investigation into the human element of a business might prove profitable.

The research work that the personnel department may undertake is quite varied, and the extent to which it may be carried on is limited only by the time and the money the management wishes to spend. The larger the number of employees and the greater the number of different types of employees, the more numerous the personnel problems that arise. The following are indications of some of the research activities in which the personnel department may engage:

1. Preparing job analyses and compiling job specifications.
2. Making studies of wage systems, including profit-sharing, that point out both the strength and the weaknesses of the various systems. A wage system that will cause the worker to want to do his best is the ultimate goal. As economic conditions change, the wage system will probably have to be revised or adjusted.
3. Studying methods of eliminating unnecessary noise and vibration, which may be injurious to the health and the working efficiency of employees.
4. Studying the best methods of heating, lighting, and ventilation.
5. Investigating the causes of accidents and working out plans for prevention in the future.
6. Designing plans for training employees.
7. Making time and motion studies of various employees.
8. Making studies on fatigue and the effect of monotony on the employee.

Much of the personnel research will be carried on within the company's own organization, but some of it will be based upon what other similar businesses are doing. Activities carried on by one company can often be adopted, with perhaps slight modification, to good advantage by another company.

QUESTIONS FOR DISCUSSION

1. How can a new employee be given general information about the business?

2. Why should the personnel department make a follow-up of a new employee?

3. Explain why it is desirable to keep the labor turnover as low as possible.

4. What is meant by a procedure manual?

5. State some advantages of procedure manuals.

6. What are some of the methods used by businesses in obtaining training for their employees?

7. What is the purpose of a motion and time study?

8. Suggest some activities that a business might include in its health program.

9. Classify the causes of accidents.

10. What are some of the activities that a business might include in a safety campaign?

11. What is meant by personnel research?

12. State some research activities that might be carried on by a personnel department.

13. How are motion-picture cameras used for motion study?

14. What advantage is there in transferring individuals from one department to another instead of discharging a person in one department when he is not needed and hiring a new person in another department?

15. Explain the two methods of computing labor turnover.

16. Give four reasons why labor turnover is costly.

17. What, in your opinion, is the advantage of a health program from the point of view of a business?

PROBLEMS AND PROJECTS

1. Select some job with which you are familiar, and prepare a job specification card for it. The card may be similar to the one shown in Illustration No. 171 on page 409.

2. Look through the classified-advertising section of a newspaper to see if businesses are advertising for employees. Make a list of the businesses and the types of work for which employees are required.

3. If you have ever applied for a job, give a detailed report of the procedure you had to follow.

4. The Henry Manufacturing Company pays employees on a piece-rate basis that varies according to the number of pieces produced each day. The basic rate is 15 cents a piece. This rate is paid if the employee produces exactly 40 pieces a day (40 × 15 cents = $6). If the number of pieces produced in a day exceeds 40, the employee's basic rate on *all* pieces is increased ¼ cent apiece for each piece exceeding 40 (for example, 42 × 15½ cents = $6.51). If the rate of production is below the normal rate of 40 pieces a day, the rate on all pieces is decreased ¼ cent apiece for each piece under 40 (for example, 36 × 14 cents = $5.04). What should be the pay for a day if an employee completes (a) 38 pieces? (b) 44 pieces?

5. The profit-sharing plan of a certain company provides that each employee who has been working for the company five years shall receive a cash bonus of ½ per cent of his five years' earnings for each dollar of dividends over $3.50 that were declared to the stockholders. How much would an employee who has earned $2,000 a year receive if—
   (a) The dividends to stockholders were $5.50?
   (b) The dividends to stockholders were $8?

6. Referring to the income security plan of General Motors given on page 422, assume that an employee's standard weekly earnings are $30. During certain successive weeks his earnings are $14.50, $16.20, $18.60, and $29.50. What amount will he actually receive each week? (Disregard unemployment compensation and old-age pension.)

7. The number of employees of a certain company averages 180; the number of employees who have left the company is 12; the number of employee replacements is 9. Compute the percentage of labor turnover by each of the two methods given on page 430.

8. Visit some business and obtain a poster or posters used in promoting a safety or accident-prevention campaign. This project might be correlated with Safety Week.

CHAPTER XVIII

BUSINESS RISKS AND INSURANCE

Purpose of the Chapter. Every business is confronted with certain types of risks. Some of these can be overcome by good business management. Others must be overcome by various forms of insurance. The purpose of this chapter is to explain the various risks and to show how a businessman may obtain protection from them. The following are some of the questions that will be answered:

1. What are the different types of business and economic risks?
2. How can a businessman overcome some of these risks by good management?
3. How does insurance protect a businessman from risks?
4. What types of insurance are available to the businessman?
5. What function does life insurance serve in business?

General Types of Risks. Risks are of many varieties. They are sometimes classified as natural, personal, and social risks. They may be classified in general as follows: floods, storms, fires, robbery, strikes, riots, forgery, racketeering, panics, price fluctuations, taxes, tariffs, laws, changes in demand, and economic changes.

Special Types of Risks. The businessman is particularly concerned with certain special types of risks. For instance, anyone who has operated a business has discovered that people change in their needs, desires, and wants. These changes cause serious business risks. Most products are produced in anticipation of sale. If the needs, desires, and wants of consumers change, however, those who have produced goods are liable to suffer a loss.

Fashions, particularly in women's clothing, change frequently. Manufacturers and merchants of such clothing are sometimes stocked heavily at a time when styles change

440

or when buyers fail to accept new styles. Whoever is stocked with the merchandise therefore suffers a loss and probably has to sell the goods at a special sale. A wise merchant will watch his purchases carefully to be sure that he does not overstock. He will see that slow-moving style merchandise is disposed of through some special sale.

Methods of heating, transportation, and lighting cause serious business risks. For instance, the owner of a store that was thoroughly modern a few years ago may find all his customers going to another store that has recently had air-conditioning equipment installed. New decorations and new lighting equipment may attract customers away from an old, established store. Improved methods of transportation may give one type of business an advantage over another. For instance, busses may eliminate the need for streetcars, or private passenger automobiles may injure the business of bus companies. There are numerous such changes going on regularly. Probably the most recent significant change has been the introduction of the radio, which at least temporarily caused piano and phonograph manufacturers to lose sales. It is possible that in the future the development of television may cause a serious business risk to manufacturers of ordinary radios and, in turn, may cause motion-picture producers and theaters to suffer a loss.

The changes in the weather are sometimes serious business risks. For instance, a delayed summer season may prevent manufacturers and stores from disposing of summer clothing. A cool summer may injure the business of pleasure resorts because people may stay comfortably at home.

The fluctuation in business conditions is another serious risk. It can be overcome to some extent by studying business conditions and by planning carefully in anticipation of changes in business. Therefore, a knowledge of economics is valuable to a businessman.

Within any business community there are numerous local risks, such as the relocation of highways, which may cause customers to change their sources of supply to more con-

venient ones; the development of new highways, which
may take customers to larger communities to do their
shopping; the improvement of streets, which may make
one location better than another and therefore draw customers away from an old location; parking restrictions and
the establishment of no-parking zones, which may cause a
bad effect upon certain types of businesses; the shift in
population and the types of population in a community,
which may make it necessary to move businesses. These
and several similar risks must be considered by every businessman. Unless he recognizes them, he may wait too long
and find that his business has been totally or partially
destroyed.

None of these risks can be controlled, and there is no
protection from them in the form of insurance; but a keen
knowledge of business will help the businessman to avoid
some of them. These examples are pointed out as a warning
to the person who may contemplate entering business. He
is constantly faced with these problems, and he can solve
them only through careful management.

Hedging. *Hedging* is a term that is applied to the practice
of buying so-called *future contracts*. Hedging is especially
practiced in the commodity markets, such as the grain
exchanges. Speculators in those markets make it possible
for legitimate manufacturers to reduce their risks. A professional speculator is a person who spends all his time in
forecasting price changes. The speculator, as will be seen
in the following explanation, provides protection to the
manufacturer.

Here is how a manufacturer of flour, for instance, can
protect himself through a speculative future contract: A
producer of flour agrees to deliver a certain amount of
flour in four months at a specified price. He wants to begin
producing the flour in two months. In order to protect
himself from the risk of rising prices of wheat, he must
enter into a future contract to buy wheat for delivery in
two months. He buys this wheat at a specified price quoted
by the speculator. The speculator who takes the order

agrees to deliver the wheat, hoping that the price at which
he can buy the actual wheat two months later will assure
him a profit. The two points that concern the flour producer are (a) that he can definitely obtain the wheat when
he wants it and (b) that he knows the exact price he must
pay. He therefore can figure his profit accurately and can
sell the flour for future delivery without gambling on an
indefinite price of wheat. The producer of flour therefore
passes the risk on to the speculator.

It is possible for manufacturers to follow the same plan
in the purchase of many other commodities so that they
need not take the risk of fluctuations in prices.

We ordinarily associate the term *hedging* with examples
similar to the one mentioned above. Many businessmen,
however, follow essentially the principle of hedging. For
instance, a producer of canned goods may contract to sell
canned peas for future delivery at a certain price. He may
then immediately contract in advance for peas to be delivered to his cannery at harvest time. By contracting in
advance, he knows the selling price and the cost of the
peas, and therefore he has some reasonable assurance of
a profit. Genuine hedging, however, takes place through
a speculator on some established market.

Economic Cycle. There is probably no risk in business
that is so hazardous as the change in business conditions.
For instance, when business conditions are at their best
and there is a period of so-called prosperity, numerous new
businesses are started; but many of these do not become
well established before a period of decline begins. The
period of decline may therefore force a large number of
them to go out of business. A more detailed discussion of
the business cycle, or economic cycle, is given in Chapter
XXV.

Types of Insurance Companies. Insurance companies
collect from policyholders amounts that are called *premiums*. A premium is a payment for protection against
some risk, such as fire, sickness, accident, or death. Pre-

miums are paid weekly, monthly, quarterly, semiannually, or yearly, the time of payment depending upon the nature of the insurance, the type of policy, and the kind of insurance company. The funds collected from policyholders are used by the company in somewhat the same manner as cash deposits are used by banks. In other words, with the funds paid by policyholders, insurance companies make investments that earn an income. An insurance company must, of course, keep a reasonable amount of cash available to pay the claims of policyholders in case of fire, accident, death, ill health, or other similar happenings. The way that an insurance company handles its affairs is governed by law.

There are two general types of insurance companies. One is known as the *stock company;* and the other, as the *mutual company.* The stock company is a corporation that is formed according to the laws of the particular state. The stockholders own the company and operate it although they are not necessarily policyholders. An insurance company of this type obtains money from the sale of stock to stockholders, as well as from the collection of premiums from policyholders. The profits of the company are paid to the stockholders, who are the owners of the business. In some companies the policyholders also share in the earnings after the stockholders have been paid a stipulated amount.

A mutual company must also be organized under the laws of the particular state. The policyholders in such a company are, however, the owners. Each person or business that is insured in a mutual company becomes a member of the company and is entitled to a share in the ownership, the control, and the earnings. The ownership of the members is not evidenced, however, by shares of stock, as it is in a stock company.

Although the policyholders do not own shares of stock, they are in a sense partners or members of a co-operative organization. The only way in which they can exercise their power of control or management is for a sufficient number of them to register a protest or to act as a group in demanding changes in the management or the operation

of the business. Of course, the insurance departments of
the various states look after the interests of policyholders
and therefore scrutinize the management of these companies.

Policyholders in mutual companies usually pay premiums
at a predetermined fixed rate, comparable to the rate established by stock companies. The policyholders in mutual
companies, however, may receive dividends or have to pay
assessments. If the company makes a profit, each policyholder shares in proportion to the amount of his policy.
If the company fails to make a profit, each policyholder
(except those in most life insurance companies) is assessed
a certain amount so that the income of the company will
be equal to its expenditures. Usually the maximum amount
of an assessment cannot exceed the original premium.

It is to the advantage of a mutual company to select
carefully those risks on which insurance is to be issued.
The company can thereby establish a low percentage of
loss. If the percentage of loss is low, the net rates are
correspondingly low. For instance, if the buildings insured
by a mutual company are seldom damaged or destroyed by
fires, the net rates of that company are very low. If there
are many fires, however, the rates are high. It is, furthermore, of particular advantage to a mutual company to
increase fire-prevention activities and thereby to reduce
the number of fires. Some mutual companies are not particularly careful in selecting risks. Others do, however,
select only high-grade risks, while some confine their insurance to restricted localities, to particular types of
industries, or to selected groups of individuals. If a businessman is going to insure in a mutual company, he should
be sure that the company selects its risks carefully.

How Insurance Rates Are Established. Insurance rates
vary according to the risk that is involved. For instance,
if there is a large number of robberies in a particular
community, theft insurance is high in that community. If
fire protection is bad, buildings are not fireproof, and fires
are frequent in a certain community, the fire insurance

rates are high in that community. Rates charged for insurance are based upon the past experience of the insurance company in distributing losses over all the property that is insured. The rates established for any particular year are therefore in anticipation that the losses for that year will be essentially the same as those of the previous year. Naturally, when risks are reduced, rates can be reduced.

An insurance company must not only pay the claims of its policyholders who have suffered losses, but must also obtain enough to cover all expenses and, particularly if the company is a stock company, to ensure a profit as well. Sometimes the carefully selected risks of a mutual company result in such low costs of operation that those insured in the company have returned to them some of the profits. Some stock companies also follow the practice of returning to their policyholders a certain amount of the profits.

The following factors, for instance, are taken into consideration by an insurance company in establishing fire insurance rates on property:

1. Water supply
2. Fire department
3. Fire-alarm system
4. Police system
5. Building laws
6. Hazards
7. Structural conditions
8. Climatic conditions
9. Correlation between the water supply and the fire department
10. Fire-sprinkler system

For example, two businesses occupy buildings, side by side, in which all the conditions are equal. If one of these businesses installs a sprinkler system, it will thereafter pay a lower insurance rate than the one without such a system. In the case of fire insurance the businessman will find it advantageous to consider the various factors affecting the rates. He may save considerable money by installing a fire-sprinkler system or a fire-alarm system. In considering two pieces of property for rental, a businessman may wish to select the one on which the insurance rate is the lower.

Fire Insurance. Fire insurance provides funds to replace buildings, furniture and equipment, machinery, raw ma-

Cincinnati Salvage Corps.

*Illustration No. 181—A Salvage Corps Reduces
Fire Losses*

terials, and finished goods that have been destroyed by
fire. Insurance on a building usually does not cover equipment, machinery, and stock. Ordinarily separate policies
are required to give full protection from fire loss. The
owner of a building should be interested in insurance to
protect his investment. The occupant of a rented building
should be interested in insurance to protect his business.
In buying insurance one should know just what is covered
by the policy.

The actual loss in property destroyed by fire is not the
only loss to a business. The interruption to business until
a new place can be obtained and operations can be resumed
will result in a loss of profits and considerable incidental
expense. Special types of insurance can be obtained to
cover such losses caused by the inconvenience of a fire.

Features of Fire Insurance. When a businessman is
buying fire insurance, he should know what he is buying
and how he will be protected. He should give careful consideration to the amount of his protection, the kind of
protection, and special clauses in the policy. Illustration
No. 182 shows a typical fire insurance policy.

STANDARD FIRE INSURANCE POLICY

MANUFACTURER'S MUTUAL FIRE INSURANCE COMPANY
CINCINNATI, OHIO

No. 927653

Replaces No.

CASH PREMIUM POLICY

$ 5,000

NON-ASSESSABLE POLICY

Amount **$5,000** Rate **$1.50** Annual Premium **$75.00**

In Consideration of the Stipulations herein named and of

_____ Seventy-Five and 00/100 _____ Dollars Annual Premium

Does Insure _____ Queen City Printing Company _____

[Insert here P. O. address if location of risk is different ☞] 13 West Third Street, Cincinnati, Ohio

and legal representatives, to the extent of the actual cash value (ascertained with proper deductions for depreciation) of the property at the time of loss or damage, but not exceeding the amount which it would cost to repair or replace the same with material of like kind and quality within a reasonable time after such loss or damage, without allowance for any increased cost of repair or reconstruction by reason of any ordinance or law regulating construction or repair and without compensation for loss resulting from interruption of business or manufacture.

FOR THE TERM OF **Five Years**

from the **tenth** day of **October** 19**39**, at noon,

to the **tenth** day of **October** 19**44**, at noon,

against all DIRECT LOSS AND DAMAGE BY FIRE and by removal from premises endangered by fire, except as

herein provided, to an amount not exceeding **Five Thousand** Dollars,

to the following described property while located and contained as described herein, or pro rata for five days at each proper place to which any of the property shall necessarily be removed for preservation from fire, but not elsewhere, to-wit:

$5,000.00 on furniture and fixtures, office supplies, typewriters, adding machines, iron safes, etchings, cuts, electrotypes, metal plates, tools, implements, and appurtenances to their business, all while contained in the six-story and basement, brick and stone, approved roof building, situate 13 West Third Street, Cincinnati, Ohio, and occupied by the assured for printing plant, warehouse, and office purposes.

CO-INSURANCE CLAUSE

In consideration of the rate and/or form under which this policy is written, it is expressly stipulated and made a condition of this contract that the insured shall at all times maintain contributing insurance on each item of property insured by this policy to the extent of at least .....90.% of the actual cash value at the time of the loss, and that failing to do so, the insured shall to the extent of such deficit bear his, her or their proportion of any loss.

WAIVER OF INVENTORY OR APPRAISEMENT CLAUSE

If this policy shall be subject to the conditions of a Co-Insurance Clause, it is also made a condition that in the adjustment of any loss hereunder, provided same does not exceed 2% of the total insurance carried, it shall not be a part of compliance with the conditions of a Co-Insurance Clause to inventory and/or appraise the undamaged property.

If this policy be divided into two or more items the foregoing conditions shall apply to each item separately.

AUTOMATIC SPRINKLER CLAUSE NO. 1
(WITH SUPERVISORY SERVICE)

This policy being written at a reduced rate, based on the protection of the premises by automatic sprinklers, it is a condition of this policy that, in so far as the sprinkler equipment and the water supplies therefor, and in connection therewith the approved Central Station sprinkler supervisory service complete, are under the control of the insured, due diligence shall be used by the insured to maintain them in complete working order, and that no change shall be made in said water supplies and/or the Central Station sprinkler supervisory service complete without the consent of this company in writing.

This Policy is made and accepted subject to the foregoing stipulations and conditions, and to the following stipulations and conditions printed on back hereof, which are hereby specially referred to and made a part of this Policy, together with such other provisions, agreements, or conditions as may be endorsed hereon or added hereto; and no officer, agent or other representative of this Company shall have power to waive any provision or condition of this Policy except such as by the terms of this Policy may be the subject of agreement endorsed hereon or added hereto; and as to such provisions and conditions no officer, agent, or representative shall have such power or be deemed or held to have waived such provisions or conditions unless such waiver, if any, shall be written upon or attached hereto, nor shall any privilege or permission affecting the insurance under this Policy exist or be claimed by the insured unless so written or attached.

MUTUAL POLICY CONDITIONS: The assured, by accepting this Policy, becomes a member of this Company, and agrees to pay it the premium, as hereinbefore set forth. This Policy is Non-Assessable, and participates in the Profit.

In Witness Whereof, the said, Manufacturer's Mutual Fire Insurance Company, has caused this Policy to be signed by the President or Vice-President, but same will not be valid until attested by the Secretary, in the

city of Cincinnati and State of Ohio, this **tenth** day of **October** A. D. 19**39**

C J Morton Secretary _L H Dixon_ President

Illustration No. 182—A Fire Insurance Policy

No businessman has any advantage in being overinsured. As a matter of fact, he will save money by keeping his insurance down to an amount that actually equals the value of the property. Policies when renewed should therefore be revised in amount so that they cover the real value of whatever is being insured. It is therefore important to check the policies carefully before they are renewed.

In most states the actual amount of the loss is paid, rather than the insured value. In some states there are so-called "valued policy laws." These laws require the face value of the contract to be paid in the event of a total loss, regardless of the value of the property at the time of the loss. In the case of items such as manuscripts, rare books, rare pieces of art, and other similar articles, the value must be determined and agreed upon between the insurance company and the policyholder at the time the policy is purchased.

An ordinary insurance policy provides that the insurance company must repair or replace the damaged property within a reasonable time, but it does not cover any loss due to interruption to business. Business interruption insurance is presented later in this chapter.

Instead of paying only for the damage to a replaceable article, the insurance company may exercise the right given in the policy to take all or part of the insured article at an appraised value. In such a case the company may repair, rebuild, or replace the damaged property with other property of like kind and quality within a reasonable time. In the case of a building that is insured, the insurance company may likewise repair, rebuild, or replace the damaged property. Insurance companies ordinarily do not exercise this option but usually follow the practice of compensating for the damage and letting the policyholder take care of the property.

The policyholder is required, according to the contract, to be responsible for the property that has been damaged. In other words, he may not abandon it to the insurance company, for it still remains his property until an adjustment has been made. The policyholder cannot assume that, immediately after the fire, the insurance company is responsible for the damaged property.

In every fire insurance policy the property that is covered should be clearly identified as to description and location. The property included in the policy and the property excluded should be definitely understood. In the event of a fire, property may be moved to another location for protection. In this location it is covered by the insurance for a certain amount of time, usually about five days.

Remington Rand, Inc.

Illustration No. 183—Records Should Be Safe from Fire

The standard insurance policy usually excepts or omits such items as accounts, bills, money, notes and other evidences of debt, deeds, and securities. This fact emphasizes the necessity for keeping such items safely. It is difficult to establish a value for most of them; and, as they are not covered by an ordinary policy, extreme care should be exercised in protecting them. Even if such items are insured, the difficulty of replacing them still remains the prime consideration in their protection.

Special clauses in an insurance policy or special policies may protect the items mentioned above. A lower rate can be obtained on this type of insurance if the insured person or business agrees to keep in a safe place duplicates of such items as plans, maps, and invoices.

A fire insurance policy is a contract between the policyholder and the insurance company whereby the policyholder is to be indemnified for any loss traceable to fire. The honesty of the policyholder is an important factor in connection with such a contract. As the contract is a personal one between the policyholder and the insurance company, it cannot be transferred to another person without the consent of the insurance company.

The policyholder must have an *insurable interest* in the property. An insurable interest is generally defined as any interest in property that will suffer a possible financial loss if there is a fire. The interest in property to be insured must be specifically indicated in the policy. For instance, a person who has a mortgage on a piece of property has an insurable interest in the property. A person who has purchased a piece of property but has not paid for it also has an insurable interest. A person who uses a building as a warehouse has an insurable interest in the building, even though he does not own the building. Other factors that affect the contract are a change in the interest in the property, other insurance on the property, and mortgages.

In every fire insurance policy there are restrictions as to increases in the hazards. For instance, after an insurance contract has been written, the hazards may undergo changes because of physical changes in the property, alterations or repairs, changes in the use or the occupancy of the property, or the addition of explosives, gases, or the like.

Fraud or the concealment of facts may void any insurance policy.

Features of Coinsurance. To understand coinsurance, one must understand the reason for it. Losses naturally determine the rates of insurance. For example, assume that among 50,000 buildings there will be an estimated 1,000 fires during any particular year. The table in Illustration No. 184 shows the ratio of the loss to the entire value of each piece of property.

RATIO OF LOSS TO VALUE	NUMBER
Between 0% and 10%	751
Between 10% and 20%	107
Between 20% and 30%	47
Between 30% and 40%	30
Between 40% and 50%	20
Between 50% and 60%	16
Between 60% and 70%	12
Between 70% and 80%	9
Between 80% and 90%	5
Between 90% and 100%	3
Total number of fires	1,000

Illustration No. 184—Average Percentage of Loss for Each 1,000 Fires

It is evident that most of the losses from fires are small losses. For instance, in 751 cases out of 1,000, the loss from fire will amount to 10 per cent or less of the total value of the property. If one buys regular insurance, he will pay the same rate per thousand dollars of insurance, regardless of whether he has complete coverage or only partial coverage. It is obvious, therefore, that under ordinary insurance, the person who carries complete coverage is penalized by paying a high rate. For example, if a person buys a straight insurance policy covering 100 per cent of the value of his property, he pays the same rate per thousand as a person who carries only a small amount of insurance. There is very little likelihood, however, that the former will ever have a total loss. In other words, straight insurance does not give any inducement to carry a large amount of insurance.

Under coinsurance, however, the insurance company says, in effect, "If you take out more insurance, we'll charge a decreasing rate as you go up the scale in the amount of insurance that you carry." Under coinsurance the amount of insurance carried is stated in terms of a percentage of the total value of the property. The percentage carried will depend largely upon the custom in the community and the nature of the property being insured. Usually this percentage is approximately the percentage of total destructible loss that is possible. For instance, if it can be assumed that only 80 per cent of the property is destructible by fire (a certain proportion of the masonry and concrete work being indestructible), the policy should carry an 80 per cent coinsurance clause and thereby provide insurance covering 80 per cent of the value of the property. The rate is calculated on this basis. The premium rate on buildings is, on the average, reduced 10 or 15 per cent by coinsurance. If the insured person, however, is not willing to carry insurance up to 80 per cent of the value of the property, he may carry whatever amount he wishes but will have to assume part of the risk. The insured person may carry insurance equal to the total estimated loss or may carry less. The following are examples of how 80 per cent coinsurance clauses operate:

EXAMPLE A

When insurance exceeding 80% of the value is carried.

Value of property	$10,000
Insurance required	8,000
Insurance carried (face of policy)	9,000

All losses up to $9,000 are paid in full.

EXAMPLE B

When insurance equal to 80% of the value is carried.

Value of property	$10,000
Insurance required	8,000
Insurance carried (face of policy)	8,000

For losses exceeding $8,000, the face of the policy ($8,000) is paid.
All losses under $8,000 are paid in full.

EXAMPLE C

When insurance of less than 80% of the value is carried.

Value of property	$10,000
Insurance required	8,000
Insurance carried (face of policy)	5,000

For losses exceeding $8,000, the face of the policy ($5,000) is paid.
All losses under $8,000 are paid in the proportion that $5,000 bears to $8,000, which is $\frac{5}{8}$.

All these examples of coinsurance can be summarized in one formula:

$$\frac{\text{Amount carried (face)}}{\text{Amount required}} \times \text{Loss} = \begin{array}{l}\text{Amount recoverable from the in-}\\\text{surance company, which, however,}\\\text{must never exceed the face of the}\\\text{policy.}\end{array}$$

Illustration No. 185 is a table showing in detail how various 80 per cent clauses operate. Other clauses operate in a similar manner.

Value of Property	Percentage Required by Policy	Amount Required by Policy	Actual Percentage Carried	Amount Carried	Loss	Amount Paid by Insurance Company	Loss Borne by Insured
$10,000	80%	$8,000	80%	$8,000	$9,000	$8,000	$1,000
10,000	80%	8,000	80%	8,000	8,000	8,000	0
10,000	80%	8,000	80%	8,000	5,000	5,000	0
10,000	80%	8,000	60%	6,000	6,000	4,500	1,500
10,000	80%	8,000	60%	6,000	9,000	6,000	3,000
10,000	80%	8,000	90%	9,000	9,000	9,000	0

Illustration No. 185—How Coinsurance Clauses Operate

The coinsurance clause is usually attached to an ordinary fire insurance policy. Illustration No. 186 shows a typical coinsurance clause.

Coverage for Bad Risks. In many communities it is impossible for any particular business to obtain all the insurance it desires through one insurance company. Insurance

COINSURANCE CLAUSE

In consideration of the rate and/or form under which this policy is written it is expressly stipulated and made a condition of this contract that the insured shall at all times maintain contributing insurance on each item of property insured by this policy to

the extent of at least____80____% of the actual cash value at the time of the loss, and that failing to do so, the insured shall to the extent of such deficit bear his, her or their proportion of any loss.

If this policy be divided into two or more items, the foregoing conditions shall apply to each item separately.

This clause, at the request of the insured, is attached to and forms a part of Policy No.__36600__of the

__Fire and Marine__Insurance Company of__Minneapolis, Minn.__

issued at its__SHELBYVILLE, KY.__Agency   Dated__June 20,__19.39

S. S. Johnson Insured.

C. A. RANDOLPH & CO.   Agent.
SHELBYVILLE, KY.

NOTICE.—This clause, when attached to policies covering in whole or in part on realty, must be signed by the insured, and in duplicate, one copy to be attached to policy, the other to daily report sent the Company. Agent must sign in all cases.

Illustration No. 186—A Coinsurance Clause

companies follow a policy, particularly in certain high-risk districts, of insuring only a certain percentage of the value of property. There are two ways, however, in which a businessman may obtain complete coverage. One is by obtaining two or more policies that together cover the entire value of the property. The other is by purchasing complete coverage from one insurance company, which in turn will reinsure part of the value of the property with one or more other insurance companies. When any particular insurance company issues a large insurance policy, it usually sells or reinsures part of the risk with other companies. This practice is considered good management on the part of the insurance company because it distributes the risk among a number of companies. Any particular large loss might seriously embarrass a single company; but when it is distributed over several companies, it is not so significant. In other words, several insurance companies bear the loss instead of one company.

Features of Use and Occupancy Insurance. Use and occupancy insurance is sometimes referred to as *business interruption insurance*. For instance, after a fire in an office, a factory, or a store, the business suffers an additional loss because it cannot carry on its operations in the normal manner. Some of its expenses continue in spite of the fire. These are such expenses as interest on notes, taxes, rent, royalties, certain insurance, advertising, telephone service, and certain salaries. The business may lose not only the normal income from sales but also its customers, who may go to other sources and never come back. On the other hand, during the period when the business may be shut down because of the fire, it may save the salaries of certain employees and a few other miscellaneous expenses. The purpose of use and occupancy insurance is to protect the businessman from loss during the interruption and to enable him to get back into normal operation as soon as possible. Several different plans of insurance are provided to cover the losses resulting from business interruption. These are as follows:

Plan 1. Concerns having reasonably even daily earnings may carry insurance providing for a daily payment not exceeding 1/300 (or 1/365 if the business is operated on Sundays) of the face of the policy. This clause may be written to cover two years.

Plan 2. Businesses in which the daily earnings are not even may take out insurance providing for weekly payments amounting to 1/52 of the amount of insurance carried.

Plan 3. Businesses in which the earnings are not even from day to day, week to week, or month to month may obtain insurance that provides protection when it is needed but withdraws it when it is not needed. A canning factory that operates during the berry-canning season in the spring and the vegetable-canning season in the early fall is an example of such a business.

Plan 4. In addition to the choices indicated above, coinsurance clauses may be inserted in these policies. The policyholder may consequently be required to carry insurance equal to 80 per cent, 90 per cent, or 100 per cent of the actual use value of the business. These clauses operate for use and occupancy insurance in essentially the same manner as they do for fire insurance policies.

Let us assume that the use and occupancy insurance carried by a particular business amounts to $300,000 and that the business is not operated on Sundays and holidays. Under the first plan the payments would not exceed 1/300 of $300,000, or $1,000, a day.

Plans 1 and 2 are basic. Plan 3 can be used with Plan 1. For instance, assume that the greatest risk occurs between July 1 and January 1. The payments might be:

	PER DAY	NO. OF DAYS	INSURANCE
January 1 to July 1.......	$ 500 ×	150	$ 75,000
July 1 to January 1.......	1,500 ×	150	225,000
Total		300	$300,000

Plan 2 is a basic weekly plan. Under it the weekly payments would not exceed 1/52 of $300,000, or $5,769.23, a week. If the fluctuating form in Plan 3 is used with Plan 2, the payments could be arranged as follows:

	PER WEEK	NO. OF WEEKS	INSURANCE
November 15 to June 6....	$ 6,000.00	× 29	$174,000
June 6 to August 1.......	10,000.00	× 8	80,000
August 1 to November 15..	3,066.66	× 15	46,000
Total		52	$300,000

In determining the amount of such insurance to carry, the businessman should consult an insurance representative. He will find it advisable to prepare a list of items that are customarily considered as fixed charges, and to make an estimate of his normal profit, taking into consideration past experience and future expectations. When such an estimate has been made, a record should be kept of the method of computing the estimate so that these figures can be submitted in justifying a claim.

Features of Burglary and Robbery Insurance. Many businesses, especially stores, need protection from loss due to burglary, robbery, theft, and larceny. Some policies provide for (a) divided coverage or limited coverage, (b) blanket coverage, or (c) full blanket coverage. To understand these coverages, it is necessary to read the details of the clauses in the particular policies.

Various policies provide protection from loss due to personal holdup, robbery of merchandise, robbery of safe, robbery of paymaster, messenger robbery, and interior office or store robbery. Because of the differences in the types of businesses and the methods of operating businesses, the risks vary considerably. Consequently, the rates also vary considerably. Individual policies may be obtained to cover different risks, or one policy may be obtained to cover several risks. The rate on the latter type of policy will depend upon the number of risks covered.

Store owners need protection from shoplifting and therefore carry such insurance. It is often a better policy for merchants to employ a detective agency to check on shoplifters than it is to expect their employees to watch customers and accuse those guilty of shoplifting.

Coinsurance may be obtained with various forms of burglary and robbery insurance. For instance, a coinsurance clause is often used in burglary insurance policies on open-stock merchandise. In burglary insurance, as in the case of fire insurance, usually only a limited loss is sustained at any particular time for seldom is all the merchandise stolen. The greater number of coinsurance clauses are therefore confined to smaller percentages. If the policyholder is willing, however, to insure for 90 or 100 per cent, he will obtain more complete protection at a lower rate.

Transportation and Cargo Insurance. *Marine insurance,* or *transportation insurance,* has many uses. If a shipment is sent by water, the person who owns the goods will want protection against damage, theft, and complete loss. The person who owns the goods may obtain this insurance, or the company that transports them may provide it as a part of the cost of transportation. The transportation company may insure all its shipments through an insurance company, or it may assume its own risks and pay its own losses.

In sending a shipment by railway freight, the shipper need not declare the value; but if the shipment is lost or damaged, he may file a claim and recover the full amount of the loss. The insurance cost in such cases is included in the rate charged for transportation.

When a shipment is sent by express, the value need not be declared if it does not exceed $50, for the express company assumes, without extra charge, responsibility for any loss up to $50. It will also assume, without extra charge, responsibility for any loss not exceeding half the value of the shipment. If the declared value is greater than $50 or greater than one half the value of the total shipment, the shipper may purchase additional insurance at 10 cents on each additional $100 of the value.

Parcel-post packages may be insured by the Post Office Department upon the payment of an extra fee, or they may be sent uninsured.

Certain other forms of transportation, such as motor-truck, require insurance. Such insurance should definitely identify the merchandise and indicate its point of origin, its destination, and the route of travel, for the merchandise is protected only during the process of transportation.

Common carrier trucking companies must carry cargo insurance. Illustration No. 187 shows a form that must be submitted by the insurance company to the Interstate Commerce Commission whenever a policy is issued on a cargo.

Form B. M. C. 34
To be sent to—
INTERSTATE COMMERCE COMMISSION
BUREAU OF MOTOR CARRIERS
Washington, D. C.
Received and approved:
Date ....

MOTOR CARRIER CARGO LIABILITY CERTIFICATE OF INSURANCE
FILED WITH
INTERSTATE COMMERCE COMMISSION
BUREAU OF MOTOR CARRIERS
Washington, D. C.
(Executed in Triplicate)

Docket Number
....

THIS IS TO CERTIFY, That the ..... The Tower Mutual Insurance Company .....
(Name of Company)
(hereinafter called Company) of ..... Carew Tower, Cincinnati, Ohio .....
(Home office address of Company)
has issued to ..... Ajax Motor Service, Inc. ..... of ..... 131 Walnut Street, Cincinnati, Ohio .....
(Name of Motor Carrier) (Address of Motor Carrier)

the policy of Cargo Insurance herein described which, by the attachment of endorsement, form number B. M. C. 32, approved by the Interstate Commerce Commission, has been amended to provide compensation for loss of or damage to all property belonging to shippers or consignees and coming into the possession of the Insured in connection with its transportation service under certificate of public convenience and necessity issued to the Insured by the Interstate Commerce Commission or otherwise under the Motor Carrier Act, 1935, and the pertinent rules and regulations of the Interstate Commerce Commission, regardless of whether the motor vehicles, terminals, warehouses, and other facilities used in connection with the transportation of such property are specifically described in the policy or not The liability of the Company extends to such losses or damages whether occurring on the route or in the territory authorized to be served by the Insured or elsewhere, except as follows:

..... none .....
(Name as exceptions only States in which the Insured's operations are covered by other insurance)

Whenever requested by the Commission, the Company agrees to furnish to the Commission a duplicate original of said policy and all endorsements thereon.

The endorsement described herein may not be canceled without cancelation of the policy to which it is attached. Such cancelation may be effected by the Company or the Insured giving thirty (30) days' notice in writing to the Interstate Commerce Commission at its office in Washington, D. C., said thirty (30) days' notice to commence to run from the date notice is actually received at the office of said Commission.

Policy No. ..... F0-67069 ..... Effective from ..... May, 1939, ... to ..... until canceled .....
12:01 a. m., standard time at the address of the Insured as stated in said policy.
Countersigned at ..... Cincinnati, Ohio, ... this ..... first ..... day of ..... May, ... 1939.

..... J. M. Blake .....
Authorized Company Representative.

Illustration No. 187—A Form Submitted to the Interstate Commerce Commission

Automobile Insurance. Automobile insurance may cover loss caused by fire, theft, collision, bodily injury, property damage, tornado, windstorm, rain, or the like. Bodily-injury insurance was formerly referred to as public-liability insurance. There are also several other special types of protection that can be obtained.

Almost every owner of an automobile agrees that protection from fire and theft is desirable. There are relatively few automobile owners who do not carry this protection. The insurance rates are therefore low because the risks are spread among a great number of automobile owners.

It formerly was the custom for insurance companies to issue policies in which they agreed to pay a fixed amount in case of loss or damage due to fire or theft. The most common practice now is to issue policies which state that the market value of the automobile at the time of the loss will be paid. For instance, a new car may be insured on January 1 for its actual value, or cost, of $980. If it is stolen six months later, the amount that the insurance company is obligated to pay is only the market value of a secondhand car of that particular age and kind. Most policies are worded in such a manner that the insurance company may replace the car with a similar one or pay the market value at the time of the loss, regardless of the amount of insurance carried on the car. When there is only a partial loss, the insurance company repairs the damage or pays an amount of cash equivalent to the cost of repairs. Most policies include protection against fire and theft while an automobile is being transported on a boat or a railroad.

Collision insurance is usually meant to be protection against damage to one's own car. This type of insurance is becoming somewhat unpopular because it is costly and because some unscrupulous people damage their own cars to collect insurance.

Although fire and theft insurance are the most widely used forms of automobile insurance, bodily-injury and property-damage insurance are probably the most important. Some states have passed legislation that makes it necessary for automobile owners to take out these types of insurance before they can obtain licenses for their cars.

Property-damage insurance provides protection against damage to the automobile or to some other property of another person, while bodily-injury insurance provides protection against an injury to any living person. These two forms of insurance are often sold jointly in the same policy, although they can be bought separately. They are important because the hazards of not carrying bodily-injury and property-damage insurance are unknown and potentially great. On the other hand, the hazards from fire and theft are definitely known and are not particularly great.

The so-called "five and ten clause" in an automobile insurance policy refers to $5,000 of bodily-injury insurance for injury to one person and $10,000 for injury to two or more persons in the same accident. These amounts are usually the minimum amounts for which bodily-injury insurance should be carried, but it is common practice to carry $10,000 and $20,000 of protection. The additional protection costs only approximately 20 per cent more than the lesser protection, although the amount of protection is twice as much. The reason why the additional protection costs only a small amount is that most of the damage claims for bodily injury are of small amounts.

Most claims can be settled within the limits of $10,000 and $20,000. If $10,000 worth of bodily-injury insurance is carried as protection against a single injury, the person who is injured can collect from the insurance company an amount not exceeding $10,000. If more than one person is injured, the total amount that can be collected cannot exceed $20,000. The amount of the damages must be determined by a court or established by an agreement between the injured person and the insurance company. A good insurance company will take care of all legal details; but if the amount of injury exceeds the amount of the insurance, the insured person will have to pay the difference.

Ordinarily it is considered wise not to carry less than $5,000 worth of property-damage insurance. If an automobile driver who carries $5,000 worth of property-damage insurance damages the automobile of another person or the front of a store, for instance, the person whose property has been damaged may collect damages from the insurance company to the extent of $5,000.

Insurance against such hazards as tornado, windstorm, and rain is used less frequently, although the rates for such protection are low. The rates are low because the chance of loss from these hazards is relatively small.

Unless otherwise specified, the insurance on one's car covers its operation within the United States and for the purposes specified in the policy. For instance, the insurance on a car may cover the use of the car for both business and pleasure, for business alone, or for pleasure alone. Although the insurance is always issued to an individual, the policy covers a particular car and anyone operating that car. Ordinarily the policy does not cover the individual when he is operating the uninsured car of another person. In buying automobile insurance, however, the purchaser can have inserted in the policy a special clause covering himself when he is operating a car other than the one insured.

Automobile insurance rates are generally considered somewhat unfair because the reckless driver, if he can obtain insurance, pays for it at the same rate as the careful driver. Furthermore, rates are based upon localities. For instance, the rates on various types of automobile insurance are not the same in Chicago and in San Francisco. Some companies have attempted to offset this unfairness by selecting carefully those whom they insure and thereby providing insurance at lower rates.

In the state of New York, careful drivers are now rewarded with lower rates for bodily-injury and property-damage insurance. To those who have had not more than one accident involving property damage within the last two years, a classification known as Rate A is given. Such persons are given the basic rate, which is the lowest. To those who have had not more than one accident involving property damage and one accident involving personal injuries, a classification known as Rate B is given. Such persons are required to pay a premium that is 10 per cent greater than that paid by those in the Rate A classification. To those who have had two or more accidents involving either property damage or personal injury, a classification known as Rate C is given. Such persons are required to pay a premium that is 15 per cent greater than that paid by those in the Rate A classification. The insurance company may refuse to insure those persons who have had many accidents.

Special Store Insurance. Businessmen operating retail stores or dealing directly with the public in other ways usually find it necessary to carry various forms of special insurance, such as insurance providing protection from loss due to the personal injury of customers. A claim may result from a customer's being injured by slipping on a floor, falling down steps, being caught in an elevator, or harmed by an employee or by some other customer. Damage claims may also result from the use of merchandise that was sold by a store. For instance, the dye in some clothing may cause a skin infection. A cosmetic may result in injury to a user. A piece of machinery may be defective and cause personal injury. Claims can result from all these cases, but there is insurance available to provide protection against them.

Even though insurance is carried as protection against such claims, the owner or the management has an important responsibility to prevent accidents. When an accident occurs, it creates ill will. The prevention of accidents is therefore really as important as insurance providing protection against them.

Surety Bonds. Surety bonds, which are used in business, are really a form of insurance. For instance, when a person employed by a bank will be required to handle money, he must be bonded by a surety and bonding company. Then, in case the employee later embezzles or steals money from the bank, the bonding company is required to make good the loss provided the employee is not able to return the money. Some banks pay the cost of the bond, but others require the employee to pay it. Bonds are issued only on the basis of reputable character. The rate is dependent upon the risk involved. For instance, a person handling a small amount of money will not require a large bond and the rate will probably be reasonably low. On the other hand, if the person handles a large amount of money, the bond will probably be rather large and the rate therefore higher.

Performance Bonds. These bonds are also commonly used in business. They are in a sense a form of surety bond. For instance, if one obtains a contract to construct a building or to furnish merchandise at a specified price and under specified conditions, it may be necessary for him to give a bond. If the contract is not carried out according to its terms, the bond is forfeited and the company that issued it must pay damages to the person for whom the building was being constructed or the merchandise was being produced. Bonds are used quite generally in business. For instance, if a company establishes an agency, the agent may be required to give a performance bond. Sometimes when merchandise is sent on consignment, the person who receives it is required to give a bond.

Life Insurance in Business. Ordinarily people do not consider life insurance as having a place in business, but it does have a very important place. For example, a businessman who carries life insurance may be able to borrow on the policy to help finance his business. He may carry a life insurance policy so that, when he dies, the proceeds will pay for the business, permitting it to be turned over to a son or to some other successor. It is quite common for the owner of a small business to insure his life so that, in case of his death, a debt, such as a bank loan, can be repaid without jeopardizing the business. Important executives are commonly insured. The theory behind this plan is that, if a key executive dies, the progress of the corporation will be impaired, but the proceeds from the insurance will help the corporation to make any adjustments that are necessary until a new executive can be obtained.

The so-called group insurance plan has a prominent place in business. The business and the employees share in the payment of the premiums. When an employee dies or becomes incapacitated, the insurance company pays an indemnity based upon the clauses in the policy. Under this plan, insurance is provided for many employees who could not individually obtain insurance because of their health. From the point of view of the employee the insurance is available usually at a relatively low rate. The employer is relieved of some responsibility when an employee dies.

QUESTIONS FOR DISCUSSION

1. Name at least five examples of general business risks.
2. Point out some examples of risks that have recently developed or that may develop in the future.
3. Why is the risk of style changes so important in a business selling women's clothing?
4. A company is organized to manufacture and sell butter, as well as to manufacture and sell oleomargarine. What, in your opinion, are some of the advantages of this combination?
5. Explain the differences in ownership between the mutual insurance company and the stock insurance company.
6. Name at least five factors that are taken into consideration in determining fire insurance rates.
7. Does a fire insurance policy on a building usually cover the equipment and the materials in the building?
8. Is there any advantage in carrying fire insurance for a greater amount than the actual value of the property?
9. Why is it advisable to keep in a fireproof vault such items as accounting records, plans, and maps, even though these items are insured?
10. Does a person who rents a building have an insurable interest in the building?
11. Under a coinsurance fire insurance clause, why are the rates per thousand dollars of insurance lower than they are under ordinary insurance?
12. Explain the formula for computing the amount that is recoverable under a coinsurance clause in a fire insurance policy.
13. Why is business interruption insurance a desirable form of insurance for some businesses?
14. Name the various types of protection or coverage in burglary and robbery insurance policies. May coinsurance be obtained on these policies?
15. How is insurance handled on (a) railroad freight shipments? (b) railway express shipments? (c) parcel-post shipments?
16. What are the options of an insurance company in paying for the loss caused by the theft of an automobile?
17. What is bodily-injury insurance?
18. What is the significance of the so-called "five and ten" bodily-injury clause?

PROBLEMS AND PROJECTS

1. The following are the details of an 80 per cent coinsurance policy:

    Value of property $8,760
    Insurance carried 5,000
    Loss 4,000

    Compute the amount that will be paid by the insurance company.

2. The following are the details of a fire insurance policy with a 90 per cent coinsurance clause:

    Value of property $21,560
    Insurance carried 19,000
    Loss 6,000

    Compute the amount that will be paid by the insurance company.

3. Obtain a sample of some kind of fire insurance policy for a business. Study its clauses and regulations. Write a report on it.

4. Make an investigation of the local rates for theft, property-damage, bodily-injury, and fire insurance on automobiles. Compare these rates with those in other communities. Write a report summarizing your findings.

5. Obtain an automobile insurance policy of some kind. Study its clauses, and make a report on its features. Point out some of the ways in which the automobile owner may not be protected adequately by the policy.

6. In Illustration No. 185 on page 454 is a table constructed for coinsurance clauses. Assume that each policy carries a 90 per cent coinsurance clause but that all the other facts remain the same. Compute the amounts for the last two columns.

7. If a business carries $200,000 worth of business interruption insurance under Plan 2 explained on page 456, how much insurance could be collected weekly because of business interruption?

8. A business concern wishes to carry $200,000 worth of business interruption insurance. Assume that its business is divided as follows: 20 per cent in May, 20 per cent in June, and approximately 6 per cent in each of the other months. Construct a table showing how the amounts of insurance should be distributed weekly to provide adequate coverage.

CHAPTER XIX

FINANCIAL RECORDS NEEDED IN BUSINESS

Purpose of the Chapter. Under conditions of modern competition, a business cannot succeed indefinitely unless it follows sound methods of management. One of the most important aspects of business management is the use of adequate financial records. Using financial records means not only the preparation of them but also the interpretation of them.

A knowledge of accounting is a valuable asset to every businessman. It cannot be assumed, however, that everyone who reads this chapter will have a knowledge of accounting. The information presented here is not based upon the assumption of such a knowledge. The purpose of this chapter is largely to point out the necessity for financial records, to give examples of them, and to demonstrate their use. The following are some of the questions that will be answered:

1. What financial records are needed?
2. How can accounting records be used for managerial control?
3. What information is needed daily?
4. What information is needed monthly?
5. What information is needed yearly?
6. What information is needed for income-tax purposes?
7. What records are needed for social security taxes?

Use of Accounting Records. No business can be operated successfully unless books are kept and accounting statements are prepared. No one should start in business without a knowledge of bookkeeping or the aid of someone who has such a knowledge. Some of the information that a business manager should expect from accounting records is as follows:

1. Kinds and values of assets
2. Amount of cash sales
3. Amount of cash received from credit customers
4. Amount of credit sales
5. Amount of C.O.D. sales
6. Amount of cash deposited in the bank
7. Amount of cash withdrawn from the bank
8. Amount of debts that are owed by the business
9. Amount owed to the business
10. Bills that are paid
11. Total amount of expenses
12. Amount of merchandise bought
13. Transportation charges paid
14. Amount sold by each salesperson
15. Profit or loss
16. Percentage of profit or loss

Sales, accounts receivable, payments on account, expenditures, and cash balances should be tabulated daily. The information listed above should be compiled monthly or at least semiannually. Modern accounting records are not difficult to keep up to date. Machines, special books, and files can be utilized for this purpose.

Double-entry bookkeeping is the accepted standard in modern business. It is distinguished from *single-entry bookkeeping* by the use of offsetting entries to record each transaction. The totals of all offsetting entries must always balance. Double-entry bookkeeping provides a better proof of correctness than single-entry bookkeeping.

Control Through Accounting Records. The study of the financial records is the main means of control in the management of a business. Businessmen use the statement of profit and loss and the balance sheet as part of the means of controlling their operations. Every business should have these two statements prepared no less than once a year, but preferably every six months or even every month. In many cases they are prepared every month.

Let us consider the grocery business that is operated by Mr. H. J. Brooks. The statement of profit and loss of this business is shown in Illustration No. 188. It provides Mr. Brooks with an analysis of the results of his business opera-

H. J. BROOKS
STATEMENT OF PROFIT AND LOSS
FOR SIX MONTHS ENDING DECEMBER 31, 194/-

Income from Sales:				
Sales			24,956	34
Cost of Merchandise Sold:				
Mdse. Inventory, July 1	2,165	42		
Purchases	20,504	73		
Total Cost of Mdse. Available for Sale	22,670	15		
Less Mdse. Inventory, December 31	3,495	35		
Cost of Merchandise Sold			19,174	80
Gross Profit on Sales			5,781	54
Operating Expenses:				
Salaries and Wages	2,630	00		
Advertising	332	15		
Donations	25	00		
Supplies Used	80	65		
Miscellaneous Office Expense	34	75		
Telephone and Telegraph Service	47	50		
Delivery Expense	305	15		
Taxes and Insurance	160	05		
Rent	600	00		
Heat, Light, Water	147	12		
Loss from Bad Debts	270	16		
Interest Paid	60	00		
Repairs and Depreciation	150	00		
Other Expense	122	23		
Total Operating Expenses			4,964	76
Net Profit			816	78

Illustration No. 188—A Profit and Loss Statement

tions during a period of six months ending on December 31. The information reported on this statement was obtained from the accounting records. The statement discloses the fact that a net profit of $816.78 was made during the six-month period.

Illustration No. 189 is a balance sheet that was prepared at the same time as the statement of profit and loss. The purpose of the balance sheet is to show the condition of the business on December 31. According to this statement the net worth, or capital, of Mr. Brooks is $3,638.50. On July 1 his net worth had amounted to $3,612.37. During the six months between July 1 and December 31, Mr. Brooks withdrew $790.65 for his own purposes. If he had

H. J. BROOKS
BALANCE SHEET
DECEMBER 31, 194–

Assets				
Current Assets:				
Cash	630	90		
Notes Receivable	43	50		
Accounts Receivable	614	00		
Merchandise Inventory	3,495	35		
Total Current Assets			4,783	75
Deferred Charges:				
Supplies	39	50		
Insurance	44	00		
Total Deferred Charges			83	50
Fixed Assets:				
Equipment	500	00		
Less Depreciation Reserve	105	00		
Total Fixed Assets			395	00
Total Assets			5,262	25
Liabilities				
Current Liabilities:				
Notes Payable	649	50		
Accounts Payable	974	25		
Total Liabilities			1,623	75
Proprietorship				
H. J. Brooks, Capital, July 1	3,612	37		
Net Profit 816.78				
Less Withdrawals 790.65				
Net Increase in Proprietorship	26	13		
H. J. Brooks, Capital, December 31			3,638	50

Illustration No. 189—A Balance Sheet

not made these withdrawals, the net worth would be
$790.65 more.

The following is a list of items of information that was
prepared by Mr. Brooks on December 31. Similar information is obtained from the records every day. This list gives
information on cash receipts, cash payments, cash deposited in the bank, and cash balance.

Total cash received	$ 50.57
Cash sales	40.15
Cash received on accounts	10.42
Credit sales	16.10
Purchases on account	72.04
Payments for purchases (made by check)	30.46
Payments for miscellaneous expenses (made with cash)	3.12
Cash deposited in bank	47.45
Bank balance	630.90

Interpreting Financial Statements. The simple financial statements that have just been presented are not always sufficient to enable the manager to interpret the condition of the business. An accountant can prepare numerous ratios that will help to analyze the business. For instance, he may compute a ratio to show the relationship between current assets and current liabilities. Such a ratio helps to determine the ability of the business to pay its current debts. For example, if a business has $3 of current assets for every $1 of current liabilities, it is apparent that the business is better able to pay its liabilities when they become due than it would be if the ratio were two to one or one to one. There is no ratio that can be set as a standard because some types of businesses do not require as large a ratio as others.

Another important ratio is the relationship between sales and cost of sales, an analysis of which is usually handled by an accountant. The manager of the business must understand something about accounting in order to understand these figures. For instance, even though the businessman may not be sufficiently familiar with accounting procedure to prepare the financial statements, he should be able to look at them and understand the figures. As an example assume that during one year the cost of sales amounted to 80 per cent of the gross sales and that during the next year the cost of sales amounted to 85 per cent of the gross sales. Obviously, therefore, the manager should be concerned with figuring a way of reducing the cost of sales or of increasing the selling price. Otherwise the trend indicates that eventually net profit will be eliminated.

Quite often it is important to compare the results of one year with those of the previous year. For instance, the profit and loss statement of one year is tabulated alongside the profit and loss statement of the preceding year or the statements of several years. At a glance one is then able to make a comparison of various items for two or more years. Similar comparisons are made of balance sheet items for two or more years. For example, Illustration No. 190 shows a comparative balance sheet of Mr. H. J. Brooks. It

H. J. BROOKS
COMPARATIVE BALANCE SHEET
DECEMBER 31, 194–, AND JUNE 30, 194–

Assets	December 31				June 30			
Current Assets:								
Cash	630	90			785	22		
Notes Receivable	43	50			59	61		
Accounts Receivable	614	00			693	57		
Merchandise Inventory	3,495	35			4,012	23		
Total Current Assets			4,783	75			5,550	63
Deferred Charges:								
Supplies	39	50			54	75		
Insurance	44	00			49	00		
Total Deferred Charges			83	50			103	75
Fixed Assets:								
Equipment	500	00			700	00		
Less Depreciation Reserve....	105	00			175	00		
Total Fixed Assets			395	00			525	00
Total Assets			5,262	25			6,179	38
Liabilities								
Current Liabilities:								
Notes Payable	649	50			665	22		
Accounts Payable	974	25			960	31		
Total Liabilities			1,623	75			1,625	53
Proprietorship								
H. J. Brooks, Beginning Capital..	3,612	37			3,638	50		
Net Increase in Proprietorship.	26	13			915	35		
H. J. Brooks, Ending Capital.			3,638	50			4,553	85

Illustration No. 190—A Comparative Balance Sheet

is obvious that during the six months ending June 30, the business has been in a better condition than it was during the six months ending December 31. The total liabilities are approximately the same, but the total assets are greater. The capital, or proprietorship, of Mr. Brooks is therefore greater.

On comparative statements of profit and loss it is helpful to show, by means of percentages, the relationship of the various items for one year to the sales for that year. For instance, Illustration No. 191 shows the latest profit and loss statement of Mr. H. J. Brooks with such percentages. If such a statement is prepared each year, the manager is able to make a definite analysis of the operations of the business from year to year. For example, if the per-

H. J. BROOKS

STATEMENT OF PROFIT AND LOSS

FOR SIX MONTHS ENDING DECEMBER 31, 194–

Income from Sales:					
Sales			24,956	34	100.00%
Cost of Merchandise Sold:					
Mdse. Inventory, July 1	2,165	42			
Purchases	20,504	73			
Total Cost of Mdse. Available for Sale...	22,670	15			
Less Mdse. Inventory, December 31	3,495	35			
Cost of Merchandise Sold			19,174	80	76.83%
Gross Profit on Sales			5,781	54	23.17%
Operating Expenses:					
Salaries and Wages	2,630	00			10.53%
Advertising	332	15			1.33%
Donations	25	00			.10%
Supplies Used	80	65			.32%
Miscellaneous Office Expense	34	75			.14%
Telephone and Telegraph Service	47	50			.19%
Delivery Expense	305	15			1.22%
Taxes and Insurance	160	05			.64%
Rent	600	00			2.40%
Heat, Light, Water	147	12			.59%
Loss from Bad Debts	270	16			1.08%
Interest Paid	60	00			.24%
Repairs and Depreciation	150	00			.60%
Other Expense	122	23			.49%
Total Operating Expenses			4,964	76	19.89%
Net Profit			816	78	3.27%

Illustration No. 191—A Profit and Loss Statement with Percentages

centage of gross profit on sales has increased, but the selling expenses have increased in a greater proportion, there is an indication that something is wrong with the efficiency of the operation of the business. If the selling expenses continue to increase at the same rate, the business may eventually cease to earn a profit. Something should be done to adjust these expenses so that they will be in the proper relation to the sales and the gross profit.

Sometimes financial statements like those presented previously do not provide sufficient detail to enable the manager of the business to get a clear picture of the situation. He must therefore have subsidiary reports. Subsidiary reports are often prepared for notes receivable, accounts receivable, merchandise inventory, and many of the other items on the balance sheet or the profit and loss statement.

For example, the following is a subsidiary report of the accounts receivable of Mr. H. J. Brooks:

ACCOUNTS RECEIVABLE

Elite Baking Company	$ 73.40
Maryvale Rural School	95.72
Mr. A. F. Walker	27.61
Mr. John S. Morse	63.59
Mrs. Allen Roper	80.25
Mrs. R. E. Williams	59.56
Mr. James O. Arnold	24.91
Mr. E. R. Welch	66.80
Blue Bird Cafeteria	15.02
Mills Grocery Company	107.14
Total	$614.00

Such subsidiary reports may be more useful to the manager if they provide a more detailed analysis. For instance, a report of the accounts receivable may show how long each account has been outstanding, in order that the manager can determine whether some special procedure should be established to collect some of the accounts before they become too old.

Comparative Operating Costs. The businessman is wise if he compares his results with the results obtained by other similar types of businesses. From the Federal Government it is possible to get figures on the operating costs of various kinds of stores in all types of communities. Information can also be obtained from other sources, such as chambers of commerce, Dun and Bradstreet, Incorporated, the Merchants Service Bureau of the National Cash Register Company, and various trade magazines. For example, the table in Illustration No. 192 shows some operating costs of hardware stores in cities with a population of more than fifty thousand. These figures are classified according to the sales of each store. The profitable stores are distinguished from the general group. The value of a study of these figures arises from the ability of the businessman to adjust some of his costs that seem to be out of line with those of other businessmen. Similar figures for retail meat markets and for retail grocery stores are shown in Illustration No. 193.

	SALES UNDER $25,000		SALES $25,000 TO $40,000		SALES $40,000 TO $60,000	
	Group Average	Profit Makers	Group Average	Profit Makers	Group Average	Profit Makers
NUMBER OF STORES REPORTING	47	30	33	28	29	24
NET SALES .....:......	100.00%	100.00%	100.00%	100.00%	100.00%	100.00%
COST OF GOODS SOLD..	66.84%	65.14%	68.35%	67.99%	70.26%	69.53%
MARGIN	33.16%	34.86%	31.65%	32.01%	29.74%	30.47%
EXPENSE:						
Salaries, Management and Buying	3.21%	2.87%	2.70%	2.56%	2.99%	2.97%
Salaries, Selling	12.46%	11.97%	10.74%	10.52%	9.82%	9.37%
Salaries, Office	1.77%	1.82%	1.74%	1.70%	1.64%	1.54%
TOTAL SALARIES	17.44%	16.66%	15.18%	14.78%	14.45%	13.88%
Office Supplies and Postage	0.28%	0.28%	0.46%	0.44%	0.48%	0.46%
Advertising	0.74%	0.69%	0.83%	0.89%	1.07%	1.00%
Donations	0.09%	0.09%	0.11%	0.13%	0.09%	0.09%
Store Supplies	0.29%	0.27%	0.24%	0.23%	0.32%	0.32%
Telephone and Telegraph	0.65%	0.65%	0.43%	0.41%	0.35%	0.36%
Losses on Notes and Accounts	0.38%	0.37%	0.58%	0.58%	0.54%	0.52%
Delivery Expense (incl. deliv. wages)	1.84%	1.98%	1.70%	1.50%	1.83%	1.78%
Depreciation Delivery Equipment	0.30%	0.30%	0.35%	0.31%	0.24%	0.26%
Depreciation Furniture, Fix. and Tools	0.53%	0.49%	0.44%	0.38%	0.30%	0.29%
Rent (incl. taxes, ins., depr. and int.)	5.09%	4.90%	3.80%	3.66%	3.50%	3.24%
Repairs	0.23%	0.28%	0.25%	0.17%	0.13%	0.12%
Heat, Light, Water, Power	1.00%	0.91%	0.85%	0.85%	0.83%	0.79%
Insurance (ins. on bldg. incl. in rent)	0.68%	0.55%	0.63%	0.60%	0.55%	0.56%
Taxes (taxes on bldg. incl. with rent)	0.87%	0.89%	0.77%	0.79%	0.57%	0.54%
Interest on Borrowed Money	0.25%	0.25%	0.25%	0.25%	0.27%	0.25%
Unclassified	0.40%	0.36%	0.39%	0.37%	0.63%	0.66%
TOTAL EXPENSE (Int. on invest. not incl.)	31.06%	29.92%	27.26%	26.34%	26.15%	25.12%
EARNINGS ON SALES..	2.10%	4.94%	4.39%	5.67%	3.59%	5.35%
Cash Disc. and Int. Rec'd (pctg. on sales)	1.10%	1.16%	1.25%	1.31%	1.15%	1.15%
TOTAL EARNINGS	3.20%	6.10%	5.64%	6.98%	4.74%	6.50%
Credit Sales (percentage of total sales)	29%	34%	42%	43%	50%	51%
Days' Credit Bus. on Books —End of Year	45	48	64	60	65	65
Capital Turn Times	2.29	2.25	2.29	2.33	2.65	2.84
Stock Turn Times	1.94	1.91	2.36	2.45	2.56	2.83
Owning Real Estate	13%	13%	9%	7%	17%	13%

Hardware Retailer.

Illustration No. 192—Operating Costs of Hardware Stores

Retail Meat Markets	Average of all Stores	All Stores with Sales Under $40,000	All Stores with Sales Over $40,000	Group A Sales Under $20,000	Group B $20,000 to $30,000
Percentages to Sales					
Gross Margin	24.4%	26.0%	23.9%	27.7%	26.3%
Total Expense	20.5	23.6	19.5	24.4	26.1
Net Profit	3.9	2.4	4.4	3.3	0.2
Analysis of Expense:					
Wages	12.5	13.4	12.1	14.1	14.2
Rent	1.9	3.2	1.5	3.0	4.9
Heat, Light, Power,					
Water, Ice	0.8	1.2	0.7	1.6	1.3
Wrappings	1.0	1.0	1.0	0.9	1.0
Advertising	0.9	0.5	1.0	0.4	0.4
Insurance	0.5	0.5	0.5	0.5	0.6
Depreciation	0.9	1.4	0.8	1.4	1.3
Miscellaneous	2.0	2.4	1.9	2.5	2.4
Sales per Clerk per Week ..	$297	$254	$314	$247	$236
Average Sale Transaction ..	78.0¢	66.7¢	82.3¢	53.3¢	59.1¢
Stock Turnover (times per year)	43.4	40.1	44.6	...	...
Average Inventory (Mdse.).	$992	$474	$1,580	...	...
Results per Pound (cents):					
Selling Price	23.2¢	25.0¢	22.9¢	...	...
Cost Price	17.6	18.4	17.5	...	...
Gross Margin	5.6	6.6	5.4	...	...
Total Expense	4.7	6.0	4.4	...	...
Net Profit	0.9	0.6	1.0	...	...

Meat Dealer and Butchers and Packers Gazette.

Retail Grocery Stores	All Groups	Group I Net Sales Over $75,000	Group II Net Sales $50,000 to $75,000	Group III Net Sales $25,000 to $50,000	Group IV Net Sales Under $25,000
Number of Concerns	63	14	16	17	16
Typical Net Sales	$45,500	$116,000	$60,000	$37,700	$16,100
Average Inventory	2,800	6,082	3,150	2,500	1,150
Annual Inventory Turnover.	13.7	15.9	13.7	12.6	11.5
Operating Statements (In percentage of sales)					
Net Sales	100.0%	100.0%	100.0%	100.0%	100.0%
Cost of Goods Sold	81.5	80.9	80.4	80.8	84.1
Gross Margin	18.5%	19.1%	19.6%	19.2%	15.9%
Operating Expenses:					
Rent	1.3%	1.1%	1.2%	1.3%	1.5%
Heat, Light and Water ..	.7	.5	.7	.9	1.0
Taxes and Licenses	.5	.3	.5	.6	.3
Insurance	.2	.1	.2	.2	.2
Depreciation of Fixtures..	.5	.5	.5	.5	.5
Employees' Salaries	5.5	6.3	7.1	4.9	1.8
Proprietors' Salaries	4.0	2.4	4.0	4.0	6.6
Advertising	.6	.6	.6	.7	.5
Delivery Expense	.6	1.1	.6	.7	.6
Loss on Bad Debts	.6	.9	.5	.6	.9
Miscellaneous Expense ...	1.1	1.2	1.2	.9	.7
Total Operating Expense ...	15.6%	15.0%	17.1%	15.3%	14.6%
Net Operating Profit	2.9%	4.1%	2.5%	3.9%	1.3%

Bureau of Business and Government Research, University of Colorado.

Illustration No. 193—Operating Costs of Retail Meat
Markets and Grocery Stores

Records for a Small Business. A small business, especially a retail store, does not need elaborate records. A retail store can use the cash register as a basis for obtaining most of the information for its financial records. Models of such records can be obtained from the manufacturers of some cash registers. Some associations, such as oil dealers, plumbers, and dentists, have standard forms that they recommend for their members.

When a cash register is used, it is common practice to prepare a daily balance slip, the two sides of which are shown in Illustration No. 194. In addition to this daily balance slip, a summary is made. The two sides of this slip are shown in Illustration No. 195.

A simple system of record-keeping based upon the cash register can be learned easily by a person who is not

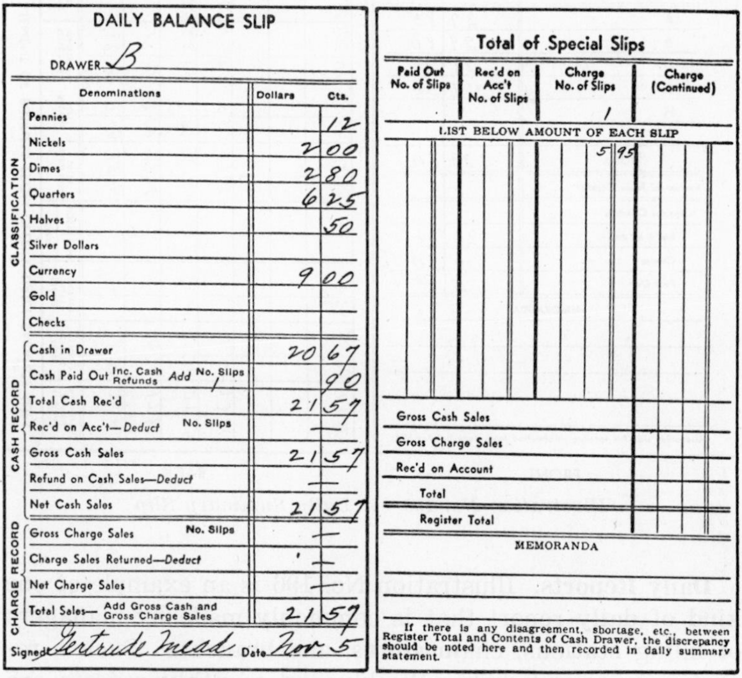
DAILY BALANCE SLIP

DRAWER B

	Denominations	Dollars	Cts.
CLASSIFICATION	Pennies		12
	Nickels	2	00
	Dimes	2	80
	Quarters	6	25
	Halves		50
	Silver Dollars		
	Currency	9	00
	Gold		
	Checks		
CASH RECORD	Cash in Drawer	20	67
	Cash Paid Out Inc. Cash Refunds Add No. Slips 1		90
	Total Cash Rec'd	21	57
	Rec'd on Acc't—*Deduct* No. Slips		—
	Gross Cash Sales	21	57
	Refund on Cash Sales—*Deduct*		—
	Net Cash Sales	21	57
CHARGE RECORD	Gross Charge Sales No. Slips		—
	Charge Sales Returned—*Deduct*		—
	Net Charge Sales		
	Total Sales— Add Gross Cash and Gross Charge Sales	21	57

Signed Gertrude Mead Date Nov. 5

Total of Special Slips

Paid Out No. of Slips	Rec'd on Acc't No. of Slips	Charge No. of Slips	Charge (Continued)
		1	

LIST BELOW AMOUNT OF EACH SLIP

5 95

Gross Cash Sales
Gross Charge Sales
Rec'd on Account
Total
Register Total

MEMORANDA

If there is any disagreement, shortage, etc., between Register Total and Contents of Cash Drawer, the discrepancy should be noted here and then recorded in daily summary statement.

FRONT BACK

Illustration No. 194—A Daily Balance Slip

familiar with accounting. A knowledge of accounting is, however, helpful in keeping such a set of records.

It is usually possible to hire someone to come in daily, weekly, or monthly to prepare the records and the financial statements that are necessary. If such a plan is followed, the daily summary slips, as well as certain other information, are kept. These slips are then turned over to the bookkeeper who is hired to prepare the records and the statements. Summary slips are kept by chain-store managers, filling-station operators, and other businessmen.

Daily Summary Statement of Register Totals

Date October 22, 194_

DRAWER	AMOUNT Dollars	Cents
A	27	85
B	29	80
D	28	35
E	47	30
H		
K		
TOTAL	133	30
Amount of Main Counter		
Special Counters		
Rec'd on Acc't.	30	00
Charge	30	70
Paid Out	5	35
MEMORANDA		

Use other side for totaling information from daily balance slips.

FRONT   BACK

Illustration No. 195—A Daily Summary Slip

Daily Reports. Illustration No. 196 is an example of one kind of daily report that is commonly made by managers of filling stations, chain stores, and branches. Such a report is prepared daily. Weekly and monthly reports are also sometimes used.

Opened 7:00 A. M.

Closed 11:00 P. M.

Street Address 206 Park Avenue

VALVOLINE OIL COMPANY

DAILY FILLING STATION REPORT

Station No. 1761

Town Louisville, Kentucky

Date January 9, 1940

	OPENING INVENTORY	QUANTITY RECEIVED	TOGETHER	CLOSING INVENTORY	TOTAL TO ACCOUNT FOR	— OVER OR + SHORT	CHG. SALES QUANTITY	CASH SALES QUANTITY	CASH SALES MONEY
GASOLINE—REGULAR	700	500	1,200	750	450		300	150	27 00
MAGNET	300	200	500	400	100		75	25	4 50
HITEST	400	250	650	495	150	+ 5	60	90	18 00
ETHYL	500	1,000	1,500	905	600		300	300	63 00
TOTAL GASOLINE	1,900	1,950	3,850	2,545	1,300		735	565	112 50
KEROSENE—	50		50	35	15	+ 5	5	10	2 00
OILS—									
VALVOLINE—SAE	75	25	100	65	35		15	20	5 00
MAGNET—SAE	25	15	40	20	20		15	5	1 50
"									
TOTAL OILS	150	40	190	120	70		35	35	8 50
GREASE— LBS.	100		100	90	10		17	3	1 05
LBS.	75	25	100	80	20		15	5	2 00
TOTAL GREASE	125	25	200	170	30		22	8	3 05
ALCOHOL	50	50	100	45	55		10	45	13 50
TOTAL SALES (Cash)									137 55

COLLECTIONS—NAME	AMT.
H. A. Ashby	12 50
P. O. Marks	8 50
S. E. Jones	3 05
	24 05

TOTAL COLLECTIONS	24 05
TOTAL CASH AND COUPONS	161 60
LESS COUPONS ATTACHED	13 10
BALANCE	148 50
LESS EXPENSE ITEMS—O. K'd RECEIPTS MUST BE ATTACHED	3 40
NET CASH DUE THIS REPORT	145 10
TO CORRECT REPORT OF	
CASH ENCLOSED TO COVER	145 10
ADD OR DEDUCT	

Illustration No. 196—A Daily Report of a Filling Station

This type of report is not only commonly used in filling stations, but is also commonly used in all types of businesses which operate branches. The manager of the branch not only gets an accurate picture of what has happened during the day, but the central organization also is kept informed of the operations. Many of the reports used for such purposes are much more complicated.

Large-Scale Financial Records. In a large organization more than one person is responsible for keeping the records and for compiling the statistics from these records. The customary divisions of an accounting department are as follows:

1. *General ledger section.* This section is responsible for keeping the general ledger and for preparing the periodic financial statements.

2. *Cost accounting section.* This section is responsible for keeping the records from which are obtained the cost of the product produced. This section naturally exists in a manufacturing business.

3. *Accounts receivable section.* This section is responsible for maintaining accounts with customers and for preparing statements of account for submission to customers.

4. *Accounts payable section.* This section is responsible for keeping accounts with creditors and for preparing for the signature of the treasurer the checks to be used in paying creditors.

Under some circumstances there may be a branch accounting section, a pay-roll section, a tabulating section, or the like.

Reports and Exhibits. In many large organizations numerous reports and exhibits are prepared for the benefit of executives. These types of reports are also useful in smaller organizations. Such reports may be classified as follows:

1. Reports showing the present financial condition. The standard form of balance sheet with various subsidiary schedules is used for this purpose. The balance sheet is the oldest and most commonly used report.
2. Reports showing the results of past operations in terms of income and expense. The various forms of income and expense analysis and the standard form of profit and loss statement with subsidiary schedules are used for this purpose. (See page 469.)
3. Reports showing information necessary for the daily actions of executives and employees. These reports may include a statement for the treasurer showing the accounts payable falling due on a current day; a report for the collection manager showing accounts thirty, sixty, and ninety days past due; a report for the sales manager showing the slow-moving items of stock; and hundreds of other reports of a similar nature.
4. Reports showing the anticipated results of future operations. These reports include estimates of sales, estimates of purchases, estimates of production, estimates of financial condition, estimates of income, and similar reports. These reports are statistical compilations instead of accounting summaries. A discussion of them is given in Chapter XX.
5. Reports showing a comparison between the actual results and the estimated results. These reports make possible the enforcement of budgets and provide data for use in revising the budgets when revision is necessary. Chapter XX on budgeting gives various standard percentages that enable a businessman to compare the results of his business with those of other businesses. Possibly a more important analysis is to check the budget periodically to see how the actual operating performance compares with the budgeted estimate. Illustration No. 197 shows a comparison of actual sales and advertising expenditures for the first quarter of a year with estimated sales and advertising for the same quarter. From such an analysis the manager

Items	Estimated Sales First Quarter	Actual Sales First Quarter	Estimated Advertising First Quarter	Actual Advertising First Quarter
Shoes	$ 3,000	$ 2,770	$ 55	$ 49
Women's dresses	4,200	3,605	100	87
Women's millinery	1,500	1,620	40	42
Men's clothes	4,250	4,335	75	67
Men's hats	750	695	30	25
Bedding	3,900	4,223	105	118
Furniture	4,150	4,100	135	142
Household furnishings .	2,725	2,897	75	77
Household equipment ..	3,050	2,816	60	46
Total	$27,525	$27,061	$675	$653

Illustration No. 197—A Comparison of Estimated Figures with Actual Figures

of the business may be able to adjust expenditures in order to keep them within the budget.

6. Reports providing data on conditions external to the business but affecting the plans and policies of the business. These reports are usually of a statistical nature and present data helpful in making the departmental budgets, as well as in deciding policies for the business as a whole. Many of the reports are prepared from data collected and analyzed by agencies outside the business itself. (See Chapter XXVI.)

Ratio Analysis. From the various records and reports prepared for a business, it is possible to make certain ratio analyses that are helpful in the management of the business. Illustration No. 198 shows a ratio analysis for various types of wholesalers and retailers that was prepared by Dun and Bradstreet, Incorporated. Such ratios are of interest to the businessman because he can compare his business with others. For instance, the ratio of current assets to current debts is computed by dividing the total amount of such assets as cash, accounts receivable, and merchandise by the total amount of such liabilities as accounts payable and notes payable. If a businessman has such comparative ratios prepared for his own business each month or each year, he is kept aware of his financial condition.

Line of Business	Current Assets to Current Debt (Ratio)	Net Profits on Net Sales (Per Cent)	Average Collection Period (Days)	Net Sales to Inventory (Times)
WHOLESALERS				
Automobile Parts, Accessories	3.33	1.80	48	5.2
Butter, Eggs, Cheese	2.76	0.47	26	23.3
Drugs, Drug Sundries	3.47	1.24	45	6.3
Dry Goods	2.81	2.05	65	7.3
Electrical Parts, Supplies	2.36	1.68	55	8.1
Fruits and Produce, Fresh ...	2.66	0.76	25	26.0
Furs, Skins	3.23	2.36	64	10.5
Groceries	3.12	0.92	31	8.6
Hardware	3.53	2.68	53	3.9
Hosiery	3.60	0.98	56	8.2
RETAILERS				
Clothing, Installment	3.83	3.42	172	7.4
Clothing, Men's and Boys' ...	2.90	3.65	...	3.9
Department Stores	3.31	2.66	...	6.0
Furniture, Installment	3.90	5.41	214	6.2
Lumber	3.26	2.94	87	4.7
Shoes, Men's and Women's ..	3.15	2.53	...	3.6
Women's Specialty Shops ...	3.02	3.12	...	9.6

Dun & Bradstreet, Inc.

Illustration No. 198—A Ratio Analysis

Depreciation. Every businessman should recognize the problems that result from the decrease in the value of property through use. For example, a filling-station operator buys a pump that costs $200. He knows from experience that at the end of five years the pump will not be worth any more than its value as junk, about $25. He estimates therefore that it will wear out at the rate of $35 a year. This is a common way of figuring depreciation, although there are various other more complicated methods.

The general term that is applied to such a decrease in the value of an asset is *depreciation.* Property may also decrease in value because of *obsolescence;* that is, the asset may become out of date, or it may become inadequate for a particular purpose. For all practical purposes, however, any decrease in the value of an asset can be considered depreciation. A cash register, for instance, may wear out gradually, or it may become inadequate because the business has expanded and a larger register with more complicated tabulations is required.

The loss due to depreciation is very real, although it usually cannot be computed definitely. Any businessman who fails to recognize depreciation is failing to observe good business principles. When equipment is worn out, it must be replaced. If money is not available to replace the equipment, the business enterprise may be handicapped seriously.

The depreciation of assets is part of the cost of doing business. For example, a contractor who is constructing a large building buys shovels and a concrete mixer. He expects the shovels and the concrete mixer to be worn out by the time the building is completed. The cost of the building will therefore include, in addition to such expenses as salaries and wages, supplies, and materials, the cost of the shovels and the concrete mixer. The shovels and the concrete mixer represent assets at the time they are bought; but at the end of the construction process, when they have been worn out, they will constitute an expense.

The United States Bureau of Internal Revenue sets up what are considered to be fair rates of depreciation for various types of assets. The following table shows the probable useful life of some typical assets and the rates of depreciation that are considered reasonable for them:

Type of Asset	Probable Useful Life	Rate of Depreciation
Hotel dining-room furniture	12 years	8⅓%
Carpets in theaters	8 years	12½%
Money-counting machines	10 years	10%
Sewing machines	10 years	10%
Addressing and mailing machines ...	15 years	6⅔%
Automatic scales	15 years	6⅔%
Wrapping machines	10 years	10%
Automobiles	4 years	25%
Adding machines	10 years	10%
Billing machines	8 years	12½%
Office desks	15 years	6⅔%

Illustration No. 199—Reasonable Rates of Depreciation

The rates indicated in this table are those that the United States Bureau of Internal Revenue has found reasonable in allowing deductions for income-tax purposes. In computing the profit of a business for each year, the manager must take into consideration the fact that the assets have worn out to some extent. This depreciation charge should be considered as an expense. Illustration No. 200 is an example of the schedule used in a Federal income-tax return for reporting claims for depreciation.

Schedule E.—EXPLANATION OF DEDUCTION FOR DEPRECIATION CLAIMED IN SCHEDULES C, D, F, AND G								
1. Kind of property (if buildings, state material of which constructed)	2. Date acquired	3. Cost or other basis	4. Assets fully depreciated in use at end of year	5. Depreciation allowed (or allowable) in prior years	6. Remaining cost or other basis to be recovered	7. Estimated life used in accumulating depreciation	8. Estimated remaining life from beginning of year	9. Depreciation allowable this year
Addressing machine	1-34	$ 175 00	$	$ 58 35	$ 104 98	15 yrs	10 yrs	$ 11 67
Typewriter	1-34	100 00	100 00	100 00		5 yrs		
Adding machine	1-35	125 00		50 00	62 50	10 yrs	6 yrs	12 50
Office desk	1-38	50 00		3 33	43 34	15 yrs	14 yrs	3 33

Illustration No. 200—Federal Income-Tax Deductions for Depreciation

The need for the replacement of an asset should be foreseen, and a reserve fund should be created to take care of the loss in value. Suppose, for example, that a merchant who has been using a small cash register finds that his business has expanded to the point where he needs a larger cash register with several drawers. The cash register that he is using would probably last several more years, but it would not serve the business satisfactorily. Because of changes in design and other improvements, this type of machine has gone out of style. The merchant therefore finds that he cannot obtain from the sale of the machine as much as the machine is actually worth according to its condition. If he has predicted the loss in value, however, and has accumulated a reserve fund to take care of it, he should have enough money available to pay the difference between the value of the old machine and the cost of a new one.

Registers. The accounting records provide information on such items as insurance, fixed assets, and real property; but the accounting records do not provide the detailed information that is needed with regard to these assets.

Special ruled forms that are referred to as registers are used for keeping the detailed information on these items.

PERPETUAL RECORD OF EQUIPMENT								
Description Typewriter				Class Office Equipment				
Age when acquired New Estimated life 3 years Estimated exchange value $25 Rate of annual estimated depreciation 25%								
COST				DEPRECIATION RECORD				
Date Purchased		Detail Description and Name of Firm or Individual From Whom Purchased	Amount	Year	Rate	Amount		Total to Date
1937				19				
Jan.	2	Typewriter No. 21	100 --	1937	25%	25	--	25 --
		Typewriter Exchange, City		1938	25%	25	--	50 --
		Underwood Typewriter #4034625 - 11		1939	25%	25	--	75 --
				19				
				19				
				19				
				19				
				19				
				19				
				19				
SOLD, EXCHANGED OR DISCARDED				19				
Date		Explanation	Amount Realized / Less than } More than } / Book Value / Debit Reserve	19				
1940				19				
Jan.	10	Exchanged for Type-writer No. 27	20 -- / 5 -- / 75 --	19				

Illustration No. 201—A Card Record of a Fixed Asset

For instance, a businessman may have insurance policies on equipment, merchandise, trucks, buildings, plate glass, and various other items. He therefore needs to know such information as the face of each policy, the amount of the insurance expense to be charged off each month, the date of expiration of each policy, and the like. Illustration No. 201 shows a card from an equipment register. Illustation No. 202 shows an insurance policy register. These registers provide supplementary information that is helpful to the bookkeeper and to the manager of the business.

INSURANCE POLICY RECORD

Date of Policy	No.	Name of Company	Property Insured	Amount	Expires	Premium
1940						
Jan. 2	89773	Royal	Office Equip.	500	Jan 2, 1942	70 40
2	124568	Sun Mutual	Store Fixtures	1000	Jan 2, 1942	40 80
Feb. 1	904369	Hartford	Mdse Stock	5000	Feb. 1, 1943	75 00
Mar 1	7808	American Auto	Del. Equip.	1500	Mar 1, 1941	42 78

Illustration No. 202—An Insurance Policy Record (Left Page)

Keeping Records Safe. The financial records, including the accounts of customers and all other vital information, should be kept safe. They should be protected from such hazards as fire and theft. Many records, such as the accounts of customers, would not be stolen, but they could easily be destroyed by fire. In every office, therefore, there should be a fireproof safe or vault for such records. So-called fireproof filing cabinets made of sheet metal with insulated walls are not always sure protection against fire. They will withstand heat; but if the building burns and something heavy falls upon such a cabinet, the cabinet will be crushed.

Unusually valuable documents, such as notes, deeds, leases, mortgages, and contracts, should be placed where they are secure from theft or fire. Many of these are often placed in bank safe-deposit boxes if there is no adequate protection in the office. An ordinary fireproof file often is not safe because it may collapse during a fire.

Income-Tax Records. The Federal income-tax law requires every business to keep satisfactory records so that the true income and expenses can be reported. Preparation of an income-tax return for a small business is relatively simple. The information needed for an income-tax return of a business can be obtained from any good set of business records kept under the double-entry method. The income-tax form and the sheet of instructions accompanying the form will provide most of the information needed. Illustration No. 203 shows an example of the detailed reports that must be included in the income-tax return of a business.

INSURANCE POLICY RECORD

| | | | | | Monthly Expirations | | | | | | | | Amount Carried Forward |
Jan.	Feb.	Mar.	Apr.	May	June	July	Aug.	Sept.	Oct.	Nov.	Dec.	
.85	.85	.85	.85	.85	.85	.85	.85	.85	.85	.85	.85	10.20
1.70	1.70	1.70	1.70	1.70	1.70	1.70	1.70	1.70	1.70	1.70	1.70	20.40
		2.08	4.08	4.08	4.08	4.08	4.08	4.08	4.08	4.08	2.12	52.08
			3.56	3.56	3.56	3.56	3.56	3.56	3.56	3.56	3.62	7.12

Illustration No. 202—An Insurance Policy Record (Right Page)

Schedule D.—PROFIT (OR LOSS) FROM BUSINESS OR PROFESSION.

1. Total receipts (state nature of business or profession)				$ 9,750 13
COST OF GOODS SOLD			OTHER BUSINESS DEDUCTIONS	
2. Labor	$ 2,300 00		10. Salaries not included as "Labor" (do not deduct compensation for yourself)	$ 522 18
3. Material and supplies	115 00		11. Interest on business indebtedness	161 00
4. Merchandise bought for sale	1,620 19		12. Taxes on business and business property	1,002 42
5. Other costs (itemize below)	302 40		13. Losses (explain below)	100 50
6. Plus inventory at beginning of year	1,050 00		14. Bad debts arising from sales or services	375 00
7. Total (lines 2 to 6)	$ 5,387 59		15. Depreciation, obsolescence, and depletion (explain in Schedule E)	72 17
8. Less inventory at end of year	865 10		16. Rent, repairs, and other expenses (itemize below or on separate sheet)	2,060 05
9. Net cost of goods sold (line 7 minus line 8)	$ 4,522 49		17. Total (lines 10 to 16)	$ 4,293 32
Enter "C," or "C or M," on lines 6 and 8 to indicate whether inventories are valued at cost, or cost or market, whichever is lower.			18. Total deductions (line 9 plus line 17)	8,815 81
			19. Net profit (or loss) (line 1 minus line 18) (enter as item 9, page 1)	$ 934 32

Illustration No. 203—Federal Income-Tax Profit and Loss Statement

Social Security Taxes. Under the Federal Social Security Act the employer must keep a detailed record of the compensation paid to every employee. The information required is as follows:

1. The employee's name, address, and social security number

2. His occupation

3. The gross amount of his earnings, the time of payment, and the period of service covered by each payment

4. The amount of his taxable wages

5. The amount of the employee's tax withheld from his wages

The Social Security Act also requires that any employer subject to tax under the Act must keep such permanent records as will provide the following information:

1. The total amount of remuneration payable to employees. The following amounts must be shown separately: (a) the total remuneration payable for excepted service (employment not covered by the Act), (b) the total remuneration payable for service performed outside the United States, and (c) the total taxable remuneration payable.

2. The amount of contributions paid into state unemployment funds. The following amounts must be shown

separately: (a) the contributions of the employer and (b) the contributions of the employees.

3. The information required on the prescribed return and the total tax liability.

The record in Illustration No. 204 shows the form required in reporting wages paid. In addition to such records, an individual record must be kept for each employee. Illustration No. 205 shows the form of record suggested for keeping the following information on each employee:

1. The name, social security account number, occupation, rate of wages, and other general information pertaining to the employee.

2. The pay-roll period, the time worked, the regular earnings, and the excess earnings for overtime. In this particular illustration it is assumed that employees are paid twice each month. There are consequently twenty-four lines so that an entry can be made for each of the twenty-four paydays during the year. At the end of each quarter, there is a line provided to record quarterly totals.

3. All deductions for the employee's income tax, state unemployment compensation, and group insurance. If other deductions are made besides the ones listed, additional columns could be included in the record.

4. The net amount paid to the employee, including the number of the check that was used in making payment.

5. The taxable earnings under the various titles of the Social Security Act.

6. The totals at the end of each quarter and at the end of the year. This information facilitates the preparation of quarterly and annual reports.

Every employer must furnish to each of his employees a written statement or statements showing the wages paid to the employee during the year. Each statement must be suitable for permanent retention. It may cover one, two, three, or four quarters of the year. Each statement must be furnished to the employee not later than the last day of the second calendar month following the period covered by the statement. Each statement should be retained as a permanent record by the employee.

EMPLOYER'S TAX RETURN	For Quarter Year Ended March 31, 1939

Form SS-1a (Rev. July 1938)
TREASURY DEPARTMENT
INTERNAL REVENUE SERVICE

UNDER CHAPTER 9, SUBCHAPTER A, INTERNAL REVENUE CODE (FORMERLY TITLE VIII, SOCIAL SECURITY ACT)

1. Number of TAXABLE employees (from Item 15) 10
2. Total taxable wages PAID (from Item 22) ...... $ 4,929.70

EMPLOYER'S TAX

3. 1% of Item 2 ...... $ 49.30
4. Credit or adjustment ...... $ None
5. Total employer's tax ...... $ 49.30

EMPLOYEES' TAX

6. 1% of Item 2 ...... $ 49.30
7. Credit or adjustment ...... $ .01
8. Total employees' tax ...... $ 49.31
9. Total tax (total of Items 5 and 8) ...... $ 98.61

11. I swear (or affirm) that I have examined this return, that it is made in good faith, and that to the best of my knowledge and belief all entries made herein, and contained in each schedule or statement attached and made a part hereof, are true, correct, and complete; and in accordance with the law and regulations applicable hereto.

(Signed) M. O. Johnson
(Title) President

Sworn to and subscribed before me this 29th day of Apr., 1939.
L. M. Willenborg
Notary Public

If paid by check or money order, make payable to "U.S. Collector of Internal Revenue."

CASHIER'S STAMP
(Do not use this space for seal)

12. Date quarter ended March 31, 1939

Taxpayer will NOT use this space
Total tax ...... $
Penalty ...... $
Interest ...... $
Total ...... $

Johnson Millwork Co.
2100 Broad Street
Canton, Ohio
31-0450660

10. Enter in this space employer's name, address of principal place of business, and identification number.

DO NOT DETACH SCHEDULE A FROM ABOVE TAX RETURN
SCHEDULE A—EMPLOYER'S REPORT OF TAXABLE WAGES PAID TO EACH EMPLOYEE
(List all employees to whom taxable wages were paid during the quarter)

READ INSTRUCTIONS CAREFULLY

Johnson Millwork Co.
2100 Broad Street
Canton, Ohio
31-0450660

14. Date quarter ended March 31, 1939

15. Number of taxable employees in your employ on last working day (or last pay roll) of quarter 10

If there is not enough space to list all employees below, use Schedule A continuation sheets (Form SS-1b). Each such continuation sheet must show a page number, beginning with number 2. (See instruction on back of continuation sheet.)

16. Total number pages of this return, including continuation sheets attached ...... one

13. Enter in this space employer's name, address of principal place of business, and identification number.

Do Not Use This Space	EMPLOYEE'S SOCIAL SECURITY ACCOUNT NUMBER (17)	NAME OF EMPLOYEE (18)	TAXABLE WAGES PAID TO EMPLOYEE DURING QUARTER (19)	SEPARATION DATE (20)	STATE If employed outside the State of residence of principal place of business, show State in which employed (21)
	550-07-6199	Roy A. Nelson	$412.50		
	873-04-1984	Clifford King	750.00		
	284-09-9043	Frank Wisenecker	658.20		
	675-05-3452	Virgil H. Platte	548.50		
	495-06-4173	William Barker	485.00		
	949-02-3671	Charles Eberhardt	587.00		
	749-01-5791	James Edward Egan	410.00		
	313-13-3131	Russell G. Hall	328.50		
	787-24-2634	Carol Ann Smith	450.00		
	531-23-7246	Marjorie Louise Cox	300.00		
	TOTAL FOR THIS PAGE—Total taxable wages paid		$ 4,929.70		
	22. TOTAL FOR THIS RETURN—Total taxable wages paid		$ 4,929.70	(This total must be the same as Item 2 above)	

THIS FORM MUST BE FILED WITH U.S. COLLECTOR OF INTERNAL REVENUE ON OR BEFORE THE LAST DAY OF THE FIRST MONTH FOLLOWING THE CLOSE OF THE QUARTER YEAR

Illustration No. 204—Pay-Roll Report Form

	19 40 PERIOD ENDING	TOTAL WORKED		REGULAR EARNINGS		ADDITIONAL EARNINGS FOR EXCESS HOURS WORKED			DEDUCTIONS			NET PAID		TAXABLE EARNINGS	TIME LOST
		DAYS	HOURS	HR. RATE	AMOUNT	HOURS	RATE	AMOUNT	O. A. B.	STATE U. C.	GROUP INS.	CHECK NO.	AMOUNT		
1	Jan. 15	10	80	40	32 00				32			6143	31 68	32 00	
2	Jan. 31	12	96	40	38 40				38			6592	38 02	38 40	
3	Feb. 15	11	88	40	35 20				35			6980	34 85	35 20	
4	Feb. 29	10	80	40	32 00				32			7274	31 68	32 00	
5	March 15	11	88	40	35 20				35			7533	34 85	35 20	
6	March 31	11	88	40	35 20				35			7846	34 85	35 20	
QUARTER TOTAL		65	520		2 08 00				2 07				2 05 93	2 08 00	
1	Apr. 15	10	80	40	32 00				32			8035	31 68	32 00	

SEX M	DEPARTMENT Sales	OCCUPATION Stenographer	WORKS IN (STATE) Ohio	S. S. ACCOUNT NO. 791-20-3481	NAME – LAST Martin FIRST Eleanor MIDDLE Ann	COMPANY NO. 53124

Illustration No. 205—Record of Employee's Earnings

QUESTIONS FOR DISCUSSION

1. Enumerate the types of information that the manager of a business should expect from his accounting records.
2. What does a profit and loss statement show?
3. What does a balance sheet show?
4. What is meant by comparative financial statements?
5. Which would be considered the better ratio: (a) $2 in current assets for every $1 of current liabilities, or (b) $1 in current assets for every $2 of current liabilities? Give your reasons.
6. If a cash register is used in a business and each clerk has a drawer, what should the daily balance slip show?
7. In a large business what are the common sections of an accounting department?
8. Besides the balance sheet and the profit and loss statement, what are some financial reports and exhibits that are often prepared for the benefit of business executives?
9. What is meant by the term *depreciation*? Is there any difference between depreciation and obsolescence or inadequacy?
10. Why is depreciation a part of the cost of doing business?
11. How is depreciation determined? Is there a standard rate of depreciation?
12. What are some of the items of information that are recorded in an insurance policy register?
13. What types of businesses must file Federal income-tax returns?
14. What information with regard to each employee must the employer keep in order to conform to the Federal Social Security Act?

15. What information with regard to wages must the employer give to each employee? In what form must the information be given?

PROBLEMS AND PROJECTS

1. What laws have been enacted in your state to correlate with the Federal Social Security Act?

2. On the basis of the income-tax depreciation schedule on page 485, list the information that would be placed in the nine columns for an adding machine that cost $105 on January 1, 1938. The report is for the year 1939. Use the depreciation rate accepted by the United States Bureau of Internal Revenue. (See page 484.)

3. Mr. J. A. Watkins, who operates a grocery store, reports the following income and expenses for the year:

Total sales, $28,150.34
Cost of goods sold, $21,654.80
Salaries and wages, $3,000
Advertising, $156.10
Donations, $123.05
Supplies used, $90.45
Office expense, $33.15
Telephone and telegraph service, $41

Delivery expense, $410
Taxes and insurance, $150.05
Rent, $624
Heat, light, and water, $123.15
Loss from bad debts, $205.44
Interest paid, $52
Repairs and depreciation, $289
Other expense, $123.04

Compute the gross profit on sales, the total operating expenses, the net profit, and the percentage of each item in relation to the total sales, which represent 100 per cent.

4. Mr. C. W. Alexander, the operator of a drugstore, obtains the following information from the bookkeeping records kept by an assistant:

Sales, $22,475.42
Merchandise inventory at the beginning of the period, January 1, $3,275.14
Purchases made during the period, $18,244.85
Merchandise inventory at the end of the period, June 30, $3,989.55

Salaries and wages, $1,965.20
Advertising, $235.15
Supplies used, $75.40
Telephone service, $96.50
Delivery expense, $400
Taxes and insurance, $185

Rent, $500
Heat, light, and water, $152.12
Loss from bad debts, $126
Repairs and depreciation, $290
Miscellaneous expense, $115.14

These items provide information on the operations of the business from January 1 to June 30. Prepare a statement of profit and loss, similar to the one on page 469.

5. On June 30 the records of the business of Mr. C. W. Alexander disclose the following information on assets, debts, and ownership:

Cash, $728.92
Notes receivable, $75
Accounts receivable, $398.10
Merchandise inventory,
    $3,989.55
Supplies, $42.15
Insurance, $39.60
Equipment, $800

Depreciation reserve, $16
Notes payable, $650
Accounts payable, $865
C. W. Alexander, capital, January 1, $3,737.85
No withdrawals during the period

Prepare a balance sheet as of June 30, using the statement on page 470 as a model.

6. Mr. J. B. Coland has the following assets: (a) a new automobile truck that cost $800; (b) a store building that he had constructed five years ago at a cost of $10,000, not including the value of the land; and (c) store equipment that cost $2,000 and was installed at the time the store was built. Assume the following conditions with regard to depreciation: (a) The automobile will last four years and, at the end of that period, can be traded in for $200; (b) the building decreases in value to the extent of 2 per cent a year; and (c) the store equipment decreases in value to the extent of 3 per cent a year. The depreciation of the automobile will be charged equally to the several years. What will be the values of the assets at the end of two more years?

7. Rule a model of income-tax Schedule D shown in Illustration No. 203 on page 488. Using the following figures, fill out this schedule:

Total receipts, $9,109.41
Labor, $2,229.56
Material and supplies, $167
Merchandise bought for sale, $1,654.02
Other costs, $294.43
Inventory at beginning of year, $1,250
Inventory at end of year, $955.07
Salaries not included as "labor," $502.99

Interest on business indebtedness, $94
Taxes on business and business property, $861.24
Losses, $90
Bad debts arising from sales or services, $298.47
Depreciation, obsolescence, and depletion, $51
Rent, repairs, and other expenses, $1,809.11

8. From the following information taken from the daily balance slips of the clerks, prepare a daily summary statement:

Drawer	Cash in Drawer	Paid Out Including Cash Refunds	Received on Account	Cash		Charge Sales Returned	Gross Charge Sales
				Short	Over		
A	$15.21		$ 3.25				$ 7.62
B	22.64	$1.15	10.60	.15			8.31
D	19.75	3.40	15.50			$2.50	13.75
E	20.08		5.35	.25			5.22
G	36.29	2.05	2.20				7.46

CHAPTER XX

BUDGETING IN BUSINESS

Purpose of the Chapter. It is unwise and unprofitable to purchase or to produce more goods than can be sold within a reasonable time. To do so results in tying up capital. In planning purchases or production, the manager of a business must therefore take into consideration sales expectancies. On the other hand, it is unwise to sell goods in excess of the possibilities of supply. Loss may arise from the ill will created by disappointed customers. Sales, purchases, and production must therefore be correlated. An additional problem is the providing of capital and cash at the proper time to prevent unnecessary borrowing. This chapter will attempt to answer such questions as the following:

1. What procedure should be followed in preparing a budget?
2. How is a budget used in controlling a business?
3. What is a good cash budget?
4. Why is it necessary to make adjustments in the budget?

Preparing the Budget. During the process of preparing and adjusting the budget, each branch of the business should know the plans of the other branches. For instance, the plans of the sales department must be known to the purchasing department so that the latter department will have on hand the proper materials when they are needed. The production department must know what the sales department is planning so that the products to be sold will be manufactured from the materials that have been purchased and will therefore be on hand at the time they are needed. The traffic department must know the plans of the sales, production, and purchasing departments so that it can anticipate traffic requirements. The treasurer must be

494

acquainted with all these plans so that he can estimate the financial requirements. The office manager must know something about these plans so that he will be able to handle all the work in the office. In a small business these duties are often combined. The preparation of the budget is therefore simplified.

The following is the relative order of procedure in preparing a complete budget for any departmentalized business:

1. The estimate of sales is based upon past experience and future expectations. As will be explained later, there is more than one method of making this estimate.

2. The advertising budget is based upon the expected sales and the amount that can be afforded in promoting new products and in opening new territories.

3. If the business is a manufacturing one, the production plans should be based upon the expected sales of the individual products. It is therefore necessary to take into consideration the production capacity and the equipment needed.

4. The purchasing requirements are based upon expected sales and production. Purchases must be made far enough in advance to allow time for production. It is therefore necessary to be familiar with the times of the year when the sales are greatest.

5. In a large manufacturing business it is necessary to anticipate the labor requirements. The budget of labor must therefore be based upon the production requirements.

6. The budget of administrative costs, office costs, and the cost of supplies must be based upon all the previously mentioned factors.

7. The mass budget is made up after all the preceding budgets have been made.

8. The cash budget, which is explained later in this chapter, is a budget that shows the manager of the business or the treasurer what cash balance he can expect at any particular time. Such a budget is necessary to anticipate borrowing.

An analysis of the preceding procedure will show that most of the individual budgets rest upon sales. At some times, however, in some types of businesses, either the production capacity or the financial capacity must be determined first. The sales and all other estimates are then based upon this budget.

It can also be seen that the traffic manager, the office manager, the employment manager, and the engineer in a large production plant must be acquainted with all the individual budgets because their departments are affected by the budget requirements. The small businessman, obviously, will not have such a detailed budget as that described previously. He will in all cases, however, be concerned with budgeting sales, purchases, expenses, and cash.

Control Through Budgeting. Accounting records of some kind are necessary in order to provide the information needed in budgeting. Because of the intricate business relations in modern civilization, budgeting has become extremely important. A study conducted by the United States Department of Commerce reveals the fact that stores that budget their financial operations are more successful than stores that do not budget. The stores that are most successful are those that (a) keep double-entry bookkeeping records, (b) have their accounts audited by an experienced accountant, (c) take an inventory of merchandise more than once a year, and (d) operate under a financial budget.

Budgeting means the estimating of income and expenditures. In other words, it means planning operations so as to be sure that expenditures will not exceed income.

Illustration No. 206 shows a simple budget that Mr. Brooks prepared after the close of his business on June 30. His budgeting process consisted in (a) tabulating the items from his statement of profit and loss; (b) computing percentages on the basis of the total sales; (c) comparing his experience with the experiences of other grocers by using the standard percentages of a large group of others; (d) estimating for the next six months each item on the statement of profit and loss on the basis of his past experience and his plans for the future; and (e) calculating the percentages of his estimates to see how his budget compared with standard conditions. After computing his estimated percentages, he might have found one of his figures to be considerably out of line with his previous experience or with the standard percentage. He would then have deemed it advisable to revise the budget in this respect and to try to operate within the new limit.

The operations of the business should be checked periodically, preferably monthly but in some cases weekly, to determine whether the business is making a profit and

H. J. BROOKS
BUDGET FOR SIX MONTHS ENDING DECEMBER 31, 194—

Income, Expense, Profit	Amounts for Past Six Months	Percentages of Sales	Standards for Comparison	Amounts Budgeted for Next Six Months	Estimated Percentages
Total Income from Sales....	$24,956.34	100.0%	100.0%	$32,000.00	100.0%
Cost of Merchandise Sold...	19,174.80	76.8	81.7	26,166.00	81.8
Gross Profit on Sales.......	$ 5,781.54	23.2%	18.3%	$ 5,834.00	18.2%
Salaries and Wages........	$ 2,630.00	10.5%	9.5%	$ 2,500.00	7.8%
Advertising	332.15	1.3	.8	360.00	1.1
Donations	25.00	.1	.1	35.00	.1
Supplies Used	80.65	.3	.4	75.00	.2
Misc. Office Expense	34.75	.1	.2	32.00	.1
Telephone and Telegraph Service	47.50	.2	.2	48.00	.1
Delivery Expense	305.15	1.2	1.4	295.00	.9
Taxes and Insurance	160.05	.7	.7	160.05	.5
Rent	600.00	2.4	1.9	500.00	1.6
Heat, Light, Water	147.12	.6	.6	147.16	.5
Loss from Bad Debts	270.16	1.1	.7	224.00	.7
Interest Paid	60.00	.3	.1	60.00	.2
Repairs and Depreciation...	150.00	.6	.6	150.00	.5
Other Expense	122.23	.5	.4	122.23	.4
Total Operating Expenses...	$ 4,964.76	19.9%	17.6%	$ 4,708.44	14.7%
Net Profit	$ 816.78	3.3%	.7%	$ 1,125.56	3.5%

Illustration No. 206—An Income and Expense Budget

whether the budget is being followed. If the budget is not being followed closely enough to ensure a profit, it may be necessary to reduce some items of expense or to find new ways of promoting business.

Control of Expenses. After a businessman has a sufficient amount of income available to operate his business successfully, he must next control his expenses actively and carefully. Financial statements, ratio analyses, and charts will help him to do so; but it may be helpful for him to compare his figures with those of other businessmen.

The information in the following table was compiled by the United States Department of Commerce to show the average percentages for various types of expenses incurred by retail stores of several kinds. For instance, this study discloses that the rent of grocery stores averages 2.7 per cent of the net sales of such stores.

Item	Percentage of Net Sales				
	Grocery Stores, and Grocery and Meat Stores	Drug-stores	General Stores	Furniture Stores	Department Stores
Rent	2.7	4.7	2.5	5.2	3.0
Heat, light, and power...	.8	1.5	.3	.6	.7
Taxes and licenses	.7	1.4	.8	1.0	.9
Insurance	.3	.5	.3	.6	.7
Interest	.6	.5	.4	1.0	.7
Telephone and telegraph service	.3	.4	.2	.5	.4
Boxes, wrapping paper, and other packing materials	.4	.3	.3	.2	.3
Postage	.1	.3	.04	.1	.5
Maintenance and depreciation of delivery equipment	.9	.8	.5	1.8	.2
Depreciation other than that on delivery equipment; repairs	.6	1.0	.3	1.3	.5
Collection costs	.9	.1	.3	1.1	.1
Bad debts	.25	.89	.17	.8	.62
Advertising	.4	.7	.4	1.0	1.7

Illustration No. 207—Average Percentages for Various Expenses

Figures such as these can be obtained for practically every type of business and should be used for comparison. In addition, other tables can be obtained from such sources as the National Cash Register Company, the Harvard Bureau of Business Research, and various trade associations.

Illustration No. 208 is a table showing a comparison of the operating expenses, the gross margin, and the net profit of various kinds of independent grocery stores. The businessman should compare such information with similar information gathered from his records.

Item	Service Grocery Stores	Cash Grocery Stores	Complete Food Markets
Salaries and wages (including the owner's)	9.5%	6.5%	12.9%
Advertising	.8	1.0	.8
Donations	.1	.1	.1
Supplies	.4	.3	.6
Office expense	.2	.2	.8
Telephone and telegraph	.2	.1	.2
Delivery	1.4	.4	2.2
Taxes and insurance	.7	.5	.6
Rent	1.9	1.3	1.4
Heat, light, and water	.6	.4	.7
Loss on bad accounts	.7	.....	.5
Interest paid	.1	.1	.2
Repairs and depreciation	.6	.6	.9
All other expenses	.4	.4	.6
TOTAL OPERATING EXPENSES	17.6%	11.9%	22.5%
GROSS MARGIN	18.3%	15.7%	22.9%
NET PROFIT	.7%	3.8%	.4%

From "Operating Expenses," Merchants Service Bureau of the National Cash Register Company.

Illustration No. 208—A Comparison of Operating Expenses and Profits of Independent Grocers

Sales Budget. The sales budget is strictly a forecast of the sales for a month, a few months, or a year. Estimated sales may be computed on the basis of sales territories, salesmen, branch offices, departments, or particular commodities. Sometimes independent estimates are made on all these bases; and, after some compromises, a final sales budget is compiled. Sometimes sales estimates are prepared with the idea of developing sales quotas for salesmen and territories. These estimates provide a goal for the sales department, as well as a basis for preparing the merchandising, purchasing, and other operating budgets.

Illustration No. 209 shows sales estimates determined in three different ways for the same company. As the three sets of estimated figures are not the same, someone must be responsible for combining them into one satisfactory estimate that can be followed.

BUDGET BASED ON ANALYSIS OF SALESMEN

Salesmen	Sales 1938-39	Estimate 1939-40
R. J. Mason	$ 17,836	$ 19,000
T. L. Wilson	17,419	18,000
J. H. Lancey	23,562	22,000
M. O. Burns	22,147	22,000
F. R. Jacobs	21,349	22,000
J. O. Kinsey	20,418	20,000
Total	$122,731	$123,000

BUDGET BASED ON ANALYSIS OF DEPARTMENTS

Departments	Sales 1938-39	Estimate 1939-40
Department A	$ 36,142	$ 40,000
Department B	23,456	25,000
Department C	63,133	66,000
Total	$122,731	$131,000

BUDGET BASED ON ANALYSIS OF PRODUCTS

Products	Sales 1938-39	Estimate 1939-40
Electric Ranges	$ 32,142	$ 34,000
Electric Heaters	10,116	10,000
Electric Fans	9,463	9,000
Electric Lamps	10,468	10,000
Electric Refrigerators..	60,542	65,000
Total	$122,731	$128,000

Illustration No. 209—Three Ways of Budgeting Sales

Factors That Influence the Sales Estimate. Numerous factors influence the making of the sales estimate. General business conditions have an important bearing, although one concern may enjoy good business while another, at the same time and under the same economic trend, may suffer a decline in business. If a good harvest and favorable prices for the produce are anticipated in a certain section, there should be good prospects for selling farm machinery in that section. A retail store located in such an area should expect good business. A flood or a drought may affect certain businesses adversely but others favorably. These are examples of some of the influences that should guide one in making a sales estimate.

Merchandising and Purchasing Budgets. The merchandising and purchasing budgets, which are prepared after the sales budget, must be closely correlated. The kinds of stock to have on hand and the time when they should be available are determined. Maximum and minimum supplies are established. Purchases are planned, and information is passed on to the financial department so that the financial requirements can be estimated. Sources of supply are checked, and delivery dates are scheduled. The production department and the receiving department are notified. Requisitions and orders are tentatively planned. Orders are sometimes placed in advance, subject to cancellation later; or minimum orders are placed, subject to increase later.

Advertising Budget. Advertising should be kept within some reasonable bounds, for it is a fallacy that sales will always be in direct proportion to advertising. In other words, if the estimated sales are pretty well known, it would be unwise to spend an unusual amount for advertising. Such a plan might result in a loss. On the other hand, a special advertising campaign, properly planned, might increase the sales of a certain product; and the advertising budget would consequently have an influence on the sales budget. These two budgets should therefore be planned together. Likewise, the person in charge of finances should be aware of the plans for advertising in order to control those expenses and to have the necessary cash at the proper time. Illustration No. 210 shows an advertising budget based upon estimated sales.

Cash Budget. Budgeting cash is sometimes referred to as providing working capital. Working capital comes from either or both of two sources: (a) from the income of the business or (b) from borrowing. When money is borrowed, it must eventually be paid back. In the cash budget, therefore, borrowed money should be included as a special item under receipts. When it is to be repaid, it should be included in the cash budget under disbursements.

The form in Illustration No. 211 was prepared as a result of a survey made by the Metropolitan Life Insurance Company. It may be used for the cash forecast or budget of a small business. This type of budget, however, should be prepared by every business, regardless of size. It should show the anticipated necessity of borrowing and the possibilities of repaying borrowed money. For instance, it is possible for a business to make plenty of profit; but at some particular time during the year the business may not have enough cash for its operations and may therefore have to borrow.

Administering the Budget. After having budgeted sales, purchases, and the other items indicated above, it is relatively simple to estimate the profit or the loss. If a loss is indicated, the manager should review the expenses to determine what can be done to reduce them. If such economies are not apparent and the forecasted sales volume appears as high as it can be conservatively anticipated, he will have to consider drastic adjustments, such as a reduction of rent, the elimination of part of the personnel, or the elimination of certain purchases.

Economies can be effected by budgeting the inventories carefully to avoid the buying of unnecessary new merchandise and the carrying of an excess quantity of old items. The careful control of the inventories will conserve the cash supply. Purchasing should be checked carefully with the inventories to avoid unnecessary expenditures.

Items	Sales 1938-39	Advertising 1938-39	Percentage 1938-39	Estimated Sales 1939-40	Estimated Advertising 1939-40	Percentage 1939-40
Shoes	$10,394	$ 246	2.37%	$11,000	$ 250	2.27%
Women's dresses	15,156	542	3.58	15,000	500	3.33
Women's millinery	4,283	200	4.67	4,000	200	5.00
Men's clothes	16,418	390	2.38	18,000	350	1.94
Men's hats	3,011	100	3.32	3,000	100	3.33
Bedding	10,146	365	3.60	12,000	350	2.92
Furniture	12,596	395	3.14	13,000	400	3.08
Household furnishings...	10,145	250	2.46	9,000	240	2.67
Household equipment....	12,462	240	1.93	12,500	260	2.08
General advertising		1,250			1,250	
Total	$94,611	$3,978	4.20%	$97,500	$3,900	4.00%

Illustration No. 210—An Advertising Budget Based upon Estimated Sales

CASH FORECAST

3 months beginning April 1

	April	May	June
Cash on hand at beginning of month	$ 2,325	$ 1,425	$ 2,085
Receipts:			
Collections from accounts receivable	15,026	16,592	15,227
Other receipts	2,142	3,061	2,958
Total receipts	$17,168	$19,653	$18,185
Total Cash Available	$19,493	$21,078	$20,270
Disbursements:			
Pay roll	$10,462	$10,704	$10,823
Production materials	5,860	6,092	6,411
Supplies and expenses	246	197	329
Construction and plant additions	500		
Other disbursements (repayment of loan, etc.)..	1,000	2,000	500
Total disbursements	$18,068	$18,993	$18,063
Estimated cash at end of month	$ 1,425	$ 2,085	$ 2,207

Policyholders Service Bureau, Metropolitan Life Ins. Co., New York, N. Y.

Illustration No. 211—A Cash Budget

Adjusting the Budget. No budget or quota can be followed exactly. One must remember that a budget is an estimate and that it therefore cannot be exact. It is merely a guess of what may happen. If the sales increase more than was anticipated, all elements of the budget can be adjusted, particularly purchasing. If the sales decrease more than was anticipated, economies must be put into effect before it is too late. The possibility of looking ahead prevents serious losses. Watching the budget carefully enables one to make adjustments before it is too late.

QUESTIONS FOR DISCUSSION

1. What are the suggested steps of procedure in preparing a complete budget for a departmentalized business?
2. Why is it necessary for the production manager to know something about the sales budget?
3. Why is the cash budget so important from the point of view of the treasurer of a company?
4. Why is budgeting considered such an important factor in management?
5. In what way are figures based on the past experiences of other businesses of the same type helpful in preparing a budget?
6. Name some bases on which it is possible to estimate the sales of a business.
7. Why is the sales budget so important in most businesses?
8. What are some of the factors that must be taken into consideration in making a sales estimate?
9. Let us assume that, two months after a budget was established, a checkup on the budget shows that the actual sales are 20 per cent less than those which were anticipated. What would you recommend to the manager of this business?

PROBLEMS AND PROJECTS

1. Prepare a budget for a committee working on a class play. Estimate the income and then budget all the costs.
2. Prepare a simple budget of the income and the expenditures of some group or society of which you are a member. If possible, use actual figures based on past experience. If you cannot do so, at least use the proper titles of the income and the expenditures.

3. Refer to the figures in the first column of Illustration No. 206 on page 497. Using these figures as a basis, prepare a budget for Mr. Brooks for the six months ending June 30. Assume that his expected sales for the six months are $21,000, the cost of merchandise sold will remain 76.8 per cent of the sales, the supplies used will be .3 per cent of the sales, and the loss from bad debts will be 1.1 per cent of the sales; but that all the other expenses will be exactly as they were during the past six months. (Disregard the figures in the fourth column of the illustration.) Indicate for each item its estimated percentage of sales.

4. Draw a form for a cash budget like that shown in Illustration No. 211 on page 503. Starting with the balance at the end of June, enter the budgeted figures for July, August, and September, assuming that the receipts and the disbursements for July will be the same as those for June, but the receipts and the disbursements for August and for September will be 10 per cent less than those for June.

5. Refer to the three budgets on page 500 showing sales estimated on the bases of salesmen, departments, and products. Assume that the estimated sales of products are considered correct and that these figures are based upon the retail prices. How much cash must be available for purchases if the wholesale purchase prices of these items are 70 per cent of the retail prices and the following is the schedule of purchases for the year?

> Electric Ranges: one fourth in January, one fourth in August, one fourth in September, one fourth in December
>
> Electric Heaters: one fourth in January, one fourth in October, one fourth in November, one fourth in December
>
> Electric Fans: one half in May, one fourth in June, one fourth in July
>
> Electric Lamps: one fourth in January, one fourth in May, one fourth in September, one fourth in December
>
> Electric Refrigerators: one fourth in May, one fourth in July, one half in December

6. Obtain a copy of a budget of your city, county, township, or some other political subdivision, and analyze it in a written report. If any parts of it are not clear to you, try to get the proper official to explain these to you so that you can put the explanation into your report.

CHAPTER XXI

BANKING AND FINANCIAL PROBLEMS

Purpose of the Chapter. Every businessman, large or small, must establish some banking relationship. This relationship usually involves the safekeeping of deposits, the handling of a checking account, and the borrowing of money. No attempt is made in this chapter to discuss the details of writing checks and handling other minor transactions; but an attempt is made to answer many questions, some of which are as follows:

1. What are the factors that determine the selection of a bank?
2. What kind of financial advice can be obtained from a bank?
3. Upon what bases are loans made by banks?
4. What are the different ways in which money can be borrowed?
5. Does the bank or the depositor suffer a loss if a bad check is presented for collection?

Selecting a Bank. Convenience in banking facilities is important, although safety should not be sacrificed to convenience. When deposits are guaranteed, one bank is essentially as safe as another. There are, however, ways of determining the safety and conservativeness of a bank. The most common means is through an analysis of the bank's financial statements. The ratio of cash and government bonds to the deposits in one bank may be compared with the same ratio for another bank. The bank that has the higher ratio is essentially the safer and more conservative bank.

Even though the deposits of a bank may be insured in some way, a person should not be relieved from the responsibility of selecting a bank that meets his requirements. He should not trust to luck or depend entirely on conven-

506

ience of location. Integrity is the important factor to be considered in choosing a bank. He should therefore choose a bank that is sound, that has officers who are known for their honesty, and that, above all, meets his needs. If he utilizes normal banking facilities, it is important for him to deal with bankers whom he can consult confidentially and who will give honest advice.

Deposit Insurance. In spite of some unfortunate occurrences during periods of economic depression, the majority of banks are safe and sound. Most banks now are insured by The Federal Deposit Insurance Corporation. Each depositor in a bank that carries this insurance is protected from loss to the extent of $5,000. The fact that most banks now carry this insurance discourages depositors from withdrawing their funds in a panic. The insurance therefore serves as a stabilizing influence.

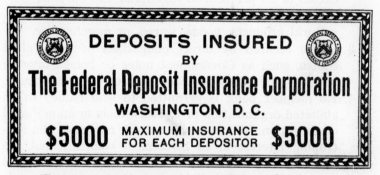

Illustration No. 212—A Sign Announcing That a Bank's Deposits Are Insured

Size and Type of Bank. In some communities there is an advantage in placing an account in a small bank because the officers and the personnel of such a bank learn to know each customer and appreciate his business. The advantages of a small bank, however, are sometimes offset by those of a larger bank. Dealings with a large bank may be impersonal, but such a bank can offer facilities that are not otherwise available. Small banks may not be able to make a loan under a favorable rate or may not be able to make as large a loan as is desired. The businessman who has many dealings in other cities may find the larger bank more efficient because it may have better connections in those cities and can therefore handle transactions more conveniently.

Federal Reserve Regulations. State and Federal laws limit banks, according to their classification, in the types of loans that can be made. State banks are governed by the laws of their respective states. Members of the Federal Reserve System are governed by the following restrictions:

1. The Federal Reserve Board has power to fix the percentage of loans that the banks in any Federal reserve district can make with bonds and stocks as collateral. No member of the Federal Reserve System may, however, lend to any person or business an amount in excess of 10 per cent of its capital and surplus.

2. Member banks may make loans secured by staple agricultural products, goods, wares, or merchandise.

3. Loans secured by direct obligations of the United States, such as Government notes or bonds, may be made to individuals, partnerships, or corporations.

4. No member bank is permitted to lend money to an affiliated organization or to individuals in an affiliated organization. For instance, a bank may hold the controlling interest in an investment company, but the bank is not permitted to lend money to this affiliated organization or to individuals in that organization. It may not accept securities of an affiliated organization as collateral for a loan if the loan exceeds 10 per cent of its capital and surplus.

5. Loans can be made on improved real estate, including improved farm land. Such a loan must not, however, exceed 50 per cent of the actual value of the real estate offered for security and must not extend for a period greater than five years. Only a limited amount of the funds of a member bank may be used for loans on real estate.

Underwood & Underwood.

Illustration No. 213—Consult Your Banker for Financial Advice

Financial Advice. The best place to seek financial advice and to obtain loans is always the banking institution with which contacts have already been established. If credit relations have been established with the bank, the obtaining of a loan should be simple. Most bankers will give advice to those who apply for credit.

A wise banker will not make a loan to anyone if he believes that the loan cannot be repaid or if he thinks that the repayment of the loan will place an undesirable hardship upon the borrower. Regardless of the character of the borrower or the security that has been pledged to the bank, the making of a loan in such a case may result in financial disaster. The businessman should therefore consider carefully any necessity for a loan.

Types of Loans. A loan may be classified according to the basis on which it is made. It may be based (a) on confidence, (b) on security, or (c) on the indorsement of another person. If the conditions for a loan seem unusually favorable, the banker may not require security but will rely upon the borrower's character and capacity to pay. Conservative commercial banks, however, usually require security in some form of property. In other words, this property is pledged to the bank as a guarantee that the loan will be repaid according to the agreement. This property can be

---

FINANCIAL STATEMENT

INDIVIDUAL—PROPRIETORSHIP
MANUFACTURING OR MERCANTILE LINES

NAME John Davidson

BUSINESS Cincinnati Wholesale Shoe Company   ADDRESS 751 Main Street, Cincinnati, Ohio

STATEMENT FOR

CONDITION AT CLOSE OF BUSINESS............March 31,.........1939.   FILL IN DATE

(left margin, vertical text): LEAVE NO BLANKS. INSERT "0" OR WORD "NONE" WHERE NECESSARY TO COMPLETE INFORMATION

ASSETS	DOLLARS	CTS.	LIABILITIES	DOLLARS	CTS.
CURRENT			CURRENT		
CASH ON HAND	50	00	NOTES PAYABLE—TO BANKS (SCHEDULE 1)	600	00
CASH IN BANKS—(SCHEDULE 1)	1 717	50	BANKERS ACCEPTANCES—MADE FOR MY ACCOUNT		
U. S. GOVERNMENT OBLIGATIONS	4 000	00	NOTES PAYABLE—COMMERCIAL PAPER BROKERS		
TRADE ACCEPTANCES—CUSTOMERS			NOTES PAYABLE—OTHERS		
NOTES RECEIVABLE—CUSTOMERS—(SCHEDULE 2)	750	00	NOTES PAYABLE—FOR MERCHANDISE		
ACCOUNTS RECEIVABLE—CUSTOMERS—(SCHED. 2)	2 190	00	TRADE ACCEPTANCES PAYABLE		
MERCHANDISE—FINISHED GIVE FULL	12 220	00	ACCOUNTS PAYABLE—NOT DUE	4 402	00
MERCHANDISE—IN PROCESS DATA ON			ACCOUNTS PAYABLE—PAST DUE		
MERCHANDISE—RAW PAGE 3			ACCOUNTS PAYABLE—OTHER		
			PROVISION FOR FEDERAL TAXES		
TOTAL CURRENT ASSETS—	20 927	50	ACCRUED INTEREST, OTHER TAXES, ETC.	85	00
CONTROLLED AND AFFILIATED CONCERNS—			DEPOSITS OF MONEY WITH ME		
INVESTMENTS IN (SCHEDULE 3)			MORTGAGE OR LONG TERM DEBT—PAYMENTS DUE WITHIN ONE YEAR		
DUE FROM {FOR ADVANCES (SCHEDULE 3)			DUE TO CONTROLLED AND AFFILIATED CONCERNS— (SCHEDULE 3)		
{FOR MERCHANDISE (SCHEDULE 3)					
TOTAL					
INVESTMENTS					
STOCKS, BONDS & INVESTMENTS (SCHEDULE 4)					
REAL ESTATE NOT USED IN BUSINESS (SCHED. 5)			TOTAL CURRENT LIABILITIES	5 087	00
MORTGAGES RECEIVABLE (SCHEDULE 7)			DEFERRED—(DUE AFTER ONE YEAR)		
CASH SURRENDER VALUE LIFE INS. (SCHED. 8)			MORTGAGES OR LIENS ON REAL ESTATE (SCHED. 5)		
			CHATTEL MORTGAGES—(DETAILS ON PAGE 3)		
TOTAL INVESTMENTS			LOANS ON LIFE INSURANCE (SCHEDULE 8)		
FIXED ASSETS					
LAND (SCHEDULE 5)	2 000	00			
BUILDINGS (SCHEDULE 5)	5 000	00	TOTAL DEFERRED		
MACHINERY, FIXTURES AND EQUIPMENT	3 000	00	RESERVES		
			RESERVE—FOR DOUBTFUL RECEIVABLES	470	00
TOTAL FIXED ASSETS	10 000	00	RESERVE—DEPRECIATION—BUILDINGS	850	00
MISCELLANEOUS ASSETS			RESERVE—DEPRECIATION—MACH. FIXT. EQUIP.	975	00
PREPAID INTEREST, INSURANCE, ETC.	600	00	RESERVE—OTHER—(ITEMIZE)		
MISCELLANEOUS MATERIALS AND SUPPLIES	434	50			
MISCELLANEOUS DEPOSITS—(WATER, POWER, ETC.)					
DUE FROM—OTHER THAN CUSTOMERS (SCHED. 6)					
DEFERRED EXPENSE, ETC.					
GOODWILL, PATENTS AND TRADE-MARKS					
TOTAL MISCELLANEOUS	1 034	50	NET WORTH (SEE PAGE 2)	24 580	00
TOTAL ASSETS	31 962	00	TOTAL	31 962	00
CONTINGENT LIABILITIES					
LIABILITY UPON TRADE ACCEPTANCES AND/OR NOTES RECEIVABLE DISCOUNTED OR SOLD					
LIABILITY UPON TRADE ACCEPTANCES AND/OR NOTES RECEIVABLE ASSIGNED OR PLEDGED					
LIABILITY UPON CUSTOMER'S ACCOUNTS SOLD, ASSIGNED OR PLEDGED					
LIABILITY UPON ACCOMMODATION PAPER OR ENDORSEMENTS OR UPON NOTES EXCHANGED WITH OTHERS					
LIABILITY AS GUARANTOR FOR OTHERS FOR NOTES, ACCOUNTS OR CONTRACTS—BONDS, ETC.					
ANY OTHER CONTINGENT LIABILITIES					
			TOTAL CONTINGENT LIABILITIES		

Illustration No. 214—The First Page of an Application for a Loan

taken over and sold by the bank to protect itself in case the borrower cannot pay the loan when it is due. In a sense, an indorsement is a form of security. If a person indorses a note in order to aid a borrower in obtaining money, the indorser is held responsible for the payment of the note in case the borrower is unable to pay.

Commercial Loans. Warehouse receipts and mortgages on real property are common forms of security. For instance, a person who wishes to borrow from a bank may have placed one thousand bushels of wheat in a grain elevator. If he has receipts for this wheat, he may turn these receipts over to the bank, thus transferring to the bank the right of ownership to the wheat in case he does not pay his loan when it becomes due. Likewise, a person may borrow money on real estate and grant a mortgage that gives the lender the right to take possession of the real estate if the loan is not paid.

Borrowing on Bonds and Stocks. Bonds and stocks are frequently used as security for loans. When stocks or bonds are pledged as security, the loan is commonly spoken of as a *collateral loan*. In other words, the bonds and stocks serve as the collateral.

Any stock or bond that has a value can usually be used as collateral. Some banks prefer stocks and bonds that are listed on recognized exchanges because such bonds and stocks can be marketed easily if they must be sold to pay the loan. A bank will ordinarily lend about 50 per cent of the value of a good stock or a good bond. Suppose, for example, that a loan of $200 is required for three months and that the bank charges 6 per cent interest. Good bonds or stocks with a market value of approximately $400 may be used as security. In making the loan, the bank will deduct the interest in advance as follows:

Amount to be paid to bank in three months $200.00
Six per cent interest deducted in advance 3.00
Amount of cash given to borrower $197.00

In this example the interest charge is actually more than 6 per cent, for $3 is being charged for the use of $197 for three months. If the loan is not repaid in three months, the bank has the privilege of selling the securities to obtain the $200. Suppose that, at the end of three months, this

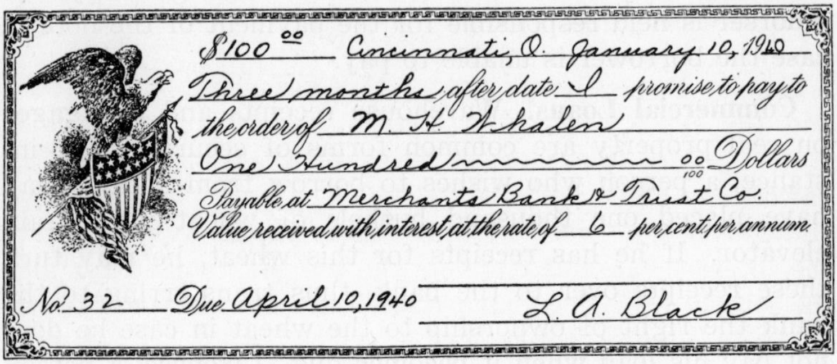

Illustration No. 215—An Ordinary Note

loan has not been repaid. It may be possible for the borrower to have the loan renewed by paying $3 interest in advance and by signing a new note to take the place of the old one. Or he may pay $100 and sign a new note for $100 after paying $1.50 interest in advance on the new loan.

If the securities are sold to protect the bank, more or less than the amount of the loan may be obtained, depending upon the fluctuation of the market prices of the securities. Suppose that, in the preceding example, nothing is paid on the loan and the bank sells the securities at the end of the three months for $300. The additional $100 will go to the person who obtained the loan. If the securities are sold for only $175, however, the person who obtained the loan still owes the bank $25.

Borrowing on Insurance Policies. Most insurance policies have a cash value and a loan value. These values are usually the same. An insurance policy can be used as the basis of obtaining a loan, usually at 6 per cent interest. The policy must be given to the insurance company as security, and the loan can be repaid when it is convenient. If death occurs before the loan is repaid, the amount of the loan is deducted from the payment due the beneficiary.

The amount that can be borrowed on an insurance policy depends entirely on the face of the policy and the length of time the policy has been in force. A bank will occasionally lend on an insurance policy in the same way as an insurance company.

Interest Rates. Interest rates vary according to the states and the types of lending institutions. Statutes in most states govern the interest rates of such institutions as pawnshops and loan associations. The state banking laws and the rules of the Federal Reserve System govern largely the interest rates of banks, although the demand for and the supply of money have much influence on the interest rates on bank loans.

In nearly every state there is a *legal rate* and a *contract rate* of interest. In the absence of any agreement as to the interest rate, a bank may charge the legal rate. A special agreement may be made to permit a bank to charge the contract rate, which is limited in most states.

Illustration No. 216 shows the maximum interest rates of the various states and territories. These rates are determined by law and are changed from time to time. If an individual wants to know the maximum rates in his state, he should consult the latest law on this subject.

Computing Interest. When a short-term loan is obtained from a banking institution, the interest is usually deducted in advance. The amount that is credited to the borrower's account is therefore the amount of the loan less the interest charged. For example, on a loan of $5,000 for ninety days at 6 per cent interest, there would be a deduction of $75. The borrower would therefore have $4,925 credited to his account or would receive that amount in the form of a check.

Paying a Loan. Bankers have found that borrowers will pay long-time obligations with less difficulty if some provision is made for paying off the loan at intervals instead of in one amount at the expiration of the loan period. If

States and Territories	Legal Rate (Per Cent)	Contract Rate (Per Cent)	States and Territories	Legal Rate (Per Cent)	Contract Rate (Per Cent)
Alabama	6	8	Montana	6	10
Alaska	6	10	Nebraska	6	9
Arizona	6	8	Nevada	7	12
Arkansas	6	10	New Hampshire	6	Any rate
California	7	10	New Jersey	6	6
Colorado	6	Any rate 1	New Mexico	6	10 2
Connecticut	6	12	New York	6	6
Delaware	6	6	North Carolina	6	6
District of Columbia	6	8	North Dakota	4	7
Florida	8	10	Ohio	6	8
Georgia	7	8	Oklahoma	6	10
Hawaii	6	12	Oregon	6	10
Idaho	6	8	Pennsylvania	6	6
Illinois	5	7	Porto Rico	6	9 3
Indiana	6	8	Rhode Island	6	30
Iowa	5	7	South Carolina	6	7
Kansas	6	10	South Dakota	6	8
Kentucky	6	6	Tennessee	6	6
Louisiana	5	8	Texas	6	10
Maine	6	Any rate	Utah	6	10
Maryland	6	6	Vermont	6	6
Massachusetts	6	Any rate	Virginia	6	6
Michigan	5	7	Washington	6	12
Minnesota	6	8	West Virginia	6	6
Mississippi	6	8	Wisconsin	6	10
Missouri	6	8	Wyoming	7	10

Illustration No. 216—Legal and Contract Rates of Interest

the average borrower is given the privilege of waiting until a specified date to pay the entire amount, he may carelessly or intentionally utilize his income for other purposes and not have available the proper amount of money when the loan becomes due. The property that was given as security may by this time have depreciated so much that the bank will not have adequate protection on its loan.

Some borrowers have a tendency to borrow money without giving specific thought as to when and how it can be repaid. They assume that, if they cannot repay a loan when it becomes due, they may renew it and continue to pay the interest without making payments on the principal. Bor-

---

1 When any rate is permitted for contracts, there usually is a limit on a small loan of approximately $300 or less, although this limit may be as high as 3 per cent a month.

2 When a loan is unsecured by collateral, the contract rate may be 12 per cent.

3 When the amount is more than $3,000, the maximum contract rate is 8 per cent.

rowing without a definite intention and specific plan of paying off the principal is a dangerous practice for both the borrower and the lender. It will eventually result in catastrophe for those involved. The borrower will be forced into bankruptcy; the banker will be unable to collect the debt and may consequently be unable to pay his depositors.

Cost of Operating a Checking Account. Obviously, the service provided by a checking account costs money, for it must be remembered that the bank not only provides a place of safekeeping for the depositor's money but also is responsible for all the bookkeeping necessary in keeping the records up to date. Furthermore, as the checking account provides a convenient means of making payments to other persons and to business concerns, the bank must use the services of a local clearinghouse and of clearinghouses in other parts of the country. Because the bank has to pay expenses incurred in rendering all these services, it must earn something from the checking accounts. Consequently, in most communities there is a charge for small accounts. As the size of these accounts varies, the tendency is to base the charge upon the actual cost of operating such an account. In states in which there is a tax on deposits and on checks, the bank may or may not pay the tax. If it pays the tax, it must realize enough profit from the accounts to compensate for the tax as well as for other expenses involved.

The clearinghouse associations in various cities and the individual banks set up charges for the handling of checking accounts. The following are examples of the charges made in one large city under a uniform plan established by the clearinghouse:

Analysis Formula for
Accounts with Balances of Less than $500

For accounts with balances of less than $500, a simple form of analysis has been adopted so that each customer can readily determine for himself, on the basis of the balance he maintains, the charge, if any, on his account. The analysis is applied as follows:

1. Average balances:

   Less than $100: Charge is $1 a month; allowance, 15 items.

   $100 to $199: Charge is based on the cost of activity.

   $200 to $299: Charge is based on the cost of activity; 5 items without charge.

   $300 to $399: Charge is based on the cost of activity; 10 items without charge.

   $400 to $499: Charge is based on the cost of activity; 15 items without charge.

2. Items in excess of the number permitted without charge are to be charged for at the rate of 3 cents each, but no charge is to be recorded unless it amounts to at least 15 cents.

Analysis Formula for
Accounts with Balances over $500

A detailed analysis is used on accounts in this classification to determine the charges for maintaining them. The accounts are analyzed monthly as follows:

1. From the average daily ledger balance for the calendar month, a deduction is made to take care of the average daily amount of float (deposited items that are in the course of collection) for the period under analysis.

2. On the net balance thus determined, a service credit of $1.50 a thousand dollars per month is allowed. (This is the equivalent of 2.4 per cent a year less 25 per cent to cover legal, cash, and bank reserves.)

3. The cost of operating the account and of other services is charged against the service credit according to the following schedule:

   (a) On debits to the account the following charges are made:

   First 400 items, 3 cents each.

   All items over 400 items, 1½ cents each.

   (b) On credits to the account the following charge is made:

   City and foreign deposited items, 1½ cents each.

(c) A maintenance charge of 35 cents a month is made on each account.

(d) The cost of all other services rendered the depositor during the period under analysis are made against the service charge, unless such cost has been charged directly to the customer's account or has been paid in cash.

(e) When the deduction of float in any account creates an overdraft in the net funds available for investment, an interest charge at 1 per cent above the customer's current lending rate is made.

4. When the service credit is insufficient to cover the cost of operation and of other services, a deficiency charge to cover the indicated loss on the account is made to the customer's account at any time during the following month that the bank may consider convenient. The minimum charge so made is 15 cents a month.

Reconciliation of Bank Statements. Illustration No. 217 shows a typical bank statement. Not all banks use the same form, but they do use forms that are similar. For instance, all statements have a column for indicating the amounts of checks that have been drawn, another column for indicating the amounts of deposits, and another column for indicating the balance on particular days of the month.

A businessman, as well as an individual, should obtain his bank statement at the end of each month and should compare it with his checkbook stubs, canceled checks, and deposit slips to be sure of its accuracy. The following procedure is suggested:

1. Verify the checks recorded on the bank statement by comparing them with the canceled checks accompanying the statement.

2. Determine from the checkbook stubs which checks were outstanding on the date of the bank statement.

3. Verify all deposits by checking those on the bank statement with those recorded in his bankbook and on the check stubs or deposit slips.

4. Use the following method in reconciling the balance on the bank statement with the balance shown in the checkbook:

(a) Cash balance indicated by the bank statement $1,407.23

(b) Total of checks still outstanding....... 132.50

(c) Cash balance in the checkbook $1,274.73

After the checks still outstanding have been deducted from the balance on the bank statement, the cash balance should agree with the balance in the checkbook. If there has been a service charge or a tax on checks, it should be shown as a separate deduction on the bank statement. Such deductions on the bank statement should also be subtracted

FIRST NATIONAL BANK
CINCINNATI, OHIO

VOUCHERS RETURNED___ 11 ___

A. M. Fulton
1026 Gilbert Avenue

DATE___ March 31-39 ___

DATE	CHECKS	DATE	DEPOSITS
	BALANCE BROUGHT FORWARD ☞		1,325.61
March 1-39	121.50	March 2-39	70.00
March 4-39	30.00	March 8-39	125.50
March 8-39	86.00		
March 11-39	141.85	March 15-39	202.75
March 14-39	18.90	March 19-39	151.00
March 16-39	60.25		
March 17-39	37.50	March 21-39	91.25
March 22-39	159.75	March 25-39	146.00
March 27-39	10.00		
March 30-39	7.05	March 30-39	39.42
March 31-39	71.50		

PLEASE EXAMINE AT ONCE

IF NO ERROR IS REPORTED IN TEN DAYS THE ACCOUNT WILL BE CONSIDERED CORRECT

BALANCE ☞   March 31-39 1,407.23

Illustration No. 217—A Bank Statement

from the checkbook balance so that the balance on the checkbook stub will agree with that on the bank statement.

When there are several items to be considered in making the reconciliation, it is desirable to use a more detailed method than the one given on pages 517 and 518. Illustration No. 218 shows a frequently used method.

BANK STATEMENT RECONCILIATION

CHECKBOOK	BANK STATEMENT
Balance $1,372.00	Balance: $1,600.00
Deduct charges:	Deduct checks out-
Service charge	standing:
made by bank... 2.00	#563 $30.00
$1,370.00	#587 27.50
Credits to be added:	#588 77.50
Deposits made but	#589 10.00 145.00
but not recorded	
in the checkbook. 85.00	
Adjusted checkbook	Adjusted bank state-
balance $1,455.00	ment $1,455.00

Illustration No. 218—A Bank Reconciliation

Certified Check. It is sometimes desirable to transfer money by using a certified check. A certified check is useful when the person receiving it must be assured that the drawer of the check has sufficient money in his bank for the payment of the check. Such a check certifies that it will be paid upon presentation. As soon as the cashier of the bank certifies the check, he charges the amount to the

Houston, Texas July 5   19 39
CERTIFIED
PAYABLE ONLY AS ORIGINALLY DRAWN
AND MUST PROPERLY ENDORSED
The Public National Bank 35-73
Pay to the
order of B. E. Alcott & Co JUL 5 - 1939 $45 10/100
                    PUBLIC NATIONAL BANK
Forty-five and   HOUSTON, TEXAS   10/100 Dollars
                    E. M. Gray ...ASST. CASHIER
                    DO NOT DESTROY N. C. Jameson

Illustration No. 219—A Certified Check

depositor's account. The amount cannot then be utilized for any other purpose, unless the certified check is canceled.

For instance, Mr. A must make a down payment of $1,000 on the purchase of a home at the time the contract is signed. He goes to Bank X and writes a check on his account in the bank. The check is presented to the cashier for certification. Immediately the bank impounds or earmarks in his account $1,000. This amount is thus held for the payment of the check upon presentation to Bank X.

Bank Draft. A bank draft is a check that a bank draws on funds deposited to its credit in some other bank. A bank draft is a convenient means of transferring money when the individual who is making payment is not known in the part of the country to which the remittance is to be sent. He may obtain the draft by purchasing it from a bank.

FIRST NATIONAL BANK
56-906

CAMDEN, OHIO, ___JANUARY 17___ 19 40 ___ No. 169

PAY TO THE ORDER OF ___EVERETT & SONS___ . . . . $ 500.00

REGISTERED $500 AND 00¢ _____ DOLLARS
R-6637

TO
FIRST NATIONAL BANK   } _William H. Jackson_
13-1 / 4   CINCINNATI, OHIO   CASHIER

Illustration No. 220—A Bank Draft

For example, Mr. A, who lives in Dallas, wishes to make a payment of $2,000 in New York City. As Mr. A is not known in New York City, his personal check will not be accepted. Mr. A therefore buys from Bank X in Texas a draft that Bank X draws on Bank Y in New York. When the draft is presented to Bank Y in New York, it is paid as any other check would be paid.

Cashier's Check. One may buy a cashier's check in somewhat the same way as a person buys a bank draft. The cashier's check is a check on the bank that issues it, payable to the person designated by the purchaser of the check. Banks also use cashier's checks to pay their own debts and expenses.

For example, Mr. B's personal check for $1,000 may not be acceptable. He therefore purchases from Bank X a cashier's check made out to Mr. C. Mr. B pays Bank X $1,000 plus a fee. Mr. B presents the check to Mr. C, who in turn presents it to Bank X for payment.

Collection Service. Banks provide a collection service for such items as notes, drafts, trade acceptances, checks, and interest and principal on bonds. For instance, when a note that he owns becomes due, a businessman may turn it over to his bank for collection. He may also have his bank take care of the collection of drafts, trade acceptances, and checks that he holds. The bank charges a fee for this service. Charges for the collection of checks have been explained previously.

Many bonds have on them coupons that are to be torn off and submitted for collection when interest on the bonds is due. A bank will perform this collection service. Likewise, when the principal of a bond becomes due, the bank will act as the collecting agent. Sometimes there is no charge when such collections are made locally, but in most cases there is a charge. Banks will also take care of the collecting and the exchanging of securities, such as stocks and bonds. A service charge and a shipping charge are included in the fee for handling securities. Such a charge can be deducted from the depositor's account.

Negotiable Instruments. The relation of borrowing and lending centers largely around a *negotiable instrument*. A negotiable instrument is a written evidence of some contractual obligation and is ordinarily transferable from one person to another by indorsement. It is frequently referred to as *negotiable paper* or *commercial paper*.

The most common forms of negotiable instruments are (a) promissory notes and (b) checks. A promissory note is an unconditional written promise to pay a sum certain in money, at a particular time or on demand, to the bearer or to the order of one who has obtained the note through legal means. The one who executes a promissory note, that is, the one who promises to pay the amount specified in the note under the terms indicated, is the *maker*. The person to whom the note is payable is known as the *payee*. A check is a written order on a bank to pay previously deposited money to a third party on demand. The person who writes the check is the *drawer*. The person to whom the check is payable is the *payee*. The bank that is ordered to pay the check is the *drawee*.

The maker of a note or the drawer of a check is unconditionally required to pay the amount specified. This obligation assumes, of course, that the transaction represented by the instrument has been proper and legal. The drawer of a check is required to pay the amount of the check if the drawee (the bank) does not pay it. There are, however, certain limitations on this rule in many states.

The person who indorses a negotiable instrument and transfers it to someone else is known as the *indorser*. The person to whom he transfers the negotiable instrument is referred to as the *indorsee*.

Bad Checks. A bad check is one that is not honored when it is presented to a bank for payment. It may not be paid because there are insufficient funds in the account on which it is drawn, or because it was written by a dishonest person who does not have an account in the bank on which it was drawn. In either case there are laws in every state that make it possible to prosecute the person who has written the check.

Ordinarily banks and business people are courteous and considerate whenever a person unknowingly writes a check on an account in which there are insufficient funds. Both the person who drew the check and the person to whom the check was issued are notified. Ordinarily no legal action is taken if the matter is cleared up satisfactorily. On the other hand, if there is an apparent intention of fraud, the person to whom the check was issued is usually responsible for starting any legal action.

When a check or any other negotiable instrument is presented to a bank for payment but is not paid, it is returned to the one who submitted it. Accompanying it is a form called a protest. Such a form is shown in Illustration No. 221. The bank makes a charge for protesting payment. It

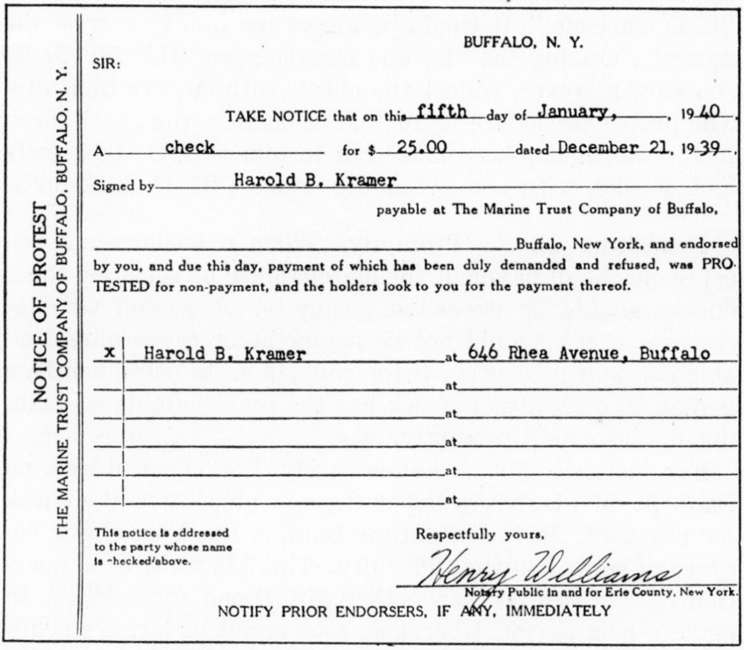

NOTICE OF PROTEST

THE MARINE TRUST COMPANY OF BUFFALO, BUFFALO, N. Y.

BUFFALO, N. Y.

SIR:

TAKE NOTICE that on this fifth day of January, 1940.

A check for $ 25.00 dated December 21, 1939.

Signed by Harold B. Kramer

payable at The Marine Trust Company of Buffalo,

Buffalo, New York, and endorsed by you, and due this day, payment of which has been duly demanded and refused, was PROTESTED for non-payment, and the holders look to you for the payment thereof.

x	Harold B. Kramer	at 646 Rhea Avenue, Buffalo
		at
		at
		at
		at
		at

This notice is addressed to the party whose name is checked above.

Respectfully yours,

Henry Williams

Notary Public in and for Erie County, New York.

NOTIFY PRIOR ENDORSERS, IF ANY, IMMEDIATELY

Illustration No. 221—A Protest Form

is therefore advisable to avoid submitting to a bank any item that probably cannot be collected. It should be borne in mind that, when a bank accepts a check for deposit, it is acting only as the collecting agent until the check has been collected. If the bank cannot collect the check, it deducts the amount from the account of the depositor.

Forgery and Alterations. It is illegal to forge another person's name. In other words, it is illegal for one to sign another person's name unless he has been authorized to do so and unless the substitute signature is recognized as acceptable. The changing of a signature is likewise illegal. Furthermore, it is illegal to change the date, the amount, or any other significant information on any legal instrument, such as a check or a note.

Let us assume, for instance, that Mr. H. O. Jackson receives a check that has been issued to him in the name of "B. O. Jackson." It would be illegal for him to correct the name by erasing the "B" and inserting an "H." Mr. Jackson can, however, collect the check without any difficulty. The proper procedure is for him to endorse the check, first, in the way it has been made out to him ("B. O. Jackson") and, second, with his correct signature ("H. O. Jackson").

Depositing Checks Promptly. When a businessman accepts checks in payment for merchandise or services, those checks should be deposited promptly. A person who receives a check should not be negligent or cause unreasonable delay in presenting it for collection. In other words, a person who receives a check has the responsibility of cashing it reasonably promptly.

For instance, Mr. A issues to Mr. B a check drawn on Bank X. Mr. B delays thirty days in presenting the check for payment. In the meantime Bank X has been closed because of some financial difficulty. There is some legal question in this case as to whether Mr. B can force Mr. A to make a new payment because, as a result of Mr. B's negligence, the check was not presented for payment within a reasonable time. On the other hand, if Mr. B had not been negligent, Mr. A would probably be legally bound to make a new payment.

Collection Between Banks. When there are only a few banks in a city, the process of exchanging checks among them is simple. Suppose, for example, that there are only two banks in a particular city. Customers of Bank No. 1 make deposits during the day. Some of the deposits are in cash, but many of them are in the form of checks. At the end of the day Bank No. 1 has in its possession ten checks amounting to a total of one thousand dollars. These are drawn on the funds of individual depositors in Bank No. 2. A messenger from Bank No. 1 takes these checks to Bank No. 2. After an investigation discloses that the depositors who wrote the checks have enough money to pay them, Bank No. 2 approves the checks, cancels them, and either pays one thousand dollars in cash to Bank No. 1 or gives credit for that amount to Bank No. 1. If Bank No. 2 finds that any particular depositor does not have enough money to pay his check, the check is returned to Bank No. 1. Bank No. 2 follows the same procedure in connection with checks it has that are drawn on Bank No. 1. The average collections between the two banks will probably be about equal. Variations will not be large unless some unusual transactions are made during a particular day.

In large cities a system such as this would be cumbersome, slow, and costly. *Clearinghouses* have therefore been organized to facilitate collection between banks. A clearinghouse represents an association of banks. At a certain hour of each day clerks from all the banks meet at the clearinghouse. In most cities two clerks represent each bank. One clerk delivers the checks that the bank received during the previous day and that are to be collected from other banks. With the checks is a list showing the amount due from each bank and the total amount due on all the checks. The second clerk receives from the other banks checks that are to be collected from his bank.

A clerk from each bank then quickly determines the difference between the amount his bank owes all the other banks and the amount that all the others owe his. If his bank owes more than the amount due from other banks, it pays the difference to the clearinghouse. If the other banks owe his bank more than it owes them, the clearinghouse pays the difference to his bank. Under this system the collection between banks takes only a short time. Small banks that do not belong to a clearinghouse association have their checks cleared through a bank that is a member of the association.

The Federal reserve banks perform an important function in the clearing of checks between cities. A Federal reserve bank will accept from the member banks in its territory all checks that are to be collected from banks in other cities. These checks are sent by the Federal reserve bank to the clearinghouses in the other cities. The procedure is quite detailed, but the Federal reserve bank acts essentially as the agent of member banks in collecting checks drawn on banks in other cities.

Banks that are not members of the Federal Reserve System may, in some cases, have their checks cleared through the Federal reserve banks by a special agreement.

Some banks clear their out-of-town checks through *correspondent banks*. For instance, Bank A in Chicago and Bank A in New York have arrangements for the exchange of checks. Bank A in Chicago has a check for collection on Bank B in New York. Bank A of Chicago presents this check to Bank A of New York. Through the clearinghouse procedure in New York City, Bank A of New York makes collection and either credits the proceeds to the account of Bank A in Chicago, or sends a draft, a check, or the actual funds to the latter.

QUESTIONS FOR DISCUSSION

1. What is the limit of insurance on each account deposited in banks carrying Federal deposit insurance?
2. What may be the advantages of dealing with a large bank?
3. What may be the advantage of dealing with a small bank?
4. On what three main bases do banks lend money?
5. What is the negotiable instrument that a businessman must always sign when he borrows from a bank?
6. What is meant by the word *collateral?*
7. How is the interest on a short-term loan usually handled by a bank?
8. Why is it necessary for many banks to make a service charge on checking accounts?
9. What is a certified check?
10. What is a bank draft?
11. What is a cashier's check?
12. Give examples of the most common types of negotiable instruments used in business.

13. What is the term applied to the person who signs a note and thereby promises to make a payment?

14. What is the term applied to the person who writes a check?

15. Is there any crime involved if a person writes a check on insufficient funds in his account, or writes a check on a bank in which he has no account?

16. If a check is made out incorrectly to an individual, does that person have the privilege of correcting the name?

PROBLEMS AND PROJECTS

1. On the basis of the analysis formula in this chapter for computing the service charge on checking accounts, consider the following facts:

   (a) The net average daily balance (after float has been deducted) is $800.
   (b) The number of checks written during the month is 30.
   (c) The number of checks deposited is 70.

   Compute (1) the service credit, (2) the total service charge, and (3) the difference between the two items.

2. On the basis of the analysis formula in this chapter for computing the service charge on checking accounts, consider the following facts:

   (a) The net average daily balance (after float has been deducted) is $1,500.
   (b) The number of checks written during the month is 25.
   (c) The number of checks deposited is 80.

   Compute (1) the total service charge, (2) the total service credit, and (3) the difference between the two items.

3. Assume that you are in business and have an invoice for $576.50 on which the terms are 2 per cent ten days, net thirty days. You wish to take the discount, but find it necessary to borrow money at 6 per cent until the end of the month in order to pay the invoice. You will need to borrow $500. How much money will be saved by borrowing the money for twenty days in order to obtain the discount?

4. Assume that you borrow $100 from a bank for sixty days at 6 per cent interest, deductible in advance. At the end of thirty days you are able to pay off the debt. The bank is willing to accept payment and to allow you credit for the remaining thirty days of interest. How much will you pay back?

5. Consider the following figures on a bank statement:

CHECKS		BALANCE
No. 20	$20.00	$1,005.20
No. 21	5.00	DEPOSITS
No. 22	15.06	$30.50
No. 24	25.50	7.75
No. 25	9.00	42.25
No. 27	30.75	10.00
No. 28	22.50	10.00
		15.20

(a) Reconcile the bank statement, taking into consideration the following additional facts:

Checks outstanding: No. 23, $10.50
                       No. 26, $52.40
Checkbook balance: $930.19

(b) If the checkbook balance were $928.21, what procedure would you recommend?

6. Mr. J. A. Pendery borrowed from the Merchants National Bank $1,000 on a 90-day note. The bank gave him cash for the face value of the note less interest at 6 per cent for 90 days. (a) How much cash did he receive? (b) How much cash did he pay at maturity?

7. Go to your own bank or to a bank with which you believe you would like to deal, and obtain the following:

(a) All forms necessary for opening a checking account
(b) A list of the regulations governing a checking account
(c) Samples of all the forms used by depositors, such as a bank statement, a bankbook, a regular check, a counter check, a deposit slip

Make a report on the method of opening a checking account and on the regulations governing such an account.

8. Assume that you are the manager of a book store and are authorized to borrow money to finance the operation of the store. Write a note according to the proper form, making it payable to a local bank and signing it with your signature.

CHAPTER XXII

RELATIONS OF BUSINESS WITH GOVERNMENT

Purpose of the Chapter. If one expects to go into business, he should have a clear understanding of the fact that government tends not only to aid business but also to control business. In other words, business operates under a set of laws that both aid and control. In order for government to operate, there must necessarily be taxes to finance it. There are so many different types of taxes that one's tax relations with the government are particularly important.

The purpose of this chapter is to seek answers to many questions, some of which are:

1. What rights does government grant to business?
2. What limitations are placed on business rights?
3. To what extent may we do as we wish in business?
4. What are the so-called fair trade laws?
5. What are the advantages and the disadvantages of the fair trade laws?
6. What departments of the Federal Government tend to influence and control business?
7. How do states control business?
8. How do the various types of taxes affect business?

Section I

Governmental Control of Business

What Is Private Property? *Private property* is the name applied to goods or rights controlled by one or more individuals. A private-property right is the right to control some goods, whether they be in the form of real estate or an automobile. The right to own private property is fundamental and so essential that we ordinarily do not think of it as depending upon the consent of the members of society.

In this country the right to own property has been recognized since the first white settlers arrived.

We may have the right of possession, the right of use, and the right of ownership. A person may rent a house and have the right of possession and the right of use, but he does not own the house. An individual may use a park or a street, but he does not have the right of ownership except as one citizen among many.

Various rights to property are undergoing slow but constant modification. The right to inherit property, for instance, has undergone considerable change through taxation. To some extent one loses the right of inheritance because of laws that enable the government to share in the inheritance through the process of a tax. Taxes on income also represent a change in the right of ownership. The fact that a person has earned an income is no assurance that he has the right to use all of it; he must share part of it with the government.

Limitations on the Use of Private Property. In the United States, where the people theoretically grant powers to the government, the people have the right of use of private property. Society, or the government, through its right to form laws, has the power to deprive individuals of certain privileges. It therefore has the right to govern the use of property. The imposition of a tax is one of the first actions of society in governing the use of private property by individuals. Society, through its laws, may authorize the government to take property in time of an emergency such as a war, or for the public good as in the widening of a street or the building of a new highway. This right is referred to as that of *eminent domain*. When property is taken in this manner, the government must prove that the taking of the property is for the general welfare of society.

During the World War the Federal Government, when it found a need for camps in which to train soldiers, exercised its right of eminent domain by taking suitable sites and paying the owners a fair compensation. If, in such a case, the value of the property is questionable, it is established through a court decision. If a city government needs land to widen a street, it may insist upon buying the land; it may condemn the property and, through legal procedure, establish a fair price. States may exercise the right of eminent domain in taking land for the construction of roads and bridges.

The Federal Government has given railroad companies the right to obtain the possession of land when they have proved that the railroads will serve a useful purpose for society in general. For example, if a railroad company has been granted permission to extend a line from New Orleans to St. Louis, it can choose the most convenient route, establish a fair price for the property, and offer payment to the owners. If the owners refuse payment, the railroad company may bring a lawsuit to have a fair price established. The price established by the court is the one that must be accepted.

Under rules established by society, the right to property may revert to the government through fines levied as a penalty; through forfeiture due to some failure to comply with the law (for instance, the failure to pay taxes); or through the death of an owner who leaves no legal heirs.

The government also limits the rights of individuals in the use of property. Federal laws, state laws, and local laws prohibit the use of private property in maintaining a public nuisance or in promoting some unlawful enterprise. For instance, governments are permitted to seize and to sell automobiles used for transporting illicit liquor. A person can be prohibited from allowing his radio to annoy other people. An individual can be prohibited by law from permitting his cattle to trespass on or to damage other people's property. A businessman may be prohibited from using a certain kind of signboard.

Special Property Rights. Society, through its governmental agencies, grants certain exclusive privileges as a reward for services rendered it. These privileges are a special form of private property. Among the most important of these privileges are *franchises, patents,* and *copyrights*.

A franchise is a contract that permits a person to use public property for private profit. No individual member of society, however, has any special right to use public property except through some special grant by society. Cities frequently give private companies and individuals the right to use the streets for operating streetcars or busses, or for stretching electric power lines or telephone lines. These are temporary rights that are governed by written agreements. Such an agreement limits the use of the public property and usually specifies some compensation that must be paid to the government which granted the authority. The contract that permits the company or the person to use the public property is a franchise.

A patent is an agreement between the Federal Government and some member of society, which becomes legal evidence that the latter has developed an original article or process. A patent is an official Federal document that grants to an inventor, for a term of years, the exclusive right to make, to use, and to sell his invention under a legal form of monopoly. Through the laws of the government the patentholder can seek protection in case some other person infringes upon his right. This protection is a reward for his services in making his patent available for the general use of society. He is permitted to profit by this protection; and other members of society are prohibited, for a certain period of time, from duplicating the article or the process covered by the patent.

A copyright is similar to a patent in that it is an official Federal grant of the exclusive right to reproduce, publish,

PATENTED
December 21, 1915; July 15, 1919; April 5, 1921; August 6, 1929.

KWIKSTIK COMPANY
Chicago, Illinois

Notice of a Patent

Copyright, 1932
Copyright, 1938
By SOUTH-WESTERN PUBLISHING CO.
Cincinnati, Ohio
All Rights Reserved

The text of this publication, or any part thereof, may not be reproduced in any manner whatsoever without permission in writing from the publisher.

Notice of a Copyright

Illustration No. 222

and sell literary or artistic work. It is not possible to copyright abstract ideas; but it is possible to copyright literary or artistic work of a physical nature.

Sometimes trade-marks are copyrighted in order that they may be protected from copying. One can protect an unregistered trade-mark, however, by proving the prior use of it. If he has his trade-mark registered or copyrighted, on the other hand, he has a better means of proving his prior use of it.

Limitations on Individual Initiative. A principle upon which our economic society is founded is freedom of initiative; that is, of one's right to control and to operate one's own enterprise. This right is, however, subject to limitation. As yet there is no law to restrain anyone from initiating a legitimate enterprise in most fields of endeavor. One can open a store, a lumber yard, a manufacturing plant, or a printing shop.

Cincinnati Street Railway Co.

*Illustration No. 223—A Form of Transportation Operating
Under a Franchise*

The regulation of enterprises is, however, increasing. Cities and states have exercised the right to control the number of transportation lines as a means of protection for those whose lines are already in operation. Thus, for instance, when society through a governmental agency grants a franchise to an electric railway, it protects the railway from competition.

Many of our recent state and Federal laws have tended to regulate freedom of initiative on the part of enterprises that operate unfairly toward labor, society, or competitors. The Federal and state governments have attempted to lay down certain rules within the limits of which citizens can exercise their freedom of initiative so long as they do not infringe upon the rights of others.

Society, through its governmental agencies, is gradually changing the rights of those who operate enterprises. However, except in the field of public utilities (railways, power plants, and the like), there is, in general, no restriction on one's right to start a business.

Theory of *Laissez Faire*. During the early days of trade there developed a system that was referred to as *mercantilism*. During that time those who were engaged in business and those who were largely responsible for forming public laws were of the opinion that business could be conducted most effectively if it were regulated closely by the government. Nations therefore granted monopolies of many kinds. They regulated the relations between business operators and their workmen. They restricted importations and exportations and the use of money. There were some leaders, however, who believed that business could be conducted much more effectively by permitting each individual to operate his business to his own advantage. This theory was called the *laissez faire* theory. It was named from the French expression equivalent to our phrase, "Let one do as he pleases."

The early commerce of the United States was operated on a *laissez faire* basis. Fundamentally, commerce still operates on this basis, but with more and more regulations.

It is assumed that each person has the right to operate his business to his best advantage. The government, however, has stepped in to protect labor and the public and in some cases has regulated competition with the purpose of eliminating certain abuses.

Business today operates fundamentally on a competitive basis. For instance, two or more merchants try to sell their goods to the same person. Each merchant tries, as a matter of fact, to obtain the highest price that he can, although competition tends to regulate the upper limits of prices. In recent years, however, as will be explained later in this chapter, laws have been passed permitting manufacturers to control the resale price of merchandise. Nevertheless business is still operated fundamentally on a competitive basis; for even though prices in such instances are controlled, each businessman must compete against others in service, location, and other factors.

It can be seen that, although the theory of *laissez faire* is the fundamental basis of the operation of American business, there is a gradual trend away from this theory. Every new governmental regulation and every new law breaks it down. For instance, until recent years the buyer of foods and drugs was largely responsible for looking after his own interests. Recent legislation, however, requires more information to be placed upon the labels of foods and drugs, and thus enables the buyer to select his merchandise more wisely.

State and Federal Control of Business. Under the Federal Constitution the Federal Government is given the right to regulate commerce among the states, and no state is permitted to impose duties on imports or exports. Every year the Federal Government passes new laws regulating commerce among the states. Every year the various states pass new laws regulating business within those states. Furthermore, in recent years there has been considerable state legislation that tends to obstruct the flow of commerce among the states. The following are the results of some of these restrictive state laws:

1. Use taxes, which are equivalent to a sales tax and are charged when goods are bought in one state and used in another.
2. Oleomargarine taxes, which are in a sense a license for the permission to sell the product in individual states.
3. Chain-store taxes, which tend to reduce the number of stores that a company may operate within a state.
4. Discriminatory taxes on corporations doing business within the state but incorporated in another state.
5. Discrimination against employing residents of other states or buying products from other states for local public institutions.

The fair trade laws, as well as various aspects of Federal control, will be discussed later in this section.

Monopolies. A monopoly is the control of the price or the production of some commodity or service. Monopolies are not necessarily undesirable; sometimes they represent very efficient forms of production. It is rather the question of control or use that determines whether or not monopolies are socially desirable.

The Sherman Antitrust Act and various other Federal laws, as well as many state laws, attempt to prevent or to control monopolies. Whenever there is a monopoly such as that which exists in the telephone and telegraph industry, the Federal Government reserves the right to regulate that industry.

The Federal Government grants monopolies to railroad companies. This policy is based on the assumption that the public would not be benefited, but would probably be harmed, if new railroads were built in competition with those already existing and therefore made it impossible for any of the railroads to be profitable.

The Interstate Commerce Commission establishes rates for the transportation of products and groups of products between specified points. Nevertheless the railroads compete with one another on the basis of services and conveniences. Take, for example, the railroads that operate between Cleveland and New York. No new railroad can start operation between those points without permission from the Interstate Commerce Commission. The existing railroads, however, must compete with one another. Each may have a feature which makes that road more attractive than its competitor. One railroad may have more comfortable passenger trains than another. One may take less time to travel between the two points. Another may handle freight shipments better, although the rates that it charges are the same as the rates of the other roads. It is thus evident that railroads have a partial monopoly in that no new roads can be constructed without permission. The existing railroads, however, do compete with one another by offering better services and conveniences than their competitors.

The United States Postal Service is one form of governmental monopoly. No private enterprise is allowed to compete with the governmental postal service except in the parcel-post branch. No company, for example, can establish a service to handle first-class letters, although express companies and other transportation agencies are permitted to handle shipments comparable to parcel post.

There are independent monopolies that are neither owned nor granted by the government. The Standard Oil Company at one time had practically a monopoly on world production and distribution of oil. There are claims that certain of our metal products are produced under partial monopolies. The world production of raw rubber was practically a monopoly of the businessmen of Great Britain at one time. For many years most of the raw rubber was produced by concerns owned in England. These English concerns therefore regulated the price of raw rubber. The monopoly was destroyed when new producing areas were opened and new processes were developed for producing rubber. Diamonds are produced and marketed under a very strict monopoly that regulates the supply and the price.

Under a monopoly, competition is eliminated and some of its waste is avoided. The incentive to improve services or methods changes, then, from a competitive one to a question of reducing the costs of production so that incomes and profits may be increased. Although under a truly monopolistic situation the price is controlled, this fact does not necessarily mean that the price will be the highest possible one. It means rather that the price will be established at a point which will encourage people to buy in quantities that will produce the greatest net profit.

A monopoly under some circumstances is necessary. In many instances of governmental or private monopolies, such as the postal service or railroad utilities, it would be extremely wasteful if the services were duplicated in the sense in which we have a duplication of grocery stores and restaurants. The major advantage of a monopoly is the elimination of the wastes of competition.

Fair Trade Laws. Numerous so-called fair trade laws have been enacted by the Federal Government and by state and local governments. The most important of these are the Robinson-Patman Act and the Tydings-Miller Fair Trade Enabling Act.

The Robinson-Patman Act is one that attempts to prevent discrimination in selling. It is largely the outgrowth of abuses that arose out of selling to certain preferred customers at much lower prices than to other customers. Under the Robinson-Patman Act the buyer and the seller are equally guilty if the seller discriminates in price, service, or any other way and the buyer accepts the discrimination. For instance, if a manufacturer sells to Merchant A at one price but gives a special discount to Merchant B, the manufacturer and Merchant B are both guilty of violating the Robinson-Patman Act.

The Robinson-Patman Act permits the giving of special concessions if merchandise is bought in large quantities, but there must be no special concessions between buyers who obtain the same quantity under similar conditions.

The Tydings-Miller Act is a Federal act that enables the individual states to enact so-called fair trade laws in co-operation with the Federal Government. The general provisions of the individual state laws promoted by the Tydings-Miller Fair Trade Enabling Act are as follows:

1. The state laws permit the owners of identified commodities and the wholesale and retail distributors in a state to make contracts containing price agreements.
2. They permit contracts that enable the owner of merchandise to require of any dealer to whom he may sell the commodity an agreement that the dealer will not, in turn, resell the commodity at less than the minimum price stipulated.
3. They permit the owner of trade-marked merchandise to specify the prices at which the various distributors, such as wholesalers and retailers, are to resell the merchandise.
4. They permit the owner of trade-marked merchandise to hold those distributors who have signed no contracts to the terms of other contracts in force in the state. If such a distributor "willfully or knowingly" advertises or sells any commodity subject to a state fair trade act at a lower price than that specified in a resale price agreement, the price cut is specified as unfair competition and, as such, brings the distributor within the compass of the act.
5. While fair trade acts provide for vertical price agreements on a commodity from the manufacturer through the distributor to the consumer, they specifically prohibit horizontal price agreements between manufacturers, or between wholesalers, or between retailers.
6. In general, the fair trade laws permit price cuts below the contract minimum (a) when a dealer's stock of a particular commodity is being closed out with the purpose of discontinuing that commodity; (b) when damaged, secondhand, or deteriorated goods are being disposed of and the fact is clearly made known to the public; and (c) when the goods are being disposed of by a court order.

Nearly all states now have laws that permit the manufacturer of a trade-marked article to control the resale price of the article. These laws have been enacted as a result of the Federal law.

Arguments for Fair Trade Laws. The arguments in favor of the fair trade laws enacted under the Tydings-Miller Act are as follows:

1. Small independent businessmen, especially independent retail druggists and other so-called "small" retailers, believe the protection of this law is necessary to keep them in price competition on well-known, business-sustaining items with larger distributors.

2. Fair trade laws embody for the independent retailer the idea of one price to all. The consumer feels secure in the price he pays, knowing that someone else cannot buy the same goods more cheaply at another store. This one-price-to-all idea automatically lowers sales resistance.

3. Fair trade laws tend to eliminate so-called "loss-leader" selling (selling an article below cost in order to attract customers). Loss-leader merchandising, it is true, has been found an effective policy in aggressive retailing. For the retailer with ample resources, it is merely a promotional measure for getting customers into the store, but it also keeps customers out of smaller stores. It has been claimed in some instances that the advertised item used as "bait" was not even available at the store or was available only in a limited quantity.

4. Under fair trade contracts a fair margin is planned for the price-controlled items. In this way the manufacturer gets better co-operation from the small retailer, who in turn finds he is able to meet competition on well-known brands. Manufacturers must see to it that independent retailers survive, because such distributors still do about 73 per cent of the total retail business.

5. Manufacturers who own a brand or a label, who have spent money in developing a demand for certain products, and who have improved quality standards have a right to protect their property (the goodwill represented by the label).

6. Fair trade laws affect only a small proportion of the goods bought by the consumer.

7. Manufacturers are not given a monopoly because the fair trade laws provide that there shall be no horizontal price agreements between manufacturers. All manufacturers of similar goods must therefore compete with one another on the basis of price.

8. Trade tends to flow through normal retail channels and not to be diverted into unnatural channels. When consumers are led out of their normal course, however, to buy at out-of-the-way places because of cut prices that are not available in all stores, normal retail channels are not employed.

9. Direct governmental regulation must result if the independent businessman fails to suppress distributor monopoly (resulting from the ability to cut prices) through the operation of fair trade legislation.

10. The promulgation and the observance of the principles of fair trade are vitally important to the preservation of the profit system and of our form of government and our civilization.

11. There can be no general prosperity without a prosperous body of distributors; and distributors cannot be prosperous when they are beset by wasteful and unsound competition among themselves and by warfare which so weakens them that they cannot perform the services necessary to keep the factory wheels running.

12. With the elimination of the independent dealer, producers would have to rely upon a few large distributors. Thus they would be compelled to accept low prices for their output and, receiving low prices, would have to pay low wages to workers.

Small distributors feel they have a just cause in their support of fair trade laws. A number of intelligent and responsible manufacturers join them. They believe that the consumer will be benefited by such legislation.

Arguments Against Fair Trade Laws. The following are the arguments that are proposed against the fair trade laws sponsored under the Tydings-Miller Fair Trade Enabling Act:

1. Large distributors object to the interference of manufacturers with their retail price policies. They feel that this intrusion reduces their ability to apply sound merchandising methods to their business. With minimum retail prices there is no latitude for the retailer to meet given situations as they arise. He becomes a tool of the manufacturer.

2. The manufacturer of a nationally known item may hesitate to adopt fair trade contracts because of his fear that the standardized prices on his item may encourage the use of private brands as a result of distributor or consumer resistance.

3. A large percentage of small consumer goods is sold through different types of stores with varying overhead costs. Some retailers require greater margins than others. Standardized margins may therefore not be sufficient for some retail outlets, whereas the margins may be excessive for others. Fixed retail prices subsidize the inefficient retailer at the expense of consumers.

4. There are too many stores. The total cost of distribution would be less and prices would be lower if the small and inefficient stores were allowed to close.

5. It is anomalous that the greatest drive for fair trade laws comes from small distributors in organized groups, whereas the legal basis for such laws is the protection of the property rights of producers.

6. The manufacturer who commits himself to minimum retail prices lays himself open to exploitation by competitors whose prices are not under fair trade contracts. This argument might not apply, however, in those industries in which price contracts are numerous, as in the case of manufacturers of drugstore items.

7. Those opposed to fair trade laws say that, because of the power of the producer to control prices, these measures may lead eventually to governmental regulation of prices for the protection of the public.

8. The consumer is more concerned with low prices than with social and economic reasons for higher prices. Consumers hesitate to pay a few cents more for any item. At least those consumers who are in the habit of patronizing cut-rate stores will have to pay higher prices on some of their favorite items.

9. It is expensive and troublesome for manufacturers to keep abreast of all the legal aspects of different fair trade laws, as well as to keep informed on the current litigation in each state. This task becomes especially irksome when the major portion of the manufacturers' distributive trade does not demand price contracts.

10. It takes more courage than that possessed by many manufacturers to turn down the large profitable orders of mass distributors who wish to operate on a price-appeal basis.

11. For many manufacturers the ever-present desire for an increased sales volume and the effectiveness of the price motive in moving large quantities of goods are strong arguments against fair trade laws.

12. Although the proponents of fair trade laws emphasize the "voluntary" nature of fair trade price contracts, there is nothing voluntary about the requirement that distributors who do not sign such contracts must conform to the contracts of others, whether or not they are generally acceptable to the trade.

United States Department of Commerce. The United States Department of Commerce represents the voice of business in our Federal Government. The Secretary of Commerce is a member of the Cabinet of the President and is the President's advisor on matters affecting businessmen.

The United States Department of Commerce publishes a great deal of literature pertaining to business operations, business conditions, prices, production, sales, management, and numerous other topics. It regularly disseminates the kind of information that has proved to be most beneficial to businessmen. Information about the services of this Department can be obtained by writing for a list of publications and services. Branches of the Department are established in several of the leading cities.

Illustration No. 224—National Bureau of Standards

National Bureau of Standards. The principal functions of the Bureau of Standards are those that pertain to (a) the making of tests, (b) the establishment of standards, and (c) the control of weights and measures.

This Bureau has established standards for many products. If a manufacturer wishes to produce a product according to these standards, the Bureau will furnish him with the necessary information. The Bureau publishes a list of "willing to certify" manufacturers who do produce products according to its specifications. Products meeting these specifications may be marked with a label showing how they conform to the standards.

The National Bureau of Standards has also been instrumental in eliminating miscellaneous sizes and kinds of products. For instance, a few standard sizes of bolts are advocated. Bolts made according to a certain specification are interchangeable, regardless of who may have produced them. Hundreds of miscellaneous sizes have therefore been eliminated. Many other cases of standardization could also be cited.

United States Department of Agriculture. The United States Department of Agriculture administers many laws that affect the businessman. Some of the primary functions of the Department have been to standardize nomenclature, grades, and measurements. Meat, butter, and egg inspection is conducted under the jurisdiction of this Department. Probably the most important functions that affect the businessman are those pertaining to grades and labels for canned foods and drugs.

Standard Grades for Canned Foods. The Secretary of Agriculture has the right to designate the grading standards for canned foods. The grades are designated as "Grade A," "Grade B," "Grade C," and "off grade." Prod-

Consumers' Guide.

Illustration No. 225—Graded Canned Foods

ucts that are labeled "Grade A," "Grade B," or "Grade C" are up to the standards recognized by the Federal Government. Products that are designated as "off grade" are wholesome foods, though they may not measure up to recognized standards in other respects. Standards have been established for such farm products as corn, peas, beans, and tomatoes, and are rapidly being extended to other foods. Foods canned under these standards are subject to supervision and inspection by government-paid inspectors.

Labels. The Food, Drug, and Cosmetic Act and the other similar acts administered by the Department of Agriculture are, of course, subject to periodic changes by Congress. The primary purpose of the Food, Drug, and Cosmetic Act is to prevent the manufacture, sale, or transportation of adulterated, misbranded, poisonous, or deleterious foods, drugs, and cosmetics in interstate commerce. Under this Act any drug sold in interstate commerce must conform to standard specifications or must be labeled to indicate how it deviates from those specifications. The labels of other medicinal preparations must show the contents and provide other information required by law. The United States Pharmacopoeia and the National Formulary are the basic sources of many of the specifications for products that are sold in interstate commerce under this Act. These agencies provide standards for the medical and the pharmaceutical professions. The standards are revised approximately every ten years. Besides the Federal regulations, many states have regulations with regard to the labeling of products.

The Tea Act and the Import Milk Act are concerned mainly with the wholesomeness of tea and milk. Standards of quality regulate the importation and the sale of these products.

The Insecticide Act is concerned mainly with the quality and the effectiveness of insecticides, fungicides, turpentine, and resin. When these products are sold in interstate commerce, they must meet the requirements of the Act and must be labeled accordingly.

Federal Trade Commission. The Federal Trade Commission is the outgrowth of a demand made by competing manufacturers for protection from unfair methods of competition. This Commission is therefore charged with the administration of most of the Federal laws having to do with fair competition. A businessman, for instance, may make a complaint against another on the grounds that the latter is using unfair practices in restraint of trade in order to raise prices, or that he is selling an inferior product under false specifications. In such a case the Federal Trade Commission is charged with the responsibility of conducting an investigation.

Complaints to the Federal Trade Commission. A complaint may be registered with the Federal Trade Commission by an individual, a business concern, or an association. A letter of complaint stating the facts in the case may be submitted. Some of the causes for complaint are adulteration, mislabeling, misleading selling schemes, false advertising, selling refinished goods as new, selling imitations of products, and otherwise misrepresenting an article to the extent that the competitor will be damaged or the public misled.

The procedure in laying a complaint before the Federal Trade Commission is outlined in the following example: Dealer A discovers that Dealer B is selling a product that he is misbranding and misrepresenting. Dealer B is able to undersell Dealer A and therefore causes Dealer A a loss of business. As Dealer B is selling his product in interstate commerce, he is subject to the jurisdiction of the Federal Trade Commission. Dealer A writes a complete letter of complaint to the Commission. The latter asks for such additional information as it needs; or if the complaint is serious enough, it sends an investigator to get additional facts. The case will then be called for a hearing. If the Federal Trade Commission decides, however, that there is insufficient evidence to bring an action, or if the matter is settled without necessity for an action, the case may be dismissed. If it is called for a hearing, both dealers will be called to testify. If a decision is rendered against Dealer B, the Commission will issue an order requiring Dealer B to cease carrying on the unfair trade practice specified in the complaint.

Reports of the Federal Trade Commission. A study of the annual reports of the Federal Trade Commission will give an idea of some of the unfair trade practices that are detrimental to businessmen and to consumers. The following is an example of a Federal Trade Commission report:

MISBRANDING PRODUCTS—ELECTRIC LIGHT BULBS

White-Lite Distributing Corporation and Others, New York City.— The Commission, in a proceeding against this corporation, found that it and its manager, another respondent, sold electric light bulbs marked with substantially less than the correct number of watts, indicating that the bulbs or lamps would use less electric current to operate than they actually did use, and representing that the bulbs would, therefore, be less expensive to operate than lamps of standard makes sold by competitors. For example, salesmen of White-Lite Corporation demonstrated its lamp marked "15-watt," which was actually a 27- or 28-watt lamp, against a 25-watt standard lamp of a competitor. The customer was thus led to believe that if he bought respondent's lamp, for which he paid twice the purchase price of the standard lamp, he would save in the cost of electric current the difference between the cost of operation of the 15- and 25-watt lamps, respectively. The customers purchasing "Sun-Glo" lamps from respondents thought from the marking on the lamps they were obtaining a 50-watt capacity bulb. Such "Sun-Glo" lamps were found to measure 63.6 and even 69.1 watts.

The Commission further found that Sun-Glo lamps marked 60 watts actually measured 69.8 watts and produced only 569 lumens of light, whereas a standard 50-watt lamp produced 575 lumens of light. In addition, the Commission found that to operate this Sun-Glo lamp at 6 cents a kilowatt-hour would cost $4.19 for 1,000 hours, whereas the cost, at the same rate, for operating the 50-watt standard lamp would be only $3 for 1,000 hours, or $1.19 less.

The Commission ordered the respondent to cease and desist from selling and offering for sale incandescent lamps marked with other than the correct number of watts, and further to cease and desist from representing the lamps as being manufactured to comply with specifications of the United States Bureau of Standards. Respondent was further ordered to cease and desist from representing that any trade-mark used in the sale of incandescent lamps was registered in the United States Patent Office, unless such registration had actually been made.

Federal Control of Advertising. The Federal Trade Commission Act was amended to provide for Federal jurisdiction over false advertising. Under this amendment, which became effective May 22, 1938, it is unlawful for an advertiser to disseminate false advertising to induce the purchase of foods, drugs, devices, or cosmetics, or to participate in any other unfair methods of competition. This amendment is devised to protect honest businessmen.

State Control of Advertising. There are numerous state laws that are barriers against dishonest advertising. Probably the most famous law is the *Printers' Ink* Model Statute, which is quoted here.

"Any person, firm, corporation or association who, with intent to sell or in any wise dispose of merchandise, securities, service, or anything offered by such person, firm, corporation or association, directly or indirectly, to the public for sale or distribution, or with intent to increase the consumption thereof, or to induce the public in any manner to enter into any obligation relating thereto, or to acquire title thereto, or an interest therein, makes, publishes, disseminates, circulates, or places before the public, or causes, directly or indirectly, to be made, published, disseminated, circulated, or placed before the public, in this State, in a newspaper or other publication, or in the form of a book, notice, handbill, poster, bill, circular, pamphlet, or letter, or in any other way, an advertisement of any sort regarding merchandise, securities, service, or anything so offered to the public, which advertisement contains any assertion, representation or statement of fact which is untrue, deceptive or misleading, shall be guilty of a misdemeanor."

The following twenty-five states have adopted it:

Alabama	Michigan	Ohio
Colorado	Minnesota	Oklahoma
Idaho	Missouri	Oregon
Illinois	Nebraska	Rhode Island
Indiana	Nevada	Virginia
Iowa	New Jersey	Washington
Kansas	New York	Wisconsin
Kentucky	North Dakota	Wyoming
Louisiana		

The following thirteen states have substitutes patterned after the *Printers' Ink* Model Statute; but, in the opinion of critics, the statutes in these states are relatively ineffective compared with the original model:

Arizona	Pennsylvania
California	South Carolina
Connecticut	South Dakota
Maryland	Tennessee
Massachusetts	Utah
Montana	West Virginia
North Carolina	

State and Local Control of Wages and Hours. Anyone engaged in business should become familiar with state and local regulations affecting wages and hours. In some states there are special regulations as to the number of hours that may be worked, the opening time, and the closing time of businesses. There is special control over certain hazardous industries as well as over the wages and hours of children and of women. Many of these laws give particular attention not only to the number of hours that children and women work but also to the particular hours in which they work during the day. They are forbidden in some instances to work overtime and are prohibited entirely from working in certain industries and types of businesses. There is, however, no uniformity in these state laws.

Federal Control of Wages and Hours. The so-called Fair Labor Standards Act was enacted by the Federal Government in 1938. It is often referred to as the Wage-Hour Law or the Fair Labor Law. The provisions of this Act cover only workers employed in industries that are engaged in interstate commerce or in the manufacture of goods shipped in interstate commerce. It does not attempt to regulate the wages and hours of executives, administrators, employees engaged in the professions, outside salesmen, or employees in retail and service establishments that conduct their business largely within the boundaries of a state. It also largely exempts agricultural workers and those engaged in the canning or packing of agricultural products. There are also a few other minor exemptions.

After October 24, 1940, the maximum number of hours that can be worked during a week is 40. Overtime is permitted provided employees are paid one and one-half times their regular rate. An employer may arrange rates for overtime with his employees, provided he receives the sanction of the National Labor Relations Board. No employee is permitted to work more than 1,000 hours in any 26 consecutive weeks or more than 2,000 hours in any 52 consecutive weeks. Under all circumstances, however, work in excess of 12 hours a day or 56 hours a week must be compensated for at the rate of one and one-half times the normal rate. Transportation employees are exempt because they are governed by the Interstate Commerce Commission. Certain seasonal industries, particularly those engaged in the production or the handling of perishable food products, are permitted to work their employees as much as 12 hours a day or 56 hours a week for not more than 14 weeks in any calendar year.

The minimum wage rate is 30 cents an hour or the rate fixed by the administrator. After October 24, 1945, the rate is 40 cents an hour, unless proof can be shown that this rate will curtail employment. The administrator is charged with the responsibility of raising these rates as rapidly as he can.

No producer, manufacturer, or dealer can ship or deliver in interstate commerce goods produced in establishments where oppressive child-labor conditions exist. Oppressive child-labor conditions are constituted to be the employment of children under sixteen and the employment of children between the ages of sixteen and eighteen in occupations found hazardous by the Federal Children's Bureau. Children may work for their parents in any occupations except manufacturing or mining. Children under sixteen years of age who are not legally required to attend school may work in agricultural employment. The Act exempts children employed as actors. Children between fourteen and sixteen years of age may be granted permits for work in occupations other than manufacturing and mining if the Federal Children's Bureau finds that such employment will not impair the health or the well-being of the child.

Control of Working Conditions. Nearly every state and many cities have laws governing the sanitary and healthful conditions under which employees work. Anyone going into business should investigate thoroughly the laws on this subject. In most states these laws are administered under the state industrial commission or some similar commission. The local ordinances of cities are administered by local inspectors or by the police.

State laws usually govern such items as ventilation, lighting, sanitary conditions, and safety precautions. There are detailed regulations covering certain hazardous industries. For instance, special precautions must be taken in industries in which a person may be subject to lead poisoning or to some other industrial ailment.

QUESTIONS FOR DISCUSSION

1. What is the right of eminent domain?
2. Give some examples of the ways in which government limits the rights of individuals in the use of property.
3. What is a franchise?
4. What is a patent?
5. What general types of work may be copyrighted?
6. Give at least two examples of limitations on business activities.
7. Can you justify the statement that American business operates under the theory of *laissez faire*?
8. Give at least two examples of state laws that restrict the flow of commerce between states.
9. Why is the Tydings-Miller Act referred to as an *enabling* act?
10. Under what circumstances do the Tydings-Miller Act and the state fair trade laws permit price cuts?
11. What is the essence of the Robinson-Patman Act, and why is this Act important?
12. Give at least two advantages of the fair trade laws enacted under the Tydings-Miller Act.
13. Give at least two arguments against the fair trade laws enacted under the Tydings-Miller Act.
14. Give some examples of how the United States Department of Commerce serves business.
15. Name the functions of the National Bureau of Standards.
16. In what way does the United States Department of Agriculture affect businessmen?
17. What department of the government is primarily charged with the administration of fair trade laws?
18. What is the so-called *Printer's Ink* Model Statute?
19. Under the Federal Wage-Hour Law what regulations have to do with the rate for overtime work?
20. What exceptions are made in certain industries with regard to exceeding the maximum number of hours per week?

Section II

Taxation of Business

Social Security Taxation. The Social Security Act, which was passed on August 14, 1935, levies certain taxes on employers and employees for the purpose of providing funds from which payments can be made (a) to employees in the form of old-age benefits and (b) to employees as remuneration during periods of unemployment. There are two kinds of social security taxes; namely, those for old-age insurance, or benefits, and those for unemployment compensation.

Old-Age Insurance Taxes. The Social Security Act levied a tax on employers and one on employees. These taxes, which began on January 1, 1937, are paid into a fund of the United States Treasury. Benefits are paid from this fund to properly qualified individuals. The qualifications required of those seeking benefits will be discussed later.

Under this part of the law an employer is a person who employs one or more individuals. Not all employers, however, are governed by this law. For instance, the law exempts employers of farm labor, domestic help, and school teachers, as well as employers in certain other classifications, which may change from year to year in accordance with amendments to the law. In a sole proprietorship form of business the owner is not considered an employee. In a partnership form of business the partners are not considered employees. In a corporation the officers are considered employees. A director of a corporation is not an employee unless he performs services for the corporation other than the service rendered by attending and participating in the board meetings.

The tax on employers for old-age insurance is called the *employer's excise tax*. This tax is levied on the first $3,000 of wages paid each employee during a calendar year, provided the business comes under the requirements of the Social Security Act. The rate of tax from January 1, 1937, to January 1, 1943, is 1 per cent. This rate, however, is subject to change by an act of Congress. If an individual earns $4,000 in wages during a year and the rate of tax is 1 per cent, the employer's excise tax is $30, or 1 per cent of the first $3,000 in wages. Similarly, if an individual receives $2,400 in wages, the employer's excise tax is $24.

The tax on employees for old-age insurance is called the *income tax on employees*. The rate of tax on employees is the same as the rate of excise tax on employers. In other words, an individual making $4,000 a year pays a tax of $30 at the 1 per cent rate and actually receives $3,970. An individual making $2,400 a year pays a tax of $24 and actually receives $2,376. This tax on the employee is similar to a premium that one might pay on an insurance policy, for the employee expects to receive monthly benefits in later life as a result of the deductions made from his salary.

The law requires that the employer deduct the employee's income tax in paying the wages of the employee. As soon as wages have been paid, the employer is liable to the Federal Government for the amounts deducted from the wages of his employees. The amount deducted from the employee's wages is payable to the Federal Government by the end of the month following each calendar quarter. The employer's excise tax for the quarter is payable at the same time.

Old-Age Benefits, or Insurance. An individual who has met certain requirements under the Social Security Act, including payments of the proper amounts as his employee's income tax, is eligible for monthly primary benefits after reaching the age of sixty-five years. These benefits are similar to the annuity payments that an individual would receive under an annuity insurance policy. The benefits are paid monthly until the individual dies. In other words, the taxes on the employee and on the employer for old-age insurance build up a fund from which are paid to qualified individuals a monthly benefit after such individuals retire from active employment.

In addition to the monthly primary (old-age) benefits paid to a qualified individual, the Act also makes provision for the following monthly benefit payments: wife's insurance benefits, child's insurance benefits, widow's insurance benefits, and parents' insurance benefits.

Unemployment Compensation Taxes. Under this part of the Social Security Act, an excise tax is levied on the salaries of employees in businesses that have eight or more individuals. Certain types of businesses and employment are exempt from this tax. The excise tax is 3 per cent of employees' salaries, up to and including $3,000 for each employee. The tax for the current calendar year is payable to the Federal Government by the end of January of the next year.

In addition to the Federal tax for unemployment compensation, each state has passed an unemployment compensation law under which employers are taxed on wages paid. In some states the taxes are called contributions instead of taxes. The basic rate of tax in most states is 2.7 per cent of the wages paid. The amount of wages on which the state tax is imposed varies in different states.

In paying the Federal tax of 3 per cent each year, employers are permitted to claim a credit up to 90 per cent of the Federal tax because of payments made to state governments for unemployment compensation. For example, if a particular employer has a Federal excise tax amounting to $3,000 but has paid state unemployment compensation taxes on $2,700, he may deduct the entire latter amount from the tax due the Federal Government and therefore pay the Federal Government only $300. If he has paid state taxes of $3,200, he is allowed a credit of only $2,700, or 90 per cent of the $3,000. Actually, the Federal tax in most cases amounts to only one tenth of 3 per cent, or 0.3 per cent. In most states the employer will pay a Federal tax of 0.3 per cent and a state tax amounting to approximately 2.7 per cent, or a total tax of 3 per cent.

From the amounts paid in Federal unemployment taxes, Congress appropriates each year to each state an amount to take care of administrative costs to operate the state unemployment plans. Benefits to unemployed workers are paid from the state funds.

The laws of the various states differ as to the methods of qualifying for unemployment benefits. In most states, however, if an employee becomes unemployed, he must wait a certain length of time before filing an application for unemployment compensation. There is also a limit to the length of time during which the employee can receive unemployment compensation. Because of the variations in the state unemployment compensation laws, it is not possible in this textbook to give detailed information as to the benefits paid for unemployment and the rates of taxes imposed. In a few states a tax, or contribution, is required of the employee as well as the employer.

Licensing of Businesses. City, county, and state governmental agencies have used licensing as a device for limiting and controlling those who go into particular types of businesses. For instance, one may be required to obtain a license for the operation of a certain hazardous business. In some cities businesses of all types must obtain licenses. It is particularly common to license restaurants, beauty parlors, barber shops, and other forms of service estab-

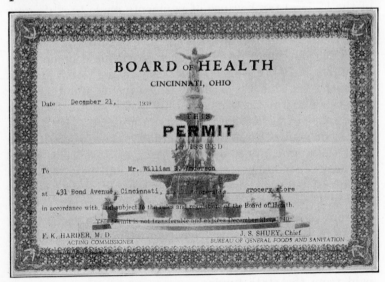

Illustration No. 226—A Business License

lishments that may particularly affect the health of the community. In most states and in many cities there are special licensing laws that regulate the sale of such items as liquor and tobacco. Under a licensing system, inspectors are required for administering the law, and revenue is provided for the support of the government. Under the system a license may be revoked if the business is not operated according to the standards specified in the law. In order to start a business that must be operated under a license, one must file an application in accordance with the law.

The control of itinerant peddlers has always been a problem because in the past many of these peddlers have been able to come into a community without paying taxes and without the normal control that is exercised over an established business. Many communities, however, have established the practice of licensing all peddlers.

Several states have enacted chain-store licensing taxes. Most of this legislation is promoted by individuals who are opposed to chain stores. The tax is graduated in most cases. The rate, for instance, in one state starts at $3 for the first store and runs to as high as $300 a store. Usually the tax that is charged depends upon the number of stores within the state.

Sales Tax. The sales tax has become quite prominent in recent years. There is now a sales tax in almost every state. Although there is no uniformity in the administration of these taxes, in nearly every case the retailer ·is responsible for the collection of the tax and in turn must pay this tax to the state government. It is therefore important for the businessman to be familiar with the sales tax law of his state so that he can be sure to collect the tax properly and to keep records that will enable him to report the tax correctly.

Property Tax. In every state there is some form of property tax, and in some states there are two or more property taxes. For instance, there may be a real property tax, a personal property tax, and an intangible property tax. A real property tax is a tax levied on land and buildings.

A personal property tax is a tax on such items as furniture and fixtures. An intangible property tax is a tax on assets such as money in the bank, notes, stocks, bonds, and other securities. The businessman should familiarize himself with all the tax laws of his state to be sure that he gets the proper forms at the right time and reports his taxes accurately. If he is delinquent in paying his taxes or attempts to avoid the payment of them, he will be subject to a penalty.

A tax on property, whether on real, personal, or intangible property, is stated in terms of a percentage of mills, or of dollars a thousand. It is most frequently quoted in terms of mills. For instance, a tax of 14 mills is $14.00 a thousand or, on a percentage basis, .014. At this rate the tax on $2,000 would be $28.00.

Income Tax. A Federal income tax is imposed upon all individuals and business establishments. Different forms are provided for the individual, the sole proprietorship business, the partnership, and the corporation. Accurate bookkeeping records are required in order that the true income can be reported and the tax computed accurately. The income-tax return gives instructions and provides a detailed form for reporting the various information that is required. Bookkeeping records of the type needed in preparing an income-tax return for a business are discussed and illustrated in Chapter XIX.

Taxes as State Barriers. Theoretically, under the Constitution of the United States, the Federal Government reserves the right to regulate commerce between the states. States may impose their own taxes, but in recent years there has been a tendency to develop special state taxation laws that constitute barriers to interstate business. Illustration No. 227 shows various state taxes that tend to regulate commerce between states but serve as state barriers of business.

Variety of Taxes. Taxation has become so complicated that the average businessman spends a great deal of time

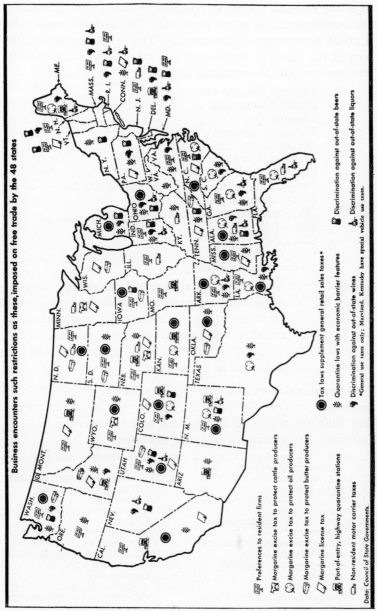

Business Week.

Illustration No. 227—State Barriers to Interstate Business

in filling out tax forms, in computing taxes, and in making
various reports. In many businesses the various taxes take
a great percentage of the income. The following are examples of the types of taxes that a business operating in only
one state might be required to pay:

> Federal income tax
> State income tax
> License fee
> Personal property tax
> Occupational tax
> Corporation tax
> Capital stock tax
> Federal social security (or excise) taxes
> State unemployment tax
> State industrial insurance tax
> Sales tax
> Use tax
> Gasoline tax
> Motor vehicle license

Furthermore, a corporation doing business in several
states will be subjected to numerous additional taxes, some
of which may be overlapping. If a business is organized in
one state, it probably will have to obtain a special license
to do business in another state and will be subjected to the
various taxes enforced in both states.

Government Services. The taxes that are collected from
business and from individuals pay for the numerous services that are rendered to business and to individuals. The
following are examples of those services:

1. Police, fire, military, and coast-guard service
2. Legal title records
3. Health protection
4. Garbage collection and sewage disposal
5. Inspection of weights and standards
6. Schools, universities, and research laboratories
7. Legislative and executive services
8. Postal service
9. Transportation service
10. Courts, prisons, and jails
11. Welfare and relief agencies
12. Street lighting and cleaning
13. Water, electric, and gas systems
14. Maintenance of streets, sidewalks, highways, and waterways
15. Parks and recreational activities
16. Civic museums, auditoriums, and libraries
17. Harbor and terminal facilities
18. Inspection of building construction
19. Regulation of admission requirements for professions
20. Forestry and reclamation service
21. Employment service

QUESTIONS FOR DISCUSSION

1. What are the two main types of social security benefits that are provided under the Social Security Act?
2. What is the income tax on employees under the Social Security Act?
3. How much will be deducted from the wages of an employee as an income tax for old-age benefits under the Social Security Act (a) if he earns $2,000 a year? (b) if he earns $4,000 a year?
4. What is the employer's excise tax?
5. What is the relation between state unemployment laws and the Federal Social Security Act?
6. Are the members of a partnership considered to be employees under the Social Security Act?
7. Are the officers of a corporation considered to be employees under the Social Security Act? Is a director of a corporation considered an employee?
8. What portion of one's salary is taxable in computing the deduction for unemployment insurance?
9. Are school teachers subject to a social security tax?
10. Give some examples of businesses that are often licensed in towns and cities.
11. Why is the licensing of businesses considered desirable and necessary?
12. How do merchants collect and pay sales taxes?
13. What is considered to be real property?
14. What is considered to be intangible property?
15. Why is it absolutely necessary for a business to keep accurate bookkeeping records?
16. Name at least five examples of different taxes paid by businessmen in your state.
17. What are some of the services that are provided by states from the funds collected through taxes?

PROBLEMS AND PROJECTS

1. List some types of businesses in your community on which there are special restrictions.
2. Are there any general restrictions in your community that are placed on all new businesses?
3. On the basis of the advantages and the disadvantages of the fair trade laws presented in this chapter, and from informa-

tion gathered from your friends and from merchants, give your conclusions as to the effects of price-control policies in your community.

4. Using the example of the report of the Federal Trade Commission presented in this chapter, show how the Federal Trade Commission is helping business in general and how the bad practices condemned by the Commission hurt all businesses.

5. Assume that the following is a brief financial statement showing the income and the expenses of a manufacturer who is paying an average wage rate of 30 cents an hour for labor. Prepare the same financial statement, using a minimum wage rate of 40 cents an hour.

Gross Sales		$30,245.50
Cost of Goods Sold		21,825.14
Gross Profit on Sales		8,420.36
Operating Expenses:		
Manufacturing Labor	$2,736.30	
Office Expense	672.50	
Advertising Expense	301.22	
Sales Commissions	598.61	
Salaries	1,650.00	
Taxes	940.80	
Depreciation	456.25	
Miscellaneous Expenses ...	270.90	
Total Operating Expenses		7,626.58
Net Profit from Operations	$	793.78

If the wage rate of 40 cents an hour is put into effect, what adjustments may be necessary for the manufacturer operating this business?

6. Assume that the wages paid the employees of a business amount to $17,256.50 during the year and no wage paid to any single individual exceeds $3,000. (a) How is the Federal old-age insurance computed? (b) How much does the employer owe the Federal Government for unemployment compensation taxes (excise taxes)? (c) How much credit does the employer get if he has already paid a state unemployment tax of $517.70?

7. Compute the tax on real estate appraised at $7,560, assuming that the tax rate is 21.4 mills.

8. Assume that a real-estate tax is assessed at the rate of 17 mills per dollar of valuation. (a) What is the tax per thousand dollars of valuation? (b) What is the tax on real estate valued at $15,422.50?

9. Using your local tax rate, compute the real-estate tax on the valuation of $15,422.50 used in the preceding problem.

CHAPTER XXIII

LEGAL RELATIONS IN BUSINESS: CONTRACTS

Purpose of the Chapter. Most of the activities in business have to do with buying and selling. These activities are important because they involve contracts either written or oral. In this chapter no attempt is made to develop technical legal aspects, but an attempt is made to provide a general understanding of the most common legal relationships in business. The following are some of the important questions that are answered in the chapter:

1. What is a contract?
2. What types of contracts should be in writing?
3. What types of contracts must be in writing?
4. What are the essentials of a contract?
5. What kinds of contracts are voidable?
6. Why should one read a contract before signing it?

What Is a Contract? A contract is an agreement, but not all agreements are contracts. For an agreement to be a contract, it must be the type of agreement that, if broken, will permit the injured person to obtain some remedy through law. The first essential of a contract therefore is an agreement. In nontechnical language, the other essentials of a contract are (a) that the consent of each party must be genuine and the agreement must be reached without threat or intimidation; (b) that the parties to the contract must be competent to enter into contracts; (c) that the purpose for which the contract is made must be legal; (d) that each party to the contract must offer or give something as a consideration; and (e) that the contract must be in the required form.

Offer and Acceptance. Whenever an offer has been made by one person and accepted by another, an agreement has been reached, provided the offer and the acceptance have been made in accordance with certain legal regulations. These regulations will be explained later in this chapter. Unless a specific date is mentioned when an offer is to be withdrawn or otherwise terminated, the offer may be accepted within a reasonable length of time. What may be considered a reasonable time will depend upon the circumstances. The interpretations of courts in such cases are not always uniform.

Oral Contracts Versus Written Contracts. For the sake of certainty and safety, all important contracts should be written. Many contracts do not need to be written, for the entire transaction is executed at the time the contract is made. Those that must be written usually pertain to real estate. In some states any contracts that require more than a year for fulfillment must be written.

In some states a contract for the sale of merchandise above a specified minimum sum must be written. Sales contracts need not be in writing when the price is less than the amount designated in the law. As a rule, the minimum amount is $500, but in some states it may be as low as $50. It varies greatly in different states, ranging from $30 to $2,500. The Uniform Sales Act prescribes a minimum of $500. In some states a sales contract must be signed by both parties, but in most states the contract or memorandum need be signed only by the party to be held to the contract. For instance, in some cases the buyer may wish to hold the seller, and in other cases the seller may wish to hold the buyer. Both the buyer and the seller should, of course, sign in order that each may have protection.

Importance of Reading Contracts. Some contracts are printed in very small type in the hope that they will not be read. The type, in fact, is so small in some contracts that it can hardly be read. Many old forms of contracts are printed in this manner, although the businesses that use them are entirely honest. A person should not be misled by a contract that is printed in small type. He should insist upon taking time to read it.

Underwood & Underwood.

Illustration No. 228—Read Before You Sign

Every contract should be examined carefully before it is signed. An honest and legitimate business will encourage the buyer to read the contract before signing, whereas an unscrupulous business may try to induce the buyer to sign before reading. An invitation to read a contract should always be accepted. The document may be presented in the hope that it will not be read. If there is any indication that an attempt is being made to prevent the reading of the contract, one should insist upon reading every detail.

Reasons for Written Contracts. In a casual oral agreement there may be some misunderstanding as to price, terms of sale, or other elements of the contract. The mere writing of a contract should cause each party to give more careful attention to the details than he could in the case of an oral agreement.

In an oral contract there may be an apparent agreement; but if the contract is to be fulfilled later, some of the terms of the agreement, such as the quantity of the product to be delivered, the terms of payment, or the obligation of either party, may be forgotten. For instance, Mr. A may agree to furnish Mr. B all the eggs that the latter needs regularly each week. If Mr. B depends on receiving these eggs at a specific time each week or in a particular quantity, he may be inconvenienced by delivery at irregular intervals or in small amounts. In the absence of a written agreement, there would be no way of determining whether or not the contract was being fulfilled properly.

One party to an oral contract may believe that he has a legitimate reason for bringing a suit to enforce the carrying out of the agreement. If the contract were in writing, however, he would know more definitely his legal rights. Litigation is often the result of misunderstandings. Written contracts help to avoid misunderstandings.

Although fraud is possible in written contracts as in oral contracts, a written contract provides better evidence in case there is an attempt to defraud. Statements in properly written contracts are enforceable, whereas statements in oral agreements are vague and often cannot be enforced.

A written contract will provide evidence in the case of the death of either party to the contract. For example, Mr. A may lend one thousand dollars to Mr. B without requiring Mr. B to sign a note. If Mr. A dies and Mr. B wants to avoid his obligation, the heirs of Mr. A will have difficulty in proving the claim against Mr. B. A written contract left by Mr. A would provide suitable evidence.

Preventing Fraud and Misunderstanding. The following suggestions are offered to prevent misunderstanding and fraud in drawing a contract:

1. Use simple words and expressions that will not be misunderstood. Do not allow the use of any word that might be misinterpreted.

2. Avoid, if possible, dealing with persons who are not honest.

3. In case of doubt with regard to a contract, consult a lawyer.

4. In the absence of substantial proof with regard to oral agreements or supplementary agreements, only the agreements stipulated in the contract are enforceable. Do not leave anything to a general understanding. Be sure that every act to be performed is stated clearly in the contract.

5. Do not sign a contract with the understanding that supplementary agreements will be made later. Be sure that these agreements are included in the contract.

6. Read the contract carefully before signing.

Essential Information Required in Written Contracts. The following is the essential information that is desired in a contract: (a) date and place of agreement; (b) names of parties entering into the agreement; (c) statement of the purpose of the contract; (d) statement of the money, the services, or the goods given in consideration of the agreement; (e) statement of the acts that are to be performed by each party; and (f) signatures. Illustration No. 229 shows a simple contract. The various elements in the contract should be observed.

GENTLEMEN:

Please enroll me as a member. It is understood that I am to receive, free, the book checked below, that I am also to receive, without expense, your monthly magazine which reports about current books, and that for every two books-of-the-month I purchase from the Club, I am to receive the current book-dividend then being distributed. For my part, I agree to purchase at least four books-of-the-month a year from the Club.

Check title you prefer to receive as your free enrollment book
(No others available at this time)

☐ AMERICAN PRINTS   ☐ JOSEPH IN EGYPT   ☐ INSIDE EUROPE
        ☐ BARTLETT'S QUOTATIONS   ☒ ANDREW JACKSON

Name Mr. Mrs. Miss } _ _MARTIN_ _REED_ _ _ _ _ _ _ _ _ _ _ _ _ _ _ _ _
                          PLEASE PRINT PLAINLY

Address _ _ _215_ MADISON AVENUE_ _ _ _ _ _ _ _ _ _ _ _ _

City _ _ _ TOLEDO_ _ _ _ _ _ _ _ _ _ _ _ _ _ _ _ State _ _ OHIO_ _ _ _

Business Connections, if any _

Please check whether you would like us to ship the current
book-of-the-month with the free book above **YES** ☒ **NO** ☐

Illustration No. 229—An Agreement That Is a Binding Contract

A simple signed order for merchandise or for any other item is a contract. For instance, when one signs an order for the purchase of an automobile, he is signing a contract. Illustration No. 230 shows a memorandum of an agreement leading to the sale of equipment on an installment plan. When this memorandum is properly filled out and signed, it becomes a contract. (Installment contracts were discussed in detail in Chapter XIV on credit.)

Bill of Sale. Bills of sale are used in selling many types of merchandise. In most states, but not all, a bill of sale is required to provide evidence of ownership. For instance, it is impossible in some states to obtain an automobile license without providing a bill of sale or a sworn statement as evidence of the ownership of the automobile. If the bill of sale has been lost, it is possible to establish the ownership by going through the legal procedure of obtaining a sworn statement of ownership. The most common type of bill of sale is that used in selling automobiles. In many states, bills of sale of different types are required for new cars and used cars. Illustration No. 231 shows a typical bill of sale for a new car.

In most states in which a bill of sale is required, the transaction is not completed and legal until the contract has been recorded by the local recorder or other designated public official. The recording of a bill of sale prevents an unscrupulous seller from selling the same merchandise again to another buyer who has no knowledge that the merchandise has already been sold.

Uniform Sales Laws. The Uniform Sales Act has been adopted by almost every state. The purpose of the Uniform Sales Act is to establish some uniformity in the provisions of the sales laws in the various states. When transactions take place between businessmen located in different states, many complications arise with regard to the contracts because of differences in the requirements and in the interpretations of the sales laws in those states.

The uniform sales laws are quite technical. When there is some question about a contract or there is a possible

MEMORANDUM OF AGREEMENT

GEO. S. WRIGHT CO.

Indianapolis, Ind.

County of __Marion__

State of __Indiana__

January 17, __1940__

Please ship to __Robert C. Bennett, 4620 Woodlawn Avenue, Clermont, Indiana__

Model __A31__ , Serial No. __71152__

(Vendor is authorized to insert the number hereafter) with __I__ agree to pay you the sum of __Seventy-Two__ Dollars all in good order, in consideration for which __used__ being allowed in exchange for. __used__ machine Model No. __A22__

as follows :—$ __12.00__ Cash herewith; $ __10.00__ being allowed in exchange for. __used__ machine Model No. __A22__

Serial No. __43095__ and the balance in __five__ __weekly__ monthly payments of $ __10.00__ each due and payable without notice or demand on the __first__ day of each __week__, month, consecutively after date until whole amount of __Seventy-Two__ Dollars as represented has been paid in full.

The above described property is and shall remain the property of you or your assigns until each and every one of said payments, and any judgment rendered thereon, shall be paid in full, and said property shall not be subject to any other person and shall be insured by the undersigned against fire for your benefit or your assigns. In default of any payment as above stipulated, or if the undersigned shall sell or encumber, or offer to sell or encumber said property, or any part thereof, or in the event of loss or damage to said property from whatsoever cause, it is hereby agreed that all the remaining payments shall immediately become due and payable at the election of you or your assigns. In default of payment of any one of said payments, or upon violation of any of the covenants herein, or on removal or attempt to remove said property from __4620 Woodlawn Avenue, Clermont, Indiana__

without your consent in writing, you or your agents or your assigns are hereby authorized and empowered, without notice or demand, to enter the premises wherever the property may be, take possession of and remove the same without legal process, and all claims for trespass or damages arising from said retaking are hereby waived, and in such case all moneys paid on the purchase price thereof shall belong to you or your assigns as liquidated damages for the non-fulfillment of this contract by the undersigned, depreciation in value of said property and for the use or rental of said property while remaining in possession of the undersigned. The loss, injury or destruction of said property shall not operate in any manner to release the undersigned from payment as provided herein. All rights of exemptions and homestead are hereby waived by the undersigned, and undersigned agrees to pay any and all charges and expenses, including $10 attorney's fees, incurred in retaking said property or in collecting the balance of amount due herein in case of default.

It is expressly agreed that this instrument shall not be countermanded by the undersigned and covers all agreements between us, all claims of verbal or other agreements between us being waived, and that nothing but acceptance in writing by your manager shall constitute an acceptance hereof on your part.

(Signed) __Robert C. Bennett__

Address. __4620 Woodlawn Avenue, Clermont, Ind.__

Witness __Donald Stitz__

REFERENCES:—

__Central Bank & Trust Company__

__Mayer Clothing Company__

Illustration No. 230—A Memorandum of an Agreement

BILL OF SALE, in Duplicate
NEW MOTOR VEHICLE
Gen'l Code, Sec. 6310-5

Know All Men by These Presents, *That* ____The Central Motor Company_____

*Residing at*_____1156 Fillmore Street_____

_____Dayton, Ohio_____

the Grantor__, do __ee__hereby execute this Bill of Sale in Duplicate and deliver to _____

_____Harry B. Jacobs_____

*Residing at*_____759 Harrison Avenue_____

_____Dayton, Ohio_____;

the Grantee__, the possession of the following described Motor Vehicle:

*Manufacturer or Maker*__General Motors Corporation_____;

*Manufacturer's (Factory) No.*_____; *Engine or Motor No.*__C2-143560_____;

*other numbers*__Chassis No. 74513992_____*Horse Power*____23.44_____;

*Description of Body*_____Coach, two-door de luxe_____

*Make*___Chevrolet_____, *Type*__Passenger Car____, *Model*___C6 (1940)_____

*Other number or marks of identification thereon or on appliances attached thereto,*_____

_____

It is mutually understood that the contents, execution, delivery, acceptance or filing of this "bill of sale" in no manner affects or governs the rights, title and interest of either the transferer or transferee in and to the vehicle herein described or referred to, or in and to any chattel mortgage, note paid or unpaid purchase price, lease, lien, insurance policy, conditional sale contract, or any contract or agreement collateral or otherwise of any kind whatsoever, concerning such vehicle, the sole purpose of this "bill of sale" being to comply with Sections 6310-3 to 6310-14, inclusive, of the General Code of Ohio, and in order to evidence the fact that possession of such vehicle has changed on this day.

IN WITNESS WHEREOF, the said____Central Motor Company and_____

_____Harry B. Jacobs_____

ha**ve**_hereunto set___t**heir**_hand this____third_____day of__January_____

19**40**__

Witnessed by   __The Central Motor Company_____

                                        __Henry Armstrong__

____Mary Meyers_____ __Sales Manager_____

____John Alford_____ __Harry B. Jacobs_____

                                                      Grantor___

                                        _____

                                                      Grantee___

Illustration No. 231—A Bill of Sale for a New Car

lack of uniformity between one state and another, the businessman should consult a lawyer.

Warranties. The seller's statements of opinion or belief as to the value or the merit of an article, as well as the commendations used to induce a purchase, are not warranties. In the eyes of the law, certain statements of a seller are *puffs*. For instance, a seller may assert that certain merchandise is "the best that can be obtained" or that a particular machine is "a thoroughly dependable machine." Such statements should be considered, not as warranties, but as puffs or *trade talk,* and should not be relied upon by the buyer.

A warranty is a statement or an implied affirmation of fact (not opinion) that the subject of a contract is as it is declared or promised to be. For example, if an oral or a printed statement with regard to a product declares that the product "will not damage silks," such a statement is a warranty. In the absence of fraud and of any special regulatory law, the principle of "Let the buyer beware" is followed. It is assumed that, if a person inspects an article before buying it and if he is not misled by fraud, he should know what he is getting.

When a buyer has an opportunity to inspect the goods, there is no implied warranty that the goods are of a particular quality. If the buyer does not inspect the goods, however, but relies largely on the judgment and the honesty of the seller, there is an implied warranty (on the part of the seller) that the goods are of a satisfactory quality. The goods therefore must be suitable for the purpose for which they are sold.

When a sample is used to indicate the kind and the quality of the goods, the seller impliedly warrants the goods to correspond to the sample in kind and quality.

When merchandise is purchased by description, such as specifications, the seller impliedly warrants the goods to correspond to the description. (See Illustration No. 232.)

Remedies for Breach of Warranty. There are various remedies in case of a breach of warranty. The following general recourses are open to the buyer: (1) to keep the goods and to deduct from the price the amount of the damages; (2) to keep the goods and to bring an action against the seller for damages; (3) to refuse to accept the goods and to bring an action against the seller to recover damages; (4) to rescind the contract and to refuse to receive the goods, or, if the goods have been accepted, to return them to the vendor and to recover the price that has been paid.

Passing of the Title. Two general rules govern the passing of the title when goods are sold, although there are exceptions in some states, especially with regard to such other goods as coal, wheat, or oil, of which any unit is considered to be the equivalent of any other unit. The two rules determining the passing of the title are: (1) under a contract to sell *unascertained goods,* the title will not pass until the goods have been ascertained; (2) under a contract to sell *ascertained goods,* the title passes at the time the parties intend it to be transferred.

GARDEN HOSE: Inside diameter—¾". Outside diameter—1³⁄₁₆". Construction—double braids of closely woven hawser twist fabric. Average bursting pressure—500 to 530 lbs. Average tensile strength of inner rubber tube—570 to 675 lbs. Average tensile strength of rubber cover—750 to 850 lbs. Average friction of the tube to fabric—14 to 18 lbs. Average friction between cover and braids of cotton fabric —14 to 18 lbs. Weight per 100 ft.—48 lbs. To be in 50'—0" lengths, including couplings.

MOP COTTONS: 16 oz. Industrial Special, 5" Band. Mop shall be subject to the following tests: *Absorption Test* — Sample shall be submerged in water at 70° temperature for five minutes, but not disturbed or worked in the water, then removed and allowed to drain for ten minutes and then weighed. The absorption at this time shall not be more than 65%. Tensile strength: Six strands taken from sample shall average not less than 48 pounds dry, or not less than 60 pounds wet.

Illustration No. 232—Purchasing Specifications

Unascertained goods are goods included in a lot of merchandise of the same general kind and are consequently not distinguishable until an actual selection has been made. When the specific goods have been selected, they are said to be ascertained.

For instance, Mr. A had agreed to sell Mr. B one hundred women's dresses at a specified price, the dresses to be selected by Mr. B from a display in Mr. A's exhibit rooms. Mr. B delayed the selection of the dresses, although he was urged to make his selection by Mr. A. In the meantime there was a fire in the exhibit rooms of Mr. A. The fire destroyed about four hundred of the two thousand dresses on display. Mr. A contended that Mr. B should pay the loss on the dresses that the latter had contracted to purchase. The contention was that the dresses had been available for Mr. B to make a selection and that, if he had made his selection on schedule, Mr. A would not have to bear the loss on those dresses. In this case, however, the title to the dresses had not passed to Mr. B because the goods had not been ascertained. Mr. B was therefore not responsible for any loss.

On the other hand, if Mr. B had selected his dresses and had agreed to call for them, the goods would have been ascertained and the title would have passed to Mr. B. In such a case the court would probably decide that Mr. B must be responsible for the loss of the dresses that he had purchased.

When goods are sold f.o.b. the shipping point, the buyer is required to pay the transportation charges, and the title ordinarily passes to the buyer at the time the shipment is turned over to the transportation company. If the goods have been sold on open account, the title does pass to the buyer at this time; but if they are sent C.O.D. or if they are to be turned over to the buyer when a draft is signed or when some other condition is fulfilled, the title does not pass to the buyer until that condition has been fulfilled. When goods are shipped f.o.b. destination, the seller pays the transportation charges. Under such a condition the title ordinarily passes to the buyer at the time the goods are delivered to the buyer by the transportation company; but, as in the preceding example, the title may not pass to the buyer until the goods have been paid for or some other condition has been fulfilled.

Place and Time of Delivery. When the place of delivery of goods is not specified, it may be the seller's place of business or it may be fixed by the custom of the trade. For instance, when products are to be delivered for sale through a commission house, the custom of the trade may require them to be delivered at a certain warehouse or placed on a railroad siding for examination. The place of delivery of steel shipped on barges may be the waterfront of the city to which the steel is being delivered.

If no time is set for delivery, the vendor must make delivery within a reasonable time.

Acceptance. The buyer is under a duty to accept and pay for the goods, provided delivery of them is made in accordance with the terms of the contract. The acceptance of the goods is indicated by (a) a specific indication that the buyer accepts the goods, (b) the use of the goods, or (c) the retention of the goods for an unreasonable length of time.

Unenforceable Agreements. In the absence of any disqualifying factors such as those indicated below, an exchange of assents constitutes an enforceable agreement, provided the assents are genuine. An agreement is not enforceable under any of the following circumstances:

1. If there is a mutual *mistake* as to the identity of the subject matter. For example, assume that Mr. French offers to sell Mr. Thomas a team of horses. Mr. French has two teams of horses of the same general color and description. He has reference to a particular team that he is willing to sell, but Mr. Thomas has the other team in mind when he accepts the offer. There is a mutual mistake as to the identity of the subject matter.

2. If fraud in the form of *misrepresentation* is present. Consider the following example: Mr. Allen intentionally misrepresents to Mr. Smith that he is acting as an agent for a certain producer of clothing. When the merchandise is delivered, Mr. Smith discovers that Mr. Allen is acting as the agent for an entirely different producer. Mr. Allen is guilty of fraudulent representation.

3. If one person makes an agreement as the result of a *threat* or an *act of violence*. For instance, Mr. A induces Mr. B to sign a contract for merchandise under a threat that Mr. B's daughter will be abducted if he does not sign the contract. This contract is not enforceable, for it has been obtained by means of a threat of violence.

4. If there has been *undue influence* to the extent that one person has not reached the agreement through the free exercise of his own judgment. For instance, consider the case of an aged woman who has inherited a small sum of money. She is besieged by several representatives of a furniture company who, after prolonged high-pressure selling, induce her to spend a large portion of her inheritance for furniture. Such a case probably represents undue influence.

Protection of the Seller. In case the buyer of merchandise fails to perform his part of the contract, the seller may sue for payment if the title has passed, sue for damages if the title has not passed, or rescind the contract. At any time the buyer and the seller may rescind the contract by mutual agreement, but the seller may rescind the contract if the buyer fails to perform his part of the contract. If the seller contemplates taking any legal action, he should, however, consult a lawyer.

Protection of the Buyer. In case the seller fails to perform his obligation, the buyer may recover the goods or the value of the goods if the title has passed. If the title has not passed, he may sue for damages or, if he chooses, rescind the contract. If he desires to do so, he may insist upon the fulfillment of the contract. Before any legal action is taken, the buyer should always consult a lawyer.

Voidable Contracts. A *voidable contract* is an agreement that may be enforceable but, because of the lack of an essential of contracts, may be made inoperative by one or both of the parties.

All contracts made by persons with unbalanced minds are voidable. A contract of this type may be rescinded by the guardian of the person with the unbalanced mind.

A minor (an individual who has not attained legal age) can void all his contracts except those for necessary things, such as food and clothing. Even in the case of necessaries, however, the minor is responsible for only a reasonable amount. The fundamental reason for permitting minors to rescind their contracts is that they need certain protection from unscrupulous persons.

Consider the following example: A youth of twenty bought an automobile. When he became of age, he returned the automobile and demanded his money. He was entitled to his money, for he had entered into the contract when he was a minor. As he disaffirmed the contract soon after he had reached his majority, he voided it. If he had failed to disaffirm the contract within a reasonable time after reaching his majority, he could not have avoided the contract.

Suppose the youth mentioned in the preceding example had agreed, while twenty years of age, to buy an automobile when he became twenty-one years of age. In this case the contract would not have been executed until after he became of age. He would therefore not have been liable unless he had ratified the contract after reaching his majority.

All contracts made with intoxicated persons are voidable. A contract made with such a person may be rescinded by that person when he becomes sober.

Bailments. Whenever one person has control over the personal property of another, the relationship is called a *bailment.* When this relationship exists, one party has possession of property for a definite purpose, and is to return the property or dispose of it in accordance with the agreement. For instance, anyone who borrows something from someone else is obligated to return it in good condition. If merchandise is sent to a businessman on consignment (to be left in his hands until it is sold or returned), this merchandise is not the property of the person to whom it has been entrusted. Until it is sold, it is considered to be the property of the one who sent it on consignment. When it is sold, payment should be made promptly according to the agreement.

Whenever a dry cleaner accepts a dress or a suit to be cleaned, a garage accepts a car for storage or repair, or a furniture storage plant accepts furniture for storage, a bailment exists. The bailee (the person accepting the goods) is responsible for due care in handling them. For instance, if a dry cleaner accepts a dress or a suit for cleaning by the normal process and does the work in a proper way, he is not responsible if the article is damaged. Sometimes special fabrics will not clean properly under ordinary methods. Hence a cleaner cannot be held responsible unless he is given some warning. A dry cleaner is responsible, however, for any damage that results from the lack of reasonable care.

Any businessman who is engaged in dealings that involve bailments should therefore study carefully his legal rights and responsibilities in the state in which he is located and should take steps to protect himself from any loss or lawsuits.

QUESTIONS FOR DISCUSSION

1. What is a contract?
2. What are the essentials of a contract?
3. If there is any dispute with regard to whether an offer has been accepted within a reasonable length of time, how may the matter be settled?
4. Why is it unnecessary to make many contracts in writing?
5. Name some types of contracts that, under various state laws, are required to be in writing.

6. Is one relieved from the responsibility of a contract if much of the printing on the contract is so small that it was difficult to read at the time the contract was signed?

7. Name the reasons why a written contract is desirable.

8. Besides the essentials of a contract previously mentioned in answer to Question 2, what information should be included in a contract?

9. What do you recommend as a wise practice when a contract that has been drawn is to be signed with the understanding that a supplementary agreement will be made later?

10. What is a bill of sale? What function does it serve?

11. What is meant by buying by inspection? What is the responsibility of the buyer in such a case?

12. If a person buys merchandise that is warranted to be of a certain quality or to be suitable for a certain purpose, what remedies are there in case the goods are not as they were warranted?

13. What are the evidences of the acceptance of goods that have been delivered?

14. Under what circumstances are agreements not enforceable?

15. What may the seller do if the buyer of merchandise fails to perform his part of the contract?

16. What may the buyer do to protect himself if the seller of merchandise fails to perform his part of the contract?

17. What is a voidable contract?

18. What is the nature of the bailment that exists when a drayage company accepts something for hauling, or a dry cleaner accepts something for cleaning?

PROBLEMS AND PROJECTS

1. Is this a contract?

> I agree to deliver to you on May 1 ten tons of coal at $7.60 a ton, payable on delivery.
> James A. Hoskins.

Give your reasons and explanations.

2. Mr. Anderson wrote Mr. Kelly on July 1, offering to sell the latter 500 tons of coal at $5 a ton. He added to his letter the instructions: "Telegraph me immediately if you accept this offer." On September 1 Mr. Kelly wrote that he accepted the offer to the extent of 300 tons. Mr. Anderson refused to fill the order, and Mr. Kelly brought a suit for a breach of contract. Do you think that Mr. Kelly was entitled to any damages for a breach of contract?

3. Mr. White agreed to construct an electric pump on the farm of Mr. Drake. The contract required Mr. White to furnish all the material, including the pipes. The contract also specified that the electric pump should be completed within a reasonable length of time and that it should furnish plenty of water for Mr. Drake's cattle. Mr. White worked only periodically on the construction. Mr. Drake complained several times. Finally, during the summer season, the dry weather caused a serious shortage of water. Because of urgency Mr. Drake notified Mr. White that he was canceling the contract. He then hired another person to construct immediately a pump that would furnish adequate water. Mr. White sued for damages, claiming that Mr. Drake had no right to break the contract. What is your opinion? Why?

4. Investigate the laws of your state with regard to the responsibility of the husband in paying debts incurred by his wife, and vice versa.

5. Obtain a copy of a chattel mortgage. Study it carefully, and list the legal responsibilities of the mortgagor and of the mortgagee.

6. Write a contract of employment between you and some employer for whom you would like to work. The contract should conform to the essentials of a contract outlined in this chapter and should contain the proper information.

7. The Atlantic Seed Company agreed to buy from Mr. J. L. Kramer certain alfalfa seed. The agreement stipulated that the seed was to be cleaned before delivery and payment of the price. The seed was not delivered, and the company brought an action for possession. Was this remedy the proper one?

8. The F. H. Bowen Company, a wholesale dealer, shipped several diamonds to Mr. A. E. Carter, of Des Moines, Iowa, to be sold for their common profit or to be returned. After receiving the stones, Mr. Carter placed them in a showcase, from which they were stolen, however, within the course of the next hour. Under what circumstances would Mr. Carter be liable for the loss?

CHAPTER XXIV

ETHICS: THE UNWRITTEN LAWS OF BUSINESS

Purpose of the Chapter. Business is not a game; but, like all other human activities, it must operate under a set of rules. Some of these rules are prescribed by law. Others are based upon unwritten moral codes, written codes, and agreements. The purpose of this chapter is to point out some of the desirable and the undesirable practices in conducting business. This chapter will seek the answers to many questions, some of which are as follows:

1. What is the moral code of business?
2. Is there any conflict between statutory laws and business ethics?
3. What are considered unfair trade practices?
4. What is the advantage of a code of fair practice?
5. What are some of the practices frowned upon in advertising and selling?

Standards of Businessmen. During times of business and social stress, there is always criticism of businessmen, such as merchants, bankers, brokers, and others. Most businessmen, like any other people, are honest, although occasionally dishonest businessmen can be found. Very few businessmen are deliberately dishonest. In many cases they may be misinformed or may commit an error because of lack of knowledge, but the standard of honesty among businessmen is similar to the standard among other people.

Honesty in Business. Many people wrongly believe that dishonesty may aid in getting ahead in business. For a short period of time dishonesty may pay, but in the long run such a policy leads to disaster. If any large number of people were dishonest, the entire business system would not work, for the whole organization of business is based upon the idea that people in general are honest. Most of the transactions of business, for example, are carried on through some form of credit. The extent to which the system succeeds or fails is determined by the extent to which people are honest or dishonest.

It is true that some businessmen are engaged in various kinds of doubtfully honest practices. Under all circumstances such businessmen should be avoided. One should be cautious in reaching a decision as to the dishonesty of another person; but whenever a negative decision has been reached, the safest practice is to find some honest person with whom to deal.

New Requirements in Business. It is probably true that, as business becomes more complicated and more competitive, businessmen will have to increase their training. The large fortunes made in the nineteenth century from monopolies of natural resources and from business enterprises developed during a period of rapidly growing population cannot be duplicated in this century or in future centuries. The businessman of this century must win in a competitive battle on the basis of training and ability in management.

The new type of businessman must learn to cut costs without reducing wages; he must learn to get the maximum output from workers without impairing their health; he must learn to deal with numerous governmental regulations and yet be able to maintain his own business on a profitable basis. Certainly the new type of businessman must be trained in finance, marketing, personnel problems, accounting, diplomacy, and other requisites of business. In the nineteenth century many businessmen made money by their wits. Today the businessman must make his gains by superior training and service.

Unfair Trade Practices. Illustration No. 233 shows some of the different types of complaints that are made in business. These complaints are based upon the unfair trade practices listed. Each unfair practice is certainly reprehensible. In most cases it is impossible to draw the line between unfair practices of a serious nature and those of a less serious nature. For instance, bribery is probably no

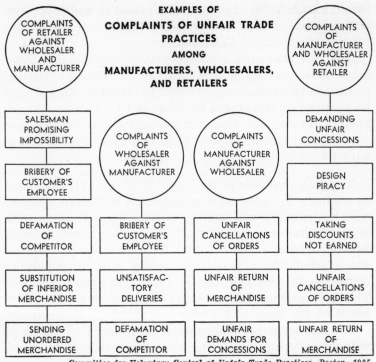

EXAMPLES OF
COMPLAINTS OF UNFAIR TRADE PRACTICES
AMONG
MANUFACTURERS, WHOLESALERS, AND RETAILERS

COMPLAINTS OF RETAILER AGAINST WHOLESALER AND MANUFACTURER

COMPLAINTS OF MANUFACTURER AND WHOLESALER AGAINST RETAILER

COMPLAINTS OF WHOLESALER AGAINST MANUFACTURER

COMPLAINTS OF MANUFACTURER AGAINST WHOLESALER

SALESMAN PROMISING IMPOSSIBILITY			DEMANDING UNFAIR CONCESSIONS
BRIBERY OF CUSTOMER'S EMPLOYEE			DESIGN PIRACY
DEFAMATION OF COMPETITOR	BRIBERY OF CUSTOMER'S EMPLOYEE	UNFAIR CANCELLATIONS OF ORDERS	TAKING DISCOUNTS NOT EARNED
SUBSTITUTION OF INFERIOR MERCHANDISE	UNSATISFACTORY DELIVERIES	UNFAIR RETURN OF MERCHANDISE	UNFAIR CANCELLATIONS OF ORDERS
SENDING UNORDERED MERCHANDISE	DEFAMATION OF COMPETITOR	UNFAIR DEMANDS FOR CONCESSIONS	UNFAIR RETURN OF MERCHANDISE

Committee for Voluntary Control of Unfair Trade Practices, Boston, 1935.

Illustration No. 233—Unfair Trade Practices in Business

worse than promising an impossibility. Each practice is certainly dishonest.

Codes of Fair Practice. During a long period in the history of American business, various associations and groups of businessmen have at times developed so-called codes of fair practice. Never, however, during any other stage in the development of American business were there so many codes as during the day of the old National Recovery Administration. Although the N.R.A. proved unconstitutional, a study of the codes developed at that time is significant. Such a study tends to illustrate what all businessmen consider to be unfair trade practices. For instance, nearly all industries consider secret allowances and inaccurate advertising to be unfair trade practices.

Illustration No. 234 shows a partial summary of thirty-six different codes written under the N.R.A.

Codes of Ethics. Many stores, associations, and other organizations develop so-called codes of ethics to which their employees or their members are pledged. For example, Rotary International, Kiwanis International, Lions International, and many other civic and professional groups have codes of ethics. Many department stores attempt to train their employees to live up to codes of ethics in dealing with the public and in dealing with other employees. An example of a code of ethics is shown in Illustration No. 235.

Ethics in Advertising. For many years there has been considerable criticism of all forms of advertising. Individuals have criticized advertising because of its dishonesty and, in some cases, its indecency. The Federal Communications Commission has been quite instrumental in controlling radio advertising, but until recent years not much has been done with regard to the ethics of other forms of advertising. Some publishers of magazines and newspapers have attempted to promote honesty and decency in advertising. The National Vigilance Committee, the National Better Business Bureau, the Association of National Advertisers, and the American Association of Advertising Agencies have also been instrumental in placing advertising on a better plane.

The Association of National Advertisers and the American Association of Advertising Agencies have established the following as criteria of unfair and unethical advertising:

1. False statements or misleading exaggerations.
2. Indirect misrepresentation of a product or a service through the distortion of details, either editorially or pictorially.
3. Statements or suggestions offensive to public decency.
4. Statements that tend to undermine an industry by attributing to its products, generally, faults and weaknesses true only of a few.

Provisions in Codes	Number of Industries Including Provision (total 36)
ADVERTISING, inaccurate; unfair	18
ALLOWANCES, secret; limits and prohibitions, goods, services, deals, etc.	25
BIDS AND BIDDING; limits and restrictions	3
BILLINGS; uniform; prescribed	2
COMMISSIONS AND FEES; restrictions	8
CONSIGNMENT shipping; restrictions	10
CONTAINERS; inviolacy guaranteed	1
CONTRACTS; to promote breach of; unfair	16
CREDIT, CREDITS; restrictions	6
DEMONSTRATORS; restrictions on use of	2
DESIGN PIRACY; controls	6
DISCOUNTS; restrictions	13
DISCRIMINATION; restrictions	6
DISPARAGEMENT; of competitor or goods; unfair	12
DISSENSION; to foment; unfair	1
ENTICING EMPLOYEES; unfair	7
EQUIPMENT sales and loans to marketers; limits	1
FREIGHT RATES, basing points, prepayment, etc.; restrictions	8
FINANCING RATES; controls	1
GAMES OF CHANCE; restrictions on use of	3
HANDLERS, kind of; defined	1
INACCURATE RECORDS; forbidden	1
LOSS LEADERS; criticized or restricted	5
MARKET CHANGES, guarantees against; forbidden	6
MARKUP, minimum; specified	4
MISREPRESENTATION of analysis, goods, specifications; barred	19
PREMIUMS, use of; limited	10
PRICE (a) cutting, opposed or controlled	17
(b) sales at less than cost, catalogue, or minimum prices; limited	15
(c) quantity price restrictions	6
(d) pooled orders, soliciting barred	1
QUANTITY STANDARDS; set, controlled, policed, or recommended	9
QUOTATIONS; duration of validity	2
REIMBURSEMENT for usual expenditures; barred	1
REPAIRS by suppliers to property of retailers or consumers; barred.	1
ROLLING STORES; barred	1
SALES TERMS (a) must be equal to all	9
(b) uniform terms are or may be prescribed	13
(c) claim of underselling forbidden	3
(d) part shipments at quantity price; barred or limited	1
SERVICES; limits on services which may be rendered	14
STYLE SHOWS; financial contributions or fees barred	1
SUBSTITUTION; limited	7
TERRITORY; inviolacy of	0
TRADE-MARKS; limits on unauthorized use of	14
TRADE SECRETS; unfair to procure	8
THREATS AND INTIMIDATION; unfair	4
UNIFORM hours of operation may be set	4
WEIGHTS, shipping; control of	2

Illustration No. 234—A Summary of Thirty-Six Codes

THE ROTARY CODE OF ETHICS
FOR BUSINESSMEN

FIRST: To consider my vocation worthy, and as affording me distinct opportunity to serve society.

SECOND: To improve myself, increase my efficiency and enlarge my service, and by so doing attest my faith in the fundamental principle of Rotary, that he profits most who serves best.

THIRD: To realize that I am a businessman and ambitious to succeed; but that I am first an ethical man, and wish no success that is not founded on the highest justice and morality.

FOURTH: To hold that the exchange of my goods, my service and my ideas for profit is legitimate and ethical, provided that all parties in the exchange are benefited thereby.

FIFTH: To use my best endeavors to elevate the standards of the vocation in which I am engaged, and so to conduct my affairs that others. in my vocation may find it wise, profitable and conducive to happiness to emulate my example.

SIXTH: To conduct my business in such a manner that I may give a perfect service equal to or even better than my competitor, and when in doubt to give added service beyond the strict measure of debt or obligation.

SEVENTH: To understand that one of the greatest assets of a professional or of a businessman is his friends, and that any advantage gained by reason of friendship is eminently ethical and proper.

EIGHTH: To hold that true friends demand nothing of one another and that any abuse of the confidences of friendship for profit is foreign to the spirit of Rotary, and in violation of its Code of Ethics.

NINTH: To consider no personal success legitimate or ethical which is secured by taking unfair advantage of certain opportunities in the social order that are absolutely denied others, nor will I take advantage of opportunities to achieve material success that others will not take because of the questionable morality involved.

TENTH: To be not more obligated to a Brother Rotarian than I am to every other man in human society; because the genius of Rotary is not in its competition, but in its co-operation; for provincialism can never have a place in an institution like Rotary, and Rotarians assert that Human Rights are not confined to Rotary Clubs, but are as deep and as broad as the race itself; and for these high purposes does Rotary exist to educate all men and all institutions.

ELEVENTH: Finally, believing in the universality of the Golden Rule, *all things whatsoever ye would that men should do unto you, do ye even so unto them,* we contend that Society best holds together when equal opportunity is accorded all men in the natural resources of this planet.

Illustration No. 235—The Rotary Code of Ethics

5. Price claims that are misleading.
6. Pseudo-scientific advertising, including claims that are insufficiently supported by accepted authority or that distort the true meaning or application of a statement made by professional or scientific authority.
7. Testimonials that do not reflect the real choice of a competent witness.

National Better Business Bureau. The National Better Business Bureau, in co-operation with the better business bureaus in numerous cities, has made a great contribution in promoting higher standards of business practice. The local better business bureaus attempt to check carefully all soliciting schemes, advertising, and other forms in which unfair trade practices might be used. The purpose of these bureaus is to protect not only honest businessmen from dishonest businessmen, but also consumers from dishonest business practices.

The National Better Business Bureau emphasizes the following business policies:

1. We believe in truth, the cornerstone of all honorable and successful business.
2. We believe there should be no double standard of morality involving buyer and seller.

At bridge parties, at dinner tables, in restaurants, and aboard trains, one hears the consumer's estimate of the businessman's printed, displayed, or broadcast sales message. Sometimes the comments of consumers are flattering, but often they are not. One cannot help noticing in these comments that the consumer has a great deal of respect for honesty in advertising. The so-called consumer movement in recent years has been another factor that has forced some businessmen to practice honesty in advertising. Advertising is definitely being improved.

Fair Trade Code. The National Better Business Bureau has issued an interesting booklet entitled *A Guide for Retail Advertising and Selling*. This book is essentially

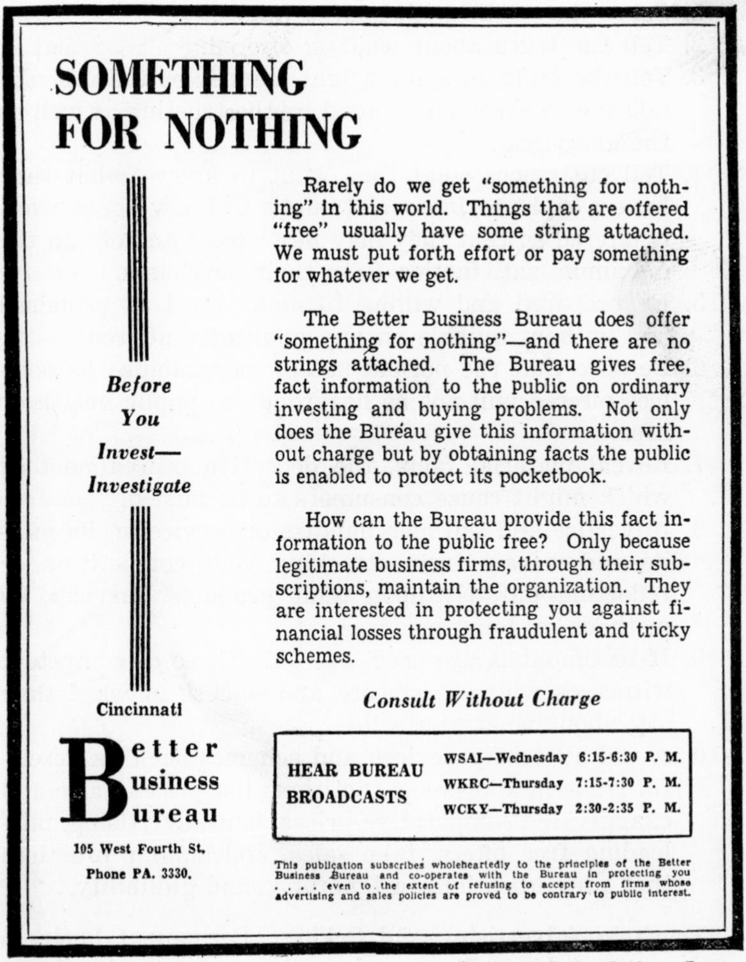

Cincinnati Better Business Bureau.
Illustration No. 236—An Advertisement of a Better Business Bureau

devoted to the ethics of advertising and selling. It is a useful guide for winning and holding the confidence of the public. The introduction of that booklet contains a "Fair Trade Code for Advertising and Selling," which has been adopted by the National Association of Better Business Bureaus, Inc. This code is as follows:

1. Serve the public with honest values.
2. Tell the truth about what is offered.
3. Tell the truth in a forthright manner so that its significance may be understood by the trusting as well as the analytical.
4. Tell customers what they want to know—what they have a right to know and ought to know about what is offered so that they may buy wisely and obtain the maximum satisfaction from their purchases.
5. Be prepared and willing to make good as promised and without quibble on any guarantee offered.
6. Be sure that the normal use of merchandise or services offered will not be hazardous to public health or life.
7. Reveal material facts, the deceptive concealment of which might cause consumers to be misled.
8. Advertise and sell merchandise or service on *its* merits and refrain from attacking your competitors or reflecting unfairly upon their products, services, or methods of doing business.
9. If testimonials are used, use only those of competent witnesses who are sincere and honest in what they say about what you sell.
10. Avoid all tricky devices and schemes such as deceitful trade-in allowances, fictitious list prices, false and exaggerated comparative prices, bait advertising, misleading free offers, fake sales, and similar practices that prey upon human ignorance and gullibility.

Truth in Advertising and Selling. Permanent business success must be built upon honesty, understanding, and fair practices. A businessman may be tempted occasionally to exaggerate or may be tempted to imitate some other competitor who seems to be stretching the truth. In the long run it does not pay, however, to break the confidence of customers.

The National Better Business Bureau has established standards to be followed in selling and advertising. Particular attention is given to misleading statements. The following paragraphs give some examples of misleading terms and statements that should not be used in selling and advertising:

Terms of purchase. Statements such as "Pay as You Please" and "Your Own Terms" are usually inaccurate, as the customer is seldom permitted to name his own terms. Credit terms should be stated explicitly.

Sales. The public construes the term "sale" to mean an offering of merchandise at a price concession.

Special sales. Special sales or offerings should fulfill the accepted meaning of the word "special," namely, "out of the ordinary practices."

Time limits on sales. Time limited sales should be rigidly observed. All offers to purchase under the terms of a time limited sale, received after the expiration of the period, should be refused. "One-Day Sale" means that merchandise either is taken off sale or reverts to a higher price on the day following the sale.

Going out of business. Such terms as "Going Out of Business," "Selling Out," and "Closing Out Sale" should not be used unless the concern so advertising is actually going out of business.

Reliability of guarantee. A guarantee is only as good as the concern that makes it. When merchandise or service is "guaranteed," the consumer has a right to expect that the terms of the guarantee will be fulfilled by the guarantor. Accordingly, a guarantee should not be made on merchandise or service unless the guarantor is in a position to fulfill the guarantee in case he is called upon to do so. In their advertising, retailers should not use statements regarding a manufacturer's guarantee unless the manufacturer is known to be in a position to carry out his guarantee; nor should retailers refer to their merchandise merely as "Guaranteed" unless they are willing to make good if they are called upon to do so.

Free offers. The common meaning of the word "free" is "without cost or obligation," or "gratuitous," that is, given without recompense or payment. The word "free" may therefore have the capacity to mislead when used in any other sense.

Derogatory statements. Statements derogatory to the price, the merchandise, or the service of competitors should not be made. Such statements not only are unethical and unfair but also destroy public confidence in advertising.

Low rent and similar statements. Low rent alone does not make low prices, and such a claim should not be used. Low rent with a low volume of sales may mean higher prices than high rent with a huge volume of sales. Likewise, the claim that a merchant's prices are lower because all his business is done on a cash basis or because he has no advertising expense is not reliable. In determining the effect of any item on prices, one must give consideration to the relation between that item and the volume of sales. For example, an expensive delivery system might overcome all the advantages of doing a cash business.

Satisfaction guaranteed. When such claims as "satisfaction or your money back" are made, the customer should be the judge of whether or not he is satisfied, and such guarantees should be honored at once. If a guarantee covers a certain amount of time, the amount of time should be specified definitely.

Tendency of Federal Control. Sometimes the dishonest and unethical practices of a few businessmen are the cause of new Federal and state regulations of business. State and Federal control of business relations has been increasing steadily. Many of the new laws force all businessmen to do what they ordinarily should do voluntarily. Chapter XXII points out some of these governmental regulations of business. For instance, the Federal Trade Commission now has control over all unfair trade practices, including unethical advertising, when such activities cross state boundaries. As explained in Chapter XXII, there are also various forms of state legislation that control trade practices within states.

QUESTIONS FOR DISCUSSION

1. Are there more or fewer dishonest people in business than in other occupations?

2. Why is the use of credit in business one evidence of the honesty of businessmen?

3. Why do the new requirements in business make ethics much more vitally important than they were in the past?

4. Name some complaints of unfair trade practices that retailers make against wholesalers and manufacturers.

5. In your opinion what reasons may be given for the fact that manufacturers complain that wholesalers sometimes make unfair demands for concessions?

6. Under the Robinson-Patman Act the customer who accepts a concession is just as guilty as the person who gives the concession. What do you think of the fairness of this part of the law?

7. Is a person permitted to copy a copyrighted textbook and mimeograph and reproduce the material for use in classroom instructional purposes? What do you think of the ethics of this practice?

8. One of the great evils in the retail trade is the returning of merchandise by customers who have no legitimate reason for doing so. Explain this statement.

9. When a 2 per cent discount is granted for the payment of cash in ten days, some businessmen deduct the discount even though they pay their invoices twenty or thirty days after the purchases were made. What do you think of such a practice?

10. Do you think that the codes of ethics of various groups are of any value?

11. What function is served by the code of ethics of a store or any other business organization?

12. What function do you believe may be served by the standards established by the Association of National Advertisers and the American Association of Advertising Agencies?

13. In general, what are the functions and standards of the better business bureaus?

14. What limitation does the National Better Business Bureau place on the use of the term "Going Out of Business"?

15. Why does the National Better Business Bureau condemn the use of the statement "Pay as You Please"?

16. To what extent does the Federal Government have control over unfair trade practices?

PROBLEMS AND PROJECTS

1. Prepare a code of ethics that could be posted as guiding principles for those operating and those dealing with a school book store.

2. Write a theme on "Good Business Ethics Are Better Than Laws Governing Business" or on "Business Laws Are Necessary Because of a Lack of Good Business Ethics."

3. Obtain from a newspaper an advertisement and check it with the criteria of unfair and unethical advertising established by the Association of National Advertisers and the American Association of Advertising Agencies. (See pages 583 and 586 for these criteria.)

4. Obtain from a magazine an advertisement and check it with the criteria of unfair and unethical advertising established by the Association of National Advertisers and the American Association of Advertising Agencies.

5. Go through one particular issue of a local newspaper, and check all the advertisements to see which ones violate the standards of the National Better Business Bureau with regard to the following: (a) terms of purchase, (b) sales, (c) special sales, (d) time limits on sales, (e) going out of business, (f) guarantees, (g) derogatory statements.

6. From your local better business bureau obtain an example of some recent work done in the community to prevent unfair trade practices.

7. Obtain from a local newspaper the code of advertising of that newspaper, and check it with the advertisements to see whether they measure up to the standards of the code.

CHAPTER XXV

GROWTH AND EXPANSION PROBLEMS

Purpose of the Chapter. Chapter XXI includes a study of banking and financial problems. This chapter deals with the financial problems that have to do with expanding a business. Obtaining the money that is needed to start a business is one problem, but obtaining money to expand a business presents some additional problems. The following are some important questions that will be answered in this chapter:

1. Why is it desirable to build up a cash surplus?
2. At what time during the business cycle is it most opportune to expand?
3. How should one estimate the advisability of expanding?
4. What are the important sources of money for use in expansion?
5. By what methods can the securities of a corporation be marketed?

Profits and Surplus. Unforeseen happenings make it necessary for the manager of a business to build up a surplus to take care of them. If the business makes a profit, the owner should not take out all the profit in the form of cash or other assets, but should attempt to leave sufficient cash for the following:

1. Replacements needed as the result of depreciation
2. Replacements needed as the result of obsolescence
3. Additions that are necessary for expansion
4. Financial protection during periods of low sales
5. Purchases of goods at times when bargains can be obtained

Even if a business is not making a profit, but is just breaking even, it should make provision for replacing the assets that decrease in value because of depreciation or

593

obsolescence. For instance, a bus company may start operations with new busses. The business may not make a profit, but there may be considerable cash available each month. If the owners of the business take out all the available cash, there will not be any funds with which to buy new busses when the present ones are worn out.

Maintaining the credit of a business is important because good credit frequently determines success. Furthermore, most businessmen have to borrow money. The business manager who is wise will conduct his affairs so that banks will be willing to lend him money when he needs it. If a banker finds, however, that the manager is taking all the profits out of the business and is not leaving a safe margin for emergencies, he will probably be skeptical about lending money to the business.

When to Expand. Any businessman who is contemplating expanding his business should consider carefully general economic and business conditions. Business conditions are judged by the so-called business cycle, or economic cycle, which is presented in the chart in Illustration No. 237. It is always possible that a few businessmen may be making a profit while business conditions in general are bad. Generally speaking, however, it is undesirable to start a new business during periods of decline or depression.

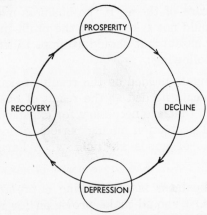

Illustration No. 237—The Business Cycle

The table in Illustration No. 238 presents an analysis of the various phases of the business cycle. During times of prosperity there are liable to be overproduction and too much expansion. These are some of the factors that cause a decline. The cautious businessman will therefore watch

PROSPERITY	DECLINE	DEPRESSION	RECOVERY
1. Labor is fully employed.	1. Profits decline.	1. Volume of business is low.	1. There is an accumulated shortage of goods.
2. Wages are high.	2. Goods are forced onto the market.	2. Buying is only for immediate requirements.	2. Most debts are paid.
3. Costs of operation increase.	3. Prices are reduced.	3. Wages are low.	3. Outlook is favorable.
4. Selling prices increase.	4. Buying is reduced.	4. Production is efficient.	4. Sales increase.
5. Stocks of goods are large.	5. Volume of business decreases.	5. Prices are low.	5. Construction increases.
6. Construction begins to decrease.	6. Unemployment results.	6. Costs of operation are low.	6. Borrowing begins.
7. Creditors begin to demand payment.	7. Businesses cease to expand.	7. Costs of construction are low.	7. Prices begin to rise.
	8. Businesses quit borrowing.	8. Stocks of goods are small.	8. Buying begins in anticipation of rising prices.
	9. Prices decline.	9. Shortage of goods develops.	9. People go back to work.
	10. Debtors press for payment.	10. Interest rates are low.	10. Business begins to operate at a profit.
	11. Failures increase.	11. Demand for loans is small.	

Illustration No. 238—An Analysis of the Business Cycle

out for such signs and will avoid overexpansion during times of prosperity. If he overexpands at that time, he may suffer a serious loss during the decline and the depression.

It is obvious that, if a businessman can definitely predict the phase of the cycle, he will know when to start a business, when to purchase generously, when to expand, or when to contract his business. For instance, the best time to start a business is when recovery starts, but it is usually difficult to determine exactly when recovery is in the process. If one waits until the peak of prosperity, he may start the business just before a serious decline. He may enjoy prosperity for a short time and then suffer a severe loss when the decline begins.

The reason it is difficult to determine the existing phase of the cycle is that there are always temporary fluctuations. For instance, in any particular month there may be a spurt in business, when prices may rise and people may go back to work; but soon conditions may grow worse. Long-time trends are those that determine the cycle.

Too Much Optimism. There is a general feeling among businessmen that small businesses of certain types may remain successful while they are small, but they will cease to be successful if they are expanded to any great extent. When a restaurant owner, for instance, discovers that he has more customers than he can accommodate and then enlarges his restaurant, he may find, to his dismay, that he cannot obtain enough new customers to fill his enlarged restaurant. This experience has been true in a great many instances although it is not universally true. Such a situation emphasizes the care that is needed to avoid too much optimism. The fact that one's business has increased steadily is no reason to believe that it will always continue to increase. Furthermore, there are certain factors to be considered in determining whether expansion is wise.

Guiding Factors in Expansion. When one is considering an expansion program, he should consider the following question: Although a substantial profit has been made on the present basis, what proof is there that profit will be made on the new basis? It is therefore advisable to make an estimated profit and loss statement showing the possible results after expansion. This statement should include the increased overhead, the debts that may be incurred, the repayment of any loan, the additional working capital that will be needed, and the distribution of profits to new stockholders in the case of a corporation.

Suppose that Mr. H. J. Brooks, whose financial statements are shown in Illustrations Nos. 188 and 189 of Chapter XIX, desires to expand his business by opening a new store. He uses his latest financial statements as a basis for making estimates of the possible profits for the next six months and of the possible additional capital requirements.

He estimates the additional capital requirements as follows:

Additional cash or working capital.........	$ 500.00
Additional investment in merchandise......	2,000.00
Additional investment in supplies..........	25.50
Additional investment in insurance.........	31.00
Additional investment in equipment........	365.00
Total..............................	$2,921.50

He decides that, in order to maintain as great a proportion as possible of the ownership of the business, he will borrow $1,500 at 5 per cent interest. He will then permit a friend of his to invest $1,421.50 in the enterprise, thus changing the business to a partnership. The agreement will be that the partners are to share the profits and the losses in proportion to their investments in the business. If the partnership begins operations on January 1 under the foregoing conditions, the capital invested by each partner will be:

H. J. Brooks	$3,638.50
P. O. Marsh	1,421.50
Total capital	$5,060.00

On the basis of the latest statement of profit and loss of Mr. Brooks's business, the statement in Illustration No. 239 is prepared to show the estimated earnings of the partnership at the end of the following June.

The estimated net profit of $894.72 must be divided proportionately between the two owners of the business. The following is the division of the estimated profit:

	CAPITAL	NET PROFIT
H. J. Brooks	$3,638.50	$643.37
P. O. Marsh	1,421.50	251.35
Totals	$5,060.00	$894.72

It is evident, therefore, that Mr. Brooks will not earn so much profit under the new arrangement as he did under the old. Of course, as the business progresses and expands, he may eventually earn more; but that possibility is one of the chances taken in expanding a business. At any rate, if he expands his business, he will have to sacrifice some earnings at least temporarily. Furthermore, out of the earnings of the business, the two owners must repay the borrowed money.

H. J. BROOKS AND P. O. MARSH
ESTIMATED STATEMENT OF PROFIT AND LOSS FOR SIX MONTHS ENDING JUNE 30, 194–

Income from Sales:				
Sales			39,900	00
Cost of Merchandise Sold:				
Mdse. Inventory, December 31	3,495	35		
Purchases	33,004	73		
Total Cost of Mdse. Available for Sale......	36,500	08		
Less Mdse. Inventory, June 30	5,560	30		
Cost of Merchandise Sold			30,939	78
Gross Profit on Sales			8,960	22
Operating Expenses:				
Salaries and Wages	4,360	00		
Advertising	532	00		
Donations	25	00		
Supplies Used	125	00		
Miscellaneous Office Expense	54	00		
Telephone and Telegraph Service	60	00		
Delivery Expense	460	00		
Taxes and Insurance	260	00		
Rent	1,000	00		
Heat, Light, Water	247	00		
Loss from Bad Debts	420	00		
Interest Paid	47	50		
Repairs and Depreciation	250	00		
Other Expense	225	00		
Total Operating Expenses			8,065	50
Net Profit			894	72

Illustration No. 239—An Estimated Profit and Loss Statement

The preceding discussion emphasizes the fact that the money for use in expanding a business must be borrowed from some source or obtained from new owners. If it is borrowed, interest must be paid on it. If it is obtained from new owners, such as partners or stockholders, these owners must share in the profits of the business. Naturally all the regular expenses will increase.

The discussion that follows will give more information on the various ways of obtaining money for expansion.

Sources of Capital. There are two types of capital needed by a business. One is referred to as *working capital,* and the other is referred to as *fixed capital.* Working capital is the cash needed for the regular operations of the business, as in purchasing merchandise and paying wages.

Fixed capital is the cash needed to buy equipment and a building and land.

The following are the generally recognized sources of capital for a business:

1. From the owners of the business, by selling new stock to the owners if the business is a corporation or by selling new shares in the partnership if the business is that type of organization. If the business is a single proprietorship, additional money is put into it by the individual owner.

2. From long-term creditors, who may be individuals, banks, investment companies, or insurance companies. A corporation may issue bonds that are purchased by such long-term creditors. Money may be borrowed, and a mortgage issued on assets or income of the corporation. Long-term notes, which are essentially bonds, may be issued to creditors.

3. From short-term creditors, who usually are individuals or banks that lend money on notes. Short-term credit, which is called commercial credit, is ordinarily considered to be from thirty to ninety days. Such credit is obtained largely to provide working capital. It is not safe to finance the purchase of fixed assets through such credit.

4. By reinvesting profits. This plan applies to any form of business.

Capital from the Owners of the Business. The individual proprietor of a business can sell some of his personal assets, borrow from an individual, mortgage his personal property, or obtain an ordinary commercial loan to finance his business. The members of a partnership may provide additional capital by investing money in the business, or new partners may be taken into the partnership upon the investment of cash or other assets. When a corporation wishes to expand, it may sell additional stock to its stockholders or to other persons. The corporation may also issue bonds or long-term notes as a means of borrowing money to finance the expansion of the business. The various procedures in bor-

rowing are described in Chapter XXI. A discussion of
stocks has been presented in Chapter III.

Long-Term Credit. Long-term credit is usually obtained
by issuing bonds, long-term notes, or mortgages. When
bonds are issued by a corporation, the corporation usually
pledges some security to the bondholders. This security is
either some specific property or a right to certain earnings.
In other words, the corporation tells the bondholders that,
if the interest on the bonds or the principal is not paid
according to the agreement, the owners of the bond can
take over the property or collect certain earnings that
have been pledged. When certain property is pledged as
the security, the bonds are called *mortgage bonds*. When
particular earnings are pledged, the bonds are called *debenture bonds*.

A long-term note has some of the aspects of a mortgage,
but it does not extend for such a long time. In other words,
money is borrowed from a bank or some other institution
and a note for sixty or ninety days or a longer period is
given.

Obtaining money by issuing a mortgage represents
merely borrowing money and pledging property as security
in case the principal or the interest on the debt is not repaid. A more complete discussion of bonds has been given
in Chapter III.

It can be seen from the preceding discussion that a sole
proprietorship cannot issue bonds and obtain the usual
long-term credit that is thus available to corporations. The
sole proprietor can obtain ordinary short-term credit from
a bank; but in order to obtain long-term credit, he must
usually mortgage his personal property or the property of
the business, or pledge some other security for the loan.

Short-Term Credit. Short-term credit is the kind of credit
ordinarily used in obtaining working capital or funds for
operating expenses. Banks are the most common source
of short-term credit. Banking procedures are explained in
Chapter XXI.

Reinvesting Earnings. Reinvesting earnings in the business is probably the most conservative means of expanding a business. Some business operators make the mistake of bleeding the business by taking out so much of the profits that there is nothing left to take care of expansion. If the owners of a business let the earnings accumulate, there will be money available for expansion without the necessity of borrowing from other sources or selling shares in the ownership.

Instead of following a policy of reinvesting earnings in the business, some business owners sell additional stock or sell shares in their partnership and thus lose sight of the fact that they are actually decreasing the income from their investments. For instance, let us assume that there are three stockholders who together have $50,000 invested in a corporation. The yearly earnings on this investment have averaged $5,000. These three stockholders decide to expand the business by selling $50,000 of additional stock to other persons. The additional investment will enable the business to make $8,000 a year, but this income must be divided among all the stockholders. As there is $100,000 of stock outstanding, the original stockholders will get $4,000 of the income instead of the usual $5,000. The expansion program will therefore cause a decrease in the income of the original stockholders.

Factors in Acquiring Capital. Two important factors should be considered in ascertaining the cost of capital: (a) the original cost of procuring the capital and (b) the interest rate. The original cost of obtaining capital from bondholders, holders of long-term notes, and stockholders is usually larger than the original cost of obtaining it from mortgageholders or short-term creditors. Considerable preliminary investigation usually has to be carried on before bonds and stocks can be sold, and considerable expense is usually incurred in doing this. Further and larger expenses are usually necessary in reaching prospective buyers. Investment banking firms that specialize in the sale of bonds and stocks will usually not sell an issue of securities of less than $500,000 in amount. They contend that the minimum expense which must be incurred on any issue is so large that a profit cannot be made on a small issue. A business that desires to obtain capital of less than $500,000 in amount will usually resort to short-term borrowing or to using a mortgage, unless it is prepared to market its own securities. This procedure, however, is usually costly. A business may, of course, have a market that it can reach with little expense. For example, the present stockholders of a corporation may be willing to purchase additional stock. They may also be willing to purchase bonds issued by the corporation. Employees may be ready purchasers of the securities of the company for which they work. Customers may be potential purchasers. Most businesses, however, have to follow the costly procedure of appealing to the public.

Interest rates vary from month to month and from year to year. A business needing money when interest rates are high may issue short-term obligations with the expectation that interest rates will be lower at the time these obligations mature. If this expectation is realized, long-term obligations may then be issued at a lower interest rate to obtain funds with which to pay the short-term obligations. By this means the high interest rate is paid for only a short period of time; whereas, if the long-term obligations had been issued originally, the high interest rate would have been paid during the whole period of their life. In following this plan, however, a business is exposing itself to the possible difficulty of procuring funds when the short-term obligations fall due.

A final factor that must be considered in deciding the source from which capital should be obtained is the authority exercised by the various contributors of capital. If short-term creditors contribute capital, they usually have no control over the affairs of the business. If the obligations are not paid, the creditors may bring a legal action to recover the amount due them; but otherwise the owners of the business are in no way restricted in their conduct of the business. If capital is obtained by the use of bonds or mortgages, the holders of these usually have a lien on at least part of the assets of the company. This lien may impose restrictions on the use of these assets, and the agreement under which the bonds or the mortgages were issued may impose restrictions on the use of the income of the company. Other restrictions may also be imposed. If new stockholders or new partners contribute capital, they thereby gain a voice in the management of the business. The original owners may not desire to relinquish any of their authority to outsiders. It is possible in most states to issue stock that does not have voting rights, but such stock may be hard to sell. Of course, if the old stockholders or partners provide the additional funds, the control of the company is not affected, provided they contribute in the proportion of their past holdings.

Marketing of Securities. After the amount of capital needed has been determined and the source of it has been selected, the next problem is to make the contract by which the capital is to be obtained. The procurement of funds from short-term creditors is usually a simple procedure. Either purchases are made from merchandise creditors, or money is borrowed from a bank or through a note broker. The procurement of funds by means of a mortgage is also a relatively simple procedure. When bonds, stocks, or long-term notes are offered to the public, however, the procedure becomes more complex. There are two methods by which these securities may be sold: (a) directly to investors or (b) through investment banking channels.

It may be desirable to appeal directly to investors in the following cases:

1. When the securities offered for sale are of a highly speculative nature because of the type of operations of the company. Mining companies frequently resort to this plan. The ethics of selling such securities is, to say the least, questionable.

2. When securities are issued by a new company that has been organized by men who have little or no standing in the financial world.

3. When small issues are made. In such cases bankers will either refuse the issue or charge an exorbitant amount for its sale.

4. When a company desires to obtain the influence as well as the investments of certain classes. For example, a business may sell its securities directly to employees with the hope of enlisting their goodwill. Again, it may sell to its customers with the hope of increasing their goodwill and patronage.

5. When the concern has a national reputation for financial success and the fair treatment of investors, and consequently has a market for the securities that already exist.

6. When the concern desires and can afford to create an investment clientele for future financing. This situation may exist if a company issues large quantities of securities periodically and has a national reputation for financial strength. The American Telephone and Telegraph Company follows this plan.

Control of the Income. The work of financial administration does not cease when the amount of capital needed has been determined and obtained and its expenditure has been efficiently controlled. The profits resulting from this investment must be correctly determined and wisely used. The correct determination of profits involves questions that are beyond the scope of this discussion. Briefly, it requires the application of conservative principles of accounting and administration to the end that profits will not be anticipated, but that all probable losses will be provided for.

The wise use of profits necessitates:

1. The setting up of proper reserves to provide for anticipated losses and to take care of decreases in the value of assets due to their use in operating the business.

2. The adoption of a conservative dividend policy so that funds which may be needed in the operation of the business will not be paid to stockholders as dividends.

3. The profitable investment of surplus so that the profits retained in the business will be made to earn the
maximum amount for the benefit of the stockholders.

Expansion through Branches. Many companies choose
to expand by establishing branches. A chain-store organization is essentially a group of branches. An organization
may also have one central office or plant and establish
offices or branches in other cities in order to render service
more effectively and thereby to increase its sales. For
instance, some companies have a central location for manufacturing. From this location various sales offices and
warehouses in other cities are supplied. These in turn
supply the customers.

Horizontal and Vertical Expansion. There are two types
of expansion that are common in business. One is known
as *horizontal expansion,* and the other as *vertical expansion.*

The typical chain-store organization represents horizontal expansion because it involves spreading out similar
units of the business. Another kind of horizontal expansion is found in the business of a manufacturer of washing
machines who acquires a plant for the manufacture of electric sweepers and another plant for the manufacture of
electric stoves. The chart in Illustration No. 240 shows an
example of horizontal expansion.

Any type of business may expand vertically. Vertical
expansion involves acquiring control over various stages
in the process of distribution. For example, a manufacturer of paper might obtain control over the source of
power, the source of paper pulp, and the source of chemicals. He might go one step farther and obtain control
over wholesale distributing branches and possibly printing
plants or publishers that consume the finished paper. A
wholesale grocer who owns some canning factories and
acquires some retail outlets is engaging in vertical expansion. The Ford Motor Company is a good example of vertical expansion, for that company controls mines, railroads,
ships, finance companies, lumber mills, forests, and various

other sources of supply from which are obtained the materials needed in the manufacture of the one product of the company.

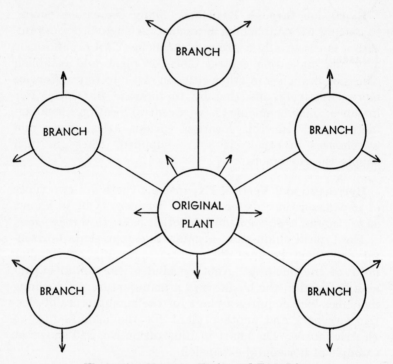

Illustration No. 240—Horizontal Expansion

There are various degrees to which a business may expand vertically. The ultimate goal of vertical expansion would be the owning and operating of all units of an organization through all steps of production and distribution until the goods reach the consumer. The chart in Illustration No. 241 illustrates the principle of vertical expansion. Some businesses not only expand horizontally, but also expand vertically. Whenever businesses expand to the extent that they have many units and cover wide areas, the problems of management become very complicated.

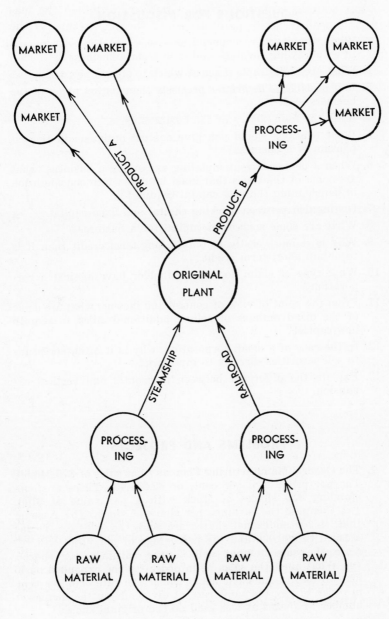

Illustration No. 241—Vertical Expansion

QUESTIONS FOR DISCUSSION

1. What would you recommend as a wise practice with regard to withdrawing earnings and cash from a business?
2. What are undesirable times at which to start a new business?
3. Is it possible to determine precisely the existing phase of the business cycle?
4. State the four phases of the business cycle.
5. What cautions would you give against optimism in the expansion of a business?
6. When a person is contemplating expanding a business, what are some of the items that must be taken into consideration in determining the new capital required?
7. Distinguish between working capital and fixed capital.
8. What are some sources of capital for a business?
9. Why is it more costly to obtain long-term credit than it is to obtain short-term credit?
10. What type of claim does a bondholder have against a corporation?
11. From the point of view of control and income, what are some of the disadvantages of selling additional stock to acquire new capital?
12. In the case of a small corporation, why is it often necessary to sell securities directly to investors?
13. Explain the difference between horizontal and vertical expansion.

PROBLEMS AND PROJECTS

1. The General Manufacturing Company has sales of $75,246.50. The net profit is 3 per cent, or $2,257.40. There are outstanding 400 shares of stock with a par value of $100. (a) Compute the earnings per share of stock. (b) Assume that, if 200 additional shares are sold, the sales can be increased to $90,000 and the percentage of net profit will remain the same. What will be the earnings per share? (c) What must the sales be in order for the expanded business to earn a sufficient net profit at the rate of 3 per cent in order to pay the same rate of dividends on the increased number of shares as was paid on the original shares?

2. Two partners who are operating a business have been earning approximately $3,600 a year, which has been divided equally between them. Each has had $10,000 invested in the business. Approximately $10,000 will be required to purchase the building instead of renting it. The partners are debating whether to borrow the money or to admit a new partner who will contribute $10,000 and will share a third of the profits. A loan of $10,000 will require interest of 5 per cent on the unpaid balance. Assume that in either case the profit for the next year will be the same and that the first year's interest on the loan will be computed on the amount of the loan obtained. Show how the earnings of each individual will be affected (a) if the money is borrowed and (b) if a new partner is taken into the business.

3. Using the figures given in Problem 2, assume that the principal of the loan is to be paid off at the rate of $1,000 a year, plus interest on the unpaid balance. Set up a table for the ten years, using separate columns for the year, the interest that will be paid, the part of the principal that will be paid, the unpaid balance, and the amount of principal and interest that must be paid out of earnings. If the two owners of this business draw a salary that is sufficient to support them, can the loan be paid off satisfactorily?

4. Assume that a small corporation decides to sell 200 shares of common stock with a par value of $100 a share. A bank has agreed to take the stock and market it at a 7 per cent discount. The miscellaneous costs, including printing and registering the stock, will amount to $1,365. What will be the net proceeds from the stock?

5. Assume that the Aladdin Corporation issues $200,000 in bonds as follows: 2,000 bonds with a face value of $100 each at 5 per cent interest, payable annually. The bonds are to be redeemed at their face value in ten years. There is a good market for the bonds; and, because of the favorable interest rate, an investment bank agrees to take the bonds at the price of $101 each. The miscellaneous costs, including printing and registering the bonds, will amount to $2,570. What will be the net proceeds from the bonds?

6. Refer to the example in this chapter in which Mr. P. O. Marsh invests $1,421.50 in the business of Mr. H. J. Brooks. Mr. Brooks decides to buy out Mr. Marsh's interest and assumes that the net profit of $894.72 will continue each half year for the next five years. Will it be possible for him to pay for Mr. Marsh's share out of the earnings if he is required to make payments at the rate of $500 each half year plus 6 per cent interest on the unpaid balance?

CHAPTER XXVI

KEEPING ABREAST OF THE TIMES

Purpose of the Chapter. After one starts a business, he must be constantly alert to changes in economic conditions and business practices that may affect his business. He must therefore keep himself well informed on these subjects. The following are some of the important questions that will be answered in this chapter:

1. How are charts and graphs useful in the management of a business?
2. What are sources of information on local business conditions?
3. What are sources of information on national business conditions?
4. What kinds of research and testing laboratories are available to serve the businessman?
5. What is meant by market research?
6. How does market research help the businessman?
7. What should be the relation of the businessman to his community?
8. What are the functions of a merchants' bureau?
9. What is the function of a better business bureau?
10. How can the businessman be served by the United States Chamber of Commerce?

Use of Charts and Graphs. Preceding chapters have pointed out the necessity of budgeting and of keeping proper financial records. These records are of no value unless they are interpreted and used. Preceding examples have pointed out some of the statistics that can be prepared from financial records. For instance, rate of merchandise turnover, ratio of current assets to current liabilities, and numerous other ratios are statistics that help to keep the businessman informed about the condition of his business.

610

Another way to analyze statistics in business is to compile the figures and arrange them in the form of graphs or charts. For example, Illustration No. 242 contains graphs that show the relationship between sales and cost of sales. Illustration No. 243 contains graphs that illustrate the efficiency of salespeople. Numerous graphs or charts can be prepared as guides in watching and interpreting the trend and the condition of a business.

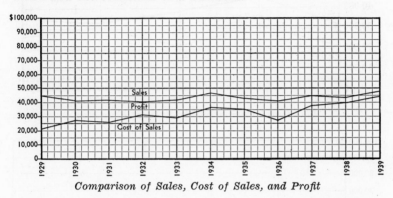

Comparison of Sales, Cost of Sales, and Profit

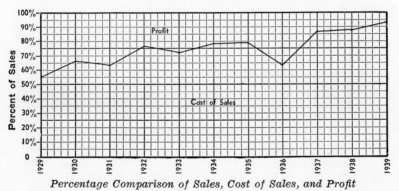

Percentage Comparison of Sales, Cost of Sales, and Profit

Illustration No. 242—Graphs Showing the Relationship Between Sales and Cost of Sales

Graphs are especially helpful in business because trends and conditions can be observed at a glance much more easily than if the information were presented in tables of figures.

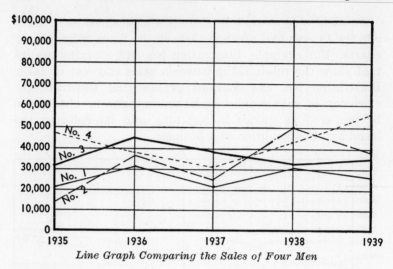

Line Graph Comparing the Sales of Four Men

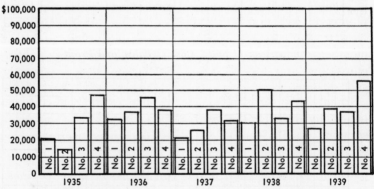

Bar Graph Comparing the Sales of Four Men

Salesperson No. 1 .... Mr. Jones
Salesperson No. 2 .... Mr. Jackson
Salesperson No. 3 .... Mr. Orville
Salesperson No. 4 .... Mr. Horton

Illustration No. 243—Graphs Illustrating the Efficiency of Salespeople

Sources of Information on Business and Economic Conditions. There are numerous sources of information on local and national business and economic conditions. It is important for a businessman to know not only local business conditions but also national conditions. Sources of information on local business conditions usually include the following:

> Newspapers
> Chamber of Commerce
> Credit bureau
> Retail merchants' bureau

The sources of information on national business and economic conditions are so numerous that not all of them can be listed, but the following are typical:

> Trade association publications
> United States Department of Commerce
> United States Department of Labor
> United States Chamber of Commerce
> Special services, such as Standard Statistics, Moody's, Brookmire, and Dun and Bradstreet, Incorporated

A trade association is an association of the businessmen in some particular trade or industry, as retail clothiers, plumbers, automobile dealers, and steel manufacturers. Nearly all trade associations issue publications for their members. There are also private publishers who publish magazines and reports that are of particular interest to such groups.

Illustration No. 244 is an example of the charts published by the United States Department of Commerce, showing an analysis of business conditions over a period of years.

Research and Testing Laboratories. Some large business organizations have their own testing and research laboratories. The testing laboratories are maintained to test both the products manufactured by the organizations and the materials purchased. The research laboratories are used in developing new products or new uses for old products, and in improving the products that are manufactured. Illustration No. 245 shows such a laboratory of the General Electric Company.

Many smaller businesses have testing laboratories to control the quality of their products. Such laboratories are particularly common in chemical manufacturing concerns.

Monthly Business Indicators, 1929–39

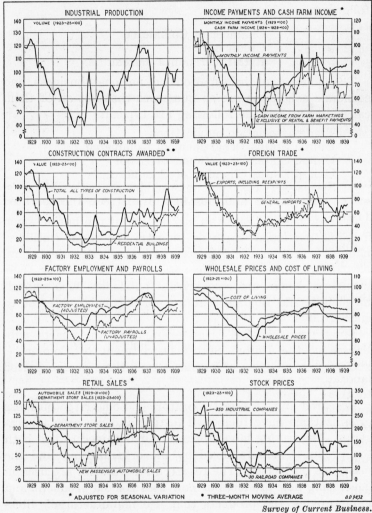

Survey of Current Business.

Illustration No. 244—An Analysis of Business Indicators

Many small mechanical manufacturing concerns also have testing departments and inspection departments.

Many universities maintain research laboratories that businessmen can use. Research problems can be submitted

General Electric Company.

Illustration No. 245—A Privately Owned Research Laboratory

to these laboratories for study. There are also other research organizations that are operated for the benefit of industry. The Mellon Institute, of Pittsburgh, Pennsylvania, is probably the most notable example. Industries that have a difficult research problem can, through an agreement with the Mellon Institute, arrange for the research to be done in that institute. Illustration No. 246 shows a picture of the Mellon Institute and one of the laboratories.

There are numerous commercial testing laboratories that can be used by anyone who wishes to submit an article for testing. The United States Department of Commerce publishes a directory of commercial testing and college research laboratories. For a certain fee, articles can be submitted to these commercial testing laboratories for testing and analysis. Stores and other business organizations use these testing laboratories, particularly in obtaining information about merchandise and materials that are being purchased and also in getting information about their own products.

The National Bureau of Standards, of Washington, D. C., will test a product for the company that manufactures it but will not divulge information to anyone who is contemplating purchasing the product. The National Bureau of Standards also establishes standards for observance in purchasing materials and merchandise for the Federal Government. The standard specifications established for various materials and products can be obtained by anyone

Mellon Institute.
Illustration No. 246—An Industrial Research Laboratory

who is interested in them. A businessman who wishes to buy scientifically can therefore obtain standards for many items. These standards can be used in making specifications for items that are to be purchased. For example, the following standards for bath towels have been established by the National Bureau of Standards:

TYPE AND GRADE
The types shall be that shown in Table I.
The grade shall be that known commercially as "firsts."

MATERIAL AND WORKMANSHIP
Material. The material shall be made of thoroughly cleaned cotton, free from waste.
Workmanship. It shall be free from avoidable imperfections in manufacture and from defects or blemishes affecting the appearance or the serviceability.

GENERAL REQUIREMENTS
Finish. The material shall be fully bleached. It shall be free from sizing.
Weave. The fabric shall consist of warp and filling ground threads and warp pile threads. It shall be woven with a terry weave except that there

shall be a border of plain cloth (without the pile) approximately 2 inches long at each end. It shall have tightly woven fast selvages, ¼ inch wide approximately.

Hemming. The ends shall have ½- to ¾-inch hem with no raw edges. The corners of the hem shall be backstitched.

Yarns. For Type A and Type C the ground warp shall be 2-ply, and the pile warp shall be a single yarn with two ends woven as one. The filling shall be single. For Type B the ground and the pile shall be 2-ply, and the filling shall be single.

TOLERANCES

Thread count. A minus tolerance of 2 threads per inch and any plus tolerance will be allowed.

Width. A tolerance of plus or minus 1 inch in the length and ½ inch in the width will be permitted.

Weight. A minus tolerance of 2½ per cent, and any plus tolerance, on a dozen towels will be permitted.

Additional information is furnished with regard to methods of sampling, inspecting, and testing.

The National Bureau of Standards publishes what is called a "willing to certify" list. On this list are the names of producers who are willing to certify that their products measure up to standards established by the National Bureau of Standards. The businessman can obtain a copy of this list. Illustration No. 247 is an example of a label used on a product that conforms to governmental specifications.

The American Standards Association is an organization that attempts to standardize the sizes and the qualities of various products, as well as the terminology used in connection with those products. Information on the standards established by this association is available.

Illustration No. 247—A Label on a Product Conforming to the Specifications of the National Bureau of Standards

Market Research. Many large business organizations have so-called market research departments. These departments study such problems as (a) the type of package that a customer prefers, (b) the buying habits of consumers, (c) desirable locations for retail outlets, (d) the price preference of particular communities or groups of customers. There are numerous other topics that are studied under the classification of market research.

Naturally, the small businessman cannot enter into such activities on a large scale, but he should always seek to keep himself informed as to the changes that are going on about him. For instance, a merchant who finds that his business is decreasing should determine the cause. The loss of sales may be due to bad economic conditions or to some other factor. Perhaps people in the community have been steadily moving away or have found some other store that is preferable. If customers have been moving away, perhaps the merchant should change his location. If they are going to another store, he should find out why and then adjust his procedure in order to regain his customers and to get new customers.

Manufacturers must likewise keep themselves informed on competitive conditions. They should watch carefully for new products, improved designs, changes in qualities, changes in selling plans, changes in prices, and numerous other factors.

Merchandising methods should be under constant scrutiny and study. Style, new products, new types of services, new types of display, and new selling plans are factors that represent constant change. For example, a manufacturer of cereals may find that a competitor, by taking an old product and putting it into a new package, is now getting most of the business in cereals. Merchants, as well as the manufacturer, are affected by the change. Likewise, new cereals are promoted and new selling plans are devised through advertising stunts over the radio. All competing manufacturers and all merchants who handle these products are affected by these changes in merchandising plans. They, therefore, may be forced to make some changes.

Business people can make numerous surveys locally and can also obtain access to surveys that have been made by the Federal Government, by universities, and by chambers of commerce. For instance, the following tabulation of information is taken from a survey of Toledo, Ohio, consumers by a professor in the University of Toledo. This information could be used to advantage by a restaurant operator in adjusting some of the practices within his business or by an individual in starting a new restaurant. The information that is tabulated is in answer to the question: "In your opinion, what should restaurants do to increase their popularity?"

Rank	Recommendation	Men	Women	Total
1	Better food	133	101	234
2	Quicker, better service	104	72	176
3	Cleaner	54	47	101
4	Lower price	57	29	86
5	More attractive surroundings	49	34	83
6	Courtesy	29	8	37
7	More variety of food	19	16	35
8	Larger portions	19	8	27
9	Better cooked food	20	4	24
10	Pleasant employees	5	16	21
11	Good music	5	11	16
12	Change menus more frequently	5	2	7
13	Attractive waitresses	6	0	6
14	Cater to individual	4	2	6
15	Increase personal comfort	4	1	5
16	Better trained employees	5	0	5
17	Advertise	4	1	5
18	Treat employees fairly	5	0	5
	Miscellaneous	55	42	97
	Total	582	394	976

Harold A. Frey (Bulletin 11 of the Bureau of Business Research, College of Business Administration, University of Toledo).

Illustration No. 248—A Survey of Consumers

The table in Illustration No. 249 shows the results of a study made by the Chamber of Commerce in Beaver Dam, Wisconsin. The following complaints were made by the people who were studied in the survey:

    19 per cent said prices were too high
    7 per cent said quality was too low
    52 per cent said larger selections were needed
    20 per cent complained better salespeople were needed

Purchases	Percentage Buying Out of Town	Where They Go		
		Other Towns	Mail Order	Peddlers
Auto Supplies	15.8%	46.2%	53.8%	...
Groceries	4.9	75.0	12.5	12.5%
Lumber	3.6	83.5	16.5	...
Drugs	14.2	57.2	28.6	14.3
Hardware	11.5	36.8	63.2	...
Dry Goods	24.3	70.0	30.0	...
Jewelry	4.9	87.5	12.5	...
Electrical Goods	11.5	36.8	63.2	...
Electric Refrigerator	2.4	100.0	...	...
Radio	6.1	30.0	70.0	...
Men's Clothing	30.3	74.0	26.0	...
Child's Clothing	33.3	69.0	31.0	...
Women's Clothing	52.7	83.3	16.7	...
Shoes	32.8	81.8	18.2	...
Hosiery	10.3	52.9	41.2	5.9
Novelties	12.7	85.8	9.6	4.7
Seeds and Feed	7.3	66.6	33.3	...
Furniture	18.8	51.7	48.3	...

CONSUMER BUYING HABITS

American Business.

*Illustration No. 249—Consumer Buying Habits in
Beaver Dam, Wisconsin*

Illustration No. 250 is an example of a questionnaire used
by the Michigan Retail Hardware Association. Many other
trade associations have used similar devices for making
community studies.

Membership in Civic Organizations. Every businessman
should enter into the business and civic life of his community. Experience in such organizations as the Rotary
Club, the Kiwanis Club, the Lions Club, the Co-operative
Club, the Optimists Club, and other similar organizations
is not only inspiring, but also profitable to those who enter
into the activity. Such groups have major civic activities
that are important to every community. Members are encouraged to take pride in the organization and in the
community. Through such groups an individual can become
acquainted with many other responsible business and civic
leaders, and has an opportunity to help set some of the
business standards of the community.

CONFIDENTIAL REPORT BY CUSTOMERS

A. COMMUNITY RELATIONS:

1. Are owners considered active in community development, charitable and civic affairs ?_____
2. Has the store a reputation for fair dealing ?_____
3. Would you call this a "progressive" store . . . one that attempts to "keep up with the times" ?_____
4. What is the general atmosphere of the store . . . do you "feel at home" when trading there ?_____
5. Does the manager or owner impress you as one who treats his employees with consideration ?_____

B. MERCHANDISE . . . PRICES AND QUALITY:

1. Do you consider the assortment of merchandise satisfactory ?_____ If not, in what lines are poor assortments carried ?_____
2. Does the store feature "new" and "seasonal" merchandise ?_____
3. Is the store frequently "out" of merchandise you would expect it to carry ? _____
4. What lines, not now handled, do you think should be carried in stock ? _____
5. Are prices generally fair ?_____. If not, in what lines do you consider that prices are too high ?_____
6. Are you generally pleased with the *quality* of goods purchased ?_____ If not, in what lines or items is the quality poor ?_____

C. STORE DISPLAY:

1. Is the store front inviting ?_____
2. Is merchandise well displayed in the show windows ?_____
3. Has the store a "modern" interior arrangement ?_____
4. Is merchandise in the store well displayed or "sloppy" in appearance ? _____
5. Are inside displays clean and free from dust ?_____
6. Is the store well lighted ?_____
7. Is the "color scheme" attractive ?_____
8. Are goods priced so that you do not have to ask prices of salesmen ? _____
9. Give general comment on "store display." _____

D. EMPLOYEES:

1. Do owners or employees greet you as you enter the store ?_____
2. Are employees alert, courteous, and helpful ?_____
3. Do you get waited on promptly ?_____
4. Are employees neat and careful of their personal appearance ?_____
5. Do employees know, and can they clearly explain, the merits of the goods they are selling ?_____ If not, on what items or lines are they weak ?_____
6. Give general comment on employees._____

E. STORE SERVICE:

1. Is "store service" satisfactory ?_____
2. Are promises kept ?_____
3. How could store service be improved ?_____

F. GENERAL:

1. Do you consider that the store has a good location ?_____
2. What general comments have you to make on this store as a place in which to trade ?_____

IT IS UNNECESSARY TO SIGN YOUR NAME

Illustration No. 250—A Questionnaire Used by the Michigan Retail Hardware Association

Activities of Trade Associations. The trade association is an important organization. As was explained previously, a trade association is an organization formed of the individuals within a certain industry or line of business. For instance, plumbers, wholesale grocers, electrical manufacturers, or other similar groups organize to promote cooperative programs within their industries. The United States Department of Commerce reports that there are at least four thousand state and local trade associations. A list of such associations is available from the United States Department of Commerce. The following are some examples: National Retail Dry Goods Association, Retail Merchants Association, National Retail Druggists Association, and the Association of Master Plumbers.

A trade association must conform to various state and Federal laws. There must be particular care that the association operates in accordance with the Federal Antitrust Laws. For instance, the following specific practices will, in many cases, determine whether the acts performed by the association are lawful or unlawful:

1. Secrecy in the reporting of data and the limitation of the information to the members of the association have been regarded as constituting one of the potent reasons for adjudging a reporting plan illegal.

2. Statistics must be compiled "fairly" and present an accurate record of "actual" transactions.

3. The report must not give more detailed or specific information than is adequate for an intelligent knowledge of the fundamental conditions affecting the industry. The names of customers or the specific facts of a sale do not ordinarily add to the general value of statistics.

4. Comments, advice, or suggestions by an official or a representative of the trade association, dealing with the production or the price policy of each individual member, seem to be regarded by the courts as a clear indication of group pressure to force the members to act in concert and in conformity with a joint plan.

5. Generally speaking, it is legal for an association to report prices on past transactions, but it is illegal to report current prices or future prices.

6. There must be no penal provision to compel each member, under duress of fine, suspension, or expulsion, to conform to group action rather than individual discretion.

7. A drastic supervisory system that amounts, in substance, to control of the individual's affairs by the association is another feature that has received judicial condemnation.

The following are some activities in which a trade association may logically participate for the benefit of its members and for the general welfare of the industry:

Collection and dissemination of information
Exchange of ideas on management
Co-operative testing
Establishment of fair trade practices
Laboratory research
Hiring of specialists to serve members
Market research

Chambers of Commerce. The chamber of commerce is not a trade association, because it is composed of any business or professional men in the community who are interested in becoming members and who are accepted into the membership. The chamber of commerce usually promotes the business welfare of the community and participates in civic activities for the general improvement of the community.

Retail Bureaus. Many chambers of commerce also include so-called retail bureaus and committees. Membership in these bureaus is usually open only to members of the chamber of commerce. The trade-promotion activities of a retail trade bureau commonly include the following:

1. Establishing closer relations with outlying trade
2. Featuring special retail sales days
3. Promoting spring and fall openings, with window displays, parades, music, and other attractions

4. Organizing salesmanship classes composed of men and women, and establishing courses in retail selling
5. General educational work

The chamber of commerce or the retail trade bureau of the chamber of commerce often promotes other activities besides trade promotion. Some of these activities are those commonly handled by better business bureaus, and are as follows:

1. Obtaining speakers to address merchants on retail trade problems
2. Prosecuting transient merchants who have not complied with local regulations
3. Warning the public against sales of goods by peddlers who misrepresent their wares
4. Championing the cause of retailers in all legislation affecting their interests, local, state, or national
5. Protecting members against advertising mediums that have no advertising value
6. Promoting co-operative delivery, uniform closing hours, and holiday agreements
7. Obtaining the adoption of uniform rules concerning the return of merchandise, the granting of discounts, and the like
8. Obtaining from organizations in other towns and issuing to its members confidential information on check forgers, shoplifters, fake solicitors, and all kinds of frauds
9. Exchanging credit information among its members

A Model Merchants' Bureau. To illustrate the purposes and the activities of a merchants' bureau, or retail bureau, the following model constitution is presented:

The Retail Merchants' Council of the Rochester, N. Y., Chamber of Commerce

ARTICLE I
NAME AND OBJECT

SECTION 1. *Name.* The name of this organization shall be the Retail Merchants' Council of the Rochester Chamber of Commerce.

SECTION 2. *Object.* The object of this council shall be to promote the interests of retail trade in Rochester and vicinity; to bring about closer relations among those engaged in retail merchandising, and to secure concerted action on their part in the improvement of existing conditions.

ARTICLE II
MEMBERSHIP

SECTION 1. *Retail Business.* Membership in the Retail Merchants' Council shall be limited to individuals or business concerns engaged in selling merchandise or services to the general public.

SECTION 2. *Admission to Membership.* Membership in the Retail Merchants' Council shall be limited to the following: (a) Persons who are engaged in selling merchandise or service to the public and who are members of the Rochester Chamber of Commerce; (b) Partnerships and corporations engaged in selling merchandise or service to the public, provided an executive officer of such partnership or corporation is a member of the Rochester Chamber of Commerce; (c) Chain stores, provided the Rochester manager is a member of the Rochester Chamber of Commerce.

SECTION 3. *Termination of Membership.* Membership in the Retail Merchants' Council may be terminated in any one of the following ways: (a) By resignation in writing to the Executive Committee of this Council; (b) By the removal of any of the conditions for membership as specified in Section 2; (c) Nonpayment of Council dues.

SECTION 4. *Dues.* Each member shall pay annually an amount proportioned to the number of employees as of November 1 of each year except that in no case shall the dues be less than $10.00.

All dues shall be due and payable January 1 of each year in advance; but if in excess of $25.00, payment may be made in semiannual installments.

SECTION 5. *Application and Acceptance.* Application must be made on form furnished for the purpose and shall be referred to Membership Committee for recommendation and final action by Executive Committee.

ARTICLE III
EXECUTIVE COMMITTEE

The supervision of the activities of this Council shall be in the hands of an Executive Committee appointed annually by the President of the Chamber of Commerce.

The Executive Committee shall have power to fill all vacancies on the Committee.

With the approval of the Officers and Trustees of the Chamber, they may adopt rules and regulations for conducting the business of the Council.

This Committee shall elect from its own number a Chairman and Vice Chairman, who shall be respectively the Chairman and Vice Chairman of the Retail Merchants' Council.

ARTICLE IV
OFFICERS

SECTION 1. *Chairman.* The Chairman shall be elected annually by the Executive Committee and shall preside at all meetings of the Council and its Executive Committee. He shall perform all duties incident to his office and advise such action as may be deemed by him likely to increase the usefulness of the Council.

SECTION 2. *Vice Chairman.* The Vice Chairman shall be elected annually by the Executive Committee and shall act in the absence of the Chairman; and in the absence of the two officials named, a member of the Executive Committee shall be chosen to act temporarily.

SECTION 3. *Treasurer.* The Treasurer of the Rochester Chamber of Commerce shall act as Treasurer of the Retail Merchants' Council. He shall receive and dispose of funds of the Council and render prior to the annual meeting an annual report to the Executive Committee.

SECTION 4. *Secretary.* The Secretary of the Rochester Chamber of Commerce shall personally, or by deputy, act as Secretary of the Retail Merchants' Council. It shall be the duty of the Secretary to conduct the official correspondence, preserve all books, documents, and communications relative to the work of the Council, keep an accurate record of the meetings of the Council, and perform any other duties incident to the position of Secretary.

ARTICLE V
COMMITTEES

SECTION 1. *Appointment.* The Chairman shall appoint all committees, subject to confirmation by the Executive Committee.

SECTION 2. *Authority.* It shall be the function of committees to investigate and to make recommendations. They shall report in writing to the Executive Committee. No standing or special committee shall represent the Council in advocacy or opposition to any project without the specific confirmation of the Executive Committee, whose action shall in turn be subject to confirmation by the Officers or Trustees of the Chamber.

SECTION 3. *Meetings.* Meetings of the committees or subcommittees may be called at any time by the Chairman of such committee.

ARTICLE VI
MEETINGS

SECTION 1. *Time and Place.* Meetings shall be held at such times and places as the Executive Committee shall determine.

SECTION 2. *Annual.* The annual meeting shall be held on the first Tuesday in December.

SECTION 3. *Quorum.* Ten per cent, but not less than twenty, of the members of the Council shall constitute a quorum.

ARTICLE VII
AMENDMENTS TO BYLAWS

SECTION 1. These Bylaws may be amended by affirmative two-thirds votes of the members of the Council voting at any meeting, in the call for which notification of the amendments shall have been made.

SECTION 2. Such amendments shall become effective only when approved by the Officers and Trustees of the Chamber of Commerce.

Better Business Bureaus. Every self-respecting business-man should be in sympathy with, and should co-operate with, the local better business bureau if there is one. He should be a member of that bureau and should support it. A better business bureau is organized to prevent unfair trade practices.

United States Chamber of Commerce. The United States Chamber of Commerce has many services available to members and literature that can be bought by nonmembers. A price list of the literature can be obtained. Much of the literature is of particular benefit to the small businessman, as well as to the large. The following are examples of some of the printed pamphlets that are available:

Planning Your Business Ahead
The Relation Between Chain Stores and Local Chambers of Commerce
Retailers' Expenses
Small Store Advertising
Small Store Arrangement
Special Sales Events
Store Opening and Closing Hours
Discriminatory Legislation Affecting Retailers
Evaluation of Territory and Customers
Burglary and Robbery Insurance
The Fire Insurance Contract
Organization Plans for Budget Control
Perpetual Inventory and Stores Control

Federal Publications. From the United States Printing Office and through the various departments of the Government, particularly through the United States Department of Commerce, there are numerous publications obtainable that are useful to the businessman. Everyone engaged in business should obtain a copy of the list of publications issued by the Bureau of Foreign and Domestic Commerce of the United States Department of Commerce. The following titles are taken from this list to indicate the types of literature available:

Causes of Commercial Bankruptcies
Credit and Payment Terms
Exclusive Sales Agreements
National Retail Credit Survey
Candy Distribution in the United States
Commercial Survey of Philadelphia Marketing Area
Aids to Retail Grocery Profits
Market Research Sources
Survey of Retail Management Practices

Business Literature. Every businessman should assume that his education has just begun. He should therefore study regularly to keep himself up to date on all subjects. One of the best ways is to subscribe to at least one trade magazine. A trade magazine is one containing information on a particular industry or line of business. For instance, there are magazines covering coal, iron, chain stores, independent stores, dry goods, pottery, electrical appliances, and practically all other lines of industrial endeavor. Many of these are specialized according to particular products or particular types of distribution.

There are published each year hundreds of books covering all phases of accounting, merchandising, purchasing, stock control, advertising, promotion, and other business activities. Some of these books should go into the library of the businessman regularly.

Many city libraries make a practice of establishing special sections devoted to business and industry. Some libraries, such as the Business Branch of the Public Library of Newark, New Jersey, publish monthly and yearly bulletins showing the literature available in the field of business.

In such libraries a businessman will find many books and magazines that will help him to keep up to date in his management practices.

Public Library, Newark, New Jersey.

Illustration No. 251—Business Branch of a Public Library

QUESTIONS FOR DISCUSSION

1. Why are graphs usually more effective than figures in giving a person information on business conditions, trends in sales, and the like?

2. What are some sources of information on local business conditions?

3. What are the two departments of the Federal Government from which one can obtain the most information on business and economic conditions?

4. What is a trade association?

5. (a) Will the National Bureau of Standards conduct a test on any item that you are interested in purchasing? (b) Will it conduct a test on a product that you have manufactured?

6. How can the various testing agencies be used to advantage in business?

7. Mention a few of the problems on which information can be obtained through market research.

8. Mention at least three activities of a trade association.

9. How does a chamber of commerce differ from a trade association?

10. What are the common functions of a retail trade bureau (sometimes a part of a chamber of commerce)?

11. What department of the Federal Government prepares literature of particular interest to the businessman?

12. Does the United States Chamber of Commerce serve nonmembers?

13. What agency in a community sometimes performs some of the functions of a better business bureau?

14. Name at least three printed indexes that are sources of information on business.

PROBLEMS AND PROJECTS

1. Using the following figures, prepare a line graph similar to the first graph in Illustration No. 242 on page 611:

SALES	COST OF SALES	YEAR
$ 9,260.50	$8,120.50	1935
10,420.14	8,550.20	1936
9,555.10	8,216.43	1937
9,100.44	8,820.14	1938
8,980.85	8,111.23	1939

2. On the basis of the figures given above, draw a graph showing the cost of sales and the gross profit (the difference between the sales and the cost of sales) in terms of percentages of sales. Consider the sales for each year to represent 100 per cent.

3. Obtain figures for school attendance, school grades, sales of the local book store, production or sales of some local business, accidents, or the figures on any other interesting topic. Present these figures in the form of a neatly drawn graph. Your original figures should accompany the graph.

4. List the various sources of information on the business conditions of your community.

5. On the basis of the questionnaire on page 621, make an analysis of a local hardware store or some other type of store suggested by your teacher. A summary of the analyses of the other members of the class will then be made available so that you can write a summary of the findings of the study and make some recommendations.

6. Make a list of the local civic and professional groups that, in your opinion, help in developing better business relations and thereby contribute something to the community.

7. Go to your local public library and find out what types of business magazines are available in the library. Write a report on your findings, pointing out the types of articles that appeared in some of the magazines.

INDEX